MEDIA, FEMINISM, CULTURAL STUDIES

The Sacred Cinema of Andrei Tarkovsky
by Jeremy Mark Robinson

Liv Tyler
by Thomas A. Christie

The Cinema of Hayao Miyazaki
Jeremy Mark Robinson

Stepping Forward: Essays, Lectures and Interviews
by Wolfgang Iser

Wild Zones: Pornography, Art and Feminism
by Kelly Ives

'Cosmo Woman': The World of Women's Magazines
by Oliver Whitehorne

The Cinema of Richard Linklater
by Thomas A. Christie

Andrea Dworkin
by Jeremy Mark Robinson

Cixous, Irigaray, Kristeva: The Jouissance of French Feminism
by Kelly Ives

The Erotic Object: Sexuality in Sculpture
From Prehistory to the Present Day
by Susan Quinnell

Women in Pop Music
by Helen Challis

Sex in Art: Pornography and Pleasure in Painting and Sculpture
by Cassidy Hughes

Erotic Art
by Cassidy Hughes

Jean-Luc Godard: The Passion of Cinema / Le Passion de Cinéma
by Jeremy Mark Robinson

Genius and Loving It! Mel Brooks
by Thomas Christie

The Comic Art of Mel Brooks
by Maurice Yacowar

Marvelous Names
by P. Adams Sitney

The Art of Katsuhiro Otomo
by Jeremy Mark Robinson

Akira: The Movie and the Manga
by Jeremy Mark Robinson

The Art of Masamune Shirow (3 vols)
by Jeremy Mark Robinson

Detonation Britain: Nuclear War in the UK
by Jeremy Mark Robinson

Julia Kristeva: Art, Love, Melancholy, Philosophy, Semiotics
by Kelly Ives

Luce Irigaray: Lips, Kissing, and the Politics of Sexual Difference
by Kelly Ives

Helene Cixous I Love You: The Jouissance of Writing
by Kelly Ives

FORTHCOMING BOOKS

Legend of the Overfiend
Death Note
Naruto
Bleach
Hellsing
Vampire Knight
Mushishi
One Piece
Nausicaä of the Valley of the Wind
Tsui Hark
The Twilight Saga
Jackie Collins and the Blockbuster Novel
Harry Potter

THE ECSTATIC CINEMA

OF

TONY CHING SIU-TUNG

Tony Ching Siu-tung is one of the legends of Chinese action cinema. A genius whose movies include the *Swordsman* series, and the *Chinese Ghost Story* series, Ching was also the action director of giant Chinese productions such as *Hero, House of Flying Daggers, The Warlords* and *The Curse of the Golden Flower*.

THE ECSTATIC CINEMA
OF TONY CHING SIU-TUNG

Jeremy Mark Robinson

Crescent Moon

Crescent Moon Publishing
P.O. Box 1312
Maidstone, Kent
ME14 5XU, Great Britain
www.crmoon.com

First published 2023.
© Jeremy Mark Robinson 2023.

Set in Helvetica 9 on 14pt.
Designed by Radiance Graphics.

British Library Cataloguing in Publication data available for this title.

ISBN-13 9781861718761

CONTENTS

**PART THREE
TONY CHING SIU-TUNG
MOVIES AS ACTION DIRECTOR**

ACKNOWLEDGEMENTS

To the authors and publishers quoted.
To the copyright holders of the illustrations.

PICTURE CREDITS

Golden Harvest. Shaw Brothers. Paragon. Cinema City. Film Workshop. China Entertainment. Paka Hill. Eastern Production. Win's Entertainment. Star East. Jing Productions. Media Asia. Beijing Polyabana Publishing. United Filmmakers Organization. China Film Co-Production. Big Pictures. China Juli Entertainment Media. Distribution Workshop. Different Digital Design. Huxia Film Distribution. New Classics Pictures.

ABBREVIATIONS

LM   *The Cinema of Tsui Hark* by Lisa Morton

倩女幽魂

只羨鴛鴦不羨仙

對月形單空相護

寸寸青絲愁華年

十里平湖霜滿天

A CHINESE
GHOST STORY I

The Swordsman 2 (1992).

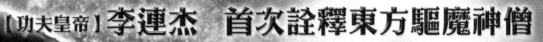

【功夫皇帝】李連杰　首次詮釋東方驅魔神僧

導演／動作指導　程小東

唯我替天行道

世間群魔亂舞

MOSTRA INTERNAZIONALE
D'ARTE CINEMATOGRAFICA
la Biennale di Venezia 2011
Out of Competition

68

THE SORCERER and the White Snake

法海

白蛇傳説

程小东作品

中國巨力影視傳媒有限公司 出品及攝製

主演 李連杰 黃聖依 林峯 蔡卓妍 文章 姜武 特別演出 徐若瑄 友情客串 楊千嬅 杜文澤 林雪
造型指導 張叔平 動作指導 程小東 攝影指導 姜國民(HKSC) 剪輯 林安兒 音樂 雷頌德
主題歌 許諾 作曲 Choi Joon Young 作詞 陳少琪 原創版權　Warner/Chappell Music Korea Inc.
製片人 王松 王岳 編劇 張炭 曾謹昌 司徒卓漢 出品人 楊子 監製 崔寶珠 導演 程小東

© 2011 中國巨力影視傳媒有限公司 保留所有權利

10月14日 翻江倒海　龍祥鉅獻 元氣無限

The Sorcerer and the White Snake (2011).

Jade Dynasty (2019)

他们谁没有偷看过

究竟何物

PART ONE

TONY CHING SIU-TUNG

1

TONY CHING SIU-TUNG: BIOGRAPHY

TONY CHING SIU-TUNG: INTRO

Tony Ching Siu-tung (b. 1953) started out as an actor and stuntman, working in movies in the late 1960s and 1970s; he moved into television as martial arts co-ordinator in the late 1970s and thru the 1980s (on several historical TV series); he moved up to directing movies with 1983's *Duel To the Death*.

Tony Ching Siu-tung's two signature works are probably *A Chinese Ghost Story* and *The Swordsman 2*. Critically, those two films (and their movie series, the *Chinese Ghost Story* series and the *Swordsman* series), have garnered the highest criticial accolades (and they were big hits financially), and *The Swordsman 2* has been the subject of numerous analyses of gender-bending issues in cinema. The sight of Brigitte Lin in drag and later fooling around with Jet Li as a 'woman' seems to drive film critics goo-goo.

Tony Ching Siu-tung has won top awards for the action choreography for *The Witch From Nepal, Shaolin Soccer, New Dragon Gate Inn, Hero* and *The Swordsman*.

Like the other famous action directors in Hong Kong cinema (such as Yuen Woo-ping, Sammo Hung, Corey Yuen Kwai and Yuen Bun), Tony Ching Siu-tung has worked with every single star in Hong Kong, every producer, every cameraman, designer, stylist, costumier, etc, and probably every stuntman and stuntwoman.

Tony Ching Siu-tung has action director credits on: *Dangerous Encounter – 1st Kind, Twinkle Twinkle Little Star, Peking Opera Blues, A Better Tomorrow 2, The Killer, New Dragon Gate Inn, Moon Warriors, City*

Hunter, Butterfly and Sword, the Krrish films, Kung Fu Dunk and The Warlords. He is an action director in high demand – for many TV shows as well as movies. Ching has worked many times with producer/ director/ dynamo Tsui Hark.

Tony Ching Siu-tung seems barely known outside of Chinese film circles, and in the West[1] his name is over-shadowed by directors such as Tsui Hark, John Woo, Wong Kar-wai, etc. Yuen Woo-ping has become known for the Matrix movies and others, and of course Jackie Chan remains a huge presence (tho' as a movie star, and not for his incredible directing skills. Few realize that Chan has directed several masterpieces, including the Project A series and the Police Story series).

But consider the achievements of Tony Ching Siu-tung – they are very impressive: two of the finest and most celebrated of Hong Kong franchises – the Swordsman movies and the Chinese Ghost Story movies. Judged solely on the basis of those two film trilogies, Ching is a kung fu master and lion dancer among filmmakers. The first two Chinese Ghost Story films are masterpieces, are the first two Swordsman films (some would include the third installment, too – it's very popular with critics and fans). Near-masterpieces would include Ching's first film as director, Duel To the Death, The Sorcerer and the White Snake, Jade Dynasty and An Empress and the Warriors. Add to those giant historical pictures his work as action director on masterpieces such Hero, Peking Opera Blues, House of Flying Daggers, A Better Tomorrow 2 and The Killer, and a host of very enjoyable pictures, such as: Butterfly and Sword, City Hunter, Moon Warriors, the Krrish films, Curse of the Golden Flower, and The Warlords. (Some of those productions were enormous – Krrish, The Warlords, Hero, Curse of the Golden Flower, etc).

Technically, the movies directed by Tony Ching Siu-tung are breathtaking – in every department of film production, Ching's movies excel. Costumes are lavish, the sets are super-detailed, and the cinematography is stellar. Sometimes you really are looking at something very close to a classical, Chinese painting, where the billowing robes that the actors wear fit in perfectly, and are spot-on equivalents for the spiritual mood of Chinese art. The floating, ruffling clothes are also practical, on-set versions of the figures in Chinese art, as if they have been animated from paintings on silk and given three-dimensional form.

Like Tsui Hark, Tony Ching is fascinated by visual effects, and his cinema contains every trick imaginable. Ching's cinema celebrates the magic of filmmaking, the artifice, the dream.

1 By the early 2000s, many Hong Kong action directors were working in the West, including Tony Ching Siu-tung, Corey Yuen Kwai, Yuen Cheung-yan and, most famously, Yuen Woo-ping.

Talking about the issue of co-direction: Hong Kong cinema has a long-established tradition of sharing duties in many areras of production, direction included.[2] The high speed of production meant that if someone wasn't available, someone else would step in; it was simply a practical solution; the idea of waiting weeks until the main director became available again, because only the main director was capable or legally authorized to shoot the film, is just silly. Most of the celebrated film directors in Hong Kong have co-directed at some time or other. Tony Ching Siu-tung was happy to collaborate with Tsui Hark, as we know – and also to share direction with Wong Jing, Johnnie To, and others.

It's common in the Hong Kong industry for film directors to also be actors, for actors to direct, for writers to be actors, and for some of the really gifted people to have multiple roles (like Sammo Hung, Jackie Chan, Tsui Hark, Eric Tsang, Wu Ma, etc).

TONY CHING SIU-TUNG: FILM CREDITS

Tony Ching Siu-tung's films as director include:

Duel To the Death (1983)
The Witch From Nepal (1986)
A Chinese Ghost Story (1987)
The Terracotta Warrior (1989)
The Swordsman (1990 – co-directed)
A Chinese Ghost Story 2 (1990)
The Raid (1991 – co-directed)
A Chinese Ghost Story 3 (1991)
Swordsman 2 (1992)
Swordsman 3 (1993 – co-directed)
The Heroic Trio (1993, co-directed)
The Executioners (1993, co-directed)
Wonder Seven (1994)
Dr. Wai In "The Scripture With No Words" (1996)
The Longest Day (1997)
Conman In Tokyo (2000)

2 A surprising number of actors and crew in the Hong Kong film industry have also directed. Actors, DPs, editors, writers and action choreographers often step into the director's chair.

Naked Weapon (2002)

Belly of the Beast (2003)

An Empress and the Warriors (2008)

The Sorcerer and the White Snake (2011)

Jade Dynasty (2019)

Tony Ching Siu-tung's work as action director/ choreographer includes 84 films up to 2011 (this is in addition to most of the movies he also helmed, where he was the action director, and not forgetting the many TV series that Ching has action directed – see below).

The following is a partial list:

The Fourteen Amazons (1972)

The Rats (1972)

Love and Vengeance (1973)

Shaolin Boxer (1974)

The Tea House (1974)

Kidnap (1974)

Lady of the Law (1975)

Negotiation (1977)

He Who Never Dies (1979)

Monkey Kung Fu (1979)

The Bastard Swordsman (1979)

The Sentimental Swordsman (1979)

Dangerous Encounter - 1st Kind (1980)

The Spooky Bunch (1980)

The Sword (1980)

The Master Strikes (1980)

Gambler's Delight (1981)

Return of the Deadly Blade (1981)

Sword of Justice (1981)

The Story of Woo Viet (1981)

Rolls, Rolls, I Love You (1982)

Once Upon a Rainbow (1982)

Swordsman Adventure (1983)

Twinkle Twinkle Little Star (1983)

Cherie (1984)

Happy Ghost 3 (1986)

Peking Opera Blues (1986)

A Better Tomorrow 2 (1987)

The Eighth Happiness (1988)
I Love Maria (1988)
The Killer (1989)
All About Ah-Long (1989)
The Fun, the Luck and the Tycoon (1990)
Casino Raiders 2 (1991)
Son On the Run (1991)
New Dragon Gate Inn (1992 – co-directed)
Moon Warriors (1992)
Twin Dragons (1992)
Royal Tramp (1992)
Royal Tramp 2 (1992)
Gambling Soul (1992)
Justice, My Foot! (1992)
Lucky Encounter (1992)
Flying Dagger (1993)
Future Cops (1993)
Holy Weapon (1993)
The Mad Monk (1993)
Butterfly and Sword (1993)
City Hunter (1993)
Love On Delivery (1994)
A Chinese Odyssey 1: Pandora's Box (1995)
A Chinese Odyssey 2: Cinderella (1995)
The Stuntwoman (1996)
Warriors of Virtue (1997)
Hong Niang (1998)
The Blacksheep Affair (1998)
The Assassin Swordsman (2000)
The Duel (2000)
My School Mate, the Barbarian (2001)
Invincible (2001)
Shaolin Soccer (2001)
Hero (2002)
Spider-Man (2002 – uncredited)
House of Flying Daggers (2004)
The Curse of the Golden Flower (2006)
Krrish (2006)
In the Name of the King: A Dungeon Siege Tale (2007)
The Warlords (2007)

Dororo (2007)

Legend of Shaolin Kungfu I: Heroes in Troubled Times (2007)

Butterfly Lovers (2008)

Kung Fu Dunk (2008)

The Treasure Hunter (2009)

Future X-Cops (2010)

Just Call Me Nobody (2010)

Legend of Shaolin Kungfu 3: Heroes of the Great Desert (2011)

Krrish 3 (2013)

Tony Ching has been the action director on many television series, including:

The Spirit of the Sword (1978)

It Takes a Thief (1979)

The Roving Swordsman (1979)

Reincarnated (1979)

Reincarnated 2 (1979)

Dynasty (1980)

Dynasty 2 (1980)

Legend of the Condor Heroes (1983)

The Return of the Condor Heroes (1983)

The New Adventures of Chor Lau Heung (1984)

The Duke of Mount Deer (1984)

The Return of Luk Siu Fung (1986)

The New Heaven Sword and Dragon Sabre (1986)

The Storm Riders (a.k.a. *Wind and Cloud*, 2002)

The Storm Riders 2 (a.k.a. *Wind and Cloud 2*, 2004)

The Royal Swordsmen (2005)

It's worth noting a couple of things about the credits of Tony Ching Siu-tung and other action directors:[3] (1) some sources have Ching as the director, confusing action director with director. (2) The action director does indeed oversee whole sequences of a movie. The director sometimes leaves action scenes (and more) up to them. Also, action direction often includes second unit work. So you could argue that some films are co-directed – especially action movies, where lengthy sections will have been overseen by the action director. (3) And some movies were officially co-directed by Ching, working as a director (often with Tsui Hark). As you can see from the credits and the dates of the movies, co-directing usually

---

3 The 'martial arts director' was a position partly created by director King Hu in the 1960s.

occurred in the ultra-busy time of the late 1980s and early-to-mid-1990s, when people were working on four movies simultaneously, and sleeping in their car.

In Tony Ching Siu-tung's case, we know that *New Dragon Gate Inn* ran into trouble, and Ching and Tsui Hark came in to oversee the direction in order to finish the movie (part of which was filmed on location in Mainland China). *The Swordsman* too had problems, with several directors contributing to it to get the whole thing done.

In the West, the division of labour includes stunt co-ordinator, who oversees the stunt team and the stunts, and second unit director, who takes up all of the material that the first or 'A' unit hasn't time to do. In Hong Kong, the action director tends to combine the role of the stunt co-ordinator with that of the second unit director (many of the big name action directors have their own stunt teams – Jackie Chan's guys being the most famous).

How could Tony Ching do so much work in action direction – often several movies in the same year? The answer is the action director or stunt co-ordinator will be hired for short periods, sometimes even a day, to deliver particular effects. Even if they oversee several action sequences, they won't be on board for the whole schedule (for the talky scenes, for instance). Some productions call for a lot more action, of course, which will take longer; but many films hire several action directors (plus assistants). Thus, the action scenes can be filmed simultaneously.

In addition, action teams are often collaborating with the same people on film after film, so they develop a shorthand way of working; they are used to working fast; they often work long hours (without film unions); and they sometimes work on other shows at the same time (having several action directors means that some can be working in the studio, while others are on location).

Tony Ching Siu-tung had provided action direction for Tsui Hark, Johnnie To, John Woo, Wong Jing, Ringo Lam, Zhang Yimou, Peter Chan, Andy Lau, Kevin Chu, and Stephen Chow, among others. That is, practically all of the major filmmakers in China. (Ching has worked many times with a group of directors that include Tsui, Jing, To, Chow, Zhang and Chu. Ching has worked with Jing more than anyone else, except perhaps Tsui). There's no doubt whatsoever that one of the reasons those directors are celebrated by critics and fans around the world is because their action sequences were overseen by Ching and his contemporaries.

We might wish, selfishly, that Ching Siu-tung had directed more movies, as with Jackie Chan (13 or so), rather than providing action direction for other filmmakers. However, 22 features as director or co-director, between 1983 and 2019, is a solid career – some of those movies are masterpieces (22 films is more than celebrated directors such as Orson Welles and Luchino Visconti).

TONY CHING SIU-TUNG: BIOGRAPHY

Tony Ching Siu-tung – often known as Tony Ching or as Ching Siu-tung[4] – was born on October 30, 1953, in Anhui, Showhsien province)[5] Ching is a genius of action cinema.[6] No one in the West can touch him, and only his contemporaries among Chinese action choreographers, such as Yuen Woo-ping, Corey Yuen Kwai and Yuen Bun, offer serious competition. Ching is the director of two of the great recent fantasy franchises in Chinese cinema: the *Chinese Ghost Story* series and the *Swordsman* series – two trilogies of pure cinematic bliss.

If these two film trilogies were better-known, Tony Ching Siu-tung would be celebrated like the greats of cinema – Renoir, Rossellini, Mizoguchi, Hawks, and, yes, even Murnau and Griffith. Ching 'demands to be ranked with the most idiosyncratic visionaries in film history', Howard Hampton[7] asserted (*pace The Swordsman 3: The East Is Red*).

Tony Ching Siu-tung[8] has helmed 22 movies (*A Chinese Ghost Story* was only his third feature as director), and has been the action choreographer on some of the very finest action movies of recent times, including *Hero, House of Flying Daggers*, *The Curse of the Golden Flower*, *Shaolin Soccer, Moon Warriors, Peking Opera Blues, New Dragon Gate Inn, City Hunter, The Killer, A Better Tomorrow 2* and *Twinkle Twinkle Little Star* (Ching's first action dir. credits go back to 1972's *The Fourteen Amazons* (his first credit as action director, for a film directed by his father, Ching Gong), and he was an actor in classics such as *Come Drink With Me*, 1966).

---

4 As usual in China, there are many variants on his name, including: Xiaodong Cheng, Cheng Sao Tung, Ching Ting Yee, Cheng Bao-shan, Cheng Hsiao-tung and Shao-Tung Cheng.
   The names in Chinese cinema are confusing: there are at least two and often more for each person: a Chinese name, and an Angelicized name. Further, names in Cantonese and Mandarin are different. There is also some confusion about first names and surnames or family names – names're often printed with the surname first. And a single vowel change can mean a different name: Chang or Cheng, for example. So it's easy to be confused by the many Wongs, Laus, Leungs, Cheungs and Yuens!
5 Other sources say it was Hong Kong.
6 'The world's greatest wire-rig wizard', said Lisa Morton (LM, 88).
7 Quoted in F. Dannen, 338.
8 Cheng Xiaodong in pinyin.

Tony Ching won Golden Horse Awards for *New Dragon Gate Inn* and *Shaolin Soccer*, Hong Kong Film Awards for *The Witch From Nepal, The Swordsman* and *Hero,* as well as the awards for *A Chinese Ghost Story*.

Ching Siu-tung has returned to work in television from time to time. For ex, in 2002 and 2004, he was the action choreographer on the long-running series *The Storm Riders,* also known as *Cloud and Wind.* This Taiwanese production of 45 episodes was based on a comic (known in China as *manhua*) by Ma Wing-shing called *Fung Wan.*

Tony Ching Siu-tung's father is Ching Gong (b. April 7, 1924, also known Cheng Kang), a writer and director at Shaw Brothers. Ching senior was directing Cantonese films occasionally from 1951 onwards, shot 2nd unit for Shaws in the 1960s, became a full director in 1967, and his output (of some 30 titles) includes many swordplay movies. He was very active in the 1950s-1970s as a writer – he's known for films such as *The Magnificent Swordsman* (1968) and *The Fourteen Amazons* (1972). His last film as director was *Gambling Soul* (1992).

Ching junior worked at Shaws as a stuntman,[9] sometimes on his Dad's movies; he grew up on film sets. Later, Ching acted as action director on several of his father's films. (Unfortunately, as with so many Hong Kong movies, many of them are not widely available).

Ching Gong was a writer for many years before directing – he has an impressive list of credits. However, the desire to write didn't transfer to his son – Ching has very few writing credits.

Tony Ching trained for seven years in Peking Opera and in *kung fu* in the Northern Style, at the East Drama School, run by Tang Ti.

＊

Sidenote on the Shaws: the Shaw Brothers Studio at Clearwater Bay in Hong Kong was launched in 1957 by Sir Run Run Shaw (Shao Yifu). Dubbed 'Movie Town', the 49-acre complex included eleven sound stages, fifteen standing sets on the backlot (featuring old Chinese settings), post-production, dubbing and editing facilities, print laboratories, dormitories and apartments for the casts and crews, and its own film school. (Run Run Shaw was in Singapore before this, overseeing distribution and acquiring properties. He came to Canton to take over the business from his brother, Runde).

Shaw Brothers kept players and talent on contracts, as in the Hollywood system (some 1700 workers).[10] The pay was famously low. Altho' the Hong Kong operation was regarded as Shaw Brothers, each brother oversaw companies within the empire. Shaws wasn't just a

---

9 As Ching was small, he sometimes doubled for women.
10 At its height, the Shaw Brothers operation had 1,500 actors and 2,000 staff, an 80,000 wardrobe dept, a drama school (of 120 students), and in-house magazines.

production facility/ studio, it had a distribution network.

Run Run Shaw spent HK $800,000 (= US $103,000) per movie; they were filmed in colour and in widescreen (Shawscope). Shaw was a canny and energetic businessman. He made deals with overseas producers, such as Italian producers, and the British Hammer studio (a famous investment was $7.5 million for foreign rights in the Warner Brothers/ Tandem/ Ladd Company movie *Blade Runner*).

＊

One of Tony Ching Siu-tung's specialities is wire-work (there is plenty in the *Chinese Ghost Story* series); another is swordplay. Ching can fly actors and stunties with a blissful disregard for anything as everyday as gravity. The speed, invention, spontaneity, timing, rhythm, and acrobatic dynamism of Ching's action scenes are truly marvellous. Also worth remarking upon is the visual style of Ching's films: they have a highly romantic, luxurious look, with particular attention to art direction, costumes and textures. His films exploit props and the physical environment to a striking degree (this is true of many Hong Kong action movies). But Ching seems to go further than anyone else in evoking mystery, beauty and romance. Ching is an all-round filmmaker, and his mark is everywhere in his movies. Even amongst many similar films in Hong Kong cinema, Ching's stand out. Ching has said that entertainment is the highest priority for him as a filmmaker – like Tsui Hark, he is a supreme example of the Filmmaker As Showman.

Tony Ching Siu-tung is also a master of visual effects – no doubt he learnt plenty from Tsui Hark and Film Workshop, but visual effects and practical effects are a key ingredient in the Chingian style of filmmaking. If there's a cinematic trick available, Ching will use it. 'I like being unconventional', he remarked.

The movies of Ching Siu-tung foreground the tricks and visual effects of cinema; Western filmmakers who also use this approach include: Orson Welles, Jean Cocteau, Walerian Borowczyk, Sergei Paradjanov, Tim Burton, Vincente Minnelli, Powell & Pressburger, Ken Russell and Francis Coppola. Films of Ching's such as *A Chinese Ghost Story* are filled with visual effects (the influence of producer Tsui Hark is clear in this production).

Only in Hong Kong has the kind of action choreography delivered by Tony Ching and his contemporaries been possible. Nowhere else on this planet has action direction this complicated, this fast, this imaginative and this entertaining, using wires, rigs, harnesses, pulleys, cranes and ropes, been seen in movies.

Ching Siu-tung was promoted to martial arts coordinator in movies in the '70s, and worked in television (at Commercial Television) as a martial arts coordinator (at the invitation of Anthony Leung). Ching was the chief martial arts adviser on the 1979 TV series *Meteor, Butterfly, Sword*. He worked for Rediffusion Television on TV series such as *The Spirit of the Sword* (1978), *It Takes a Thief* (1979), *The Roving Swordsman* (1979), *Reincarnated* (1979), *Reincarnated 2* (1979), *Dynasty* (1980) and *Dynasty 2* (1980).

Tony Ching continued to work in television throughout the 1980s, including Hong Kong Television Broadcast series such as: *Legend of the Condor Heroes* (1983), *The Return of the Condor Heroes* (1983), *The New Adventures of Chor Lau Heung* (1984), *The Duke of Mount Deer* (1984), *The Return of Luk Siu Fung* (1986) and *The New Heaven Sword and Dragon Sabre* (1986). This extensive work in television partly explains the gap of three years between the feature productions *Duel To the Death* and *The Witch From Nepal*.

Tony Ching's first full-length, theatrical film as director was *Duel To the Death* (1983), which was, of course, a *wuxia pian*. Ching's first collaboration with Tsui Hark on a feature film was *Dangerous Encounter – 1st Kind* in 1980, tho' they had already worked together in television.

Tony Ching has moved into North American movies (with *Belly of the Beast* (2003), a Steven Seagal actioner), worked uncredited on *Spider-man* (2002), has choreographed the Indian superhero movie *Krrish* (2006), and the sequels, produced the pop video *L'Âme-Stram-Gram* (1999) for French pop star Mylène Farmer, and contributed to the 2008 Beijing Olympics (at the invitation of director Zhang Yimou).

Tony Ching has been an actor many times, taking lead roles in *Monkey Kung Fu* (1979) and *The Master Strikes* (1980). Ching launched his own production company in 1993, China Entertainment.

Tony Ching Siu-tung's directing credits (22 features up to 2019) include *Dr Wai, The Sorcerer and the White Snake, Jade Dynasty, Wonder Seven, An Empress and the Warriors, Belly of the Beast, The Terracotta Warrior, The Raid* (co-directed), *The Witch From Nepal* and *The Executioners*. Ching's credits as action director (84 films up to 2011!) include *Butterfly Lovers, The Warlords, Shaolin Soccer, Invincible, In the Name of the King, Holy Weapon, Spider-man, Moon Warriors*, the *Royal Tramp* films (sometimes credited with co-direction), *Peking Opera Blues, Krrish, Butterfly and Sword* (sometimes credited with co-direction), *Bloodmoon, Hero, House of Flying Daggers, The Curse of the Golden Flower, The Royal Swordsmen* (TV series), *The Duel, Chinese Odyssey,*

Kung Fu Dunk, City Hunter, Twin Dragons, Future Cops, The Killer, A Better Tomorrow 2, The Storm Riders (a.k.a. *Cloud and Wind*, TV series, 2002/ 2004), and *Twinkle Twinkle Little Star*.

Altho' John Woo, Yuen Woo-ping and Tsui Hark receive many of the accolades from film critics (and fans) for their depiction of action on screen, I am struck with awe at the imagination and magnificence of Tony Ching Siu-tung's work. He is the equal of Tsui, Woo, Yuen *et al*, and in some respects he out-does them (he has also of course worked as an action choreographer for all of the big names in Hong Kong action cinema). For action with a high fantasy component, Ching can't be beat – look at his work in *Hero* or *The House of Flying Daggers* or *Moon Warriors*, for instance. (And let's remember that Ching worked as action director for many Hong Kong directors, including John Woo: one of the reasons that the *Better Tomorrow* movies or *The Killer* are so good is because it's Ching choreographing the action. And it's often the action that critics rave about in those Woo-helmed movies).

Producer Terence Chang said that Tsui Hark and Tony Ching Siu-tung complemented each other: while Tsui was enamoured of the historical pictures from the Shaw Brothers, Ching actually worked on them: 'they complemented each other and were tied together by their shared romantic vision', Chang remarked.

Indeed – of all of Tsui Hark's many, many creative collaborations, the ones with Tony Ching Siu-tung are among the most productive: they seem to have sparked each other to greater imaginative heights, as evinced by the *Chinese Ghost Story* series and the *Swordsman* series (both made in the busy late 1980s/ early 1990s period).

Jeff Yang noted that Tony Ching Siu-tung was about the only director able to work with Tsui Hark consistently, maybe because he got along with Tsui, or because he was happy to let Tsui take all of the glory (2003, 97). Also, directors in Hong Kong are happy to share director credits – most of the major directors have done it.

Maybe Tony Ching Siu-tung was able to accommodate Tsui Hark and his tendency to wade in heavy and strong to a film project and not get freaked out by it. Maybe Ching realized that the movies they were producing were extraordinary (so a bit of aggro didn't matter, and aggro doesn't last anyway). Maybe Ching was easy-going enough (where other filmmakers in this period found it just too difficult to work with Tsui, and some walked out).

Because Tony Ching Siu-tung clearly threw himself 100% into the three *Chinese Ghost Story* movies (and the *Swordsman* movies). These are film productions that literally *roar* with fire and energy and humour and action and sweetness and tenderness and mind-boggling eccentricity. There's *so much* energy on screen, these movies are like a conflagration.

As a director, Ching Siu-tung's career has been a tad uneven: low-points include *Naked Weapon* and *Belly of the Beast*, two mean-spirited films that Ching directed which were not worthy of his talents. However, in 2002 and 2003 Ching also action directed two sublime examples of action cinema: *Hero* and *House of Flying Daggers* (plus the great comedy *Shaolin Soccer*, and the TV series *The Storm Riders*). Soon after that, Ching provided the action direction for *Krrish* and *The Curse of the Golden Flower* (both 2006), and took up the directing reins in 2008 for his masterpiece *An Empress and the Warriors*.

PEKING OPERA.

Tony Ching trained in Peking Opera, a breeding ground for many future Hong Kong and Chinese stars. Peking Opera is known as *jingju* = theatre of the capital. The four performance skills in Peking Opera are *da* (acrobatics and martial skills), *chang* (singing), *nian* (reciting) and *zuo* (acting).

In Chinese Opera, as in many theatrical traditions, men play women's roles (so that only men're on stage). Yam Kin-fai and Pak Suet-sin, for instance, played across the gender divide in the Opera movies of the 1950s and 1960s. In Cantonese Opera, the fighting instructor was called *longhu* (= Dragon-Tiger Master).

The Peking Opera approach to entertainment was characterized thus by Bey Logan:

> extravagant costumes, bright full-face makeup, Olympic-class gymnastics, and both weapon and empty-handed combat, as well as a rich tradition of character, music and drama. (9)

Beijing Opera is the most well-known form of Chinese Opera, but it's not the only one. There are 100s of Opera styles, including Cantonese Opera. Acrobatics, extravagant costumes, make-up, singing, music, and stylized gestures constitute the performance style. Most of the performers have traditionally been men. The heyday of Chinese Opera was the 1930s. Following its decline in the 1960s and 1970s, performers moved into the film industry.

Peking Opera's most famous academy was the one run by Sifu Yu Jim Yuen in Hong Kong, the stern taskmaster who oversaw the performance troupe that included Jackie Chan, Sammo Hung, Yuen Biao, Yuen Tak,

Yuen Wah, Yuen Bun and Yuen Kwai (Corey Yuen). They were known as the Seven Fortunes (tho' there were fourteen of them). Their upbringing at the academy was immortalized in the 1988 movie *Painted Faces* (with Hung playing the *sifu*). As Hung, Chan, Biao and others have often remarked, the regime overseen by Yu was so harsh, no one would believe them! (Even though in the *Painted Faces* movie what the boys have to undergo is pretty tough).

HONG KONG CINEMA IN CRITICISM.

The critical response to Hong Kong cinema in recent years tends to celebrate the same movies, and the same filmmakers are enshrined by the critical academy: Tsui Hark, John Woo, Yuen Woo-ping, Wong kar-wai, Johnny To, Lau Kar-leung, Peter Chan, Stanley Kwan, Corey Yuen Kwai, Sammo Hung, Ronny Yu, Ann Mui, Ringo Lam, and of course Jackie Chan. Tony Ching Siu-tung is part of that list.

The same actors are exalted: Jackie Chan, Jet Li, Chow Yun-fat, Tony Leung, Andy Lau, Leslie Cheung, Sammo Hung, Yuen Biao, Donnie Yen, Stephen Chow, Leon Lai, Jacky Cheung, Simon Lam, Joey Wong, Zhao Wenzhou, Zhao Wei, Chingmy Yau, Anita Mui, Michelle Yeoh, Maggie Cheung, Brigitte Lin, Michelle Reiss, Carrie Ng, Cherie Chung, Rosamund Kwan, Sally Yeh and Zhang Ziyi.

The much-discussed Hong Kong movies include the *Once Upon a Time In China* series, the *Police Story* series, the *Project A* films, the *Armor of God* films, the *Better Tomorrow* series, the *Stormriders* series, the *Fong Sai-yuk/ Legend* series, the *Lucky Stars* series, the *Bride With White Hair* series, the *On Fire* series, *Rouge, Mr Vampire, Rumble In the Bronx, Zu: Warriors From the Magic Mountain, Peking Opera Blues, Painted Faces, Infernal Affairs, Dragons Forever, Drunken Master, Snake In Eagle's Shadow, Iron Monkey, Moon Warriors, The Spooky Bunch, Bullet In the Head, The Killer, Hard-Boiled, God of Gamblers, Chungking Express, Ashes of Time, Aces Go Places, Wicked City, City Hunter, Naked Killer, Sex and Zen*, etc. And of course every critic also cites the Bruce Lee movies, and the Shaw Brothers classics.

Tony Ching has several movies that're part of that list: the *Swordsman* series and the *Chinese Ghost Story* series; he has worked on many classics directed by others, too: *New Dragon Gate Inn, Moon Warriors, A Better Tomorrow 2, Peking Opera Blues* and *The Killer*.

You try finding a study of Chinese cinema or Hong Kong cinema between 1980 and today that *doesn't* mention *any* of the above movies or directors or actors! So it's a narrow group of film classics, in short.

REMAKES AND UPDATES.

Much of Ching Siu-tung's cinema comprises updating and remaking previous movies and stories. Hong Kong filmmakers know their history, and how their industry is constantly recycling and updating earlier movies. As Ching notes, you have to be contemporary, you can't be out of date. As an action director, Ching has worked on many remakes and updates of earlier films: *A Better Tomorrow* was a remake of *Story of a Discharged Prisoner* (a.k.a. *True Colors of a Hero*, 1967), *New Dragon Gate Inn* updated the King Hu-helmed movie of 1967, and *The Warlords* was a remake of *The Blood Brothers* (1973).

In thriving film cultures, like France, Japan, Korea or the U.S.A., it is completely expected and normal to remake movies and stories all the time. *New actors in old stories* is one of the definitions of the Hollywood movie machine in the glory days of the 1930s thru 1960s, but the phrase still sums up a large proportion of the output of any flourishing filmmaking centre. Often, the remakes and updates are simply old stories dressed up in new clothes, with some new gimmicks to help sell them (such as 3-D, or visual effects, or a postmodern spin on an old chestnut).

CHING SIU-TUNG AND TELEVISION.

Television nurtured the New Wave filmmakers in Hong Kong – becoming something like a Shaolin Temple for cinéastes, as critic Law Kar put it. They worked at stations such as C.T.V. (Commercial Television), R.T.H.K. (Radio Television Hong Kong) and T.V.B.[11] (Hong Kong Television Broadcast, Ltd.). Selina Chow, a TV executive, was instrumental in hiring the 'New Wave' filmmakers in television.[12] They were also a film school generation: the New Wave directors studied at film schools abroad partly because they didn't really exist in Asia (the Chinese State film school, Beijing Film Academy, didn't re-open until 1978).

Ching Siu-tung worked a good deal in television, from the 1970s onwards. Before he helmed his first feature, *Duel To the Death* in 1983, Ching had already been an action director for TV shows such as *The Spirit of the Sword* (1978), *It Takes a Thief* (1979), *The Roving Swordsman* (1979), *Reincarnated* (1979), *Reincarnated 2* (1979), *Meteor, Butterfly, Sword* (1979), *Dynasty* (1980) and *Dynasty 2* (1980). Ching returned to television production periodically – in 2002 and 2004, for example, Ching action directed the *Storm Riiders* TV series (a.k.a. *Wind and Cloud*).

---

11 T.V.B. was the television arm of Shaws.
12 Lisa Morton, 221.

TONY CHING SIU-TUNG * 32

THE HONG KONG NEW WAVE.

Ching Siu-tung was not one of the New Wave of Hong Kong filmmakers who went to film school overseas – instead, Ching grew up in the film industry: his father Ching Gong was a film director at Shaws. However, Ching worked on many of the New Wave productions – three in 1980, for example: *The Sword, Dangerous Encounter* and *The Spooky Bunch.*

Many of the Chinese New Wave filmmakers were film school graduates: Ann Hui and Yim Ho studied in London; Tsui Hark in Austin, Texas; and Ringo Lam in Toronto (York University). They studied in the West, or in Western-style institutions in Hong Kong. They could speak English with critics, which no doubt helped, because they'd spent time in the West. And they were familiar with the art film traditions of Europe and the U.S.A.

Following film school, they went to work in television. (Hui, Ho and Tsui were part of the first wave of the New Wave, along with Allan Fong, Patrick Tam, Kirk Wong, and Tony Ching Siu-tung); the second wave included Stanley Kwan, Alex Law, Clara Law, Cheung Yuen-ting, Jacob Cheung, Wong Kar-wai, and Eddie Fong.

The Hong Kong New Wave did not have a style or an approach: it took on aspects of youth: 'school, sex, drugs and other travails of growing up in a materialistic society, misunderstood by parents and adults in authority', according to Stephen Teo (1997, 156).

It was no surprise that many of the first films of the Hong Kong New Wave were thrillers or crime stories – because they are a staple of Hong Kong cinema, and of cinemas the world over, because they tend to be cheap to make, because the genre was versatile, and because a huge proportion of source material was in the crime or thriller genre.

For Stephen Teo, the two strands of the Hong Kong New Wave cinema – realism and genre conventions – developed towards the latter: the New Wavers started out tackling realism but lent towards genre filmmaking (1997, 149). The forms and conventions of genre were updated for modern audiences in the 1980s. (The first official, Hong Kong New Wave film was *The Extras* (1978), but the unofficial film that launched it, according to Cheuk Pak-tong, was *Jumping Ash* (1976). In 1979, some of the first New Wave films included *The Secrets* (dir. Ann Hui), *The Butterfly Murders* (dir. Tsui Hark), *The System* (dir. Peter Yung) and *Cops and Robbers* (dir. Alex Cheung)). By contrast, Ching Siu-tung's first film as director was the high fantasy swordplay movie *Duel To the Death* in 1983.

At the height of the 1990s New Wave, actors and crew were commonly rushing from one movie set to another. Andy Lau Tak-wah slept in his car while filming a movie a month in 1991, and according to rumour making four movies in four locations at the same time. (Chinese filmmakers became geniuses at stretching footage of actors who could only give them a day or so, by using doubles, re-arranging scripts, focussing on reaction shots, etc).

You'll see the same actors and directors in the New Wave of Hong Kong and Chinese cinema, continuing up to the present day. The actors include: Jet Li, Jackie Chan, Brigitte Lin, Tony Leung, Leslie Cheung, Michelle Yeoh Chu-kheng, Zhao Wei, Donnie Yen, Maggie Cheung, Jacky Cheung, Zhang Ziyi, Yuen Biao, Chow Yun-fat, Josephine Siao, Stephen Chow, Gong Li, Rosamund Kwan, Zhao Wenzhou, Kent Cheng, and Xiong Xin-xin.

And directors such as Tsui Hark, Ronny Yu, Ringo Lam, King Hu, Sammo Hung, Zhang Yimou, Ann Hui, Wong Jing, Yuen Woo-ping, Wong Kar-wai, Stanley Tong and John Woo. Tony Ching Siu-tung is part of that group.

The second wave of Hong Kong filmmakers occurred in the mid-1980s, and included filmmakers such as Stanley Kwan (*Rouge, The Actress*), Wong Kar-wai (*Ashes of Time, Chungking Express*), Clara Law (*The Reincarnation of Golden Lotus*), Tony Ching Siu-tung (*The Swordsman, A Chinese Ghost Story*), Mabel Cheung (*An Autumn's Tale*), Lawrence Ah Mon (*Gangs, Queen of Temple Street*), Alex Law (*Painted Faces*), Eddie Fong, and Jacob Cheung.

✳

Hong Kong is a city of seven million or so. The filmmaking community is small: everybody knows or has heard of everyone else. Over its history, the cast and crew of Hong Kong movies would've met many times at the Shaw Brothers' studios at Clearwater Bay, or the Golden Harvest studios in Diamond Hill, or the television studios at Hong Kong Television Broadcast, Ltd. They would visit the same vars and restaurants. Some American filmmakers prefer to shoot outside of L.A., because if you film in Tinseltown everybody knows what you're doing. No chance of avoiding that in Hong Kong!

You'll see the same downtown areas of Hong Kong, the same harbour fronts, the same strips of forest or beaches, and the same standing sets of 19th century China, in movie after movie. (And, with the problems of obtaining film permits, shooting on location on the streets often means guerilla-style filmmaking, which Hong Kong crews are experts at).

Ching Siu-tung on set.

2

ASPECTS OF THE CINEMA OF TONY CHING SIU-TUNG

'MORE POWER!': SOME OF TONY CHING SIU-TUNG'S MOTIFS

Tony Ching Siu-tung's on-set mantra is, 'more power, more power!' Among the many motifs and techniques in Ching's style of action direction are:

• an emphasis on the beauty and flow of bodies in motion (Tony Ching Siu-tung is probably the most painterly of Hong Kong action directors);

• fluttering, flapping robes, banners and flags (fans are continually blowing on a Ching set);

• mass battles – chaotic movement everywhere; typically, someone will bounce on a hidden trampoline across the camera;

• extremely rapid swordplay accompanied by jumps and acrobatic spins, and often moving across the ground, covered in tracking shots;

• the lone swordsman entering the fray, weapon extended, like Superman;

• groups of figures lowered on wires – it might be the heroes arriving at a scene, or henchmen (*Krrish*), or some ghoulish characters (as in *A Chinese Ghost Story*);

• water explosions – multiple fountains of water from oil barrels, often erupting behind a magician (as in the *Chinese Ghost Story* series, *Moon Warriors*, the *Swordsman* films and *Royal Tramp 2*);

• long distance airborne travel – a palanquin complete with footmen hurtling thru the tree-tops at speed;

• ærial flight gags – ninjas[1] flying on kites;

• visual effects – these are everywhere in Tony Ching Siu-tung's cinema, combined with action;

[1] Bey Logan calls the ninjas that regularly pop up in the films of Tony Ching 'Chinjas'.

- charas (often ninja) diving into frame from either side of a rapidly-tracking camera;
  - exiting a scene by soaring upwards and crashing thru a roof;
  - hidden attacks from high above, sword pointing down;
  - horror movie gags (giant tongues);
  - gross-out gags – people or horses[2] split apart; people exploding in a flurry of blood and rags;
  - massive gags and stunts – disintegrating wooden platforms, flying logs, collapsing buildings, crazy monsters, enormous explosions.

ELEMENTS OF CHING SIU-TUNG'S CINEMA

The 22 films directed (and co-directed) by Ching Siu-tung (up to 2019) feature the following elements:

- They all have Chinese casts (with one or two exceptions).
- They all use Hong Kong and Chinese crews.
- They are all set in Asia, and usually in China or Hong Kong.
- They are all Chinese stories (with one or two exceptions).
- They are all produced in China (with the odd overseas trip).
- They draw heavily on Chinese tradition and history.
- About half can be classed as swordplay movies (or *wuxia pian*). The rest are thrillers or action-adventures.
  - Two-thirds are historical movies; one third are contemporary-set.
  - Comedy is a significant element in at least half of the films.
  - All of the films climax with a giant action scene.
  - Ching Siu-tung has action director credits on all of them.

These elements speak for themselves: most of Ching Siu-tung's films have been about China, set in China, with Chinese stories featuring Chinese characters, using Chinese crews and casts, and two-thirds have been historical movies.

---

2 If you love horses and don't like to see them harmed – even if you know it's movie fakery – don't watch Hong Kong action movies! Horses are punched and wrestled to the ground (*An Empress and the Warriors*), decapitated (*Burning Paradise*), pushed down steep slopes (*Seven Swords*), and sliced in two (Tony Ching Siu-tung's films).

Tony Ching Siu-tung told the Hong Kong Film Directors' Guild:

> I like beautiful, romantic things, and have an almost extreme and idealized sense of perfectionism regarding the films I make, and strive to achieve the kind of poeticism found in traditional Chinese paintings.

Keep those things in mind when considering Tony Ching Siu-tung's cinema: romance, idealization, perfection, painting and poetry. (And remember, too, that Ching trained in Peking Opera for 7 years).

Altho' Ching Siu-tung is known as an action director and a film director who showcases action, romance, comedy and a painterly vision are also key elements of his cinema. For instance, his first big hit movie was a romance (*A Chinese Ghost Story*), and romance was an important ingredient in the *Swordsman* films, in *The Terracotta Warrior* and more recent films, such as *An Empress and the Warriors* (which features a lengthy romantic idyll).

Tony Ching Siu-tung said he liked to try new ways of approaching storytelling, and he enjoyed taking on fantasy forms. Why? – 'Because I'm not a normal person. I think it's fun to shoot something different, something unusual'.

When he was asked what the secret was of being a good action director, Tony Ching Siu-tung replied:

> The secret is to stay young. Your ideas can't age with you – although we're getting older, what we film has to feel young. It's not okay to be outdated.

Tsui Hark on action:

> Action is not just by itself; action always comes with a story, it also comes with a style, it comes with extra information about what the director wants to show to the audience. These sorts of things are always with me. (2011)

Tony Leung Siu-hung noted that action choreographers have to imprint their style on a scene: 'All comes from your mind, your imagination. You then have to share it with your assistant. It's the same with Tony Ching Siu-tung; after he's finished working on a choreographed scene, it's eventually Ching Siu-tung's imagination which appears at the end. (A. Lanuque, 2006)

When he's directing, Tony Ching Siu-tung is amongst the actors and crew, not hiding in a video village off to one side. He is interacting directly with the cast, including all of the principals, showing them how to perform the action, often at a micro, beat-by-beat level. (That's partly because an action director can't hide behind a bank of monitors and assistant directors, they have to be in the thick of things). Ching also operates the camera himself, so we are often seeing Ching's own compositions and camera moves in his films.

One of Tony Ching's early assistants, Tony Leung Siu-hung, remarked: 'I really admire some of his creations. He's got no limitations! He really knows how to use camera angles and camera movement' (A. Lanuque, 2006).

One of the hallmarks of Tony Ching Siu-tung's form of action cinema is excessive, fantastical violence, action so quick, intense and extreme it borders on the comical. Such as Ching's penchant for warriors being ripped in half by swords in mid-air, or bodies being sliced apart from head to toe and the two halves falling away. In a Ching swordplay flick, victims are decapitated with a single swish of the blade and the heads spin thru the air.[3] It all happens so rapidly, and without showers of blood, it seems 'unrealistic'. But how can you test 'realism'? – like, when was the last time you saw a warrior in full battle armour being torn to pieces by a slashing swordsman – while both of them were in mid-air, at night, in a forest?

Wire-work: the signature image of Tony Ching Siu-tung's cinema is a swordsman flying through the air, sword arm extended, robes fluttering in the breeze. Ching has several motifs in his wire-work which recur: one is flying several characters at the same time, in groups (a great example occurs in the *Chinese Ghost Story* movies. What you don't see are forty guys off-stage hauling on the ropes and cables,[4] and the enormous cranes).[5] Another is a gentle, romantic flight over a long distance (often it's two lovers, embracing and smiling at each other. Sometimes they're on horseback). Another is the rapid exit from a interior scene by zooming upwards, smashing through the roof. When a swordsman enters or exits a scene of combat, they always spin quickly in the air, and also dive and tumble (these moves are very Peking Opera-ish, emulating the way that performers make their entrance on stage. A flashy entrance is a big deal in Peking Opera). Halfway thru a sword fight, a warrior will disappear – then they materialize far above the opponent, and descending swiftly, sword arm stretched out.

3 Pre-dating *Sleepy Hollow* (1999) by many years.
4 It requires several people to fly one actor.
5 Photos or detailed descriptions of just how Ching and his crews achieve their effects are hard to find – because they want to keep it secret.

Inanimate objects: the wire-work in Hong Kong action movies is puppeteering the environment extensively: walls topple, tables spin, benches are smashed apart, ladders, columns and logs fly thru the air as weapons, and entire buildings collapse. In a Hong Kong action flick, the whole environment can come alive. Special wire-work in Tony Ching Siu-tung's output includes his penchant for very extravagant deaths – victims are torn apart by sword slices or magic.

While we're celebrating the outrageous stunts and wire-work of Hong Kong action directors, we must also remember that they have whole teams of very clever engineers and talented craftsmen who can build all of those rigs, cable systems, scaffolding, cranes and all the rest (and a bunch of burly guys to hang into the wires and the ropes). Stunt gags require plenty of prep work – building breakaway sets or props, for ex, or manœuvring the cranes into the right position. It's one thing you *don't* see in any 'making of' documentaries – just how those complex rigs work. (Partly, perhaps, because sometimes film crews like to keep one or two tricks of the trade secret).

Ninjas! No other film director, in the West, the East, the North, the South – or on Mars – has been so crazy about ninjas and putting them on film (outside of *anime*). Tony Ching just adores those mysterious, black-clad warriors of stealth and cunning. If there's a chance to include some tumbling, running, super-soldiers in a scene, Ching will take it. (And Ching is especially fond of inventing all sorts of incredible gags for the *shinobi* to perform). It's a pity, perhaps, that Ching hasn't (yet) directed a whole movie about *shinobi*. (If you were going to produce a live-action version of a Japanese ninja tale, such as *Naruto,* Ching is definitely your man).

One of Tony Ching's talents is to make actresses look fantastic when they're in action. Hong Kong cinema has a long tradition of female fighters, but many of the actresses in Ching's films (and others of the 1970s through 2010s) are not professional or trained martial artists (and neither are most of the men). But Ching can make them look incredible: Maggie Cheung, Anita Mui, Sharla Cheung, Fennie Yuen, Zhang Ziyi, Kelly Chen, Michelle Reiss, Brigitte Lin, Flora Cheung, Meng Meiqi and Tang Yixin.

Although the Hong Kong film business is male-oriented and masculinist, like all film centres around the world, some of the movies of Tony Ching and his contemporaries have been written by women. Sandy Shaw Lai-king, for instance, wrote *The Heroic Trio, The Executioners* and *Dr Wai* (Shaw's other credits include *Once a Cop, My Father Is a Hero, The Mad Monk, Justice, My Foot!, Twinkle Twinkle Little Star* and *It Runs In the Family. Some of those movies were directed by or starred John Woo and

Stephen Chow).

Many of the movies that Tony Ching works on are cast young – film producers often have an eye on attracting a young audience. Being young, the actors don't have much – or any – experience with complicated stunts, or doing wire-work, or co-operating with visual effects (effects that are created in front of the camera or added later in post-production).

Thus, one of Tony Ching's jobs on any new movie production is training – to teach the young actors how to work with cables and rigs and visual effects. (This is a key reason why some film directors like to work with the same people, who're often veterans of many movies, precisely because they *don't* have to go through the explanations and training each time).

If you look at the movies that Tony Ching has chosen to do as an action choreographer, you can see that he is one of those people who thrives on new challenges and working with young people. As he says, films and filmmakers have to stay up to date.

All of Ching Siu-tung's movies as director, and most of those as action director, climax with a giant battle. No matter what the movie has been about, the ending is always a massive sequence of incredible action.

Tony Ching Siu-tung doesn't employ slow motion nearly as much as some of his contemporaries. And some of the directors he's worked for as an action choreographer over-use slo-mo, which spoils the sequences he's devised. (However, having said that, I've just watched the group of movies made in the early 2000s again – *Invincible, Hero, Naked Weapon* and *Belly of the Beast* – which do employ a good proportion of slo-mo per fight).

Many Chinese action movies employ slow motion, and also step-motion. Indeed, step-motion (a.k.a. step-printed film) occurs just as much as slow motion. True slow motion is of course filmed on the set, with the camera running at higher speeds (48 frames per second or 96 f.p.s. being typical speeds). But step-motion is created after the fact, in the editing room and by optically treating the celluloid in the processing lab (where you can also select different kinds of step-motion). Sometimes Chinese action movies play whole beats of an action scene in step-motion, but with heightened sound effects (and usually a big music cue). Incidentally, Tony Ching often films action scenes slightly under-cranked (at 22 f.p.s.), to give them an extra ziiip.

Let's not forget, either, that *comedy* and *humour* is *absolutely funda-mental* to the action direction of Tony Ching Siu-tung. Oh yes, Ching is not a dour, old curmudgeon who never cracks a smile, who never allows a smidgen of humour to infect movies with wall-to-wall grimness and frowningness.

In fact, many of Tony Ching Siu-tung's finest works in action are comedies, or feature comedy as a key ingredient, like *Shaolin Soccer*, *A Chinese Ghost Story*, *City Hunter, Krrish, Jade Dynasty* and *Heroic Trio;* And his two famous series – the *Swordsman* series and *Chinese Ghost Story* series – are stuffed with humour. Ching has worked many times with comedy directors and actors such as Wong Jing and Stephen Chow.

For some critics, the emphasis in the marketing of Chinese and Hong Kong movies in the West on action, violence, energy and weirdness has put it back into a pigeon-hole, which ignores many other kinds of cinema coming out of Hong Kong, Shanghai or Beijing.

Comedy is certainly one of the staple (and lucrative) genres of Hong Kong cinema, often ignored or derided by Western critics. For instance, between 1950 and 1970, 25% of films from Canton were comedies (of the 3,000 films produced). An industry like Hong Kong only produces that many comedy movies if it knows they are going to find an audience. And they do.

In the West, in the U.S.A., martial arts films, action films and art films are the biggest financial successes (and with the film critics), but in Hong Kong, it's *comedies* that have ruled the local box office. Nine out of the ten bestsellers in the 1980s and 1990s in Canton and Taiwan were comedies. Often they are combined with other genres: vampire comedies, *kung fu/* martial arts comedies, cookery comedies, gambling comedies, historical comedies, detective/ thriller comedies, etc. (But comedies, as we know, are hampered by problems of translation, dubbing, and cultural specificity. So that giant stars in Asia like Stephen Chow or Michael Hui are still largely unknown in the West. Instead of Adam Sandler or Ben Stiller, try some Stephen Chow for a change).

❀

Tony Ching Siu-tung is not a screenwriter, other people write the scripts that he directs (Ching has only two credits as screenwriter – *Duel To the Death* and *Wonder Seven*). He is also not a film producer (he has only 4 producer credits and 2 writing credits). Ching comes to cinema from the practical, organizational side of things, graduating from acting and stuntwork to action choreography and direction.

Tony Ching is thus not an *auteur*, in the manner of filmmakers who write and direct (and also produce) their own material. Much of the time, Ching is a director for hire, someone who's offered scripts and projects – which's how most directors operate (the proportion of film directors who write their own material *and* originate it *and* it's not based on any existing property is *very* small).

Yet Tony Ching Siu-tung's stamp is all over the movies he directs, and his action choreography is instantly recognizable when he works on other productions (especially his style of fantastical swordplay). Certainly, Ching is as natural filmmaker as any in film history. And tho' not an *auteur* with issues he explores in film after film, he does have recurring themes and motifs. Romance is uppermost, as is action. If something can be expressed in choreography (not always action or military choreography), Ching will try it. This is the Peking Opera form of filmmaking, where gesture and movement, alongside costume and make-up, do the storytelling. In Peking Opera, as soon as an actor steps onto the stage, the audience knows who they are by their clothes, accessories and make-up – and their movement and gestures. Applied to movies, the Peking Opera approach is all over Hong Kong cinema (and Chinese cinema), and informs much of Ching's work (he trained in it for seven years).

Tony Ching Siu-tung is not known for being a firebrand political filmmaker, tho' there are numerous, self-conscious political statements throughout his work.

He's not known for delivering complex narrative structures, but his films are, like many movies, actually more complex narratively than they first appear. This applies to so many movies: film critics routinely call a plot 'simple', when it clearly isn't. Parts of a plot may seem simple (revolving around single words like 'revenge' or 'romance'), but how the plots are portrayed is seldom simple (even in Hong Kong cinema, where the quality of the screenplays is derided in Western film criticism).

Many actors and crew are happy to work with Ching Siu-tung, partly because they know that their work will be seen potentially by millions of people. Which's what it's all about. They also know that Ching is one of the great talents in action cinema, and that working on a Ching movie raises their own profile. And Ching will make them look very cool.

Also, movies directed by Ching Siu-tung will get released, a lot of people will see them, they won't be re-cut by studios or backers (or censored – usually), and there's a good chance that the marketing and promotion will be effective, and that they will be reviewed, and that they will have an after-life on TV, cable, DVD, etc. (All actors, East, or West, have been in or know about projects that were sat on for years, or never got released, or were distributed poorly, or were hacked about by distributors or studios.)

ASPECTS OF CHINESE ACTION MOVIES.

The following items are some of the aspects of Chinese and Hong Kong action movies, compared to Western (North American and European) action cinema:

• Acrobatic and athletic: one of the most obvious differences between Chinese and Western action cinema is the emphasis on acrobatic movement, on portraying the body in movement in space, on action like dance choreography and ballet, and action like circus performers, trapeze artists, jugglers, and street entertainers. (In Western choreography, acrobatics is part of the 'flash').

• Naturalism/ realism vs. fantasy: even the most 'realistic' of Chinese action movies contains more fantasy than most Western fantasy movies! Chinese action filmmakers never feel constrained to stick to notions such as 'realism' or 'naturalism'. A Chinese action scene can fly off in all sorts of directions.

• Humour: even in the grisliest and nastiest and most violent scenes in a Chinese action movie there might be humour. This is one aspect of Asian cinema that really jars with Western audiences, who like their serious moments to stay serious. Asian filmmakers (and Japanese animators in particular) are happy to mix in humour with drama, to pop melodramatic bubbles with laughs.

• Editing: Chinese action movies tend to be cut faster than Western action movies; but they don't resort to four angles of the same action (an irritating recent trend in Western cinema and TV).[6]

• Pacing: Chinese action movies are *much* faster, in terms of storytelling and pacing, than Western action movies. Yet there are many scenes where moments are expanded way beyond the requirements of the drama (emotional moments, for example, or, most famously, big action scenes which go far beyond the dramatic requirements of the scene).

• Cutting: the cuts occur in a different place in a Chinese action movie compared to its Western counterparts, and there is a different emphasis of the flow of movement, rhythm and of timing.

• The camera is very wild in Chinese action cinema: it doesn't stay on the horizontal, it is often tilted, it is often continually moving, and it is often at a low angle.

• The freedom of the camera: Chinese action filmmakers emphasize a feeling of total freedom to put the camera *anywhere* on the set.

• Framing: Chinese action movies tend to compose each shot for a specific movement.

---

[6] One reason is they haven't got *time* to film four shots of someone raising a glass to their mouth to drink.

• Shots: Chinese action cinema tends to construct its action scenes using short, individual shots, each one tied to a specific beat or movement or gesture, rather than master shots. In the West, master shot filmmaking is a standard approach, with the crew then moving in for close-ups, medium shots and inserts.

• The Chinese action team will film each individual moment, then turn around the camera and the lights to shoot the reverse angles, then go back again to continue with the first side.

• Whole body shots: Chinese action movies typically include all of the body in their action scenes, rather than chopping it up into bits (a frustrating tendency in Western action cinema).

• Some shots are set up to be wildly over-the-top.

• Slow motion is everywhere (and at times filmmakers have had to slow down the martial arts performers because they are too fast for the camera to record their movements).

• Movement and reaction: Chinese action cinema is absolutely brilliant at evoking the impact of hits, the reactions of bodies in movement, the thud of a stunt guy on the ground. In Chinese action cinema, you see people *really* slamming into each other or the wall or the floor. There is always time taken for the reactions and the consequences of a particular movement or gesture.

• Visual effects: most Chinese action movies are filmed live, on the set, without resorting to post-production techniques. By contrast, since the 1990s, Western movies often include a lot of post-production technology. Budgetary reasons are key here, because Chinese action movies have a far lower budget than North American action movies (and visual effects are *very* expensive).

• In front of the camera: Chinese action cinema recreate everything in front of the camera, and emphasize atmospheric elements, such as wind machines, smoke machines, fire, explosions, candles, and a host of wire effects and practical effects.

• Wirework: Chinese action filmmakers are without question the masters of using cables and movement of any cinema anywhere.

• Movement is much bigger and freer in Chinese action cinema compared to Western action cinema: bodies float, spin, leap and contort to an extraordinary degree in Chinese action cinema.

• Props: no filmmaking centre uses props as imaginatively as Hong Kong film crews (with a star like Jackie Chan, one of the all-time masters at deploying props in a fight scene).

• Weapons: in a Chinese action movie, anything in the immediate surroundings can be used as a weapon (including clothes and props like hats and umbrellas).

• Sound: Chinese movies tend to be filmed without live sound. The sounds that are added later mix punches and whooshes very high, but only use a few channels of sound; the movies also deploy sound effects in a different, highly stylized and definitely non-realistic manner. Western action movies, if they have the time and budget, often cram action scenes with large quantities of sounds, which tend to promote 'realism'/ 'naturalism' (and fight with the music).

• Budgets: Hong Kong movies in the 1980s typically had budgets between US $100,000 and US $1,000,000.[7] The New Wave cinema of the early 1990s helped lead to rising costs, sometimes up to US $4 million (which was regarded as big budget), tho' around US $1.2 million was typical (as was $650,000 – which was the budget of *A Chinese Ghost Story*). Needless to say, these are *very* low budgets compared to Western and Northern American budgets (similar American movies would cost 20 or 30 times more. When you see what Hong Kong filmmakers can do with 1.2 million US dollars, it is simply astounding).

SCRIPTS.

Almost all Hong Kong movies employ conventional narrative structures, including those of Ching Siu-tung. Altho' a common view among Western critics is that Hong Kong movies ignore conventional script structures, and focus on, say, action at the expense of narrative form, in fact they adhere to conventional structures. First acts climax just where you'd expect, for instance, and the finales begin right on cue.

Instead of applying the three-act model to all movies, a better way of thinking of acts in film scripts is to see them as 25-30 minutes narrative units (following Kristin Thompson in her book *Storytelling In the New Hollywood*). Thus, a two-hour movie will have *four*, not *three* acts (otherwise, you'd have a middle act lasting an hour). However, in Hong Kong, the industry usually releases films of 85-90 minutes, so that, yes, they are *three-act movies*. (And thus, for the action movies of Hong Kong, the *second act* is the big challenge – because any decent action movie can deliver a couple of great action scenes in the first act, and a Big Finale for the third act. But coming up with something in the middle which keeps the movie (and the audience) afloat is trickier).

One of the pluses of Chinese action cinema is that it tends to come in at 80 or 90 minutes. Whereas Western action movies of recent times tend to add an extra half-act or another whole act (i.e., 15 minutes or 25-30

7 The budget for *The Big Boss*, a 1971 Bruce Lee picture, was $50,000.

minutes) to a movie, so they feel bloated and over-blown, Chinese action movies wind up the story in an hour-twenty or an hour-thirty. Because we've got people to meet afterwards, right? And dinner dates! And more movies to see! And *things to do*. Life in Hong Kong, for many citizens, is fast-paced, so a 2h 20m movie is simply *too long*.

Thus, Hong Kong and Chinese action movies are based on a three-act model – with each act running the customary 25-30 minutes. Altho' some critics complain that Hong Kong/ Chinese movies (in any genre) don't have decent scripts or stories, they do. In fact, they conform very much to traditional narrative structures. The first act, for example, is as conventional as in cinema from anywhere else.

MORE ON THE NARRATIVE STRUCTURE OF HONG KONG MOVIES.

Hong Kong movies are generally three-act movies running 80-90 minutes. The first act is typically the regular length (25-30 minutes), but the second act in an action movie is often shorter (20-25 minutes, rather than 25-30 minutes). This is partly because the second act usually explores characterization, back-stories and subplots, which can take a movie too far from action (it's also because the second act is by far the most challenging to write). Thus, the third and final act in an action movie might run for 35-40 minutes – partly because action movies are all about action and climaxes.

An action movie will typically have three big action set-pieces and three additional, smaller set-pieces – this applies to Hollywood action movies as well as Hong Kong action movies:

Act 1 climax
Act 2 climax
Act 3 climax
In addition, there will be further action sequences:
• The opening scene.
• Halfway thru act one.
• Halfway thru act two.

The finale of act three is often a reprise of the first act finale (on a bigger scale, with more at stake). The act two action set-piece might push the heroes back, have the villains triumphant for a moment, with all being staked in the final showdown. (They might steal the MacGuffin, or kidnap one of the heroes).

Action movies which open with an action set-piece sometimes use it to introduce the characters, and sometimes it will be a stand-alone sequence. After it, the exposition is delivered, as well as the narrative set-up or quest. This will be played out in the act 1 climax.

The action sequence halfway thru act one is often a reversal of fortunes for the heroes (it might split them up or injure one of them). If the movie didn't start with action, this is usually the first big action scene.

The action sequence halfway thru act two is often a chase or a raid or a heist – something to bring the heroes and the villains together. But nobody is a clear winner, and no one is sacrificed (sometimes more action scenes are added to act two).

POLITICS.

The social-political backgrounds of many Hong Kong historical pictures (including those of Tony Ching) can be reduced to simple components, like:

Hong Kong	versus	Mainland China
Capitalism		Communism
Westernization		Eastern values
The new		The old
Modernity		Tradition

And a good deal of the political and ideological content of historical Chinese movies boils down to simple dramatic oppositions:

West = technology (bad) ⋯ East = tradition (good)
West = guns (bad) ⋯ East = martial arts (good)
West = modern medicine (bad) ⋯ East = Chinese medicine (good)
West = exploitation (bad) ⋯ East = mercantile capitalism (good)
West = individualism (bad) ⋯ East = communities (good)

Thus, in film criticism of Hong Kong and Chinese cinema, the same simple oppositions are often employed:

Hong Kong	People's Republic of China
Hong Kong	Beijing
Hong Kong	North America
Hong Kong	Britain
Capitalism	Communism
Right-wing	Left-wing

Chinese culture	Western culture
Home	Exile
China	Chinatowns around the world
Chinese	Foreigners

So it's not only the *movies* that offer 'simplified' versions of politics, the *critics* do too.

CHING AND CHINA.

As an action director, Ching Siu-tung has overseen the action on many Western and non-Chinese productions; but his movies as director have tended to gravitate towards Chinese or Asian subject matter. Most of Ching's movies as director have been set in China, or are about Chinese characters. (And when he's directing a North American production, such as *Belly of the Beast*, the story is brought to Asia). As with the films of Tsui Hark, there is a celebration of Chinese tradition and culture in Ching's movies as director.

Stephen Teo, one of the better critics on Chinese cinema, pointed out that Tsui Hark's movies employ some of the icons and clichés of Chinese culture (such as acupuncture, martial arts, Peking Opera), in order to help make the movies appealing to outsiders. Yes – but as Tsui himself has noted, in the New Wave of Hong Kong cinema, the filmmakers were producing movies for the *local market*, and *not* for the global market (that came later).

This also applies to Ching Siu-tung's films, which celebrate traditional Chinese culture and practices. It's true that you could see that as a way of presenting the clichés and icons of China back to the home audience (just as every American cowboy flick contains numerous iconic elements which sell the Western/ frontier lifestyle back to the American audience).

Stephen Teo also talks of 'cultural nationalism', more an emotional desire among Chinese people living abroad for Chinese culture. Chinese nationalism, Teo asserts, is found everywhere in Chinese cinema, from *kung fu* flicks to New Wave films, from Mandarin historical epics to Cantonese melodramas (1997, 110-1). In the *kung fu* movies of the 1970s, Teo identified an abstract nationalism in which *kung fu* heroes were using traditions (often from Shaolin) to fight foreign Manchus to restore the Chinese race (1997, 113).

Ching Siu-tung doesn't go as far as Tsui Hark in celebrating Chinese culture and society (that is one of Tsui's passions), but Tsui has certainly been a huge influence on Ching's form of cinema, and the cinematic nationalism in Tsui's work has definitely inspired Ching, too.

WUXIA PIAN.

Some eleven of Tony Ching's 22 films as director (from 1983-2019) can be classed as swordplay movies or *wuxia pian* (and also a good proportion of his films as action director). Thus, Ching can be regarded as one of the great experts of recent times in depicting swordplay on screen.

Wuxia[8] means swordsman/ martial fighter/ knight-errant (*wu* = military or armed; *xia* = hero, chivalrous. Known as *Mo hap* in Canontese. *Pian* = movies). [9] Thus, *wuxia pian* were swordplay pictures, and they tended to be filmed in Mandarin (shifts in the popularity of Mandarin versus Cantonese have occurred in the industry over the years).[10] *Kung fu* films referred to fist fighting, were usually made in Cantonese (with the *Wong Fei-hung* movies as the typical local product). There's a North (Mandarin) vs. South (Cantonese) divine, too.

Wuxia movies were regarded as more historical and 'authentic' than *kung fu* movies; their trademarks included fantasy, the supernatural, performers flying,[11] 'Palm Power' (lightning bolts from the hands in the Taoist tradition), and visual effects. David Desser defined swordplay movies as 'period films, historical epics, mythological tales of magic, or action-spectaculars with colorful costumes' (2002, 31). *Kung fu* movies (from Canton) tended to be more 'realistic', emphasizing training and the body.

Jiangzhu means 'rivers and lakes': the term goes back at least to the 12th century and *The Water Margin* novel. *Jiangzhu* refers to the 'martial world' (and *wulin* to the 'martial forest'), in which the code of honour, of chivalry, of brotherhood, prevails. It's the code of living honourably that's invoked in the *jiangzhu*.

The *jiangzhu* and the *wulin*, the wandering world of a China that never really existed, is a mythical realm that Tony Ching has explored many times.

MORE ON *WUXIA PIAN.*

The genres of Chinese movies in the 1920s were largely defined by the Shaw Brothers (then known as Tianyi Film Company). Shaws was

8 *Wuxia*, according to director Chang Cheh, comes from *wu* = martial arts, and *xia* = chivalry.
9 Some titles of Hong Kong and Chinese movies are vague and generic – you'll see these words crop up time and again: *legend, story, hero, cop, dragon, weapon, dagger, sword, swordsman, warrior, butterfly, gambler,* etc.
10 Martial arts movies shifted in the early 1970s to Mandarin cinema, as Cantonese dwindled to nearly nothing in 1971-72. Martial arts movies, in Mandarin, dominated the box office. (Cantonese cinema declined in the middle to late 1960s, down to nearly nothing by 1972: 35 Cantonese films in 1970... in 1971, only one film... and in 1972, not a single one).
11 The powers of the floating warriors in *wuxia* films come from their martial arts skills, their *chi* – but they're not supernatural or superhuman powers.

founded in 1925 by Runjie Shaw. The popular genres of the time were *wuxia pian* (swordplay epics), *guzhuang pian* (classical, Chinese costume dramas), and *baishi pian* (historical movies).

Wuxia pian rapidly became popular in the 1920s: 250+ films were produced between 1928 and 1930. One of the most famous was *The Burning of Red Lotus Temple*[12] (Zhang Shichuan, 1928), regarded as the first martial arts masterpiece, which led to 18 sequels in 3 years. In the 1950s, Shaws was making fifty+ swordplay pictures a year. That meant they were releasing a film a week – incredible productivity – and most were in the martial arts genre.

Wuxia pian are typically set in ancient times, often in dynasties and courts, with chivalrous knights. The swordplay genre was associated with the Mainland, with Shanghai, while *kung fu* was a Southern, Hong Kong form. The *kung fu* genre is more 'realistic', often set in the Qing Dynasty, with foreigners as the villains. The heroes of Southern, *kung fu* movies include Wong Fei-hung and Fong Sai-yuk. When a swordsman is about to perform one of their special techniques, they often announce it: 'Flying Sword!'

COSTUMES.

The films of Ching Siu-tung are costume dramas even when they're set in the present day. Chinese, historical movies, historical martial arts movies and *wuxia pian* foreground *clothes* and *costumes*. Outlandish costumes are pretty much mandatory in a Chinese, historical movie, and of course this is also a big part of the Peking Opera tradition. Bright colours, tons of red and gold, rich blues and the brilliant yellows of Buddhism, are everywhere in Chinese, historical movies. And when it comes to depicting royalty or wealth, out come the luxurious frocks, the braid and embroidery, with an obsessive attention to detail (and as many action movies focus on guys, the costume, hair and make-up people seize upon the one or two female actresses with enthusiasm, lavishing attention on them). Purely as displays of costume design, Chinese, historical movies (and many action flicks), are sumptuous. And the films of Ching are some of the finest – one of his hallmarks is a feeling for flowing clothing flapping in the breeze as a swordsman (or swordswoman) makes yet another flying leap.

The wardrobe is also a significant ingredient in the action in a Chinese, historical movie: sometimes characters use clothing to attack opponents (Wong Fei-hung rushing thru a street brawl, for instance, using his jacket to whack people, in *Once Upon a Time In China 3*). In flying scenes,

---

12 It was adapted from the martial arts novel *Legend of Strange Heroes*.

clothes're whipped by high wind, with the sound of flapping, twisting clothing mixed high (the sound of the wind is one of the fundamental sounds of the mysterious and the supernatural – not only in cinema, but anywhere). The shapes that the clothing makes are beautiful (especially in slow motion). The layers of loose, richly-hued clothing recalls the costumes that the Virgin Mary wears in Renaissance paintings in the West: painters in Europe in the 1400s-1600s had to learn how to depict robes and cloaks with deep, shadowy folds; it was part of the mythology of Christian art. And angels in Renaissance art also had billowing robes, emphasizing their spiritual energy as they descend from the heavens down to Earth).

Clothes are part of the stances and motion of martial arts, of course: flying scenes feature clothes flapping and billowing; in fights on the ground, clothes are grabbed, or they twist around bodies, or're used as weapons; when Jet Li's Wong Fei-hung prepares to battle, he flicks his outer garments back around his right leg, to leave room for movement.

And along with costumes, the hair and make-up in Chinese, historical movies is technically dazzling, but often also extravagant. There's no holding back in some of the fantastical, historical movies, which take place in the *jiangzhu*, the mythical China of yore. Then beards become so long you can trip over them, and wigs become so hairy they become a character in themselves (in fantasy flicks like *The Bride With White Hair* series, hair is a series of weapons in itself).

TEXTURES.

It's common in Hong Kong cinema to add textures in front of the camera, using practical effects: smoke is everywhere, for instance. Smoke in Hong Kong cinema is not a pretty effect that drifts in the background of a scene to enhance the lighting – it is used as a setting in itself, a real, physical presence in the scenes. Sometimes smoke provides the whole environment of a scene (and, yes, sometimes that billowing smoke is used to hide things). Items such as dust, earth, and leaves are thrown in front of the camera just before a take (sometimes petals, feathers, and dripping water). On a Tony Ching set, electric fans are always near the camera – clothes must flap and billow. And if it's a calm night, those fans will add the essential movement. (All sorts of fans – handheld, desk fans, larger fans, fans blowing down tubes to get the air close to the actors, etc.)

Hong Kong cinema developed the Akira Kurosawa School of Filmmaking – plenty of natural, elemental material on screen – rain, fire, smoke, wind, leaves, torchlight, candlelight, and more fire and more rain. Creating those textures also means filming outdoors in sometimes tough conditions (plus many night shoots). It means leading the production team up mountains and across rivers. And for the actors it means quite a bit of hardship (luxurious trailers are *not* usually part of a Hong Kong film production!).

To achieve those Kurosawan effects requires stamina, determination, and, perhaps above all, patience[13] (plus the resources of a fully-equipped studio with its technical staff). This is perfectionist filmmaking, getting every detail right, composing scenes and frames teeming with incident and gesture.

AVAILABILITY

A *major* problem with approaching the cinema of any Hong Kong or Chinese film director is availability. You will stumble into the issue of availability as soon as you try to see anything other than the movies released in the Western world. Most of the films (and TV work) directed or action directed by Ching Siu-tung were produced for a Chinese market: the markets of Hong Kong and Mainland China are absolutely crucial.[14] This doesn't mean, tho', that the movies travel outside of China, either in their original form or in dubbed versions.

The language issue – Cantonese, Mandarin, English, whatever – is a minor one compared to general availability (subtitling is yet another issue). It's true that some of the key works directed by Ching Siu-tung are easy to obtain in the West – the *Swordsman* series, for instance, or *An Empress and the Warriors*.

But many movies are not easily available in the West, such as: *The Witch From Nepal, The Terracotta Warrior, The Longest Day, Conman In Tokyo* and *Belly of the Beast*. And gems of China cinema that Ching action-directed, like *Peking Opera Blues,* should be available in supermarket racks like Disney cartoons.

Even some of movies featuring big stars such as the two Chows – Chow Yun-fat and Stephen Chow (Chow Sing-chi) are not easily obtainable

---

13 Patience may be the number one requirement for a film director – the dogged determination to wait until you get what you're after.
14 Hence, Hong Kong films are usually released with a Cantonese and a Mandarin soundtrack, which's the norm in Chinese cinema.

in the Western world. You should be able to find *Royal Tramp* or *Fight Back To School* anywhere.

That means that plenty of Tony Ching's films as an action director of the 1970s are not widely available, nor his films as an actor. Consequently, some movies directed by Ching Siu-tung, have not been explored fully in this study, including many released before 1980.

The issue of availability affects many celebrated filmmakers – you simply can't find many of their key works. The issue of quality is another consideration: many movies are only available in substandard prints, with bad soundtracks, or in butchered versions (some Hong Kong movies look like they were copied from beat-up release prints that have been kicking around Central for years, then re-dubbed onto video and back again). Despite new distribution systems like the internet, or streaming, or DVD and Blu-ray (or older ones like video, or broadcasting on television), it's amazing how many jewels of cinematic art remain in limbo, or are lost, or can only be bought in crappy versions from dodgy, one-eyed former Buddhist monks in the scuzzy end of town (for extortionate prices).

Another issue is that the international and Western versions of Hong Kong and Chinese movies sometimes change the following: the music; the dialogue; the scripts (scripts are rewritten during dubbing); add new sound mixes; and whole scenes are dropped.

Thus often the Western/ international cuts of Asian movies are *not* in the form the filmmakers preferred. Tsui Hark, for instance, has complained many times that distributors have altered his movies for releases overseas.

The practice of dubbing the sound on afterwards in Chinese movies also extends to the stars: it was many years before Chinese movie audiences heard the real voices of Jackie Chan and Jet Li, for instance. Another consequence of dubbing is that the same group of actors tend to be heard in every movie. For international releases, scenes are often added, or cut, and music is altered, as is dialogue.

For research online, the Hong Kong Movie Database and Hong Kong Cinemagic are excellent (they have photos of the cast and crew, for instance – very helpful when Chinese movies are filled with unusual names (and alternative names and multiple spellings) in both Mandarin and Cantonese).

Making Jade Dynasty (2019), this page and over.

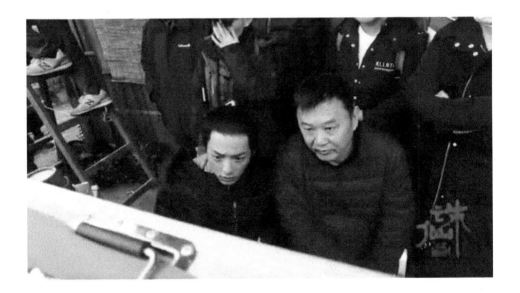

小战战与河水结下了深刻的革命友谊

[是他抢我的棍子]

PART TWO
TONY CHING SIU-TUNG
AS DIRECTOR

1

DUEL TO THE DEATH

Sang Sei Kyut

INTRO.

Duel To the Death (*Sang Sei Kyut* a.k.a. *Sheng Si Jue,* 1983) was produced by Raymond Chow Man-wai. Exec. producer: Catherine Chang Si-Kan. Production company: Paragon Films. Distributor: Golden Harvest. Script: David Lai, Manfred Wong and Ching Siu-tung. Action dirs.: Ching and Lau Chi Ho. Music: Siu-Tin Lai. DPs: Yu-Tang Li and Hung Kuan Liu. Editing: Peter Cheung. Sound: Shao Lung Chou and Ping Wong. Art dirs.: Mai Ho and Chin Sam. Costumes: Kung Chuan-Kai and Chu Sheng-Shi. Make-up: Chan Kok-Hong. Released Jan 13, 1983. 86 mins.

In *Duel To the Death* there are two main characters:

• Hashimoto, the Japanese[1] samurai (Norman Chui Siu-keung)[2]

• Bo Ching[3] Wan, the Shaolin swordsman (Damian Lau Chung-yan)

And three secondary charas:

• Sing Lam, the warrior princess (Flora Cheung)[4]

• Master Han, her stern patriarch of a father (Paul Chang-chung)

• Kenji, the wily Shogun operative (Eddy Ko-hung)

Also in the cast[5] were: Yeung Chak-lam, Kwan Yung-moon, Casanova Wong, Hon Gwok-choi, Stephan Yip, Wilson Tong, Gam San, and Cheng Mang-ha. (Some of the cast, such as Norman Chui, had already worked

---

[1] Yes, *Duel To the Death* is another movie where Chinese actors are playing Japanese characters (this occurs everywhere in Hong Kong cinema). It irks some audiences.
[2] Eddy Ko and Norman Chui appeared in films not long before *Duel To the Death* such as *We're Going To Eat You* (Tsui Hark, 1980). Over their long careers, all three of the leads – Ko, Chui and Lau (b. 1949) – appeared in 100s of films.
[3] We note that Bo Ching Wan is given the director's name.
[4] Flora Cheung trained with the Royal Ballet in Albion. *Duel To the Death* was her only martial arts movie. Like many actresses, she married, had children, and left the business.
[5] Some of the actors in *Duel To the Death* had already worked with Tony Ching Siu-tung on his TV series.

with Tony Ching before – in *The Sword* in 1980, for instance).

According to the cast, photography on *Duel To the Death* wended on for 6 months, a long time for a Cantonese movie. Tony Ching Siu-tung was under pressure to deliver, and asked for re-takes to get everything just right.

It's a movie that is important in the Tony Ching Siu-tung *œuvre*: it's his first as a director to be released theatrically; and it's a movie in which he has a rare co-writer credit (with two other writers – with Manfred Wong and David Lai). And of course, Ching was action choreographer (along with Lau Chi Ho).

It's pretty cool to have your first theatrical released movie working as a film director (aged 30) turn out to be a masterpiece. Such is *Duel To the Death*.

So *Duel To the Death* is Tony Ching Siu-tung's first film as director with a cinema release,[6] yes, but let's not forget that by this time Ching had already been the action director on 19 movies, and also oversaw the action choreography on several important TV series (and he was continuing to action direct TV series in this period). No novice, then: if you look at the action and the wire-work in *Duel To the Death*, you can see that it is already very accomplished (and already *way* beyond anything in Western cinema).

Thirty at the time of the release of *Duel To the Death*, Tony Ching Siu-tung was, if you think about it, extremely confident and talented in putting action on screen. *Duel To the Death* is also a movie on a big canvas, and is full of location shooting (filming in real locations is one of the hallmarks of Ching's cinema).

STYLE, LOOK, ACTION.

Duel To the Death reveals Tony Ching Siu-tung in full effect: everything is here: the *wuxia pian* or swordplay movie genre,[7] the rapidity of the action, the wire-work, the visual effects, the supernatural/ fantasy/ horror elements, the crude humour, the emphasis on costumes and the look, exquisite photography, romance, heroism, a geo-political back-ground/ context, disguises (crossdressing), and an exhilarating joy of making movies.

Once again, *Duel To the Death* displays that giddy feeling that *anything is possible*. Even if we know it's not, even if cops, governments, teachers, doctors, and scientists insist to us that *no*, some things are impossible, films like *Duel To the Death* persuade us that we might be

6 The box office at home was disappointing.
7 Eleven of Tony Ching's features as director or co-director are *wuxia pian*, and he has action-directed many more (and TV series, too).

right. We should be right. We *must* be right!

Duel To the Death is another movie where anything can happen in any corner of the frame. Nowhere is out of bounds for a human to fly to, land on, or move through. We burrow underground, we crash through ceilings, we slip through walls, we zoom across courtyards. Photographically, *Duel To the Death* is masterful, revealing the director's insistence on lush visuals which complement the crucial romanticism of his films (especially his historical films). Technically, *Duel To the Death* is a delight – Ching's movies are definitely cameraman's movies, where the cinematography is foregrounded. Consider the very precise compositions and the use of the camera in *Duel To the Death.*

Duel To the Death is a Kitchen Sink Film – no, not a dreary socialist-realist movie about dour coal miners in grim, North England from the early 1960s, but a movie where everything plus several kitchen sinks are chucked into the mix. The settings, for ex, run from beaches, rocky clifftops, forests and rivers to Buddhist temples, underground dungeons, and aristocratic, Japanese palaces.

Duel To the Death boasts a marvellous use of locations. And they don't have the appearance of the same locales used in 100s of Cantonese movies, which we're very familiar with (even tho', yes, *Duel To the Death* was filmed in some of the same spots, such as the forest and the beach near Hong Kong). Exteriors, including the Chinese temples and the Japanese settings, were filmed in Korea and Taiwan. The grand temple that's meant to be the famed Shaolin Temple is in Korea.

The art direction and textures in *Duel To the Death* are impressive – like the roses placed beside the waterfall, for one of the romantic scenes; like the Fall leaves scattered on the bridge at the Holy Sword House; like the dripping water in the sword cave; like the Chinese art in the reception hall of Holy Sword House; and like the calligraphy[8] employed against white for the main titles (which occur some minutes into the picture).

The score – by Siu-Tin Lai – features the expected percussion (much timpani, and martial patters on the snare drum), simulations of Chinese folk music, and some unusual choices (electric piano), and gloomy synthesizers. It isn't a wholly successful score, but the film generously allows the music to play thru for lengthy periods without the distractions of dialogue or sound effects.

Tony Ching Siu-tung is fond of horror movie ingredients (especially if it means he can orchestrate some intricate visual effects, too). The scene where the Chinese warriors have been captured and drugged and suspended on ropes in the dungeon below Master Han's school is a typical

8 The calligraphy was by Kit-Luen Lee.

piece of Chingian horror.

No individual can claim credit for developing wire-assisted stunts in Hong Kong action movies (around the late 1970s and early 1980s), but Tony Ching Siu-tung was certainly one of the first to do so, and, much more significantly, one of the first to fully exploit all the possibilities. Ching as a wire-master has no superior and very few peers.

❀

Tony Ching Siu-tung likes to open his movies with a BANG! *Duel To the Death* is no different: the first 5 or 6 minutes comprise an elaborate raid on the Shaolin Temple by the Shogun's ninja (to steal sacred scrolls, a recurring motif of the *wuxia pian* genre),⁹ followed by a giant bust-up between Buddhist monks and the *shinobi*.

Chinese *kung fu* experts versus ninja warriors is one of the staples of Asian action cinema. So we have many gags that Tony Ching is very fond of: warriors performing the same movements in a row at the same time; black-clad agents tumbling thru open windows and landing on the floor;¹⁰ *shinobi* flying on kites; rapidfire magical transformations (into smoke, a naked woman, a giant, etc).

Duel To the Death is almost wall-to-wall action. *Almost* – because there are many scenes not only of talk, but also of contemplation. There's the romantic subplot, for instance (which runs over several scenes); the scenes between Bo Ching and his *sifu* Hon; scenes at the Shaolin Temple; scenes where Hashimoto is in Nihon, talking with his master (and carousing with the lads); a cemetery scene; and two scenes where the heroes visit the underground memorial to the former participants in the martial arts world.

A movie of many set-pieces, one of the grandest (and the most costly) in *Duel To the Death* is the festival which climaxes act one: filmed at night in a huge setting, with 100s of extras in costume, this is where the main female character, Sing Lam (Flora Cheung) is introduced (with a classy entrance – floating into the crowds over a great distance. The flying swordsmaster is a staple of the genre).

Of the many lively bits of business in the festival sequence, the puppet show is a delight. In Punch and Judy style, we see Bo Ching and Hashimoto fighting non-stop. We don't need to see the rest of the movie – it's all done with two puppets beating each other with sword-sticks. (What is a live-action movie but a bigger and costlier version of a puppet show? And many aren't as good! And a puppet show can get across all of the

9 And, in a nifty variant, to take an impression of the scroll on paper. It's also popular in Japanese animation.
10 A classic Chingian shot occurs early on: a rapid dolly shot backwards, with the ninja tumbling into frame on either side.

same points – quicker, funnier, sillier).

Thus, immediately following her entrance, Sing Lam is given a piece of action to express her characterization as a righteous figure – she dispatches the associates of the man who ran through the puppeteer because the show ridiculed the Japanese fighter (the man himself falls onto the blade that the dead puppeteer's wife (Cheng Mang-ha) is holding). The action is swift and decisive, and it's economical, too – Sing takes cares of the villains with minimum fuss, barely seeming to move. (Sing also meets Bo Ching here – he too is clad in white).

❖

Duel To the Death is wholly a manly, masculine movie, with only one significant female character – Sing Lam. Every other woman is either a servant (in the Holy Sword House), a geisha, or a wife (of the puppeteer).

Hong Kong cinema, like Chinese cinema, reflects the patriarchal nature of its society: altho' women are sometimes portrayed as super-beings, as Bey Logan noted (149), they are also depicted as romantic interest or they are objectified sexually. Aside from the work of filmmakers such as Tsui Hark and Wong Kar-wai, much of Hong Kong and Chinese cinema is almost anti-feminist.

It's typical of the swordplay genre that Sing Lam has to crossdress in order to appear as a swordsman in public (crossdressing is a recurring motif in Ching Siu-tung's cinema, most flamboyantly in the astonishing *Swordsman* movies, where Brigitte Lin is the first and last word in transgender characters in Hong Kong film).

Bo Ching Wan mentions (in the romantic forest conflab) that Sing Lam might be benefit from dressing in a more feminine manner. Instantly, we cut to a slow motion scene of Sing in her chamber dressing herself (once again foregrounding costumes in a Tony Ching movie).

Bo Ching Wan's *sifu* is Hon Gwok-choi, appearing in only one sequence, set in a forest, performed wholly for comedy (the rest of the movie is played straight). The scene, complete with a silly talking cockatoo, is a nod to the drunken master sort of character (can this really be Ching's *sifu*?!). [11] It's also meant to contrast with the heaviness of the Japanese scenes, where, before he leaves Nippon, Hashimoto kills his *sensei* (by accident). [12]

ACT TWO AND THE NINJAS.

Act two of *Duel To the Death* is a classic 'complications' plot, after the initial introductions and set-up in act one: complication [1]: Japanese

11 He has one of the ugliest hair-do's in cinema.
12 Leaping into the path of a warrior on tenterhooks dressed in a pink fright wig might lead to some injury!

ninjas attempt to foil the plans for the duel by attacking the competitors in many scenarios (in a cemetery, on a beach, in a forest, even at the dinner table of their host, Master Han). Complication [2]: the romance (or at least, the mild flirtation) between Bo Ching and Sing Lam is opposed by the patriarch Master Han. Complication [3]: Han bemoans the ailing fate of the family, and makes Sing painfully aware of her shortcomings (i.e., she's a woman!). Complication [4]: warriors in China are being captured and imprisoned.

Duel To the Death has a lot of fun with cooking up spectacular gags for the Japanese ninja (the 'Chinjas' pop up in many subsequent Tony Ching outings): they burst out of the soil; they vanish in puffs of smoke; they disappear in the blink of a missing frame; they sail beneath paper kites; they combine to form a towering giant; and the funniest stunt: they turn into naked women (like Naruto's erotic *ninjutsu* in Masashi Kishimoto's *Naruto manga*).[13]

And another gag that Tony Ching Siu-tung has made his own: warriors carrying palanquins *in the air, through the tree tops.* It's a gag that seems fiendishly difficult to accomplish. And to make it look good. (In a later scene, the *shinobi*, led by Kenji, are schlepping the palanquins through a stony riverbed – at speed. Another scene which looks tricky to film).

In one of the ninja scenes, Bo Ching Wan and Sing Lam fight them together, on the beach at night (the ninja have returned to collect the scrolls they buried in the sand. This doesn't quite make sense – presumably, they didn't carry off the scrolls so they wouldn't get wet. But if they're so brilliant, surely they'd have a means of keeping paper dry?).

Anyway, first Sing Lam and then Bo Ching Wan take on the ninja (Bo Ching leaps into the fray to rescue Sing). This is the moment where Sing is injured, leading to the familiar scene of healing (beside a waterfall), which in the action-adventure genre (and in *wuxia pian*) always means a flirtation scene (and it's always the one being healed who realizes how tender the other one is).

CHINA VS. JAPAN.

Duel To the Death is set in the Ming dynasty (16th century). What's a stake? Honour, 'face', pride – personal pride which's overridden by community and national pride. (Vital ingredients in both Japanese and Chinese historical stories).

The background story of *Duel To the Death* is a simplified version of a long-festering antagonism between the two superpowers: China and Japan

---

13 Being Japanese *shinobi*, they have to use throwing stars (which embed themselves in tree trunks via pixillation). And they have many special skills.

(a political backdrop that has been mined in 100s of Chinese movies, and will likely keep storytellers going for another thousand years at least). It is delivered in a colourful, cartoony format of oppositions: China<->Japan, two rival martial arts schools and styles, two artistic cultures,[14] and two guys, Bo Ching and Hashimoto. Xenophobia, us and them, nationalism, etc.

So, yes, there *is* a duel in *Duel To the Death* – uhh, wait a minute! there are *hundreds* of duels in *Duel To the Death*! No, I mean the duel of the title, a national (and nationalistic) competition between China and Japan, where they send their finest sportsmen to compete. Around this simple narrative structure of us and them (like many sporting events, it's dopily simplistic), *Duel To the Death* builds a more complicated narrative of warring schools of martial arts, and the cunning Shogun using undercover agent Kenji and his band of ninja to nobble the Chinese warriors and capture them. The goal? Oh, the usual one in action-adventure genre of using weapons or warriors to Rule The World.

Yes, it's the Chinese who're the heroes here, and the Japanese are the sneaky guys who pretend to send their best swordsman (a samurai) on the one hand, while with the other claw they're attacking the Chinese fighters.

Duel To the Death contrasts the more humane Chinese with the unbendable sticklers for rules Japanese, with their adherence to orders, hierarchies, and servitude. Bo Ching Wan is the 'Lord of the Sword', but he also knows when to quit;[15] Hashimoto won't quit, and won't admit defeat. Even tho' the duel contest has been corrupted with kidnapping and killing, Hashimoto insists that he and Bo Ching duel as promised.

But hang on a sec, instead of painting the Japanese as the out-and-out villains, *Duel To the Death* is more ambiguous: instead, there are nefarious deeds on both sides. The Shogun puts the operation to attack the martial arts participants into effect, but the Chinese (including Master Han) aid them (the contemporary resonances of collusion behind the scenes, among high ranking officials, are obvious).

This is a foundational aspect of martial arts movies: that there are sections of the Chinese community who will sell out their compatriots. Thus, Master Han appears at first as a dependable and upright[16] citizen (and he's the strict tho' genial host of the contest), but he is collaborating with the Japanese Shogun to capture warriors, drug 'em, sling 'em in

---

14 The plum blossom of China is contrasted with the cherry blossom of Japan in the reception hall scene (Hashimoto mentions the *mono no aware* (= transience) symbolized by *sakura*, and Bo Ching notes that plum trees are hardy, tenacious trees).
15 Bo Ching notes that death is the ultimate victor in a duel.
16 Upright, but not so 'upright' – he has two wooden legs, which he employs to fool Bo Ching Wan.

dungeons, and ship 'em East.

Also, Hashimoto is humanized in the first act of *Duel To the Death*, where he's not depicted as a cold, rule-bound rival. But the pressure to live up to the task set by his countrymen is intense. As the rules of his *dojo* state, you have to try everything to win.

The concept of sacrifical suicide among Japanese is also invoked in *Duel To the Death*, when some of the ninja hurl themselves at their opponents, carrying explosives, which they set off when they grasp the victim.

The scenes in Japan are impressive: largely filmed in the studio, they reproduce Shogun-era Nippon economically but successfully. They have the formal, ritualized aspects of Japanese society down pat. The scenes also introduce us to the figure of Hashimoto, who's initially portrayed as a more carefree character than Bo Ching Wan: he's depicted watching children practice with wooden *katana* in the *dojo*, and carousing with his chums on the night before he leaves.[17] (But when he's put on the spot, and dealing with stern father figures like Master Han or Kenji, he is all-business, and a stickler for following the rules to the bitter end – which means, in his eyes, that the duel is likely to end in d-e-a-t-h).

Yes, *Duel To the Death* is yet another Hong Kong martial arts movie which draws on the myth and legend of the Shaolin Temple – a place that because it appears in so many films, if it didn't exist, filmmakers would've invented it. The Temple setting allows for the mandatory training scenes (i.e., fighting), and the mandatory dramatic confrontations (i.e., fighting), and the opening scene, where the Japanese ninja infiltrate the Temple at night (i.e., more fighting).

THE LAW OF THE FATHER.

The Law of the Father is everywhere in the *jiangzhu,* the martial arts world, as we know well: patriarchs who expect to be obeyed, son figures who devoutly carry out their wishes, an unbreakable hierarchy of power, and severe punishments for anybody who dares to go against the status quo.

Thus, Sing Lam defies her father and is run thru by his sword for her trouble (albeit in a kind of mishap, when Master Han aims for Bo Ching and he dives out of the way). And woe betide anyone who thinks they can oppose the Shogun (as Hashimoto does). In this picture, of course Master Han and Kenji have to expire, but it's cruel that Sing Lan does too.

Fathers and sons, the older generation and the younger generation,

---

17 This is where we see the first female charas in *Duel To the Death* – they are, inevitably, courtesans (geisha).

and the fiercely patriarchal structures of both nations are grandly and cruelly portrayed in *Duel To the Death*. In which case, there's only space and time for one significant female character – Sing Lam (who, of course, has to dress as a guy to be deemed worthy of warriorhood. Master Han's disappointment that the clan's hopes rest in the hands of a mere woman are foregrounded in their every scene together).

Later, of course, Tony Ching Siu-tung would bolster up the roles of women in his movies, to the point that in some flicks they are the main charas (*The Heroic Trio, The Executioners, Naked Weapon, An Empress and the Warriors*, etc).

THE FIRST HALF OF THE FINALE.

The duel btn the two heroes closes *Duel To the Death*, but actually there are multiple conflicts exploding everywhere prior to that: there are the two scheming patriarchs to deal with first, for example. Thus, Master Han tricks Bo Ching Wan with his severed legs, but he has wooden ones and is a perfectly accomplished swordsman. In the reception room of the Holy Sword House we have several superb duels – between Master Han and Bo Ching, between Bo Ching and Sing Lam, and a three-way bust-up.

In a moment of tragedy much loved by Chinese cinema, the father slays his daughter (while aiming for Bo Ching). His punishment? To have his daughter expire in his arms. Sing Lam's death is but one of multiple deaths at the end of *Duel To the Death*.

Kenji the Japanese double agent must die, in movie-movie moral terms (and as the emissary of political power in Japan, the Shogun). The finale of *Duel To the Death* is certainly unusual in several respects in this part of the plot: it has Master Han keeping captured warriors strung up and drugged in an underground dungeon; Bo Ching also falls into the trap, until he's rescued by Sing Lam (after she's defied her father); Kenji and the ninja re-take the warriors, carrying them off in palanquins along a riverbed (to make tracking them more difficult, one supposes); but Hashimoto is waiting for them.

The expected smackdown between Hashimoto and Kenji takes place once again in the forest (after starting in the stream). Now the editing (by Peter Cheung) assumes a lightning-quick pace, with blink-and-you-miss-it shots – Hashimoto cutting off Kenji's arm, Kenji leaping up into the trees, Kenji hurling explosives at Hashimoto, and finally Hashimoto beheading Kenji. (This includes a gag of Kenji continuing to issue orders when he's just a head hanging from a tree, a typical piece of Chingian horror).

THE ENDING.

With Kenji decapitated (and finally silent), with Sing Lam dead and Master Han a broken man, Bo Ching Wan seems completely justified in wanting to return to the Shaolin Monastery, with the surviving monk, his uncle, Kwan.

But *Duel To the Death* doesn't end, as might be expected from the political-historical background pitting China against Japan, with the death of Hashimoto on the cliffs. No: the ending has both of them surviving (tho' Bo Ching Wan is now armless and fingerless). Because, as Tony Ching Siu-tung insisted, *Duel To the Death* wasn't about heroes and villains, with the Japanese typed as the 100% bad guys.

At the end, following the river and forest fights, Bo Ching Wan is carrying back the injured second-in-command of the Shaolin Temple, Kwan Yung-moon. But Hashimoto still insists that they will still duel; after failing to persuade the weary Bo Ching with arguments, he kills the monk to force Bo Ching's hand. Extreme, but it does the trick.

The finale of *Duel To the Death* takes place on a rocky cliff[18] right above the ocean – as if the filmmakers challenged themselves to seek out the most demanding (and dangerous) location possible.[19] The grips and stage hands who had to lug the gear up there must've cursed the producers under their breath (and the mechanisms for wire-work are very heavy, too).[20]

No rubbish green screens here and stage hands off-screen throwing buckets of water in a film studio, this is the real deal – and it looks spectacular. The finale has both Bo Ching and Hashimoto worked up to intense levels of rage, hurling themselves at each other, and cutting each other to bits. As well as lopped-off arms (with a bit of one-armed swordsman business), the ending also includes literal cliffhangers as the warriors hang off a cliff above the ocean (this is where stuntmen have to *really* trust those cables!).

The 'duel to the death' of the title actually comprises several beats – from the standing far apart and glaring at each other, through the multiple clashes of sword-on-sword, to added complications, such as rising fog, the collapse of part of the cliff, the two swordsmen hanging off the cliff, and the frenzied final lunges and slashes, leaving both participants bloody and maimed.

The film closes with a shot of both warriors in the frame, somehow still standing, on the cliff, as the credits roll. Bo Ching Wan has wanted to end

18 The cliff was later used in *Moon Warriors*, which Ching also choreographed.
19 The cast remembered that *Duel To the Death* was a tough movie to make.
20 Indeed, the wire stunts gained an added *frisson* by being above the sea on rocks. Actor Norman Chiu recalled that he had eight stunt guys hanging onto his wire.

the fight several times, and he walks off in disgust once, only to have Hashimoto attack him again. Hashimoto simply won't quit, until he's in no condition to continue.

IN SUM.

Duel To the Death would be a masterpiece without a solid script, because it boasts enough stellar elements – including of course action. But it's actually the script that makes everything else really catch fire, as nearly always in movies. Indeed, *Duel To the Death* spends some time with the two main characters away from duelling and the circus of continuous action.

There's nothing 'new' here, story-wise or character-wise: the elements of patriarchal power exerting its cold, unyielding control, the struggle of son and daughter figures to come up to the mark (but always destined to disappoint their elders), the tug of war between individual and community, warrior and school, self and nation, are all very familiar components of *wuxia pian.*

Duel To the Death is riddled with clichés, for sure, but the *way* those clichés are delivered, the casting choices, the technical elements, the combination of new techniques and old skills, makes for a superbly realized piece of entertainment.

Oh, sure, *Duel To the Death*'s characterizations are stereotypical and upper-level only: if you want Dostoeivskian/ Chekhovian/ Tolstoyan/ Shakespearean depths, darling, you're better off renting another movie. It's not going to happen! Not in this movie.

In fact, you can't even really describe the characters in *Duel To the Death* as conventional characters – they are more like attitudes or energies that're being orchestrated in this tale of a nationalistic bust-up.

Duel To the Death isn't flawless – but it's pretty close. The music seems a little unimpressive and undistinguished at times (as if it can't decide whether to modernize or go for a period feel), and the comical skit with Bo Ching's *sifu* and that bloody bird seems out of place (altho' it's typical of Hong Kong movies to include such scenes. Indeed, in a Wong Jing version, there would be crude humour, some farce, and some contemporary references).

Duel To the Death features 100s of special effects, and most of them are in front of camera effects (tho' there is some animation),[21] including running the film backwards, freeze frames, optical superimposition, pixillation, and of course wire-work and trampolines. As in other Tony Ching Siu-tung films, the environment itself is being puppeteered as well

21 In the scene where the giant ninja breaks apart into regular ninja.

as the characters – objects are being manipulated off-screen by cables to interact with the characters.

And, as in Tony Ching Siu-tung's cinema as a whole, there is a child-like delight in *Duel To the Death* worthy of the early pioneer of cinematic magic, Géorges Méliès, in the delivery of the visual effects. Ching never seems to get tired (as with, say, Tsui Hark, Walerian Borowczyk and F.W. Murnau), of the trick shots that cinema provides. A big part of Ching's filmic make-up is a magician, a director who relishes the magic show aspects of cinema (and when you combine that with the Peking Opera elements, and the martial arts and wire-work elements, you have a thoroughly magical form of cinema).

2

THE WITCH FROM NEPAL

Kei Jyun

INTRODUCTION.

The Witch From Nepal (*Qi Yuan* in Mandarin, a.k.a. *The Nepal Affair/ Affair From Nepal/ A Touch of Love*, 1986) was prod. by Anthony Chow for Golden Harvest/ Paragon Films, wr. by Chui Jing-Hong, action dir. by Alan Chui Chung-San, Phillip Kwok Chun-Fung, Lau Chi-ho and Tony Ching, art dir. by James Leung Wah-Sing, DP: Tom Lau Moon-Tong, ed. by Peter Cheung Yiu-Chung, costumes by Cheung Chi-Yeung, and music by Sherman Chow Gam-Cheung and Violet Lam Man-Yee. In the cast were Chow Yun-fat, Emily Chu, Yammie Lam, Ng Hong-sang and Dick Wei. Released Feb 27, 1986. 89 mins.

The Witch From Nepal won the award for Best Action Choreography at the Hong Kong Film Awards (where it was competing against *Peking Opera Blues, Royal Warriors, Martial Arts of Shalion, Righting Wrongs* and *Twinkle Twinkle Lucky Stars*).

There are three main characters in *The Witch From Nepal*:
• Joe Wong – Chow Yun-fat, an architect
• Ida – Yammie Lam, his girlfriend
• Sheila – Emily Chu, the witch

Providing the supernatural threat is the cat-like demon, played by Dick Wei.

CHOW YUN-FAT.

This is Chow Yun-fat's movie: he appears in almost every scene, and the story is all about him. Chow is a spectacular presence in movies, even in something like this, which is rather a pot-boiler (tho' expertly done).

Tony Ching had already worked with Chow Yun-fat several times before *The Witch From Nepal* – as action director for films such as *The Story of Woo Vet*, and he would work with him again (including in much later movies, such as *The Curse of the Golden Flower*).

1986 was a very good year for Chow Yun-fat: he married his second wife (Jasmine Tan) and appeared in a very successful movie that made him an even bigger star: *A Better Tomorrow*. Inevitably, *The Witch From Nepal* has been over-shadowed by *A Better Tomorrow* (along with other movies of 1986 which featured Chow, such as *Dream Lovers, Love Unto Waste, The Seventh Curse, Rose, The Lunatics,* and *A Hearty Response*. That's 8 movies in a year!).

STYLE.

Costume designer Cheung Chi-Yeung has surrounded Chow Yun-fat with white throughout the movie: white shirts, white pants, a white house, a white car, white paper, white ornaments, white walls, etc. Chow looks very good in white (he can wear a white shirt better than anybody. Hell, Chow looks great in anything!).

The Witch From Nepal is stuffed with special effects, like most of Tony Ching's movies: stopmotion, puppeteered objects, explosions, optical processing, and animation. The movie plays some of the supernatural elements in a lighthearted manner – such as when Joe manipulates sugar lumps and milk on a table using telekinesis, when he's having a polite coffee with his girlfriend.

The stunts in *The Witch From Nepal* include full-body burns, explosions, and several impressive car stunts.[22] Having a demon who acts like a cat enables the filmmakers to use plenty of wire-work, so that the demon can leap from walls, ships, and bridges. There are some gross gags in *The Witch From Nepal* – like the cat-demon tearing apart a guard dog that dares to yap at him.

The score of *The Witch From Nepal* (by Sherman Chow Gam-Cheung and Violet Lam Man-Yee) isn't the finest to appear in a Tony Ching movie. It's mainly electronic, and sounds too cheap and too run-of-the-mill.

THE STORY AND SCENES.

The Witch From Nepal opens with a big nighttime action sequence – which's how many Hong Kong action pictures start (Tony Ching has used the device several times). Opening like this announces to the audience

---

[22] The car stunts were probably by Bruce Law, who oversaw many car gags in Hong Kong cinema.

that this is an action film, full of atmosphere, and threats in the night, including of a supernatural kind (captions after the main titles remind us that there are beyond-human entities in the world).

The opening action sequence introduces characters such as one of the chief heavies in *The Witch From Nepal*, the cat-demon. The action itself includes Chingian staples such as tussles with knives, diving about, and wire-assisted leaps.

Just as significant, however, is the atmosphere and texture of the opening action sequence – the nighttime setting of an exotic temple lit by flickering torches, the gathering of devotees, the evocations of religion and supernatural forces, etc. The opening scene takes us immediately into an Eastern, unworldly, strange and uncertain environment – we're not in downtown Hong Kong here, in a shopping mall, or a restaurant, or on a bus, or in someone's apartment.

Opening a movie with scenes such as this is a way of shifting the audience into a different frame of mind – and it's striking just how many Hong Kong action movies begin not only with action but with outlandish or sensational material in a nighttime setting. And it can be so much more appealing for a viewer than the standard method of 1. Long shots of a location, 2. Shots of the environment, and 3. Gradual introductions of the main characters. Instead of boring long shots or helicopter shots of the setting of the movie, *The Witch From Nepal* gets right into it.

After this, and the main titles, *The Witch From Nepal* introduces the main character – Chow Yun-fat's architect Joe, on vacation in Nepal with his girlfriend Ida. The couple are depicted as happy and enjoying multiple touristy experiences – trying the food, buying gifts, admiring the view, driving hired cars in busy streets, etc. The experiences are presented in a montage format, establishing the main characters as regular people (tho' well-off).

Chow-Fun-fat's Joe is no underdog: he is a wealthy architect with a spiffing home (a fancy, modernist building with impressive views across the bay. No doubt the architect designed it himself). Joe is also an ardent sketcher from nature: he carries a sketchpad and draws on his travels. As the fantasy plot kicks in, Joe discovers he's been drawing scenes of temples and fights (which we saw in the prologue). He also takes to sketching the mystery woman.

The first act of *The Witch From Nepal* continues with the travelogue approach to the story, when Joe and Ida ride some elephants in the countryside (spotting rhinos, for instance). The summery, sunny scene turns nasty when Joe has an accident, falling off an elephant and breaking his leg (the mysterious woman – Sheila (Emily Chu) – prompts this event).

As act one of *The Witch From Nepal* progresses, with Joe laid up in hospital, a romantic/ mystery triangle develops – Joe in between two women, his girlfriend Ida and the witch Sheila. Act one climaxes with a classic Chingian scene – two characters in flight: Joe and the witch plummet from the hospital balcony; the sorceress saves Joe, and magically heals his injury. Soon after this, she transfers magical power to Joe. (The witch is but the first of many powerful women in Tony Ching's cinema).

Act two of *The Witch From Nepal* develops the themes of act one, and recycles several scenes: further scenes of supernatural powers; scenes with Joe and his girlfriend; more of the romantic triangle between Joe, Ida and Sheila; another nighttime visit to the hospital (with Joe and Sheila escaping the hospital orderlies by leaping from roof to roof; meanwhile, the cat-demon arrives at the docks in grand style (bursting out of the side of a ship onto the dockside at night) to liven up the proceedings even further.

Some of the scenes with Joe and Sheila are played with a child-like quality, as if they're teenagers on a nighttime date, relishing being let off the leash from home life with their parents. In one sequence, they pass a storefront stocked with still cameras (a very 'Made In Hong Kong' setting), and Joe sets off the cameras so they all flash together and print out the Polaroids of Joe and Sheila looking at them. Scenes like this play into Chow Yun-fat's media image as an all-round sweet guy (and a romantic lead). It's so cute the film shouldn't get away with it; but it does.

Actually, director Tony Ching is a real softie sometimes in his movies: there are similarly adolescent and twee scenes in films such as *A Chinese Ghost Story* and *Jade Dynasty*. In fact, Ching is not afraid to slap plenty of cheese into his movies. There are twee scenes, cute scenes, silly scenes, and plenty of romantic scenes.

Thus, at times, *The Witch From Nepal* resembles supernatural/ romantic comedies, where characters encounter ghosts, such as *Ghost*, *Always* and *City of Angels.*

◆

The Witch From Nepal builds up to the inevitable smackdown between Joe and the cat-demon. Before we reach that duel, the movie heads off into zombie horror territory, when the car driven by Joe is jinxed (by the cat-demon) and crashes into a graveyard. Tony Ching is fond of characters emerging from the earth (often they're ninja or swordsmen); here, it's zombies, crawling out of graves to menace the heroes in the car.

This section of *The Witch From Nepal* looks forwards to Tony Ching's best-loved work as a director, the *Chinese Ghost Story* movies: it's full-on Gothic material, with smoke billowing through a cemetery at night, women being terrorized by zombies, and plenty of stunt gags.

To provide some dramatic juice, the witch, Sheila, races to aid Joe and co. but is fatally injured, expiring in Joe's arms back at his place. Thus, Joe goes into action against the cat-demon partly as revenge for Sheila. (Joe is really on the war-path now, and he's become an action hero. In one scene, he dives right thru the plate glass window of a storefront, so he can chase the cat-demon. Ever tried to dive thru a plate glass window? It's not that easy!).23

The duel in *The Witch From Nepal* is a massive action sequence, starting down on the street (with the cat-demon on a horse), and moving up to the roof of a nearby skyscraper. Elevators that are cut and hurtle towards the ground, and then zoom upwards out of the roof of the building are included in the numerous physical stunts.24 Joe and the cat-demon spar against a bank of lights on the roof. An unusual setting is used for the climax of the fight – a series of power generators near the top of the skyscraper (partly so that the movie can have its mandatory explosions).

Oh yes, stuff is blowing up, lightning bolts are zigzagging, smoke is billowing, and stunt guys are crashing into glass windows, or hanging off buildings, or falling heavily to the ground. In fact, *The Witch of Nepal*'s finale features the full arsenal of Tony Ching's favourite action choreography, from the inanimate (breakaway sets and puppeteered props) to guys on wires and some *kung fu*. (We don't have swords here, however: Joe is armed with a magical knife, and the cat-demon has a club made from a bone25).

In the *dénouement* of *The Witch From Nepal*, the golden couple of cinema (the hero and his girl) are re-instated, with Joe and Ida on the steps of the temple (where Joe has returned the magical totems, and paid his respects). Joe has his arm in a sling, but looks remarkably relaxed and fresh-faced, considering he's been beaten to a bloody pulp in a massive fight in a Hong Kong action movie. Well, he *is* Chow Yun-fat, after all, as remarkable an actor as any who've appeared in the history of film.

---

23 I've seen people bump into a glass door in New York, on the street in the old Virgin Megastore, and end up on the floor with a bloody nose.
24 Some of the flow of the action doesn't quite make sense.
25 It resembles the magical stick in *Jade Dynasty*.

Duel To the Death (1983).

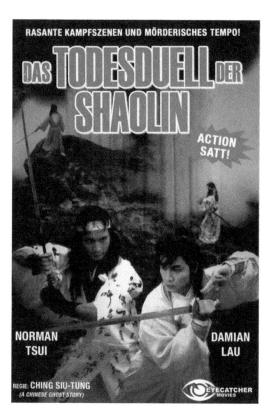

RASANTE KAMPFSZENEN UND MÖRDERISCHES TEMPO!

DAS TODESDUELL DER SHAOLIN

ACTION SATT!

NORMAN TSUI

DAMIAN LAU

REGIE: CHING SIU-TUNG
(A CHINESE GHOST STORY)

EYECATCHER MOVIES

DUEL TO THE DEATH

FROM THE ACTION DIRECTOR OF THE BOX OFFICE SMASH HIT 'HERO'

DUEL TO THE DEATH

HONG KONG LEGENDS

18

SPECIAL COLLECTOR'S EDITION

DUEL TO THE DEATH

A HONG KONG CLASSIC

STARRING   NORMAN TSUI   DIRECTED BY   CHING SIU TUNG
演員   徐少強   導演   程小東

DAMIAN LAU
劉松仁

FLORA CHEUNG
張天愛

生死決

DUEL TO THE DEATH

The Witch From Nepal (1986).

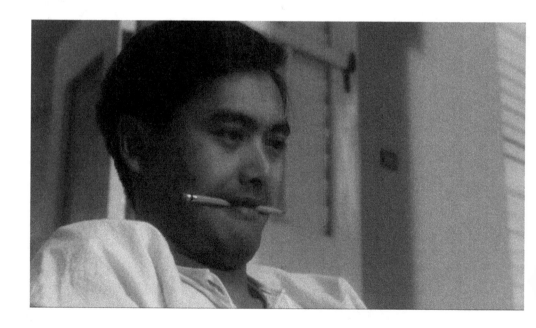

3

THE TERRACOTTA WARRIOR

Chin Yung

The Terracotta Warrior (*Chin Yung/ Gu Gam Daai Zin/ Yon Qing* in Cantonese, a.k.a. *Fight and Love With a Terracotta Warrior,* 1990) is a top-of-the-line, Chinese action-adventure movie with a romance and time travel theme, based on the novel by Lillian Lee. It was headed up by three of the greatest directors of action in world cinema: Tony Ching Siu-tung, Zhang Yimou and Tsui Hark. Art & Talent Group Inc. produced; Pik Wah Lee scripted; exec. producer: Kam Kwok-Leung; the producers were Tsui Hark, Zhu Mu and Hon Pau-chu; Peter Pau and Lee San-yip were DPs; Marco Mak Chi-sin edited; art dirs.: Kenneth Yee Chung-man[1] and Lau Man-Hung; costumes by Bruce Yu Ka-On; make-up: Man Yun-Ling; hair: Peng Yen-Lien; dialogue ed. by Pei-Ru Chang; sound ed.: Leung Ka-Lun; special fx by Siu-Lung Ching; music by Romeo Diaz, James Wong and Joseph Koo; and Ching was of course action director (along with Bobby Woo Chi-lung, Andy Ma, Jack Gao, Lau Chi-Ho, with stunts by Jinghua Zhang). Category II. Released Apl 12, 1990. 106 mins. (145 mins).

In the cast were Zhang Yimou, Gong Li, Yu Rongguang, Wu Tian Ming, Cheung Jun Ying, Luk Shu Ming and Chiu Chi Gong. (The movie was remade by Jackie Chan and Stanley Tong in 2005 as *The Myth*).

Lilian Lee Bik-dut (b. 1959) is a Chinese novelist best-known for *Farewell My Concubine*; her fiction has provided the basis for several projects from Tsui Hark, including *Green Snake* and *A Terracotta Warrior*. Other Lee books have been adapted, including *Reincarnation of the Golden Lotus*, *Temptation of a Monk*, *Red and Black*, *Sheng Si Qiao* and *Tales From the Dark*.

---

1 Tony Ching worked with Yee Chung-man many times – *Kung Fu Dunk, The Curse of the Golden Flower, An Empress and the Warriors, Jade Dynasty*, etc.

In *The Terracotta Warrior,* Zhang Yimou stars as the First Emperor's (Lu Shuming) bodyguard, General Mong Tianfang, who has a forbidden love affair with one of the Boss Man's concubines, Dong'er, played by Gong Li. Zhang is impressive as the strong, silent type, who holds a flame that never goes out for the concubine Dong'er. (Zhang is not so accomplished as the comical touches, where the fish out of water aspect of time travel is explored. There, in the remake, Jackie Chan wins). And Gong is as appealing as ever, with her open features that seem purpose-built for cinema. Gong is one of those actresses who lets all of her emotions flash across her face: she is perfect to play doomed lovers who look forlorn and weep at the slightest provocation. (One of Gong's techniques, which she seems to employ in every role, is quivering with sadness and bursting into tears).

Meanwhile, Yu Rongguang plays the nefarious Bai Yunfei, a playboy type and actor who, underneath that handsome exterior, is a nasty piece of work. All three actors form an appealing central cast in *The Terracotta Warrior.*

✳

The Terracotta Warrior portrays, once again, that mythical China, that Ancient China, that China of the *jiangzhu,* the martial arts world, that never existed – but that *should've* existed – and if it did exist, it would look like *this*!

The Terracotta Warrior is thoroughly *Chinese* – it is a film made in China, set in China, and all about China and Chinese history. But the form draws heavily on Western and Hollywood models.

The Terracotta Warrior is proudly Chinese: it portrays a famous part of Chinese history, and takes in several famous settings, including the Great Wall itself (much later, Zhang Yimou directed a movie entitled *The Great Wall* in 2016).

This is grand, operatic filmmaking, with gutsy, sometimes hysterical forms of performance (and not only from the actors, the music, the sound effects, the visuals, the costumes – they're all bold).

The cinematography in *The Terracotta Warrior* – by Peter Pau and Lee San-yip – is absolutely spectacular. This is one of Tony Ching's finest-looking films, embodying his goal of maximum romanticism. The film has everything, photographically, including one of Hong Kong's cinema's great specialities – ravishing nighttime imagery. Nobody else can photograph night scenes like Chinese technicians. In addition, *The Terracotta Warrior* boasts sunsets and dawns, crystal-clear noonday scenes, and all sorts of fires, candlelight and natural light.

The Terracotta Warrior is a masterclass in cinematography. It's a riot of textures – of rain, of smoke, of floating leaves, of flickering flames. The interior of the Imperial Palace, for example, is exquisitely lit with diffuse light through hanging white scrims, coupled with light arcing through windows and plenty of smoke.

The costumes in *The Terracotta Warrior* were by Tsui Hark's regular costumier, Bruce Yu Ka-On, with make-up by Man Yun-Ling and hair by Peng Yen-Lien. *The Terracotta Warrior* is a handsome-looking production all-round, with the hair, make-up and costumes being especially fine (the crew clearly enjoyed coming up with exciting wardrobe ideas for Gong Li in her 1930s incarnation – heavy on the dyed fake fur and extravagant hats).

Musically, *The Terracotta Warrior* was written by Romeo Diaz, James Wong Jim and Joseph Koo – between them, they seem to have scored every Hong Kong movie of the 1980s-2000s. So we're in good hands. *Very* expert hands. If you hire James Wong to compose your soundtrack, you won't have to worry about it – it'll be just fine. Together, Wong, Diaz and Koo provide the expected traditional, Chinese instrumentation and musical cues, as befitting a romance set partly in Ancient China. They'll bring the movie up to date with electronic and synthesized sounds (but less appealing, I think, compared to the traditional, Chinese orchestration). But there's no doubt that Wong, Diaz and Koo contribute immensely to the big emotional moments in *The Terracotta Warrior*, when the operatic film-making requires operatic music.

✳

The first act of *The Terracotta Warrior* illustrates a love affair out of Chinese mythology – the soldier and the courtesan, with the Emperor as the third main character, the patriarch, the authority who embodies the law (and the reasons why the lovers can't be together).

The romance is very conventional, but the clichés are delivered with such panache, we go along with it. Both Ching and Tsui (and Zhang) have returned to this sort of traditional romantic scenery many times. Partly because it works, and because it's perhaps the central narrative element of cinema (and because they're softies at heart).

✳

The first act of *The Terracotta Warrior* climaxes with the death of the lovers, in a spectacular fashion: Dong'er is burnt alive, while General Mong is buried alive under clay (he's the terracotta warrior of the title). The second act of *The Terracotta Warrior* cuts to the 1930s in China, to the glamorous world of movies and archaeological digs (with more than a few nods to the *Indiana Jones* series). The 1930s setting would appeal to Tsui Hark – it's the era of one of his great films of a few years earlier, *Shanghai Blues*.

The first act of *The Terracotta Warrior* is a mini-epic of its own, featuring the grand setting of the ancient capital of China, courtly intrigue, a cast of thousands, plenty of swordplay and action, romance, gorgeous costumes, impeccable make-up, and luscious lighting (the visuals in *The Terracotta Warrior*, as usual in a film helmed by Tony Ching Siu-tung, are outstanding). *The Terracotta Warrior* has got the back-lighting, the drifting, Autumnal leaves, the slow motion, the billowing smoke at night, the flickering firelight, the candles and lamps, the hangings a-fluttering, and plenty of rain scenes – all of the textures of Chinese, historical movies. (Once again, Chinese cinema demonstrates that it is the finest when it comes to staging historical extravaganzas, despite fierce competition from Western cinema, such as that of France).

In 36 or so minutes (it's a long first act), *The Terracotta Warrior* squeezes in grand processions, horse fights, an assassination attempt on the Emperor, a hunting scene, a budding romance (and love scene), a suicide bid, the induction of the concubines into the court, lyrical interludes, sword practice, political shenanigans behind the throne, and a grand dual death scene.

And, in typical style for a movie directed by Tony Ching Siu-tung, *The Terracotta Warrior* opens very big, with vistas of a huge, Imperial scheme, Ching's version of the building of the Pyramids or the Great Wall (the hauling of enormous artworks with ropes and wooden trolleys was used again as the opener for *Dr Wai* in 1996). This is followed by a royal hunt sequence, where the Emperor is attacked by an assassin – which means, of course, a ton of swordplay and daredevil horse-riding. The equestrian games and the royal hunt allow for plenty of action, of the acrobatic kind (including many horse falls for the stuntmen), plus some images of soldiers and riders out of Akira Kurosawa.

An important scene is seemingly modest, dramatically: Dong'er taps some bowls filled with rainwater to make musical sounds, while nearby General Mong practices his swordplay, with classic Tony Ching moves (in a courtyard filled with floating, Autumn leaves, a fundamental form of Chingian, poetic cinema. Electric fans, needless to say, are blowing on set throughout this movie).

The scene is a musical montage: it cuts between the two characters, using music (and editing) as the link: both Ching and Zhang would return to this form of filmmaking several times – most notably in their collaboration in 2002's *Hero.* The music and the sounds that connect the characters are enhanced by the editing: the film fuses the lovers together even when they're apart. (And it's typical, too, that the music begins simple and diegetic – we hear the sounds of Dong'er tapping the bowls – but then it becomes more orchestrated, with other instruments joining in).

✳

After such an inspired opening act, the second act of *The Terracotta Warrior*, set in the 1930s,[2] is a little less riveting in a few areas. For example, Gong Li's modern-day character Zhu Lili is allowed to squeal and over-act too much.

The second act brings Mr Brown and Bai Yunfei into play: Bai is a handsome playboy and actor who's cheesy and attractive on the outside, but the shiny, suave exterior hides the villain underneath. Bai reveals his true colours in a scene at an archaeological dig, where his disappointment with progress is expressed by beating up one of his underlings, and then stabbing him. This is where the clumsy goof Zhu Lili stumbles into the scene, and seems to have witnessed the murder (or maybe not).

Anyway, Bai Yunfei and his crew dealing with Zhu Lili leads to the big action sequence which ultimately brings General Mong the terracotta warrior back to life. The action scene is stuffed with visual effects (including models and explosions), and is centred around a plane flight. Up in the air, Bai is planning to bump off Zhu Lili, but by accident she shoots the pistol, damaging the plane, which crashes (after Bai has bailed out).

Following many preposterous bits of business, the plane falls into the underground chamber where the terracotta warrior Mong Tianfang was sealed in mud. The film is now in rollercoaster mode, with one scene hurtling into the next – Mong and Zhu Lili encountering each other, Mong fighting Bai's henchmen, Bai and Mong duelling, etc.

A charming aspect of *The Terracotta Warrior* is the evocation of filmmaking in the Thirties in China, complete with makeshift snow and rain (from watering cans on ladders above the actors. Things haven't changed much). Pik Wah Lee wrote the film, but these scenes were likely the suggestion of Tsui Hark – he is very fond of the mechanics of movie-making and theatre, and enjoys putting them on screen. General Mong has to deal with bewildering modern technology – cars, electric lamps, medicine, cameras, radio, steam engines, etc.

✳

The uneven second act is soon forgotten, because the third act of *The Terracotta Warrior* ramps up to the expected mayhem, swordplay,

2 The shift from the ancient world to the Thirties is indicated with a shot of a propellor-powered plane landing. The image offers a striking contrast to the epic romance of the first act, and also depicts the new-fangled technology of flight.

explosions and outrageous stunts. Fights on trains, inside planes, snakepit scenarios with walls closing in, colossal explosions – *The Terracotta Warrior* compacts a hundred years of action-adventure movies into 25 minutes.

Some of the gags in the climax of *The Terracotta Warrior* are distinctly Tsui Harkian: the heroes escaping ancient booby traps (*à la Indiana Jones*), the raising of the terracotta army from underground up to ground level, and the use of the plane (crashing into the temple and statuary).

The finale employs miniature photography extensively (courtesy of Cinefex Workshop), in order to capture the wild stunts of planes careening through the terracotta army, and the whole compound levitating to the surface.

This is bold, confident filmmaking, at once quaint and old-fashioned (reminiscent of, say, an Irving Allen disaster movie of the 1960s or 1970s), but filmed with a feeling for texture, light and atmosphere that shlocky adventure films seldom attain. The biggest scene is undoubtedly where the whole terracotta army, plus statues and a staircase, rises.

Tony Ching and Tsui Hark would return to this sort of grandiose finale several times (in the *Chinese Ghost Story* films, for instance). It's kitchen sink time – thrown in everything you've got.

There are many memorable beats in the finale of *The Terracotta Warrior*. General Mong on horseback, sword drawn, facing the approaching plane; several sword versus gun duels; Mong mowing down henchmen on the train, etc.

✳

Narratively, all plays out as expected – the villain meets his come-uppance, the heroes escape, but with a bittersweet outcome: Zhu Lili expires (cue an emotional death scene, filmed in trembling close-ups, with Zhu Lili dying in General Mong's arms). Mong climbs free of the wreckage of the collapsed resting-place of the terracotta army, but we cut to a coda, set in the present day. This was filmed at the real museum in Xian in Shaanxi province. Now Gong Li plays a student visiting the museum with a coachload of tourists. And working on cleaning the famous statues is none other than Mong, now in a modern guise. (Thus, not only is Dong'er/ Zhu Lili reborn in the form of the student, Mong continues, too. It's a cute, upbeat ending, which leads into the customary montage of highpoints from the film, accompanied by a pretty ballad sung by Sally Yeh and composed by Joseph Koo, with lyrics by James Wong Jim).

4

THE RAID

Chok Suk Hi Wang Chin Gwan

The Raid (*Choi Suk Ji Wang Siu Chin Gwan,* 1991) was co-directed by Tsui Hark and Tony Ching Siu-tung. Tsui produced for Film Workshop and Cinema City; Tsui co-wrote with Yuen Kai-chi, from a story by Michael Hui Koon-Man; Tony Ching and Ma Yuk-sing were action dirs.; art dir. by Chung Yee-Fung; make-up by Man Yun-Ling; costumes by Lee Pik-Kwan; hair by Gloria Lam Wai-Lok; sound: Foo Leng Luk Yam Sat; music: James Wong Jim and Romeo Diaz; editor: Marco Mak Chi-sin; and DPs: Arthur Wong and Tom Lau Moon-tong.

The Raid starred Jacky Cheung, Dean Shek, Tony Leung, Paul Chu-kong, Fennie Yuen, Chiu Man-yan, Lau Siu-ming, Corey Yuen Kwai, and Joyce Mina-godenzi. Released: Mch 28, 1991. 100 mins.

Uncle Choi by Michael Hui Koon-Man, a comic, was the basis of *The Raid* (it was published in Hong Kong from 1958 to the mid-1970s). In a nod to its origins in comicbookland, the movie deployed treated still photographs and optically altered footage in little snippets, as segues between scenes (and for the main titles).

The Raid is an adventure comedy, drawing on earlier Tsui Hark outings such as *Peking Opera Blues* and the *All the Wrong Clues* films, and Hollywood models like the *Indiana Jones* series. It is also reminiscent of *The Terracotta Warrior*, which Ching Siu-tung helmed in 1989.

The concept of *The Raid* – an aged, Chinese soldier-doctor using healing to do the right thing in the run-up to the Sino-Japanese War in the Thirties – is perfect for Tsui Hark (it's another reworking of a Wong Fei-hung motif, another very Chinese story, and another political context), while the emphasis on comedy and action is Tony Ching Siu-tung's *forte*.

Genius director Corey Yuen Kwai pops up in a cameo in *The Raid* as the big-nosed gangster, one of his rough-and-ready characterizations (he mainly has scenes with Jacky Cheung, which involve lots of shouting and bickering). And a big scene with Dean Shek, hanging off the cliffs we've seen in 1,000s of Hong Kong movies (which also involves plenty of arguing and yelling).

The lovely Fennie Yuen plays Tina, the main female chara amongst the heroes in *The Raid*: she is another Tsui Harkian woman – large glasses, short, dark hair, slight and skinny and tomboyish, like a female Tsui Hark (and also a dab hand with the long spear).

There are numerous Tsui-isms in *The Raid* – like the bust-up in the tent in act one, when everybody is suddenly armed, crowding around the heroes, and the heroes're dodging flying axes (it recalls the comical brawls in *We're Going To Eat You*). And visual effects a-plenty, with miniatures.[3]

✳

In act two *The Raid* stages a bedroom farce, with characters on the bed, someone knocks at the door, a character dives to hide under the bed, and so on. Tsui Hark had delivered this sort of adolescent desire-and-embarrassment scenario in *Shanghai Blues* (and much better, too). Another slice of farce has a love letter being read by several charas, who think it's for them (a classic piece of Tsui-ian humour). These sections are definitely directed by Tsui Hark, not Tony Ching.

The set-piece that climaxes act two of *The Raid* contains several classic Tony Ching Siu-tung moments: ninja brandishing swords leaping off a bi-plane onto railroad tracks at night, for instance. Logistically, these set-pieces are a nightmare, where moving aircraft have to be hung from cranes and cables. But Ching and the crew make them look so easy. However, in this set-piece there aren't enough shots or angles to make it flow satisfyingly, and again the low budget (or the too-tight schedule) cuts into the production. (Ching and Tsui hark had already done these sort of stunts in *The Terracotta Warrior* – and twenty years later, in *The Taking of Tiger Mountain*, Tsui was staging the same sort of gags with planes).

✳

The finale of *The Raid* plays out exactly as expected: fire-fights, outrageous stunts, the hero and the villain tussling, and everybody gets their moment to shine. In a beat that seems very bad taste, yet is also part of the action-adventure genre, and has been used many times before and

---

[3] The action beat involving a bi-plane attacking Uncle Choi hanging from a water dam is cribbed from *Indiana Jones and the Last Crusade*, down to the use of a model for the plane.

since, the heroes are rounded up and thrust into a sealed chamber, where they are gassed. The allusion to the death camps is clear and crude (and also, historically, *The Raid* is set in the 1930s).

Brother Big Nose redeems himself by helping the heroes to escape; guns are fired all over the place; actors are diving for cover every 30 seconds; stuff blows up; and the villain and the vamp expire in a giant explosion.

✳

This time, the critics were right about *The Raid*: somehow, despite all of the elements being present and correct, before and behind the camera, it doesn't quite work. The cast is great, the production personnel are the best in the business, and the technical elements are superb... but... the characterization of Uncle Choi doesn't really compel (and the way that Dean Shek plays him, like an older Tsui Hark with a white beard, isn't appealing, either).

Tsui Hark and Tony Ching Siu-tung have trod these action-adventure trails before (and since), and with much more satisfying results (prior to *The Raid*, in *Shanghai Blues* and *Peking Opera Blues* for Tsui, and *The Terracotta Warrior* and *The Witch From Nepal* for Ching; and afterwards in *The Taking of Tiger Mountain* and *Shanghai Grand* for Tsui, and *Wonder Seven* and *The Heroic Trio* for Ching). The Chingster and Tsuister should be able to pull this movie off, with this cast and these resources, but it remains still-born.

The Raid is wrestling with its too-low budget as well: it's trying to deliver *Indiana Jones and the Last Crusade* (1989), which cost U.S. $55.4 million, using under 2 or 3 million dollars. There are many scenes which are noticeably cutting corners.

5

THE HEROIC TRIO

Dung Fong Saam Hap

Michelle Yeoh, Maggie Cheung and Anita Mui... Let me repeat that cast list: Anita Mui, Michelle Yeoh and Maggie Cheung. And that's all you need to know!

But when you add that they are starring as superheroes, in a giant, action comedy choreographed by Tony Ching Siu-tung and co-directed by Ching and Johnny To Ke-fung – well, this is pure Hong Kong action cinema bliss!

The Heroic Trio (*Dung Fong Saam Hap*) was produced by China Entertainment Films and Paka Hill Productions; producer: Tony Ching; wr. by Sandy Shaw Lai-king; DPs: Tom Lau Moon-tong and Poon Sang Hang; ed. by Kam Wah; costume design: Yeung Gam-jan and Sin Pik-ha; with music by William Wu Wai-lap. Released Feb 12, 1993. 83 mins.

Sandy Shaw Lai-king (b. 1960) scripted films such as *The Execut-ioners, The Mad Monk, Project S, Justice, My Foot!, Twinkle Twinkle Little Star, Dr Wai, Shanghai Grand, My Father Is a Hero, Sky of Love* and *CJ7*. She worked for directors and stars such as Stephen Chow, Tsui Hark, Tony Ching and Johnnie To. For Ching, Shaw wrote *Dr Wai, The Heroic Trio* and *The Executioners*.

Ah, 1993... What a Miracle Year that was for Chinese action cinema! *Once Upon a Time In China 3, Fong Sai-yuk 1* and *2, Iron Monkey, Green Snake, City Hunter, The Bride With White Hair, The Swordsman 3, Flying Dagger, Butterfly and Sword, Kung Fu Cult Master* and *Last Hero In China*.

And *The Heroic Trio*. Which starred Michelle Yeoh Chu-kheng (as San), Maggie Cheung Man-yuk (as Chat) and Anita Mui Yim-fong (as

Wonder Woman), three of the hottest, funniest and finest actresses on the Hong Kong cinema scene (also in the cast were Damian Lau Ching-wan, Anthony Wong Chau-sang, James Pak, Paul CHun, Yen Shi-kwan, Chen Xuoxin, Jiang Haowen and Lee Siu-kei).

Who cares about the story, when the stars were so radiant, and the action was so superlative? (but folks, *The Heroic Trio* is definitely more fun than the dreary dreck of *Charlie's Angels* (2001), which it is sometimes compared to – even if Yuen Cheung-yan was the action choreographer for *Charlie's Angels*).[4]

Ah, but there *is* a story to *The Heroic Trio:* you've got three *very* sexy, young stars, right? So what're they going to be fighting over? What is at stake in this story? Only babies! Yes – someone is stealing new-born babes from a hospital ward (a very comicbook, superhero concept). Once you have the three superbabes protecting tiny tots, you have to concoct a super-villain with a master plan. This involves a dark lord (of the Ancient, Chinese, Ming, eunuch type), Evil Master – Yen Shi-kwan, who's carrying away babies (male, of course!) in order to create a new Emperor for China.

Michelle Yeoh Chu-kheng is San a.k.a. Ching a.k.a. Invisible Girl (the one who's stealing the babies); Anita Mui Yim-fong is Tung a.k.a. Wonder Woman, a superhero (and demure wife, married to a hapless cop, Inspector Lau), and Maggie Cheung Man-yuk is the maverick Chat a.k.a. Thief Catcher, who once worked for the villain lord.

But enough guff about the story in *The Heroic Trio* – how about the amazing wire-work stunts? How about the super-cool arrival of Maggie Cheung as Chat on a motorcycle, in a to-die-for, fitted, black leather costume?[5] How about the heart-shaped pout on Anita Mui's lips (and that incredible, clinging dress)?! How about the extraordinary fight scenes in which one of the participants is invisible?

Oh, the glory of Hong Kong action cinema is something to see! – when you've got such appealing actors, fantastic costume design (by Yeung Gam-jan and Sin Pik-ha), cool props like motorcycles,[6] ninja throwing stars, Batman masks, truly inventive and thrilling action, and a visual style which pumps every shot with smoke, back-lighting, and a gorgeous, glossy, comicbook look.

Once again, *The Heroic Trio* is another Hong Kong movie in which the *tone* is absolutely spot-on: it's that energetic aim to entertain combined with bags of colourful, comicbook style and just the right note to the

---

4 Even Hong Kong action choreographers as skilled as Yuen Cheung-yan couldn't make the feeble actors in *Charlie's Angels* convince as kick-ass heroines (altho' they did train beforehand with Yuen).
5 Maggie Cheung is at her vampiest and sexiest in *The Heroic Trio,* with hair teased into back-combed fluffiness, and a punk-Goth make-up.
6 In one scene, a motorcycle spins thru the air, round and round, with the riders still on the bike!

humour (some of which can be gross and/ or weird), and jammed with incendiary action sequences.

When you've seen a few Western/ North American movies and you come back to a Hong Kong picture, you're amazed at just how enthusiastically the Chinese filmmakers deliver the goods, how keen they are to entertain you, how *astonishing* they are at putting on a show, how *incredible* is their action (leaving *everyone else* far, far behind), how *fast* their storytelling is, and how much *fun* their movies are!

Hell, anything else is just *lame* after a Hong Kong movie. So serious, so po-faced, so sombre, so stuck/ mired in 'realism'/ 'naturalism' (like a swamp of *un*invention and *un*imagination).

Lighten up North America! Lighten up Europe!

The finale of *The Heroic Trio* is a stops-all-out rampage with our three heroines finally agreeing to work together. The action choreographers (Tony Ching Siu-tung *et al*) chuck in everything, as so often at the end of a Hong Kong action pic: there are many cliffhangers, as the actresses dangle from cables over rocky cliffs or tower blocks; sweeping wire-work, with the actresses and their stunt doubles flying all over the place; gags involving horses and motorcycles; and sword duels and flying stars.

The super-villain, Evil Master, proves to be a formidable opponent, who can take on all comers and survive. Even when the sucker's blown up and burns in another of Thief Catcher's bombs, he comes back to life as a frazzled skeleton (this section is a steal from *The Terminator 2* (1991), when morphing cyborg T-1000 emerged from the fire). *The Heroic Trio* has great fun turning Evil Master into a creature that merges with Michelle Yeoh's Invisible Girl, clinging to her back and taking control of her body – resulting in many unusual stunts.

Wow, the girls *really* take a battering in this 1993 movie! There's no holding back from the filmmakers, as the heroines're strangled, punched, kicked, and cut. This is a *lot* more'n receiving a little scratch on the cheek for the lead actress in the finale of your average, Western action-adventure pic! Oh no, there's blood spouting from mouths, the actresses're hurled to the ground and winded, and fall to their doom from on high.

The Heroic Trio garnered some poor reviews (from Asian critics who felt they'd seen it all before), but also some raves: several Western critics put it in their 'best of' lists. Howard Hampton loved it: 'Pop-art entertainment, a fairytale with live ammunition', and Barry Long admitted that *The Heroic Trio* was 'one of the films that hooked me on Hong Kong cinema' (F. Dannen, 338, 365).

6

THE EXECUTIONERS

Xian Dai Hao Xia Zhuan

The Executioners (*Xian Dai Hao Xia Zhuan*, a.k.a. *The Heroic Trio 2*, 1993) was produced by China Entertainment Films and Paka Hill Film, and co-directed by Tony Ching Siu-tung with Johnnie To Ke-fung. It was produced by To, Ching and Yeung Kwok-fai. It was written by two women – Susanne Chan and Sandy Shaw Lai-King (Shaw also has story by credit).[7] Music: Cacine Wong. DP: Poon Hang-sang. Eds.: A. Chik and Jue San-Git. Costumes: Yeung Gam-Jan and Sin Bi-Ha. Hair: Lee Lin-Dai and Kennedy Lau Kam-Hung. Make-up: Jeng Fung-Yin and Kitty Ho Wai-Ying. Art dirs.: Bruce Yu Ka-On and Raymond Chan Kam-Ho. Sept 30, 1993. 97 mins.

In the cast were Anita Mui Yim-fong, Michelle Yeoh Chu-kheng, Maggie Cheung Man-yuk, Damian Lau, Takeshi Kaneshiro, Paul Chun, Anthony Wong, Lau Ching-wan, Kwan Shan, Eddy Ko Hung and Sze Ning (that's a superb cast. Most had worked with Tony Ching before, and would do again).

The Executioners was a follow-up to *The Heroic Trio* (1993), with the same trio of super-women in the lead roles: Maggie Cheung Man-yuk, Anita Mui Yim-fong and Michelle Yeoh Chu-kheng, an incredible trinity of stars in a movie if ever there was one. (*The Executioners* shamelessly exploits its cast – Mui, Yeoh and Cheung are depicted naked in a giant bath in an early 'fan service' scene, by some ten minutes into the film.)

The Heroic Trio and *The Executioners* were filmed back-to-back at the 'Coca Cola factory', as a new studio in Hong Kong was dubbed (other films made there included some John Woo classics, and *Moon Warriors*). The same sets were used in both pictures.

---

7 An action movie written by two women is unusual in commercial cinema anywhere.

※

This time, we're in the future following an apocalypse, and what's at stake is water and the water supply, with our superheroes battling the capitalist crooks (from the Clear Water Corporation) who're controlling supplies in a futuristic society. So it's water this time, not money, or treasure, or drugs, or a super-weapon. Meanwhile, a Colonel (Paul Chun) is trying to take over the government, and the regime is incredibly repressive (there are armed cops and guards seemingly everywhere). This is what the heroic trio are fighting.

The premise is unusual, depressing, and not wholly compelling. Selling water that's not contaminated by radiation as the MacGuffin, rather than something aspirational like money or drugs, is trickier, even tho' water is infinitely more important to life than money or drugs or treasure or pretty much anything else. You can survive without most things, and even food for some time; but not water.

But the villains and what's at stake are only part of a Hong Kong action movie. And with actresses as strong as Anita Mui, Michelle Yeoh and Maggie Cheung in the foreground, and an action director like Tony Ching Siu-tung overseeing the stunts and the choreography, the plot takes a back seat, and is forgotten.

Assassinations occur with depressing regularity in *The Executioners* – the holy man Chong Hon is killed, Inspector Lau is gunned down at a railroad station, a masked man unloads bullets into civilians at a public protest meeting – nobody is safe and nowhere is secure in the world of *The Executioners*. The possibility of being injured or worse from a terrorist's bomb or a cop's gun are high.

There's also a hunchback survivor of Evil Master from the first film, Kau (Anthony Wong), whom Wonder Woman has taken under her wing (partly to atone for her misdeeds during her time working for Evil Master). And Takeshi Kaneshiro plays Chong Hon (a.k.a. Coda), a modern messiah in white robes.

※

Maggie Cheung is on delightful form as Thief Catcher, the cynical, money-hungry bounty hunter Chat: Cheung's uppity, cocky characterization comes from her astonishing turn as the innkeeper Jade in *New Dragon Gate Inn*: she struts about like she owns the city, a tomboy girl of the streets who can handle herself in amongst the men. (Especially enjoyable in *The Executioners* are Cheung's regular spats with fellow bounty hunter Ah Te (Lau Ching-wan), as they squabble over the same prey). Thief Catcher always gets the upper hand because she's – well, because she's played by Maggie Cheung!

Chat announces her cocky, rebellious manner in her first scene, with her dynamic, choreographed movements. She is not a girl to sit still. When Chat visits Wonder Woman, and tells everybody that it's time to have a bath, she walks in carrying a fireman's hose turned on full. Even though water is precious, she happily squirts it everywhere (this leads to the scene of the girls taking a bath).

Meanwhile, Anita Mui seems to have given up being Wonder Woman, and is now caring for her precious daughter, Cindy,[8] at home. (Her Wonder Womanness does emerge periodically, however, like when she trounces a thief stealing water in a back alley with some simple moves). In its crude fashion, *The Executioners* explores the issues of contemporary women in China finding a balance between home and work, motherhood and a career, being economically independent and economically dependent (Tung is married to the hapless but well-meaning cop, Inspector Lau; the film evokes their marriage and domestic life as the main sub-plot. Instead of a romantic sub-plot, it's a huband-and-wife sub-plot, and a family sub-plot. Lau's trying his best, but that's not enough in this tough socio-political climate). Let's remember that although *The Executioners* is a very macho and patriarchal movie, depicting an oppressive and repressive political regime, it was written by two women (Shaw and Chan), and stars three women (Yeoh, Mui and Cheung).

✳

The *mise-en-scène* of *The Executioners* is the rough-and-ready world of your typical post-apocalyptic flick (tho' on a small budget – indeed, one of the reasons that filmmakers choose post-apocalyptic scenarios is precisely because they can use trashy materials and existing locations).

Smoke and backlighting, military trucks and jeeps, wire fences, down-at-heel office blocks; everyone has a cigarette in their *bouche*; guards with rifles are all over the place (rather than a post-apocalyptic Hong Kong, it looks, as so many futuristic scenarios do, more like WWII. Of course – WWII is an all-purpose apocalypse still within living memory). The look of *The Executioners* resembles pictures such as *Brazil* (1985), *Escape From New York* (1981), and *The Terminator* (1984). Or maybe it's how the film reckons Hong Kong will look lioke after the Hand-over.

The Executioners is one of those studio-bound films in the thriller or horror or fantasy genres where you never seem to see the sky. So there is never a breather from the claustrophobic, oppressive atmosphere. We're always stuck in one cramped room or another. In addition, the miasma of political repression hangs over everything, and life can never be free and

---

8 Charlie in the English dub.

easy anymore. In this respect, *The Executioners* is a successful depiction of political oppression, which permeates every aspect of society. In *The Executioners*, the oppression weighs so heavily on everybody there's no possibility of life being anything other than a struggle for survival.

The Executioners moves into pop music promo territory (as Hong Kong movies often do) in some of the action scenes as well as the contemplative scenes. For ex, when Inspector Lau is gunned down by the Colonel's mob (with the Colonel leading the charge), *The Executioners* shifts into slo-mo, Sam Peckinpah-style, accompanied by a pop song (the songs in *The Executioners* included the theme song of *The Heroic Trio*, 'A Woman's Heart' (composed by Lo Ta-yu and Albert Leung), and were sung by Anita Mui, the 'Madonna of Hong Kong').

Inspector Lau had been implicated in the murder of Chong Hon by the authorities, giving them the excuse they need to get rid of him. Lau tries to flee the city with his daughter Cindy – but from the main rail station, which seems a little silly, when he's being hunted by the Colonel's lackeys.

✳

The plot of *The Executioners* isn't cast aside by the filmmakers, however: despite the criticisms of the critics: *The Executioners*, believe it or not, is actually telling a story.

And *The Executioners* is consciously political: the scenes of public protests against the control of the water supply which descend into riots and gunshots are clear references to Tiananmen Square, and the 1993 movie is obviously speculating on how things might be after the Hand-over.

There's a further riot at the railroad station, as everybody tries to flee the city (and there aren't enough tickets, or enough trains). This is one of the clearest dramatizations of the uneasy feelings in Canton about the Hand-over to control by the People's Republic China in 1997: *get out of Hong Kong!* is the loud and clear message. In the rail station, the crowd is hysterical, jostling, shouting, waving their tickets in the air, with the authorities firing tear gas and then bullets. (Anyone who slips through unauthorized towards the trains is shot).

✳

The Executioners is nihilistic, with several groups resorting to senseless violence. This is the depressing thing about *The Executioners* – the underlying, political context is harsh and uncompromising. Civilians are gunned down regularly, no matter what the heroes try.[9] So even with the heroes emerging triumphant, the victory is at a great cost in terms of human lives.

9 The doctors looking after the injured President, for example, are executed in cold blood.

The Tiananmen Square massacre resonates in *The Executioners*; it is an angry film, but it's not sure where to direct that anger. Hong Kong movies couldn't make direct critiques of the government of the People's Republic of China (before the Hand-over, and definitely not after it); thus, the frustration they felt at being intimately involved with Mainland China had to be channelled into other cinematic forms (this partly explains the ultra-violence and bloody battles of Hong Kong films). A movie like *The Executioners*, with its overtly political plot, is all about Hong Kong in 1993, halfway between Tiananmen Square (1989) and the Hand-over (1997). It's the sort of movie that would be tougher to make after the Hand-over, when scripts had to be submitted to the authorities.

The critics didn't warm to *The Executioners*, and compared it unfavourably with *The Heroic Trio* (which many critics, particularly Western ones, really liked). Both movies were regarded as impressive but depressing (which was also the view of Michelle Yeoh).

It might also be due to the more confused plotting of *The Executioners*, and the need to find things for the characters to do when there are a few too many characters. *The Executioners* is a little over-stuffed with characters, some of whom are not required to tell the story. Consequently, parts of *The Executioners* feel a little rushed – in Hollywood, and produced today, it would be a four-act movie, running over two hours. Three acts is not quite sufficient to do justice to the issues and themes as carried by so many characters.

7

WONDER SEVEN

7 Jin Gong

An action comedy thriller directed by Tony Ching Siu-tung and starring Michelle Yeoh Chu-kheng – that's all you need to know! There's nothing better than watching Ching let loose with wild action – nobody can deliver motorcycle stunts (including flying bikes) like Ching, and Yeoh is a sensational screen presence if ever there was one.

The credits of *Wonder Seven* (*7 Jin Gong*, 1994) are: prod. by China Entertainment Films; producer: Catherine Hun; wr. by Charcoal Tan Cheung, Elsa Tang Bik-yin and Tony Ching (one of his two writing credits – indicating that the project had some significance for Ching), with a story credit for Manfred Wong Man-Chun; Xiong Xin-xin, Deon Lam Dik On and Lau Chi Ho were action dirs., along with Ching, of course (the car and motorcycle stunts were by Bruce Law Lai-yin); art dir. by James Leung Wah-Sing; make-up and hair by Cheng Wai-Fong; ed. by Poon Hung; DPs: Poon Hang-Sang and Peter Ngor; costumes by Silver Cheung Sai-Wang and Chan Sau-Ming; and music by Barry Chung, Ta-Yu Lo and Fabio Carli. Released: Apl 1, 1994. 888 mins.

With a terrific cast (that included Kent Cheng, Xiong Xin-xin, Li Ning, Kwan Shan, Chin Ho, Vincent Lau-tak, Elvis Tsui, Roger Kwok, Chi Ming Lau, Kam-Kong Wong, Hilary Tsui, and Andy Hui), and a superb technical team, *Wonder Seven* has a simple narrative set-up: a band of seven special forces agents from the People's Republic of China (Superman, Shaolin Monk, Dragon, Coach, Steelbar, Fatty10 and Tiny), are working undercover in Hong Kong, fighting crime (and, in particular, political/

---

10 Called Nanny in the subtitles – perhaps because he is the doctor among the group.

terrorist crime. The criminal underworld in China is buying American weapons to sell to Chinese terrorists). The run-up to the 1997 Handover lurks behind this movie, and the uneasy relations between Canton and the Mainland. The team's job is to patrol the borders[11] – the robbery that opens the movie has some crooks heading for the Mainland in a van following a heist, with the Wonder Seven in pursuit. The background of *Wonder Seven* is thus explicitly political, even if this is a movie in a comicbook vein.

There's a McGuffin (a special card device for money deals), which's a mere pretext for multiple firefights, acrobatic duels, motorcycle chases, and more than enough flying stunts for any action fan. (Hollywood movies such as *James Bond, Diehard* and *Lethal Weapon* are some of the films that *Wonder Seven* is sending up).

Wonder Seven is a popcorn movie, an over-the-top action comedy in the Jackie Chan[12] vein, another comicbook outing, like *City Hunter* (1993), but with seven heroes fighting political exploitation and bad guys instead of one. In Tony Ching Siu-tung's action formula, a team of seven means seven times more stunts, more motorcycles, and more action! (It's a kind of expansion on the *Heroic Trio* movies of the year before – superheroes on motorcycles, but this time it's seven instead of three).

Wonder Seven is one of those casual/ throwaway action movies where villains[13] whip out a gun at the slightest provocation and blow someone away at close range – whether they're a henchman who's flunked, a rival boss, or even a Buddhist monk. Like it doesn't matter. Like stuntmen in a scene exist solely to be slain in two seconds.

The only two significant women in this very boysy picture are Michelle Yeoh and Hilary Tsui. Of course, as the top-billed player, Yeoh overshadows Tsui (and everybody else). As the only female member of the Wonder Seven, Tsui's Tiny Archer is a small, modest, tomboy type (the polar opposite of Yeoh's slinky assassin, so as not to clash with her).

Michelle Yeoh's wardrobe (by Silver Cheung Sai-Wang and Chan Sau-Ming) is a delight – silk pant suits with flared trousers (scarlet in the first act, white in the second act). With her dark glasses (of course) and fitted jackets, Yeoh cuts a glamorous, slinky figure throughout the movie. No wonder that Oliver Stone, when he met her in the 1980s, reckoned that Yeoh was the sexiest woman in movies.

*

11 The costs of working for the security services for the People's Republic of China are not ignored: Superman dies, and Dragon is severely injured.
12 Chan is among the jokes.
13 Chin Ho plays the super-villain Chun with a cackling exuberance, a cartoon bad guy who kills a monk at point blank range simply because he gets in the way.
  To Chun, it's a crazy game, and getting hurt or shot is simply part of life's surreal carnival. Yet henchmen're being wasted by the hundred, with gouts of blood; but the jokey tone remains.

Wonder Seven opens with a giant action sequence lasting six minutes, where the special forces team of seven show off their stuff, their quippy repartee, their personalities, their way of operating, and their teamwork (Tony Ching Siu-tung is fond of of opening very big very quickly – getting into a balls-to-the-wall action scene without even any build-up or preamble or pretty 2nd unit shots of a location. *Wonder Seven* opens directly with a noisy heist). The sequence is like a *wushu* hunt and fight scene (the heroes chasing down robbers), but with (motor-cross-style) bikes instead of horses, and with guns instead of swords: the tone is set by Ching's highly entertaining mix of stunts and comedy, of thrills and beauty. (The robbers burst onto the scene like outlaws in a cowboy flick – guns blazing, filmed from inside looking outside, as if from a saloon).

None of this is taken straight or seriously – instead, there are 100s of stunt gags crammed into the sequence. Like Tiny Archer bringing down a crook with a bow and arrow (made from a *qi* stringed instrument), while riding her bike, as if she's a samurai in an Akira Kurosawa movie; like thieves being chased into pig farms (and landing – splat! – on top of pigs and into pig-doo); like Nanny crushing his back after the fence jump; like motorcycles diving into flocks of geese (there are a surprising number of animals in *Wonder Seven*. There are still farms in the New Territories).

The motorcycle stunts in *Wonder Seven* are incredible – Bruce Law has to be one of the greatest car and motorbike stunt co-ordinators ever. There's a wildness and devil-may-care attitude to the stunts that's reminiscent of the stuntwork in the silent movie era. You can see Law's work in many films by the great Hong Kong directors, such as Ringo Lam, Tsui Hark and John Woo.

✳

When the film reverts to conventional storytelling, we meet the Wonder Seven team. Some of the scenes in act 1 of *Wonder Seven* involving the group of special forces agents are a little too cute, too smug and too pat:[14] like, they all live on a funky barge next to a pier; like, they josh like teenagers rather than professional military men; like, they dream about buying a restaurant (so they are all pitching in to buy it); like, they punish one of their own who's transgressed by making them walk the plank while they pelt them with vegetables (another bit of *Arrrgh! Avast!* pirate business for Ching Siu-tung, after the third *Swordsman* flick, which featured piratey goings-on a-plenty).

It's all too cutsie – as if *7 Gin Gong* was originally conceived for 15

---

[14] There's something a little off about this 1994 movie in its attitude towards the material – the jokey tone is maintained throughout, particularly in the joshing amongst the heroes. But there's a smugness about it, and an adolescent, inane quality to this bunch of people. They're not teenagers, they're not 'ordinary' people, they're trained professionals, but they act like a goofy group of kids.

year-old kids, as if the Goonies suddenly became Chinese operatives brilliant at *kung fu*. Only when their boss Colonel Yim Tung (Wong Kam-kong) turns up to deliver the customary exposition and give them their assignment does the Wonder Seven group knuckle down to acting like adults.

Meanwhile, another twee, naïve scene has Michelle Yeoh Chu-kheng's Fong-ying encountering Ning Li's[15] Yip Fei at the waterside (at Tsimshatsui Pier). Their flirtatious relationship begins with falls into the sea, a gag that's repeated later on (and it really is Yeoh who takes high falls into the briny). Such adolescent frolicks seem out of kilter with the contemporary setting – you can get away with this sort of hokum easier in the historical genre.

The flirtatious relationship between Yip Fei and Fong-ying is the romantic sub-plot in *Wonder Seven*, pitting the leader of the Wonder Seven troupe with the gangster's moll. Fong-ying is part of the Chinese gang chasing the special card device, but she reverses her allegiance when she encounters Fei (she also has an on-off relationship with the mad dog in the crime syndicate, Chun Ho – Chin Ho).

Like Tsui Hark, Tony Ching Siu-tung is fond of evoking traditional, Chinese customs and folklore – thus, the big action sequence in the first act of *Wonder Seven* takes place at a Lion Dance and a festival at the Cultural Center (which, like many a Hong Kong action movie, soon dissolves into the chaos of a running battle as the two sides clash and the public scatter screaming).

The Lion Dance sequence is skilfully staged as the sort of chaotic festival that the *James Bond* movies used to deliver, where the villains are hidden in amongst the performers and the lively crowd. (Every shot is a long lens shot, to emphasize the fragmentation of space, so that no one can see the whole area and it's disorientating, and also to make the setting look so much bigger).

Give some action directors teams of lion dancers and they'll come up with the sort of wild action we've seen in the *Once Upon a Time In China* series or the *Fong Sai-yuk* series. *Wonder Seven* is no different: the place erupts in chaos (following the baddie, Chun Ho, killing the corrupt businessman), and our heroes're chasing the villains while continuing to dance. Yip Fei and Fong-ying have another of their many spats – flying way up high as Fatty uses a crane to lift Fei into the sky.

❂

Wonder Seven rolls along at a cracking pace, and only stutters in a few areas. One is the second part of the second act (between 45 and 60

15 Li was an Olympic gymnast.

minutes), which loses momentum somewhat; also, Michelle Yeoh is under-used (that mightbe due to scheduling).

Act two of *Wonder Seven* comprises the usual content of an action-adventure yarn in a three-act narrative form: skirmishes between the heroes and the villains. The settings range from a hospital (a staple of Hong Kong cinema), a junkyard at night, a golf course, a stadium, and a forest at night (*Wonder Seven* features *a lot* of night shooting). What's impressive here is how the filmmakers have opted to feature a series of smaller-scale set-pieces instead of one big one in the middle of the second act and a big one for the climax of the act (as is usual in Hong Kong cinema and action cinema in general). That means there's more variety in the types of action, in the combinations of characters, and in the settings.

Some of the act two set-pieces are more successful than the others. No action director could shoot a duff sequence in a hospital, with all those spaces to explore (staircases, elevators, corridors, glass partitions, curtained-off wards, etc), plus all of those props (wheelchairs, stretchers, beds, medical machinery), and the staff and patients caught in the middle). In *Wonder Seven*, pretty much everything is employed (including a fire hose to lower down the injured Dragon (Vincent Lau Tak) in a stairwell), as the heroes and the villains tussle over capturing him, and taking him to safety.

In the hospital set-piece there are some classic Chingisms – like the spokes of a wheelchair being fired at a heavy, ninja-style, like multiple knives, and Yip Fei using throwing knives instead of a gun. The hospital also features several groups of authorities clashing – the Wonder Seven, the Hong Kong detectives, and some officials from the People's Republic of China (they all distrust each other).

The stadium set-piece (filmed in the Queen Elisabeth Stadium) is notable for the image of Dragon being shot by mistake by Yip Fei as he falls onto an enormous red flag. Meanwhile, Colonel Yim is sniped by an unknown assassin (Dragon is injured when he chases him).

The golf course set-piece sees Yip Fei going alone to meet Fong-ying (rather foolishly); the scene rapidly escalates into another intense fire-fight, led by Yeung's boys. Yet again, the pacing is brisk, managing to squeeze in a kicking-punching duel between Fei and Fong-ying, noisy fire-fights (where Fei is out-gunned by a host of henchmen), conversations about that darn card device, and some more flirtation between the film's golden couple, Fei and Fong-ying.

The night forest sequence introduces a new complication: the introduction of Coach (played by veteran Elvis Tsui), the commander of the special forces who yells at Yip Fei then dukes it out with him with knives, then with empty-handed *kung fu*. The scene includes some impressive nighttime photography involving helicopters, hunting dogs, flashlights and searchlights (there's no doubt that Hong Kong cameramen are the kings in all cinema of filming at night. The key is not using *lots* of lights, but knowing exactly how to use the lamps, and where to place them in relation to the action and the camera).

To remind the Wonder Seven who's boss, Coach and his lackeys set fire to their pier-side den, providing the mandatory explosion in a Tony Ching movie. Actually, that isn't only the explosion in this part of *Wonder Seven*: the team convene on their motorcycles for another over-the-top action sequence: riding alongside a truck and setting off explosives so it leaps off the truck and careens down the road. Why? Because Yip Fei has been the fall guy for the team and is being hauled back to the People's Republic of China (no, no, don't ask why a political captive is being carted off to the Mainland in a shipping container strapped to a truck!).

✳

The climax of act two of *Wonder Seven* seems not quite big or spectacular enough: it's a face-off in a car yard at night. Yeung has brought a phalanx of henchmen on motorcycles, who take on the Wonder Seven (or, rather, the Wonder Six – Dragon is injured, remember). The addition of banners on the bikes is a typical Chingian touch, reminding us that this is in part a cowboy or samurai picture (it's a bit of Akira Kurosawa, but on bikes).

So we expect something a little wilder than the fire-fight that ensues: the motorcycles are positioned in rows, like two armies facing each other on the battlefield. Instead of the expected acrobatics with motorcycles, it's back to gunfire again.

Anyway, in the chaos, Yeung unleashes an explosion which takes out Superman (Andy Hui) in an avalanche of falling cars. The movie exaggerates and reverses the too-cutsie sentiments in act one by allowing the rest of the Wonder Seven to dissolve into hysterics.

The artificially-produced pathos and woe results in the bizarre funeral ritual for Superman: he's strapped to his motorbike, sent into the air above a cliff, and exploded by remote control. It's the gang's crude and simple-minded way of honouring Superman. Paul Bramhall at the City On Fire website summed it up in 2019:

> *Wonder Seven* deserves some kind of award for the most ridiculous funeral scene ever committed to celluloid. I mean, why go for a burial or cremation, when you can have your buddies straddle your lifeless

corpse to your motorbike, rig it to the nines with dynamite, and then send you full speed over the edge of a cliff before detonating mid-air to send you up in the mother of all fireballs? ...It's moments like these that serve as a reminder of the days when you never knew what a H.K. flick was going to assault you with next, and movies from this era were really the beginning of the sunset on this unique brand of H.K. styled insanity.

✳

The finale of *Wonder Seven* involves – inevitably! – many motorcycle stunts (flying motorbikes, motorbikes in elevators, up stairs, etc), helicopters and cranes hanging off the side of skyscrapers, fire fights a-plenty, and more. Oh, Michelle Yeoh looks so cool on a motorcycle soaring thru the air while shooting up henchmen!

Wonder Seven's climax is one of the more ridiculously over-the-top outings in Tony Ching's cinema. It looks as if the movie aimed to pack in as many cliffhangers and snakepit scenarios as possible in 25 minutes. In fact, it's a whole *History of Action Cinema*, with pretty much every gag and stunt that has ever been put film.

There are multiple sections to the finale: most of them are staged in the villains' skyscraper. The face-off in the underground car lot is merely the opening barrage of numerous fire-fights and running battles (by the time the movie's over, we've visited every area of the building).

The Wonder Seven (or Five) arrive on their dirt bikes, of course, reminding us that this is a preposterous comicbook movie. For some reason, Mr Big is playing a drumkit when the heroes turn up, and acts like a TV game show host – to him, it's all a game, and human life itself is absolutely worthless, only useful in terms of how many thrills it can add to the game. Chun Ho isn't even interested in the special cards or the money – those are simply gimmicks to get the game moving. When hostilities begin, the motorcycles're employed in some manic flying stunts. (Some of the stunts come from cowboy flicks – like when Ying's motorbike catches on fire and she hops onto Fei's bike).

Then it's all hands into the service elevators, and up we go – to the security room, to the office balcony, to the rooftop, to elevator shafts, to stairwells, to corridors, and finally to Chun Ho's secret heli-pad.

Every inch of the building is exploited: among the OTT gags are Coach and Yip Fei fighting on a crane hanging over the side of the building; a face-off between the four principals – Fei, Ying, Chun and Coach (Fei, Ying and Coach are injured by bullets); the Wonder Seven finish off the crooked Mainland general (they all fire at him at once, in a circle); the team fleeing the building (Monk slides down a cable in the elevator shaft); and an intense fire-fight amongst the elevators, with many high falls (including the mandatory gag of a victim getting chopped in half by the elevator mechanism). If you find elevators scary, don't watch *Wonder Seven*!

In between the many extravagant gags are fire-fights and fist fights, as the Wonder Seven encounter Chun Ho's henchmen, and then Coach's team (Coach gives his boys an order to blow up the skyscraper, to add a countdown to the already frenetic activity in the climax).

The finale runs thru so many bits of business as if it's trying to pack the endings to ten or twenty movies into a single picture. The final action scene of *Wonder Seven* is a big helicopter stunt (echoing the 1978 *Superman* movie and its many imitators). There's another duel, between Yip Fei on the floor and Chun Ho in a helicopter (which he uses like a battering ram, pushing Fei into an elevator, which he then blows up with a grenade. Ying has been taken hostage by Chun). Quick-thinking Monk creates an explosion way down below, to prevent an elevator containing Fei to hit the ground (it shoots out of the elevator shaft, into the sky, crashing into Chun's chopper).

Here we have the final cliffhanger (of many), and the demise of the super-villain in the customary high fall: the helicopter falls from the sky, upside-down, catching a runner on part of the crane. Yip Fei saves Ying and, to his credit, Chun Ho slips the cards MacGuffin to Ying before the chopper slides off the skyscraper, crashing onto the street below.

There's nothing here we haven't seen before, but for a fraction of the budget of similar Hollywood productions, *Wonder Seven* is highly entertaining. It hits all the expected narrative beats, adds some twists of its own, and all the while the movie simply ignores the fact that this is all crudely artificial.

Michelle Yeoh's Fong-ying has less to do in the finale of *Wonder Seven* – maybe Yeoh's schedule didn't allow for more time. Instead, much of the action is given over to Li Ning as Yip Fei, who gets to battle with Coach, then Chun Ho (with Ying being taken hostage by Chun). Altho' Li is accomplished enough for action scenes, he doesn't have the star power and charisma of Michelle Yeoh, whom we'd much rather see battling Chun (tho' Fei has to take on Coach, his boss, of course).

The Terracotta Warrior (1989).

张艺谋 GONG Li
巩俐 Zhang Yimou

古今大战秦俑情
TERRACOTTA WARRIOR

The Raid (1991).

The Heroic Trio (1993).

The Executioners (1993).

Wonder Seven (1994).

8

DR WAI IN "THE SCRIPTURE WITH NO WORDS"

Yale: Mo Him Wong

Dr Wai In "The Scripture With No Words" (*Yale: Mo Him Wong*, a.k.a. *Mao Xian Wang*, 1996) is an action-adventure comedy starring Jet Li and directed by Tony Ching Siu-tung. Produced by Tsai Mu-ho, Wong Sing-ping and Charles Heung Wah-keung for Win's Entertainment and Eastern Production; exec. producer: Tiffany Chen Ming-Ying; wr. by Lam Wai-Lun, Roy Szeto and Sandy Shaw Lai-King; DPs: Tom Lau Moon-tong and Edmond Fung Yuen-man; music by Frankie Chan; ed. by Marco Mak Chi-sin and Angie Lam; art dirs.: Jason Mok, Kenneth Yee Chung-man and Fu Tak-Lam; hair by Chau Siu-Mui; costumes by Mok Kwan-kit, William Fung Kwun-Man and Chan Gai-Dung; make-up: Man Yun-Ling and Xu Qiu-Wen; and action dirs.: Ching and Ma Yuk-shing. Released: Mch 14, 1996. 87/ 91 mins.

The teaming of Ching Siu-tung and Jet Li as actor and director has produced some of the finest moments in recent, Chinese cinema – *Hero, The Warlords, The Swordsman 2, The Emperor and the White Snake*, etc (Ching brings the best out of Li, and Li inspires Ching to ever-greater filmic heights). *Dr Wai* features terrific support from Rosamund Kwan, Takeshi Kaneshiro, Charlie Yeung, Ngai Sing, Billy Chow and Law Kar-ying.

The production of *Dr Wai* was set back by a fire[1] which ruined film sets (that cost HK $10 million – a lot of money in the Hong Kong film industry). *Dr Wai* globetrots – from the desert in Xian to Shanghai to the Great Wall of China (some of the film was shot in and around Beijing).

[1] It's scary just how many fires occur in every film production centre on Earth, even today.

A higher budget outing than your average Hong Kong picture, you can see the Hong Kong dollars being burnt up on the screen as a railroad engine careens thru a crowded downtown area (and thru the facades of several buildings), sending stunt guys flying in all directions, as a prehistoric, mechanical Golden Ox out of Homer's *Odyssey* goes haywire (in the prologue), and later buildings are collapsing, characters smash through brick walls, and so on.

A historical adventure set in the 1930s in Shanghai, during the Japanese Occupation, *Dr Wai* doesn't labour its political elements, because they are already shining in neon (particularly when *Dr Wai* was released a year before the 1997 Hand-over). An oppressive regime – no, *two* oppressive regimes are here! – Japan and Mainland China! And quite a bit of time is spent with a newspaper that's struggling to keeping on reporting the news in the face of aggressive social and political forces, a commentary upon governments suppressing the media. The newspaper is run by an editor called the Headmaster, played by Hong Kong veteran Law Kar-ying. (And during the finale, a vision of the future is shown to the heroes, in the form of newsreel footage of the fall of Japan in WWII and the atomic bombs. To put those serious issues into a goofy action-adventure yarn is unusual).

However, Chinese cinema, and Hong Kong cinema, has mined the political conflicts between China and Japan many, many times. You can bet that ever since the 1930s the issue has appeared in several films in every year. It is a very familiar political background, which can be evoked instantly in a shorthand manner. The audience knows exactly where they are. (And, like all explosive situations or war zones, you can plump your characters down in the midst of it all and generate instant drama).

Dr Wai is portrayed as the superhero-ish, all-round adventurer of a million movie serials – he can ride horses (and leap from them), he can wisecrack, he can flirt with women, and he can beat up henchmen like it's nothing. And nothing is ever seriously in jeopardy because, as with those million adventure movies, we know that the hero will always prevail. But we go along for the ride.

It works also because of the casting – the role was clearly written by Roy Szeto, Lam Wai-Lun and Sandy Shaw Lai-King knowing that Jet Li would be playing Dr Wai and Chow Si-Kit in the present day. Similarly, the romantic subplots work because they are built around the sort of characters that Rosamund Kwan plays (in particular opposite Li, as in the *Once Upon a Time In China* series).

Dr Wai In "The Scripture With No Words" is a counterpart (and a kind of sequel) to *The Terracotta Warrior,* which Tony Ching Siu-tung directed in 1989: both are comical adventures in the Hollywood Hokum style, which travel between the past and the present (tho' the present day in *The Terracotta Warrior* is the Thirties, and here we go back from the present – 1996 – to the Thirties. And back even further, to set up the MacGuffin, the magical box).

Dr Wai In "The Scripture With No Words" shamelessly steals from the *Indiana Jones* series,[2] just as *The Terracotta Warrior* had done (and Jackie Chan did in his *Armor of God* films): Dr Wai is an archæologist adventurer who's charged with finding a magical box from ancient times (the box leads to the scripture). So there's a comical sidekick, a *femme fatale* among the Japanese, outrageous action set-pieces, and our hero's pitted against numerous henchmen as he fights for the Right and the Good.

Dr Wai In "The Scripture With No Words" is more Hong Kong hokum, delivered with a breezy touch which makes the Hollywood action movie counterparts look like rusty tanks mired in mud. So light, so fast! – *Dr Wai* hurtles along like the out-of-control steam engine in one of its very expensive set-pieces.

And the wonder of *Dr Wai* is of course Jet Li – and Li as directed by the amazing Tony Ching Siu-tung, a director who never lets mere physical laws hold back his performers or his movies. If Ching wants to place an actor *right up there*, he doesn't let anything or anyone stop him doing it! And Li moves with the grace of Gene Kelly or Fred Astaire at their very best. The man is a cinematic dream, a man who exudes more charisma and charm than a whole army of wannabe stars.

Dr Wai is a counterpoint to Wong Fei-hung in the Jet Li cinematic canon of the Nineties era – again, he's clad in white and pale colours (and one of the only guys wearing a hat, so you can spot him anywhere). At one point, he uses an umbrella as a weapon, as he does in the *Once Upon a Time In China* series.

Once again Jet Li has a flirtatious relationship with Rosamund Kwan, his co-star in the *Once Upon a Time In China* series (and other movies, such as *The Swordsman 2*). In the present day, Kwan is Chow Si-Kit's wife in the process of a fractious divorce with Chow; in the past, Kwan plays a formidable Japanese agent, Cammy.

And the teaming of Jet Li with the gorgeous Takeshi Kaneshiro as his comical sidekick Shing is a winner – Kaneshiro gamely goofs it up for the camera (stepping away from his familiar serious dramatic roles,[3] or his

---

2 And from Dr Wisley Wei by Ni Kuang.
3 Is this the same Takeshi Kaneshiro who smoulders so impressively in *The House of Flying Daggers?* It's hard to believe!

soap operaish parts). The 1996 movie contains two flirtatious relationships – between Dr Wai and Cammy, and between Shing and Yan-yan.

One of the delights of *Dr Wai In "The Scripture With No Words"* is seeing familiar Hong Kong stars cutting loose a little – Rosamund Kwan, under-rated by some Western critics as pretty and pert but merely adequate as an actress, gets to play a woman who conducts dodgy laboratory experiments on men! This includes the sight of Kwan playing Cammy as a dominatrix in black wielding a whip. (Kwan is more game for trying new things than critics giver her credit for. Look at her in *Assassins* (Bill Chung Siu-hung, 1993), for instance. And any actress is going to jump at the chance to fling a whip about, clad in clingy black dress like a 1930s Catwoman, and perform martial arts stunts that run rings around the guys).

Another scene where actors let their hair down – literally – has Messers Kaneshiro and Li dragging up as two of mobster Hung Sing's many concubines. They're in glitzy drag so that they can perform another staple of the action-adventure genre – the comical heist (to snaffle a document from the Japanese Embassy in Shanghai during a high-class function). The Embassy party gives us the ritzy setting for a picture set in Shanghai in the 1930s.

The scene where Dr Wai and Cammy are in a near-clinch in the office with the safe in the Embassy seems especially Tsui Harkian in its evocation of crossdressing – a man in drag is almost-about-to seduce a woman. (It's funny also because it draws on the characters that Kwan and Li have played together. Earlier, Kaneshiro and Li deflect the amorous attentions of two guys).

✻

Once again, Tony Ching Siu-tung demonstrates his mastery of visual effects in *Dr Wai In "The Scripture With No Words"*. Indeed, he may be the finest film director of visual effects in Hong Kong, even including Tsui Hark. Models, optical effects, digital animation, special make-up, and 100s of practical effects, *Dr Wai* is virtually a whole history of visual effects filmmaking.[4] Exploding buildings, collapsing walls, a sword duel with giant, flaming swords – *Dr Wai* has got the lot. Jet Li fights Sumo wrestlers (!), grapples a giant rat, parachutes out of a crashing plane with Rosamund Kwan, and dispatches henchmen by the score.

There are rivals after the godly box, as in the usual treasure seeking plot – such as the gangster Hung Sing (a.k.a. Hung Hung Sing Sing, played by Colin Chou). The heroes have several tussles with Hung Sing – the finest one climaxes act two, and features Dr Wai using wire in the ninja

---

4 Thomas Weisser enthused: 'the most impressive collection of special effects ever amassed for one movie' (58).

fashion fired from fountain pens (because he's an author, right? And the pen is mightier than the sword). In a warehouse setting, the participants smash into piles of iron pipes, scaffolding and the mandatory ingredient of any Hong Kong action scene: large glass windows. Dr Wai gallops into the fray on a horse and carriage, and Hung Sing uses a huge steel pulley to smash it to pieces and knock out the horse.

This is one of the great duels in Jet Li's film career – it's played in the comical action style, but that doesn't make it less impressive on a physical and practical level. The King of Adventurers tops every move or gadget that Hung Sing produces – a rifle, a pistol, etc. In a send-up of *Once Upon a Time In China*, Dr Wai fires the spines of an umbrella at Hung, piercing him like a pin cushion. Dr Wai doesn't finish off Hung (he escapes), but he does save the newspaper editor, the Headmaster.

Another action sequence in act two of *Dr Wai* sees a bunch of heavies storming the newspaper offices to beat up the Headmaster and threaten the operation (the Headmaster turns out to be a martial artist as well as a journalist fighting for free speech). Charlie Yeung – very cute in bunches and overalls – receives her finest moment in *Dr Wai* when she takes on the hoods out in the street.[5] Tiny and skinny she may be, but with Tony Ching directing the film, Yeung can be portrayed as kicking ass (including with several kicks). Yeung is good – but Jet Li is better, entering the fray and demonstrating once again why he's such a wonderful action movie star.

Yet another action scene – which tops act two – sees the King of Adventurers taking on Sumo wrestlers, of all things. It seems to be a case of the writers answering the question: who *hasn't* Jet Li battled yet in a movie? (There is a connection, albeit tenuous – some of the villainous forces in *Dr Wai* are Japanese).

While Shing wisely hides during the fights (in the role of the cowardly sidekick), Dr Wai dispatches the Sumo wrestlers. And before that, he tackles the famous 'Chinjas', Tony Ching's version of Japanese ninjas. It's not a Ching movie without a bunch of stunt guys dressed in black, Japanese *shinobi* outfits: here, Dr Wai employs sneaky moves of the *James Bond* sort: frying the ninjas with electricity as they're connected by metal chains to a wire fence, for example (the same wire fence that Dr Wai had used to deflect their throwing stars).

＊

One half of the final act takes place in a plane flying towards the Great Wall of China. Many of the gags in the aircraft are self-consciously old-fashioned – this might be a Bob Hope and Bing Crosby *Road To...* movie

---

5 Dr Wai comes up the idea of having everybody carrying fake boxes, and splitting up outside, to put the heavies off the scent.

from the 1940s. Hung Sing is by now the all-purpose villain, exploding into the scene from the floor of the plane, and continuing into the temple finale. Plus we have that very dangerous box, and explosives, too, and people switching sides – so there are plenty of ingredients for the writers to use to keep the adventure bubbling along. The plane has to crash, and our heroes have to bail out – this is an *Indiana Jones* type of movie. The budget of *Dr Wai* was enough to film real aerial footage and freefall images not often seen in Hong Kong cinema.

In the second half of the finale of *Dr Wai* – in the usual setting of the Big Set (statues, a temple, sand, flickering torches) – there are four heroes – Jet Li, Rosamund Kwan, Takeshi Kaneshiro and Charlie Yeung. They make an appealing group, and you look at them and think, wait a minute, it's two guys and two women! It's nearly always several guys and one woman in the finale of any action-adventure flick (if the female chara is included at all, or she's a hostage to be rescued).

Hung Sing returns to create mayhem in the underground temple, battling each of the heroes in a series of farcical fights as they struggle to keep hold of the magical box. The to-ing and fro-ing is rapid and complicated: every part of the set is used for bits of comical business.

The flaming swords duel is a marvellous combination of practical effects and optical animation: the swords flail like whips, scorching the ground, and send out sparks when they clash. The magic box performs plenty of work in the finale, too: it's opened several times and transforms the characters into æthereal forms, including being composed of little, steel balls (these are early versions of computer-aided effects).

Dr Wai is funny, too. Our heroes ask to see the future from a wise sage who materializes when the box and the scripture are re-united, look on a wedding scene: when Shing asks to see his finest achievement in the future, it's the same scene (much to Yan-yan's dismay). Meanwhile, Dr Wai carries the romantic subplot – the estrangement from his wife, Monica (so that the stories in the past and the present day scenes continue to mingle).

✳

The 1996 movie for some versions included additional footage over-seen by Tsui Hark and Gordon Chan.[6] The scenes created a framing story set in the present day, with Jet Li as Chow Si-Kit, a writer, and his sidekicks. Tsui's influence on *Dr Wai In "The Scripture With No Words"* is obvious, from the look, the pace and the visual fx to the casting and the story (Tsui has explored the same era several times). The movie featured some of the same crew that work regularly with Tsui.

6 Some say it was for the Hong Kong version, others for the international version.

And yet, the reception/ perception of *Dr Wai In "The Scripture With No Words"* in the West has been hampered by poor print quality, and an English dub which doesn't always clarify the time-jumping plot. *Dr Wai In "The Scripture With No Words"* deserves to be better known as a nimble, funny and occasionally spectacular outing. (Unfortunately, shoddy prints with bad audio harm the impact of too many Hong Kong movies. They look like they were tossed away after they'd been used for a month in the theatres, and somebody picked up the film cans from the garbage. These sorts of pics really do need vivid, sharp prints and bright, clear sound).

Dr Wai In "The Scripture With No Words" is a time travel movie, a movie with two time zones, and a movie with real sections and fictional sections (in the Cantonese version). The gimmick that ties it together is that the hero, Chow Si-Kit, is a writer, and the movie portrays his stories. So we are cutting back and forth between the 'real' present day and the fictional past. In the present tense, as well as writing his novel, Chow is struggling with the divorce of his wife Monica Kwan (Rosamund Kwan). In the past, multiple stories are related: the main one is the quest/ chase narrative of the magical scripture and the special box.

A third time travel layer in *Dr Wai* involves the back-story of the Pandora's Box: it's part of a ferocious battle sequence featuring the Salt Gang with swords, guns and horses (their descendants in the Thirties are searching for the box). In the flashback, the box is opened and all Hell breaks loose (white light bursts out, as always, and the warriors are frazzled. It's another Ark of the Covenant-style sequence from *Raiders of the Lost Ark*).

Knitting the skittering narrative structure together in *Dr Wai* are several voiceovers, and the actors playing dual roles, in the manner of *The Wizard of Oz*. So Chow Si-Kit the writer also plays Dr Wai, the King of Adventurers, in the past. His assistant, Shing (Takeshi Kaneshiro) appears as the goofball Shing, his other assistant, the punky Yvonne (Charlie Yeung), is Yan-yan, and Monica, Chow's soon-to-be-ex-wife (Rosamund Kwan), is also Madame Cammy, a Japanese agent.

It sounds complicated because it *is* complicated, but the 1996 movie delivers the narrative structure in a light-hearted, comical-adventurous (and comicbook) manner. Once the film has cut back and forth a couple of times, the narrative structure is easy to follow. (Several movies more recently have approached fantasy and writing in the same way, with the reality and the fantasy intermingling, and commenting upon each other).

As the story progresses in *Dr Wai*, the characters change from input from Chow Si-Kit: Cammy, for instance, starts the movie as a Japanese agent dominatrix but becomes more genteel towards the end, dressing in a traditional *kimono*. (Both Shing and Yvonne have been adjusting the story while Chow is away or asleep; Chow also alters their take on the plot when he sees what they've written. And while Chow is in hospital, and Monica visits him, she rewrites the ending of his story).

The framing story receives a happy ending, with the estranged husband and wife agreeing not to sign the divorce papers. They appear in the final shot, on the streets of downtown Hong Kong.

Dithering about in the present day is a trifling matter of little significance – as Chow Si-kit gets writer's block and can't think of any new plots, and battles with his dissatisfied wife Monica.

The 1930s action-adventure parts of *Dr Wai* are far more compelling than the present-day scenes: the comical antics of Chow, Shing and Yvonne in the newspaper office, and the angry encounters between Chow and his wife Monica, are over-shadowed by the 1930s sections. The editing between the two time zones is slick – *Dr Wai* was cut by the two finest editors in Chinese cinema – Marco Mak Chi-sin and Angie Lam, but the modern-day scenes are just too routine, and they don't exploit the potential of the four actors (Li, Kwan, Kaneshiro and Yeung). And the addition of voiceovers to explain things as we hop between now and then aren't necessary.

But this might be because framing stories are seldom as gripping as the main story, as in two Tim Burton pics, *Edward Scissorhands* (1991) and *Alice In Wonderland* (2010). Not every movie can be *The Wizard of Oz*, where the framing story is essential.

✳

As usual with over-the-top, Hong Kong comicbook movies, the usual critics didn't go for it, and the usual critics enjoyed it (you know who they are – is it worth quoting them again?). So the grumpy critics complained about the lack of story, the paper-thin characters, the adolescent tone, etc, and the positive critics enjoyed the self-conscious hokum, the vivid photography, and the visual effects.

Dr Wai In "The Scripture With No Words" is not a movie to resist or to fight, as with a Hollywood musical movie, or forerunners like *Romancing the Stone* and *Indiana Jones*. You're wasting your time.

For fans of Hong Kong action cinema, there is plenty to enjoy here – not least in seeing Jet Li in a non-serious role (except perhaps in the angry divorce scenes with Rosamund Kwan). Li, as his portrayal of Wong Fei-hung showed, is a very appealing action hero. And when he sends himself up (as in his Wong Jing-directed films), it's even better.

9

CONMAN IN TOKYO

Chung Waa Dou Hap

Conman In Tokyo (*Zung Waa Dou Hap,* 2000) was prod. by Wong Jing for Star East and Best of the Best[7] and Partners, wr. by Law Yiu-fai,[8] ed. by Poon Hung, action dir. by Tony Ching and Lee Tat Chiu, with sound by James Tse Yiu-Kei, art dir. by Andrew Cheuk Man-Yiu, make-up by Maggie Choi Yin-Jing, costumes by Ng Tin-Sang, with music by Cheung Shung-kei and Cheung Shung-tak. Released Aug 31, 2000. 103 mins.

In the cast were: Louis Koo, Nick Cheung, Athena Chu, Christy Chung, Ben Lam, Bryan Leung, Yasuaki Kurata, Joe Cheng, Wong Tin-lam and Zuki Lee.

Conman In Tokyo is a comedy, a comedy which is part-drama (a war between gamblers, with a woman caught in the middle), and part-action movie (involving triads and gangsters). The influence of the ever-present Wong Jing is all over *Conman In Tokyo* (it is a very Wongian comedy – which means it's flashy, brash, crude, sexist, and very silly[9]). It's another of the many collaborations between Tony Ching and the producer/ writer.

Conman In Tokyo is part of Wong Jing's *Conman* series, though for this outing the casting was switched around. But it's the same premise of a group of youngish characters in contemporary cities (Hong Kong and Tokyo) getting involved with minor crimes (and gambling, one of Wong's passions). Other *Conman* films from the Wongster include *The Conman* (1998), with Andy Lau, *Conman In Vegas* (1999), and *Conman* (2002), directed by Aman Cheung Man (which also features Nick Cheung, like this film). The casting required some juggling in the script, so we have Anthea Chu playing Ching's twin Karen, and Koo replacing Andy Lau.

---

7 Wong Jing's company.
8 He wrote the Jackie Chan film *Gorgeous* of the year before.
9 It's a movie where characters're called Banana, Cool, Fatty and Turkey.

Comedy is an under-appreciated element in the works of many Hong Kong directors – Tsui Hark, John Woo, Yuen Woo-ping, etc. They've all produced comedy films, and have also included humour in many other films (it's true, tho', that Woo seems to have left comedy behind when he began his most celebrated works of the late 1980s onwards. And film critics and fans in the West have almost completely neglected Woo's comedies – they prefer the blammy-blammy Woo, shootin' with two guns while divin' thru the air, and lookin' extremely cool while doin' it). Tsui Hark, meanwhile, has incorporated humour throughout his entire *œuvre* (recently, in the 2008 film *All About Women* or *Journey To the West*, 2017).

Tony Ching has featured comedy in many of his movies as director, and lots more in his films as action director (in the many Stephen Chow and Wong Jing comedies, for example).

You have to admit that a movie such as *Conman In Tokyo* is below Tony Ching's talents. While it's always encouraging to see an important director taking on a comedy (the most under-valued of all genres), this one is only amusing in parts. *Conman In Tokyo* also seems about 8 years past its time – it feels like an early 1990s movie, with its evocations of gamblers and gambling. (And the script has the appearance of being reworked to include certain characters and comedic elements).

Conman In Tokyo is edited (by Poon Hung, who's worked many times with Ching Siu-tung) like a drunken night in Kowloon or Shinjuku – no shot lasts longer than two or three seconds.[10] The cutting gives *Conman In Tokyo* a juddery, nervous feel, creating a viewing experience where there's no time or place to relax (look at how many reaction shots, for instance, are jammed into the action scenes by editor Hung).

The editing, as with the music, seems like another too-desperate attempt to be 'contemporary' or 'urban' or 'slick'. Yes, the score of *Conman In Tokyo* (by Cheung Shung-kei and Cheung Shung-tak) does feature several pastiches of hiphop and 'urban' musics.

Along with the too-flashy, hyped-up style (which includes lurching camerawork and scarlet-walled clubs), the performance of Nick Cheung as Jersy is similarly over-the-top (tho' he also steals the movie). Cheung's punky, pumped-up turn was disliked by some critics, but his up-for-it, party persona does offer a lively contrast with the under-played, unemotive Cool (it's also a staple of the action-adventure genre to give the grim, silent, restrained hero a humorous sidekick).

✳

The background of *Conman In Tokyo* is gambling, one of the staples

---

10 The horse racing research scene is a very rapidly-cut montage, apeing the flashy approach of a Las Vegas caper movie.

of Hong Kong movies (and daily life)[11] – and comedies in particular. Wong Jing, as we know, is very fond of gambling. Gambling inevitably means lots of card games, and gangsters, and cute girls hanging on the arms of said mobsters, and the glitzy, downtown world of clubs, nightclubs, pool halls and bars.[12] It also means action gimmicks with playing cards (cards as weapons, cards as knives in victim's arms, etc). Tony Ching had already been involved with many gambling films by the time of *Conman In Tokyo* (going back to early 1980s films such as *Gambler's Delight*, 1978), and his father (Ching Gong) made gambling films, too (such as *King Gambler*, 1976, *The King of Gambler*, 1981, *The Casino*, 1981, and *Gambling Soul*, 1992).

The fetishization of gambling is everywhere in *Conman In Tokyo* – we've got horse racing, poker, bowling, dice, soccer, you name it. Parts of *Conman In Tokyo* feel like one of those modern updates of Hollywood caper movies or heist movies, where a scam or robbery is being planned by a group of cool crooks in Las Vegas.

Many of the motifs in *Conman In Tokyo* are *very* Hong Kongian: money (getting it, keeping it, and also spending it), gambling (of all kinds), erotic/romantic desire, and 'face' (maintaining it, trying not to lose it). Wong Jing includes most of those motifs in almost every movie he produces, writes or directs (though Wong didn't write this movie, Law Yiu-fai did). The boys want to gamble, the girls want to go shopping, and both want to party (all except Cool. He plays the retired warrior or *ronin* of swordplay movies, who's moved to Tokyo to run a restaurant, preferring the quiet life. Until, that is, Jersy tracks him down. But he still resists getting involved).

Conman In Tokyo is also yet another Hong Kong movie which takes up Japanese culture, flattering and playing to one of Cantonese cinema's primary markets. (There is some second unit photography in Tokyo, including famous spots like the much-photographed road crossing in Shinjuku outside Shibuya Station, surrounded by advertizing hoardings and neons). Much of the 2000 film seems to have been produced back in Hong Kong, however.

✳

And there's dancing – yes, dance in a Tony Ching movie (but his action scenes are often dance-like). In a comedy, all sorts of other forms of performance are allowed, and encouraged. So some guys at a gambling table jump up to perform a banana song (making the phallic undercurrent of macho posturing obvious), and Cool and Karen decide to dance after

---

11 Wong Jing has overseen several gambling movies.
12 In its use of existing locations in Hong Kong, *Conman In Tokyo* does capture the lively atmosphere of the city. It definitely feels like a brash, Hong Kong production.

successfully nobbling a gangster and his boys.13 (This occurs in the lengthy flashback which climaxes act one).

Being a contemporary-set movie, and an urban movie, the action of *Conman In Tokyo* is more grounded *kung fu* and gunplay, rather than floaty warriors on wires. It's stunt guys crashing thru glass, or landing hard on tables which break. And the film has fun coming up with special gags for the attacks by Cool using playing cards – mainly using them like flying daggers. (However, Ching Siu-tung manages to squeeze in ninja-like fights, flashing swords and black-clad ninja-ish warriors in the finale).

The romantic triangle subplot is linked to the main plot of *Conman In Tokyo*, comprising the gambling and gangsters plot, Cool and Tetsuo pitted against each other for the title of the Number One Gambler In Asia.

Structurally, for an action comedy, *Conman In Tokyo* is unusual: it features a flashback structure in the first act, where we discover the central character of Cool (Louis Koo) through the eyes of Jersy (Nick Cheung), who worships him.

＊

Conman In Tokyo is a boys' movie – the girls are second bananas here (the girlfriend of Jersy is even called 'Banana'. Her nickname in a Wong Jing-produced film can only refer to one thing!). Yes, it's a movie where guys snarl at each other, or josh and snark with each other, or attack each other. (It's male peacock time, strutting-around-looking-cool time).

However, Christy Chung as Jersy's girlfriend Banana is allowed to cut loose, such as adding her own manic bits to the fights. Banana is also given a smattering of a personality in the script, which goes beyond being a one-dimensional characterization. She is not merely the pretty girlfriend of one of the two male leads. For ex, Banana constantly upbraids Jersy for not being up to the mark as a boyfriend or as a man, and she's involved directly in many scenes (many comprise Jersy, Banana and Cool), and not relegated to the background. (Some of this is down to Chung, a consistently impressive actress, who brings more weight to what is essentially a lightweight role). These are the most entertaining sections of the movie.

It's true that the character of Jersy and his funky girlfriend Banana are superfluous to the story of *Conman In Tokyo*: because this narrative is really all about Cool. He's the one who's lost his lover to a venal schmuck, and the one who contended with Tetsuo for the title of Number One Gambler In Asia. (Asia's a pretty big place, but the Number One Gambler

---

13 However, the camera performs a move in the dance scene that should be outlawed from all films – the 360 degree tracking/ Steadicam shot.

can only be in Hong Kong or Macau). /////

So the characters of Jersy and Banana seem to have been either added to the project at the behest of a producer or actor, or to have their roles bumped up. Jersy is only necessary, structurally, as an occasional sidekick for Cool (to lighten the glum mood). But the 2000 movie benefits from the lighthearted characterization of Jersy (even if the way that Jersy's played by Nick Cheung is similar to the hyped-up party animals that Jacky Cheung played in the early 1990s, with a bit of Anthony Wong mania added).

∗

If you're waiting for *Conman In Tokyo* to move on to something more dramatically 'substantial' after the goofy humour, soapy emotions and frantic pace of act one, you're watching the wrong movie. *Conman In Tokyo* is a throwaway action comedy, with some thriller/ gangster elements, so it's never going to become *A Better Tomorrow* or *Chungking Express* half-way through.

Actually, though, in act two of *Conman In Tokyo*, the dramatic material takes over, as the back-story of Cool unfolds: now the schemes of the truly venal Yeung Kwong (Ben Lam) are unveiled: violent maltreatment of Karen (Athena Chu), including an assassination attempt at their wedding (intended for Cool). This goes horribly wrong, when Cool rushes up and Karen hurls herself in front of him, to protect him, receiving a paralyzing bullet to the spine (the treatment of Karen is awful in *Conman In Tokyo*).

Thus, the romantic triangle between Cool, Karen and Yeung Kwong is fraught with seething resentments and thoughts of revenge. Yeung in particular is a thoroughly nasty piece of work. When Karen expresses doubts about marrying him, for instance, right before the ceremony, he gives her a vicious kick in the torso which throws her across the room. And in her paralyzed state, Yeung further abuses Karen (unbeknownst to Cool, who takes to spying on Karen from afar, using binos in trees. But it's OK for Cool to act like a besotted stalker, because he's the hero of the movie, right?).

It's pretty vile stuff, which Tony Ching explored even further in *Naked Weapon*. Again, this is likely the influence of Wong Jing (who also wrote and produced *Naked Weapon*) – because this sort of violence against women doesn't occur with same viciousness in other Ching films (but it is, sad to say, quite common in Asian cinema, including Chinese cinema).

Certainly the wedding and the assassination in *Conman In Tokyo* are ridiculous and artificial, as narrative and dramatic constructions. And altho' *Conman In Tokyo* appears at first to be a manic comedy, the slide into violence seems schizophrenic. But that's typical of Hong Kong cinema – goofy laughs one minute, and a mobster threatening someone with losing an arm the next. As Tsui Hark has pointed out, Cantonese audiences know that a Hong Kong movie isn't going to be a conventional movie. And Wong Jing is especially fond of mixing elements in a jarring manner (crude humour in the midst of extreme violence, for instance).

✳

Act two of *Conman In Tokyo* climaxes with the confrontation between Cool and Tetsuo (Yasuaki Kurata) over who's got the biggest package (pack of cards, that is), or the biggest gambling skills (or the best flying cards skills), plus Cool's rescue mission to save Karen.

In the first action sequence in act two of *Conman In Tokyo*, on Tetsuo's home turf, Cool barges in to save Jersy, who's being tortured with hot wax.[14] The tussle between Cool and Tetsuo is staged as a flying cards duel – a flurry of kicks are exchanged above the green poker table amidst cascades of playing cards. Here, Tony Ching depicts more of the gravity-defying action which is one of his mainstays as an action choreographer. The bust-up ends in a stalemate, the familiar 'to be continued' note (thus, we can guess that this scene will be repeated in the finale – which it is – Hong Kong action cinema often simply revives the climax of act one or the climax of act two for the finale of act three).

In the second action sequence in *Conman*'s second act, another rescue mission for Cool, Ching Siu-tung squeezes in one of his beloved ninja motifs. This being a contemporary-set movie, we can't have ninja dressed all in traditional black, but this is as near as. The female bodyguard looking after Karen just happens to be armed with an endless supply of *shuriken* (as ninja always are) – so we have flying stars versus flying cards in a traditional, Japanese home complete with *tatami* (mats)nearly all and *fusama* (sliding doors).

No Ching Siu-tung movie is complete without some swordplay – so, tho' it's indulgent and unrealistic, we have Cool taking on further body-guards using a Japanese *katana*. It's a piece of the *Swordsman* series in the midst of the contemporary era.

✳

For the finale, *Conman In Tokyo* becomes a different movie, shifting into *James Bond* territory. So, where do you think that Tetsuo, the Number One Gambler In Asia, is going to hold his grand tournament against the hero, Cool? In his plush club in Tokyo? Or that staple of Hong Kong action movies, the dockside or warehouse?

---

14 Tho', in typical Wong Jing style, Jersy also slyly admits that he might be enjoying it.

No – an aircraft carrier![15] Yes, an aircraft carrier (to take advantage of being in international waters, presumably, and to make a change from Macao); and it's filmed at night, to make it more challenging (and more expensive). Now we can see why the rest of *Conman In Tokyo* was a little cut-corners, budget-wise, because renting an aircraft carrier can't be cheap![16]

So, yes, it's ridiculous, but Tetsuo has his own ship, his own navy, and his own aircraft. And anyone who gets too close, they are fired upon with missiles. Well, it makes for an unusual setting in which to stage the inevitable Giant Battle that's the climax of nearly all (no, all) of Ching Siu-tung's movies.

✳

The finale of this *Conman* movie, as often in Hong Kong action cinema, is in two halves: the first half is the gambling smackdown (involving European soccer and a card game), as Tetsuo and Cool butt heads at the gambling table. When this has been exploited to the full (lots of glaring and frowning and taunts, and flashy card tricks – but with the outcome left dangling), the second villain/ rival appears – Yeung Kwong.

A 'what the hell!' attitude prevails, with *Conman In Tokyo* becoming an all-out action epic: it depicts Yeung Kwong's guards storming the aircraft carrier, and an enormous fire-fight erupting between them and Tetsuo's private navy.

Thus, Ching Siu-tung gets to have his black-clad ninjas after all (including the familiar Chingian wire-work gag of raising some stunt guys at the same time, in a row). The blammy-blammy dust-up is an accomplished piece of action filmmaking, the sort of scene that every director in Hong Kong seems to have tackled at one time or another (or, if you're John Woo, or Tsui Hark, or Ching, many, many times).

Following the *Action-Adventure Movie Genre Handbook*, the first half of the second part of the finale of *Conman In Tokyo* culminates with the resolution of the Cool and Tetsuo plot – Tetsuo is wounded by Yeung Kwong, and expires (thus, Cool becomes the Number One Gambler In Asia by default. It's fitting that Yeung, not Cool, kills Tetsuo).

There are also dramatic revelations: Karen, it turns out, is really her twin sister, hired by Yeung Kwong for revenge on Cool. In a typical piece of over-cooked melodrama, Cool discovers this just as the twin is dying in his arms (after being shot by Yeung as he leaves – another of his revolting acts, killing an unarmed woman at point blank range). But Cool has already

---

15 There's also a chance for Cool to wield a length of rope like Jet Li (because there's always rope on a ship, right?).
16 And for the many night shoots. Extra lighting is employed to give the vessel the look of a swanky resort.

foreseen this, and has been tricking Yeung (he has placed Karen out of harm's way).

✳

The second half of the second part of the finale of *Conman* is of course the Big Fight Between the Hero and the Villain. This takes place all over the aircraft carrier's flight deck – there are gags with stairs, with ladders, with helicopters, with guns, with parachutes, with missiles, with high wire stunts, and with jets (which blow up, of course). It's a rough-and-tumble sequence of continuous kicking and punching and grappling (and for the stunt team, it's in an unwelcoming and downright uncomfortable environment of damp metal and wind and cold and nighttime).

The finale is one of those action scenes where characters become superhuman, enduring excessive violence which would flatten any regular person after a punch or two. The outcome is as set in stone (or cold, hard steel) as it always is in the action-adventure genre: Yeung Kwong must die at the hands of Cool. However, not before every inch of the setting has been exploited by the stunt team.

The fighter jet is employed to great effect – having Cool and Yeung fighting even when they're flying in the air below a parachute (after ejecting from the cockpit).[17] The villain is dispatched when he's sucked into the air intake of the jet (don't try this at home, folks!). And then the aircraft explodes. (The finale employs some miniature work and computer-aided animation – such as helicopters and missiles).

Just as preposterous as all of this hokum is the sudden appearance of Banana pushing the real Karen in a wheelchair into the scene. That the two girls materialize out of nowhere is dramatically necessary for the kissy-kissy reunions of the main characters, of course (Cool and Karen, Jersy and Banana, and the final bow to the audience). Cool and Karen depart in a chopper, while Banana and Jersy share a kiss.

---

17 A similar gag appeared in the *James Bond* film *Golden-Eye* (1995).

Dr Wai (1996).

Jet Li
Dr Wai

EASTERN PRODUCTIONS LTD. présente
un film de CHING SIU-TUNG «DR. WAI IN THE SCRIPTURES WITH NO WORDS»
avec JET LI, ROSAMUND KWAN, TAKESHI KANESHIRO et CHARLIE YOUNG
photo TOM LAU montage MAK CHI-SIN
producteurs CHARLES HEUNG et ALEX WONG
scénario SANDY SHAW, ROY SZETO et LAU WAI-LAM
réalisé et chorégraphié par CHING SIU-TUNG

이연걸   관지림

최고의 스펙터클 액션어드벤쳐!

모험왕

1월 29일, 전설의 모험이 시작된다!

It should be my turn to decide how to gamble this time

Did someone assassinate him?

Conman In Tokyo (2000).

It's unfair to both of us

中華賭俠

CONMAN IN TOKYO

10

NAKED WEAPON

Chek Law Dak Gung

Naked Weapon is Tony Ching's nastiest and most problematic film. *Naked Weapon* (*Chek Law Dak Gung*, 2002) was produced by Wong Jing and John Chong for Media Asia and Jing Productions. Wong also has script credit. Tony Ching Siu-tung was director and action director; Lau Chi-ho was also action dir. DP: Choi Sung Fai. Music: Ken Chan and Chan Kwong Wing. Prod. des.: Sung Pong Choo. Costumes: Pik Kwan Lee. Yu Lai Cheng: make-up. Wai Hing Lau: hair. Sylvia Liu: 1st A.D. Felix Sze Ming Chung: music editor and sound effects editor. Editor: Angie Lam. (The crew of *Naked Weapon* features some superstars: for instance, Angie Lam is one of the genius editors on the Hong Kong scene. Her CV includes the *Once Upon a Time In China* movies, *Iron Monkey, Xanda, Seven Swords,* etc. And Hong Kong legend Cheng Pei-pei plays the heroine's mother). Released Nov 15, 2002. 92 mins.

In the cast were Daniel Wu Yin-cho, Anya Wu, Maggie Q, Cheng Pei-pei, Almen Wong Pui Ha, Jewel Li Fei, Andrew Lin-hoi, Dennis Chan Kwok San, Monica Lo Suk Yee and Marit Thoresen.

The production went to Manila in the Philippines (for the training camp scenes, and the downtown Rome scenes). Filmed partly in English (tho' dubbed, too), and Cantonese; the Cantonese version was, as usual, looped.

The gross at the Hong Kong b.o. was very poor – HK $700,000, one of the lowest for a Tony Ching Siu-tung movie.

The concept of *Naked Weapon* is silly, completely unbelievable, and offensive in parts: a ruthless organization kidnaps forty girls to train as assassins. For years the girls are put thru hell in a training camp on an island somewhere on Earth (filmed in the Philippines). It's *Full Metal Jacket* for teenage girls (and of course the commanding officer is also a woman, Madame M. played with aloof venality by Almen Wong,[1] while Drillmaster Augustin Aguerreberry runs the training regime).

The notion that an organization would pay to train 40 people over many years and kill most of them in order to produce that One, Special Assassin, is utterly stupid.[2] You might as well have Lord Buddha materializing beachside atop a dragon and achieving world peace with a single, nonchalant wave of the hand.

Naked Weapon's script doesn't convince in many areas, largely stemming from the ridiculous underlying concept. But even when you put that aside (accepting that this is a Hong Kong production, and a Wong Jing production), and buy into the movie as a movie (and a very movie-movie sort of movie), it still contains elements that're just plain dumb.

Daniel Wu plays Jack Chen, a Chinese American working for the Central Intelligence Agency in the New World. Like the other male charas, there isn't anything slightly arresting about Chen. He is simply the detective trying to solve the case of the 'China Dolls' murders. Wu's agent Chen represents the normalizing, moralizing aspect of Western society, to bring the vicious, Oriental assassination scheme to justice, to catch the crooks, etc. But *Naked Weapon* isn't invested in him or the moral guardians of society at all: it's fascinated, rather, by watching a group of cute girls go thru Hell, and putting them into over-the-top, dangerous, criminal scenarios.

Naked Weapon is in part a gimmick (and it's a typical Wong Jing gimmick): a tough, military-style training camp – but for girls! Yes, not sweaty guys in combat gear this time, but girls in short-sleeved Tee shirts and tight shorts!

So we've got the girls assembling pistols and shooting them in a firing range (an ultimate *otaku/* geek moment – girls handling naked weapons!). We've got girls wriggling under barbed wire. Girls doing press-ups in the surf. Girls jogging (and bouncing) in shorts. Girls in the shower. Girls in bunkbeds. Girls hugging. (The highly artificial narrative set-up also evokes the women in prison genre, and the prisoner of war camp genre, and shifts into death match and *Battle Royale* territory).

Naked Weapon is also a classic Wong Jing outing in stealing from recent Western cinema – *Naked Weapon* is a nasty take on *Charlie's Angels*, 2000), a truly cretinous grrrl power film (which, ironically, used

1 She was the nasty Japanese assassin in *Shanghai Grand*.
2 Do you know how much it would cost to raise, feed, house and educate 40 people over 6 years?!

Hong Kong action director Yuen Cheung-yan);[3] it takes up the humourless, abused female assassin from *Nikita*;[4] it has the fight-to-the-death arena from *Gladiator* (2000); it includes death matches from *Battle Royale* and post-apocalyptic movies; and it takes up one of the staples of Asian cinema: fighting girls (Japanese *anime*, for example, has a whole sub-genre devoted to beautiful warriors fighting – *Queen's Blade, Manyuu Hiken-Chou, Kampfer, Dirty Pair, Sekirei, Samurai Girls, Burst Angel, Vandread, The Qwaser of Stigmata*, etc. Indeed, sometimes it seems as if Wong is producing live-action versions of Japanese animation).

Wong Jing has always followed the hits in Hollywood very closely, and produced his own knock-offs for a fraction of the cost (sometimes very soon after the Hollywood movies have been released).

The marketing hook of girls as savage assassins in *Naked Weapon* is Wong Jing at his worst – and yet, it's also Wong at his best! You have to admire Wong's guts, his business *chutzpah,* after all – it's like Russ Meyer filming big-boobed women in leathers as killer pussycats (completely mindless and chauvinist), or Roger Corman squeezing another dime out of cheapo movies that he's had some eager film school graduate re-cut and re-shoot.

So *Naked Weapon* is a high class exploitation picture, with a calibre of filmmakers (Angie Lam, Choi Sung Fai, Tony Ching Siu-tung) far, far more talented than necessary (this story, these characters, these scenarios, you have to admit, could have been covered by an average action crew).

At the technical level, *Naked Weapon* is a classy piece of filmmaking. And it looks fabulous, like all of Tony Ching Siu-tung's pictures. And the action is outstanding.

✳

From the *risqué* title on down, Wong Jing's influence is all over this picture. For a start, it's an exploitation movie. It is what snobbish critics, and those who dislike Wong, deride as 'trash'.

As 'trash' or 'exploitation', *Naked Weapon* is way below the talents of Tony Ching Siu-tung, a director who can stage outrageous fantasy action and incredible battles, whose films are thrilling in their invention and imagination.

But Tony Ching Siu-tung and Wong Jing have worked together before on *Flying Dagger* and *Conman In Tokyo*, for example (indeed, Wong has worked with pretty much everybody in the Hong Kong film industry, as has

3 Yuen Cheung-yan went to Tinseltown to action choreograph the *Charlie's Angels* movies (helmed by Joseph 'McG' Nichol); altho' I find the *Charlie's Angels* movies smug, self-satisfied, boring and irritating (Cameron Diaz, for starters), David West pointed out that they are actually conceived like a Hong Kong movie, constructed as a series of set-pieces that switch between action, comedy and musical numbers (247).
4 Maggie Q. starred in the *Nikita* TV series (2010).

Ching). Whatever Wong's reputation amongst intellectuals, journalists, and taste-makers, Ching took on the directorial duties of this picture which's written and produced by Wong.

So it is Wong Jing who came up with the concept, the approach, the characters and the script, *and* who produced the movie (which included casting). Even if Wong *didn't* perform some of those functions on this movie (Wong-detractors often criticize him for not fulfilling the job of direction of production, but assigning jobs to others), this is *still* very much a 'Wong Jing production'; you can spot Wong's distinctive approach in the concept and the screenplay, for example (remember that Wong enjoys writing most of all in filmmaking). And, despite the astonishing talents of Tony Ching Siu-tung as a director, this particular flick seems more a Wong Jing Show than a Tony Ching Siu-tung Show.

On the DVD audio commentary, Maggie Q. (Margaret Quigley, b. 1979) whinges more than any actor or crew I've heard on any commentary: she complains to Bey Logan about Wong Jing, the movie, the script, the objectification of women, the toughness of the filming, and other topics (she seems to have hated every minute of making this film). Maggie Q. said she brought in a scriptwriter from L.A. (producer Andrew Loo) to polish Wong Jing's script, asked for scenes to be changed (such as the lesbian clinch in the shower, which Wong wrote but Quigley wanted out), threatened a lawsuit for the cover of the DVD release, and a host of other gripes. [5]

Polishing a Wong Jing script or the dialogue, however, does not change the fundamental concept, or significantly alter the characters, or the story, or the themes, or the issues. It shows how much the production wanted the services of Maggie Q. that they let her bring in a writer to adjust the script. After all, Wong Jing was a veteran of literally hundreds of movies by this time (2002). There was nothing you could teach Wong about screenwriting or how to make movies!

Because, you have to admit, this *is* a movie with numerous sleazy elements and some brutal scenes. Girls in their early teens are gunned down; several die trying to escape; as late teens, the girls are forced to kill each other, in a preposterous bloodbath (slitting throats with knives, stabbing with broken toothbrushes and the legs of a bunkbed, using straps for strangling, etc).

I don't attack Wong Jing like so many critics do (and people in the film industry). In fact, I enjoy many of his movies. There's no question that he

[5] With all of those complaints, it does seem that this particular production was one that the actress should've passed on (she initially refused it). Many of the elements are right there in the screenplay, so you can see what you will be asked to do and what the film is about in the script.

is a brilliant film producer, with a keen eye for what audiences enjoy, and what will make mon$y. And he's a great director. *Really?* Can Wong *really* be classed as a great director? Oh gosh, yes: purely for his contributions in comedy, he is a master. He has coaxed some fantastic performances from stars such as Chow Yun-fat (*The God of Gamblers*). There are some duds, of course, some misguided flops, but plenty of hits, too (not to mention all of the other genres that Wong's taken up).

Wong Jing has become a punchbag or focus for what people don't like about Hong Kong movies: too crude, too crass, too stupid, too sexist, too violent, too nationalistic, too racist, etc. But everything that critics don't like within Wong's movies can be found in *all* of the other directors in the Hong Kong film industry, including the Great and the Good (John Woo, Tsui Hark, King Hu, Chang Cheh, Lau Kar-leung, Sammo Hung, Jackie Chan, Ringo Lam, Peter Chan, Gordon Chan, etc – and, yes, even the other Wong – Wong Kar- wai).

✳

The photography (by Choi Sung Fai) is outstanding – it's particularly good at lighting and filming the close-ups of so many actresses. Tony Ching's staples of back-lighting and lots of smoke and wind machines are everywhere. The visual approach seems both gritty and naturalistic and extremely heightened and stylized (the hair and make-up is crucial in this movie, as always in a Ching movie, with so many performers acting out vulnerable and volatile scenarios. Yu Lai Cheng did the make-up, and Wai Hing Lau did the hair). The women look both naturalistic and glamorous.

The editing (by Angie Lam) is a masterclass in maintaining a vibrant sense of pace. Disregarding the over-reliance on fashionable editing tricks in the fight scenes, *Naked Weapon* moves along at a cracking pace. There's no doubt that Lam is one of the greatest editors of action in the entire history of cinema.

✳

Let's look at some of the scenes: the opening sequence of *Naked Weapon* sets up the tone of the movie: the assassination of a high-ranking mobster in Rome. A sleek woman, Fiona Birch (photographic model Marit Thoresen), clad in a revealing silver dress, arrives in a sports car and slinks into a hotel. After tupping the target (providing the mandatory T. and A. in a Wong Jing picture), she kills him (tweaking the spine as she pretends to massage him!), and flees in a hail of bullets and punchy-kicky action, as she takes on the wise guy's bodyguards. (Only to be blown to bits in her car moments later by a rocket launcher, in a big pyro stunt). The prologue also introduces Madame M. as the overseer of this operation:

and when it all goes cock-eyed, Madame M. kills her injured pet assassin from her stretch limo.

The prologue sets up the theme of the 2002 movie, the concept of deadly female assassins, of Madame M. commanding the scheme (and why she needs fresh blood), and of the Central Intelligence Agency operatives on the ground trying to run them down (Jack Chen is at the scene, but is too late to stop Madame M. roaring away in her limousine). It also inaugurates the mass abduction of children undertaken by Madame M.'s business, which Chen is tracking down back in Washington, D.C. (the film shifts in time 6 years).

When a contemporary thriller like this moves into slow motion within the first minutes, accompanied by dance music, for the simple act of a person walking into a hotel, it can come across as smug arrogance, a desperation to be cool and hip and trendy Later, slo-mo is over-used in the many fight scenes, where it becomes jarring. And of course each swooping movement in slow motion is accompanied by those annoying whooshes and drones. Since when does an arm moving thru the air go *whoooooop*? This is a Hong Kong movie playing too much to an international/ North American audience (but then, Hong Kong movies have always added effort sounds to punch up their action).

Naked Weapon is a movie that wants to be as cool as a *James Bond* movie, or whatever is regarded as the latest classy item (in 2002, that might be a Quentin Tarantino or Tom Cruise pic).

Ah, but Tony Ching Siu-tung is so much *better* than this! Ching can turn out a movie like this in his sleep. It's not a step backward, but it's the bleakest installment in a stellar career in cinema (along with *The Executioners*).

And when the girls're set against each other as competitors in fights to the death, in the cage, we're in Roman arena territory, or futuristic prison camp territory (Madame M. even sits on a throne to enjoy the proceedings). And then, as a parting gesture, the girls are drugged and gang-raped! Talk about sleazy.

The arena battle is the highlight of *Naked Weapon* from an action point-of-view, with numerous inventive tussles between girls clad in shirts and shorts. The action is staged with many Chingian flourishes as the girls grapple each other with a variety of weapons. It's a tough form of choreography, where the actors are falling on hard concrete.

The three survivors – Katt, Charlene and Jewel – are brought together by Madame M. for a celebratory dinner, which turns into gang-rape after they've been drugged by the wine. Following this horrible scene, one of the nastiest in Ching's cinema, *Naked Weapon* shifts into a series of rapid montages of the 'China Dolls' performing assassinations all over the world. Each vignette is given its own style of action (the girls are able to use any object to main or kill, including the lens of their sunglasses, or their fingers). *Naked Weapon* is more brutal than it needs to be. But, hell, that applies to thousands of movies!

This section of *Naked Weapon* is Tony Ching working in his favourite place – action choreography in elaborately staged scenarios. Before we reach the finale of act two of *Naked Weapon*, however, there is an extended seduction sequence, with Charlene dancing and preening in front of the mobster – it's the Tease before the Kill. For some reason, the fancy apartment is filled with wind machines which blow Charlene's hair and clothes like she's in a shampoo commercial – and there's slow motion everywhere. This part of *Naked Weapon* is more Wong Jing than Tony Ching (like the close-up where Charlene slips off her panties), though there are many scenes of erotic seduction in Ching's *œuvre.*

A massive fire-fight is unleashed in this assassination sequence, when Charlene attempts to kill the gangster (with the grip on the spine), and finds herself under attack from every stuntman in Hong Kong. The running battle includes numerous gags, including Katt coming to Charlene's rescue in the corridor and hauling her up through the ceiling.

The action choreography is sharp and punchy, reminiscent of the work that Tony Ching did for directors like Tsui Hark and John Woo in films such as *A Better Tomorrow 2, Peking Opera Blues* and *The Killer.* The sisterhood theme is appealing, too – when Katt tells Charlene to leave in an emotional moment (and in heavy rain). The sequence has to end with big explosions, and it does: Katt hides in a metal cabinet then shoots out a gas pipe to ignite the fumes (a classic, Hong Kong gag).

✳

In the third act of *Naked Weapon,* all of the more intriguing aspects of the first half are normalized, heterosexualized: firstly, Madam M. is replaced by Ryuichi (Andrew Lin-hoi) as the chief antagonist. Now Charlene has to best Ryuichi in the finale (not, as would be so much more fitting and more compelling, dramatically, Madame M.). So, it's a girl against a guy.

Secondly, Daniel Wu's character, Jack Chen, replaces Charlene's best friend, Katt[6] – as a lover and aide. Again, this normalizes the concept of *Naked Weapon,* so that the third act plays out entirely predictably: Charlene and Jack make out, and the final duel is between Charlene and

6 Jing (Jewel Lee) is also a survivor of the training regime (she is portrayed as an unruffled, cold-blooded professional).

Ryuichi.

Ryuichi is an off-the-peg *yakuza* boss, picked straight out of the Hong Kong Action Cinema box of tricks, like a plastic toy figure, exactly the same as 1,000s of others. (Actually, all of the cast of *Naked Weapon* are figurines, like the 'China Dolls' themselves).

Ryuichi displays gangster attributes so stereotypical Andrew Lin-hoi isn't able to do anything with them. That he's a psycho goes with out saying: he springs a trap for the 'China Dolls', reeling them in, and capturing Katt in the process (with a whip! Just as Katt is hopping over a balcony. That's a classic Chingism!).

∗

In yet another mad moment – in a movie stuffed with them – Ryuichi has Katt strung up like a puppet, with ropes hanging above her (tho' piercing her limbs). Ryuichi taunts Charlene at length, on the other side of some bullet-proof glass in a ghastly display of sadomasochism. He decapitates Katt with a samurai sword, in front of Charlene – which's what *yakuzas* do, of course. The camera films through the glass which's drenched with dripping blood, playing over Charlene's agony as she's helpless to prevent the murder of her best friend.

Towards the end, *Naked Weapon* is riding over so many bumps in the story, so many stupider-than-stupid turns in the plot, nothing seems to matter anymore.

There are several corny, awkward and mindless snakepit scenarios. In one, in a true Wong Jing moment, the heroine is drugged with an aphrodisiac. Like that was needed to bring the hero and the heroine together! On the beach! At night! And they tup in the surf, in a Hong Kong tribute to *From Here To Eternity* (1957).

Sometimes the editing by the great Angie Lam takes a curious approach to the flow of action in the fight scenes especially, lopping off what you'd expect to be the beginning and the ending of shots, so the audience fills in the rest of the action. It doesn't always work. And when you combine that with the over-use of slow motion, and those horrible whooshes and whoops, some of the action scenes judder. Yet many scenes offer fine examples of the Tony Ching Siu-tung style of action cinema.

The hero and the heroine get to know each in, of all things, an ice cream truck. Which might work in a Jackie Chan[7] flick, but here?! Yes, in classic, Wong Jingian terms, they have to snuggle up to keep warm in the refrigerator in the truck, surrounded by cardboard boxes of Magnum lollies. (And this is right after Charlene has perpetrated yet another hit – at

7 Daniel Wu's character is called Jack Chen, as close as you can get.

a favourite Hong Kong ritual, the Dragon Boat Race (see in *The Killer*).[8]
And in front of her mom, Faye Ching (Cheng Pei-pei), too.

The heroine's relationship with her estranged mother Faye Ching is a touching element in *Naked Weapon* – its significance is enhanced by the casting of a much-loved actress in Hong Kong cinema, Cheng Pei-pei. Jack Chen takes to staking out Faye's (rather plush) digs, and just happens to be nearby when Jewel, of all people, turns up to kill her.

This is another action set-piece (towards the end of act two), with the filmmakers building it up with some music video flourishes: flashes of lightning, big windows, billowing curtains (the wind machines on this production were blowing in almost every scene, as usual with a Tony Ching movie).

First we have Jack Chen versus Jewel (he drops his pistol in the garden, so the fight becomes hand-to-hand and foot-to-foot), and then Charlene just happens by, so we also get the last of the girl-on-girl fights. It's a furious duel which foreshadows the final smackdown, between Charlene and Ryuichi. Visual effects were included in post-production to augment the practical effects (such as flying glass, which Charlene flings at Jewel, puncturing her face).

✳

The movie finishes off Madame M., the Queen of Death, by stringing her up, and maiming her, then cutting her loose so she falls – in front of Charlene and Katt. It's a cruel and grotesque demise, but somehow apposite for a woman who's been the Empress of a revolting regime for training female assassins.

Incidentally, Madame M. is part of the (second) trap set by Ryuichi to lure Charlene and Katt to his lair: he wants revenge on the 'China Dolls' for nobbling one of his criminal cohorts, the mobster that Charlene was sent to dispatch.

✳

The finale of *Naked Weapon* is set in the absolutely mandatory setting for all Hong Kong Action Cinema products: the dockside. Yes, and at night, too – the stage for 1,000s of Hong Kong movies.

For a change, however, the filmmakers place the two fighters away from the usual props and furniture, in a space of their own. And they have them duel unarmed. So there's a lots of punchy, kicky, lungey, divey, flying bits of business.

The final fight took a week and two days to film. You can see why: the duel runs through several phases, and involves numerous complicated

---

8 The Boat Race scene includes some traditional Chinese culture in the form of lion dancers.

stunts with wires. Both actors and their stunt doubles are working hard to sell the fury of the duel (Maggie Q. said she was hit so hard in one stunt she cried). At the end of it, Charlene finishes off Ryuichi with the pincher grip to the spine as he flies past her, reprising the memorable opening sequence.

There are some 3-D animation visual effects[9] in *Naked Weapon* (for the finale when Charlene, temporarily blinded, attunes her senses to work out where her enemy is. She imagines herself standing still and calm on a lake, sensing where the enemy is by his movements. The film evokes ripples on the lake in darkness, a poetic way of evoking the perception of sound).

✻

The ideology promulgated in *Naked Weapon* is nihilistic: according to the life-philosophy of Madame M., the world is a cesspit, and you have to kill to survive. Don't expect anything (least of all love). Don't trust anyone.

Yet altho' *Naked Weapon* exhibits a mean-spirited and cruel streak, there are many memorable moments: many scenes are played in an inventive, physical manner, exploiting the terrain (on the beach, or in the shallow water); a girl, Jing (Jewel Lee) performs a routine in the *wushu*-style at sunset; and we see many creative, Chingian ways of using weapons (whips, flicked glass, pipes, etc).

It's worth noting that this movie has a female in the lead role, a woman as the chief antagonist (until she's bumped off and replaced), and many women in the secondary roles (including the best friend and the mother). Actually, that has been part of Tony Ching Siu-tung's cinema – *The Heroic Trio* and *The Executioners*, for instance, and the later movie, *An Empress and the Warriors*. It's not a self-conscious drive towards featuring women in important roles movies that you find in the work of Tsui Hark (Tsui is a special case in Hong Kong cinema), but it is significant.

Detractors of *Naked Weapon*, and of the work of Wong Jing, can once again point out that Wong is marketing exploitation, and women as titillation, that Wong isn't a fervent radical feminist (!) who's promoting roles for women in cinema with the hope of revolutionizing all of the societies on Earth. *Naked Weapon* is a movie where girls in tight tanktops and tight shorts are wriggling under barbed wire, loading guns, kick-boxing, getting raped, and lapdancing atop sleazy crooks.

Another flaw in *Naked Weapon* is its humourlessness – the script by Wong Jing contains comedic elements, but they are pulverized by the too-serious direction and the po-faced performances. Maggie Q. in particular is grim throughout, and keeps us outside her predicament. She acts as if

9 Ringo Lee was visual effects supervisor and Mil Leung was visual effects team leader.

it's assumed and taken for granted that we'll know how she's feeling. (As in, if you were in this situation, you'd feel like this, right?).

On a plus note, the sisterly relationship between Charlene Ching and Katt is touching (inevitably, Wong Jing wrote a lesbian relationship. And he got one). For critics looking for lesbian material in *Naked Weapon*, there is plenty already; the movie doesn't need lesbian kisses or clinches for critics to crawl all over it and find lesbian elements crammed into every scene. (Even the gang rape can be turned around symbolically, so that it contains a lesbian defiance to the imposition of a violent heterosexual act by the regime of Madame M.).

And the fans were disappointed: touted as a follow-up to *Naked Killer* (and *Raped By an Angel*), *Naked Weapon* disappoints; marketed as an exploitation picture, fans also found *Naked Weapon* underwhelming (because there is too little nudity and 'fan service' of the kind that fans enjoy).

(Critics noted that the concept of female assassins who get close to their prey thru seduction was close to the theme of *Naked Killer*. So *Naked Weapon* is a kind of updating of the original *Naked Killer* of 1992. Even so, producer Wong Jing had *already* explored the *Naked Killer* idea with several sequels – tho' they were titled *Raped By an Angel*).

11

BELLY OF THE BEAST

Belly of the Beast (2003) was produced by G.F.T. Entertainment/ Salon Films/ Studio Eight Productions/ Emmett/ Furla Films. Dis. by Columbia. Prod. by: George Furla, Gary Howsam, Jamie Brown, Randall Emmett, Steven Seagal and Charles Wang. Script: Thomas Fenton and James Townsend. Story (uncredited): Steven Seagal. Music: Mark Sayer-Wade. DP: Danny Nowak. Editor: David Richardson. Released Dec 30, 2003. 91 mins.

In the cast were: Steven Seagal, Byron Mann, Monica Lo, Tom Wu, Sara Malakul Lane, Patrick Robinson, Vincent Riotta, Norman Veeratum, Eilidh MacQueen, Chan Siu-tung, Kevork Malikyan and Pongpat Wachirabunjong.

The production filmed in Thailand (based in Bangkok), where many Hong Kong and Chinese productions have ventured. Principal photo-graphy ran from Feb 3 - Mch 17, 2003 (42 days), on a budget of U.S. $14 million. A significant aspect of *Belly of the Beast* is that it was filmed in English.

Belly of the Beast was Tony Ching Siu-tung's first American movie as director, tho' he had already worked on American productions (as action director, such as *Spider-man*, the year before). Ultimately, it's a minor entry in Ching's output, competently achieved, but far below his talents. (Let's also remember that Ching is a director-for-hire here, though he does perform action direction, too. Ching didn't write the script, or originate the idea, or the characters. So although the proprietary credit comes up in the opening credits – 'A Tony Ching Siu-tung Film' – you can't call *Belly of the Beast* that).

Belly of the Beast is one of a group of movies which used second-rank, Western action stars in Hong Kong movies (or Chinese movies, or American-financed movies made in Asia).[10] Jean-Claude van Damme, Dolph Lungren and Steven Seagal were typical action stars of the Asian-American hybrid flicks. One reason is obvious: American movies could be produced much cheaper in Asia, but with American stars (*Belly of the Beast* cost $U.S. 14 million, but it would've been far more in the U.S.A. In the Hong Kong industry, the budget would've been much less. In the 1980s and 1990s, Ching and his contemporaries could deliver a movie like this for under U.S. $1 million).

Belly of the Beast is one of these hybrid movies – there were many Asians in the crew and the cast, it filmed primarily in Asia, but with a Hollywood star, and part-American finance. (Steven Seagal had moved from theatrically-released movies to direct-to-the-consumer projects: in 2003, Seagal was also in two other sell-through movies: *The Forgeiner* and *Out For a Kill*).

✳

Belly of the Beast is a post-9/11 political movie: it pits the U.S.A. against Islam, the Land of the Free against Islamic fundamentalists (the Abu Karaf group). In essence, it's another replay of the trauma of the attacks on Gotham and D.C. by Osama bin Laden and company, but it does what Hollywood movies always do: it crystallizes big, political issues in the form of individuals, it dramatizes abstract concepts in the form of people that are relatable (and played by well-known actors). And it adds the drugs trade and the arms trade to the nest of political corruption (while quietly ignoring the fact that the biggest manufacturer and merchant of arms on Earth is the U.S.A. It spent $778 billion on the military in 2021. That's 39% of the global expenditure of every nation).

In the story of *Belly of the Beast*, we have a former Central Intelligence Agency operative, Jake Hopper (Steven Seagal), whose beloved daughter Jessica (Sara Malakul Lane) is kidnapped by the Islamic fundamentalists Abu Karaf while on vacation in Thailand (the political group is after the daughter of U.S. Senator John Winthorpe, Jessica's friend, Sarah Winthorpe (Eilidh MacQueen), and takes both of the girls, after killing their boyfriends).

So it's a kidnapping and hostage scenario placed in the midst of a political tug-of-war between North America and Islam/ Asia/ Thailand. And it's a plot which reveals, in the usual thriller mode, wheels within wheels, so that the Mr Big behind the kidnapping isn't the Abu Karaf after all, but the super-villain General Jantapan (Tom Wu).

So the corrupt General Jantapan is the mastermind behind the plot of

10 Many were financed/ distributed by Columbia.

Belly of the Beast: he's been exploiting several groups, including the Abu Karaf and the Thai police, to gain the upper hand in the drugs and arms trade.

The ideological/ ethnic confusions of *Belly of the Beast* are intriguing: it's an American production with a white, American star, but it's set in Asia, with an Asian film director at the helm (and a part-Asian cast and crew), and the white Westerner is beating the hell out of Asians. Ah, but only the nasty, corrupt Orientals, you understand, not the good, obedient, Buddhist Orientals.

Also, the dubious ideological aspects of *Belly of the Beast* are tempered a tad by the portrayal of the white, Western hero as an Orientalized individual. He can speak the lingo, he prays at Buddhist temples, he greets people with a respectful clasping of the hands, and his fighting style is Asian.

✳

There are two problems with *Belly of the Beast*:

(1) The script.

(2) Steven Seagal.[11]

ITEM 1: The script (by Thomas Fenton and James Townsend) is too bound by the rules of the thriller genre, too formulaic, too predictable, and too unimaginative. The characterizations are paper-thin, none of the characters develop at all, and at the centre of the piece there's a really boring man that we don't root for.

Well, this is the issue with 99.99% of mainstream, commercial cinema: the scripts. If a movie isn't soaring, it's nearly always the screenplay that's the primary cause.

And we've seen this movie before.

Hell, we've seen this movie *thousands and thousands of times before*! OK. Nothing wrong with that – what is cinema and television but the same ten stories being told over and over again? Repetition is the rock bottom foundation of the global media. And audiences happily lap up the same yarns time after time.

But *Belly of the Beast* doesn't attempt to tell a very familiar tale in especially inventive ways.

ITEM 2: Steven Seagal. He looks like a bouncer at a nightclub or a fat[12] teamster. The bloated features, the little, piggy eyes, the bulky, beefy frame (Seagal is of course the beast's big belly of the film's title).[13] I know that the Seagalster has his action fans, but not me; I find him

---

11 Replacing Seagal would improve the picture, but as this was a star vehicle tailor-made for Seagal, it might not exist without him.
12 There's a joke about Hopper not over-eating, which might be a dig at Seagal's rather portly stature: his daughter Jessica has put post-it notes all over the grub in the fridge.
13 The legendary Sammo Hung is a famous tubby actor who can fight like a demon.

ridiculous.

And like some other action stars, Steven Seagal is not known for being a terrific dramatic actor. But here in *Belly of the Beast* he is wooden.[14] It's an attempt that many American stars make of apeing the laconic, cool, wry style of Clint Eastwood, Robert Mitchum or Steve McQueen – seeming to do or say very little (and to mumble lines *à la* Marlon Brando), but still being charismatic and watchable. But Seagal is not Mitchum or Eastwood; he's just dull.

It's a passionless performance of going through the motions from Steven Seagal (even tho' he is co-producer and apparently provided the initial story). Seagal's investment in this movie seems to be suffering through it so he can take the money and leave as soon as possible.

Seagal (b. 1952) was a former martial arts teacher (he trained in Japanese *aikido*), and a somewhat controversial figure in his professional career. He is best-known for the *Under Siege* movies (1992 and 1995), his biggest hits, and later flicks such as *On Deadly Ground, The Glimmer Man, Fire Down Below, The Patriot, Exit Wounds*, and *The Foreigner*. Seagal tended to play cops or agents (or a Navy Seal, in *Under Siege*) who battle drug lords, gangsters and villains (often with a sidekick, such as U.S. rapper DMX in *Exit Wounds*). Seagal's character Hopper in *Belly of the Beast* is in the same mold.

The role of Jake Hopper rescuing his daughter from kidnappers could've been played by any number of Hollywood stars *circa* 2003: Bruce Willis, Mel Gibson, Tom Cruise, Harrison Ford – all the usual suspects (actors such as Liam Neeson in the *Taken* series and Denzel Washington in *The Equalizer* mined similarly territory).

There were rumours of Tony Ching and Steven Seagal not agreeing on how to film the action sequences: Ching had filmed some of the action scenes without Seagal, so that he could be included later. A disagreement saw Ching walking off the set with his stunt team (for a director as professional and hard-working as Ching to abandon a film is very unusual, so it must have been something major).[15]

✳

However, *Belly of the Beast* is technically and cinematically a solid piece of work. It's got the flashy, glossy look of an urban thriller down pat. It has the funky nightclub settings (with scantily-clad dancers for the T. & A. quotient),[16] the tough streets of the Big, Bad City, the teeming markets and stalls, the run-down, industrial zones, and the odd slice of exotica (the

14 Acting honours in *Belly of the Beast* go to Byron Mann, terrific as Sunti, the hero's Buddhist sidekick (he was in *Invincible*).
15 Seagal has a reputation of being difficult to work with.
16 And the two hostages are attractive, young women who play the whole film in bikini tops and cut-off denim shorts.

Buddhist temple). Plus some All-Americana – a scene set in the Central Intelligence Agency's HQ in D.C. (which sets up the political background of the story).

The photography (by Danny Nowak) is vivid and nimble – it keeps up with the hectic pace of Tony Ching's direction. Some of the creative choices seem unusual – what *is* Steven Seagal wearing when he reaches Bangkok? (It looks like a blue tent cut up into a sort of kimono. Katrina McCarthy was costume designer. Dressing Seagal must be an uninspiring gig for a designer: it's the big, shapeless clothing of Marlon Brando in his super-size phase.)

Remember the music in *Belly of the Beast*? You won't, because it is utterly forgettable. Mark Sayer-Wade composed such an empty soundtrack you won't be able to remember a single cue, melody, or texture.

A very obvious element lacking in *Belly of the Beast* compared to a Hong Kong cinema version of the same plot is humour. There are no laughs here, and few smiles. Maybe, at most, a wry grin (lasting 1.25 seconds). If this was a Hong Kong production, some goofing around would be included (though maybe not in a John Woo version. But even Ringo Lam, in some ways tougher than Woo in outlook, included some humour in his thriller films).

As for Tony Ching Siu-tung's input – there are many punchy, blammy action scenes: they combine open-handed *kung fu* with Hong Kong thriller fire-fights (everybody has a gun, and the ammo, as in a John Woo or Ringo Lam actioner, never runs out).

Action-wise, *Belly of the Beast* is a companion piece to the previous year's Ching-directed *Naked Weapon*; but, altho' parts of that movie were crudely exploitative and downright repulsive, the action set-pieces seemed more galvanizing, and livelier. One can see how in *Naked Weapon* putting vulnerable, young women into the familiar gritty action movie setting and having them fight for their lives inspired the filmmakers. Having Steven Seagal struggle to save his daughter from kidnappers doesn't quite have the same dramatic potential. (The outcome, after all, is 100% certain: he'll rescue his daughter, neither of the moppets will die, and he'll fight global corruption at the same time).

The action in *Belly of the Beast* is the urban thriller kind – plenty of gunplay, of stunt guys diving and firing pistols, along with open-handed combat, and some bigger gags. Hong Kong action cinema has been coasting along with this kind of action for decades: but it works, it's entertaining, and it's superbly achieved. After all, even when Tony Ching is coasting along, he is very, very good.

This is rough-and-tumble action, featuring young guys in tee shirts hurtling along alleys or corridors, wielding guns and yelling. The opening action sequence includes Hong Kong staples like stunt guys leaping through glass windows, jumping off balconies, and diving onto the ground. The action style is *kung fu* (hand-to-hand-combat) rather than the swordplay and wire-work which is Tony Ching's signature style.

You'll notice that Steven Seagal in combat scenes is filmed mainly in medium close-ups, of the upper body, with fewer wide shots or medium long shots, presumably to make the aikido martial arts style look more effective. This approach is also used to hide a performer who isn't a martial artist, cutting to stunt doubles for the bigger moves.

✳

The script of *Belly of the Beast*, while unengaging in many areas, does include scenes evoking the political background of the plot – a discussion of the issue from the point-of-view of the U.S. government, in Washington, and a scene at an airbase in Thailand where Army choppers deliver the wounded and the dead from the terrorist bomb supposedly committed by the Abu Karaf (the scene is impressive, full of soldiers in formation, medical trucks, etc. The scene might be bigger if the budget had allowed for it, but it's plenty big enough. Also, a bigger budgeted film might have shown the terrorist bomb scene. Instead, it is referred to in dialogue, in these scenes of returning injured soldiers, and in that old, cheapo staple of all movies everywhere – the fake newspaper).

The 2003 film seems better when you see it again – then you notice some of the extra narrative work, after you've got the story and the action (and if you can simply ignore the fact that Steven Seagal is in it. Difficult, because he's in pretty much every scene).

✳

Belly of the Beast is set in Bangkok and Thailand: Bangkok is the most-visited city in the world, along with London (with something like 20 million tourists per year. For a comparison, New York City has around 13 million). But this is not the sensational, sleazy Thailand of movies, nor quite the exotic Sin City that some tourists hope to encounter (apart from the dancing girls in the nightclub). Jake Hopper is no party animal (he barely cracks a smile thru the entire picture. Seagal's idea of wit is so dry it's brittle and frail). He'd rather be praying in front of a golden statue of the Buddha in a temple than carousing in the fleshpots of downtown Bangkok. (We see Hopper lighting incense and praying to a photo of his dead wife, and later kissing his wedding ring.[17] So there'll be no fooling around for him,

17 Which's parallel-cut with a scene of Jessica praying to her mom! Talk about cheesy!

and no romantic subplot (a typical ingredient of action thrillers such as this, and probably the most common subplot in all cinema). Indeed, in an unbelievable bit of business, a Thai hooker, Lulu (Monica Lo – thirty years younger), latches onto Hopper after he saves her from some troublesome guys in the nightclub (in another fight scene). Soon she's buying him food and getting all friendly like (encouraged by Fitch McQuoid). But saintly, Buddhist monk Hopper brushes her off repeatedly (there is a brief love scene, however, when Hopper finally caves in. The sex scene is clothed, of course, and filmed in the usual semi-abstract, partial-close-ups manner. And it lap-dissolves into a shot of the ocean, of all things, followed by a sunset! So the film goes all coy and clichéd where love's concerned, but it's happy to depict henchmen being shot to ribbons multiple times).)

Jake Hopper is played as a familiar character type in Chinese cinema – the man who's as spiritual and ascetic as a Buddhist monk, who does the right thing, and isn't interested in girls[18] – i.e., he's Jet Li not Stephen Chow).

Jake Hopper is acting on his own – instead of sitting at home fretting beside the phone while the authorities rescue his daughter, he's out in the field. The movie explores a little of just what an individual can do when faced with a tough challenge (like finding someone in a faraway country), but not too much; it would slow the plot down. Besides, Hopper is a former C.I.A. agent, and the star of an action movie, so we know that he can take charge (and he has contacts he can call on for aid).

Belly of the Beast is an action thriller where the romantic, idealized aspects of the cinema of Tony Ching Siu-tung seem thin on the ground. However, there are a surprising number of scenes which celebrate Buddhism: Jake's chum, Sunti, joins a Buddhist temple to recuperate after leaving the Central Intelligence Agency (and to atone for shooting a woman by mistake); Buddhist artefacts are shot to bits in the finale; Jake prays to his dead wife in the Buddhist manner; he visits Sunti at the temple and also prays; later, he receives a lucky charm from his Buddhist Master (and also spiritual aid during the final smackdown); and finally there's a Buddhist funeral procession (complete with elephants).

There's some *James Bond* glam in *Belly of the Beast* (Tony Ching had already filmed many *Bond*-like movies by this time, and some *James Bond* movies had been filmed in Bangkok – such as *The Man With the Golden Gun* in 1974): the title caption of *Belly of the Beast*, for instance, plays over an image of a naked woman (Malin Moberg) swimming in a pool. Several times Hopper performs *Bond*-ish moves – for instance, he's a cat

---

18 Indeed, Hopper's interest in Lulu is partly because she's the girlfriend of Fitch McQuoid (Vincent Riotta), an arms dealer.

burglar in one of the opening scenes, like 007 (that scene includes the woman in the pool).

Belly of the Beast doesn't go as far as Wong Jing and Tony Ching Siu-tung did in the previous year's *Naked Weapon*, but there is some gruesome material in *Belly of the Beast*: the boyfriends, for ex, are slaughtered in front of the girls when they're kidnapped. One of the heavies slides along a stall of frozen fish in ice into a meat cleaver. And there's a rape scenario in the prison, with the jailers and the girls (plucky Jessica stabs the assailant repeatedly with the guy's giant knife, and seems to kill him).

✳

As a location, Bangkok has it all – although *Belly of the Beast* doesn't trawl the shadiest parts of the city, it does feature some wonderful location shooting – from the mandatory scenes filmed in a boat travelling along the famous rivers and watersides, to the exotic temples and the downtown markets (actually, Bangkok is surprisingly like Hong Kong in many respects, a Westernized city of Asia).

There's no doubt that one of the strengths of Hong Kong movie-making is its feeling for texture and atmosphere: Hong Kong filmmakers really know to exploit a location and bring out its beauty or its danger (it's partly a necessity, because Hong Kong cinema usually doesn't have the luxury of working on giant backlots of modern city streets, so productions have gone out onto the streets of Canton and filmed it guerilla-style).

Belly of the Beast follows the formula of narrative structure for an action film of both Hong Kong and Hollywood: it opens with an action sequence (set in the past, in 1994); the kidnapping comprises a minor action scene; the first big action scene occurs in a busy food market, halfway through act one (a traditional setting and a moment in the movie for this kind of scene); a minor fight scene is set in a nightclub, when Hopper encounters the hooker Lulu (who befriends him); and the first act climaxes with the hero evading an attempt on his life by the heavies.

From time to time we cut back to the girls in their jail, to remind us what's at stake. Jessica is a Daddy's girl through and through (as heroines in action movies always are): she is certain that her pa is going to sort everything out.

One of the heavies in *Belly of the Beast* is the androgynous, clawed Mongkol (Pongpat Wachirabunjong), who might've stepped out of a Shaw Brothers actioner of the 1960s (which the Tony Ching might've appeared in as a child).

The mid-film shoot-out (halfway thru act two) occurs at the Sangkom train yard. It starts off as an arms delivery and escalates into a blam-blam, shoot-em-up sequence. Here's where the budget kicks in: this scene should really take place at night (as it might do if it was made in Hong Kong). But that costs more. So we have the silly sight of guys with weapons parading atop disused railroad carriages in daylight, within sight of downtown.

The 2003 movie shifts into several beats of slo-mo deaths amidst exploding squibs, a form of action cinema which the Hong Kong industry has exported globally. Some of the big stunts here include high falls, and Seagal's double diving out of a train window in slow motion, while firing his trusty weapon.

Act two of *Belly of the Beast* climaxes with an artificial action sequence: our heroes (Hopper and Sunti) arrive at a lumber warehouse rendezvous to find a bunch of crooks already dead. It's a trap (the villains exit in their Jaguar, as they did in the train yard sequence).

So a group of henchmen materialize atop piles of timber, wielding two swords each. Yes, it's 2003, and when you want to bump off two American agents, you send in black-suited guys with swords! And you order them to preen and pose before they leap in for the kill. So Tony Ching squeezes swords yet again into a contemporary thriller, and they're a version of his 'Chinjas'.

Unfortunately, the warriors spend more time showing off their sword skills, twirling them like cheerleaders, allowing Sunti and Hopper to make mincemeat of them. (Altho' the ex-Central Intelligence Agency guys are armed, they set about the swordsmen using martial arts. After all, it's not fair to shoot people using archaic weapons, is it?).

✳

The finale of *Belly of the Beast* is certainly entertaining, from a spectacle and action point-of-view. No matter how lacklustre the scripts are that Tony Ching Siu-tung has worked from (and some have been decidedly patchy), he always finds something to latch onto in the climax. And in action cinema, and most definitely in Hong Kong action cinema, scripts're tossed away in a hail of bullets, and cinema becomes all about cinema.

Here, it's the spiritual side of Asian religion which Ching Siu-tung and Hong Kong cinema have exploited many times: the super-villain (General Jantapan) visits a shaman in a temple[19] to ask for aid in defeating Jake Hopper, while Hopper receives a gold chain and the support of his Master at the other (Buddhist) temple, where Sunti found sanctuary.

19 Decked as a movie-cliché Temple of Doom with scary statuary, scorpions, spiders and flickering red light.

So, during the Big Fight at the end of *Belly of the Beast*, between the hero and the super-villain, the voodoo doll pricked by the evil shaman in the temple disables Hopper, but the Buddhist monks are chanting and challenging the shaman's magical influence. It's a piece of filmic hokum, Oriental exoticism, resembling the ending of Hong Kong fantasy flicks such as *Green Snake* (1993) and the remake which Ching helmed, *The Emperor and the White Snake*. (This takes *Belly of the Beast* into fantasy territory, but the evocations of religious elements have been featured throughout the movie. Both Sunti and Hopper pray before embarking on the rescue mission, for example).

Yes, the set-piece of the finale of *Belly of the Beast* is the storming of the super-villain's compound by the heroes. Yes, it's two guys versus countless stuntmen and extras. Yes, the heroes never run out of ammo. Yes, two men're able to waste everyone in sight. Yes, the two girls, hauled about in bikini tops and denim skirts, aren't injured (even in the midst of heavy machine gun fire). And, yes, the hero is separated from the others to have the obligatory one-on-one duel with the super-villain.

Having their cake and eating it – which's what filmmakers like best: so *Belly of the Beast* shamelessly includes a duel of multiple archaic weaponry, which the museum-like building the super-villain General Jantapan calls home just happens to have lying about. So we have spears, swords, bows and arrows, etc (with several bullets vs. arrows gags), plus the mandatory empty-handed combat which's Steven Seagal's speciality (plus plenty of kicking). And, this being a Hong Kong-style actioner (or a Hong Kong-North American hybrid), glass is being shattered, parts of the set're collapsing, walls're exploding, and squibs're going off everywhere. The villain is dispatched by a body blow, falling across the room into a glass display case.

Belly of the Beast closes with a touching *dénouement* scene, a Buddhist funeral for Sunti (daughter Jessica and hooker Lulu are included in the procession, wearing white). And we even have elephants. Hopper scatters Sunti's ashes on the river (using more slow motion, and a superimposed image of Sunti in happier days). It's pure cheese – but you wouldn't expect anything less from a movie like this.

And that's all we become – just dust.

Naked Weapon (2002), this page and over.

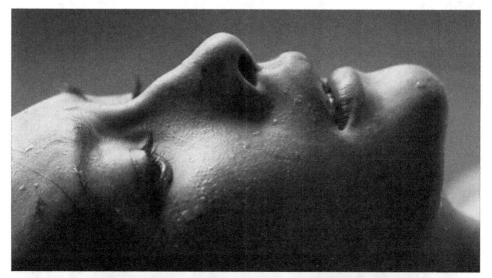

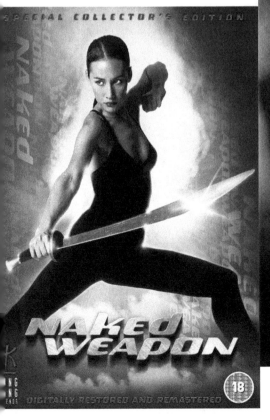

Belly of the Beast (2003)

STEVEN SEAGAL

BELLY OF THE

BEAST

Steven Seagal

A fenevad gyomrában

GFT ENTERTAINMENT and LUMINOSITY MEDIA present an NU IMAGE production STEVEN SEAGAL "BELLY OF THE BEAST" BYRON MANN, MONICA LO and TOM WU
sound by WAYNE BROOKS costume design by KATRINA McCARTHY cinematography by DANNY NOWAK
executive producers DANNY DIMBORT, AVI LERNER, TREVOR SHORT
written by STEVEN SEAGAL and JAMES TOWNSEND directed by SIU-TUNG CHING

SPI
INTERNATIONAL

NU IMAGE

12

AN EMPRESS AND THE WARRIORS

Jiang Shan Mei Ren

INTRO.

...A dying King of a Chinese kingdom...

...The Imperial court squabbling over succession and power...

...A princess caught between two attractive warriors...

No, *An Empress and the Warriors* is not re-inventing the wheel, but it is a moving love story and war/ courtly drama with a vast, quasi-historical background and storming, rampaging action sequences. This is Tony Ching Siu-tung at the height of his powers. It's one of the finest of Ching's later works.

An Empress and the Warriors (*Jiang Shan Mei Ren* = *The Kingdom and a Beauty*, 2008) was produced by Beijing Polyabana Publishing Co./ United Filmmakers Organization/ China Film Co-Production Corp./ Big Pictures, Ltd. It was written by James Yuen, Tan Cheung and Tin Nam Chun; produced by Claudie Chung Jan, Gin Lau Sin-hing, Peter Chan and Dong Yu; exec. prod. by Eric Tsang and Kuo Hsing Li; costumes by Dora Ng and Huang Bao-Rong; art dir. by Kenneth Yee Chung-man; prod. des. by Ben Lau; music by Mark Lui; the DPs were: Zhang Mu Liu, Ze Xie and Xiaoding Zhao; ed. by Tracy Adams, Poon Hung and Ki-Hop Chan; hair by Tam Ying Kwan; make-up by Siu Wai Ngok; sound by Lei Wang, Terry Tu and Xiao Hui Hou; vfx sup. was Brian Ho; Tony Ching, Ma Yuk-Sing and Wong Ming-Kin were the action dirs. (Many in the crew had worked with Ching before). Filmed in Mandarin. Released Mch 19, 2008. 99 mins.

In the cast were Kelly Chen Wai-lam, Leon Lai, Donnie Yen, Xiaodong Guo, Zhenhai Kou, Weihua Liu, Shan Zhang, Zhi-Hui Chen, Jie Yan and Bo Zhou. The box office for *An Empress and the Warriors* was estimated at HK $100 million.

Tony Ching Siu-tung didn't originate the production of *An Empress and the Warriors* – it was another job for hire. United Filmmakers Organization came to him with the script. Ching knew producer Claude Chung (from the days of *A Chinese Ghost Story*), which was 'a decisive factor' for him (there are several links to the *Chinese Ghost Story* movies). Ching also fancied trying something departing from his usual type of film: 'As for the subject, I wanted to try a different style from my usual repertoire' (2008).

Of all of Ching Siu-tung's recent movies as director, *An Empress and the Warriors* is one of the most satisfying – as entertainment, it's hugely enjoyable, and as movie-making, it's outstanding. The combination of the narrative ingredients is spot-on, the love story is genuinely moving, it features three terrific leads – Chen, Lai and Yen – and it puts a woman in an action role at its heart, and makes that really work. (And it does it all in 99 minutes – no need for a 2h 30m running time).[1]

An Empress and the Warriors is a bigger budget version of movies that the Hong Kong industry – and Tony Ching Siu-tung – had been making for decades. Ching has been here before with films such as *Butterfly and Sword, New Dragon Gate Inn,* the *Swordsman* movies, and all of those TV series made in Hong Kong for which Ching oversaw the martial arts.

So there's more money sloshing around – so the production can film in Mainland China, so there are more extras in the battle scenes, so the sets are bigger, so the production can shoot with actors underwater, and build chariots for the final battle, etc.

But the story and the filmmaking is very traditional, conventional, etc, despite the new tricks of computer-based or digital visual effects. After all, *An Empress and the Warriors* is a romance, which is about the most traditional and conventional and conservative form of a story going.

Romance against a dramatic, historical background had been the essence of Zhang Yimou films such as *Hero* and *The House of Flying Daggers*. *An Empress and the Warriors* can thus be seen as Ching's version of a Zhangian romantic drama.

An Empress and the Warriors is not a historical documentary, it's not a social realist rant promoting Maoism to the masses, it's not an instruction manual on how to build tract housing in Beijing – no, it's unashamedly a romantic confection in amongst sword swinging and war-

1 More on this below.

mongering. It doesn't claim to be 'realistic' in any shape or form. It features a romantic idyll in a flying balloon! It has a tree-house designed by Disney! It has a girl beating off a band of assassins underwater![2]

William Shakespeare is one of the ingredients in *An Empress and the Warriors* – the murder of the King from *Hamlet*, for example, and the tussle over the inheritance and leadership of *King Lear* (with Yan Feier as Goneril). This is Shakespeare inspired by the way that the Bard was channelled thru the cinema of Akira Kurosawa – an Orientalized version of the tragic Shakespeare plays.

KELLY CHEN.

Known as 'the diva of Asia', Kelly Chen Wai-lam (born Sept 13, 1972, Hong Kong) brings enormous star power to *An Empress and the Warriors*. Kelly Chen is a Chinese pop singer and actress; she has recorded many albums (38 up to 2017), toured extensively, appeared in numerous TV commercials, and has a huge following (including in Japan, where she spent part of her education). She was the highest-earning female star between 2005 and 2007 in the Chinese region (and only Jackie Chan and Andy Lau earned more).

Kelly Chen was appearing in films from 1995's *Whatever Will Be, Will Be* – her movies include: *Infernal Affairs, Tokyo Raiders, It's a Wonderful Life, All's Well, Ends Well, Breaking News, Hot War, Love Under the Sun*, and *The Monkey King*. Altho' Chen played the Princess in *An Empress and the Warriors* in her early twenties (and she looks it, too), she wasn't young at the time – she was 36 years-old.

One reason that Tony Ching Siu-tung said he cast Kelly Chen was to put a very contemporary actress in a period drama.[3] Sometimes that can jar, and actors will often be passed over during casting precisely *because* they look too contemporary or have too many contemporary associations (meanwhile, some actors are perfectly suited to period dramas). In *An Empress and the Warriors* it works, tho' – we buy the Princess as a young woman who's out of her depth amidst the intense squabbles in the royal court (all those serious-looking men!), who's the only girl in amongst hundreds of guys, who has to grow up rapidly, and who rises to the challenges of her political role.

There is also the fascination with watching a young, skinny actress grappling with almost impossible things – like moving in that ornate, multi-layered armour (even if it's painted plastic, it's still going be cumbersome)… like being able to fight in training scenes with Donnie Yen

<hr>

2 Ever tried swimming in full battle armour?!
3 Casting Donnie Yen and Leon Lai was a no-brainer for a martial arts epic.

(galloping on horses and firing arrows, swordfighting atop spinning tree trunks)… like beating off a host of assassins…

Kelly Chen has the intriguing assignment of being the only significant female character in amongst hordes of men – old men, young men, middle-aged men, soldier men, minister men, doctor men, men of all kinds… and just her. (There is only one speaking role for women in *An Empress and the Warriors* – and that's the Princess. Also, I can't recall even a close-up of any female charas in *An Empress and the Warriors* apart from Chen's Yan Feier. There's a small girl in a flashback (Yiyi Jiang), but that's the young Princess.4 So this really is a one-girl-among-the-boys movie).

It's a to-die-for role, then – the sort of role that actresses will fight to get. Poor, dear Kelly Chen, she has to contend with the appealing personages of both Leon Lai *and* Donnie Yen pining for her!

And you can see it was tough, too – sword fights, training scenes, horse riding, underwater fights – the full complement of Chingian and Hong Kongian action, where you've got to be fit to survive it. Kelly Chen really throws herself into the role, and is an appealing heroine.

However, in some of the scenes where Kelly Chen has to play a leader of men, she is not completely convincing. And in some of the high drama scenes she is rather shrill and hysterical rather than emotionally believable.

STYLE.

Decking the principals out in fancy armour in *An Empress and the Warriors* is almost distracting it's so fussy and elaborate. Chinese, historical pictures have always gone overboard on costuming5 (even in the lowest budget productions – it's one area where you can suggest luxury with one or two sumptuous costumes). If you're pricing up a historical production, costumes are almost number one among the items to make from scratch (you can't buy this stuff!). For military fetishists, movies like *An Empress and the Warriors* are goldmines (even if the practicality of the full armour is uncertain).

The armour was designed by art director Kenneth Yee Chung-man (who stamps his fingerprints on other aspects of the production. Tony Ching Siu-tung said that it was Yee who suggested that he direct the movie. Yee had worked with Ching before, on productions such as *Dr Wai* and *A Chinese Ghost Story*).

As Tony Ching Siu-tung explained, the decision to *not* situate *An Empress and the Warriors* in a particular time or place gave the filmmakers

4 This is a hyper-cute scene, with the young Feier giving Murong a pebble for good luck (which he's always kept).
5 Ornate armour had been an element in *The Curse of the Golden Flower*.

more latitude. Thus, the locale is Yan, a fictional state in mediæval China (which has a long-running feud with Zhao). Well, whatever – it's still the familiar China of movie myth as well as real history, the China of vast palaces, military might, stately power, courtly intrigue, and unswerving allegiance to the ruler. It's also the familiar China of beautiful forests and rivers, Kurosawan rainstorms, armies on horseback, giant suns (a rising sun forms the opening shot), and elaborate costumes (that armour!).

Cinematographically, *An Empress and the Warriors* is a very handsome production (as pretty much *all* historical Chinese pictures are. Zhang Mu Liu, Ze Xie and Xiaoding Zhao were the DPs). It features the full complement of Chingian romantic effects, from sunsets to moonlight to heavy rain to candlelight and firelight (a Chinese, historical film is a gift to cinematographers, with all that natural light, firelight and candleshine). There is slow motion, of course (at several speeds), speed ramping within shots, step-motion, etc. (Tracy Adams, Hung Poon and Ki-Hop Chan were the editors).

As expected, *An Empress and the Warriors* contains the familiar treasure chest of Chingian effects and textures – rain, flowing water, flickering flames, backlight, slow motion, and of course air or wind blowing through every shot. One of the signature images of *An Empress and the Warriors* is the lingering close-up: the camera dwells at length on the faces of Chen, Yen and Lai as they emote.

THE CHARACTERS.
An Empress and the Warriors revolves around three main characters:
• The Princess – Yan Feier – Kelly Chen
• The General – Murong Xuehu – Donnie Yen
• The Doctor – Duan Lanquan – Leon Lai
Much of the 2008 movie comprises scenes with one or two of the principals: the Princess and the General, the Princess and the Doctor, the Princess on her own, the Princess and the General again. And so on. Chen is in most scenes, and often she's playing against either Yen or Lai.

Never under-estimate how much romance and romantic desire floods thru the cinema of Tony Ching Siu-tung. 'I like beautiful, romantic things', Ching confessed, and these are found in plentiful supply in *An Empress and the Warriors*. If you think of Ching's cinema, romance is everywhere (and comedy, in addition to action). In *An Empress and the Warriors*, the context might be mediæval China in a time of warring states, but romance is actually the main plot (as suggested by the film's title – *An Empress and the Warriors* = a woman and two men). Indeed, Ching defined *An Empress and the Warriors* as 'essentially a love story with a period background' (as Ching put it, Yan Feier was yearning for an epic romantic experience, and she'll even give up the leadership of the nation for it).

Narratively, in this very traditional piece of storytelling, one of the most intriguing moments is when Yan Feier moves into 'take charge' mode, and abdicates (this occurs towards the end of the second act, following the defeat of the Zhao army). The look of shock and horror on General Murong's face says it all:[6] *you just don't do that!* Not if you're a princess and part of a royal court.

It's a very modern moment: a girl wants to take control of her life and *not* do what is expected of her: she simply leaps onto a horse and departs to Follow Her Dream. And in a Tony Ching Siu-tung movie, her dream is course the possibility of Eternal Happiness In Love.

It's pure wish-fulfilment and escapism – it's a moment out of women's romantic fiction, it's what we all wish we could do, even if we were the Empress of an entire nation. *Right! That's it! I've had enough! I'm off!*[7]

One of the references in *An Empress and the Warriors* is to the famous female leader of China, Empress Wu (subject of many historical movies, and appearing in the *Detective Dee* romps from 2010 onwards).

It's evil schemer Yan Wu Ba (winningly played by Guo Xiaodong) who is driving much of the plot of *An Empress and the Warriors* (at first, at least, and in his function as the arch villain): it's nephew Wu Ba who kills the King Yan, who opposes the accession of the Princess to the throne of Yan (how can you have a female leader? is a view voiced several times), and who sends assassins to do away with her – all of which gets the plot of *An Empress and the Warriors* moving.

Several scenes are highly artificial in *An Empress and the Warriors*, partly to keep things in motion: the arguments over leadership, for instance, in the Hall of Swords, following the King's death. The scene is played at a loud, hysterical pitch, which is necessary in order to sell this very contrived moment (the notion of a female leader is raised, but only briefly). It's also highly unlikely that the King, pierced by an arrow, would be left alone without some aides and servants in the main battlefield tent (but this is so that Yan Wu Ba can dispatch him without anybody seeing).

And another instance: the *Empress* movie takes huge liberties with Chinese history and Imperial politics – the key scene, which we have to buy wholesale, is the tussle in the palace state room over the accession, after the opening battle and death of the monarch. The King wanted

6 Donnie Yen has to play surprise/ disappointment several times in *An Empress and the Warriors*. The camera is right in his face, and he delivers a range of confused, sorrowful and aching looks.
7 It also echoes many actresses in Chinese cinema – they reach a point where they marry and create families.

General Murong as his successor (much to Wu Ba's ire), but Murong hands the torch over to Yan Feier. It takes some narrative work from the screenwriters (James Yuen, Tan Cheung and Tin Nam Chun) to make this fly. Just don't think about it too much.

EDITING.

Not known for being too complicated in the narrative structure of his films, actually many of Tony Ching Siu-tung's works *do* have complex narrative elements. Here in *An Empress and the Warriors*, for instance, the exposition is parcelled out within flashbacks. The Big Battle is used as the hook for the audience – look! there's a Big Battle! Thrills! Excitement! Action! But the exposition is wedged in around it – the General and the Princess talking after the battle in the Hall of Swords, for instance.

However, one of the flaws of *An Empress and the Warriors* is the pacing and the editing: editors Tracy Adams, Hung Poon and Ki-Hop Chan seem to have sliced out two or three shots in many areas where more would be expected – presumably to keep the running time down, and to maintain the headlong pace. But the flow of the narrative is juddery – in some places *An Empress and the Warriors* slows to nonchalant quasi-real time (in the healing sequence at Duan Lanquan's camp, for ex), while at others it whizzes through numerous plot points too quickly.

The editing of *An Empress and the Warriors* looks as as if one or two minor subplots have been omitted: on the other hand, that's all to the good if it brings the running time down and keeps the pacing sprightly. A romance set against a war and history background doesn't need to run to two hours, and is often better if it doesn't (*An Empress and the Warriors* clocks in at 99 minutes. It's a three act film; in the West, this movie would almost certainly run over two hours, and it would be a four act film. And if it was a prestige picture, it might go to five acts, with more subplots and more characters added. No need for that – you can say everything in one and a half hours, as *An Empress and the Warriors* does).

The first act of *An Empress and the Warriors* looks as if some subplots were dropped; for example, the film rushes to the encounter between the Princess Yan and Duan Lanquan, so they meet around the 20-minute mark. Usually, this sort of dramatic turn in the narrative would occur after the first act (between 25 and 30 minutes, the usual place for a first act ending).

Additionally, the editing style departs from the usual form of Ching's cinema by including several examples of parallel action. For instance, short scenes are crosscut into longer scenes, to remind us of the other subplots. A key editorial decision is selecting where and when to cut back from the tree house romance to the court and General Murong.

THE TREE-HOUSE OF LERRVE.

An Empress and the Warriors delivers plenty of the familiar Chingian romanticism and lyricism – the 2008 movie is more interested in the romance between Duan Lanquan and Yan Feier than in the war/ battle/ palace scenes. So, after 20 minutes of battles, Imperial courtly intrigue, and personal training for Feier, the movie shifts into 20 minutes of poetry and romance.

Duan Lanquan is a former New Moon warrior (and the only survivor – the rest were destroyed ten years ago in a purge. This is portrayed in a flashback which is staged in impressionistic images. The New Moon flashback includes the moment when Duan fled the purge and ended up in the forest. He thrusts his sword into the ground, which is where years later General Murong finds it).

Now Duan Lanquan is a reclusive inventor/ healer living in an extravagant encampment in the wilds. It's an Ultimate Tree-House, the sort constructed at theme parks, with a water wheel, movable walkways, multi-level platforms, towers, ladders, and wooden logs and ropes everywhere. It looks great at sunset, great in torrential rain, great in moonlight, and great with masked assassins crawling all over it. (Is this film *really* going to get away with Leon Lai as a hermit who's built the Ultimate Tree-House in an amazingly pretty forest?).

Well, anyway – here is one of the many romantic idylls in the cinema of Tony Ching Siu-tung – this is a filmmaker who's in love with the concept of being-in-love, and has found a whole treasure box of cinematic images and motifs with which to express the beauty, the magic, the sweetness, the bitterness and the total impossibility of falling in love. It's a fantasy of a fantasy, a heightened, highly stylized representation of something that only exists in the movies, in art.

In the action-adventure genre, when a character is healed and tended by another, it's often a preamble to romance (the closeness, the partial nudity, the faces only inches away from each other, one character at the mercy of another, etc). *An Empress and the Warriors* teases with that concept (extracting some comedy from Feier forbidding Duan Lanquan to look at her), and delays the sexual consummation for the second time that Yan Feier visits Duan Lanquan. Here, the preposterous motif of a hot air balloon is employed to provide the customary scene of lovers loving each other. The trope of flying is once again wheeled in by a movie to stand in for the love scene (smiles, shining eyes, shared glances, beautiful vistas, with a fire burning to keep the whole shebang in the air). Then the movie says, what the hell, and features a more conventional love scene anyway (with, yes, firelight in the background. However, this is a more reserved version of a love scene, focussing on close-ups of kisses and heads).

Yes, *An Empress and the Warriors* is a love triangle, with Donnie Yen getting the fuzzy end of the lollipop (someone's got to lose out – who would you choose? Leon Lai or Donnie Yen?). It's one of the oldest stories on the planet, and it will thrive for millennia more.

ACTION.

The action sequences in *An Empress and the Warriors* are of course outstanding. Even tho' the filmmakers seem conscious that audiences were getting tired of wire-work (as Tony Ching Siu-tung noted in an interview), there is plenty of it in *An Empress and the Warriors*. In the finale, there's a nod to being 'anti-wires' when Donnie Yen plays part of the one-man-versus-an-army sequence on the ground, twisting and kicking down opponents (see! you don't need wires! you can wrestle in the dust and still fight to the death!).

An Empress and the Warriors opens with a huge battle already in progress (the editing places the duologue between Yan Feier and General Murong in the Hall of Swords *after* the battle, so the battle – and the King's murder – are actually flashbacks). It's a big production number, in heavy rain, with tons of extras, swords, horses, etc). The rapid montage style of the editing puts the death of the King in amongst the battle and the struggle for leadership.

The battle between the nations of Yan and Zhao that climaxes act two of *An Empress and the Warriors* is a wild scene which includes chariots, as Tony Ching Siu-tung does his version of *Ben-Hur*. So, how would soldiers bring down chariots hurtling towards them? The stunt team came up with a novel solution which clearly demanded a *lot* of rehearsal from the performers: the soldiers dive to the ground, and hold up their shields, to form a makeshift ramp. The chariots fly up on one wheel, and topple over. In a real battle, it would surely be almost impossible, but – hell – it looks great!

THE FINALE.

That the 2008 movie is going to finish with a Big Battle, and the duel between the hero (or heroine) and the villain is expected; *An Empress and the Warriors*, however, shifts its genre slightly to incorporate tragedy (a favourite form in Chinese culture – Chinese movies like nothing better than slaughtering all of the principal characters in the final reel). Now Duan Lanquan expires from poisoned[8] darts from Yan Wu Ba's assassins, General Murong collapses after a stunning scene where he fights off hordes of warriors, Minister Teng is decapitated, and the scheming nephew Wu Ba is slain by the heroine. (It takes some narrative juggling to get the heroine to face off in a duel to the death with the villain while surrounded by hostile troops. This is meant to be an Empress in Ancient China, after all. But as this is a very heightened, romantic movie, such a scene is necessary, and welcome).

Leon Lai and Donnie Yen of course cross swords – in a unusual setting – a weir in a wide river. So Duan and Murong swing their swords while splashing knee-deep in water. (The subtext? They're fighting over Yan Feier, of course – it's the old macho, phallic tussle over a woman). Tony Ching has been filming this sort of action scene for decades.

Another impressive action scene in *An Empress and the Warriors* is an unexpected twist on the betrayal of the villain, Yan Wu Ba, in the finale. General Murong approaches the palace alone on horseback at night; Wu Ba orders his men to finish him off (from a cowardly position, standing where the sentries watch above the gate); some of Murong's faithful troops rush out of nowhere to protect the General; they all expire defending the gate.

For portraying glorious, old-fashioned heroism and dynamic action, few actors can best Donnie Yen in the contemporary era. *An Empress and the Warriors* is a brilliant example of Yen's unstoppable energy[9] and grim determination.[10] Yen is given a massive action sequence where he takes on a zillion soldiers, mowing them down left, right and centre, clutching a whole armful of spears and staffs, and wielding two swords (including the fabled Swallow Sword). You do *not* want to get in the way of Yen when he's on the warpath!

By the end of *An Empress and the Warriors* – which rightly ends on a close-up of Kelly Chen (in Imperial robes, now the queen overlooking her queendom) – we have enjoyed the full wagonload of Chingian action. Swords have been swung (a *lot*!), chariots have crashed in the dust... warriors have been trained... rivals have clashed... horses have galloped (and riders have fallen, repeatedly)... But also the full jade box of love letters of Chingian romance – eyes have shed tears, lovers have kissed in front of a roaring fire (and flown on the breeze), sunsets have glowed, and all three principals have stared longingly into space...

8 Poison is everywhere in Chinese, historical movies.
9 In one gag, he wrestles a horse to the ground.
10 And no doubt Yen contributed his own ideas to the scene, as he likes to do.

13

THE SORCERER
AND THE WHITE SNAKE

Baak Se Cyun Syut Zi Faat Hoi

Demons, giant snakes, swirling clouds, vortexes of water, beautiful but dangerous women, huge statues of Lord Buddha, temples in the mountains, epic vistas, waterfalls, talking mice, flying swords, outstanding visual effects and razor-sharp martial arts... *The Sorcerer and the White Snake* has all of that and more: it's a very entertaining slice of Ancient Chinese mythology starring Jet Li.

The Sorcerer and the White Snake (*Baak Se Cyun Syut Zi Faat Hoi*, a.k.a. *The Emperor and the White Snake*, a.k.a. *Madame White Snake*, a.k.a. *It's Love*), was produced by China Juli Entertainment Media/ Distribution Workshop/ Different Digital Design Ltd., the producers were Chui Po Chu, Chi Wan Tse and Yang Zi; exec. producer: Pang Yau-Fong; written by Charcoal Tan, Tsang Kan Cheung and Roy Szeto Cheuk-hon; DPs: Wai-Nin Chan,[11] Venus Keung Kwok-Man and Tony Lam Tak-Ming; music: Mark Lui; ed. by Angie Lam; action dirs. Tony Ching and Ming Jian Huang; art. dir by Tao Zhai and William Chang Suk-Ping; costumes by William Chang; special make-up by Cherlynn Koh; make-up: Man Yun-Ling; hair: Tam Ying-Kwan; sound: Gang Wang; and vfx by Next/ Visual Studio. Released Sept 28, 2011. 100 mins.

In the cast were Jet Li, Huang Shengyi, Raymond Lam, Charlene Choi, Jiang Wu, Miriam Yeung, Chapman To, Law Kar-ying, Wen Zhang and Vivian Hsu.

---

[11] Wai-Nin Chan had been the lighting gaffer on many of Tony Ching's films (including Ching's work as an action director). *The Sorcerer and the White Snake* was one of his first movies as DP.

2011 was a busy year for Jet Li in fantasy *wuxia pian* – he also starred in *Flying Swords of Dragon Gate*, directed by Tsui Hark, with whom Li had worked many times. This was a partial remake of the 1992 *Dragon Gate* movie, which Tony Ching Siu-tung had also worked on.

Principal photography ran from Sept 10, 2010 Jan 16, 2011. The budget was rumoured at HK $200 million (= US $25.8 million – one of the biggest budgets that Tony Ching Siu-tung has had as a director).

▼

Extravagant visuals, crisp, saturated cinematography, eye-popping visual effects, incredibly rapid action sequences, fabulous stunts, and plenty of humour adds up in *The Sorcerer and the White Snake* to a wonderful ride. It's fantasy time, where everything is out-size and played to the hilt, it's a Chinese version of *The Arabian Nights*, and it's a romp.

White Snake was not a *wuxia pian*, Tony Ching Siu-tung explained, but a fantasy: 'For this movie, we're aiming to make a fantasy, whereas in the past, we were making *wuxia* films'. Thus, instead of the fights occurring with swords and spears, it's magic and energy (as demonstrated in the opening battle – which does, however, include some of Jet Li's signature *wushu* work with a long spear, and there is a sword duel between Li and the snake-girls later).

As Tony Ching Siu-tung explained in a *Time Out* interview in 2011, his version of the White Snake myth altered the characterization of the monk (making him righteous, and not the villain), and invented new characters for the romantic subplots. When you hire Jet Li, scripts are often rewritten – there are things that play to Li's screen image, and other things that he'd prefer to avoid, or that the audience won't buy him doing. (For instance, the subplot of Green Snake's liaison with the monk Fahai is simply transferred to his sidekick, the assistant Neng Ren. Why? Perhaps because it was decided that the sidekick could carry the romantic subplot. However, sexy women are often placed alongside Buddhist monks in Chinese fantasy movies, with the usual expected results – as in the fox-demon sequence in the bamboo woods).

The Sorcerer and the White Snake was another version of the famous *Legend of the White Snake* (a.k.a. *Madame White Snake*). As well as the 1993 movie *Green Snake* (dir. by Tsui Hark), there have been two TV series of the mythology, plus other live-action versions (such as *Madam White Snake*, 1962). The 1980 film *Legend of the White* sold an incredible 700 million tickets in China.

Meanwhile, one of the early Japanese *animé* movies, a landmark in animation, was *The Tale of the White Serpent* (a.k.a. *Panda and the White*

Serpent, Taiji Yubushita & Kazuhiko Okabe, 1958). *The Tale of the White Serpent* greatly impressed the greatest animator of recent times, Hayao Miyazaki, when he saw it as a 17 year-old youth.[12]

The Sorcerer and the White Snake could be regarded as a remake of 1993's *Green Snake* – the depiction of the Buddhist monk Fahai draws on the depiction of Fahai in *Green Snake* (as played by Vincent Zhao, who, by the way, had replaced Jet Li in the *Once Upon a Time In China* series). The characterization of the two snakes, Green and White, seems to consciously evoke Maggie Cheung and Joey Wong (even down to the way they lie beside each other when they watch the humans at the beginning). Meanwhile, some of the action set-pieces in *The Sorcerer and the White Snake* (such as the battle on the canal) seem to employ scenes in *Green Snake.*[13]

The look of *The Sorcerer and the White Snake* certainly draws on the cinema of Tsui Hark, apart from *Green Snake* – it has the appearance of *The Legend of Zu,* the 2001 digital remake of 1982's *Zu: Warriors of the Magic Mountain.* We're talking infinite vistas of mountains, lush, green valleys, waterfalls, lakes of lilies, Buddhist temples, multi-coloured skies, etc. Meanwhile, several in the crew were Tsui regulars – such as editor Angie Lam and writers Charcoal Tam and Roy Szeto.

What's not to like?! Jet Li plus martial arts plus Chinese legends plus a love story plus delightfully wild visual effects, couched in the fantasy adventure genre. In *The Sorcerer and the White Snake,* Jet Li plays a demon-busting Buddhist monk called Fahai who, with a younger sidekick (Neng Ren – Wen Zhang) battles demons (but not killing them – instead, they're imprisoned by magic inside a pagoda, where, in true Buddhist, religious style, they have to contemplate their wickedness and acknowledge their punishment. Sounds like school? Yes, a lot of religions're like school!).

Meanwhile, two mythical creatures, snake-women (a green snake and a white snake), played by Huang Shengyi as White Snake (a.k.a. Susu) and Charlene Choi as Green Snake (a.k.a. Qingqing), become enamoured of the human world (and of men in particular). Much of *The Sorcerer and the White Snake* comprises a *Beauty and the Beast* and *The Little Mermaid* sort of fairy tale, portraying a romance between a human and a demon: in this case, White Snake falls in love with wannabe herbalist and doctor Xu

12 Miyazaki recalled: 'I can still remember the pangs of emotion I felt at the sight of the incredibly beautiful, young female character, Bai-Nang, and how I went to see the film over and over as a result. It was like being in love, and Bai-Nang became a surrogate girlfriend for me at a time when I had none.' (*Starting Point, 1979-1996,* tr. B. Cary & F. Schodt, Viz Media/ Shoga-kukan, San Francisco, CA, 2009, 19)
13 The casting in *The Sorcerer and the White Snake* is not quite as strong as in the 1993 version of the snake-and-man folk tale. No complaints about Jet Li, of course, but somehow Huang Shengyi and Charlene Choi weren't quite as compelling a duo of snake-babes as Maggie Cheung and Joey Wong.

Xian (Raymond Lam), and Green Snake has a flirtatious relationship with Fahai's apprentice, Neng Ren.

Plus a host of monsters and demons: Cat Devil, Chicken Devil, Bat Devil, Toad Monster, Rabbit Devil, Ice Harpy, etc. The 2011 movie takes full advantage of digital animation to create a batch of fantasy monsters – so this is partly a monster movie, with righteous monks taking on demons and capturing them. (And as the monsters're interacting with humans, we have computer-aided versions of Jet Li *et al*).

Oh, and we also have talking animals, in the Walt Disney manner – mice, rabbits, tortoises, toads, etc. The mouse might've stepped out of the *Narnia* films, *Alice In Wonderland* or *Stuart Little*. It's another comical sidekick (for Susu) – and the mouse and its pals attack the monks in the Buddhist temple, and it also leads the scholar to the pagoda.

The Sorcerer and the White Snake makes European and North American attempts at playful fantasy movies look so tame and pedestrian by comparison. The *Twilight Saga, Snow White and the Huntsman, Nim's Island, The Hobbit* – all locked into 'realism' and 'photorealism', death to artists and creativity in filmmaking. These movies hobble along, crouch-backed and nearly lame.

Meanwhile, there's a very inspiring feeling of *freedom* and *possibility* in Chinese action movies, as in Japanese animation, that just doesn't exist anymore in the Western world. You've got to be feeling *very* confident to deliver a movie like *The Sorcerer and the White Snake* (or *Flying Swords of Dragon Gate* or *Hero* or *Detective Dee*). And you also need enormous resources, which includes a filmmaking team fuelled by energy and immense talent and knowledge.

The characterization of the relationship between the monk Fahai and his sidekick Neng Ren is depicted in the usual respectful plus a little jokily argumentative manner of genre films. Neng is somewhat cocky, but when he gets into trouble (as with the Bat-Demon), he calls on his Master.

The Sorcerer and the White Snake opens with a prologue portraying the monks Fahai and Neng Ren in action – taking on the Ice Harpy (Vivian Hsui), in a Winter Wonderland setting (high up in snowy mountains and falling snow). The prologue sets out the high fantasy and extensive visual effects approach that the rest of the movie pursues (as well as introducing the main star, Jet Li, and showing who he is by what he does).

Neng Ren and Fahai battle the Ice Harpy, with Neng rushing in and demonstrating his lack of experience (he's rapidly frozen by the Ice Harpy). Fahai duels with the Ice Harpy with his spear and magical energy. The *wushu* moves are combined with Tony Ching's trademark effects:

billowing clothes, wind machines, slow motion and flying actors. If this is violence, it's very pretty, romantic violence.

Yes, this is Ye Olde China, the China of myth and legend that never existed, but that should've existed.

Bells and sound are one of the carriers of magic in *The Sorcerer and the White Snake:* a giant bell is tolled on the mountain, Neng Ren summons his Master with a handbell, and Neng uses hand cymbals to polish off the bats. (Added to that are more alarm bells adorning the temple, plus the familiar parp and drone of Tibetan horns).

Design-wise, *The Sorcerer and the White Snake* presents several unusual choices: one is the portrayal of the Snake Women: as so much in *The Sorcerer and the White Snake* is digital animation, it's expected that the snake-sections of the characters would be animation. But not the upper part of the costumes. But here, yes: so that actresses Huang Shengyi and Charlene Choi play their roles topless (or near as), but visual effects blend their forms with the snake forms (in a painterly effect). Secondly, the Snake Demons don't slither along the ground – they float gracefully thru the air. (In Tony Ching Siu-tung's cinema, everything seems to want to fly – and with the magic of visual effects and wire-work, everything *can* fly).

▼

A human man and a magical woman – yes, it's another human-beast tale, like the ghost stories in Chinese cinema. *The Sorcerer and the White Snake* is thus an update of the *Chinese Ghost Story* films, which Tony Ching Siu-tung helmed, and which Tsui Hark produced (coincidentally, a remake of *Green Snake* was released in 2011, the same year as *The Sorcerer and the White Snake*). And two of the writers of *The Sorcerer and the White Snake* – Charcoal Tan and Roy Szeto Cheuk-hon worked on the *Chinese Ghost Story* films (and many similar films). And a remake of Ching's first *Chinese Ghost Story* film also appeared in 2011.

The Sorcerer and the White Snake is Tony Ching Siu-tung at his most romantic – it's Fairy Tale Time in Chinese cinema, with romance in the air (and in the water). Act one contains two underwater kisses, for instance – presented in the dreamy, colourful manner of romantic fiction. (The underwater kiss is a reprise of the famous moment in *A Chinese Ghost Story* featuring Leslie Cheung and Joey Wong).

'And then they kiss' – as Tony Ching says, he likes very romantic, very stylized things, and *The Sorcerer and the White Snake* is a supreme example of that all-encompassing romanticization and poeticization of the world. There's no holding back here, from a filmmaker who first hit the big time with *A Chinese Ghost Story,* back in 1987. (The kiss, for instance, is milked – it's the pivotal moment in the romance, after all. And it is reprised several times. In the finale, for example, when Susu kisses Xu Xian, it reminds him who she is).

And, like previous versions of the narrative, including the 1993 *Green Snake,* it is the women who are driving the story (at least initially), with their desires to explore the human world. And in the finale, too – when Xu Xian has forgotten who White Snake is, it's White Snake's desire that drives the narrative.

The Sorcerer and the White Snake is also in part Tony Ching Siu-tung's animated movie – there're sections of *The Sorcerer and the White Snake* which're nothing but animation – not only the snakes, the ocean and the sky, but also the actors (including a digital double for Jet Li). And yet, animation has been one of the tools that Ching has deployed from the mid-1980s – *A Chinese Ghost Story* used animation, for instance (stopmotion, as well as optical effects).

The sheer volume of visual effects and animation in *The Sorcerer and the White Snake* means that this is a movie partly produced by whole teams of visual effects folk – producers, supervisors, designers, animators, photographers, technicians, etc.

Tony Ching Siu-tung said there were 1,800 shots in *White Snake,* and of those 1,500 were visual fx shots. Which, for a Hong Kong or a Chinese movie, is huge (actually, it's huge for any movie, from anywhere).

In several technical respects Chinese movies are superior to their Western counterparts in the use of digital visual effects. One is their approach is much broader, and not tied to notions of 'realism'. Another is their eagerness to try things that Western movies don't do. Another is the vast arsenal of mythologies and legends they draw on. Another is the genius of their action and staging. Another is the interactivity of the environment with the creatures (Chinese cinema is brilliant at puppet-eering inanimate objects to evoke energy and monsters).

Altho' the digital animation is something that audiences sometimes complain about, there are 100s of practical effects in *The Sorcerer and the White Snake,* plus lots of model work. Oh yes – the flood is partly achieved in the same way that catastrophes have been produced in cinema for a hundred years: with real water pouring across miniature landscapes.

There is a surprising amount of underwater photography in *The Sorcerer and the White Snake:* Xu Xian first encounters White Snake after falling into a lake in the mountains, and again during the pavilion scene.

Meanwhile, the whole Buddhist temple is flooded in the finale. Fahai is in the water, as are the monks.

Striding thru it all, clad in white, monastic robes, and with a shaved head, Jet Li is, as always, totally marvellous. What a superstar! Can Li do no wrong? Well, I haven't seen him take a misstep yet (tho' *The Kiss of the Dragon* (2001) ventured into some dodgy ground, as Li bravely sent up his iconic status). Li is supreme as the Buddhist monk Fahai (earlier in his career, he might've played the scholar).

Jet Li summed up working on *The Sorcerer and the White Snake* thus:

> After fighting the White Snake, fight the Green Snake. After fighting the Green Snake, then fight the Demon. After fighting this Demon, then fight another Demon. After fighting this Demon, then fight the Water Monster. Everyday on set I was letting out a big sigh.

Like *Forbidden Kingdom* (2008), *The Sorcerer and the White Snake* depicts Jet Li in his stately, wise wizard role, a Wong Fei-hung who's matured into a Confucian philosopher and mystic, but who can still kick-ass better than anyone when necessary.

Because, once again, watching *The Sorcerer and the White Snake* is another reminder of just how wild and imaginative Chinese action movies are. When you come back to a Chinese action film, after watching some North American flicks, you're reminded once again just who the Kings of Live-Action Spectacle are: the Chinese film industry.

And there are images in *The Sorcerer and the White Snake* that you haven't seen anywhere else: for instance, a giant snake beating on the doors of a Buddhist temple that's completely underwater, to get at her lover, who's in the throes of demonic possession, in the lap of a huge statue of Lord Buddha, while rows of monks inside chant, holding the protection spell in place.

The incredible scenes keep coming in *The Sorcerer and the White Snake:* the Lantern Festival, for instance, in act one, delivers a colourful spectacle which the Chinese film business can do finer than anyone else. And, in the midst of it, the filmmakers stage crazy duels, in the water and in the air – between Neng Ren and bat-demons (he uses hand cymbals to vanquish the critters), and between Fahai and the flying Bat Demon (which ends up in the heart of a volcano! Fahai pursues the Bat Demon across the skies and into the mountains (to accomplish the usual change-of-a-setting for a duel). But their destination – into a volcano, amidst lava – is unexpected).[14]

We're back in yet another bamboo forest in Tony Ching Siu-tung's *œuvre* for a stunning face-off between white fox-demons and Fahai and his Buddhist buddies. These're demons that change into attractive, scantily-clad sirens that writhe around the celibate, Buddhist monks, who close their eyes to such temptations, and chant frantically. The sight of Jet Li among the bamboo stalks enveloped in acres of female flesh is worth the price of admission alone (this also provided memorable imagery for the publicity of *The Sorcerer and the White Snake*).

This time, instead of filming bamboo as weaponry, Tony Ching has the vixens emerging from the bamboo stalks to tantalize the Buddhist monks (they slide their legs and arms from the poles). Like the snakes in the finale, they converge on Fahai, while he wards them off with religious chants.

More and more: tho' *The Sorcerer and the White Snake* is not a swordplay movie, it's too much to expect Tony Ching Siu-tung and co. not to include one sword duel at least – this occurs between the Snake Women and Fahai, at the gates of the temple. This time, as Ching and the team have delivered literally 100s of swordplay scenes (on TV as well as in movies), plenty of swooshing visual effects're added, to make the flashing blades more akin to blows of energy (as expected, many of the images are filmed in slow motion, turning the swordplay into a romantic dance).

Yet another scene: Fahai versus White Snake in the back streets of the local town, as they demolish buildings and use the environment to attack each other. Here, Fahai gives Susu a chance to redeem herself, and to disappear back to her homeland. This act two finale is replayed, as often in Chinese action movies, in the act three finale).

The out-size finale of *The Sorcerer and the White Snake* features the expected showdowns between Fahai and the Buddhist monks and the two Snake Women. Fahai's tussles with White Snake are repeated several times – on the ocean, alongside Green Snake; again on the sea, with Fahai channelling his Buddhist spirituality; on the cliffs, at the pagoda, and so on.

The finale of *The Sorcerer and the White Snake* is, as you'd expect, a constant barrage of action and spectacle. Among the stand-out set-pieces are Fahai taking on the Snake Women in a sword duel; the flood – a Biblical-sized deluge that engulfs the mountains and the Buddhist temples; the monks chanting while underwater; Fahai duking it out with the

14 Parts of this scene allude to the *Lord of the Rings* series, where Gandalf fought with the Balrog.

giant snakes on the ocean; White Snake battering at the spell-protected doors of the temple; swimming mice, no less, biting the monks to break their concentration (which allows Susu to enter the temple); Fahai battling Green Snake, and being swallowed, etc.

Image-wise, these are some of the biggest scenes in the cinema of Tony Ching Siu-tung (or are they? Because Ching has been grandiose from the outset! Look at *Duel To the Death* or *The Witch From Nepal*).

But certainly the latter section of the duel in *The Sorcerer and the White Snake* , where Fahai is resting atop a sunken statue of the Buddha battling White Snake nearby, are pretty spectacular. White Snake launches multiple attacks – airborne snakes, and water, and rocks. Fahai repels them all, by focussing his Buddhist spiritual *chi* (Fahai is swamped by swarming snakes, and bitten and poisoned. Susu continues by firing missiles of spiralling water shaped like snakes at him, an inventive means of turning water into weapons. She also enchants rocks to form further projectiles).

This is marvellous visual effects photography, with superimpositions of a golden Buddha over/ behind Fahai, and godly light emanating from the boiling skies. The motif of the Buddhist palm of energy, here given a golden glow, is marvellous (sometimes there are multiple golden palms warding off White Snake's attacks; later, two giant hands are used).

This is Jet Li playing a hero at his most righteous and unstoppable: Li makes a superb incarnation of Lord Buddha. No one stands a chance, not even a deity like White Snake.

Once the action components of the finale have played out, with White Snake defeated, the romantic section closes the 2011 movie: here comes the slo-mo photography, the anguished looks of the two lovers, and the theme song (a duet).

Oh, this is Tony Ching Siu-tung at his most indulgently romantic – this is a director who's well-known for crunching action scenes with guns blazing and bombs exploding, but he's really a big softie at heart.

The ending is the tragic separation of the lovers, as at the end of the *Chinese Ghost Story* movies: Xu Xian and Green Snake have to part, being, as Fahai explains, people from different worlds. Redemption is a key ingredient here, couched with the Buddhist religion: Fahai gave White Snake a chance at redeeming herself at the end of act two, when they fought in the town. But when Susu has been imprisoned in the pagoda, she surrenders, and begs to have the chance to see Xu Xian one more time.

Fahai grants her wish – by lifting the whole pagoda up, no less, so that White Snake can scurry out to have that final, tearful embrace with Xu

Xian. Two lovers and a prohibition is all that's needed for a love story –
here, Fahai embodies the beast-and-human taboo.

The love scene is played out in the familiar manner of Chinese drama –
operatic, over-blown, weepy, accompanied by a pop song featuring two
voices (Raymond Lam and Eva Huang).

Once the tragic romance has played out, there is a brief *dénouement*
scene featuring Fahai and his sidekick Neng Ren (now a flying bat demon,
his curse for rushing in too soon and not listening to his *sifu*). *The Sorcerer
and the White Snake* closes in the classic manner, with Fahai walking off
into the sunset (and no ordinary sunset, but a lavish image of mountains
and clouds in heightened colours).

One of the valuable aspects of *The Sorcerer and the White Snake* is
that it cuts down on time spent on the subplots, and keeps the running
time to a tight 100 minutes. The temptation to drag out the movie is rightly
resisted. There's absolutely no need for a movie of this kind to run for two
hours or more (as they do in the West).

An Empress and the Warriors (2008), this page and over.

A "REPÜLŐ TŐRÖK KLÁNJA" rendezőjének lebilincselő új filmje

DVD VIDEO

DONNIE YEN   KELLY CHEN   LEON LAI

AZ URALKODÓ HARCOSAI

AN EMPRESS AND THE WARRIORS

The Sorcerer and the White Snake (2011),
this page and over.

14

JADE DYNASTY

Zhu Xian

THE PRODUCTION.

Tony Ching[1] made a welcome return to film directing with the September, 2019 release *Jade Dynasty (= Zhu Xian*; number '1' was added to the posters, hinting at a sequel[2]). *Jade Dynasty* was produced by Huxia Film Distribution/ New Classics Pictures/ Shanghai Taopiaopiao Film Culture/ Youku Pictures/ I.Q.I.Y.I. Pictures; the producers were Ning Li (producers), Huang Qunfei, Jia Xu and Tony Ching (line producers); wr. by Shen Jie and Song Chaoyun, and based on a novel by Xiao Ding (a.k.a. Zhang Jian, born in Fuzhou). (The 2003 book had already been adapted into a TV series in 2016 (*The Legend of Chusen*, a.k.a. *Noble Aspirations*), so this is kind of the big screen version of the TV show; however, only Tang Yixin from the television series appears in *Jade Dynasty*).

Two of the greatest film editors ever, Angie Lam and Marco Mak Chi-sin, cut the film; Chen Weiian was DP; music by young, Hong Kong composer Zhu Yunbian and veteran Teddy Robin; prod. des. by Kenneth Yee Chung-man; art. dir by Liu Minxiong; vfx supervisor Annie Ng;[3] sound sup. by Sergei Groshev; visual effects by V.H.Q. Hong Kong (Malaysia, Beijing and Singapore), Worldwide FX, Leyard, Hezhong Film Co., Digital Idea, W.T.W. Films, and Postmodern Digital; and action dir. by Ching, Xiong Xin-xin and Wu Zequan. Theme songs were sung by Xiao Zhan, Meng Meiqi and Zhou Shen (and composed by Teddy Robin). Filmed in

1 In China, Ching is known as Cheng Xiaodong.
2 Suggesting that the producers had market research or favourable previews and knew that the film was going to do well.
3 Vfx were by V.H.Q. Hong Kong in Singapore and Malaysia.

Mandarin. Released Sept 13, 2019. 101 mins.

Pop and TV star[4] Xiao Zhan[5] (27) heads up a truly superb cast which included many veterans from Hong Kong cinema, many of whom have worked with Tony Ching before (including Norman Chui,[6] David Chiang, Cecilia Yip, Xu Shaoqiang, and Chen Liwei). Three actresses shine bright here: Meng Meiqi, Tang Yixin and Li Qin. Also in the cast were Anthony Bao, Hsin-chih Chiu, Xu Dai, Zhengting He, Ka-Yan Leung and Benyu Zhang.

Jade Dynasty is an entertaining romp of a fantasy/ historical costume movie, filled with lighthearted moments as well as the expected high drama, incredible action and spectacle (Chinese audiences are very familiar with this sort of material – TV series are produced every year, for instance, and there was a TV show adapted from Xiao Ding's novel). Story-wise, *Jade Dynasty* is a familiar mix of Chinese mythological motifs, Peking Opera performance style, swordsmen (and women) flying thru sunset skies, intense (and very graceful) swordplay, magnificent settings, and very contemporary humour (there's a good deal more humour in *Jade Dynasty* than usual in a Tony Ching-directed *wuxia pian*, and in many other swordplay films of the era). We're in the familiar mythological, *jiangzhu* territory of *The Stormriders,* of the *Zu: Warriors of the Magic Mountain* remake, and projects Tony Ching worked on, such as *The Sorcerer and the White Snake* and the *Wind and Cloud* TV series.

Everything works here: the 2019 movie is easy to like, exquisitely crafted, featuring many memorable images, and a terrific score by Teddy Robin and Zhu Yunbian. (*Jade Dynasty* is easy to like because you are right with the hero from the outset, as the ordinary guy in amongst a world of gods and heroes – and because the tone is lighthearted in the main, without the weary cynicism, the snarky comments masking hostility, and the grumpy frowns of too many action and fantasy movies. The way that characters interact in so many contemporary action-adventure-fantasy films is just off-putting after a while).

Jade Dynasty was filmed in Winter, 2018-19 (principal photography began on Oct 17, 2018): you can see how very cold it was in most of the outdoor scenes (no need to add digitally animated cold breath here). In the enjoyable 'making of' documentary, Tony Ching looks like he's wearing several jackets against the cold (as he usually does. Even in the studio, Ching is wrapped up).

Jade Dynasty was aimed at a local audience – it was filmed in

---

4 Ching has used pop idols before, of course – in his previous movie as director, for instance – Kelly Chen, or the great Leslie Cheung in the *Chinese Ghost Story* films.
5 The role was played by Li Yifeng.
6 Norman Chui was the star of Ching's very first film as director, *Duel To the Death.*

Mandarin, in Mainland China (in Beijing, Hebei, Henan and Sichuan), though many in the team were regulars in the Canton film industry. The cast were mostly Mainlanders. The film was a hit, grossing some $56 million.

Jade Dynasty is another example of Tony Ching's insistence on keeping movies fresh and new: being out of date, or being boring, or being old-fashioned is simply no good, Ching reckons. The young cast, the sprightly pacing, the contemporary humour and the barrage of visual effects strive to keep this 2019 production up-to-date. Yes, this kind of movie is something that Chinese cinema and Hong Kong cinema has been churning out for decades. Swordplay fantasies have been a staple of Chinese, Mandarin-speaking cinema since the late 1920s, when Shaws and others made more than 250 swordplay films between 1928 and 1930.

CHARACTERS.

So we're back in the *jiangzhu* of myth and dream, ladies and gentlemen – but this is the god-level incarnation of the martial arts world, populated by deities[7] and superheroes rather than grizzled swordsmen or embittered anti-heroes (no unshaven, grubby characters here: these are clean-cut, scrubbed faces, with the girls exhibiting exquisite, porcelain skin and make-up). It's the movie genre of Ancient Chinese mythology updated with visual effects and pretty, young actors for the 21st century, building on the *Stormriders* films, *The Legend of Zu* and similar ilk of the late 1990s (which in turn drew upon the 1983 Tsui Hark epic *Zu: Warriors of the Magic Mountain*). It's that combination of supernatural soap opera (family dynamics are in full force in *Jade Dynasty*), with floaty, breezy action, and vistas of a truly grandiose China of myth and dream.

Jade Dynasty's characters are a combination of god-like personas and movie-movie performances: they're gods but they're played by Chinese actors – and they're Chinese actors but they're playing gods. *Jade Dynasty* knows it's a piece of entertainment, and everybody acts accordingly. So there's a soap opera quality to the melodramatic relationships, and the tone is light (however, when we reach the finale, out come the teardrops, the hysterical acting, and the quivering, agonized close-ups. It's not a Chinese, historical movie unless several people dissolve into weeping hysteria).

For instance, the first time we're introduced to the Taoist Masters who live in the heavens up on Dazhu Mountain, they're zooming around the

7 The veteran actors in *Jade Dynasty* playing the Taoist Masters spend most of their time pontificating in a palace sitting on divans, or overseeing the development of their students from hilltops.

skies in a game of mystical tag, led by Tian Linger trailing pink banners. The movie opens with vast views of clouds upon clouds upon clouds – how Asian artists love clouds! The art direction provides suitably awe-inspiring images of billowing, white clouds. The camera floats dreamily and shoots into the sun. It's an astonishing sequence, where the evocations of effortless flight across endless, airy spaces is very attractive. (The opening scene also introduces a recurring motif: height and verticality. We are far above the ground (and above the clouds), amongst the peaks of sacred mountains. Following that scene, the film is filled throughout with characters ascending to the skies, or descending from on high, or standing way up on cliffs or ledges. Characters spend their lives flying in or out of very high places, like birds, or they stand on the edge of abysses, just about to leap off).

The scenes of the Tian Clan soaring through the heavens also take place in the hero's mindscreen: Zhang Xiaofan is imagining himself in a clinch with his beloved Tian Linger (thus establishing his romantic longings from the outset). When *Jade Dynasty* cuts from the idealized fantasy to a shot of Xiaofan dreaming, it performs one of the great clichés of fiction, the desire and the reality, the dream and real life. It also establishes the tone of *Jade Dynasty* – wistful fantasy rather than bitter fantasy, comical fantasy rather than serious fantasy.

But when we meet the Qingyun Sect up close (when the flying warriors come in to land at their home), there's a lengthy comical skit revolving around food – meat speared on swords (which continues into the dinner table scene). Food is a great leveller in Chinese cinema – even superheroes and gods have to eat, right? And the first time in *Jade Dynasty* that we meet our hero Zhang Xiaofan, he's cooking (yes, *cooking*). In fact, Xiaofan is typed as a kind of Cinderella figure, rustling up nosh for the family of supernatural beings (and having to clean up after them).

So while the 2019 movie is couched within the high fantasy genre, where pretty much every character possesses supernatural powers (and it starts out like that), humour is introduced very quickly (it's the Heaven and Earth motif in Chinese culture: the two go together. Heaven, yes, but also Earth – or, here: clouds but also cooking).

Tian Buyi (Qiu Zinzhi) is the leader of the Qingyun Sect; his wife is Su Ru (Hsiao-hsuan Chen). Tian is a stern patriarch, always encouraging his charges to train, train, train and develop their *chi*. But he's also portrayed in a comical manner. For example, in the dinner scene, when everybody only gets rice (the Qingyun Sect is a little down on its luck), Tian has squirrelled away a chicken for himself (which he eats in front of his drooling family). These lighthearted touches continue in the movie (Su Ru gently mocks her husband, for example).

The dinner scene also introduces a key concept in *Jade Dynasty* and in all Chinese, historical cinema: energy (*chi* or *qi*): Tian Buyi tests Zhang Xiaofan's *chi* at the table, gradually pushing him over. Linger helps secretly from the other side (and then her brothers do, too).

Jade Dynasty vividly foregrounds the anxious relations between the younger generation and the older generation, a common theme in movies aimed at a younger audience (the casting of *Jade Dynasty* certainly indicates that the producers and backers were going for a young audience). The Elders pontificate in their luxurious palace up in the heavens, but it's the younger generation who have are immersed in life.

Another theme in *Jade Dynasty* is a vague proto-feminism – the inclusion of strong, young women in *Jade Dynasty* plays into the target market, of course (the producers want girls to come see this movie as well as the usual male audience), but it also counters the usual patriarchal slant of swordplay and historical movies in China. A little, at least – I mean, the world of *Jade Dynasty* is still thoroughly, completely patriarchal and massculinist (despite the token gesture of including one woman amongst the Elders, Shui Yue). And the hero is a guy, and *sifu* Tian Buyi rules the Qingyun Sect household. And all of the villains are male.

STYLE.

The art direction in *Jade Dynasty* (by one of Tony Ching's regular production designers, Kenneth Yee Chung-Man, and art director Liu Minxiong) is luxurious eye candy all the way: the actors, the faces, the skin, the hair, the costumes, the props, the settings, the lighting, the visual effects, the whole schmeer. The over-riding mantra seems to have been:

Let's just make everything BEAUTIFUL.

The art direction is a delightful and indulgent slice of Ye Olde Chinese Mythologee – light-filled, airy palaces, huge, golden bells, mountainous eyries, exquisite lakes, and of course those endless vistas of mountains. With 3.6 million square miles of land, there's no shortage of amazing places in Mainland China to use in films. The Hong Kong movies that filmed in Beijing in the 1980s and 1990s barely scratched the surface. (Since then, film companies have trekked into areas such as Sichuan and Dunhuang. Films such as *Hero* have drawn attention to the outstanding natural wonders of China).

This is a sun-lit film – there are night scenes, such as when Lu Xueqi punishes Xiaofan for peeping, or when Zhang Xiaofan finds Lu Xueqi near death in a ravine), but most scenes are lit by the sun (and many of the outdoor scenes are filmed against the sun; Tony Ching is very fond of backlight). Scenes that cry out for nighttime, such as the appearance of the Ghost King and his henchmen, are also filmed in daylight.[8] The cinematography – by Chen Weiian – is masterful.

Jade Dynasty's pacing is as a nimble as one of Tony Ching's Japanese ninjas – and with Angie Lam and Marco Mak Chi-sin overseeing the cutting, you can't go wrong; Lam and Mak have between them edited numerous masterpieces, and many of your favourite Hong Kong movies. Indeed, one of the reasons that *Jade Dynasty* is so entertaining is the editing and the pacing. That applies to Hong Kong and Chinese cinema in general: the cutting is a major technical contributor to the overall impact of the movies.

In the West, a prestige historical fantasy movie like this would run over two hours – likely coming in at 2h 20m or more. Not *Jade Dynasty*: one of the delights of Chinese cinema, and Ching's cinema, too, is that it can say all it wants to say, and do all it wants to do, in 90 or 100 minutes, as here (*Jade Dynasty* runs 101 minutes). Thus, *Jade Dynasty* is a three-act movie, which's perfect for this genre. Four acts simply aren't required (as for five acts, forget it!).

Like many similar Chinese fantasy movies, the sound of *Jade Dynasty* includes many whooshes and zings which are highly exaggerated compared to Western action-adventure films. The sound team (Sergei Groshev was sound supervisor) created a sound effects environment which helped to give *Jade Dynasty* its comicbook quality.

COSTUMES.

'I like beautiful, romantic things' – this phrase of Tony Ching's comes to mind so often when viewing his films. *Jade Dynasty* is a movie of stylized, floaty, semi-transparent costumes (pink, white, cream) shot in slow motion and blown about by wind machines (every single shot has a breeze blowing the hair and costumes of the cast).

The costume design – by, I think, Kenneth Yee Chung-man – goes full tilt into exaggerated beauty; sometimes it seems as if Tony Ching is the Chinese equivalent of Vincente Minnelli or Josef von Sternberg – he loves exquisite beauty. And with actors like the four principals to dress up, make-up and light – Xiao Zhan, Meng Meiqi, Tang Yixin and Li Qin – Ching has a pretty stunning ensemble. *Jade Dynasty* exploits the radiance of the

---

8 There are schedule and budgetary concerns – night shoots are more expensive.

cast to the full (make-up and hair are perfect; the stars have blemishless, smooth skin and immaculate hair-do's).

So, no, we don't have scruffy swordsmen here, or struggling peasants in rags,[9] but, in the main, beautiful people. This is a heightened, classy, comicbook interpretation of the mythology of Ancient China where everyone is dressed impeccably.

VISUAL EFFECTS.

The visual effects work in *Jade Dynasty* is once again such a pleasure to watch – no one here bothers with those pesky Western concepts of 'realism' or 'reality', which have the visual effects industry in Hollywood and Hollywood-type productions mired in trying to be naturalistic or 'real', using motion capture performances to drive animation and smothering everything in that really boring photorealistic visual approach.

Not here: *Jade Dynasty* is a marvel of sweeping vistas of mountains, of clouds, of smoke, of lakes, of palaces perched atop colossal peaks, of vast fields of white flowers, of endless rockfaces leading to black abysses, of high cliffs, of playful water dragons, and of several groups of supernatural beings who just happen to be either pop star cuties or movie star cuties.

A memorable image in *Jade Dynasty* has the moon being cut in half – it occurs when Lu Xueqi meets her *sifu*, Shui Yue (Ye Tong = Cecilia Yip), at night, by a lake: the enormous reflection of the moon in the water is sliced in two by a sword (an example of visual effects being used in a romantic, poetic manner. It's not all martial arts duels in *Jade Dynasty*).

The vast Imperial Army behind the making of *Jade Dynasty* is the enormous number of visual effects technicians, producers, layout artists, storyboard artists, photographers, animators and managers. The visual effects were put together in Beijing, Hong Kong, Kuala Lumpur, Singapore, Malaysia and other locations: V.H.Q. Hong Kong S.E.A., Worldwide FX, Leyard, Hezhong Film Co., Digital Idea, W.T.W. Films, and Postmodern Digital were some of the companies involved in *Jade Dynasty*.

It's not all green screens or blue screens or backgrounds tricked up in computers in Malaysia, Beijing or Hong Kong: there is lots of location shooting in *Jade Dynasty*. The film has a thoroughly outdoorsy feel, even in the interiors of the palaces, staged in the studio, because they are designed as spaces open to the elements (thus, wind – air – is blowing in every single shot in *Jade Dynasty*).

However, much of *Zhu Xian* was filmed in the studio in Beijing – due to

9 Except in the ten years ago flashback.

the complexity of many sequences, the need to control complicated elements, and because this is a high fantasy movie, which is more effectively and efficiently recreated in the studio.

ONE BOY – MANY GIRLS.

For pop idol and TV star Xiao Zhan, this is a major acting role, where you get to do everything – and Zhan is in most every scene. (And it's exhausting, too, as many actors find who come from other disciplines, such as pop music. This is a Tony Ching-directed movie, and that means tons of physical acting every day. The production schedule looks as if Zhan was fitted into a flying harness every single day. Even more modest physical gags required wire-work. Zhan is hurled across the ground several times in *Jade Dynasty*. Plus he's dunked in water, falls under water, flies upside-down, acts with a monkey, and is repeatedly slapped in the face).

The way that Xiao Zhan plays Zhang Xiaofan is the familiar goofy youth and underdog who finds himself in the midst of extraordinary people and landed in unusual circumstances; he's gentle (in a world of warriors), humble, and modest. It's a character type found in many Chinese films. It's a version of the comical persona of Leslie Cheung Kwok-wing in the *Chinese Ghost Story* movies, one of the great comedy roles in recent Chinese cinema; you could regard *Jade Dynasty* as a kind of *hommage* to Leslie Cheung and *A Chinese Ghost Story*, and maybe you could even regard it as *A Chinese Ghost Story 4*.

Indeed, like Leslie Cheung Kwok-wing in *A Chinese Ghost Story*, Xiao Zhan is playing the hero Xiaofan Zhang younger than his years: he's 27 but playing Xiaofan as about 18 or 19, just as Cheung did with Ning Choi-san in *A Chinese Ghost Story* (and both of them get away with it). Like Ning Choi-san in *A Chinese Ghost Story*, Xiaofan in *Jade Dynasty* is surrounded by beautiful girls, is hurled about all over the place, is forced to fight fearsome opponents (including some of those beautiful girls), and finds himself in plenty of trouble and at the centre of a fierce conflict between powerful adversaries. Xiao Zhan is one of the reasons that *Jade Dynasty* is so enjoyable: he's in most every scene, and he contributes immensely to making this picture soar.

The fairy tale allusions in *Jade Dynasty* are obvious: Xiaofan Zhang is Cinderella or Snow White; he cooks, he stays home and keeps house; he's surrounded by six brothers (and a sister); he is left out of the family activities; they're all great warriors, but he is not (he can't fly – mandatory if you live in the heavens); he's the son who's always left out of the scheme, the least favoured one (yet he always find himself the centre of attention); and he is the feminized, maligned man of farcical comedy.

Many scenes in *Jade Dynasty* pair up Zhang Xiaofan with Tian Linger (Girl 1), winningly played by Tang Yixin (she also appeared in the TV series of Xiao Ding's book). Linger is the unattainable sister in a family of brothers in a folk tale, but Xiaofan is fond of her. (However, some romantic jealousy emerges when Xiaofan sees Linger with a rival, Qi Huo).

Tian Linger speeds through the heavens, but she's portrayed as a much more poetic and dreamy prospect than Superman: she's dressed in a pale pink gown, and trails several very long, pink pieces of cloth (which are animated by wind machines (or artists in Malaysia or Beijing using computers) to create the impression of a floaty, mystical being of the air).

Lu Xueqi (Girl 2) is an appealing characterization by Li Qin – an ice-cold, haughty princess (who is also of course impossibly beautiful), surrounded by her entourage of adoring, sword-wielding maidens, as unreachable and unapproachable (for the hero Zhang Xiaofan) as the highest, snowiest mountain peaks. Lu is the snooty, head girl type, and the adored pop idol type, who thinks herself to be way ahead and above everyone else (because, in ability at least, she is).

For a while Zhang Xiaofan is thrown together (in act two) with the mysterious Biyao (Girl 2), the third of the pixie-like, young women in *Jade Dynasty*. Biyao is after the Fire Stick, but discovers that she can pick it up but not carry it far from Xiaofan. Biyao is the punky rebel type, winningly played by Meiqi Meng.

The lighthearted, flirty scenes between Xiaofan and Biyao are a Chinese movie staple, recalling Leslie Cheung and Joey Wong in the *Chinese Ghost Story* films, or Jet Li and Rosamund Kwan in the *Once Upon a Time In China* series. They are small-scale, domestic moments when it's the man who's the embarrassed, put-upon one.

It's one boy surrounded by girls – but this isn't a harem story.

The three girls have troubled relations with their parents. Poor Biyao has the Father From Hell, the King of the Demon Cult, and Lu Xueqi has a problematic relationship with her over-bearing mother and *sifu*, Shui Yue (both Tian Linger and Biyao are father complex girls, as are most young women in fantasy fiction of any kind).

(The Fire Stick[10] (the phallic MacGuffin of *Jade Dynasty*) provides plenty of comedy – how Zhang Xiaofan acquires it, how Biyao repeatedly tries to steal it, and how it acts as a sword (instead of a magical sword, Xiaofan gets a short, wooden stick). Part of this is played as physical, knockabout comedy (with Biyao miming the stick's mind of its own). An

10 The Taoist immortal who gives Xiaofan the stone is Jiang Dawei.

extended gag has Biyao trying to slip the stick away from Xiaofan while he's asleep at night, putting our hero and heroine into several intimate clinches, while Xiaofan remains resolutely asleep. The scenes with the monkey,[11] linked to the Fire Stick, are also played for comedy. Yes, this is another Chinese movie with a monkey as a minor character. The monkey isn't solely an animal – it leads Xiaofan to the ailing Lu Xueqi in a ravine. Initially, the magic bead is called the Blood-Devouring Pearl, and then it combines with the Fire Stick).

Other scenes are played for comedy: when the brothers sneak out to peep on Lu Xueqi and her troupe performing acrobatics, they encounter other groups of inquisitive lads trying to do the same thing (of course Xiaofan accidentally stumbles and is caught by Lu Xueqi). When Xiaofan and Biyao hole up in a cave, he thinks she's cooked their faithful dog (food, as ever, is a recurring motif in Chinese cinema). For these scenes, composers Zhu Yunbian and Teddy Robin provide a gentle, jaunty cue, to remind us that we are in the realm of goofy comedy.

ACTION.

The action in *Jade Dynasty* is choreographed with Tony Ching's usual flair and imagination (aided by Tsui Hark's regular action director, Xiong Xin-xin, plus Wu Zequan). We have, as we'd expected, many examples from the Tony Ching Cinema Circus: wire-work is everywhere (and some scenes really do look like circus acts, recalling the silk rope acrobatics you can seen regularly in Beijing, tumbling down wires). Instead of a bamboo forest, a glorious three-way fight between the leading ladies is staged in a silver birch wood (with the hapless Zhang Xiaofan in the middle, out-matched as usual).

Other Chingian motifs in *Jade Dynasty* include a swordsman descending from on high on a victim; a group of warriors lowered to the ground *en masse*; spinning, tumbling entrances and exits for charas; victims thrown a *long* way, tumbling to the ground; and the poetic, slo-mo drift of a character up in the trees (for Lu Xueqi).

When Zhang Xiaofan and his six brothers spy on the enigmatic idol Lu Xueqi training outdoors, it's another air-borne sequence played as a dreamy, breezy performance of acrobatics. Gauzy costumes trail thru the air in slow motion (and backlit), until Lu discovers the peepers in the reeds and is furious. Xiaofan, inevitably, is singled out for punishment – by being repeatedly thrown off a cliff on a rope, a *long* way. (It's not easy being the hero in a Chinese, historical fantasy movie! Xiaofan is also slapped in the

---

11 *Jade Dynasty* features several animals in the foreground: a monkey, a dog, and a dragon. (There's a gag about cooking the dog – when Xiaofan returns to the cave and sees Biyao roasting an animal on a stick.)

face by Biyao – repeatedly).

The martial arts games, a major action sequence (taking up much of act two), are also played for comedy (with Zhang Xiaofan defending himself with his Fire Stick. Xiaofan is able to beat even super-swordsmen: the stick flies out of his hand and does the work for him, spinning, attacking, and beating opponents down). This part of *Jade Dynasty* resembles *kung fu* comedies such as *Kung Fu Hustle* and *Shaolin Soccer* (which Tony Ching worked on), with several pairs of contestants pitted against each other, while the other participants look on from the sidelines and cheer (the girls have their own competition – Lu Xueqi versus Tian Linger is staged to emphasize the billowing, flowing costumes of the swordswomen).

We re-join the martial arts trials later: in round two,[12] Zhang Xiaofan is pitted against Lu Zueqi herself – he is out-matched, and is repeatedly beaten down by her (using her fists, legs and the sheath of her sword). When Lu draws her blade to strike Xiaofan, of course the Fire Stick comes to the rescue. (This motif will be replayed in the finale, when *sifu* Shui Yue commands Lu to kill Xiaofan – she tries repeatedly, eventually lunging at him with her sword).

In the Zhang Xiaofan versus Lu Zueqi duel, Tony Ching reprises many of his favourite swordplay moments – and by thus time (2018-19), Ching had been directing sword fights for over forty-five years! One of Ching's beloved motifs is the swallow-diving swordsman from on high. Usually, it's a swordsman diving onto someone on the ground. In *Jade Dynasty*, both participants are airborne, with Lu Zueqi rushing upwards towards Xiaofan (with the Fire Stick, Xiaofan is now able to fly).

The giant bell in the Taoist Masters' temple is an expensive prop just to be rung once or twice – so it's inventively re-used as the setting for Zhang Xiaofan's imprisonment by the elders: he's strung up underneath it, making a change from the usual dungeon or prison sets. (Biyao, in her Chingian ninja guise, rescues him. We find out later that it's because she is the errand girl for her father, the Ghost King, who wants the magic sword-stick).

THE FINALE.

The climax of *Jade Dynasty* is a colossal action sequence involving 100s of beats: it's a kitchen sink section of the 2019 film, with everything thrown in. Why hold back now? You get the feeling that Tony Ching really savours tackling on the final act of his movies, when all of the narrative

---

12 Everybody in the Qingyun Sect has been beaten, but *sifu* Tian is delighted that Xiaofan has somehow survived into the final round.

work of the previous acts pays off. Ching is a genius when it comes to delivering spectacular endings: his movies seldom waver towards the end (unlike many similar outings in the action and martial arts genres). There's no feeling of exhaustion, or things petering out: this movie has energy – *qi* – to spare.

It should be noted that the finale of *Jade Dynasty* isn't only a massive effort from the stunt team, the practical effects crew and everybody else on location and in the studio, but also from 100s of visual effects artists, who earn their Yuan with truly eye-popping imagery.

The Ghost King (Benyu Zhang) swoops into the finale of *Jade Dynasty* to provide the fearsome super-villain for the heroes do battle against: he's introduced with a variation on Dracula riding a carriage with horses in a forest, when the whole shebang bursts out of the ground (a stunning variation on the Chingian staple of ninjas jumping out of the soil. We've seen pirate ships surging from beneath the ocean,[13] but not often a carriage and horses. (It really should be a night scene, but the climax occurs in daylight). The Ghost King has superpowers to spare: it takes all of the seven Taoist Masters to take him on, and even then it's up to our hero, Zhang Xiaofan, so finish off the job (tho' the Ghost King manages to scoot away, hinting at a sequel).

The films of Tony Ching relish portraying evil and skilled villains, from the giant-tongued Tree Monster in *A Chinese Ghost Story* to the horrifically brutal regime in *Naked Weapon*. *Jade Dynasty* adds several gruesome henchmen to the tally: a creepy, wrinkled puppeteer with a wooden doll that can slice up swordsmen when he takes control of a victim and puppeteers him; a warrior who literally absorbs victims into his body (the image of the heads of the victims struggling to get out is pure Ching – it echoes the Essence Absorbing Stance in *The Swordsman 2*); a guy who flies with sharp, circular shields attached to his feet, which spin and cut up his opponents (another very Chingian concept – recalling the Japanese ninja riding spinning blades, also in *The Swordsman 2*); and finally a grotesque pig-man (a man with a boar's head).

These four henchmen are introduced in a rapid montage of action part-way through act three (as they set upon swordsmen from other clans). Their appearance announces the opening of hostilities and the start of the finale of *Jade Dynasty*. (It's true that the Ghost King plot seems included in *Jade Dynasty* just so we can have a Big Finale, whereas much of the movie has been concerned with other events, such as the martial arts contest, and Zhang Xiaofan getting into trouble with beautiful girls).

Yes, as expected, the finale of *Jade Dynasty* is a stops-all-out battle

---

13 *Harry Potter* and *Pirates of the Caribbean,* for instance.

between the Taoist Masters and their students and the Ghost King and his Demon Cult mob. The scenes of warriors zooming through the skies *en masse*, like rebel angels making an assault on Heaven, are truly wonderful. It's like seeing an illustration of Dante Alighieri's *Divine Comedy* by Gustave Doré come to life.

Tony Ching has been filming flying swordsmen (and swordswomen) for decades: here, with the aid of an army of computer artists and technicians in Asia, he can stage just a few more than six guys on wires! A battle in the skies, Ching-style, means warriors leaping onto their flying blades and soaring through the air in massive formations.

Another Chingian moment has the sword warriors combining mid-flight to create circular blades – so maybe thirty of them form a human version, forty feet wide, of the curved, sharp-edged discs found in Japanese *manga*. That's pretty out-there on its own – but then the human wheels pursue the Ghost King through a mountain, soaring thru rocky caverns, smashing into rocks, and out the other side.

And this is just one of numerous action beats in the climax of *Jade Dynasty*: the Ghost King responds with a flurry of bolts of energy and flames which take out the warriors. The Demon King provides plenty of opposition in the finale – going up against the seven Elders, who combine forces to try to defeat him. Zhang Xiaofan joins in the effort, too (aided by the Fire Stick). The visual effects animation enhances the proceedings with marvellous evocations of *chi* energy and Taoist magic, enlarging the duel with smoky, fiery effects in scarlet and black for the Ghost King, and blue and white for the seven Elders.

But the Ghost King is not the only super-being around: our hero Zhang Xiaofan is consumed by anger when he discovers the truth about how his parents died (it seems that someone amongst the Elders was responsible for the decimation of his home village, because they use the same thunder-and-lightning magic). Altho' this had been signposted earlier, the abrupt switch in Xiaofan's characterization – from a nice but rather hapless boy to a murderous, bulgy-eyed, cackling villain doesn't quite convince.

But it does provide the expected overblown, operatic psychological elements to the ending of a Chinese, historical fantasy picture, when everything becomes chaotic and melodramatic. So now Zhang Xiaofan is turning on his adopted family, his father, and even his beloved sister, Tian Linger (Xiaofan torturing the frail Linger is a disturbing image). Ultimately, Linger brings Xiaofan back to himself (with a loving touch), but at the cost of her life, when she sacrifices herself to save her father Tian Buyi (she throws herself between Xiaofan and her father, but takes the blow from the Fire Stick on her head). The movie includes a moving montage of previous scenes involving Xiaofan and Linger, as he is brought back to his senses (and his scornful, Gothic appearance returns to normal).

With Zhang Xiaofan as the enemy, Lu Xueqi is ordered to finish him off by her injured mistress, Shui Yue (all of the Taoist Elders have been beaten to the ground, so now it's up to the younger generation to Save The Day). Lu tries, repeatedly, to dispatch Xiaofan with her flying sword (one of Xiaofan's adopted brothers steps in the first time, and his surrogate father Tian Buyi the second time. This is a moving depiction of sacrifice and protection, and just how much Xiaofan is cherished by his adopted family).

The finale of *Jade Dynasty* includes further action sequences – such as Zhang Xiaofan versus the Ghost King when he emerges from his carriage; a reprise of the three-way warrior women fight with Tian Linger, Lu Xueqi and Biyao; the Ghost King injuring his daughter Biyao; and the repeated efforts of the Elders to defeat the Demon King.

A sequel to *Jade Dynasty* is suggested in several ways by the very final moments of the 2019 picture: the super-villain isn't destroyed, but flees; the plot of just who attacked Zhang Xiaofan's village isn't resolved; the ultimate fate of the Elders and their families isn't shown (is Tian Linger dead?); and lastly, the movie ends on an unbalanced note, when Xiaofan takes up the body of Biyao and flies away on the Fire Stick. The final minutes thus possess a 'TO BE CONTINUED' feeling.

Jade Dynasty (2019), this page and over.

JADE DYNASTY

诛

2019 9/12

还会连累师姐被罚

禁制诸般烦恼

THE *CHINESE GHOST STORY* MOVIES

15

A CHINESE GHOST STORY

Sin Nui Yau Wan

INTRODUCTION.

The *Chinese Ghost Story* movies are:

A Chinese Ghost Story (1987)
A Chinese Ghost Story 2 (1990)
A Chinese Ghost Story 3 (1991)
A Chinese Ghost Story: The Tsui Hark Animation (1997)

A Chinese Ghost Story was remade in 2011 (and dedicated to Leslie Cheung).

INTRO TO *A CHINESE GHOST STORY*.

A Chinese Ghost Story (1987, Mandarin: *Qiannu Youhun = Sien: Female Ghost*, a.k.a. *Fair Maiden, Tender Spirit*), was one of those movies where everything works, and the mix of elements is just gorgeous. This is a golden, 100% killer of a movie.

A Chinese Ghost Story has everything going for it: it is among the finest fantasy and action movies ever; it boasts a finale as grand as any in cinema; it tackles the most profound themes; it possesses a perfectly achieved tone and attitude; it features two incandescent stars; it is helmed by two of the greatest action directors in history; and it is brilliant filmmaking.

A Chinese Ghost Story was produced by Film Workshop/ Cinema City written by Yuen Kai-Chi, produced by Tsui Hark, Claudie Chung Jan and Qianqing Liu, exec. prod. by Zhong Zheng, and directed by Tony Ching Siu-tung. Music was by the great James Wong Jim,[1] Romeo Diaz, David Wu and Dai Lemin, editing by David Wu, production design by Hai Chung-Man, art dir. by Kenneth Yee Chung Man, costumes by Shirley Chan and Kitty Ho Wai-Ying, hair by Peng Yen-Lien, make-up by Renming Wen and Man Yun-Ling, visual fx by Ma Xian Liang, sound by Xiaolong Cheng, David Wu and Qun Xue, with photography by Poon Hang-Sang, Sander Lee, Tom Lau Moon-tong, Wong Wing-Hang, Yongheng Huang, Jiaogao Li and Putang Liu. Action directors[2] were Tony Ching Siu-tung, Philip Kwok Chung-fung, Lau Chi-ho, Alan Tsui Chung-sun and Bobby Woo Chi-lung. Released July 18, 1987.

In the cast were Leslie Cheung Kwok-wing, Joey Wong Jo-yin, Wu Ma, Lau Siu-ming, Lam Wai, Xue Zhilun, Wong Jing, Huang Ha, Yeung Yau-cheung, Shut Mei-yee, Elvis Tsui and David Wu. The budget was HK $5.6 million (= US $650,000). It was showered with awards (including Fantafestival Rome, Fantasporto Porto Film Festival, and Avoriaz Fantastic Film Festival, and Hong Kong Film Awards for best score, best song and best art dir.), took HK $18.8m gross, and it ran for a blissful 98 minutes.

A Chinese Ghost Story is very much in the same mold as *The Bride With the White Hair* and similar Hong Kong films. It's a romantic tale couched in horror / fairy tale/ fantasy movie packaging, an impossible romance between a human man and a supernatural woman.

Tsui Hark produced *A Chinese Ghost Story*, and his stamp is all over it: he was involved in developing the project, in creating the script, in the casting, in the visual effects, etc (as Tsui remembered: 'actually, I was thinking of [directing] all of them!'). It was produced by his Film Workshop company (with Cinema City), and his Cinefex Company created the visual effects. The frenetic pace is clearly something close to Tsui's filmic sensibility. It's safe to say that *A Chinese Ghost Story* is very much a Tsui Hark concept (and production). However, he says that it was Tony Ching Siu-tung who directed it, and that he helped out, and directed some parts. As well as Ching's contribution as director, it's also worth noting that the screenplay credit goes to Yuen Kai-Chi: one of the reasons that this movie is so good is because of the tight script.

A Chinese Ghost Story marks the first of the really great Tsui Hark

---

1 This was the first James Wong contribution to Tsui's movies (along with *Shanghai Blues*).
2 Jin Guo, Zhilong Hu, Zhihao Liu and Zhongxin Xu are also credited as martial arts directors.

and Tony Ching Siu-tung movies: no doubt about it, the two trilogies – the *Chinese Ghost Story* and the *Swordsman* films – are among the finest in fantasy and action cinema, and one of the greatest collaborations in the history of cinema between a film director and a film producer.

It's not bad going, either, for Tony Ching to have a masterpiece as his third film as director – and a much-loved film, too (altho' some critics, including me, would count *Duel To the Death* as a masterpiece, too). Thus, Ching is the man behind not one but two greatly admired and enjoyed series of films – *A Chinese Ghost Story* and *The Swordsman*.

Tsui Hark said that Ching Siu-tung had been reluctant to accept the directing assignment, partly because his previous movie, *The Witch From Nepal*, which also had supernatural and fantasy elements, hadn't done well at the box office. Ching wasn't feeling great about helming another movie, including one which was a romantic story. As they continued to talk, Tsui said, Ching eventually agreed to do it.

A Chinese Ghost Story was important in Tony Ching's career because it was a hit – his pet project, *Duel To the Death*, hadn't set the box office aflame, and *The Witch From Nepal* had fared poorly, too. But *A Chinese Ghost Story* did great business.

According to Tsui Hark, *A Chinese Ghost Story* went through some reworking: after the film had shot for some 30 days, and had been cut together, they looked at it and decided that it needed more elements in certain areas. The ending, for instance, was revamped: Tsui, with his producer's hat on, decided that the movie required something bigger. (And yet the giant battle between the Tree Demon and our heroes would be plenty for many movies. *A Chinese Ghost Story*, however, is definitely Something More).

THE PRODUCTION.

A Chinese Ghost Story was based on the 17th century (Ming Dynasty) stories (found in *Strange Stories From a Chinese Studio*)[3] by Pu Songling (Pu-Sing Ling, 1640-1715), known as 'Master Liaozhai', tho' much altered (Liaozhai lies behind the Chinese horror tradition).[4] They were also the basis for *A Touch of Zen* (1971). Songling's stories are all about the human body (which makes them perfect for Chinese action movies, which foreground the body constantly), about keeping the body intact (for reincarnation), and about ghosts/ spirits seeking bodies for reincarnation.

3 The stories have also been published as: *Strange Tales From Liaozhai, Strange Tales From the Liaozhai Studio, Strange Tales From Make-do Studio* and *Strange Stories from the Lodge of Leisure*.
4 For Chinese audiences, the beliefs and superstitions presented in horror movies aren't fake: 'Hong Kong horror films reflect the genuine beliefs and fears of a superstitious people', pointed out Bey Logan (101).

(Tsui Hark had considered a movie based on Pu Songling's works since 1978; he had pitched it to the T.V.B.). The movie changed Pu Songling's stories – to the point where it didn't look much like the story, Tsui commented (LM, 75).

The 1987 movie also references ghost stories from Japan (such as *Ugetsu Monogatari* (1953), and is a remake of *The Enchanting Shadow* (Li Hanxiang, 1960), which gave *A Chinese Ghost Story* its title). *Dragon Gate Inn* (1967) and *Legend of the Mountain* (1979) might also be influences (certainly when Tsui Hark came to direct movies such as the *Once Upon a Time In China* series and *The Blade*, the nighttime scenes especially have a *Chinese Ghost Story* feel).[5] Forerunners such as the wonderful Sammo Hung comedy horror flick *Spooky Encounters* (1980) are also in the mix.

Chinese ghost stories pivot around the theme of reincarnation, and Hong Kong horror movies are defined by ghost stories. It's the *whole body* that's important in the Chinese philosophy of reincarnation (as in Ancient Egyptian religion). Thus, shape-changing or missing limbs is not good, and the body must remain intact (so that decapitation is a major setback, because it means no reincarnation).

The female ghost is one of the principal characters of the Chinese ghost story: typically, the woman is young and unmarried (so that she has no son or husband to burn incense and give offerings so she can find a decent spot in the after-life). The female spirits search for the romance among the living that they didn't experience when they were alive. So that Chinese ghost stories tend to be romances, between human men and ghostly women. Two figures usually crop up as well: the Taoist monk, who tries to protect the man from the ghost (and from his own earthly desires), and a demon or monster, who wants the ghost for itself.[6]

The female ghost or spirit is a *juli*, a seductress, and sometimes a *xian*, a fairy (she is usually beautiful, proving the necessary eye candy, and also suggesting 'she was a victim of a love that went wrong').[7] The man tends to be an effete, harmless, goofy guy.

There were two sequels to *A Chinese Ghost Story*, as well as the inevitable quick cash-ins from rival Hong Kong film teams. In *Portrait of a Nymph* (a.k.a. *Picture of a Nymph*), for instance, released the following year (1988), some of the same cast (including Joey Wong and Wu Ma), run thru exactly the same story (some prefer it to *A Chinese Ghost Story*). As a partial tribute to Leslie Cheung, *A Chinese Ghost Story* was re-released in a restored version in 2011 (and there was a special screening, which

---

5 Hong Kong critics said that *A Chinese Ghost Story* looked like a TV commercial; quite a few movies of the 1980s drew on this look (as well as pop promos and MTV).
6 J. Yang, 2003, 76, 77.
7 S. Teo, 1997, 222.

cast and crew attended).

The *Chinese Ghost Story* sequels added cast members such as Jacky Cheung (another pop music icon in China). Cheung, one of the four Canto-pop stars (and dubbed 'the King of Canto-pop'), is wonderful in *A Chinese Ghost Story 2*, and also appeared in many other movies in this period, including action thrillers (such as *Bullet In the Head*), and Tsui Hark's films, such as *Wicked City*. Meanwhile, Tony Leung Chi Wai took over Leslie Cheung's role for the second *Chinese Ghost Story* sequel of 1991. A remake of *A Chinese Ghost Story* (a.k.a. *A Chinese Fairy Tale*), was produced in 2011 by Golden Sun Films.

In 1987, when the top-grossing movies around the world were *Fatal Attraction, Beverly Hills Cop 2* and *The Living Daylights*, *A Chinese Ghost Story* is a hugely enjoyable flick which can compete favourably with anything released that year (or any year). For example, the movies in the horror and fantasy genre in the U.S.A. of 1987 included *Predator, RoboCop, The Witches of Eastwick, Nightmare On Elm Street 3, Batteries Not Included, The Lost Boys, Innerspace* and *The Running Man*. Sure, we've all seen all those movies (and enjoyed them!), but *A Chinese Ghost Story* trounces them for imagination, style, wit and action (and beauty – what actors in those North American flicks can compete with Joey Wong and Leslie Cheung?!).[8]

By comparison with North American ghost romance pictures of the same period, such as *Ghost* (1990) and *Always* (1989), *A Chinese Ghost Story* is marvellous. It doesn't have time for anything approaching 'realism' or everyday reality (why bother? you're surrounded with it!). *A Chinese Ghost Story* is a movie-movie that celebrates its movieness with every shot. In *A Chinese Ghost Story*, 'the story of undying love and Good vs. Evil is told in the style of an American horror film on speed', as Lisa Morton put it (LM, 72).

A Chinese Ghost Story is a feast of a movie, deliberately corny, popcorny, cheesy, silly, over-the-top, and it doesn't take itself seriously for a second. It's glorious fun, the movie equivalent of a pantomime, or a fancy dress party. The pacing and editing is spot-on: just enough is spent on establishing the hero Ning[9] Choi-san's character, for instance, but not too much; the action scenes are stuffed with beats and gags, but the action is pinned to the central conflicts of each scene, and never allowed to run on simply for the sake of more action, and the 1987 movie has plenty of time to explore the intimate, romantic moments between Ning Choi-san and Nip Siu-shin.

8 'Where *A Chinese Ghost Story* is way ahead of its American counterparts is in its use of romance and sensuality', noted Lisa Morton (LM, 72).
9 Some translations used the name Ling.

If you rush the slower scenes in your haste to get to more action or more horror, the audience hasn't spent enough time with the characters, or their relationships, or the situations. It is, after all, the *characters* and their *relationships* and the *story* which really makes a comedy work. Great comedy comes out of the drama and the characters and the situations (as all of the major comedy filmmakers assert); *A Chinese Ghost Story* follows this all-important tenet (which Tsui Hark wholly understands). But that also applies to great horror movies or great action movies or great romantic movies.

Or put it like this: *A Chinese Ghost Story* has a terrific, cleverly written script that hits all of the right notes at the right time. Oh, it's not *The Cherry Orchard* or *Twelfth Night.* But it's not meant to be! It's a piece of candy, but brilliantly executed.

The script of *A Chinese Ghost Story* is once again constructed along classical lines: act one, for instance, climaxes with the Swordsman Yin versus ghost battle; act two has a similar but bigger conflict between Yin and the monsters, but closes instead with the comical courtroom scene (and Ning Choi-san and Yin agreeing to join forces). The court scene (where Ning reports a murder) lightens the proceedings, providing a farcical breather before the two finales in act three. The court scene is important, too: after it, the relationship of Ning and Yin is cemented: now they are resolved to combat the ghosts and monsters.

As Thomas Weisser put it:

> this is a brilliantly conceived fantasy featuring two very likable Asian performers, Leslie Cheung and Joey Wong. But the real star is Ching Siu Tung and his extraordinary camerawork. (40)

Ric Meyers summed up *A Chinese Ghost Story* thus:

> Ching Siu-tung's splendid fantasy of a thousand-year-old unisex tree demon with a mile-long tongue, pimping a beautiful spirit for 'the big evil'. Sit back – you literally haven't seen anything like this before.[10]

Kozo in Love HK Film reckons that

> the most compelling thing about *A Chinese Ghost Story* is probably its sheer cinematic energy. People fly, jump, and engage in situation comedy with little pause for breath… *A Chinese Ghost Story* is primo eighties Hong Kong Cinema, which means a complete disregard for any attempt at realism. Everything here is so hyperrealistic and over-the-top it makes Hollywood musicals look like the very model of

10 Quoted in F. Dannen, 373.

restraint.

THE CAST.

There are three main characters in *A Chinese Ghost Story*:
• Ning Choi-san, the hapless scholar and debt collector
• Nip Siu-shin, the beautiful ghost (*kuei*) of the story
• Yin Chik-ha, the Taoist demon hunter[1]

The cast of *A Chinese Ghost Story* is terrific, headed up two of the most beautiful people in Chinese cinema of recent times: Leslie Cheung Kwok-wing and Joey Wong Jo-yin. You can look at these two lovely actors all day. They are simply sensational. Cheung is especially fine with the comedy in *A Chinese Ghost Story* (always an attribute that's under-valued by film critics), but he's also prime leading man material: Cheung is *hot*!

LESLIE CHEUNG.

Leslie Cheung[12] was a much-revered star in both the pop music and film worlds. In Asia, pop stars regularly move into movies and television (just as they do in the West). Somehow, the stigma of a rubbish pop idol trying to achieve plaudits in cinema isn't attached to Asian stars – many of the most memorable turns in recent Asian cinema are from pop stars.

Leslie Cheung was born on Sept 12, 1956 in Hong Kong (his father was a tailor). Sadly, he committed suicide in 2003 by jumping from a 24 storey Hong Kong hotel. He suffered from depression. His suicide note said he'd had enough (altho' he had been seeing doctors). Cheung appeared in many movies, some of them first-rate, including *Ashes of Time, A Better Tomorrow 1 & 2* and *Happy Together*. At the time of *A Chinese Ghost Story*, Cheung also appeared in the critically acclaimed *Rouge*, as well as *A Better Tomorrow*. Cheung was often paired with fellow pop star and actress Anita Mui. Cheung's sexual identity was a focus of attention; he dated both men and women, and said it was best to describe him as bisexual (some of his film roles explored his queer media image, such as *Farewell My Concubine* and his films with director Wong Kar-wai).

Educated in England (like many Hong Kong actors), in Norwich and Leeds, Leslie Cheung began his pop singing career in 1977. He worked for the R.T.V. network in Canton (many future stars of Hong Kong cinema started out in television). Cheung gave up singing in 1989,[13] to concentrate on acting ('as an actor, you can go much further – travelling back and forth in time, playing different characters. It's like having more

11 The *fat-si* is a Taoist priest or shaman who has spells and magic to deal with ghosts and spirits. The *fat-si* takes on physical and scientific as well as religious tasks.
12 Leslie Cheung's name in Cantonese is Jeung Gwok-wink and Zhang Guorong in Mandarin. He is sometimes billed as Leslie Cheung Kwok-wing.
13 After giving sell-out concerts on 33 consecutive nights at the Hong Kong Coliseum.

lives during your lifetime', he explained).[14] Cheung returned to live performance, embarking on several successful tours.

A Chinese Ghost Story is one of Leslie Cheung's most enjoyable performances (he was really hitting his stride at this time – he also delivered a scorching performance in *A Better Tomorrow,* the year before *A Chinese Ghost Story*). Cheung's Ning Choi-san is well-meaning but cowardly, naïve (even simple) and unremarkable. He's the everyday guy hero, the ordinary guy who finds himself in extraordinary circumstances.[15] He doesn't want to be where he is, and he wants to stay out of trouble. He's poor, and doesn't like his job, but does it anyway (all attributes that everybody can identify with! Ning is a very Tsui Harkian characterization).

Leslie Cheung is carrying *A Chinese Ghost Story* for long stretches – where he's the only character on screen (for instance, in the earlier scenes which are essentially a guy in a haunted house scenario. And just one guy, not a couple or a group). This is a *tour-de-force* comedy turn: one of the reasons that the *Chinese Ghost Story* films are so effective and so entertaining is down to Cheung's performance.

The 1987 movie also gleefully delivers gender reversals, too – by having Ning Choi-san play a feminized role (to the point where, in the 1990 sequel, he's taking a bath when the monster appears, a cliché of the horror genre, where it's usually an opportunity to see a starlet unclad).

Amazingly, Leslie Cheung looks about 18, altho' he was 30[16] at the time of the first *Ghost* movie (Cheung also plays Ning Choi-san much younger than his real age, 20 instead of 30, but he carries it off). Like Maggie Cheung, Brigitte Lin and Chow Yun-Fat, Cheung is an ageless actor.

JOEY WONG.

Meanwhile, Joey Wong is... Joey Wong! A face that can melt the lens, the 20 year-old Wong (b. Jan 31, 1967, Taipei, Taiwan) needs to do nothing except just stand there to be incredible (tho' she does plenty more'n that in *A Chinese Ghost Story*! Critics unfairly carped that thankfully all Wong has to do is show up; but no, she is acting her socks off too! And she is terrific in other Tsui Hark-related movies, such as *Green Snake* and *The Swordsman 3*).

Joey Wong Jo-yin would later appear as one of the snake-women in *Green Snake* (1993), a movie which's essentially the same plot as *A*

14 However, Tsui Hark said that Cheung had been reluctant to take on the role, because he'd had bad experiences in playing in period roles (in TV).
15 Lisa Morton describes Leslie Cheung's Ning Choi-san as 'idealistic without being naïve, clumsy without being foolish, romantic without being maudlin, and frightened without being weak' (LM, 73)
16 He's 11 years older than Joey Wong.

Chinese Ghost Story.[17] (Casting the female ghost was probably the toughest casting job in *A Chinese Ghost Story* – finding character actors to play mad, Taoist monks or scary Tree Demons isn't so difficult! But the actress selected to play Nip Siu-shin had to be other-worldly and convince as a ghost, but also be attractive, and a good actor. Sounds easy to find? Trust me, having done casting myself, it's not that easy! What you find with casting is that if you have five boxes to tick, many actors you see will cover three or four of the requirements, but not all five).

Incidentally, Joey Wong was not Tsui Hark's first choice for the ghost in *A Chinese Ghost Story* – he thought she looked too contemporary and too tall – she's 5' 8" (his choices included Japanese singer Akina Nakamori and May Lo). But when Tsui and the team saw Wong in the costume, it was obvious she was perfect.

Ching Siu-tung wanted Joey Wong and Leslie Cheung for *A Chinese Ghost Story* precisely because they were very contemporary actors: they would revive the genre with new blood. (Ching took the same approach by casting singer and TV actress Kelly Chen in *An Empress and the Warriors*, another of his big, romantic movies).

The actors in *A Chinese Ghost Story* throw themselves into the roles – it's very physical stuff. Apart from the action scenes, the actors're drenched with rain, wading waist-deep in water, close to fire, or falling into the sea (Leslie Cheung gamely does this a number of times – not counting the takes we don't see!). A Chinese action movie is no easy ride for the cast, as many visiting Western performers have found out.

THE SECONDARY CHARACTERS.

And – this is also perfect casting – Wu Ma plays the Taoist monk hunting down the spirits. Wu Ma (1942, Tianjin – 2014), sometimes known as Feng Wuma, is a veteran of literally hundreds of movie appearances (around 250), as well as a prominent film director (A.D. to Chang Cheh, and directing from 1970 onwards).[18]

Wu Ma steals every scene he's in. His introduction, for instance, is genius: instead of having Ning Choi-san encounter Yin Chik-ha creeping around the temple at night, or stumbling upon him in the village by day, Ning Choi-san runs into Swordsman Yin in the midst of an epic sword duel with an arch rival, Hah Hau (played by Lam Wai). So, cleverly, the screenwriter (Yuen Kai-Chi) weaves in exposition about the temple and the spirits in the middle of a juicy slice of furious swordplay and wire-work. And

17 Joey Wong became a favourite for Tsui – perfectly cast in *The Swordsman 3* and *Green Snake* as doomed, tragic heroines.
18 Wu Ma has directed movies with similar man-and-ghost romances to *A Chinese Ghost Story*, including *Picture of a Nymph* and *Burning Sensation*.

we see Yin in his element, at work, *showing* us what he does (instead of him *telling* us about it).

On this same crazy night, the rival swordsman Hah Hau encounters Ning Choi-san in the wilds, in the midst of another swordplay scene; later, the rival swordsman becomes one of the ghost's sorry victims (as he nurses his wounds beside a campfire; Nip Siu-shin materializes as a seductive water nymph, and Hah Hau is soon engulfed in a monstrous tongue and sucked dry).

A Chinese Ghost Story is happy, too, to portray a powerful and predatory woman. Nip Siu-shin is depicted seducing and tupping two victims before she meets scholar Ning Choi-san. However, the movie lets the beautiful ghost stay this side of murder, when the lovemaking scenes cut to a point-of-view, Steadicam shot (the classic, subjective monster shot of 1980s horror cinema) of the thing or monster approaching rapidly. While Siu-shin looks on, it's the monster that does the actual killing (it's not revealed in full until later).

CASTING POP STARS.

In casting many performers from the world of pop music, and in relation to *A Chinese Ghost Story,* Tsui Hark said he and his production teams did that partly because they were seeking acting styles that were different from the stylizations of the old Shaw Brothers movies (which they grew up on), and different from the stylizations of television acting. And, besides, it didn't hurt that pop icons already had a built-in audience and fan base (including teens). Also, pop stars were used to performing and expressing themselves: as Tsui explained:

> I like to use singers in my films because they are already experienced in communicating their feelings to an audience. [19]

Cantopop stars include Alan Tam, Andy Lau, Karen Mok, Aaron Kwok, Jacky Cheung, Leslie Cheung, Anita Mui, Ekin Cheng and Leon Lai (most of whom have appeared in Tony Ching's movies).

The 'Four Golden Kings' – singers Leslie Cheung, Andy Lau, Jackie Cheung and Leon Lai – were hugely popular in the 1980s and 1990s. And, as Bey Logan noted, and as we know well, the 'Four Golden Kings' have appeared in numerous Hong Kong movies. In the West, Logan reckoned that it would be like the Osmonds and the Jackson Five uniting for a remake of *The Wild Bunch* (179).

In Asian cinema, casting pop stars has worked so many times. There

---

19 Quoted in B. Logan, 181.

isn't the stigma attached to using pop musicians as there is in the West (even so, Western cinema has cast from the world of pop and rock numerous times, with some incredible results: Mick Jagger in *Performance*, Kris Kristofferson in *Pat Garrett and Billy the Kid* and *Heaven's Gate*, and David Bowie in *The Man Who Fell To Earth*).

One should also note here Tsui Hark's genius with casting. Rarely commented upon by critics (tho' discussed endlessly by fans), casting is enormously important in a movie. And it's not an easy job. Tsui certainly has a knack for finding new talent, for getting the right people for the roles (he has also created roles specially for certain actors), and also for filling in the secondary roles and the character roles with suitable people. In *A Chinese Ghost Story*, everyone can agree that Leslie Cheung was the perfect choice.

Tony Ching has used many pop stars in his films as film director – the ones produced by Tsui Hark, obviously, but also his more recent works, such as Kelly Chen appearing in *An Empress and the Warriors*, and Xiao Zhan in *Jade Dynasty* (both Chen and Zhan are wonderful, and being the main characters, they have to be).

ROMANCE AND HORROR.

Nip Siu-shin is enslaved to the Tree Demon, a.k.a. Old Dame (Lao-lao): she is forced to procure men for the Tree Demon by having sex with them: the Tree Demon then rushes in to suck out their energy – with a giant tongue! (presumably their *chi* is high during lovemaking). It's a grotesque version of a sadomasochistic, master-and-slave, pimp-and-prostitute arrangement.

The horror genre aspects are the packaging in *A Chinese Ghost Story*, as Tsui Hark explained, that covers what is really a romance story. Horror and romance would be plenty, but, this being Cantonese cinema at its finest, two other elements're added: action and comedy. Getting the *mix* right is *so* important, and *A Chinese Ghost Story* is perfectly pitched in terms of tone and attitude as well as its balance between action + comedy + romance + horror.

And notice how each element complements the other: there are genuinely creepy moments in *A Chinese Ghost Story* (it is a perfect Hallowe'en movie), but they are always balanced by comedy before and after. The romance, meanwhile, is genuine (there is definitely a chemistry between Leslie Cheung and Joey Wong), but again the humour lightens it (and inevitably interrupts it). Meanwhile, the action, as one might expect, is truly extraordinary – in live-action, Chinese filmmakers have *no competition* from *any* filmmakers anywhere on Earth.

A Chinese Ghost Story is also the first grand expression of the importance of romance and romantic desire in the cinema of Ching Siu-tung (it was a subplot in his previous two movies as director). It's surprising just how much romance is a key ingredient in Ching's films, even tho' he's known as one of the premier action directors on the planet. One of the memorable aspects of *A Chinese Ghost Story* is the lovers crying 'Ning Choi-san!' or 'Siu-shiiiin!' to each other.

The romantic plot in *A Chinese Ghost Story* reaches a heightened point in the finale, when the lovers share a final moment together, and then Nip Siu-shin is gone. Forever.

When a movie gets the *balance* between horror and comedy right,[20] it's very satisfying. In *A Chinese Ghost Story*, the filmmakers might have had recent (pre-1987) outings in the U.S.A. such as *Ghostbusters* or *E.T.* or *The Evil Dead* in mind. More recently, the humour in the *Pirates of the Caribbean* series hits a very similar tone (lavish vistas, great visual effects, and spooky moments, but not too gory or nasty – and, at the heart of it, a well-meaning but klutzy guy. In fact, Johnny Depp has affinities with Leslie Cheung, in the way that Depp played Captain Jack Sparrow in *Pirates*. And in the *Chinese Ghost Story* sequel of 1990, when Cheung has his beard and moustache, he's even more Depp-ish).

COMEDY.

A Chinese Ghost Story is very funny. In the bustling village scene (mandatory in any historical movie, East or West, always in the first act), everybody regards Ning Choi-san as a doofus. When he asks about the temple where he wants to spend the night because he's broke, everyone mutters behind his back that he's a dead man, very much in the Mel Brooks mold when someone mentions Dracula's Castle (and Tsui Hark is very fond of such comical crowd scenes). There's some inventive comedy using rain and water: the debt collector's account book is a soggy mess of smeared black ink, and Ning Choi-san has charms against spirits imprinted on his back when he's pushed against a store display (again, it's likely that Tsui Hark was behind these gags).

As so often in Chinese, fantasy movies, there's some pantomime-style crossdressing in *A Chinese Ghost Story*: the Tree Demon, Old Dame, is played by Lau Siu Ming, a veteran of numerous *kung fu* movies (and like many supernatural foes, s/he has an imperious, echoey voice).

And, just as in a pantomime, there is a lengthy comical sequence

---

20 The humour in *A Chinese Ghost Story* is perfectly pitched – it's very funny, but it doesn't detract from or stop the story, and it doesn't lessen the atmosphere of dread.

where the Mother-In-Law From Hell comes to visit: the Tree Demoness pays a visit to Nip Siu-shin's chamber, announcing that she's got to marry the Lord of the Black Mountain in three days. Siu-shin, meanwhile, hides Ning Choi-san in a wooden bathtub (so that the Old Dame can't smell him – this's also why Siu-shin meets her lover out on the water, in the pavillion). Comedy, farce, hiding lovers from stern, parental figures – it's all delightfully silly (Ning catches glimpses of Siu-shin half-dressed... her sister Siu Ching, is on her case... and the Old Dame catches the scent of the human Ning several times). And it's sexy – the moment when the topless Siu-shin leans down into the water to kiss Ning underwater is iconic.21 And *A Chinese Ghost Story* is absolutely jammed with memorable images like that.

TECHNICAL ASPECTS.

Technically, *A Chinese Ghost Story* is a marvel. The production design, the costumes, the hair, the make-up, the editing, the cinematography, the sound design – all departments are working at their optimum. There is a wonderful use of props, for instance: Swordsman Yin has his anti-demon charms and a magical sword, and much is made of the painting of Nip Siu-shin which Ning Choi-san spots in the village market (that prop does a *huge* amount of narrative work in the first two *A Chinese Ghost Story* movies).22 Meanwhile, texts and words are everywhere – from the cemetery stones and the wayside markers, to the paper charms deployed by the Taoist monk and Ning's soaked tax account book. There's even time for the lovers to indulge in some Chinese calligraphy during one of their (all too brief) sojourns together.

All of the *Chinese Ghost Story* films, like many historical movies, are costume movies: *A Chinese Ghost Story* is filled with flapping, floating and very long pieces of material (Shirley Chan and Kitty Ho Wai-Ying were the costume designers). Joey Wong, as the chief female star of the movie, receives the most lavish treatment from the hair, make-up and costume departments: Wong's Nip Siu-shin is more a bundle of white or red cloth fluttering in the wind than a former human being now ghost.23 The movement of the clothes, one of the hallmarks of Chinese, historical movies, perfectly embodies her in-between status, in a limbo between life and death. (In Chinese costume dramas, clothes don't hang statically on the body, they are photographed in motion, which enhances their beauty).

21 'One of the loveliest kisses in all of modern cinema' (Lisa Morton 73).
22 When Nip Siu-shin's not on screen, it's a reminder of her; Ning sees the picture before he meets Nip; Ning goes back to buy it; it's handed back to Ning by Nip; the art dealer tells Ning Choi-san that the model has been dead a year; it reminds Ning of Nip at the end of act two; Siu-shin tells Ning to keep ahold of it, and it's the only memento of her he'll have; and, yes, he's clutching it in the final scene.
23 The filmmakers use several techniques to give Siu-shin a gliding, floaty motion.

The acting style and the staging in *A Chinese Ghost Story* is inventive and, by Western standards, unorthodox. For example, characters standing and spouting dialogue, the default performance style in Western TV and film, is only part of the mix in *A Chinese Ghost Story*. Just as common are scenes where a character leaps up into a tree, or performs a weepy, emotional scene lying on the floor,. The Peking Opera style of performance, beloved of Tsui Hark, is displayed throughout *A Chinese Ghost Story*, and not only in characters such as the Tree Demon and Nip Siu-shin.

Seven cinematographers worked on *A Chinese Ghost Story* (probably more if you count second unit and visual effects teams – and some celebrated names, such as Tom Lau Moon tong, Poon Hang-sang, etc), but the result is completely unified[24] – and absolutely gorgeous. This 1987 movie is a photographic feast, and it's got the lot, technically: lamplight, candlelight, firelight, sunset, dawn, night (many ways of lighting a night scene), lightning, explosions, and visual effects.

The sound editing, mixing and dubbing (by Xiaolong Cheng, David Wu and Qun Xue) on *A Chinese Ghost Story* has had a little more time and energy spent on it than your average Hong Kong movie (in any genre). There are some wild sounds in *A Chinese Ghost Story*: tapping, bubbling sounds for the creatures in the temple; loud, echoing voices for the demons; every variation on whooshes for the swordplay and aerial flights; comical, spooky noises when Nip Siu-shin uses her ghostly magic; and extraordinary screams in the underworld sequence.

The score – by James Wong Jim, Romeo Diaz, David Wu and Dai Lemin – includes the expected traditional Chinese music, and electronica and breathy synthesizer effects for the supernatural scenes.

Editing orchestrates the boundaries between life and death in *A Chinese Ghost Story*: several times, it's simply a single cut, and not a grand visual effect accompanied by 50 channels of noisy sound effects, that takes someone away (to death) or brings them back (to life). For instance, our heroes pick up a bunch of funeral urns, each containing a ghost. Swordsman Yin asks the ghosts to take their urn and leave – they do, and in a cut to the reverse angle, they have already gone. Similarly, when Nip Siu-shin appears to Ning Choi-san in the inn, there's a cut to the reverse angle and Siu-shin is already there, standing behind the scholar. Finally, in the deeply moving climax of the movie, Nip Siu-shin disappears in between the shots, as the camera stays on Ning and we hear Yin's voice off-screen: 'she's already gone'.

---

24 No matter how many photographers shoot a Hong Kong movie, the results always seem to be in sync.

Forget wild (and expensive) visual effects, whooshing sound effects, wreathes of smoke and flashing lights, the most formidable effect in cinema, as all good filmmakers know, is the simple cut. With just one cut, you can create – or destroy – anything.

VISUAL EFFECTS.

A Chinese Ghost Story is another of Tsui Hark's visual effects feasts. The visual effects were delivered by his company, Cinefex Workshop, and overseen by Ma Xian Liang. Altho' the visual effects budget was in the region of $160,000 (!), they are marvellous, because of the way that they are integrated into the storytelling. That is, the $160,000 spent on the visual effects in *A Chinese Ghost Story* was more successful by far than the million$ spent solely on effects in Hollywood blockbusters such as *Snow White and the Huntsman*25 or *Where the Wild Things Are*. Because those movies stink! And *A Chinese Ghost Story* simply *sings*.

Among the notable visual effects in *A Chinese Ghost Story* are the stopmotion animated creatures, very much in the Ray Harryhausen mold (and marvellously integrated with the live-action). There are also matte shots, miniatures, animation, and optical printing (the movies of Tsui Hark are especially fond of integrating matte paintings with live action, to create those impossible, vast vistas vital to much of fantasy cinema). And, with all those inanimate objects to animate, like giant tongues or swords or tree roots or tentacles, there is a lot of on-set puppeteering in *A Chinese Ghost Story,* plus some animatronics, and special make-up.

Many of the effects were of course created on the set, in front of the camera. *A Chinese Ghost Story* is, like *The Blade* or *The Bride With White Hair*, a fantastically sexy movie in its evocation of *texture* and *atmosphere*. Rain effects, fire effects, smoke effects, lightning effects, wind effects and wire effects – *A Chinese Ghost Story* has got the lot. Every shot has smoke billowing through it (and leaves), wind machines blowing clothing, and, for the lighting, deep blues for the nighttime scenes and reds and orange for the fires and the lamps and the candles.

ACT ONE.

Let's have a look at some of the scenes: –

A Chinese Ghost Story opens with a pre-credits teaser featuring the Chinese ghost of the title, in the form of Joey Wang, preying upon a hapless scholar working at his books late at night (one of those places where the windows are always open, where drapres're always fluttering,

25 *Snow White and the Huntsman* cost an astonishing $170 million! What a shocking waste of money! Just think what the Chinese film industry could do with $170 million – in 1987 – or now!

where the art direction and lighting is exquisite). The spectre appears outside the room, then moves inside to seduce the scholar. The dreamy atmosphere is enhanced by the flapping, white drapes, and the female voice singing.

Ning Choi-san is introduced travelling on his own through the countryside on his way to collect taxes (a thankless job). The rigours of travel (and Ning's characterization) are evoked with some basic realities of life – food (inedible) • and theft (unavoidable) • and death (instant) • and terrible weather (cold-and-wet).

Sheltering from a rainstorm, Ning Choi-san finds himself witnessing a savage and bloody running battle, with a swordsman pursing and nobbling several thieves (this is a kind of send-up of Akira Kurosawa's cinema – rain, countryside, swords, sudden violence, etc).[26] The scene evokes the proximity of comedy and violence, which's a recurring feature of the *Chinese Ghost Story* movies.

After delineating Ning Choi-san's characterization and predicament (as a lowly but diligent tax collector), *A Chinese Ghost Story* continues with the marvellous bustling village sequence. It's packed with incidents – selling paper charms,[27] an art dealer,[28] a street brawl, looking for somewhere to stay, finding something to eat, tax collecting, the search for wanted men,[29] the superstitious crowd, and the painting of the ghost.

The rapid shift from day to night[30] takes us into horror movie territory, with Ning Choi-san heading for the Hotel From Hell, the Lan Yeuk Temple, through a forest of wolves. All of the clichés of the horror genre are included with such charm and ingenuity, no one minds if we've seen this hokum 1,000s of times before.

The Lan Yeuk Temple is the setting for the introduction of the third major character in *A Chinese Ghost Story*, the Taoist sword master, Swordsman Yin. Once again, Ning Choi-san has the habit of stumbling into trouble; wherever he is, things go wrong. The staging of the scene is masterful, with Ning caught in the frenetic battle between two ancient, fierce rivals, Yin and Hah Hau – he's trapped literally between the two of them, at sword-point. (Here, one of Ning's only weapons – talk – doesn't quite work, tho' Hah Hau storms off in the end).

We're still only part-way through act one of *A Chinese Ghost Story*,

26 Ning might be starving, but after the swordsman's left, he immediately throws the gift of some bread away.
27 Folklore and superstition are evoked throughout *A Chinese Ghost Story*.
28 There's a great gag of the art seller turning all of his wares away from onlookers when he discovers that Ning is poor.
29 The belligerent and dim cops armed with swords looking for the criminals on the wanted posters are a classic running gag (very Tsui-ian). Later, a guy's dragged in who's the spitting image of Swordsman Yin. (Tsui used the gag later, with the impostors in *The Swordsman 3* and in *Iron Monkey*).
30 Via some optical wipes.

because we haven't even got to the nighttime romance yet, or the conflict between Swordsman Yin and the monsters. *A Chinese Ghost Story* doesn't feel rushed, yet it is also racing along at the frantic pace of the city of the Hong Kong itself.

For example, *A Chinese Ghost Story* has time to depict an exposition scene between Ning Choi-san and Swordsman Yin, a scene of Ning bedding down in the Temple, the awakening of the corpses in the attic above, the demise of swordsman Hah Hau, and the beginning of the romance of Ning and Nip Siu-shin in the waterside pavillion.

A romance between a human man and a spirit woman is a sub-genre of Chinese romance tales (but it's also found in Western folklore and fairy tales – men and mermaids, for instance). In *A Chinese Ghost Story*, it's staged as a highly stylized scene out of a mediæval painting, unreal and dreamy (torches placed in the water as well as in the pavillion is a great touch, and Nip Siu-shin plays a *qin*), but also delightfully comical.

The climax of act one of *A Chinese Ghost Story* is also the finale of both act two and act three, as usual in many movies. That is, it's a conflict between Swordsman Yin and the monsters, with Ning Choi-san caught in the middle (at this point, Ning doesn't quite know who or what Nip Siu-shin is).

Swordsmen and ghosts leaping up trees (and down them, and through them, and around them, and between them), is a form of action that Ching Siu-tung has been delivering for decades. Ching is the King of Forest Fights, of wire-work amongst leaves and branches.

The finale of act one of *A Chinese Ghost Story* is fast and frantic, but also includes several romantic clinches (Ning Choi-san lands atop Nip Siu-shin with his hand on her breasts, a Japanese *animé* joke, for instance), and some crude comedy (Swordsman Yin pisses in the bushes where Ning is hiding).

ACT TWO.

Act two of *A Chinese Ghost Story* repeats many of the elements we've already seen in act one: more romantic scenes btn Ning Choi-san and Nip Siu-shin, more of Swordsman Yin (his comical song), more of Ning in the scary temple (and the undead), Ning in the woods again (now with three lanterns), Nip snaring another victim, etc.

But there are complications – the biggest is Ning Choi-san coming face to face (or to nose) with Old Dame, the Tree Demonness, and her entourage. If the Old Dame isn't enough as a potential problem to overcome, there's Nip Siu-shin's sister Siu Ching (Sit Chi-Lun), who suspects that Nip is hiding something (or someone).

This lengthy sequence, where Ning Choi-san is hidden by Nip Siu-shin in a bathtub, is played chiefly for laughs (there are many bits of actorly business, as Ning is nearly-but-not-quite-discovered, taking *A Chinese Ghost Story* into romantic farce or comedy of manners territory. Tsui Hark (likely the creator of this part of the film) had already delivered variations on this sort of scene in both *Shanghai Blues* and *Peking Opera Blues*).

But there's also barely suppressed aggression, too. For ex, Old Dame whipping[31] her daughter Nip Siu-shin (and it's not the first time that Nip has been punished). We also see the monsterish side of the Tree Demonness, with glimpses of the giant tongue (tho' the two aren't put together in a single shot yet).

Comedy, aggression – and romance (the first time that the lovers kiss is when Nip Siu-shin gives Ning Choi-san air under water in the tub (a bath scene in movies is also often an excuse to have the lead actress undressing, as here, and kissing under water to give someone air is a common motif. Tony Ching used it recently in *Jade Dynasty*, 2019).

In the resuming of the romantic scenes, Nip Siu-shin and Ning Choi-san consummate their love in the water pavillion, filmed, as always with the pavillion scenes, with drapes fluttering in front of the camera. There's a second song here (following Yin's Taoist song), which turns the love scene into a montage of the lovers' courtship (and a 'Story So Far' summary of the film).

This is a very common narrative device in Hong Kong movies, where an ecstatic moment is riven with evocations of nostalgia and sadness. The lovemaking in the present tense seems overwhelmed by memories, set to a melancholy tune ('Let the Dawn Never Come', sung by Sally Yeh). The song and the montage editing transforms the present moment into a sum of the past, turns lovemaking into memory, and reminds us that although this is sort of the happiest of times, it is also the saddest, because the lovers cannot stay together.

The romance in *A Chinese Ghost Story* has, after all, one of the biggest obstacles you can imagine between two lovers: one of them is dead. They're not from rival clans, not from different social classes, but separated by death.

Hence the bitter poignancy of the scene at the end of act two, when Ning Choi-san and Swordsman Yin visit the cemetery, and Ning confronts the cold, hard fact by the light of day: Nip Siu-shin's gravestone, with her name on it. These are tried and tested ingredients of folklore, bringing together love and death, and they always work.

---

31 The whip neatly links to the giant tongue.

ACT THREE.

A Chinese Ghost Story isn't content with one finale: it has two! And both *rock*, big-time. Indeed, *A Chinese Ghost Story* has a final act as stupendous as any other movie ever made. The ending of *A Chinese Ghost Story* is a *tour-de-force* of filmmaking; it features a barrage of practical effects and visual effects which overwhelm the audience with thrills and invention. As a series of gags and ideas, the final act of *A Chinese Ghost Story* is truly remarkable – but these are not just effects for the sake of effects, they are all tied to the storytelling. And yet, they are not the true ending and resolution of the whole movie: that occurs in the scene in the inn, over two or three close-ups of three people in a room.

The finales of *A Chinese Ghost Story* incorporate every trick and visual effect in film history – pixillation, puppeteering, optical printing, superimpositions, slow and speeded-up film, animation, animatronics, special make-up, and wire-work.

And let's not forget the editing (by David Wu), which cuts the ending within an inch of its life, yet gives everything its proper weight and place, and doesn't shred it with pointlessly rapid editing (as so many other movies do). The two finales of *A Chinese Ghost Story* are cut very fast (as usual in a Tsui Hark movie), but the pace is in sync with the storytelling and the performances.

In the first half of the finale of *A Chinese Ghost Story*, the Taoist monk Yin Chik-ha and the hapless scholar Ning Choi-san go up against the dreaded Tree Demon, Old Dame. What are they fighting for? Why, the luscious Nip Siu-shin, of course! Only she just happens to be a ghost! (But by this time, Ning has promised Siu-shin that he'll make sure her spirit is laid to rest, which involves digging up her remains in a nearby grave. Swordsman Yin is resistant to the notion: ghosts and humans do not mix, he reckons. But Ning, realizing at last that Siu-shin is a supernatural creature (she acknowledges this to his face), and there's no hope they could be together for long, does the right thing, as a romantic die-hard).

A well-meaning but useless scholar, a crazy, old, Taoist monk, an out-size Tree Demon villain (who has the longest tongue[32] in history), and a beautiful princess who's dead – ahh, it can only be a Chinese, fantasy-action-comedy-horror-romance movie based on a 17th century tale and centuries of superstition and folklore.

◆

The first finale of *A Chinese Ghost Story* would be enough to cap any movie (but the filmmakers, considering what they'd shot, opted to go back

---

32 That tongue is 'horror and high camp, kung fu and special-effects fantasy, it is hyperactive, pathological and multi-dimensional', noted Stephen Teo (1997, 228).

and add some more). It's centred around the Lan Yeuk Temple, but also takes in much to-ing and fro-ing to the water pavillion (where Ning Choi-san and Nip Siu-shin tryst), and running around the woodland, with occasional visits to an over-grown cemetery (all set at night, of course, with blue lighting, smoke, wind, and flickering flames). The action is spell-binding, with the visual effects, the stunts, the flashing swords, the explosions, and the wire-work coming thick and fast. It's fantastically fantastic fantasy filmmaking, one of those set-pieces where the movie-makers chuck in everything they can get hold of, not caring whether it looks 'real', whether it's 'believable', or whether it even makes sense! Who cares? It's simply sublime!

But, folks, this is not miraculously achieved action and visual effects for the sake of it – the filmmaking is always telling a story, is always dramatizing the struggles between the four protagonists: the young scholar Ning Choi-san who just wants to save Nip Siu-shin and be with her (and help her achieve a peaceful quieting of her restless spirit); the Taoist demon-buster Yin Chik-ha, who wants to vanquish the monsters for once and for all; Siu-shin who hopes that her soul can be laid to rest (and be free of enslavement to the Tree Demon), but also to be with her lover; and the fiendish monster Tree Demon, who wants to slaughter anyone who opposes it (and who won't let Siu-shin go without a fight!).

The scenes in *A Chinese Ghost Story* of the colossal tongue slithering around the temple so it envelops it are brilliant updates of schlocky, 1950s monster movies. There's a Wall of Tongue out there! ('Don't let it get in your mouth!' the heroes yell at each other. Damn right! No French kissing with that demon!).[33] Once the tongue's inside the building, the gags and stunts are amazing – amazingly *rapid*, too, and very funny (As director Ching Siu-tung explained, it took a *lot* of work to make that giant tongue look good. But it was worth it).

As a sequence of in-front-of-the-camera practical effects, this is one of the finest in all cinema, worthy of the maestros of German silent cinema like F.W. Murnau or Fritz Lang. There is the same energetic, try anything spirit of 1920s German cinema, and the levels of imagination and skill on display are astounding.

Yes, when it comes to puppeteering an entire environment, with breakaway props, walls, floors, ceilings, rafters, tables, windows, and pillars, Hong Kong cinema has no equal. It's as if Hong Kong action cinema is always part-animation, but these guys are animating real things, not drawings or pixels – *whole buildings* as well as people and props and

---

33 We've already seen a ghostly point-of-view shot of the tongue entering a victim's body and sucking the life out of it.

monsters!

Anything can move in Hong Kong action cinema – and frequently does. You thought that chair was just going to sit there quietly throughout the scene? No, Jackie Chan is going to spin it, bounce it to and fro on a victim's head, and then break it over him. You thought that at least the walls might survive intact – no, that giant tongue is smashing through them.

The filmmakers of *A Chinese Ghost Story* also deliver inventive variations on the monster that can transform – so they are throwing tentacles at the audience, then roots that slither along (and under) the ground, then branches that leap at the hero, then a giant beak, and even then the monster doesn't – won't, can't – die (another horror movie staple).

The creature is slithering into and out of a hole, sliding under the ground, grasping Yip Siu-shin, and Ning Choi-san, and the Swordsman (at different times), and performing impossible transformations. The filmmakers worked tirelessly to make a giant tongue appear as a fearsome opponent, and they succeeded. It's ridiculous – a giant tongue! Everyone knows that, but one of the tricks in making it work was to approach the whole thing with just the right tone and attitude (the *tone* of *A Chinese Ghost Story* I reckon is absolutely perfect). Thus, there are comical touches, but not too many (the threat is not deflated with laughter); the humour is delicately balanced with the thrills and suspense.

So Swordsman Yin is comically covered with goop but he could still die at any moment. So Ning Choi-san is desperately trying to avoid the tip of the tongue entering his mouth in a comical manner, but it looks like he might lose.

✦

The second finale of *A Chinese Ghost Story* starts when the heroes visit a new locale, another inn. Here the lovers are re-united (following some business with the multiple funeral urns, which contain ghosts of young women, sort of Nip Siu-shin's sisters. This is played for both comedy and pathos). There are some sweet touches, too – such as Swordsman Yin's embarrassment when he sees the lovers together.

The second finale in *A Chinese Ghost Story,* producer Tsui Hark explained, came about when the filmmakers decided what they had initially scripted wasn't satisfying (the script went thru a number of variations). As they didn't have the $$$$$ for a Big Set (where most action movie finales take place – often it's the super-villain's lair, which is destroyed at the end), they decided they could place the climax in a spaceless space. That is, just a piece of ground (at night, of course), which, with the aid of *tons* of smoke and clever lighting (and slow motion, and a battery of visual effects), they could persuade the audience that it was the underworld (of course, audiences can be easily persuaded: if an actor tells them they're in the underworld, the audience believes it. There's no point not buying into it – especially this late in the movie. And, anyway, who knows what the underworld looks like?).

There are so many imaginative ideas erupting all over the place in the second finale of *A Chinese Ghost Story*, it's impossible to cite them all. Many of the images and beats are memorable: the running, galloping army that's transparent (carrying Nip Siu-shin in a palanquin[34] to her wedding)... Swordsman Yin kicking Ning Choi-san to soar over the army towards Siu-shin (a p.o.v. shot shows him flying over the army below)... the skull motif – the skulls in the inn, and the mountain of skulls that the Black Mountain demon stands on... Siu-shin and Ning Choi-san flying through the air, as she rescues him yet again... Ning and Siu-shin crashing into a cliff and being engulfed by clutching arms... Yin taking on the whole army single-handed (and later with a sword crackling with energy)... Yin writing heaven and earth spells on his palm in blood and firing them at the enemy... the Black Mountain demon's knight disappearing and re-appearing behind Swordsman Yin's back... the screaming heads that shoot out from underneath the Black Mountain demon's cloak, flying at Siu-shin and biting her...

The *confidence* of the filmmakers, their *invention* and *creativity*, and the *joy* they have in entertaining the audience, are very infectious in *A Chinese Ghost Story*. You can't help but be blown away by it, swept along by it, and energized by it. The *spirit* of this movie, its *tone* and *attitude*, are so appealing (sometimes you can't believe just how many marvellous scenes the film team have produced in *A Chinese Ghost Story* – but the montage of the movie's highlights that plays over the end credits reminds you, while Leslie Cheung sings the theme song).

And there is a *genuine* feeling of movie magic in *A Chinese Ghost Story* – of filmmakers who're delighting in the magical effects that cinema can create, just like Géorges Méliès was over-joyed like a child when he discovered what movies and cameras could do back in the early 1900s (Méliès would've utterly *adored A Chinese Ghost Story*! This is a Mélièsian movie if ever there was one!).

✦

Let's look at the climactic scene in the inn, when our heroes make it back from the underworld after the battle with the monsters and demons

---

34 Tony Ching is very fond of galloping palanquin scenes – they appear in his first film, *Duel To the Death*.

and army of the dead – how they crawl out of thin air into the shadowy interior of the temple just before sunrise (a special effect very reminiscent of *The Wizard of Oz*, *The Invisible Man* or *Stairway To Heaven*). Look at the staging of the scene – how the three actors are exhausted, on the floor,[35] until Ning Choi-san moves to the window, where the sun is streaming in (sunlight is fatal to Nip Siu-shin, like a vampire). Ning can't bear to turn to look at Siu-shin, because he knows he's got to say goodbye to her forever. He faces the window and the light, turned away, and tells her to return with her ashes. A final medium shot of Siu-shin lying on the floor... Then there's a brilliant use of off-screen dialogue, and a cut – when Yin Chik-ha says, 'she's already gone'. And in the blink of an edit made on 35mm celluloid, it's over, the romance is ended.[36]

This scene, not the giant battle in the underworld, resolves the primary plot of *A Chinese Ghost Story* – the love story. Notice how poignant it is, how effective, and how economical – it's played largely over close-ups of the principal actors. And notice too that it's very short, and all the more emotional for it. Many comparable movies, especially in the 21st century, would milk and milk that scene. I find the ending very moving – partly because we are mourning the loss of a much-loved star, Leslie Cheung.

Parts of the window's wooden blinds crumple, letting more light in – the human-and-ghost romance has ended (as it has to), but the light caught on film says otherwise: it is a rich, juicy, orange light, so vibrant you could bathe in it. It's the light of morning: there's no need to draw attention to the countless symbols that the light of sunrise embodies. And *A Chinese Ghost Story* as a whole doesn't really want or need spiritual or religious or metaphysical interpretations. But they are certainly there if you want to evoke them. (And yet there is something so luscious about the golden light flooding into the inn, and the way that it has been photographed, that's mysterious and sensual. Like many Chinese, fantasy movies, *A Chinese Ghost Story* is in love with light. It's a movie which uses light itself as a primary dramatic device, like films such as *Close Encounters of the Third Kind*[37] or *Princess Mononoke*).

35 A previous conversation btn the lovers was also played on the floor – in the midst of the giant tongue attack.
36 The movie closes with our heroes galloping away under a rainbow (several Hong Kong action movies of this period close with the heroes on horseback, including *Peking Opera Blues, New Dragon Gate Inn* and the *Swordsman* movies).
37 The deep orange of the sunlight recalls the ball of light on the other side of the door that the child Barry opens in *Close Encounters of the Third Kind* (1977). When he was asked to provide an example of a 'signature shot' or 'master image' in all of his films, Steven Spielberg chose the shot in *Close Encounters of the Third Kind* of the bright orange UFO light outside: 'that beautiful but awful light, just like fire coming through the doorway. And he's very small, and it's a very large door, and there's a lot of promise or danger outside that door'.

WE ARE ALL GHOSTS.

There are many poignant moments in *A Chinese Ghost Story*: sure, it's a stops-all-out, fantasy rollercoaster ride, but it also exhibits an acute awareness of issues like time passing and death, like the fleetingness and impermanence of human existence, like the frailty of love and romance. There are scenes in *A Chinese Ghost Story* where the headlong rush of the narrative halts, for instance: such as when Taoist monk Yin Chik-ha has a crisis of conscience, and wonders what the hell he's doing (remarking that he's set himself outside of life, but he's not a ghost, either: he's lost somewhere in-between. To humans, he deliberately appeared as a ghost, but when he's among ghosts, he is the human who wants to vanquish them).38

And there's time for a jokey courtroom scene: Ning Choi-san is beaten on the floor while the judge and his assistant berate him (the assistant's played by one of the movie's composers and a major creative talent in Hong Kong cinema, David Wu, and the judge is Wong Jing, one of the moguls of Cantonese cinema).

A Chinese Ghost Story also has time in its jam-packed 98 minutes for some musical montages. There's a delightfully bonkers scene where Swordsman Yin delivers a musical rap about Taoism ('Dao, Dao, Dao, Dao!') as he performs a marvellous sword dance (a set-piece also in the 1960 film). As the lovers make love, we have the customary slow ballad ('Let the Dawn Never Come' by Sally Yeh) playing over close-ups of two beautiful people, Leslie Cheung and Joey Wong. In many a movie, these MTV-a-like39 montages of lovemaking and togetherness have no dramatic or emotional heat at all, but in *A Chinese Ghost Story* they are delicious.

Because we are all ghosts.

Because we are all here for a moment, then we're gone.

A great fantasy movie, like *A Chinese Ghost Story*, can evoke those spiritual issues so magically, exploring them, yet somehow also offering a kind of emotional/ religious catharsis.

This is great storytelling.

---

38 In *A Chinese Ghost Story*, one of the Taoist swordsman's tasks is to keep the world of ghosts, the *yin*, separate from the world of humans, the *yang*.
39 Ching Siu-tung said the design of *A Chinese Ghost Story* was 'like watching a Chinese MTV'.

A Chinese Ghost Story (1987), this page and over.

A Chinese Ghost Story film posters.
(This page and over).

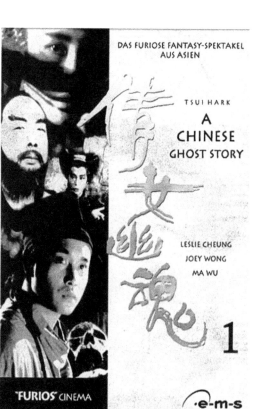

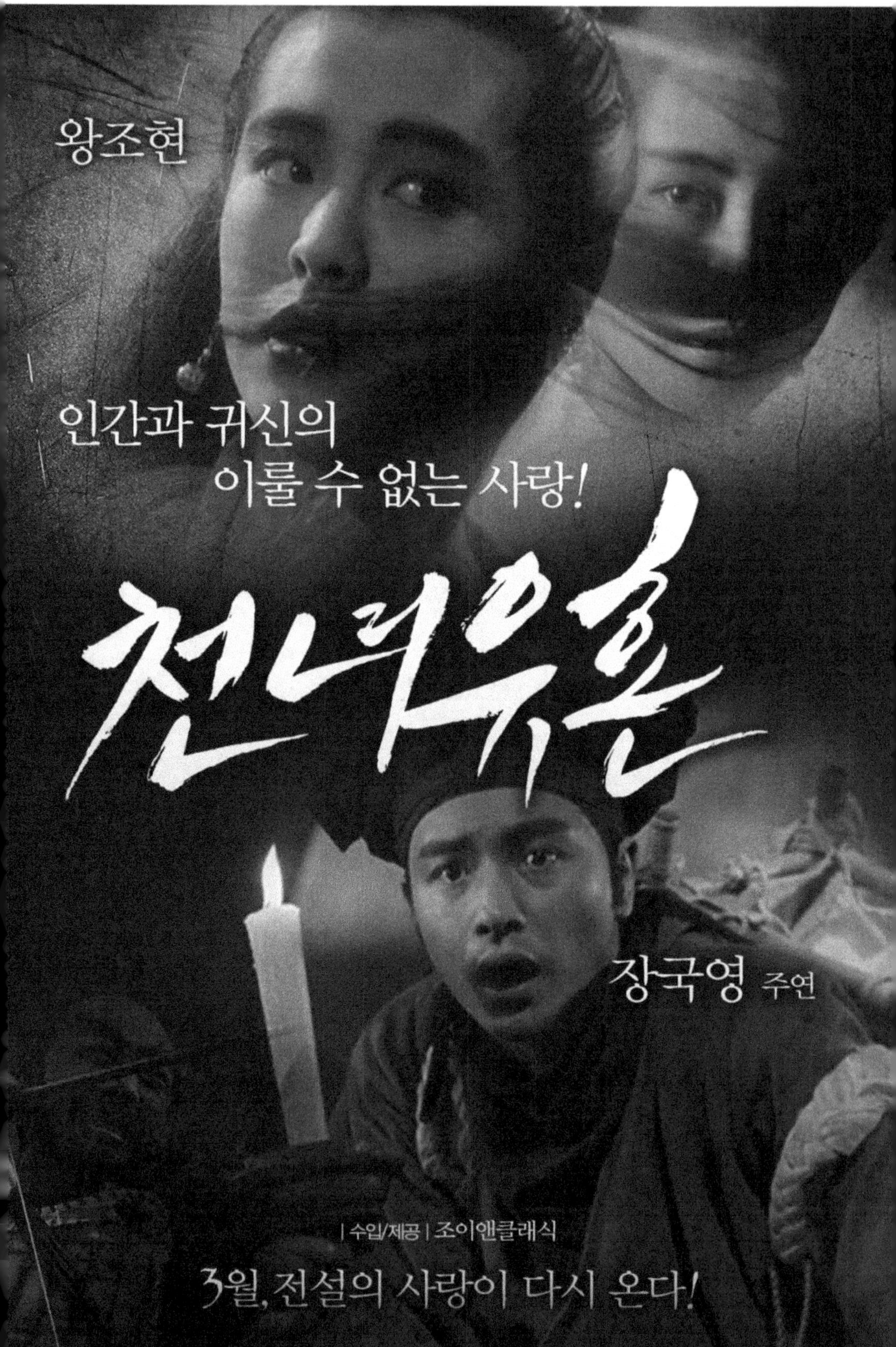

왕조현
인간과 귀신의
이룰 수 없는 사랑!
천녀유혼
장국영 주연
| 수입/제공 | 조이앤클래식
3월, 전설의 사랑이 다시 온다!

16

A CHINESE GHOST STORY 2

Sin Nui Yau Wan II – Yan Gaan Do

Most of the principals of the first *A Chinese Ghost Story* movie returned for the first sequel, including the director, producer and stars. *A Chinese Ghost Story 2* (1990, *Qiannü Youhun Zhi Renjian Dao* in Mandarin = *Sien Female Ghost II: Human Realm Tao*) was written by Lau Tai-mok, Lam Kei-to and Leung Yiu-ming (with a story co-credit for Tsui Hark and Yuen Kai-Chi), with the same cast (Leslie Cheung Kwok-wing, Joey Wong Cho-yin, Wu Ma, and Lau Slu-ming), plus newbies Jacky Cheung (as Chi Chau/ Autumn), and Michelle Reiss (a.k.a. Li, as Yuet Chi/ Moon.) Also in the cast were: Ku Feng, Waise Lee Chi-hung, Lau Shun, Wong Fue-chun, Do Siuy-chin, Johnny Koo, Fei Sing, Wong Hung and Ng Kwok-kin. (Ching Siu-tung directed all three *Chinese Ghost Story* movies, and Tsui Hark was producer on all three). DP: Arthur Wong, editor: Marco Mak Chi-sin, art dirs.: William Chang Suk-Ping and Ho Kim-Sing, sound: Miu Gik Luk Yam Sat, Kwok Wing-Kei, Lam Wing-Cheung and Wong Choh-Keung, costumes: Kitty Ho Wai-Ying, hair: Chau Siu-Mui and Peng Yen-Lien, music: James Wong Jim, Romeo Diaz and Tang Siu-Lam, special fx by Nick Allder and David Watkins, make-up: Man Yun-Ling, and the action dirs. were Cheung Kan Chow, Ching Siu-tung, Bobby Woo Chi-lung, and Lau Chi-ho. Released in July 13, 1990. 98/ 104 minutes.

Produced for around HK $7 million (= US $1 million)[1] – an impossibly tiny budget! – *A Chinese Ghost Story 2* is a typical sequel: More Of The Same, tho' slightly different (however, it develops the Chinese ghost plot into the future, rather than, like many sequels, and most in Hong Kong

---

[1] Bey Logan reckoned the budget was US $7 million, but that seems too high; it might stem from the confusion between Hong Kong and North American dollars. In fact, the first movie cost $650,000, so a step up to $1 million seems correct.

cinema, re-hashing the same elements but with a new yarn). The first movie was a ghost story and romance; the second focusses on more human issues, or morals and ethics.[2] Altho' film critics made their usual complaints about A Chinese Ghost Story 2 being less successful than the first movie, I'm sure it played well with viewers (I bet an audience in a multiplex theatre in Kowloon in 1990 enjoyed the scares, the jokes, the romance and the swordplay. It's a perfect Friday Night Movie). After all, you get more Leslie Cheung Kwok-wing (and that's enough for many fans!), and you also get more Joey Wong, and you get Jacky Cheung, and you get Wu Ma! What's not to like?!

Like many sequels, A Chinese Ghost Story 2 not only draws on the first film in every way, it quotes directly from it, in the form of several montages. A Chinese Ghost Story 2 opens, for instance, with a montage of images which summarize the story of the first outing. In the middle of act two, to evoke the tragic romance of Ning Choi-san and Nip, there's another montage, which includes the iconic scene of the underwater kiss. Joey Wong sings on the score, along with a female chorus.

Altho' Tsui Hark, among others, were part of the high-powered team of collaborators working on A Chinese Ghost Story 2, this is still a Tony Ching movie. And not only in the action scenes: many of the romantic scenes in A Chinese Ghost Story 2 are far more indulgent, stylized and dreamy than those in the work of either Tsui. A Chinese Ghost Story 2 doesn't feature just one image of the lovers in a close embrace, but many. Often these're filmed in slow motion, with exaggerated lighting. Backlit, floating, the lovers drift across the set or have their faces pressed together on the ground. The camera lingers long over the incredible faces of Joey Wong and Leslie Cheung (and Michelle Reiss).

Ching Siu-tung's cinema pushes romantic motifs into extreme stylization, holding on slow motion images of the lovers far longer than similar movies. The *mise-en-scène* is intricately art-directed, carefully composed, meticulously costumed, with perfect make-up and exquisite lighting. These images have had a lot of time and energy expended in staging them.

Technically, A Chinese Ghost Story 2 is absolutely amazing: with Arthur Wong heading up the photography department, this is one of the most ravishing looking of all Hong Kong movies. A huge proportion of the show occurs at night or dusk, requiring a massive amount of lighting

2 There were many meetings Tony Ching recalled, as they decided what to do in the Chinese Ghost Story sequel.

equipment. And as it's a historical fantasy, there is plenty of opportunity for highly stylized lighting schemes.

It wasn't easy, though: Arthur Wong recalled an incident on this movie:

> I was hanging from a big crane set above a 100-feet deep cliff. I had to move away form the edge. But they wrongly calculated my weight and when I was in the harness, with the camera and the batteries, I was too heavy. When I just took off, I was upside-down, head down. Wow, it was very scary. And it was very hard to get me back once I was upside-down. People had to come to the edge of the cliff and grab me. (D. Vivier)

All of the departments in charge of the visuals are stellar: costumes by Kitty Ho Wai-Ying, hair by Chau Siu-Mui and Peng Yen-Lien, make-up by Man Yun-Ling and art direction by William Chang Suk-Ping and Ho Kim-Sing (many of whom worked for Tony Ching and Tsui Hark on other productions).

The editing of *A Chinese Ghost Story 2* keeps the movie in perpetual motion, yet with many opportunities for reflective interludes, and emotional montages. Tsui's regular editor, Marco Mak Chi-sin, cut this film. One of the chief reasons that *A Chinese Ghost Story 2* is so satisfying is because it is so well-edited.

Finally, the score, by James Wong Jim, Romeo Diaz and Tang Siu-Lam, should be cited as a key ingredient in the success of *A Chinese Ghost Story 2*: as with the *Once Upon a Time In China* films, *A Chinese Ghost Story 2* employs a traditional, Chinese score in the main. As it's also a fantasy movie and a horror movie, however, it uses electronica for suspense. Also, there are several songs in *A Chinese Ghost Story 2*, sung by Leslie Cheung, Joey Wong and a chorus.

✦

One of the delights of a sequel is seeing how the filmmakers employ the elements of the previous movie/s. In *A Chinese Ghost Story 2*, these included finding inventive ways of bringing back props like the painting of Nip Siu-shin, or using the charms, or the demon fights, or the eye candy (male and female) and semi-nude bathing scenes.[3] But a sequel doesn't usually change *everything*, if it's got sense (if you change too much, it's not a sequel, it's a different movie). The trick with a sequel of this kind of fluffy, commercial, popcorn cinema is to give the audience something that

3 The 1990 movie decided that fans would want to see Leslie Cheung taking a bath. So, in the Righteous Villa, Ning Choi-san pops into a wooden bath which's handily nearby. And that's when the monsters show up, just as in a horror movie when the heroine's taking a shower. It's here too where the rap version of *Tao Te Ching* is reprised from the first movie, with Ning singing it now as a protection against evil spirits.

seems 'new' yet is also exactly the same (because that's also what the audience want).

It's a tricky balancing act that inevitably means that you keep many ingredients just the same. So in *A Chinese Ghost Story 2* many of the elements are straight repetitions from the first movie: thus, Ning Choi-san is back as the hapless debt collector with his backpack, arriving in a town on his travels; there's a visit to a haunted house, a creepy night spent there during a storm (with a monster appearing), a rough restaurant, wanted men posters, the painting of Nip Siu-shin, another mad Taoist monk, a procession, an arranged marriage, comical bathing scenes, farcical/ partial nudity scenes, romantic kisses, more battles with monstrous foes, more swordplay, etc.

After all, the filmmakers involved in producing *A Chinese Ghost Story 2* are Hong Kong veterans. They are out-and-out capitalists, experienced showmen who aim to *make money* from their movies. Yes – *money!* So *A Chine$e Gho$t $tory 2* is a wholly commercial proposition. Yes, and once the end credits start to roll, the house lights are already up, and you're being hurried out of your seat to make way for the next showing (common practice in Hong Kong!).

Among the most pressing challenges in *A Chinese Ghost Story 2* was what to do with Joey Wong's character, Nip Siu-shin, who eventually received the peace she desired (a proper death and burial for her soul) in the finale of the first movie. Instead of reviving the character (a cinch to do in a fantasy flick – especially one about life and death and ghosts!), which must've been tempting, the writers and producers opted to have Joey Wong appear as a new character, Windy (who's pretty much the same, of course, but not so wan and pale and ethereal – tho' just as beautiful).

Windy is part of a group that follows Elder Chu – so she is very human, very not-ghostly (but she does have a supernatural moment), and is introduced brandishing a sword which she holds up at Ning Choi-san (thus she is now one of the many female warriors in Hong Kong cinema). They meet following an extravagant nighttime fight scene outside the Righteous Villa, where the rebels dress up as ghosts in white and duel Autumn (halfway thru act one). This fight scene contains stupendous images – like the would-be ghosts floating down behind Ning.[4] And when Ning catches a glimpse of Windy, he does a double-take, as do we – actors like Joey Wong are literally breathtaking.

A Chinese Ghost Story 2 is a haunted house movie – we spend *a lot*

[4] One of the many marvellous images in *A Chinese Ghost Story 2* features the introduction of the rebels: dressed as ghosts in white, in a forest night scene, they are lowered into the frame out of focus behind Leslie Cheung as if they're corpses hanging from ropes from trees. It's a genuinely creepy image, and the *Chinese Ghost Story* movies are full of such scenes.

of time in the shadowy Righteous Villa, and far less outdoors, as in the previous *A Chinese Ghost Story* outing. *A Chinese Ghost Story 2* is part comedy horror movie, part *wuxial* martial arts movie, part romantic drama, and part farce.

As Windy inevitably falls for Ning Choi-san (and who wouldn't when he's played by the divine Leslie Cheung?!), she agrees at times to pretend to be his lost love, Nip Siu-shin. Ning, meanwhile, spends part of *A Chinese Ghost Story 2* in exhausted or altered states, imagining that Windy is really Siu-shin.

And while Ning Choi-san pines for Nip Siu-shin (even when the wide-awake side of him knows that he'll never see her again – they said farewell forever at the end of the first flick), *A Chinese Ghost Story II* includes a few scenes where both Windy and Moon are looking at Ning lovingly, from afar. The scenes play into the celebrity status of Leslie Cheung, of course – he's the kind of super-babe actor that fans at film premieres scream over. In some scenes in *A Chinese Ghost Story 2*, there isn't even a reverse angle depicting what the women're looking at: instead the camera stays on Moon and Windy, bashing their heads together in their eagerness to try to get a better glimpse of Ning. (As the movie progresses, Moon seems to accept that Ning seems more interested in Windy than her. She sulks and pouts, but in the finale becomes more attached to the Taoist monk Autumn, even tho' this relationship is also doomed. Because when Autumn revives the couple by kissing *chi* back into them, he avoids Moon because she's a woman. A romance between a woman and a Taoist monk is never going to fly in a Chinese action movie! Even when that monk is played by the appealing Jacky Cheung!).

And *A Chinese Ghost Story 2* is funny. Putting Ning Choi-san in prison with a wily, old coot played by Ku Feng (who's also near-crazy) was a fun skit on *The Count of Monte Cristo* (and the prison genre). Having Ning then being mistaken for Elder Chu, a highly-respected scholar and philosopher, was wonderful (Ning grows a beard in jail, as you do – he's in there for months – so he looks like the Elder. Later, he shaves it off to become the familiar Ning and Leslle Cheung without a beard). In a second the beardy guise switches the hierarchy of the relationships around, and now Ning is elevated to the leader of the pack, instead of being the rather hopeless youth who's just trying to get along and stay out of trouble. The gag is extended to a scene where Ning shaves off his 'tache, only to find that the rebel group dismiss him as just anyone – without those whiskers, he's a nobody! (Director Ching Siu-tung remarked that he was thinking of Tiananmen Square and the suppression of political rebellion in the personality of Elder Chu, a writer who's imprisoned for apparently politically subversive works (which aren't at all).)

Certainly the political/ ideological opinions of the writers, and Tsui Hark, can be heard in the speech that the old man gives in the cell – he mentions that if he writes history, he's accused of criticizing the present, and if he writes fairy tales, he's charged with purveying superstition (i.e., whatever he does as an artist/ writer, the powers-that-be will find some fault with his work). The Communist ideology of Mainland China is critiqued here.

✦

One of the finest scenes in *A Chinese Ghost Story 2* had the group of rebels eavesdropping on Ning Choi-san and Windy talking following their amazing encounter in the forest. Here is the brilliant use of the painting prop – the calligraphy that Ning and Nip Siu-shin performed in the first *A Chinese Ghost Story* movie (and spoke in voiceover), drawn into the painting, is now switched about. Now the rebel group is thrilled to think that Ning is going to recite some amazing poetry, and they get to hear it. Which he does! And lo and behold, the poem contains clues which the rebels decipher as referring to their Master and the water pavilion (it must've taken some time for the screenwriters to work this out! The comedy, complete with group reaction shots, is very Tsui-ian, as is the mistaken identity gag).

Wu Ma only appears towards the end of *A Chinese Ghost Story 2*: instead, it's Jacky Cheung who takes up the role of the crazy, Taoist demon hunter and companion to Ning Choi-san in the adventure. One of the four pop singers known as the 'Four Golden Kings' (along with Leslie Cheung, Andy Lau and Leon Lai), Cheung is terrific in the comic/ action/ sidekick role of the priest Autumn (he has the same charms and protections against the demons, but he can also burrow under the ground at speed – one of the ninja techniques that Tony Ching is fond of). Cheung gets the tone of these movies spot-on, revelling in the OTT masquerade of it all (*A Chinese Ghost Story 2* is like a Chinese *Abott and Costello* picture – tho' certainly made with more visual panache!). A year later, Cheung was back in a comical role for Tsui Hark, as 'Buck Tooth' So in *Once Upon a Time In China,* and after that in *Wicked City*.

✦

The script of *A Chinese Ghost Story 2* is dense with subplots: the romance between Ning and Windy, the erotic triangle of Ning, Windy and Moon; the romantic rivalry between Windy and Moon; Moon's fondness for Autumn; the Imperial persecution of Windy's father, Lord Fu; the mistaken identity of Ning as Elder Chu; the conflict between the rebels and the government; Official Hu realizing the Imperial court is corrupt; the introduction of the High Priest and his lackeys, and so on.

Multiple identity is another theme in *A Chinese Ghost Story 2* – Ning Choi-san is mistaken for Elder Chu by the rebels (despite his protestations); Windy isn't Nip Shui-sin (but Ning wants her to be); and the High Priest turns out to be a demonic Buddha and then a mad monster.

The narrative in the second act of *A Chinese Ghost Story 2* replays many moments from the first *Ghost* picture (act two is the trickiest part of any commercial movie), but you barely notice it. The characters, motifs and scenarios are switched around, but played for similar sorts of comedy, farce, awkwardness, embarrassment, suspense, etc.

The filmmakers, for instance, milk every ounce of thrills and comedy from a bunch of youths trapped inside a haunted house (the Righteous Villa). They squeeze every cent out of the giant monster and its animatronic head (it spooks Ning Choi-san and Autumn, with a series of gags about the freezing palm charm; it spooks Windy taking a bath; it creeps up on Moon. The monster fights continue outside, with the Imperial official taking it on, as well as Autumn. In some scenes, there's a flying monster hand or just the torso attacking the rebel group).

The filmmakers take great delight in dumping a ton of nasty gunk on their beautiful, leading lady, with Joey Wong's Windy turning into a demon for some fun visual effects battles reminiscent of *The Exorcist* (1973), until she's kissed back into reality by Ning Choi-san, as the lovers spin and spin in the air. This provides both a supernatural scene for Joey Wong, where she's ghost-like as in the first flick, but she's a nasty spectre who breathes out snakes, and our Movie Kiss between the two main stars, a reprise of the first film, as a series of cuts show Windy becoming more'n more human. At the end, the lovers drift gently to the floor and Ning seems blissed-out – only for Autumn to exchange his *chi* – it's OK for a Taoist priest to perform mouth-to-mouth on a guy, isn't it?

One bathing scene isn't enough. So the filmmakers have their other main star (Joey Wong) undressing and taking a bath (to wash off the goop the prop department have dumped on her). And of course the giant monster is still lurking around. And of course there's French sex farce comedy when Ning Choi-san tries to cover Windy's modesty from the rest of the rebel gang (this is a replay of the scene where the Old Dame appeared in Siu-shin's chambers in the first film). Ning goes to great lengths to preserve Windy's virtue. Woven into this is the romantic rivalry between Windy and Moon.

Another ingredient added to *A Chinese Ghost Story 2* were the cannibal outlaws: Ning Choi-san is hapless enough to stop over at their inn and restaurant not once but twice! Cue images of severed hands and toes mixed in the stew, and a dog with a hand in its maw. Yuk! (One can imagine that this part of the script came from Tsui Hark; he had made much of mad cannibals in *We're Going To Eat You*).

Either you buy into the comedy or you don't – the sex comedy stuff, the French farce stuff, the cannibals stuff, the monster creeping around and nearly-but-not-quite grabbing the heroine, and the women drooling over a man stuff. But you have to admire the light-hearted spirit in which this 1990 movie is delivered: this is a film that knows it's a pile of fluff, and revels in it. It's a Friday night, popcorn and candy and yelling at the screen sort of movie. It's the movie equivalent of a theme park ride, a haunted house ride at the fairground (plenty of Western movies are like this, and some, like *Pirates of the Caribbean* and *The Haunted Mansion*, are even based on theme park rides!).

A new character, an Imperial official, Hu (played by veteran actor Waise Lee), thickens the plot of *A Chinese Ghost Story 2*, arriving at the end of act two – by first pursuing our heroes into the haunted Righteous Villa, then switching ideological sides when he sees how brave they are, and, when he encounters the super-villain High Priest, how corrupt the Imperial circle is. Hu is a thematic character, then – not essential to the central plot, but he exposes the corruption of the Imperial government. *A Chinese Ghost Story 2* was made not long after Tiananmen Square. (Hu is part of an Imperial guard escorting Windy's father, Lord Fu, to his execution; his scene is filmed, once again, at the stony cliffs and dirt track in the New Territories. The scene features Hu going up against the Taoist priest Autumn).

The sequence where Hu enters the High Priest's lair in *A Chinese Ghost Story 2* is genuinely imaginative and chilling: it's a palace arrayed like a court of law lit by flickering torches where Imperial ministers have been kidnapped and eviscerated, so that only hollow husks remain. It's a terrific satire on the 'hollow men' who rule the land – the literal emptiness and nothingness of civil servants and governments. They're not even corpses, they're just shells. (Meanwhile, out back, Hu stumbles into the charnel pits where bits of bodies are heaped, some still partially alive. And three of the heroes have been imprisoned inside red cocoons, presumably the first stage of evisceration. Hu sets them free, which leads to the finale).

✦

TONY CHING SIU-TUNG ✦ 246

The finale of *A Chinese Ghost Story II* has to top the first movie of 1987, as sequels often try to do: it becomes a giant monster movie, when the new villain, the chief Buddhist monk and adviser to the Emperor, the High Priest, arrives in town. A formidable opponent, a self-righteous religious figure, who hides behind the paraphernalia of organized religion, the High Priest is played by Lau Shun (a Tsui Hark regular – he was Swordsman Zen in *The Swordsman 2,* the aged Asia in *The Swordsman 3,* and Wong Fei-hung's father in *Once Upon a Time In China 3*, and appeared in numerous movies of this period). Crossdressing in villains in Chinese fantasy cinema is once again evoked, when the High Priest speaks in a high-pitched woman's voice. However, that's only part of it: the High Priest is also an adept at spell-casting, reciting enchantments in Sanskrit to over-power his rivals.

When the villain turns into a giant, golden statue of the Buddha,[5] you know you are wholly within Asian folktale territory – this sort of imagery, with talking statues of gods, simply doesn't appear anywhere in Western cinema. At the climax of a North American action or fantasy movie, no villain would be allowed to turn into Jesus!

In the finale of *A Chinese Ghost Story 2*, the heroes call on the aid of the crazy, old monk Yin Chik-Ma from the first *Ghost* movie: Wu Ma makes a very welcome return as Swordsman Yin, from his bolthole in the Lan Teuk Temple from the first film.[6]

✦

The visuals in the finale of *A Chinese Ghost Story 2* are stupendous – out come the coloured lights, the glowing miniatures and matte paintings, the optically-printed bolts of magic, the smoke and fire practical effects, and actors and stuntmen are flying all over the screen. The camera is often at ground level, hurtling along. The visual effects are wild, with no holds barred: the earth is cracking open, a giant beastie emerges – a centipede![7] – and our heroes take refuge in a magic circle of flying, golden swords. Every possible visual effect and special effect and practical effect is employed, furnishing so many rapidfire gags. There is, as in the first *Ghost* movie, a joyous celebration of the trickery that cinema can conjure up.

For instance, there's a stunning battle against invisible assailants, as Hu the Imperial official duels with the High Priest's henchwomen, who hurtle at him using ninja-ish invisibility (Tony Ching had used invisible warriors before – it's irresistible to a filmmaker who enjoys the trickery of

5 The orange and gold lighting accentuates the symbolic colours of Buddhism.
6 This is one reason why Windy and Ning Choi-san get separated from the others. They're pursed by the wolves from the first film, where the mere mention of the dread name Lan Teuk Temple has the beasts fleeing.
7 Like something out of William Burroughs, a critic remarked.

cinema). The sword fight is a set-piece all of its own, with Hu playing part of it as a one-armed swordsman (a favourite staple of Chinese *wuxia* cinema), when his arm's cut off early on in the fight. There are incredible details in the scene – such as blood spattering out of invisible wounds onto the dirt (but when they're killed, the ninja lose their invisibility, then disappear).

In the same sort of rocky, threatening arena of stones and night that the first *A Chinese Ghost Story* movie used for its finale, *A Chinese Ghost Story 2* has our heroes battling a giant monster. All sorts of inventive beats and twists are concocted to surprise and delight the audience. In one memorable shot, as the monster appears, the ground erupts, forming a wall of broken stones behind our heroes (instead of the usual flames), who're running towards the camera. In another scene, the two Taoist monks, Yin Chik-ha and Autumn, are eaten by the monster (Yin dives in to save Autumn). Trapped in the yucky goop of the monster's belly, Yin reckons that they could separate their spirits from their bodies and flee. It's a suitably magical escape – a *deus ex machina* sort of escape, and a kind of cheat. But within the context of this high-powered, supernatural movie, where life and death are continually being fought over, the filmmakers get away with it. (However, poor Autumn isn't able to return to his body – there's a startling point-of-view shot, with the power and anxiety of a bad dream, when Autumn's semi-transparent spirit flies right over his body lying on the ground, and off into the black sky. Moon hurries after him, but she can't grasp his spirit).

✦

A Chinese Ghost Story II closes with an audience-pleasing happy ending (because Windy isn't a ghost or dead, our couple can be legitimately together). First, there's another elaborate street procession,[8] echoing the one in the first *Ghost* movie, where Ning Choi-san spots Windy parading thru the village. Windy, sporting an elaborate headdress[9] in a covered palanquin,[10] is going (reluctantly) to her arranged marriage (an echo of the finale of the first *Ghost* flick, where Nip Siu-shin was due to wed the Lord of the Black Mountain). Ning, hurrying into the crowd, generously wishes her well (passing his blessing to her via Moon).

Ah, but we can't leave our hero like that, can we?, watching wistfully and mournfully as the heroine is carried away by fate to a marriage she doesn't want. So the filmmakers close the 1990 *A Chinese Ghost Story 2*

---

8 Filmed on the Shaws' backlot set.
9 Joey Wong in one of her finest incarnations. The image of Wong in the headdress was employed in the marketing of the movie.
10 No one uses palanquins more than Tony Ching in cinema. Maybe Ching simply enjoys the image of a palanquin (or maybe that's how he thinks the film director should be treated on set!).

with a big reunion scene, out on the hills, staged on horseback so they can have that cliché of all movie clichés: the heroes riding off into the sunset.[11] Everything about this movie has been designed as a crowd-pleaser – the filmmakers want to entertain the audience more than anything. And they succeed! So *A Chinese Ghost Story 2* duly closes with the lovers re-united (and, please, geeks and crrritics, *don't* remind us that Windy isn't Ning Choi-san's true love, that his beloved is really Nip Siu-shin![12] We know that! And, anyhoo – he's going to be dating a flesh-and-blood woman – and she's played by Joey Wong!).

11 This occurs in several Hong Kong movies of the period.
12 Or that there'll be repercussions from the arranged marriage.

17

A CHINESE GHOST STORY 3

Sin Nui Yau Wan III: Do Do Do

A Chinese Ghost Story 3 (*Qiannü Youhun III Dao Dao Dao*, directed by Tony Ching Siu-tung, 1991) is a visual effects action comedy masterpiece. At a technical level, it is absolutely staggering. Like many Hong Kong movies (even the bad ones!), *A Chinese Ghost Story 3* is perfect fare for a rowdy, Friday night crowd in a cinema in teeming, neon-bright Hong Kong or Macau (its primary audience). *A Chinese Ghost Story 3* makes no pretence at being anything other than a straight-ahead slice of polished, incredibly sophisticated (yet grungey) entertainment. *A Chinese Ghost Story 3* is a winner in every area.

A Chinese Ghost Story 3 is a hugely enjoyable third entry in the *Chinese Ghost Story* series: it's pretty much a re-run of the story of the first movie of 1987, with two Buddhist monks taking shelter in a temple haunted by ghosts. So back come four main characters: the hapless youth, Fong, the gorgeous ghost, Lotus, the crusty, old, Buddhist monk *sifu*, Master, and the chief villain, the Tree Demon, with Jacky Cheung playing Swordmaster Yin.[13]

Many of the cast and crew of *A Chinese Ghost Story 3* had worked on the previous installments in the *Chinese Ghost Story* series (this one appeared a year after the second movie). Tony Ching Siu-tung was back directing (and he was one of the action directors, along with Ma Yuk-shing, Yuen Bun and Cheung Yiu-sing; Bruce Law handled the fire and burn stunts); Tsui Hark produced and co-wrote the script with regular

---

13 Yin makes a short speech about being trained by the older Taoist Master, to connect the two charas – altho', if this movie is meant to take place 100 years later, he would be too old (indeed, Yin says that the Master has died).

collaborator Roy Szeto; Cho King-Man co-produced; exec. producers: Chui Bo-Chu and Roger Lee Yan-Lam; music by James Wong Jim, Chow Gam Wing and Romeo Diaz; edited by Marco Mak Chi-sin; art directed by James Leung; photographed by Tom Lau Moon-Tong; costumes by William Chang, Bruce Yu Ka-On, Bobo Ng Bo-Ling and Chan Bo-Guen; make-up by Chi-Yeung Chan; hair: Chau Siu-Mui and Lee Lin-Dai; and sound by Chow Gam-Wing. Released July 18, 1991. 99 mins.

Joey Wong Jo-yin and Jacky Cheung Hak-yow reprised their roles (Cheung's Swordsman Yin was altered – now he's not a Taoist Master, but a money-hungry treasure seeker, happy to slaughter anybody foolish enough to steal his *gelt*); Lau Siu-Ming was the Tree Demon again; but Leslie Cheung bowed out, to be replaced by Tony Leung Chiu-wai (however, Cheung does appear in the opening prologue of *A Chinese Ghost Story 3*, which replays the climax of the first movie, with its giant tongue – tongues play a key role in *A Chinese Ghost Story 3*). Also appearing were Nina Li-chi (as Butterfly), Tiffany Lau Yuk Ting (as Jade), Cheung Yiu Sing, Hoh Choi Chow, and Lau Shun (as Reverend Bai Yun, Fong's *sifu*).

The tone and attitude and atmosphere of *A Chinese Ghost Story 3* is absolutely spot-on. The cast hit exactly the right note of mock seriousness, playing the adventure straight, but leaving plenty of room for the goofy helplessness of Tony Leung's Fong, the jokey asides of Jacky Chueng's Swordsman Yin, the sweet, yearning melancholy of Joey Wong's Lotus, and some of the craziest, over-the-top performances in Hong Kong cinema – from Lau Siu-Ming as the Tree Demon and Lau Shun as the *sifu* Bai Yun.

Lau Siu-Ming's Tree Demon/ Priestess is a diva of gargantuan dimensions. By comparison with the most out-there performances of actors in the West as derranged bad guys in Western action flicks, Lau is completely excessive. Robert de Niro, Ian McKellen, Mickey Rourke, Joe Pesci, Ben Kingsley, Jeremy Irons *et al* – they are well-known for playing crazy antagonists in action cinema in the West. But, accomplished as they are, and fun to watch as they are, they are utterly eclipsed by the scorchingly high energy of Chinese performers, who start big then get bigger and bigger, where the Peking Opera traditions survive in actors who can turn their own faces into wild masks of horror, terror, ecstatic glee and truly creepy sadism.

And let's not forget Tony Leung Chiu-wai ('Little Tony Leung'), with his bald pate and wide, dark eyes: a remarkable actor (who can do anything), and one of the stalwarts of Hong Kong New Wave cinema, Leung does a fine job of stepping into Leslie Cheung's shoes (a tough act to follow – because Cheung, tho' he makes it look so easy, is a truly formidable talent). Tho' Leung doesn't quite have Cheung's incandescent star quality, Leung hits just the right note of earnestness, goofiness and cowardice; he is acting his socks off. It's a terrific comic performance which gets the balance spot-on between drama and humour (that is, for the comedy to work, *A Chinese Ghost Story 3* has to function first as a story and as a drama, and you have to buy into these characters and the situations). Known for serious roles like the gangster flicks directed by John Woo (*Bullet In the Head*, *Hard-Boiled*, etc), and later on for romantic roles (in the films of Wong Kar-wai and others), it's great to see Leung playing comedy (which he has done more than you'd think).

It's impossible not to enjoy *A Chinese Ghost Story 3* – you'd have to be a really miserable, really depressed and really stick-in-the-mud so-and-so not to like *A Chinese Ghost Story 3*. Seriously. Yes: this movie is going all-out to entertain *you*, the audience, and it succeeds magnificently.

The look of the 1991 *Ghost* movie is sensational, with DP Tom Lau Moon-Tong, production designer James Leung, costume designers Bruce Yu Ka-On, Bobo Ng Bo-Ling, William Chang, and Chan Bo-Guen and all the others (in make-up, practical effects, sound, editing, casting and so on) really coming up with the goods. James Wong Jim, Chow Gam Wing and Romeo Diaz compose a suitably mysterioso score for the ghostly sequences, and jaunty pop cues for the lighter scenes. (The score supports the action at every twist and turn, almost as if the musicians are playing the music live to the picture). The action choreography (by Tony Ching, Yuen Bun, Ma Yuk-shing, Cheung Yiu-sing *et al*) is of course absolutely outstanding (with cable-work creating truly awe-inspiring flying scenes, as fluid and imaginative as in any movie in film history).

Not content with staging a single performer flying on wires – across enormous distances – the stunt team hook up a host of performers on cables (and not only people, but also numerous props, including, in the finale, giant pillars of stone which erupt from the ground). And there's a new development for this film, actors are now flying in curves and circles. There is no wire-work in cinema anywhere that comes near this!

✦

A Chinese Ghost Story 3 is another love story – between a weak, effeminate man and a ravishing female ghost (the staple format of Chinese ghost stories). Turning the two humans caught up in this tale into Buddhist monks accentuates the battle between the two realms of religion and magic on one side and evil and bad karma on the other. Fong and Lotus are thrown into the middle of the battle between Bai Yun and the Tree Demon, between Buddhism and corrupt magic, between doing the right thing and doing evil. (The duels between the monks and the ghosts in *A Chinese Ghost Story 3* allow the filmmakers to indulge in evoking numerous ancient beliefs, superstitions and practices of Chinese culture and Buddhist religion: promoting such folkloric material, even if it's in a completely hokey movie-movie manner, is one of Tsui Hark's passions).[14]

Act one of *A Chinese Ghost Story 3* includes a lesbian love scene – well, a scene that skirts very close to lesbian erotica without delving into Category III (porn) territory. In a scene that might've come out of *Green Snake*, Lotus and Butterfly are first introduced in *A Chinese Ghost Story 3* in a close embrace in their chambers (where all is pieces of floaty, coloured cloth), sharing what seems to be smoke from an opium pipe. It's girls together in a teasing, intimate set-up that's a recurring motif in Tsui Hark cinema (drugs, beautiful girls, sex, and even tattoos are laid out in a voluptuous scene lit and photographed by DP Tom Lau Moon-tong like a Chinese painting. As usual in a Tony Ching film, every single scene has wind machines billowing the hair and costumes).

The lesbian scene leads directly on to the let's-show-how-nasty-the-villains-are sequence, where the Tree Demon presides over a decadent court of ghosts who slay a band of ruffians. The centrepiece is, of all things, a pool (a more extravagant version of the wooden baths of the previous *Chinese Ghost Stories*). Lotus and Butterfly play the sirens that lure the men into their deadly domain, from which there is no escape. Out flicks the Tree Demon's tongue (in a remarkable monster p.o.v. shot, across the surface of the water), and into the gullet of its first victim. (And in a nifty piece of screenwriting, the brigands sneaked into this area in the first place because they caught a glimpse of the golden Buddha that the two monks were carrying in a restaurant; even cleverer, is it's Swordsman Yin who accidentally slices open the cloth hiding the statue).

The lure of gold in *A Chinese Ghost Story 3* brings in once again the issue of money in a Hong Kong picture, that hyper-capitalist city of, as Chinese movies have it, gamblers, gangsters, hookers and hustlers (there are two treasure-seeking groups in *A Chinese Ghost Story 3*).

Yes – this's how Swordsman Yin is introduced in the first reel of *A Chinese Ghost Story 3* (in the opening sequence) – cutting up the thieves who've stolen his money: it's the replay of the sheltering-from-a-storm scene in the first *Ghost* film, where the hapless scholar found himself in

14 The talisman in the 1991 *Ghost* movie is a golden statue of the Buddha (which performs many duties, not least reminding Fong of his spiritual calling as a Buddhist monk). The monks are transporting the precious Buddha statue, and of course the hapless Fong loses it.

the midst of a bitter feud. Comedy is uppermost, tho', as poor Fong has blood sprayed over him repeatedly and – in a classic Tsui Harkian joke – body parts too (and afterwards, he's told to bury the corpses by his *sifu* who, in a great gag, just happens to have a little hoe in his robes!).

✦

Love – and sex... *A Chinese Ghost Story 3* squeezes an entire second act out of Joey Wong's spirit Lotus trying to seduce Tony Leung's monk Fong. That's all it is, for 20 or 30 minutes: a man, a woman... one wants it, one doesn't want it... the movie happily trots out the old narrative chestnuts of a beautiful, willing woman and an unwilling (but handsome) man (that it's two famous and attractive stars of the early Nineties period, Wong and Leung, enhances the sequence no end – Leung was something of a pin-up at the time, too).

And the first act of *Ghost 3* had already delivered that scenario between Lotus and Fong – intercut with scenes of Bai Yun trying to draw out the ghosts using his Buddhist magic (Bai Yun has to be taken away from the scene, so that Lotus can go to work on Fong). Lotus attempts many times to seduce Fong, resulting in all sorts of amazingly dynamic physical acting: this is the polar opposite of a romantic comedy where two people stand and spout clever-clever quips that a team of writers have spent months re-writing. Instead of Western cinema's continual and dogged insistence on dialogue-heavy romantic comedies, and the static blocking of two actors just standing there, the Chinese action approach, steeped in Peking Opera performance styles, is gloriously kinetic and inventive.

In their first encounter, Lotus flutters into the Orchid Temple when Fong foolishly opens the front door, and wafts about in distress, crying about ghosts like a scared child. Joey Wong captures the mock fear and sneaky seduction of Lotus as she dances around Fong, trips, falls, and pulls him on top of her (repeatedly). The Peking Opera approach puts bodies in continual motion, striking amazing poses – all across the floor, and other parts of the set.

This is the Hong Kong film equivalent of a seduction scene in a Hollywood musical – musical cinema (and musical theatre) is really the closest equivalent to something like this, where movement, rhythm, timing, music, lighting, costumes, and practical effects work together to form a dazzling combination that evokes romance, beauty, comedy, and danger.

This is mesmerizing cinema, where each shot is conceived as if starting from scratch, as if each shot stands alone, as if each shot could be The One, as if each shot has the potential to become the Greatest Shot Ever Filmed.

Indeed, this is how Hong Kong cinema films action: instead of filming all of the shots from one side (from one actor's point-of-view), then adjusting everything (lights included), to film from the other side, which is the Western/ Hollywood way, Hong Kong cinema films each shot and each piece of action individually.

But the shots *are* conceived as part of a sequence, with a flow, a rhythm, a timing. Hong Kong action cinema is more compelling than many other forms of action cinema perhaps because it constructs its action sequences in this manner. The camerawork and the editing follow the rhythm and the flow of the movement as it was filmed on the set, rather than a pre-conceived series of storyboards, for example, or sticking to a rigid shot-counter-shot pattern.

So now in the second act of *A Chinese Ghost Story 3* the silly-but-fun device of the extra-long tongue that the villain deployed so memorably in the previous *A Chinese Ghost Story* movies (and seen in the prologue of this movie), becomes a motif in the seduction scene, as Lotus French kisses Fong. And French kisses him again (to get out some snake venom, she claims; snakes are everywhere in this movie. And there's the business of the lost Buddha statue (which is then found to be broken), which also adds to the comedy in act 2).

Really, all we we're watching is a couple of actors goofing around on a lavish temple set (with occasional appearances from a third actor, Lau Shun), but it's amusing, it's entertaining, it's fun. Sure, it's very conventional romance-plus-comedy, and this time not even a fervently radical film critic could link this humorous, romantic sequence to the 1997 Hand-over in Hong Kong! (Tho' that wouldn't stop them trying! There are some critics who see *every* movie made between 1982 and 1997 in Hong Kong as relating in some form or other to the 1997 Hand-over!).

But *A Chinese Ghost Story 3* is very clearly designed mainly as a piece of entertainment in which the local, Cantonese audience can *forget* about all of that, and simply watch a pantomime about ghosts and monks and demons (it's a high-class panto delivered by a team of *very* talented veterans).

A Chinese Ghost Story 3 has an impressive scope and size, with its village sets and hills, fields and forests, its temples and palaces, yet much of the film comprises only three actors: Tony Leung, Joey Wong and Lau Shun. But they are so good, you don't notice for a moment that whole scenes and then whole sections of the film slip by which feature only two actors on a single set (the Orchid Temple at night).

Act two of *A Chinese Ghost Story 3* climaxes, as expected, with a Big Action Sequence: the re-appearance of the Tree Demon, and an absolutely remarkable magical duel between the Tree Demon and Master Bai Yun – the combination of practical effects and optical effects is as inventive as any in fantasy cinema. The imagery of the Buddhist *sifu* balancing on his staff and the Tree Demon conjuring a battery of elemental forces to kill him are incredible – water effects, fire, explosions, etc (the film uses one of Tony Ching's signature images – a wall of water exploding upwards behind a sorcerous figure, also seen in the *Swordsman* series). The feeling for texture and atmosphere is so acute, you can feel the elements of fire and water as they interact with the characters. (No need for movie enhancements like I.M.A.X., or 3-D, or flight simulator platforms, or smell-o-rama, when you've got movie-making this sensuous).

Meanwhile, the more comical and romantic aspects of the battles between humans and ghosts occur in the scenes between Fong and Lotus, as a counterpart of the epic Bai Yun versus Tree Demon scenes: here's Fong hurrying about, torn between helping his Master and feeling sorry for Lotus.

The magical staff (a *khakkhara*, also known as a Zen stick and pewter staff) that Bai Yun carries is exploited inventively here – the monk throws it at Lotus, pinning her painfully to the wall of the Orchid Temple. Bai Yun calls for help from Fong, and Fong, having freed Lotus from the staff, takes him the staff. The act two climax includes numerous bits of intricate, physical business that play out very rapidly. But all of the action – and the comedy – is still fixed firmly to the fundamental characterizations of the four principal players (the two monks and the two spirits).

As Tsui Hark has explained many times, action comes with a story, and a style, and a look – it's not merely action for action's sake. Thus, the wild and over-the-top action sequences in a movie such as *A Chinese Ghost Story 3* are always rooted in the narrative context, in the characterizations, in their relationships, their conflicts, their goals and their motivations.

✦

Many, many elements in *A Chinese Ghost Story 3* are pure Tsui Hark: the scene where money-grubbing Swordsman Yin finds his coins on the ground talking back to him and scooting into a nearby pool to disappear (as charmed by Bai Yun) is pure Tsui (and pure Walt Disney). Animated in stopmotion, the coins talk back to their owner (and they also bow to prove they belong to him). Money is such an important motif in Hong Kong cinema, it's no surprise that Tsui would eventually include animated, talking coins.

Another very Tsui Harkian sequence is the crowded village scene, where everybody it seems is a sword-maker or a sword-seller (including some swords with ridiculous designs, like a convention of fantasy cosplayers and their homemade weaponry). Tsui also loves scenes where whole crowds act as one, in a humorous fashion – doing a double take altogether, for instance.

The rivalry between the two female ghosts (Joey Wong's Lotus and Nina Li Chi's Butterfly) is another Tsui Harkian ingredient in *A Chinese Ghost Story 3*. The twitching of Bai Yun's over-large ears is another Tsui-ism[15] (later, they grow and cover his eyes, when the Tree Demon captures him).

The floppy ears bit of business occurs at the close of the act two finale – really, it's a rather artificial way of delaying the final smackdown between the heroes and the villains: Bai Yun tells his pupil to hurry into town to have the golden Buddha statue fixed (it's needed to defeat the Tree Demon).

✦

So the golden Buddha statue MacGuffin is still doing some narrative work in act three of *A Chinese Ghost Story 3* – Fong heads into town to get it repaired, only to have the blacksmiths and ruffians get the better of him (there was a hint of that when they spurned Bai Yun begging for food[16]). It's here that Fong bumps into Swordsman Yin, which re-introduces Yin into the proceedings, in time for the finale. (Yin saves Bai Yun from the thugs, but for a price. He constantly calculates his fee on his abacus, while knowing that Bai Yun is penniless like him. Yin agrees to help Bai Yun rescue his Master with the promise of remuneration).

In act three of the second *Chinese Ghost Story* sequel, the French romantic farce elements are re-introduced, involving Fong and Lotus with the added complications of greedy Swordsman Yin, and the catty, resentful sister of Lotus, Butterfly (this occurs just before the action section of the finale). The many jokes include the worldly Yin, who doesn't have a problem fooling around with women, having to watch the supposedly chaste monk Fong being kissed into submission by Lotus. It's just not fair! (The humour is enhanced by the casting of pop star Jacky Cheung as Yin – a singer who's used to the adulation of girls).

Two guys, and two girls: the sequence is played like French farce and

15 'Tsui Hark's ability to make something incredible and outlandish out of ordinary facial features such as eyes, ears and tongue must mark him as a unique filmmaker', remarked Stephen Teo (1997, 229).
16 Food is another Tsui-ian motif in *A Chinese Ghost Story 3* – Fong is perpetually hungry. His Master talks about prayers and the spiritual life, but Fong can't exist on words alone.

screwball comedy: very fast, and very silly. Lotus throws herself at Bai Yun, after Butterfly has also burst into the temple to do the same. Swordsman Yin watches in disbelief as not one but two beautiful women throw themselves at Bai Yun's feet (in frustration, he performs a sword dance, this movie's version of the dance of the Taoist Master in the first film. Unusually, *A Chinese Ghost Story 3* doesn't have Jacky Cheung sing).

There's a raid on the Tree Demon's digs by Fong and Swordsman Yin, where they dash in and out rapidly, with the action as swift as a manic kids' cartoon (but with the rescue of Bai Yun put off for the finale). The stunt crew somehow depict *sifu* Bai Yun and Lotus zipping across the ground. Butterfly and Lotus are prominent here, and there's a third sister, Jade (Tiffany Lau Yuk Ting), who unfortunately gets in the way of the bitchy rivalry between Lotus and Butterfly. And the Tree Demon has his arm cut off (by Swordsman Yin) – but it grows back again.

To climax the 1991 *Ghost* installment, and all three *Chinese Ghost Story* movies, Tony Ching Siu-tung, Tsui Hark and the team conjure up a truly remarkable barrage of action sequences which assault the audience like World War Three. As with the previous two *Chinese Ghost Story* flicks, the finale is an enormous battle between the good guys (the two monks and the Swordsman) and the villains (the Tree Demon, plus the Mountain Devil, Butterfly, and their henchmen) – with Lotus as the wild card caught in the middle of the crossfire.

The action sequences in the finale of *A Chinese Ghost Story 3* are simply insane,[17] with nothing in Western cinema coming anywhere near them. By the time of this third movie, the filmmaking team had achieved a sophistication of visual effects cinema which blows everyone else out of the water.

There's so much enjoy in the climax of *A Chinese Ghost Story 3* – how about, for starters, the scene where the heroes fly on a magic carpet (made from the *sifu*'s cloak) in between stone pillars smashing upwards thru the ground? How about the insanely hysterical performance by Lau Siu-Ming as the Tree Demon, battling the heroes while poor Fong is strung up in the air with red ropes?[18] How about the Tree Demon impersonating Lotus at the night festival (so you get two Joey Wong's running in slow motion)? How about the Tree Demon's demise in an extraordinary full-body burn scene? How about the conception of the Mountain Demon as a grimacing head of dirt and dust, and a walking temple with arms? How

17 The finale of *A Chinese Ghost Story 3* employs every trick cinema has ever developed, and invents some of its own, too.
18 And Butterfly trying to seduce him – Fong is fated to have beautiful women throwing themselves at him in *A Chinese Ghost Story 3*.

about Fong being turned by his *sifu* into a man-sized, golden Buddha and flying high above the clouds to greet the sunrise and reflect the spiritual light down into the underworld built by the Mountain Devil, to dissolve the monster in a series of incredible explosions? How about the beautiful, vibrant orange colours and shafts of light to depict the sun bursting into the netherworld?

Tsui Hark inserts his beloved Lion Dancing into *A Chinese Ghost Story 3*, as he did in every historical he produced in this period. In a scene of flaming torches and a boisterous crowd, Lion Dancers perform: only after the movie shifts back to the Orchid Temple at night is it revealed that our heroes have never escaped: they've been caught in an illusion of the Tree Demon.

The welter of visual effects stomp across the finale like the Imperial Army: as soon as the giant tongue of the Tree Demon has been attacked with flying swords and bombs by the heroes, and the Tree Demon burns to death, the second villain erupts from Hell: the Mountain Devil. The sequence is a variation on the finales of both of the previous *Chinese Ghost Story* pictures, this time with a temple coming to life to stalk the heroes, who're fleeing on a magic carpet.

It sounds amazing, and it is: the combination of models, puppeteering, animatronics, and astonishing practical effects (pyrotechnics, smoke, dust, fire) is spellbinding. Whole segments of the sets are puppeteered using wires to create wild images of devastation, of crumbling stone pillars, of billowing dirt from explosions.

Even with the film sped up, the action directors (Ching, Ma, Yuen, and Cheung) conjure up remarkable stuntwork – performers are sent flying into every corner of the sets and the frame; actors slide across the ground at 50 m.p.h.; Lotus grabs Bai Yun and dives into the ground.

The pell-mell approach resembles a quickfire comedy with one gag hot on the heels of the one on the screen.

This movie simply does not acknowledge that something *can't* be done, that conventional physics would not allow the human body to travel that fast, or to bend like that. No one says 'no' to Tony Ching!

Anything seems possible here, as cinema is re-invented in scenes of breathtaking imagination. Often it's the miracle of *editing* that is making it all work: Tony Ching, Tsui Hark and editor Marco Mak Chi-sin possess a feeling for how images cut together as skilful as anyone in the history of cinema or television.

A Chinese Ghost Story 2 (1990), this page and over.

倩女幽魂 II

人間道

A CHINESE
GHOST STORY II

A CHINESE
GHOST
STORY 2

A Chinese Ghost Story 3 (1991),
this page and over.

愛は魔王に勝てるか。

THE *SWORDSMAN* MOVIES

18

THE SWORDSMAN

Siu Ngo Gong Woo

The *Swordsman* movies were adapted from *The Smiling, Proud Wanderer* by Jin Yong (Louis Cha, 1924-2018), which have been used for five or so TV series (and a Shaw Brothers movie of 1978). So the *Swordsman* films are by no means the only interpretations of the novels of Jin Yong, one of the best-known authors of *wuxia* stories. In fact, a TV series is a probably more fitting form for adaptation, because Jin Yong's stories contain a huge cast of characters and numerous events. Those depicted in the *Swordsman* movies are but one small segment (and a loose adaptation at that).

Although Tony Ching directed parts of *The Swordsman* and not the whole thing, it fits to put the entry on *The Swordsman* here with the other two *Swordsman* movies that Ching helmed. The film is usually credited to Raymond Lee (but in fact six directors are known to have worked on it, including the original director, King Hu, and Tsui Hark and Ann Hui).

The Swordsman (Cantonese = *Siu Ngo Gong Woo,* Mandarin = *Xiao Aoi Jianzhu = Laughing and Proud Warrior*), was produced by Tsui Hark, Tommy Law Wai-Tak and Chu Feng Kang for Film Workshop.[1] It was written by six people: Kwan Man-Leung, Daai Foo Ho, Huang Ying, Tai-Mok Lau, Yiu-ming Leung, and Jason Lam Kee To; costumes: Cheung Sai-Ying, Cheung Kam-Kam, Lui Siu-Hung, Shing Fuk-Ying, Edith Cheung Sai-Mei,

---

[1] According to Tsui Hark, the investor backing *The Swordsman* was not convinced about the movie, because it had been done before, and failed. Tsui insisted that he could make it work (LM, 24).

and Bo-Ling Ng; hair by Sam Biu-Hoi and Lee Lin-Dai; A.D.: Kuo-Han Yuan (and 8 other A.D.s); music by Romeo Diaz and James Wong Jim; the DPs were Andy Lam, Lee Tak-Wai, Joe Chan Kwong-Hung, Horace Wong Wing-Hang and Peter Pau; art direction by Leung Wah-sang; make-up by Lau Gai-Sing, Poon Man-Wa and Cheung Bik-Yuk; editing by Marco Mak Chi-sin and David Wu; the action choreographers were: Tony Ching Siu-tung, Lau Chi Ho, Bruce Law, and Yuen Wah. It was released on Apl 5, 1990, and grossed about HK $16 million.[2] 115 mins.

The production apparently wound on for 2 years (LM, 172). It boasts 9 assistant directors, six costume designers, five DPs, etc – and six writers. At around 115 minutes, *The Swordsman* is significantly longer than many Hong Kong action pictures (which're usually 80-90 mins, tho' this length might be not sanctioned by the filmmakers).[3] It won Hong Kong Film Awards for Best Action and Best Song and the Golden Horse Award for Best Film and Best Supporting Actor (Jacky Cheung).

✦

The Swordsman was completed by Tsui Hark after King Hu walked out (after ten days of filming), and other directors (such as Ann Hui, Andrew Kam Yeung-Wa and Raymond Lee) were tried; Tsui co-directed the remainder of the movie with action director Tony Ching Siu-tung. (Nothing remains in the film of Hu's footage, according to Lisa Morton [LM, 172]). *The Swordsman* was credited as being co-directed by Tsui Hark, Raymond Lee, Tony Ching Siu-tung and the two directors who left: King Hu and Ann Hui (Andrew Kam also appears in some credits).

For filmmakers of the Hong Kong New Wave, King Hu was a key figure, a pioneer of the martial arts movie (and of making *wuxia* cinema artistic and poetic as well as visceral and commercial). Hu's swordfighting films were typically set in the Ming Dynasty, 1368-1644 (like this one), featuring swords-men (and womon) and eunuch villains (emissaries of the oppressive Dongchang, the Imperial authorities). Hu was known for treating action as choreography as something lyrical and abstract, and stylized.

By inviting King Hu to work on *The Swordsman,* Tsui Hark and co. were expressing their appreciation for a veteran of the kind of cinema that they loved (and grew up with). However, Hu's health was failing, which didn't make the disagreements between him and the filmmakers easier (Hu died in 1997, aged 66).

✦

2 *The Swordsman* series was parodied in *Royal Tramp* (1992), directed by Wong Jing and Gordon Chan and starring Stephen Chow.
3 It's true that some of the scenes in act 3 of 4 do meander somewhat, with maybe a subplot too many.

Sam Hui Koon-kit (who had worked with Tsui Hark in 1984's OTT *Bond* spoof *Aces Go Places*, and in *Working Class* in 1985), plays the lead role in *The Swordsman*, Linghu Chong, the Hua Mountain student and swordsman.[4] Hui's Linghu is confident and calm, one of the most easy-going figures in movies of the *jiangzhu,* played with a light-hearted charm by Hui. (Jet Li continued with that light touch in the *Swordsman* sequel).

Among the supporting cast in *The Swordsman* were a bunch of Hong Kong regulars (this is a terrific cast), including: Cecilia Yip as Yue Lingshan (a.k.a. 'Skinny Boy') as Linghu Chong's sidekick (another of the many crossdressing charas in Hong Kong cinema, and another of Tsui Hark's cute tomboys); Yuen Wah plays one of his customary nasty bruisers,[5] Zuo Lengshan, a practitioner of 'dark' martial arts (Wah was also one of the action directors); Jacky Cheung Hok-yau is Ouayang Quan, eunuch Gu Jinfu's ambitious, cunning henchman; Sharla Cheung is Ren Yingying, leader of the Sun Moon Sect; Fennie Yuen is Blue Phoenix a.k.a Lan Fenghuang (Ren Yingying's aide); Wu Ma is Liu Zhengfeng, one of the retiring Sun Moon warriors; and the ever-dependable Lau Shun is Gu Jinfu, the eunuch villain from the Eastern branch of the Imperial forces. (*The Swordsman* casts three beautiful actresses to counter-balance the masculinist bias of martial arts movies: Fennie Yuen, Cecilia Yip and Sharla Cheung. Placing two women as leaders of the Sun Moon Sect – Cheung and Yuen – is very much part of Tsui Hark's project of re-instating roles for women in movies. And it's typical of a Tsui-produced *jiangzhu* movie that the sidekick of the hero is a boy played by a girl).

The casting of *The Swordsman* is marvellous, and each of the principals embodies their characters as well as popping out of them – there is always a feeling in Chinese, historical action movies of this kind that it's all a pantomime, that it's pure entertainment, and should be taken as just that – a wild show. Actors aren't allowed to wink at the camera (rightly), but the movie does. The cast play it straight – but also with plenty of Peking Operatic over-acting. They don't need to nod at the audience, because the situations are so outlandish.

The Swordsman is a gorgeous *mix* of elements: comedy, romance, spectacle, music, characterization, history/ mythology, Chinese culture – and of course action and martial arts. *The Swordsman* is also a truly inspired vision of the *jiangzhu*, the martial arts world, which Tsui Hark explored many times (in fact, *The Swordsman* marks the first major entry in evoking the *jiangzhu* which in the following decade of the 1990s became

---

4 It might've been tempting, tho', to play up to Hui's comical persona.
5 Yuen Wah was an actor and martial artist, who doubled for Bruce Lee at Golden Harvest; He was one of the 'seven little fortunes' from *sifu* Yu Jim Yuen's Peking Opera school. Yuen appeared countless times as heavies in Hong Kong movies (such as *Eastern Condors, Kid From Tibet, Dragons Forever* and *Iceman Cometh*).

home-from-home for Tsui and his contemporaries in Hong Kong); and, of course, Tsui had dived into the *jiangzhu* in his very first feature film as director, *The Butterfly Murders*, while Tony Ching had lived in the cinematic *jiangzhu* since the 1960s (working on his father's films at Shaws).

The editing of *The Swordsman* – by Marco Mak Chi-sin and David Wu (regulars in the Tsui Hark Cinematic Circus) – is fiendishly intricate. Tracking the ensemble cast and their subplots with sword-sharp precision, the cutting weaves a story stuffed with incidents and bits of business.

The theme song of *The Swordsman*, 'Chong Hoi Yat Sing Siu', was composed and written by James Wong Jim; Sam Hui performed it (several times – the film fully exploits Hui's pop star status). Like the theme music of *Once Upon a Time in China*, 'Chong Hoi Yat Sing Siu' has a sad, lyrical tone which enhances the atmosphere of nostalgia and history (and you'll be humming it immediately).

✦

The Swordsman helped to create many of the staple scenes of the 'New Wave' of historical action movies in Hong Kong cinema – the *jiangzhu;* the nighttime attack on the inn or palace; the sword fight in the trees (again at night); *ronin* warriors; the gratuitous, nude bathing scene involving a beautiful woman (plus crossdressing comedy); a wild brawl on a boat; inter-clan rivalries; a musical interlude; rebellion against oppressive/ corrupt regimes, etc.

The sequels to *The Swordsman* continued with most of the same elements and characters. Much of the cast was changed for the sequels, however, tho' returnees included Fennie Yuen as Blue Phoenix, and Lau Shun (it's not a Tsui Hark-produced movie unless Lau Shun is in it).

✦

The Swordsman teems with plots and counter-plots. Much juice is elicited, for instance, from disguises: so Ouyang Quan pretends to be Lin Pingzhi, Skinny Boy is a girl, an old man (Feng Qingyang – Han Ying-chiehj) is really a master martial artist, and Gu Jinfu and the Imperial guards are forced to act as Lam's bereaved family.

Clans and communities are a very prominent feature of *The Swordsman* (as in many Chinese, historical movies), and they're pitted against each other: the Mount Hua clan, the Sun Moon Sect, the emissaries of the Imperial Court, etc. Meanwhile, Linghu Chong and the *Sunflower Scroll* are at the centre of the tussles for power. Each group is vying for the upper-hand, imagining that the secret techniques of the *Sunflower Scroll* will give them the advantage. Within the strict hierarchy of each group (where the authority of the leaders or the *sifus* must never be questioned), there are traitors (such as Ouyang Quan). But Linghu Chong, being the hero, is of course good and straight and true (he embodies the element of righteousness that is a primary issue for Tsui Hark).

The MacGuffiin in *The Swordsman* is that old chestnut of Chinese *jiangzhu* stories, the sacred scroll (the *Sunflower Manual* contains martial arts secrets, including telekinesis and the ability to walk thru walls). In the opening scene, it is stolen from the Imperial Palace. The (nighttime, rooftop) theft kickstarts the narrative of *The Swordsman*, with the Imperial Court ordering the return of the scroll to the Imperial Library. (As is customary in Chinese, *wuxia* films, the Imperial Court scenes are placed upfront, to offer some spectacle, to orientate the movie in time and place (it's the Ming Dynasty), and to provide the impetus for part of the narrative – an Imperial order, a move against rebels, a kidnapping, or the theft of something important. But those Imperial Court scenes soon fulfil their dramatic function, and movies tend to shift rapidly to the *jiangzhu*, the martial arts world).

And the *Sunflower Scroll* is a martial arts manual which's confused in the finale for a music manuscript (a telling comment on what is important in life). The M.S. is a scroll called 'Xiao-ao Jianghu', the 'proud and laughing martial arts world' (which's the song that Liu Zhengfeng and Qu Yang sing on the boat).

The pursuit of the thieves thought to possess the *Sunflower Scroll* provides the first part of act one of *The Swordsman*, with Gu Jinfu leading the Eastern forces of the Chinese Empire. Exposition is woven into these scenes but, as the audience in this movie is chiefly a Chinese-speaking one, it contains far less exposition than movies aimed at an international market. We are thus introduced to the villains and the narrative engine that ignites the plot first, before moving on to the heroes.

We first meet the heroes Linghu Chong and Yue Lingshan (a.k.a. 'Skinny Boy') when they visit the den of Lin Zhennan, to deliver messages from the Mount Hua Sect (yes, once again a buddy duo is set up in a Tsui Hark movie, but with a lovely actress playing one of the guys). The tone of *The Swordsman* is set out here, deftly combining comedy and action, with Sam Hui's Linghu Chong played casually and humorously. For instance, to prove who he is, Linghu launches into an elaborate sword dance (the scene also demonstrates that he's an experienced swordsman).[6] (The house is one of those traditional buildings seen in 100s of martial arts movies – a large interior of wood with upper balconies, perfect for staging action all over the place. It could be intercut with the buildings in the

6 Using flames flicked from candles on the sword blade; the dance goes slightly wrong (Linghu Chong invents some of his own moves); later, there are huge explosions when gunpowder is accidentally set off.

Chinese Ghost Story flicks or *Once Upon a Time In China,* or the inn in *Crouching Tiger, Hidden Dragon*). Gu Jinfu and his henchmen soon attack, providing one of the first action sequences in *The Swordsman* (the finale also takes place here).

Zuo Lengshan, acting for Gu Jinfu and co., is a malicious piece of work all-round: in a scene of extraordinary barbarity, his heavies torture Lin Zhennan's wife by tearing out her eyes, then her tongue (the gore, including a bloody eyeball, is typical of Hong Kong cinema, but also seems unnecessary and over-the-top). Lin is nearby, listening to Zuo's taunts, and unable to retaliate because he's injured.[7] All of this takes place in long grass at night where no one can see what's going on. As if Gu Jinfu and his army aren't enough, Zuo and his thugs up the threat even more.

✦

One of the stand-out sequences in *The Swordsman* is a delightful musical interlude that occurs at the start of act two – 'Xiao-ao Jianghu' ('Hero of Heroes' or 'A Laugh At the World'), by James Wong Jim and Tai Lok-man, a song about the 'proud and laughing martial arts world' (the *jiangzhu*). Finding refuge on a boat, Linghu Chong and his sidekick Skinny Boy meet some fighters from the Sun Moon Sect, Liu Zhengfeng (Wu Ma) and Qu Yang (Lam Ching-ying), who are retiring. They sing and play the song 'Xiao-ao Jianghu', which acts as a pop promo within the movie (a not-uncommon practice in 1980s cinema, and songs and pop stars are common in Hong Kong movies). It's moving, too, that Liu and Qu are fatally wounded in the giant action scene that follows, and opt to go out in style: Liu dies, as they play the song of the *jiangzhu* one last time, then Qu sets fire to the boat, and they expire in flames on the sea. (*The Swordsman* is partly concerned with the passing of the *jiangzhu*, in common with many *wuxia* movies in this period – it's a gesture towards nostalgia, it's a swansong for the movies of a generation's youth, nostalgia for the movies that the filmmakers grew up with, nostalgia for a vanished world (that never existed in the first place, but *should* have), it's a pæan to historical as well as mythical China, plus a commentary on the state of modern China. And it's also a passing of the torch from the older generation to the younger generation).

Indeed, music is one of the most direct methods for accessing those historical, mythical, romantic realms, as filmmakers know well (the *ronin* Feng Qingyang tells Linghu Chong that emotions are more powerful than martial arts). The composers of *The Swordsman* (Tsui Hark regulars Romeo Diaz, Tai Lok-man and James Wong Jim) employ many traditional

---

7 By Linghu Chong and co. – as if Linghu unconsciously realizes that Lin Zhennan is not all he seems.

musical forms; and there's a *qin* (stringed instrument) which Linghu carries (and plays). The 'proud and laughing martial arts' song is reprised several times (including in the midst of the action finale, when Linghu sings it again, and when he is recovering from being poisoned).

Linghu Chong encounters another older, wiser figure, in the guise of Feng Qingyang (mid-way thru the movie, in the second half of the second act): as the Imperial heavies close in, a fierce battle ensues (again staged at night). Feng turns out to be a master swordsman, despite his age (at first he seems to be a weak, old man who's only interested in cooking some food): this is one of the outstanding action scenes in *The Swordsman*, definitely directed by Tony Ching Siu-tung, with its miraculous feeling for wire-work and speed and practical effects. Feng defeats one of Gu Jinfu's most vicious henchmen and his crew, with some help from Linghu; the non-stop stunts include the lightning-fast passing of swords from hero to hero, Ching's penchant for airborne swordsmen slicing through dust, and Feng and Linghu working together, culminating in the extreme (and very Chingian) physical gag of a body in flight being sliced in half. (And the sequence offers another master-pupil relationship, with Feng showing Linghu the 'Nine Swords of Dugu'. Feng also tells Linghu that all is not well in the *jiangzhu*, and that Yue Buqun (Lau Siu-ming – the Tree Demon in *A Chinese Ghost Ghost Story*), the leader of the Mount Hua Sect, is also corrupt. In the final fight of *The Swordsman*, Linghu uses the 'Nine Solitary Swords' moves to defeat the crooked leader, Yue Buqun).

✦

In the third act (using a 4-act model), *The Swordsman* travels to the exotic realm of the Sun Moon Sect in Miao: their HQ is an inn[8] in a bamboo forest. This part of *The Swordsman* is very reminiscent of the central section of *New Dragon Gate Inn* (the latter film is almost a remake of *The Swordsman*) – you've got several groups travelling in disguise, numerous cat-and-mouse manœuvres (as each group tries to gain the upper hand), creeping about at night, evocations of erotic desire (including lesbianism), eating and carousing, a powerful female leader, etc.

Each of the *Swordsman* movies comes even more to life when it depicts the Sun Moon Sect – out comes the scarlet[9] costumes and sets, the wonderful headdresses[10] (the costume design by Cheung Sai-Ying, Cheung Kam-Kam, Lui Siu-Hung, Shing Fuk-Ying, Edith Cheung Sai-Mei, and Bo-Ling Ng is outstanding), the use of wood and bamboo, the exaltation of superstition and ritual. One imagines that Tsui Hark and the

---

8 The bamboo inn is exploited to the max.
9 Red is the signature colour of this film.
10 The Miao (a.k.a. Hmong) are known for their elaborate embroideries (for wedding attire); and their jewellery – silverwork, coil necklaces, spiral earrings, and headdresses.

teams could create whole movies around the Sun Moon Clan – a band of warriors led by a beautiful, young woman who oppose corrupt regimes seems to inspire them (Tsui is especially fond of evoking ancient traditions and beliefs). But, like many exotic and unusual communities, they have a greater impact when they're set against regular, everyday folk. (However, there aren't many communities that are 'normal' in the *Swordsman* movies!).

In the Sun Moon Sect sequence, suspicion and distrust play out in the primary plot, while the secondary plots include some romantic comedy, and disguises/ crossdressing; and the poisoning of Linghu Chong. Our heroes arrive, but are treated suspiciously; Ouyang Quan appears in disguise as the dead Lin Pingzhi; and there are tussles for supremacy.

Altho' critics continually deride Hong Kong action movies for what they see as their poor scripts, the characters and their relationships are carefully worked out in *The Swordsman*: for ex, in the Sun Moon Sect section of *The Swordsman*, the antagonism between Ren Yingying and Blue Phoenix (over the leadership of the clan), between Linghu Chong and Yue Buqun (whom he now distrusts), over the secret messages from Lin Zhennan, between Linghu and Blue Phoenix, and many other charas are all evoked clearly.

Historical Chinese movies often squeeze a *lot* of dramatic mileage out of rivalries, loyalties, betrayals and disguises. The issue of loyalty and doing the right thing is vital. *Where* you put your loyalty is absolutely crucial here: are you for the Eastern branch of the Imperial Court or for the Sun Moon Sect? Or, like Ouyang Quan, are you out for yourself?

In the Sun Moon Sect part of *The Swordsman*, the struggle for the superior position politically is played out visually and dramatically in a marvellous series of kinetic scenes, with charas sneaking about, leaping thru open windows, hiding, spying, over-hearing, and occasionally fighting.

The Swordsman happily and nimbly switches genres and moods, moving from deadly serious statements about doing the right thing and opposing corrupt regimes to goofy comedy (Linghu Chong sits on Blue Phoenix and sings), romantic farce (Blue Phoenix seducing Skinny Boy), and mystical healing montages.

In the midst of it all, our hero, Linghu Chong, is poisoned (the filmmakers employ a lengthy three-shot, as poisoned cups of wine are passed back and forth in an elaborate, well-rehearsed dance). But this time, instead of the cup being knocked out of the hero's hand by accident, or something distracting the drinkers, Linghu is poisoned. Luckily, there are experts in Ancient Chinese medicine on hand (thus, Tsui Hark and the filmmakers shoehorn some more traditional, Chinese culture into a movie – altho' scenes of restoring the hero via magical and medical means are a standard trope in Chinese, historical movies).

In *The Swordsman*, Linghu Chong experiences a rough regime of healing via worms – yes, wriggly worms, administered thru pipes (by Blue Phoenix) into the nostril (ugh!). In his fever dream, Linghu thinks back to the Sun Moon Sect Elders he met, and here the footage of the song on the boat and the subsequent battle is recycled in a montage. But the recycling is not wholly shameless padding, because Linghu's visions seem to be apprehended by Ren Yingying, proving Linghu's trustworthiness (two beats before this, Ren was all for dispatching Linghu).

✦

Tsui Hark is fond of creating buddy duos, but subverting them by having the counterpart to the hero (or top-billed star) being played by an actress. The ruse works on several levels: the masculine relationship of the buddy set-up is maintained (they are 'men' in a man's world, or 'men' in public); being men, the characters can interact in the strictly patriarchal society of historical China; there's inevitable erotic attraction/ teasing between the two; and there's crossdressing and disguises (which're eventually uncovered); the crossdressing also provides opportunities for misunder-standings, embarrassments, and farce.

The quasi-lesbian scene in *The Swordsman* is pure Tsui Hark – it combines crossdressing with lesbianism. So, Blue Phoenix is given a lusty characterization (dropped from the later *Swordsman* films): she takes a shine to Yue Lingshan, Linghu Chong's companion (Skinny Boy), who travels as a man. Blue Phoenix flirts with Lingshan (who's drunk), then carries him / her into a side room and is about to have her wicked way with her/ him, only to discover that she's a woman as she rips apart her clothes. It's not the first time (nor the last!) where Tsui teases audiences with some woman-on-woman action.[11]

Further romantic elements in *The Swordsman* include Yue Lingshan's unspoken affection for Linghu Chong (witness her dismay at being ordered to marry Lin Pingzhi), and the erotic, quasi-lesbian undercurrent in the antagonism between Ren Yingying and Blue Phoenix.

One of the issues tackled in *The Swordsman* is the Sins of the Fathers, and the troubled relationship between the older and the younger generation: this is a staple of martial arts movies, and is always featured in Tsui Hark's interpretation of the genre. Thus, both Gu Jinfu and Yue Buqun

11 The comic goofing around, when Linghu Chong sits on Blue Phoenix's head when she's sneaked into his room, is another example of Tsui Hark's brand of erotic but goofy comedy.

are corrupt patriarchs (and are duly punished in the finale). Meanwhile, a good and true patriarch, Liu Zhengfeng (Wu Ma), is killed by the Imperial bruisers. The lust for power is loudly scorned in *The Swordsman*, with the crooked Elders and Ouyang Quan hungering for the *Sunflower Scroll*.

✦

With some great directors of action involved (Lee, Hu, Tsui), plus Tony Ching Siu-tung, Lau Chi Ho and Yuen Wah as action choreographers, *The Swordsman* doesn't disappoint as an action movie. Among the delights in *The Swordsman* are a fierce bust-up on a boat; several nighttime duels in smoky forests; an attack on a house; a brawl in an inn; and duels involving flying snakes and bees. The action is of the swordplay variety – fantastical and exaggerated, with much use of cables, rigs and flying, the manipulation of props, and intensely acrobatic movements out of Peking Opera. The *wuxia* genre is presented here via action with emphasizes energy and magic – there are numerous stunning evocations of high energy, and different forms of energy, in conflict with each other. (Several scenes are Chingian: the nighttime display of special swordsmanship by the hermit Feng Qingyan; the battle on the boat; and the final duel between Linghu and his *sifu* Yue Buqun, which shows Linghu Chong using the sword forms on Yue).

In the boat sequence, most of the vessel is destroyed as our heroes beat off Yuen Wah's Zuo Lengshan and his henchmen. Linghu Chong and Skinny Boy are travelling by sea with the retiring Sun Moon Sect members. Following the lovely song scene, Zuo's boat rams the ship, and an all-out battle ensues. The boat offers plenty of opportunity for stuntmen to go crashing into sails, for masts to topple, and – a Chinese speciality – characters to fly up out of the water. This is a beautiful sequence of flowing movement and inventive stunts, with a poetic use of water and light.

Yuen Wah suffers a nasty (but well-earned) death: attacking the Mount Hua house, he is set upon by Ren Yingying's bees as well as Blue Phoenix's snakes. In a disgusting, nightmarish image,[12] Zuo Lengshan's face and shoulders are crawling with bees (a call-back to *The Butterfly Murders*, perhaps). This occurs after a wonderfully staged fight in amongst the long grass once again, where Blue Phoenix and Ren are pushed to the limit against Zuo (while carrying a comatose Linghu Chong, whom Ren is trying to resuscitate even as she flies thru air, fleeing from Zuo).

As all trails lead back to the Lam house, there's the delightful sight of the Imperial eunuch and his underlings having to don disguises, and pretend to be the grieving family of *sifu* Yue Buqun. The film exploits the

12 I've had nightmares like this with bees! I can't watch this scene again!

reversal of political power as Gu Jinfu is forced to kowtow repeatedly. The tables are turned once more, before the finale, when Yue Buqun is brought to his knees and Gu Jinfu holds court again.

The action in the finale of *The Swordsman* is remarkable for its physical and technical complexity. In the small, enclosed space of the interior of the Lam household, with its upper balconies, the filmmakers stage a series of fierce battles. There's barely any room to swing a sword, let alone fly a stuntman thru the air in that building, but Tony Ching Siu-tung, Lau Chi Ho and Yuen Wah and the team deliver absolutely outstanding choreography.

Prior to the demise of the villains, the MacGuffin of the *Sunflower Manual* scroll is brought into play several times, it's repeatedly confused with the 'proud and laughing martial arts world' music scroll (and Linghu Chong gets to sing the catchy tune once more).

The Imperial eunuch, Gu Jinfu, is set upon by pistols and a rifle (brought by clever Blue Phoenix), plus swords (from Linghu Chong) and finally Ren Yingying adds the last touch, tearing the guy apart with her whip. And Linghu, in the closing duel, brings the over-bearing *sifu* Yue Buqun down a notch or two (including cutting his meridian points), using the 'Nine Swords of Dugu' forms he learnt from Feng Qingyan. Only the intervention of Skinny Boy stops the hero running her father thru with his sword.

The duel is a very Chingian swordplay scene – to portray the deadly *chi* emanating from *sifu* Yue Buqun, the environment is puppeteered – wooden fences split apart, for example, and the ground is sliced with energy lines. Tony Ching's penchant for very extravagant aerial spins and somersaults, complete with flapping clothing, is much in evidence. Ching would later make this kind of highly romantic action choreography famous in the West in the 2002 film *Hero*.

The Swordsman closes with what became one of Tsui Hark signature motifs (which he used many times): the heroes riding off into the sunset on horses under a big sky in the countryside (this time in slo-mo), as if the producers have decided to go for the most clichéd ending they can imagine.

19

THE SWORDSMAN 2

Siu Ngo Kong Woo II Dong Fong Bat Baai

THE PRODUCTION.

Jet Li plus Brigitte Lin plus superstar action director Tony Ching Siu-tung with Tsui Hark as producer and an outrageously over-the-top story combine to produce one of the great fantasy swordplay movies of recent times. It starts at full speed and doesn't let up! The prologue alone contains a horse being sliced in half, flying horses and warriors, decapitation, a swordplay battle in an Imperial palace, and a god-like being in scarlet who declaims from the tops of trees.

The Swordsman 2 is a work of genius. It's a masterpiece of pure popcorn movie fantasy, and can stand beside any of the great action movies in the history of cinema. 'Ecstatic cinema', 'giddily demented', 'eye-popping', and a 'gender-bending, gravity-defying, mystical-surreal fantasy beyond your wildest dreams' (F. Dannen, 339), are some of the critical assessments of *The Swordsman 2*.

The Swordsman 2 (Cantonese: *Siu Ngo Kong Woo II Dong Fong Bat Baai;* Mandarin: *Xiao-ao Jianghu II Dongfang Bubai = Laughing and Proud Warrior: Invincible Asia,* 1992) was directed by Tony Ching Siu-tung, and starred Jet Li, Brigitte Lin, Rosamund Kwan, Michelle Reiss (Lee), Waise Lee, Lau Shun, Chin Kar Lok, Yen Shi Kwan, Candice Yu On-on, and Fennie Yuen (that's one of the best casts in a 1990s Chinese movie). *The Swordsman 2* was a re-thinking of the first *Swordsman* movie, with the major roles being re-cast. (Others in the ensemble included: Kwok Leung

Cheung, Kwok-Ping Choi, Man-Kwong Fung, Choi-Chow Hoh, Kwok-Kit Lam, Yeung-Wah Kam and Chi Yeung Wong).

Tsui Hark was producer, Chi-Wai Cheung and Wai Sum Shia were assoc. producers, Hanson Chan, Elsa Tang Pik-yin and Tsui Hark wrote the script, Tom Lau Moon-tong was DP, Marco Mak Chi-sin was editor, music was by Richard Yuen, action directors were Tony Ching Siu-tung, Yuen Bun, Ma Yukshing, Bruce Law and Cheung Yiu-sing (plus 6 assistants), costumes: Bruce Yu Ka-on, Kwok Mei-Ling, Shiu Ching-Yee, Chan Bo-Guen, Yeung Lin-Mui and William Chang, make-up by Man Yun-Ling and Lai Ka-Pik, hair by Chau Siu-Mui and Wan Yuk-Mui, prod. des.: Yee-Fung Chung and Wah-Sang Leung, sound rec. and ed.: Kam Wing Chow.

It was produced by Film Workshop/ Long Shong Pictures/ Golden Princess. It was a big hit in Canton, with a gross of HK $34.462 million (great business for any Hong Kong movie, and one of Jet Li's biggest hits in China). Category IIB. Released on June 26, 1992. 108 mins.

The Swordsman 2 has everything – all you could desire from characters, a story, action, visuals, music and film stars. And for film critics it delivers a strong political commentary, while cultural theorists can delight in the transgender play.

Jet Li (Li Lanjie) and Brigitte Lin (Lin Ching-hsia) head up the terrific cast of *The Swordsman 2*: both have never been better, and both were at the peak of their powers. With *Once Upon a Time In China* and *The Swordsman 2*, Li established himself as a major force in Chinese cinema (*The Swordsman 2* and *Once Upon a Time In China 2*, another masterpiece, were both released in 1992). Li is at his winsome, charming best[13] in *The Swordsman 2* – yes, and he moves like a dream! He really is one of the most beautiful creatures ever put on film. (Western cinema has many male babes, pin-up stars, and great actors who're charismatic, talented and beautiful – but can they *move* like *that*?!).

JET LI.

Jet Li was born on April 26, 1963 in Beijing, China. (In Cantonese, Li's name is Lei Lin Git; in Mandarin, it's Li Lanjie). Li is short (5' 6"), but can take on anyone in movies. Li won the first national *wushu* competition in China since the Cultural Revolution (aged 9); he was the Chinese Men's All-round National Wushu Champion at the age of twelve. (*Wushu* is a form of martial arts as performance, combining Peking Opera, gymnastics, and colourful costumes, developed during the Cultural Revolution). Li moved to

13 Jet Li is not serious and dour in *The Swordsman 2*, as some critics complain – he plays a drunken warrior in an appealing manner (he's introduced riding on a horse, drinking). Indeed, Li follows how Sam Hui played the character in the first *Swordsman* film.

San Francisco with a Chinese actress (Huang Qiuyan) in 1988; they married (1987-90) and had two daughters. In the U.S.A., Li received his Green Card. Li later married actress Nina Li Chi (they have two daughters).

Jet Li first appeared in some movies about the Temple of Shaolin.[14] His break-out role was playing Wong Fei-hung in the *Once Upon a Time In China* series. Li appeared in several martial arts movies right after the first *Once Upon a Time In China* film, including *Tai Chi Master, New Legend of Shaolin* (about Hung Gar), the *Fong Say-yuk* films, *Last Hero In China*, and *Kung Fu Cult Master* (a.k.a. *Evil Cult*).

With Ching Siu-tung, Jet Li has appeared in the *Swordsman* films, *Hero, The Warlords, The Terracotta Warrior, The Sorcerer and the White Snake,* and *Dr Wai.*

BRIGITTE LIN.

Brigitte Lin is... Brigitte Lin; Lin was born in Sanchong, Taiwan on Nov 3, 1954.[15] (She is Lam Ching Hsia in Cantonese and Lin Qinhxia in Mandarin; she is also known as Venus Lin). Lin appeared in many Taiwanese films (beginning in 1973) before appearing in Hong Kong films such as *Zu: Warriors of the Magic Mountain, All the Wrong Spies, Police Story, Peking Opera Blues,* the *Bride With White Hair* films, the *Royal Tramp* films, *New Dragon Gate Inn,* Wong Kar-wai films such as *Chungking Express* and *Ashes of Time,* and the *Swordsman* cycle.

Brigitte Lin is one of the most remarkable of all recent Asian stars. She 'must certainly be one of the most fearless performers in the world' (Lisa Morton, 101). Lin, tho' straight, is known for playing lesbian and crossdressing women in films such as *All the Wrong Spies* (a lesbian disguising herself as a guy), *Fantasy Mission Force* (she shoots the clothes off a tied-up woman), *The Swordsman 3* (she's a lesbian, transsexual superhero), *New Dragon Gate Inn* (she steals another woman's clothes for herself), *Peking Opera Blues* (she wears men's military uniforms), *Boys Are Easy* (she's a lesbian cop), *Ashes of Time* (she plays both a brother and a sister), *Eagle Shooting Heroes* (she's a butch princess), and *Fire Dragon* (she's a masked male warrior).

Brigitte Lin's crossdressing or trans-gender character in the *Swordsman* movies (as Dongfang Bubai = Asia the Invincible) draws on the Peking Opera tradition (where actors can be both warriors and princesses. Indeed, the Tsui Hark movie *Peking Opera Blues* explores issues of gender[16] at length).

---

14 Li didn't make much money from his Shaolin pictures (he was paid a State subsidy).
15 Some sources say 1957.
16 Peking Opera had a huge impact on the young Tsui Hark – including the play with gender.

Brigitte Lin, according to Bey Logan, was one of the few bankable female stars in Asia: 'basically, all the ageless Ms Lin has to do is wave her arms and smile enigmatically and local audiences will pay to watch' (166).

Tsui Hark has tried to entice Brigitte Lin back to acting – for the remake of *Zu: Warriors of the Magic Mountain*, for instance, and to play the Empress Wu in *Detective Dee and the Mystery of the Phantom Flame*. Lin retired from acting in 1994, when she married businessman Michael Ying and had children.

Brigitte Lin delivers a career high with her powerful and unforgettable turn as a human-becoming-a-god in *The Swordsman 2*, Asia the Invincible. In a cinema jammed with truly insane villains/ monsters/ crime lords and all-round psychos, Lin manages to fashion a transgendered character all of her own in the world of Hong Kong movie-making. Of course, let's not forget that the role of Asia/ Dawn was actually created by the writers and the filmmakers (plus the costume designers, the hairdressers and the make-up artists. The film won the Hong Kong Film Award for Best Costumes and Make-up). But, as directors and producers and writers know all too well, they can only go *so far* in putting a character together: because, ultimately, an actor needs to embody that character on screen. And Lin achieves that magnificently.[17]

Tsui Hark said he had the idea for the character of Asia the Invincible when he was filming *Zu: Warriors of the Magic Mountain* – it was a chara tailor-made for his friend Brigitte Lin[18] (LM, 90). The character came out of Jin Yong's book, but was considerably expanded from the ten pages in the novel. Tsui told Lin not to read the book, but to read the script; he also wanted to dub her voice; Lin agreed. (However, as Tsui recalled, 'virtually everyone, including the author (Louis Cha) was vehementaly against' casting LIn).

After *The Swordsman 2*, the character of Dongfong Bat Baai became a popular gag in movies – and the next *Swordsman* movie acknowledged the popularity of the character, by building the entire plot around him/ her.

It's a wonderful fantasy of Imperial, political oppression – and if you're going to be oppressed, at least Asia the Invincible is charismatic and beautiful (if also insane and brutal). Lin's Asia makes a change, too, from the usual, Imperial tyrants in Chinese, historical movies, who tend to be twisted, eunuchized sickos.

The Swordsman 2 also conjures kick-ass roles for the other women in

17 Tsui Hark said he didn't include Asia the Invincible in the first *Swordsman* movie, because her character would've upset the balance (LM, 90).
18 Brigitte Lin as Asia may not look masculine, but her presence, her attitude and the expression of her will persuade us to accept her as male.

the cast: the lovely Rosamund Kwan, as Ren Yingying, leader of the Miaos (taking over from Sharla Cheung in the first film), gets to wield whips and daggers with an impressive confidence (and she rips assailants to shreds, too!). Michelle Reiss/ Lee is cute, naïve, playful and charming as Yue Lingshan (Kiddo), the hero's sidekick (replacing Cecilia Yip_. She's the familiar tomboy woman in Chinese cinema (and a recurring motif in Tsui Hark's films), dressing like a man, and joining the Wau Mountain Sect as one of the boys. The character of Blue Phoenix (Lan Fenghuang), played by Fennie Yuen again, is intriguing: another tomboy, who looks up to her chief, Ren Yingying (Kwan), with hints of distant, unrequited lesbian desire (tho' Blue Phoenix subsumes her emotions into the goals of her group, the Miaos).

The rest of the supporting cast of *The Swordsman 2* is very fine: Candice Yu On-on is suitably attractive and tender as Asia the Invincible's concubine Snow (a.k.a. Cici[19]), adding a running commentary on the transformation of Asia from male to female (and finding Asia becoming more diva-like and difficult as the magic of the sacred scroll takes hold). Among the guys, Lau Shun, one of the great character actors of this period of Chinese cinema (who seems to have appeared in everything, and was certainly a favourite of Tsui Hark's), is superb (as always) as swordsman Xiang Wentian (a.k.a. Zen), part of the Sun Moon Sect. Yen Shi-kwan plays the imprisoned former chief of the Miaos, Ren Woxing (a.k.a. Master Wu), with a cackling intensity. Waise Lee, another actor who is everywhere in Chinese cinema, was impressive as the *ronin* leader Fubu Qianjun (a.k.a. Hattori), who aligns himself with Dongfang Bubai. Cheung Kwok-leung was Eunuch Hong (whose fate is to be another of Asia's victims – decapitated), and Chin Kar-lok was another mad cackler, as Yuanfei Riyue (a.k.a. Saru), Hattori's henchman.

THE CRITICS.

The Swordsman 2 has everything going for it, *and then some*. The action is completely spell-binding, with the 39 year-old Tony Ching Siu-tung, the king of wire-work and flying actors and stunt people everywhere, at the top of his game.[20] Once again, one is struck by the feeling of total freedom that Ching's films as director or action choreographer possess. The sheer beauty and grace (and speed) of the movement thru the frame is gorgeous to contemplate. *The Swordsman 2* is one of Ching's finest outings – as the fantastical and exotic elements are allowed to run riot. Ching explained the approach:

19 The name of one of the only two Empresses of China.
20 'The physical effects are genuinely amazing', Lisa Morton said (LM, 88).

We tried something new in every action scene, like Brigitte Lin's *zhang feng* [palm power]. In other films *zhang feng* causes only an explosion, but I tried disintegrating an entire person.

Barry Long on *The Swordsman 2* noted:

Bordering on expressionism, this contains all of the classic elements of a Tsui Hark Film Workshop production – crisp action choreography, an ensemble of A-list performers, a visual flair this is always eye-popping, and plenty of gender confusion.[21]

Lisa Morton adds:
one of the most giddily demented films ever made... This is gonzo filmmaking, with a complexity of vision and a surety of skill that are continually jaw-dropping. (LM, 87)

Stokes and Hoover describe *The Swordsman 2* thus:

Ching plays it over the top with Dionysian abandon, creating 'ecstatic cinema' captured by multiple cameras dramatically careening at all angles and sundry color schemes of permeating blues, reds, and browns. The wire stunts come fast and furious... (104)

THE SCRIPT.

Check out the script of *The Swordsman 2*. So often critics complain about the quality of the scripts in Hong Kong cinema, insisting that they are patchy, don't make sense, and are ignored in favour of action and spectacle. Sure, many times, yes (but you try writing scripts for five or more movies per year!).

Actually, the screenplay for *The Swordsman 2* (by Hanson Chan, Tang Pik-yin and Tsui Hark) is as neatly worked-out as any good film script: the structure is rock-solid, heading from an initial crisis (Asia the Invincible taking over the Sun Moon Sect), through the reactions of the Mountain Wau Sect to the problem, up to the bloodshed and multiple deaths in the finale, as everybody converges on Asia in her/ his Imperial stronghold. Like a tragic play, the narrative in *The Swordsman 2* has an unstoppable inevitability about it – a continual descent into turmoil, you might say. The writers make sure, for instance, that the opponents and obstacles are piled up high for our heroes: not only the Imperial court, and Asia the Invincible, and the Sun Moon Sect, and Japanese ninja/ *ronin,* but even one of their own – Master Wu, Ren Woxing (who, upon his release from prison, turns out to be something of a psychopath,[22] and once Asia is

21 Quoted in F. Dannen, 36.
22 In the jail, Master Wu reveals his nasty side when he kills five guards – and Linghu Chong remarks that it's not necessary.

(apparently) vanquished, Wu embarks on a cruel programme of elimination).

Also, the script for *The Swordsman 2* is tightly-plotted and mixes up the tempo: it's not all slambang action; not only are there character-led scenes, there are musical and nostalgic interludes, humorous scenes, and a series of seduction/ flirtation scenes. There are moments, for example, when the characters stop and reflect on what it all means, and on the passing of time. (Tsui Hark said he put all of the characters onto a white board, to work out with the production team what to do with them [LM, 90]). 'What makes *Swordsman II* a great film (instead of merely an interesting curiosity) is that the emotions are as intense as the action (and the warped morality)', remarked Lisa Morton (LM, 89).

The Swordsman 2, set in 1572, continues to use the same narrative ingredients of the first *Swordsman* movie of 1990, but the new cast and the new approach makes it feel like a different story and different characters (there are rival clans, Imperial heavies, a magical scroll, a wandering warrior and his sidekick, etc). There's no doubt that Jet Li blossomed into a huge star at this time, filling the role of the drifting, drinking warrior with a wonderful, self-deprecating humour, as well as of course the agility and grace of a dancer. As Linghu Chong, Jet Li (taking over the role from Sam Hui in the first film) is a delight from his introduction onwards (swigging at a bottle on a horse, accompanied by his sidekick, Kiddo, played with sweet charm by Michelle Reiss/ Lee. So, yes, Li is playing another version of the drunken swordsman, a staple of many a *kung fu* flick. And that wine flask crops up repeatedly – and is also part of the flirtation scene between Linghu and Asia the Invincible – played out, with typical eccentricity, with both characters waist-deep in the sea).

The Swordsman 2 is also a companion to the first *Once Upon a Time In China* movie, released in 1991: there's a similar romance, for instance, between Jet Li and Rosamund Kwan (there no doubting that, in this period, Li and Kwan made a gorgeous couple – and both exude a fresh-faced, rosy-cheeked innocence that only exists in movies. If people were really like this, Earth would be Heaven!).[23]

The Swordsman 2 has time for character scenes, for love scenes, for humorous scenes, and for musical scenes: there are several musical montages:[24] music is a key component in this 1992 movie (Linghu Chong plays a *qin*, to charm Kiddo),[25] the Wau Mountain sect sing the 'Hero of Heroes' song repeatedly round the fire, and music provides the

---

23 And yet Earth *is* Heaven – we just don't realize it.
24 The Wong Jim song is 'Jek Gei Gam Woo Sin'.
25 He sings a James Wong Jim song, 'Jek Gei Gam Woo Siu'.

springboard for nostalgic and poetic interludes.[26] There's even a *Count of Monte Cristo* prison sequence, when Linghu's captured by Asia the Invincible's mob, and discovers that Master Wu is chained up in the cell opposite his (with an inventive use of rats to carry messages between the cells).

STYLE AND LOOK.

Technically, *The Swordsman 2* boasts an all-round cinematic brilliance, some lavish and intricate costumes, a battery of visual and practical effects, and incredible cinematography. This is a very, very beautiful film. The lighting is truly magical, with firelight, flaming torches, moonlight, stormlight, smoke-filled nights,[27] candles and natural light deployed with absolute mastery and lyricism. The textures and atmospheres are beyond even the celebrated Hong Kong films. *The Swordsman 2* is I think one of the greatest movies to come out of Hong Kong, and certainly one of the finest movies anywhere for lighting and photography.

Look at the use of locations in the New Territories, for instance. Even tho' fans of Hong Kong cinema will have seen some of these locations before (many times, some of us! – that same beach, that same piece of cliff and rocks, that same forest, etc), DP Tom Lau Moon-tong lends them a delightfully heightened, lush look, as if China were being re-invented all over again. The ocean, forests, mountain roads, roadside inns, and Imperial palaces – *The Swordsman 2* creates a magical dream of a China that never existed (but *should* have existed!).

The extensive night shoots out-of-doors enhance the 1992 movie with atmospheric scenes lit by burning torches and campfires. You get the impression that if the electrical power was suddenly cut for the lighting rigs, the cinematographers and the sparks would find a way of lighting the entire movie using wood fires, candles and oil-fuelled torches.

The Swordsman 2 is also a giant visual effects movie, in the Hong Kong New Wave tradition of never letting the limitations of the budget hold you back. Smoke billows thru every scene (indoor or outdoor), and the air is full of leaves, fire, kicked sand, flying snakes, branches, logs, and swords. Wind machines, rain machines, smoke machines, full-body burns, explosions, pyrotechnics, optical super-impositions, special make-up, models, animation, puppetry, and of course lots of wire-work – is there a

---

26 Linghu Chong, with his irrepressible charisma, leads the singing of the theme song ('Xiao Hongchen') of the movie in act one, at the Mountain Wau Sect's hide-out in an inn; *The Swordsman 2* seamlessly segues into the Sun Moon Sect also singing the song, as the musicians sway, while Ren waits for Linghu's return. That's clever screenwriting.
27 By this time, Hong Kong camera and lighting crews had enough light and electrical power to really make outdoor night scenes work.

visual effect that *The Swordsman 2 doesn't* use? Not really – and yet all of the effects are deployed in the service of the story and the characters. Or put it like this: *The Swordsman 2* is such a great visual effects movie because the script is solid. And most of the effects occur in front of the camera. (Again, altho' Tsui Hark is known as a master of visual effects, Tony Ching Siu-tung employs them just as brilliantly).

The Swordsman 2 is edited by Tsui Hark's regular editor, Marco Mak Chi-sin, a genius editor if ever there was one: one of the chief reasons for this movie being a masterpiece is the brilliance of the editing (which's true of many classics). Contrasts are made by cutting on visual rhymes (from one set of characters sitting around a camp fire at night to another, for example, or by cutting from one group singing a song to another). Mak doesn't simply join one scene to another: he conjures up several incredible montages – and not only poetic montages over music, but also parallel action. The most melodramatic slice of parallel action occurs when the hero Linghu Chong is making love with Snow (Candice Yu – thinking she's Asia the Invincible), while the *real* Asia is out and about wasting all of his cohorts! Wow!

How do you portray a god or demi-god on screen? The solution in *The Swordsman 2* is inventive, to say the least. Verticality and height is emphasized – Asia the Invincible stands on top of trees,[28] or in their branches,[29] as if s/he is nature itself. When s/he talks, her voice echoes around the landscape everywhere, as if the Earth is speaking.[30] Characters are rushing upwards into the sky or the branches of a tree, or diving downwards following their swords onto an opponent, or leaping into the ground. And a vast battery of practical effects are deployed to dramatize the powers that the god-like Asia possesses.[31]

ASIA THE INVINCIBLE.

In *The Swordsman 2*, Dongfang Bubai, Asia the Invincible (sometimes called Dawn), is using the sacred scroll to achieve great power. The cost? His masculinity, his male identity – or, as Master Wu chortles, his dick – he has to castrate himself (when Wu reads the sacred scroll, he roars with laughter). There's more: the characterization of Asia the Invincible not only uses the cliché of eunuchs, he is transforming into a woman (the movie tracks the change bit by bit, so that, in the finale of *The Swordsman 2*, Asia is making himself/ herself up as a woman in front of a mirror, and

28 Meanwhile, Ren Yingying and Master Wu also spend time on the roof of the inn.
29 In one amazing shot, Brigitte Lin stands in the branches of a huge tree, as Dawn converses with Master Wu in the distance.
30 But Asia doesn't move her mouth in her first encounter with Linghu.
31 Using wind machines, smoke machines, special make-up, puppetry, models, optical printing, and of course wires.

his/ her voice changes (in most of the movie Asia seems to be dubbed by a male actor; halfway thru, his voice becomes hoarser, and when the change is nearly complete, it seems to be Brigitte Lin's voice). The 1992 film plays with how people perceive leaders and political power — Asia's followers notice that his/ her voice has altered, but they still follow the commands).

The Swordsman 2 is a movie where a flirting scene between the two stars is played waist-deep in water off a sandy beach in the late afternoon. A mysterious scene, with the threat of antagonism (and violence) being put aside momentarily when Asia the Invincible finds him/ herself being instantly intrigued by this bold trespasser on his/ her realm. A scene where the anti-hero alters the weather and kills birds[32] out of the sky with his/ her new-found magical powers. A scene where the hero, in his drunken, youthful energy, spins in the air for sheer joy, flying out of the water.[33] Remarkable — it's like no other flirtation scene in cinema (especially when we know that Asia the Invincible is a demi-god, and is transforming from a man to a woman. In this scene, s/he seems to reveal herself/ himself as an attractive heterosexual prospect to Linghu Chong). And of course, the scene is performed by two of the loveliest stars in Hong Kong cinema, Brigitte Lin and Jet Li (both of whom have blurred the categories of gender, and have also played gender-bending roles). So that if the issue of homoeroticism is raised by the ruse of Asia the Invincible finding Linghu attractive, it is offset by having Asia played by a woman. So the film producers cover all bases (which they always prefer to do!).

Most of the love scenes btn Linghu Chong and Dawn the Invincible are played with Dawn staying mute, so his/ her voice doesn't give him/ herself away (it's a wry commentary on the relation between power and communication, on identity and expression, and also on gender roles — how Dawn acts the coquettish lover when s/he is still partly a man, how s/he laughs exaggeratedly, like Harpo Marx,[34] at Linghu's jokes). When Asia finally speaks to Linghu, in his/ her womanly guise, the first thing s/he says is Linghu's name.

The gender-bending in The Swordsman 2 (which continued in the sequel of 1993, of course), fascinated Western critics. Of The Swordsman 2, Raymond Murray commented in Images In the Dark: 'the film's ultimate plot twist involves Jet spending the night in Brigette's bed, before realizing it means he's had sex with a eunuchized man!' (373). And yet, of course, he doesn't — we see Linghu Chong in a clinch with Snow (a.k.a. Cici),

32 And notice how Linghu Chong and his Mountain Wau chums don't waste those dead birds! If they fell on many places around the world, they'd be cooked immediately! And the lads do just that.
33 The phallic aspects of Linghu's delight are obvious.
34 Brigitte Lin doing Harpo Marx?! Why not?!

Dawn's lover (tho' they haven't made love for 6 months, according to Snow – that is, when Asia was still a guy). Linghu Chong is not sure – he demands that Asia tell him the truth in the finale, but s/he remains, of course, a mystery.

Men meant to be men but played by women, and vice versa, and men pretending to be women, and vice versa, and the voices of men or women being dubbed by their opposite, are staples of Chinese cinema (also drawing on the theatrical tradition of all-male troupes), but seem to titillate Western film critics. Well, there *is* a tradition in the West of men playing women's roles, which Western critics keep forgetting (the history of theatre going back to Ancient Greece, for example, where everybody, male or female, on stage was played by a guy). But in North American and Western cinema, characters that're meant to be men are almost always played by men (and vice versa). But in Chinese cinema (and Japanese cinema), having women play guys, but not in a disguise or as a gender switch, is a convention.

With the *Swordsmen* movies, the fact that Brigitte Lin was doing the gender-bending added immensely to the tease for Western film critics – because Lin is a fantastically attractive woman (and also already possesses a masculine/ tomboy appeal even before she steps into men's clothes). And, in portraying three other women in strong, kick-ass roles – Michelle Reiss/ Lee, Fennie Yuen and Rosamund Kwan, *The Swordsman 2* was adding to the gender reversals (a running gag, for instance, has the boys in the Mountain Wau Sect joking about Kiddo being a woman).

◆

In act two of *The Swordsman 2*, there are seduction scenes between the hero and the heroine who's still partly the anti-hero. Linghu Chong opts to investigate Asia the Invincible's quarters (along with Swordsman Zen). This is one of several mid-film action sequences: Linghu doesn't simply sneak into Asia's palace, or knock on the front door: this is a flamboyant section of *The Swordsman 2*, involving much flitting about at night on rooftops, hanging from rafters, battling guards who erupt from underneath the ground (a classic Chingian motif), and a complex duel between Linghu and Asia the Indivisible in his/ her chambers. The editing is as nimble and swift as one of Asia's flicked needles or pebbles, and the choreography is some of the finest in a Tony Ching Siu-tung movie (notice how both characters are moving very close to the floor, never more than waist high).

To illustrate just how venal Asia the Invincible could be, Chimp (Chin Ka-lok) had already been cornered and executed earlier: Asia controls his body with a well-aimed needle at a pressure point. In a grotesque moment (which also doesn't make sense), the shape of Chimp's body is imprinted on the wall of Asia's chambers in blood (and Chimp collapses on the ground soaked in blood and very dead).

Butterflies or moths fluttering inside a paper lamp (likely a Tsui Hark addition) are one of myriad details in this sequence, and in the follow-up seduction (of course, the insect is nailed by a flying needle). Yes, those flying needles do a lot of work in *The Swordsman 2*. How wonderful is Chinese cinema in being able to turn something so domestic and 'feminine' (and *small*) – embroidery and needlepoint – into fearsome weaponry which can control the victim's pressure points. (The flying needles are reprised several times in *The Swordsman 2* – during the Linghu Chong and Asia the Insatiable seduction scenes, Linghu gets entangled in the threads,[35] a terrific *femme fatale*-as-spider motif; and in the finale, Master Wu is ensnared by a battery of needles which Asia unleashes in her/ his fury.)

And yet this elaborate scene, which displays the bodies of Brigitte Lin and Jet Li in an inventive, very graceful and tangled choreography, is only one of many packed into this part of *The Swordsman 2*, which also includes a scene of Swordsman Zen versus Hattori and his guards, Linghu Chong and his cohorts in disguise as gypsies, and Linghu carrying Asia the Invisible away from the palace, to drink with his buddies round a fire. And in this frenetically-paced movie, there is a moment where Linghu speaks longingly of a time outside of war and politics, a time when he can just drink (these anti-war, anti-oppression interludes are a recurring motif in Tsui Hark's cinema).

(This sequence also contains one of the signature romantic motifs in *wuxia* pictures of this era: the hero and the heroine flying side by side through the tops of trees, accompanied by a lush music cue – moments that become iconic, and are tailor-made for the trailers).

WOMEN IN ACTION.

The Swordsman 2 is full of women, too: there are not one, not two, not three, but four prominent female roles in *The Swordsman 2*. The clever script gives them all things to do,[36] plus goals and motivations, and none of them are simply 'girlfriend of the hero', or 'stay at home mom', or 'girl next door'. *The Swordsman 2* is a movie which foregrounds women in action – as only Hong Kong action cinema can! Each actress has her own

---

35 And there are playful jokes – like when Linghu tears the embroidery, so there are two dragons.
36 Presumably Tsui Hark, as co-writer, had some say in bumping up the roles of the women in *The Swordsman 2*. Because it doesn't really need five women – it could get by, as many action movies do, with one or two.

scene (actually several scenes) in which to shine: Rosamund Kwan[37] explodes flying warriors with her whip, Michelle Reiss takes on numerous swordsmen, spinning like a top, Fennie Yuen is an incredible snake-handler and martial artist,[38] and Brigitte Lin is, well, simply astounding as the demi-god Asia the Invincible.

Ah, how happy for Jet Li! – because each of the women in *The Swordsman 2* is in love or half in love with Linghu Chong. Thus, *The Swordsman 2* has not one romantic subplot, but several (Linghu has four admirers – a harem). And the 1992 film carefully tracks each of the women's feelings for Linghu – look at how the numerous looks and quips are integrated into the scenes (yet again negating the common view among critics that the scripts and dramas of Hong Kong movies are not carefully worked out). How, for ex, Kiddo looks at Linghu hugging Ren Yingying enviously, and how Blue Phoenix notices that (Fennie Yuen is great at sly smirks). The barely-suppressed jealousy is a delight to see in characters such as Ren (Kwan) and Kiddo (Reiss) as they squabble in the background over Linghu. (Kiddo, for instance, is keen to primp up herself to attract Linghu – the film includes humorous scenes where Kiddo's new hairstyle[39] causes surprise and pratfalls, and when her make-up is switched with ingredients for the soup. Kiddo's scene at the mirror depicts another gender reversal: Kiddo has been dressed as a man, and here feminizes herself with the aid of make-up and a new hairstyle. The comedy thus plays into the central theme of gender confusion).

Indeed, the love/ romance elements are no mere subplot/s in *The Swordsman 2*, but bear upon the main plot of clan/ political rivalry many times. Dawn the Invincible's feelings for Linghu Chong, for instance, prevent her/ him from slaying Linghu's countrymen (well, for a moment, at least!).

Jet Li and his women! – because there's another woman for Li, when Asia the Invincible coerces her lover Snow to seduce Linghu Chong (thus neatly circumventing the notion of the (apparently) straight hero of an action movie having sex with a man who's castrated himself and is transforming via magic into a woman.[40] But when that 'man'/ 'woman' is played by the incandescent Brigitte Lin, what's the problem?!).

Even more remarkable, in a movie stuffed with remarkable sequences, while Linghu Chong is taking the lovely Snow at Asia the

37 It's great to see Rosamund Kwan's demure Aunt Yee from *Once Upon a Time In China* as an action heroine. And she's given a whip! In one scene, she's pulling along a swordsman with her whip snagged on his foot, while he holds himself up with his sword, which sparks as it's dragged thru the dirt.
38 'One of the most non-traditional martial arts films ever made', opined Lisa Morton (LM 87).
39 The buns on the side of the head are a classic, Chinese hair-do, but also might be a *Star Wars* joke.
40 But why does castration equate with becoming a woman?!

Invincible's place, his cohorts are embroiled in to-the-death battles with Asia and his/ her crew. Yes, the action hero is having sex while everyone is getting slaughtered left, right and centre! (Thus, when the lights go out in Asia's chambers, and the switch of Asia for Snow occurs, it's not played for farce. It's an erotic scene, but played straight, because editor Marco Mak intercuts it with Asia demolishing Linghu's colleagues. Another detail in this sequence has Asia sensing what Snow is feeling, and perhaps regretting it).

ACTION SCENES.

It's pure pleasure all the way in *The Swordsman 2*: among the many delights are the action scenes. First up, in the prologue, there's a sword battle and escape in an Imperial palace, and a battle between Linghu Chong and Kiddo on a mountain trail with Asia the Invincible. The Japanese ninja-style attack on the inn is the highlight of act one of *The Swordsman 2* – it boasts a sophistication and invention with wire-work and movement beyond even 99% of Hong Kong filmmakers. Scenes where the warriors spin flying blades and then hop on them to soar into the building are simply astonishing. (Nothing in Western cinema has ever come close – right up to today).

There are many points in this 1992 Hong Kong movie which seem miraculous – as if we are witnessing the Birth of Cinema all over again. To achieve that (or even attempt it) is absolutely amazing. And this occurs many times in Hong Kong cinema. (This is not a pompous or pretentious statement: it *feels* like this is the Birth of Film because the filmmakers take such delight in their work; they are artists in their child-like mode, where making art has a significant and very appealing sense of *play*).

But then our heroes fight back with – what? – *snakes*. And that means snakes, Chinese-style! Draped all over the actors, whizzed on wires, and sliced to pieces by flying swords (in a huge cascade of snakes, in slo-mo). Blue Phoenix shines in this part of *The Swordsman 2* (check out the *physical* acting here, the rapid changes of pose as Blue Phoenix trills on her high-pitched whistle to call up the serpents. Tony Ching has a brilliant feeling for bodies in movement, and how the camera can frame and follow that movement). The Japanese *shinobi* respond with scorpions – so it's scorpions vs. snakes. And Linghu Chong later takes up a scorpion and puts it in his flask of wine, to enhance the flavour – this is one of the numerous comical touches woven into the slambang action sequences in *The Swordsman 2*).

The exploitation of space in *The Swordsman 2* is also exceptional –

the Chinese filmmakers use every inch of the inn, upper and lower levels, including having characters (like Kiddo) crash thru the floor, hurtle thru windows, fall from upper to lower levels, and fly up to the roof. [41] The attack on the inn continues into the forest outside, with Ren Yingying and Blue Phoenix duelling swordsmen using snakes, whips and flying swords (in *The Swordsman 2*, the participants announce their martial arts techniques, as often in swordplay films: 'Flying Sword!').

Oh, this is glorious cinema, so self-assured, so inventive – and so silly! As if being human is simply not enough for mere humans – they must be able to zoom up into the trees on cables, or disappear into holes in the ground, with their swords leaving an energy line of sparks.

The assault on Asia the Invincible's palace is another outstanding sequence: the traditional, Chinese rooms, with their veils and patterned screens, provide tight, enclosed spaces where the action choreography at times emulates lovemaking (after all, this is Linghu Chong entering Asia's chambers). The editing (by Marco Mak) is especially fine in this sequence, combining extreme close-ups of flying needles with shadowy rooms and partially-lit close-ups of the stars Jet Li and Brigitte Lin.

The penis – the sword – the needle – the canon – so many phallic tropes; there's no need to tease out the sexual subtext in *The Swordsman 2*, because the movie deconstructs itself for your pleasure in front of your eyes. Yes, this is a movie stuffed with Freudian, castration imagery, too – guys have their heads torn off, Dawn castrates himself, and both Swordsman Zen and Hattori cut off their own arms!

In a movie which reinvents fantasy swordplay yet again, as if from scratch, and also pushes what has already been achieved in *wuxia* movies even further, the Swordsman Zen versus the Mountain Wau warriors sequence is remarkable. Zen is the lone swordsman, mysterious and super-powerful (later, he's revealed to be a member of the Highlanders who's disfigured himself to elude capture. He's played by the ever-dependable, awesomely versatile Lau Shun).

So it's one man against seven or so, including Linghu Chong, and *everyone* is flying on cables (set in, of course, a smoke-filled forest at night). This is a ballet of ferocious energy and high speed. The photography and framing is another object lesson in filmmaking, the editing and rhythms have a mesmeric flow, and it's quite, quite beautiful (and details like the spinning swords, the swords rotating around the wrists, in and out of the grasp, has the vertiginous ecstasy of Japanese animation. Yes – in Chinese action cinema, it's as if all inanimate objects

41 Several characters spend time on the roof – Wu, Ren and Blue Phoenix. Indeed, roofs are a major location in many Chinese action movies – filmmakers can't resist taking the action upwards.

become alive, and the environment too is a force that can't be ignored).

In the climactic love scene in *The Swordsman 2*, where Linghu Chong arrives at Asia the Invincible's quarters and discovers that she has flattened many of her underlings, the filmmakers orchestrate space and light with a deft, skilful ease. How, for instance, Asia rapidly douses the lamps so that she can slip away and have Snow stand in for her in the love scene. How Linghu stands some way off, so he doesn't see Snow (she's behind the door).

Martial arts that can reverse the flow of blood, or momentarily paralyze the victim, is a recurring motif in the *Swordsman* series, and in many Hong Kong action pictures (in *The Swordsman 3: The East Is Red*, Koo has his blood flow reversed by Asia the Intractable, and in *The Swordsman 2*, Blue Phoenix immobilizes Kiddo during the massacre, so she can take on Asia alone[42]).

Not simply killed – victims are torn to pieces in *The Swordsman 2* in grotesquely over-the-top ways. In the massacre by Asia the Invincible in the outdoor, nighttime battles at the start of act three, the demi-god uses his/ her magic to shatter the survivors of the Wau Mountain Sect into pieces. Like a tragic play (and like many a Chinese action movie), the finale becomes wholesale slaughter – most of the Wau Mountain Sect are killed, Hattori is decimated by Master Wu, and Snow poisons herself (staying alive long enough to gloat at Asia when s/he returns).

The Swordsman 2 is stuffed with gross-out moments, too – not action, but pure horror: Master Wu's 'essence-absorbing' stance provides a few. Like, in his duel with Hattori, Wu withers Hattori's arm, and then shrinks his head to rubbery goo (while Hattori's headless corpse staggers about). To rejuvenate himself, in the impressive prison sequence, Master Wu sucks the life out of the guards, compressing the hapless victims to footballs of clothes. At the end of the movie, Swordsman Zen cuts off his own arm (in order to save face and not return to Master Wu empty-handed, so to speak, when he's sent to accost Linghu Chong and his chums, as they leave on a ship).

Asia the Invincible on her nighttime rampage is the first part of the finale of *The Swordsman 2*, and at times bests the action sequence in the Imperial palace. It contains some thrilling duels – such as (1) Master Wu against Hattori (ending in Hattori's head being shrivelled then simply yanked off Hattori's body); (2) Blue Phoenix against the Japanese ninjas; (3) Kiddo taking on the ninjas single-handed; (4) Kiddo and Ren Yingying battling more *shinobi*; (5) Asia the Invincible as a one-woman-man army, slaughtering the Mountain Wau brothers; and (6) Blue Phoenix taking on

42 Eventually, it wears off, and Kiddo returns to the fray.

Asia using snakes and poison.

The sequence, one of Tony Ching Siu-tung's finest as a director, is freighted with many memorable images, such as Asia the Incredible against a burning building... the Japanese ninjas riding on spinning throwing stars pursing Blue Phoenix crawling on the ground... and the Mountain Wau lads being literally ripped to shreds by Asia's magic...

The strength of the imagery here is far more than making pretty pictures: every single camera angle and camera set-up is designed not only to express exciting action, and to tell the story (tho' that's enough), but to create mysterious, magical events.

The sequence has a powerful dramatic countdown added to it, too – Blue Phoenix has been attacked with one of Asia the Invincible's needles, and is ailing fast (despite managing to halt the damage temporarily using pressure points). So there's a girl to save on top of everything else. (This is a reprise of the scene where Linghu Chong was poisoned in the first film.) Incredibly, Blue Phoenix has enough strength to attack Asia the Inflexible with a flying snake; when that doesn't work, she simply eats a snake and spits the poison back at Asia.

Yet *The Swordsman 2* is *not* wall-to-wall action in the finale (tho' it feels like that). In fact, there is a touching scene where Linghu Chong and his pals bury their Mountain Wau colleagues in graves (in pouring rain, of course). Linghu scratches their names on the wooden posts. Kiddo hurries back to the grave of her horse, where she left her sword, now determined to have her revenge on Asia the Invincible.

Most action-adventure movies don't have time for lengthy burial scenes – often it's just three shots lasting four seconds each for maybe two of the main characters, and then we're back to the rushing around, the yelling, the motorcycles and the explosions.

The Swordsman 2 also has time in the final act for a key scene, also between Master Wu and Linghu Chong: beside a bonfire at night they discuss the sacred scroll. Linghu is stunned to discover that to master the magic you have to lose your penis; Wu, of course, continues to laugh and laugh. (Linghu is also confused now about just who – or what – he had sex with at Asia's digs[43]).

✦

The second half of the finale of *The Swordsman 2* is set back in the Imperial palace at Black Cliffs, with Asia the Invincible single-handedly taking on the heroes. Among the many, many fantastic gags in this sequence is one where, having launched a spinning, flaming cauldron at

---

[43] If this was a Wong Jing or Stephen Chow movie, that part of the plot would be much cruder!

the heroes, Asia simply turns back to work on his/ her embroidery! It's very seldom you see the master villain in any action movie doing some needlework[44] right in the middle of a giant action scene! S/he sits there and ruminates pensively in voiceover, as if it's a sleepy afternoon of falling cherry blossom, while our heroes battle balls of fire in the air (once again, Linghu Chong rushes to Kiddo's aid).

The finale of *The Swordsman 2* features a vast battery of props that're spinning, flying and exploding across the screen – cauldrons, hooks, needles, wooden pergolas, even whole buildings. Linghu Chong of course attacks first (Jet Li is the star, after all), and manages to wound Asia the Invincible; s/he responds with multiple flying needles, as each of the heroes launches themselves at her/ him. Master Wu's life essence absorbing skill is used on Asia the Invincible repeatedly, until blood gushes out from the sword wound made by Linghu (as weapons, in an inventive touch, he brings along the metal hooks that Asia used to string him up in prison. But Asia is able to stop them with her flying needles).

The battle includes almost every gag and stunt you can think of, yet the psychodrama isn't forgotten (as when Asia the Invincible foxily lets slip that she and Linghu Chong have had sex – much to the distress and outrage of both Ren Yingying and Kiddo fighting alongside Linghu. They make catty remarks about it during the tussle). The action continues up onto a building at the end of the court, which crumbles and crashes down a cliff, topped by several more flying gags, where Linghu can't help saving Asia, even though s/he's killed his comrades (he also rescues Kiddo and Ren).

✦

Serious points are made in *The Swordsman 2*, even tho' this is very much a popcorn movie. For instance, at the end, Master Wu becomes the guy sitting on the throne in the Black Cliffs Imperial palace,[45] replacing Asia the Invincible. And what does he do? Only order the ruthless annihilation of anyone who opposes him.[46] And he cackles like a madman while heads are rolling and blood's splashing up the palace walls. So, yes, you replace one brutal head of government (Dawn the Invincible) with another (Master Wu) and, for the populace, and the law, and the nation, what's the difference? (That *The Swordsman 2* is making political comments about modern China seems obvious – but they are there if you want to take them up. After all, the background context of *The Swordsman 2* is the struggle for power in a nation riven by conflicts between warring

44 One of her needles wraps around Linghu's sword and pierces it.
45 Seen in a low angle shot which tracks into an ugly close-up.
46 Most of the victims (who appear on a list, including Linghu's), are youngish types – which we can take to refer to students and radicals in modern China.

groups. The vaguely historical context includes references to the Maindlanders, the Highlanders, and the Japanese ninjas brought in to help the Sun Moon Sect. References to the brutality of the Chinese government resonate throughout 1990s Hong Kong cinema, and to events such as Tiananmen Square).

The pursuit of Master Wu's new regime continues to a harbour, where Linghu Chong and Kiddo are preparing to leave (Ren Yingying suggests they find sanctuary for a while in Japan; she remains in China, opting to stay loyal to her father, even tho' he's turned out to be a psychotic tyrant). Zen the swordsman is sent to bring back Linghu, giving us an unexpected final swordfight on the boat and the dockside. It's here that Zen slices off his arm, so he can return to Master Wu severely injured (and this's after he's already disfigured his face![47]).

All of which ties up the plots so that the heroes can sail off into the sunset on a ship amidst drifting smoke and the final reprise of the heroic song, 'Hero of Heroes' (Ren Yingying watches from the harbour then a beach; the 1992 film cuts back repeatedly between her and Kiddo and Linghu on the boat, underlining the poignant motif of departure and change, a recurring them in Chinese cinema).

The Swordsman 2 also performs the familiar work of re-setting the characters back to their default positions: now it's Linghu Chong and his companion Kiddo on their travels again, which's how they were introduced 105 minutes ago. So they're ready for a new set of adventures in the next movie (except The Swordsman 3 decided to take a different approach, and dispensed with Linghu Chong and Kiddo altogether).

---

47 But, as he puts it, he can't fight, can he, with his sword arm amputated?

The Swordsman (1990),
this page and over.

Classic Tony
Ching imagery –
flying swordsmen.

The Swordsman 2 (1992).

20

THE SWORDSMAN 3:
THE EAST IS RED

Dong Fong Bat Baai 2 – Fung Wan Joi Hei

Move over Supergirl. Your days are numbered Wonder Woman. Asia the Invincible, the first transsexual lesbian superhero is now the reigning queen! This spectacular *kung fu* fantasy is 95 minutes of non-stop action featuring awesome special effects and enough flailing bodies and exhilarating fight sequences to keep any fan of the genre enthralled.

Raymond Murray, *Images In the Dark* (373)

The Swordsman 3: The East Is Red[1] (1993, *Dongfang Bùbài – Fengyún Zàiqi* in Mandarin = *Invisible Asia 2: Turbulence Again Rises*), was directed by Tony Ching Siu-tung and Raymond Lee Wai-man, co-written by Tsui Hark, Charcoal Tan and Roy Szeto, produced by Tsui and Lau Jou for Film Workshop/ Long Shong Pictures/ Golden Princess, and crewed by many of the same people who made *The Swordsman 2* or who were regulars in Tsui's movies of the era, including: music: William Hu and Woo Wai Laap, DP: Tom Lau Moon-tong, editing: Chun Yu and Keung Chuen-tak, set dec.: Chung-Sum Lam, art dir.: Eddie Ma Poon-Chiu, costumes:[2] Kwok-Sun Chiu, William Chang Suk-Ping, Chan Sau-Ming and Pat Tang Yu-Hiu, make-

[1] Fans and critics often refer to *The Swordsman 3* as *The East Is Red.* The title comes from an opera written during the Cultural Revolution. And *The East Is Red* is the title of a 1965 movie (directed by Wang Ping).
[2] The costumes in *The Swordsman 3* are outstanding: Kwok-Sun Chiu, William Chang Suk-Ping, Chan Sau-Ming and Pat Tang Yu-Hiu designed the wardrobe. With several Hong Kong stars to dress up, the costume dept go to town with colour and shape (plenty of loose robes for the stars, so they can float in Tony Ching's customary slow motion, aerial scenes).

up: Hon-Wan Tung and Chan Kok-Hong, hair: Jane Kwan Yuk-Chan (and 4 others), sound mixers: Wai-Luen Cheng and Kam Wing Chow, and action directors Ma Yuk-shing, Tony Ching and Dion Lam Dik-On. Category II. Released on Jan 21, 1993 (a Chinese New Year release[3] 93 minutes.

Swordsman 3 fared less well at the Canton box office (with HK $11.248 million) than *The Swordsman 2* (and it is, in the end, a lesser movie than *The Swordsman 2*, and, in a way, it's a side-story, focussing mainly on Asia the Invincible).[4]

The production of *The Swordsman 3* was 'chaos', Tsui Hark recalled, 'because we ran out of people, we ran out of actors'. Everybody seemed to be working on at least one other movie simultaneously (Tony Ching was working on two other flicks, and Brigitte Lin was shooting another film). Consequently, the picture writes and shoots around actors such as Lin who weren't always available (as well as using doubles, etc). Thus, by now in the *Swordsman* franchise Asia the Invincible has a feared reputation, so s/he can be referred to in dialogue but not seen, because the audience knows that character. And instead of the 'original' Asia, we now have impostors.

As Tsui Hark recalled, it was the backers who asked for a third helping of the *Swordsman* (because, yes, sequels and franchises are originated and orchestrated by studios and financers, not writers and directors, in the East as in the West. Sequels are usually produced in order to make money). Tsui thought he was done already with the *Swordsman* world, and with the character of Asia the Invincible (and s/he seemed to have died. However, a high fall doesn't always mean instant death – there's no shot of Asia dead on the ground (or in pieces) in the second *Swordsman* film).

So coming up with a story for a third *Swordsman* flick required some finagling with the mechanics of the narrative: Tsui Hark and his co-writers Charcoal Tan and Roy Szeto opted for a 'Death of the Costumed Swordplay Movie' concept, in which everybody is trying to cash in on the mythical status of Asia, copying her/ him (a sly dig at the rip-off ethic of the film industry in Canton, and actors playing the same role in multiple movies. The *Swordsman* movies had their own cash-in films, of course, as any box office hit does – in the West as in the East).

The Swordsman 3 is built around the usual three-act model of most Hong Kong movies (which fits an 80-to-90-minute picture). However, the problems in making the film are obvious: it really only has enough decent material for two acts (also, the film recycles both previous *Swordsman* movies in order to bump up its running time). It might've been more honest

3 To make that release date, *The Swordsman 3* would have been filming not long after the release of the second *Swordsman* movie, in June, 1992.
4 The name Dongfong Bat Baai is on everybody's lips – they repeat it all the time.

to deliver a 60-minute movie, but for a theatrical release in Canton and East Asia, that wouldn't satisfy the audience. Several of the great Walt Disney movies are a shade over 60 or 70 minutes. But audiences expect more from a live-action feature.

The Swordsman 3 is a kind of cruder, exploitative version of the previous *Swordsman* movies and of the swordplay genre: it's got sleazy scenes with hookers, gory violence, and gratuitous lesbian scenes.

The Swordsman 3 lacks a strong story to tell: there isn't an over-arching plot which compels the viewer – or compels the characters. For example, what is at stake isn't clearly defined: in *The Swordsman 2*, Asia the Incredible is a major threat because he/ she's destabilizing part of China, breaking up the clans, and ruling with a iron fist.[5] In the first *Swordsman* film, we had the brutal Eastern branch of the Imperial forces, among other villains, intent on demolishing the Sun Moon Sect.

In *The Swordsman 3*, Asia the Inconsolable seems more interested in pretending to be one of the girls in a brothel, or lording it over former lovers (like Snow), or pursuing her/ his impostors (like a multi-national corporation hunting down copyright theft and licensing pirates).

Brigitte Lin Ching-hsia was back as the great, wild, unpredictable and very dangerous Dongfong Bat Baai (who else could it be?!); Joey Wong Cho-yin played Xue Qianxun (Snow), Asia's former lover (the Cici role in the 2nd film, played by Candice Yu On-on), and now an Invincible Asia impostor (and leader of the Sun Moon Sect; however, Snow poisoned herself in *The Swordsman II*); Yu Rongguang was Gu Changfeng (General Koo), the government official tasked with discovering what really happened with Asia the Nasty years ago (he's not a replacement for Linghu Chong, tho' Koo is the main male role in *The Swordsman 3*). The rest of the cast included Lau Shun (playing Asia the Crossdresser in her/ his aged guise, whom we meet first[6]), Eddy Ko (the Chief from *We're Going To Eat You*, and one of the leads in Tony Ching's first directorial effort, *Duel To the Death*), Jean Wang, Lee Ka-ting, Dion Lam Dik-On, Lau Chi-Ming and Kingdom Yuen.

Yu Rongguang (b. 1958), a Peking Opera performer and former martial arts boxer, is I reckon a very fine actor, looks great, moves well, and is often overlooked in accounts of this period of Chinese cinema (where he's overshadowed by stars such as Jet Li, both Tony Leungs, Sammo Hung, Sam Hui, Andy Lau, Chow Yun-fat and Jackie Chan). But in movies such as *Iron Monkey, The Terracotta Warrior, Supercop 2, Rock 'n' Roll Cop* and *My Father Is a Hero,* Yu is a strong leading man, as well as a suitably

5 A fist clutching needles and colourful threads, though.
6 In the credits, Shun is known as 'Warden of the Holy Altar'.

cruel villain (however, in *The Swordsman 3*, Yu has the tough job of following Jet Li – as with Vincent Zhao in the later *Once Upon a Time In China* movies, that proves a challenge).

Yu Rongguang trained in Peking Opera performance (in Beijing – he is a Mandarin speaker). He had already appeared in movies and TV before starring in Tsui Hark productions; he was the lead in *The Terracotta Warrior*, directed by Tong Ching. Later, he moved into producing and directing.

The principal charas in *The Swordsman 3: The East Is Red* are General Koo and Asia the Incontrovertible, Snow (Asia's lover), and Dai (Snow's lover) – with Koo hoping to humanize Asia (good luck with that!), trying to tame him/ her (or at least to stop her/ him childishly, selfishly, and rather pointlessly wasting anyone who gets in her/ his way). Yet the 1993 movie wrongfoots the audience with regard to Koo – introducing him as the hero (as he leads the band of Spaniards to Asia's resting place in act one), where the real emphasis is on Asia, Snow and Dai.

The Swordsman 3: The East Is Red is a reworking of the *Swordsman*'s themes and elements: this time General Koo takes up the role of the Swordsman Linghu Chong, tho' his government official is a departure from the conception of the character in the previous movies (and in Jin Yong's stories). Koo doesn't joke around, or drink, like Linghu, for instance, and he's not the heroic swordsman, he's a government employee. Gone too is some of the rivalry between the clans and groups (tho' the Sun Moon Sect is back – and up to their usual decadent antics, with a harsh leader – Snow). And most of the characters from *The Swordsman 2* have been ditched, too, with the focus now on Asia the Insatiable and her/ his clones.

The Swordsman 3: The East Is Red politicizes the myths and legends of the *jiangzhu* by including Spanish conquistadors in the mix, as well as the Japanese military (in the form of samurai and ninja), and referencing attacks from the Dutch Navy (a caption says the film is set in 1595). Thus, once again it seems as if the adventures of swordsmen and beautiful but deadly semi-demons are being presented within a quasi-historical context which refers to the formation of early, modern China in amongst international forces (Japan and Russia on one side, and Europe on the other).

The foreigners are sent up, as usual in a Hong Kong movie (and especially in a Tsui Hark's production): the Japanese are portrayed as humourless – they go to sea dressed in full samurai armour, clad all in black. Their fiendishly clever inventions (flying ninja, a submarine) are no match for Ancient, Chinese magic. And their samurai leader is a midget.

The Spaniards are fools who don't understand the language, trailing along their witch doctor, the Catholic priest to cleanse the land.

The prologue recycles the climactic ending of *The Swordsman 2* for three or so minutes (helping to bump up the running time of this troubled second sequel): from *The Swordsman 2,* we see Asia the Invincible battling our heroes at the Black Cliffs palace, and Asia falling to her/ his doom. Notice a glaring omission from the recycled footage: no close-ups of Jet Li whatsoever (even tho' he was the most prominent chara in the finale of film two); it would mislead the audience. There's no Jet Li in this movie, folks! (This film was released in Jan, '93, seven months after *The Swordsman 2*).

General Koo and his Chinese buddies Ling and Hon Chin (Eddy Ko), for instance, arrive with the Spanish contingent on their ship (and we know that the Spaniards are after something different from the Chinese). The opening sequence takes us 23 years7 after the end of *The Swordsman 2*), with our heroes landing at the mysterious, foreboding Black Cliffs (where, the last time we saw Asia the Invincible, s/he was leaping to her/ his ruin). The Spaniards have brought along a Christian priest in order to exorcise the evil land of China – but of course European Catholicism is no match for Oriental magic! So Asia the Invincible is soon breaking loose from her/ his grave (appearing first as a wizened, slightly sinister woman with wild, white hair, played by the ever-amazing Lau Shun – Lau went from playing the evil Imperial eunuch in film one to the disfigured warrior Zen in film two to the aged Asia in film three!), before the reveal of Brigitte Lin Ching-hsia in all her glory, as a rubber mask is tossed away – another bit of Chinese Opera business. Asia also dispenses with his/ her silly white fright wig).

Thus, as Asia the Invincible is now one of the two main protagonists, she/ he is given goals to achieve and things to do: when General Koo informs her/ him that there are folk going about impersonating her/ him and debasing her/ him image, s/he flies into a rage, and vows to wipe them out (Koo's sensible pleas of 'no more killing' we know are not going to last long!). Wow! – Asia is a true diva, flying off the handle at the slightest slight (in this pumped-up sort of movie, everything is played at a hysterical level, from the performances of the actors to the visual effects, the costumes and the action). 'One of the most outrageous examinations of feminine power ever committed to film' (Lisa Morton, 99-100).

The introduction of the existence of the fake Asia the Invincibles is a clever gimmick to exploit the now-popular character with multiple versions (as well as playing to Asia's vanity, her/ his hunger for power, and ensuring that Asia's journey back from the wilderness to the centre of the story has

7 Or is it 100 years? Or is it 4 months?

some dramatic weight behind it. And it also solves the scheduling issues – if Brigitte Lin isn't always available, other actors can play one of the impostors).

It's a narrative hook that works well enough as a means of stirring up some conflict between the groups – the Chinese, the Spaniards, the Japanese, and the rivals (the Spanish declare that they too are seeking the sacred scroll).

The first Asia-as-impostor sequence features Snow and her Sun Moon Sect cohorts on a ship at sea being attacked by Thunder and his Japanese crew: the scenes of two ships shelling each other, one of the staples of the pirate genre are, in the hands of this group of filmmakers, merely one element in a panoply of visual effects, tricks, stunts and gags – including Japanese ninjas on flying kites, multiple sword fights, the Nipponese vessel turning into a submarine, and Joey Wong going into battle as Snow at her huffiest and fiercest.

Another Asia-impostor sequence (still in act one!) has Asia the Indescribable and General Koo weightlessly travelling to a forest where a more primitive, tribal form of ritual and worship is taking place (wild dancing, a roaring fire, ethnic masks, a mad mob, and sacrifical victims who are happy to be burnt as offerings to the deity Asia). Poor Koo isn't able to stand in the way of the real Asia's rage at these heathens (how *dare* they worship a fake Asia?!) – which extends to blasting out the hearts of the soldiers ranged against him/ her (one of numerous *ugghh* moments in the *Swordsman* series – including the willing sacrifical victim having *her* heart yanked out by the head priest). This ridiculous scene, which tops act one of *The Swordsman 3*, is a return of the horror genre for Tony Ching and Tsui Hark, but played for gruesome fun, like the haunted house in the funfair.8

✦

So much for the background story of *The Swordsman 3: The East Is Red* – this is 'ecstatic cinema', remember, and traditional/ conventional elements such as 'character' and 'story' and 'theme' are only part of the mix! Yes – because this is action-adventure movie directed by Tony Ching Siu-tung and Raymond Lee, and it's produced by Tsui Hark, and it's stuffed with action.

Among the numerous ecstasies in *The Swordsman 3: The East Is Red* are the many scenes filmed at sea. This is a maritime version of a *wuxia pian* (it's really a pirate movie in many respects), with ships blasting away at each other, fights in the rigging, stunt people flying about on ropes, masts toppling, and many other of the expected gags in a pirate or sea-

8 Or the second *Indiana Jones* movie.

based adventure movie (much of the *Once Upon a Time In China* series occurs at harbours – border zones between China and the rest of the world, and also stages fights on ships). But, this being Hong Kong cinema, there are all sorts of eccentric elements added to the mix: like: flying needles; like: Japanese ninja flying from ship to ship on flags like kites; like: fighters holding up cannons in one arm and firing 'em; like: Asia the Invincible riding a swordfish[9] (!); like: Asia the Inviolable collecting all of the bullets fired by the Spaniards in the air, and flicking them back, to kill them (another version of Chinese using traditional means (i.e., magic), to trump the *gweilo* invaders with their guns and bullets); like: ships running aground and also flying; like: a ship turning into a wooden submarine (yes, of course it's the fiendishly tech-minded Japanese who pull off this trick! This outrageous gag is likely a Tsui Hark idea).

For this version of swordplay-meets-pirates-meets-*kung-fu*-meets-fantasy, the filmmakers have procured some full-size boats (as well as the usual models and scaled-down sets).[10] Filming models on water is a giveaway of scale, of course, so inter-cutting with full-size sets helps a lot.[11]

The sequence where Asia the Invincible in her/ his furious god-like persona attacks Snow and her ship is simply extraordinary – the filmmakers create enormous explosions of water,[12] and place Asia rising up out of the sea on a swordfish, unleashing waves of energy (with the screen filled with sparkling, back-lit waterdrops). And all of this is filmed at night.[13]

It's like seeing a Las Vegas show combined with a Disney theme park show combined with a Japanese *manga* brought to life. Again and again, Hong Kong cinema reminds us that *anything is possible*.[14] Well, at least in movies it is!

The Swordsman 3 contains action which 'makes John Woo's *The Killer* seem like a Bergman opus', according to Raymond Murray (*Images In the Dark*, 373). 'One of the most audacious works of genius in the history of the fantasy film' (Lisa Morton, 98). '*Swordsman* is a mad, muddled and marvellous 90s update of *wuxia* films', said Stephen Teo (199).

And seeing Brigitte Lin let rip as a one-womany army is worth the price

9 Almost certainly Tsui Hark's idea – like a stag, of all things, popping as the wise oracle in *Detective Dee.*
10 The filmmakers happily have some grips manhandling a scale model ship in front of cliffs or against the sky, to stand in for the full-scale vessels they haven't got. Orson Welles did that in *Othello.*
11 The budget is still stretched, here, though it thankfully doesn't resort to the Hollywood approach of filming boat scenes in the studio, against either panoramas or green screens.
12 First seen in *The Swordsman,* but here taken to extravagant heights. In one extraordinary shot, water explodes around the whole perimeter of the ship.
13 This would've be a tough series of nights for everyone involved. Logistically, these scenes are very challenging.
14 Lisa Morton speaks, *pace The Swordsman II,* of 'the dizzying idea that human beings are capable of anything, whether it's flying or changing sex at will' (LM, 88).

of admission alone: despite the 1993 movie not fitting together narratively, or thematically, or dramatically, it features some wonderful scenes. Like Joey Wong, Lin's screen persona in many movies is of a gentle, intelligent and somewhat enigmatic actress. But Lin convinces as an arrogant, ultra-violent tyrant (partly because, as with Wong, the contrast is so extreme, and what Lin gets to do is so over-the-top. Similarly, the pert, winsome, rosy-cheeked Rosamund Kwan is dressed in dominatrix black in the *Swordsman* movies and wields a whip).

The mad laugh, the scornful looks, the sudden switches in emotion – Brigitte Lin has movie villain-dom down pat. And when s/he's standing proudly on the arm of the mast, sweeping her/ his robes to one side, looking down on everyone, Lin's Asia the Infrangible is a memorable image, an Errol Flynn or Burt Lancaster pirate gone very, very bad. Even the *Pirates of the Caribbean* films, much as we love them, with their state-of-the-art visual effects and colossal, 200 million dollar budgets (probably 100 times what *The Swordsman 3* cost), couldn't match this.

✦

For beauty, *The Swordsman 3: The East Is Red* boasts two of the great faces of recent Chinese cinema: Brigitte Lin Ching-hsia and Joey Wong Cho-yin. The filmmakers shamelessly exploit the sexual heat that their starlets generate, too, by putting them together physically as lovers. Both are women impersonating men (Wong's Snow, now pretending to be Asia), or sort-of-women that were once men (Lin's Asia). That Snow is pretending to be Asia the Invincible complicates the erotic subterfuge (and her lover Dai turns out to be a guy) – this is the kind of thing that makes postmodern critics go ga-ga. Gender-bending, transgender and lesbianism – all in one scene! *Sooo* postmodern! *Sooo* radical! Oooh, *sooo* transgressive!

It's staged as a flashback for Snow (a.k.a. Xue Qianxun), who has never stopped loving Asia the Invincible (Snow reprises the role of Cici in the 2nd *Swordsman* picture), when Asia was Dongfong Bat Baai, it seems (i.e., a man). It's intercut with Snow and *her* lover, Dai, in another lesbian, opium-sweet clinch. But on screen we see Joey Wong and Brigitte Lin (and Jean Wang) kissing, sharing opium on their tongues, and pouring wine into each other's mouths (in one of those luxurious boudoir settings, complete with painted screens and candles, exquisitely lit by DP Tom Lau Moon-tong – not forgetting the make-up by Hon-Wan Tung and Chan Kok-Hong, the costumes by William Chang Suk-Ping and others, and the hair by Jane Kwan Yuk-Chan and others. The colours in the boudoir setting are of course red and gold). The camera lingers over the faces of Lin and Wong, and Wong and Wang, in giant, glowing, back-lit close-ups – by Ganesh, these are fantastically beautiful people!

The romantic subplot of *The Swordsman 3* pays off in several ways. For a start, it is one of the few things that can humanize or redeem Asia the Inestimable (tho' not in the end!), it reminds the characters that there are other things at work and worth fighting for/ living for than taking over China as a demi-god, and of course it provides the eye candy of Joey Wong and Brigitte Lin in a Lesbian Kiss Scene, and Joey Wong and Jean Wang in *another* Lesbian Kiss Scene.

Having Joey Wong playing a jilted lover, a spurned and hurt lover, works perfectly (tho' Asia the Inexpiable isn't going to be sucked into a guilt trip! If anyone's going to be ladling out guilt, it's Asia). It plays to Wong's strengths, too, as an actress (Wong can evoke the pain of love perfectly – she can sulk and huff and pout at an Olympic Games level. Wong is terrific in *The Swordsman 3* – her screen persona is so æthereal and gentle, it makes a striking and appealing contrast when she lets fly as a tyrant). And it works well too because this side of Snow's personality is introduced *after* she was depicted as the brutal leader of the Sun Moon Sect (where her followers see her as a man. Once again, there's an important political point being made when Snow is revealed to be a woman, and the soldiers realize they've been ruled by an impostor. Yes, your leaders are never quite what you thought!).

But for an impostor of Asia the Indivisible, Snow is doing pretty well! She has many aspects of Asia down pat: the needles-as-weapons *kung fu*, the imperious, impatient, declaiming tones, the kingly demeanour, and even a devoted concubine. (Unfortunately, Dai the concubine turns out to be a Japanese ninja in disguise – his face's ripped off as a mask, revealing an ugly, middle-aged guy who's near-naked in a loincloth. Snow is, naturally, *very* enraged, and their duel, filmed amid the upper levels of the Sun Moon Sect vessel at night, and then out onto the ocean, is one of the highlights of *The Swordsman 3: The East Is Red*. It includes remarkable images such as Snow flying in slo-mo against a giant, full moon, while slicing the air with her/ his sword, and conjuring explosions out of the ocean. Like the real Asia, when Snow is crossed in love, she is *very* disgruntled!).

Two women, one man – *The Swordsman 3* again turns the tables, gender-wise, and also adds a hysterical, sadomasochistic vibe, so that Snow offers her life to Asia Indefectible when Asia's fury is unleashed when s/he finds out that Snow has been posing as her/ him, and Koo, who seems to be the hero (and casting Yu Rongguang suggests that), becomes dangerously obsessive.

In keeping with Tsui Hark's ambition to make a 'Last Of' movie (the last swordplay film, the last costume epic, etc), there's a raw, apocalyptic atmosphere to *The Swordsman 3*, which's expressed in the high energy, the multiple deaths, the insanity. (Tsui would take this martial-arts-movie-as-apocalypse even further two years later with *The Blade*).

✦

In its third and final act, *The Swordsman 3: The East Is Red* loses its way somewhat, narratively. There are several sequences which don't do justice to the premise and the themes (or the characterizations), or the goodwill that the *Swordsman* series has generated thus far (for the audience) – so that, when the final smackdown occurs (as we all know it will!), it lacks the full dramatic resonance (altho' it *is* extremely spectacular).

For instance, following the superb dust-up between Asia the Indivisible and Snow (where Snow comes off worst, as expected), the filmmakers spend maybe too much time with scenes that meander a little – like General Koo and his cohorts in a mutinous face-off with the Sun Moon Sect crew on the ship, or arguing amongst themselves, or taking care of an ailing Snow and escaping on the ship's sail like a kite, and later a wooden raft. (Some of these scenes are simply not very gripping: like, the Spanish ships approach the Sun Moon Sect's vessel, but after shelling them, they sort of vanish. Like, the scene where Koo and Snow bond on the makeshift raft runs on too long, and doesn't contain enough dramatic juice).

However, what happens is truly unexpected: the 1993 movie lurches drunkenly into a side alley marked 'Crazy-Weird' (which in Hong Kong cinema is not a tiny alley, of course, but a very wide boulevard lined with neon-drenched skyscrapers and monsters!). We follow Asia the Indefinable into, of all places, a harem of prostitutes who serve a military encampment:[15] this is Asia wondering what it's like to be ordinary and human. He/ she impersonates a mysterious woman who joins the camp – the narrative of *The Swordsman 3* is undergoing lots of sudden narrative jumps which don't quite make sense.[16] How, for example, Asia wants to be regarded as just one of the girls, only to immediately subvert that by being antsy and sly and ruthless (s/he just can't help him/ herself taking command of any situation. No one is going to boss Asia around, and Asia simply has to control everything).

15 The setting of the military encampment at night is skilfully portrayed – it's striking how much time we viewers spend out of doors, at night, where it's always breezy, and a half or full moon shines, amongst campfires, and drinking, carousing soldiers.
16 The flow of scenes judders a little, suggesting that scenes where curtailed or left out.

So there are scenes where Asia the Inequable challenges the Japanese visitors (including the midget samurai leader, Thunder) to a deadly dice game (where the stake is losing your legs! – very Tsui Hark), and also allowing her/ himself to be captured and imprisoned (and in jail, apparently, Asia realizes that to be an ordinary human sucks just as much as being a demi-god. Anyway, we don't *want* to see Asia as an 'ordinary' person!).[17]

On the plus side, this part of *The Swordsman 3: The East Is Red* allows Brigitte Lin to go all-out with the characterization of Invincible Dawn. And Lin rises to the challenge, turning Asia the Incalculable into an unpredictable force of nature – you don't know what he/ she is going to do next. For instance, nobody would guess that Asia would turn all homey and cosy and folky, when s/he picks up a *pipa* (lute) and sits by the campfire to sing a song (and the movie turns into an MTV pop promo for a minute or two, lit by flickering light, as the whores gather round to wonder who this amazing new recruit could be. It's nothing out of the ordinary, tho', for a Hong Kong movie to include several musical montages).

As wayward as the brothel sequence is, though, Brigitte Lin looks as if she is enjoying herself here – this is Lin at her most arrogant, cunning, catty and teasing. The scenes where Lin pretends to laugh along with the hookers, or to be best friends and girls together with him, are funny but also scary – we've already seen Asia the Intolerable literally tearing people apart in the Highlanders ritual scene. (The brothel madam (Kingdom Yuen) is rightly suspicious of Asia, but when she sees the newbie getting the better of the rough, demanding men, she warms to her/ him).

✦

Meanwhile, the writers – Tan, Szeto and Tsui – struggle to find new obstacles/ complications to the *Swordsman* plot and themes: anyone can spot what *The Swordsman 3* desperately lacks: a strong central plot which'll tie all of the characters together. Or to put it in simpler terms: the writers didn't have a satisfying ending.

So the authors return to the concept of multiple impostor Asia the Invincibles. Thus, now the commander of the encampment, General Tin Kai-wan (an overblown performance by Lee Ka-ting), is also having delusions of grandeur, imagining himself to be another Asia the Invincible (and having his concubines dressed up as a bunch of little Asias in red – this's where *The Swordsman 3: The East Is Red* derails itself in digressions that don't really go anywhere, and also repeat what we've already seen. Yes, it's a *second* encampment of hookers! With a similar

---

17 But has Asia forgotten what it felt like to be human? Well, it has been a long time since s/he was human!

atmosphere of drunk, out-of-control guys lurching about, ogling the prostitutes dressed as their arch enemy).

This part of *The Swordsman 3: The East Is Red* becomes Chaos Night, Topsy-Turvy Time, when things go just a little crazeee – so that even General Koo is taken over the mood of power-madness. Generals Tin and Koo are soon coming to blows as they fight over the beautiful Snow. Yes, Koo has brought Snow along with him (and his faithful aide Chin). Just by lying there looking coy and superior, and by being luscious, Snow seems to cause trouble – Tin is besotted.

The duels between Koo and Tin are deftly portrayed – using one of the staples of historical Hong Kong movies, a tall, wooden tower, just the thing for aerial combat. So once again it's night, it's smoke, it's fire, it's weightless action on wires and flailing swords.

And the action keeps coming: in the military camp scenes Snow has her moment of glory when she teases and bests the Japanese commander, Thunder, who's revealed to be a tiny guy.

The military camp sequence is a kind of free-for-all, narratively, so that anyone who has an idea for something that Snow, or Tin, or Koo could do gets their idea put in the film. Like, one of the make-up girls suggests: what if Snow arrogantly teases General Tin, like she did with Shogun Thunder? Or, one of the sparks comes up with this nugget: how about General Koo waking from delirium to discover General Tin banging a gong (!) up on the look-out tower, while Snow lolls about on his lap?

The introduction of so many narrative sidetrackings and artificial conflicts weakens *The Swordsman 3: The East Is Red* considerably in its last half-hour. Whereas *The Swordsman 2* had a tightly-controlled narrative that managed to keep the primary plot in focus as well as giving the large ensemble cast interesting (and spectacular) things to do – all the way to the Grand Finish – *The Swordsman 3* stumbles and staggers. It veers off into swordplay btn Generals Koo and Tin, into Snow horsing around with Tin (just to spite Koo, perhaps – but also because Snow remains the masochistic devotee of Asia the Unobtainable to the very end. Indeed, the filmmakers have retained Snow as a character to embody what Asia has lost – love, humanity, etc. Snow becomes the precious beauty in life which Asia has cast aside in his/ her bid for power. But they also don't quite know what to do with Snow, apart from having Joey Wong lie there and look beautiful. Which of course Wong can accomplish with ease. Thus, in the Big Battle at the end of the third *Swordsman* flick, Snow has little to do except to look pained that Asia seems to be ignoring her (and she's injured, too). Snow's strategy seems to be to sulk and pout her way back into Asia's heart).

Anyway, after emphasizing too many minor and strange elements, *The Swordsman 3: The East Is Red* hurtles around the corner of the Hong Kong Movie Race Circuit, heading for the Final Stretch – with the Finish Line in sight (10 minutes away). And just what is a Hong Kong swordplay/ fantasy/ action flick going to do? Only have scenes of Big, Wild Action! For the finale, everybody else seems to have gone home (including all of the extras), and only three charas remain: Asia the Insane, Snow the Wistful Masochist, and General Koo the Paranoid Intermediary (who just wants everybody *to stop fighting, already! And to just get along!*).

No. No – because Asia the Unpleasable is a divinity as a spoilt child who, if it/ he/ she can't get what it/ he/ she wants, is going to *destroy* it! Yes – the signs were displayed in the scene in act one of this third *Swordsman* celluloid outing where Asia attacked Snow viciously. For being an impostor, yes, but also perhaps for simply being someone who really got to him/ her, who got under her/ his skin, and whom s/he really loved. Asia is the supreme egotist (vain but vicious), who demands total servitude from his/ her lovers. *Love me or die!* might be his/ her *mantra*. So Snow must die – and it can only be Asia who kills her.

The moral teaching in the finale of *The Swordsman 3* is: recognize and love what you have, not what you desire. Very Taoist/ Buddhist: be *here* (not *there*). Or as North American schmaltz like *The Wizard of Oz* or a Disney cartoon might put it, *there's no place like home*. Ain't that right, Toto? Oh yes, ma'am, it is – especially when 'home' is a colossal nation like the People's Republic of China! (Which has a head-start on North America of several thousand years for weaving myths and legends about heroes and gods).

For the finale of *The Swordperson 3*, the filmmakers have brought back the national navies – so the smackdown takes place on wooden ships at sea. Unfortunately, we have already seen this in the incredible nighttime sequence where Asia the Naughty laid siege to Snow and the Sun Moon Sect's vessel (the finale, filmed in full daylight, simply doesn't have the same impact and atmosphere).[18] But Ancient, Chinese magic does allow for scenes not often used in the Western pirate/ maritime movie – flying ships! (Asia's magic raises ships out of the water: as well as flying boats, we have boats landing on top of each other, boats running aground, and of course, boats exploding). And other non-Western scenes – the heroes soaring on sails ripped from ships thru the sky, pounding each other with bolts of energy shot from the palms.

The finale is filled with endless bits of business in the cat-and-mouse

18 The flat, cloudy skies don't help.

tussle between General Koo and Asia the Inflammable – such as Koo wielding a cannon to fire at Asia, Asia responding by using her/ his flying needles to pin Koo to the cannon, and then Koo to the bulwark. One moment we're up in the air on the masts, the next we're in the hold. A memorable beat has Asia and Koo using sails (still attached to the square yard-arms) as weapons, striking each other with them, while hurtling thru the air.

The 'anything goes' approach to filmmaking is one of the appeals of Hong Kong cinema – here it includes Asia the Indomitable's military costume, as if he or she's the commander of an empire of one soul, her/ himself.

But this final segment of the climax of *The Swordsman-woman 3* lacks many dramatic and cinematic elements to make it convince. The staging doesn't make sense at times, as if much of the footage was achieved with stand-ins, and there wasn't enough coverage to smooth over the cracks. A giveaway is the decision to have Asia the Intractable and General Koo placed always far apart – so in the reverse angles, Koo or Asia can be a double.[19] But if the team were also making one or more films at the same time, all of this is understandable.

Yes, like many Hong Kong pictures, the ending of *The Swordsman 3: The East Is Red* has everything falling apart, emotions running wild and unchecked, and a high body count. General Koo, for ex, seems to expire in a boiling mass of fire as a ship explodes, and Asia the Inexplicable spirits the dead Snow away on a flying sail into the sunset (there's a lovely, weepy close-up of the two stars, Wong and Lin). Asia the Unstoppable, note, survives.

It's not always a convincing dramatic/ aesthetic solution, it's not always a satisfying ending in terms of narrative or thematic structure, but the Chaos + Death[20] + Shouting + Explosions ending of many a Hong Kong movie is certainly crowd-pleasing.[21] So, yes, lots of stuff blows up, fires rage, and characters die... Roll the credits!

---

19 That diminishes Asia, though: such as how s/he demands that Koo hand over Snow, from a distance, when s/he is clearly much more powerful than Koo, and can stride in and take Snow at any time.
20 'It could be argued that *everything* in *The East Is Read* leads to death, for it may be the bloodiest film with the highest death count in Tsui Hark's filmography' (Lisa Morton, 100).
21 In the noise and mad visuals, the filmmakers hope the audience will forget about the flaws in the script.

The Swordsman 3 (1993), this page and over.

PART THREE

TONY CHING SIU-TUNG

AS ACTION DIRECTOR

1

DANGEROUS ENCOUNTER – 1ST KIND

Dai Yat Lui Ying Ngai Him

At that time I was quite angry, and I tried to do something anarchistic. When you don't care what you put on the screen, a heavy burden is lifted from your shoulder, and you start to make film like a student. And that becomes effective in some way.

Tsui Hark (1997, 134)

PRODUCTION.

Dangerous Encounter – 1st Kind (1980, Mandarin: *Diyi Leixing Weixian = First Kind of Danger,* a.k.a. *Dangerous Encounter of the First Kind, Don't Play With Fire* and *Playing With Fire*) was co-written by Tsui Hark and regular collaborator Roy Szeto Cheuk Hon, produced by Thomas Wing-Fat Fung (for Fotocine Film Production Limited), with David Chung Chi-Man as DP, action directed by Tony Ching Siu-tung, and directed by Tsui. Edited by Cheung Kan Chow and Wai Wu Tsi. Art dir. by Tony Au Ting-Ping. Make-up by Man Chuen Chow. Hair by Tak-Hing Yeung. Music by Siu-Lam Tang and Leun Yu. Some of the music was from *Dawn of the Dead* (1979), composed by Goblin and Dario Argento.[1] It starred Lin Zhenqi, Lo Lieh, Tse Bo Law, Lung Tin Sang, Au Siu Keung, Ray Lui, Bruce Barron, and Richard Da Silva. Released Dec 4, 1980. 92 mins.

    Dangerous Encounter – 1st Kind is a stunning piece of work. It's an

---

[1] One of the versions of *Dangerous Encounter – 1st Kind* has an electronic soundtrack (of the usual moody synthesizers), augmented by slices of Pink Floyd (from 'Echoes'), the Alan Parsons Project and Jean Michel Jarre (from *Oxygene*).

angry, black comedy₂ featuring a disturbed, young woman, Wan Chu, a.k.a. Pearl (Lin Zhenqi/ Lin Ching)₃ who blackmails three losers in their late teens, Paul (Albert Au), Ahl Lung (Tin Sang Lung) and Ah Ko (Paul Che), into a series of hijinks and juvenile delinquency which rapidly escalate into mayhem (Wan Chu happens to be the younger sister of a cop, Tan, played by Lo Lieh).

There are thus five charas in *Dangerous Encounters of the First Kind*:

- Wan Chu – the anti-heroine
- Ah Ko – the three accomplices
- Ah Lung   "   "
- Paul   "   "
- Tan – a cop, the anti-heroine's brother

The performances of the central quartet of kids in *Dangerous Encounter* is stellar – this movie completely convinces at the level of performance (and the casting is dead-on, too). So much depends on the characterization of Wan Chu, and Lin Zhenqi nails it. She gets the tone, the subtlety, the anger perfectly. And she has attitude to spare. You buy it that she is a very dangerous character, despite being a slim-built, short girl (if she survives, and grows up, she'll be running the fiercest triad syndicate in all Asia).

Dangerous Encounter – 1st Kind benefits from some lively location shooting in contemporary Hong Kong (there are few studio sets for this low budget picture).₄ And Tsui Hark's eye for an arresting image, for moving the camera, and for using every trick that cinema offers, is very much in evidence in this his third feature movie.

Dangerous Encounter – 1st Kind is also an action movie – there are many scenes which are dramatized and choreographed in an action-based manner, using the body moving dynamically in space (way above the requirements of the narrative). One of Tsui Hark's regular collaborators, Tony Ching Siu-tung, was one of the action directors (they had already worked in television by this time; this was their first feature film together). (In a Western movie, the juvenile delinquency of Wan Chu might involve a lot more talk then a bit of action at the end of a scene; in *Dangerous Encoᵘ·ter – 1st Kind,* the actors (like the camera), are moving all the

film (it's *anybody's* darkest film)' (Lisa Morton, 44).
tress at Shaw Brothers Studio (from 1974-1982); she retired from
ngerous Encounter – 1st Kind. Born in 1955, she is too old to be a
ts away with it.
Encounter – 1st Kind was likely fairly small; there are no stars,
in characters are all young actors (i.e., dead cheap).

THE SCRIPT.

Dangerous Encounter – 1st Kind is an original concept in the Tsui Hark canon – it's not an adaptation of an ancient folktale (*The Lovers*), a remake of famous martial arts epics (*The Blade* or *Dragon Gate Inn*), or an update of a national hero's story (*Once Upon a Time In China*).

The script is, once again, classical in construction. For instance, the act one closer is dead on time: it occurs at 26 minutes and has the narrative hook of Wan Chu announcing to the boys: 'there are lots of funny things to do'. (The narrative hook perfectly sets up act two of *Dangerous Encounter – 1st Kind,* that there are lots of funny things to do).

Dangerous Encounter – 1st Kind demonstrates for all to see that the combo of Roy Szeto and Tsui Hark *as writers* is very powerful: *Dangerous Encounter – 1st Kind* explodes largely because the *script* is so solid, so inventive. First, the *concept* is granite-hard: if you start with something so good, you are most of the way there.5 Second, the narrative develops the concept with total confidence (it includes the necessary dramatic elements of, for instance, escalating violence, complicating events, unexpected twists and all the rest of the list to tick in the screenwriters' manual). Third, it performs all of the functions of a great script – it thrills, teases, amuses and startles.

From the outset, with *The Butterfly Murders*, Tsui Hark enters the world of cinema as a master showman – and by the time of the outrageously black material in both *We're Going To Eat You* and *Dangerous Encounter – 1st Kind,* his talent is almost scary it's so good. (As Stephen Teo noted, Tsui certainly has the 'devil's talent'!).

Dangerous Encounter – 1st Kind is a black comedy, but there are some moments of genuine sadism and dissidence. It's a movie made by a totally confident group of filmmakers (Tsui Hark was 30 at the time); these guys *really* know what they're doing! There's no flab or fat in *Dangerous Encounter – 1st Kind,* no meandering, no wandering off the point (and not even much milking moments for every ounce of dramatic juice). Instead, *Dangerous Encounter – 1st Kind* is too busy telling its compelling story (it's almost anti-bombastic filmmaking, avoiding the bathos and sentiment that scuppers all too many movies). And, once again, it's the *rapid pacing* that helps to prevent *Dangerous Encounter – 1st Kind* from out-staying its welcome.

'Bluntly put, *Dangerous Encounter* is probably the most nihilistic film ever made', reckoned Lisa Morton, with only *Dawn of the Dead* being comparable in terms of 'sheer, numbing, anarchic violence', making *Dangerous Encounter* 'among the most compelling 90-minutes of film in all

5 That's the biggest challenge of a movie – coming up with that initial, white-hot idea

of cinema' (LM, 41).

AN INCENDIARY MOVIE – LITERALLY!

Bombs, terrorism, rebellion, anger, anti-sociality, and anti-author-itarianism, *Dangerous Encounter – 1st Kind* sticks its finger up at a host of moral figures (including parents and adults). *Dangerous Encounter – 1st Kind* coalesces a bunch of social tensions, including the younger vs. older generation, the individual vs. the mass, femininity against masculinity, Hong Kong vs. the People's Republic of China, teens vs. authority, etc. (The rebellious, anti-social fury in *Dangerous Encounter – 1st Kind* is reminiscent of the 1960s movies of Jean-Luc Godard, when Jean-Pierre Léaud, Anne Wiazemsky, Anna Karina, Jean-Paul Belmondo and many others would get up to similar pranks, usually with a passionate Maoist, Marxist, anti-capitalist agenda).

Other movies which come to mind with a similarly bleak outlook include the zombie movies of George Romero, and *A Short Film About Killing* (Krzysztof Kieslowski, 1988). Plus some of Ingmar Bergman's angrier films (such as *Persona*, 1967). And perhaps *A Clockwork Orange* (1971).

Stephen Teo called *Dangerous Encounter – 1st Kind* 'a film made with extreme prejudice, it did not whitewash its nastiness or its vision of a miasmic social reality' (1997, 164). It was a film which placed 'youth within a society that despises youth, building up a relentless momentum of emotion in the process' (ib., 148). Lisa Morton described *Dangerous Encounter* thus: 'the bleak, nihilistic, ultraviolent and finally wrenchingly tragic film was a fireball captured on silver nitrate, one of the most incendiary films ever made' (11). Chuck Stephens called *Dangerous Encounter – 1st Kind* 'Tsui's greatest, weirdest film, a true psychotronic wonder' (F. Dannen, 409).

Dangerous Encounter – 1st Kind ran into censorship problems (including in its home territory of Hong Kong),[6] after it had been screened at the Berlin Film Festival. A re-cut version appeared in 1981 (it was thus Tsui's fourth theatrical release). Tsui and the team went back and re-edited *Dangerous Encounter – 1st Kind,* and also re-shot the plot about the foreign gun-runners, to make the piece more palatable (and also lessening the depiction of the three youths as bomb makers and teenage terrorists; new scenes involving the Hong Kong cops were included, taking

---

6 There was a coda to *Dangerous Encounter – 1st Kind* which evoked the 1967 riots in Hong Kong, which the authorities also didn't like. As Leung Ping-kwan put it, the newsreels 'provide the audience with the political and social contexts for a better understanding of the anger and anxieties expressed in the film and the raw yet daring efforts of the director to define the urban space of Hong Kong'. ("Urban Cinema and the Cultural Identity of Hong Kong", in P. Fu, 239).

the emphasis away from the kids; that Tsui was born in Vietnam and the Yanks are Vietnam War veterans is part of the political subtext of *Dangerous Encounter – 1st Kind*).

Dangerous Encounter – 1st Kind was a flop at the box office (like Tsui's other two movies as director of the time). However, *Dangerous Encounter – 1st Kind,* like *The Butterfly Murders* and *We're Going To Eat You*, showed that Tsui Hark was just getting started!

ANGER.

Like other early Tsui Hark movies, *Dangerous Encounter – 1st Kind* is much less known in the Western world than later outings such as *Once Upon a Time In China* or *New Dragon Gate Inn* (being a flop at the box office didn't help). But it's worth seeking out for its vivid, abrasive, aggressive and highly cinematic qualities, its evocation of the scuzzier, grittier sides of Hong Kong, its portrait of youngsters seeking a place and an identity in the hard and heartless Big City and the tough, contemporary, Asian world, its dramatization of the tensions between the younger and the older generations, and of course its unsuppressed social and political anger.

> I was so angry, angry with myself, angry with everybody in the industry. (Tsui Hark, LM, 45)

Like *Rome, Open City* or *The Battle of Algiers*, *Dangerous Encounter – 1st Kind* is a movie with Something To Say (tho' it is not a 'message movie', and it doesn't preach to its audience like too many Western movies branded as 'political' do).

Dangerous Encounter – 1st Kind may be 'realistic', but that is only a product of the surface element of filming on location in contemporary Hong Kong with characters that appear to be 'contemporary'. In fact, *Dangerous Encounter – 1st Kind* is very heightened, improbable and fantastical cinema.

'NO MICE WERE HARMED IN THE MAKING OF THIS MOVIE.'
Maybe – but don't bet on it!
This is a film that opens with cute, white mice having pins pushed through them, in amongst a series of gloomy-ugly images – barbed wire, a heavy storm, neighbours being pranked, shabby tenements – while a newcaster relates that day's horror stories of death and destruction (including darkly compelling news stories about schoolboys who drowned in a quarry). *Dangerous Encounter – 1st Kind* announces from the outset

that this is a horrible world, and it's horrible at home as well as outside.

WAN CHU.

At the centre of *Dangerous Encounter – 1st Kind* is the young woman Wan Chu,[7] who's full of barely suppressed rage (and a search for identity) which is exhibited in a range of anti-social behaviour. (From the opening minutes, when we see Wan Chu torturing pet mice in her den, she moves on to throwing a cat out of her fourth story window so it's impaled on a barbed wire fence and expires with monster-loud screeches. She is one nasty girl!).

That her brother Tan is a key authority figure, a cop (tho' a cool, charismatic, but not particularly successful one), is a dramatic cliché (but it works). That there are no parental presences in Wan Chu's life is significant (meanwhile, one of the three boys, Ah Lung, doesn't get on well with his folks or his home life at all).

Wan Chu is one of the most vivid portraits of a strong woman in Tsui Hark's cinema (and a gift to actress Lin Zhenqi), and the 1980 movie probably works partly because of the gender reversal. That it's three guys being manipulated by a young woman is a classic Tsui-ian approach to the story (as Tsui put it, a woman throwing a spear is just more interesting than a guy throwing it. Tsui feels very strongly about reversing the arrangement of gender in cinema).[8]

Dangerous Encounter – 1st Kind depicts Wan Chu as effortlessly ahead of the boys every time, from the moment she first meets them after their cinema prank. For ex, inviting them to her digs,[9] she pulls a gun on them. Ah, it's only a plastic toy, one of them replies. Wrong! Wan Chu has modified it so it can shoot needles, and she pulls the trigger and smashes a glass behind them as they duck. And what Wan Chu wants from the boys – this is great screenwriting – is for them to be her friends. (The lads don't know what Wan Chu is going to do or say next, but none of them were expecting that! Nor that Wan Chu would be dangling a wriggling mouse in front of them, which she's just pierced!).

A girl in a world of boys – surely the issue of love/ romance/ sex is going to raise its ugly-pretty head? It does – *Dangerous Encounter – 1st Kind* needs to get the issue of love and sex out of the way early on, to demonstrate that this movie isn't about girls and boys, and it isn't romantic

7 Placing Pearl at the centre of this bleak view of life 'flies in the face of all Western film convention' (Lisa Morton, 44).
8 Hayao Miyazaki feels the same: a woman wielding a weapon is automatically more compelling than a man, he says.
9 Wan Chu sees the lads nervously performing a prank involving a timed bomb in a crowded cinema, and she knows that she can bring them into her twisted realm. (The movie showing in the cinema is a thunderously loud war movie, cleverly reminding us that it's war everywhere in the real world).

twaddle! No, it's a ferocious, black comedy – to illustrate this, there's a scene at a basketball court on a sunny day where a cocky kid who fancies his chances ambles up to Wan Chu and slings her a chat-up line, as men have done with women for at least 500,000 years. And what does Wan Chu do? Throws a lighted cig into his shorts. Ouch! (The consequences are played for comedy – Wan Chu isn't smashed in the face, for ex (that comes later); instead, she huffs off, and the boy's buddies pour soda down their friend's shorts).

THE SET-UP.

So the narrative set-up of *Dangerous Encounter – 1st Kind* is disarmingly goofy (and unsettling): the three dweebs[10] have built a homemade bomb which they intend to set off in a crowded cinema. While a movie plays involving a battle of WW2 tanks (and soldiers using bombs),[11] the jape works far better than the youths reckoned. They manage to flee, but Wan Chu spots them, and comes after them, threatening to turn them in unless they join her in a series of crazy pranks.

That might be the set-up and hook for a charming, Hollywood comedy-action-adventure flick – *Home Alone* meets *The Goonies*, say, with fresh-faced moppets getting the better of hopeless crooks and annoying parents. Oh no, not in the hands of Roy Szeto and Tsui Hark! They push the premise to the max, announcing just how malicious they're going to go in the first three minutes, with images of the torture of animals accompanied by a catalogue of depressing events on the news.

Soon the three kids are being shown how to *really* be a nutcase in public when Wan Chu explodes a bomb in a restroom on a street, threatens a coachload of Japanese tourists with another homemade bomb, and forces them to strip (dropping them off in the middle of nowhere), and douses the boys in gasoline and tries to set them on fire!

That's it's a skinny female teenager who's manipulating the three boys without them seeming to (be able) do anything to counter her is part of the amusement. At one point, one of them (Ah Lung) can't take it anymore, leaps on top of her and throttles her. She kicks him in the balls, then threatens to jump off a high building (or allow them to push her off). Whatever the boys come up with, Wan Chu is always ahead of them, always has an answer.

Dangerous Encounter – 1st Kind is entertaining/ compelling partly because you don't quite know what Wan Chu is going to do next (so that

10 The nerdy boys all wear glasses (and so does Wan Chu – possibly taking after the lads – this is the era of very large glasses, which Tsui also sported at the time).
11 There are some wicked jokes here – a girlfriend asks her man, about the movie, 'are those bombs real?' And he replies, 'of course they are, this is a foreign film!'

the boys, and the police, are always reacting to her actions). As with other movies of mentally unstable characters (such as *One Flew Over the Cuckoo's Nest* and *The Dark Knight*), that gives the 1980 picture an unpredictable element which keeps the narrative fresh. (And not only is Wan Chu unpredictable, she is also dangerous).

If you take *Dangerous Encounter – 1st Kind* straight, you'll see a bizarre movie about a nasty, bratty girl who leads a bunch of boys astray in contemporary Hong Kong (she starts off by sticking pins in her pet mice, then gets more'n more vicious). If you clue into the humour (which is everywhere in *Dangerous Encounter – 1st Kind)*, you'll see a comedy (albeit pretty dark) in which the filmmakers use the anti-social, anti-authoritarian pranks of Wan Chu and her cohorts to attack a bunch of targets and social issues.

There is an undercurrent of anti-consumerism in *Dangerous Encounter – 1st Kind,* which pokes fun at the shallow lives of the bourgeoisie (including their idiotic consumption of television). Television is a sub-theme in *Dangerous Encounter – 1st Kind* – in many scenes TVs are burbling in the background (one shows *Tom and Jerry*). It's clear that, in the world of *Dangerous Encounter – 1st Kind,* life is so nasty the populace dope themselves up with cretinous entertainment. (Who needs L.S.D., Jean-Luc Godard said in the 1960s, when you've got colour television?).

THE SECOND AND THIRD ACTS.

So the pranks and juvenile delinquency in *Dangerous Encounter – 1st Kind* escalate until the gang of misfits encounters a North American gangster, Bruce (Bruce Baron) working for Chinese triads. At this point, *Dangerous Encounter – 1st Kind* becomes a somewhat different movie, with more conventional gangster/ thriller ingredients. (Several scenes don't quite fit with the rest of *Dangerous Encounter – 1st Kind,* dramatically or tonally. For example, there's a very ugly scene featuring a nude call-girl or girlfriend (Jenny Liang)[12] who's stabbed and killed by Bruce,[13] for no apparent reason other than he's irked that he lost the important documents being carried for the triads. Sure, the man's angry and fears for his life, but killing someone else? That's over-the-top).

However, you buy it partly because the filmmakers come up with a truly outrageous scene to bring together the wannabe terrorists plot and the adult gangsters/ thriller plot. It is one of the most out-there scenes in all of Tsui Hark's cinema: Wan Chu sets upon the boys with gasoline and

the credits, she's a prostitute.
nudity seems included purely for gratuitous reasons. It doesn't fit because
Encounter – 1st Kind has already shown us that it *won't* be about sex or male-
ns.

burning rags! This is one *very* difficult girl! She douses them with gas and chases after them with flames (a scene with very Godardian[14] aspects); in the chaos, as the lads strip off so they won't be burnt alive, they run into a hoodlum in a car. Wan Chu makes off with the precious cargo the hood was carrying, thus knitting together the world of organized crime and arms dealing with teenagers pushing at the ethical boundaries of society.

A lot of screen time in *Dangerous Encounter – 1st Kind* is given over to the repercussions of Wan Chu accidentally-on-purpose stealing the hood's booty, which includes Japanese Yen money orders, which the youths try a number of times to cash (seeking the aide of a dodgy DJ in a white suit (by name of Uncle Hark, played by Richard Da Silva) who's stepped right out of 1970s blaxploitation cinema. The scene is another pounding disco setting).

Wan Chu certainly has guts – she goes right up to this guy Uncle Hark and asks him to help her make the deal to cash in the Japanese Yen bank orders. And earlier, she approaches the youth in the basketball court, asking to see his boss. This crook was the one who came on to Wan Chu, only for her to toss a cigarette down his shorts!

As the plot of *Dangerous Encounter – 1st Kind* depicts the kids getting more'n more involved with the criminal underworld, there are inevitable run-ins with triad gangs (it's not a Hong Kong action or thriller picture unless there are triads running around with knives. John Woo built his whole career around that).

The big action scene that climaxes the second act of *Dangerous Encounter – 1st Kind* has the kids improbably out-witting and out-running a large group of triad heavies. The action team delivers plenty of running, fighting, driving and explosive gags in a basement car lot (these teen terrorists uses bombs and bottles of gasoline as their chief weapon).

Improbable this scene is, but it's also hugely entertaining – Tony Ching Siu-tung has few peers in action direction: this man is a genius at staging action. This is a textbook action sequence of startling gags and escalating mayhem. Now we see why the triad henchmen are all young guys armed with *knives* – because with a handgun, they'd be able to shoot at the kids, and this sequence is all about the kids somehow trouncing swarms of henchmen.

For the finale of *Dangerous Encounter – 1st Kind*, the violence builds to greater levels: a bodyguard is killed from one of the bombs the kids explode (at the car of a money changer); Wan Chu is menaced and

---

14 *Dangerous Encounter – 1st Kind* is reminiscent of many 1960s movies by Jean-Luc Godard, including *Bande à Parte, Pierrot le Fou, Le Chinoise* and *Weekend*.

attacked by triad heavies on the street outside her home, until she's rescued by her brother, the cop Tan (who then beats up his sister repeatedly in a nasty sequence, to punish her);[15] chained to the window by Tan, Wan Chu is set upon by some thugs who enter her apartment at night; finally, during a struggle outside, Wan Chu falls and is impaled on the same spikes that took the life of the cat she hurled out of the window in the opening reel (while Tan is also at the scene, but entering the building from the rear, so he's too late to save his sister).

Each of these scenes is a *tour-de-force* of action cinema, containing numerous memorable details – like the sight of Wan Chu flailing wildly with a knife in the midst of a bunch of henchmen in the street, and then being menaced by Uncle Hark, who sets fire to her hair.

The death of Wan Chu is an incredible scene of suspense and threat – to keep her out of mischief, Wan Chu has been tied by her brother to the window bars (by a plastic tie). Extreme, but it puts the anti-heroine in a position of high vulnerability, when the *gweilo* hoods smash their way into the apartment.

The filmmaking here, and in the rest of *Dangerous Encounter – 1st Kind,* is absolutely rock-solid – there's a clean, efficient methodology to Tsui Hark's direction. Altho' it's showy, Tsui's staging and filming of scenes is direct and to the point. Bringing Tan back home right at this point is wholly conventional, but the punchiness of the orchestration of mayhem carries it all through. How, for ex, the neighbours are brought into the action sequence at the edges (the lady next door who fumes loudly, and the blasé guy downstairs). How Wan Chu makes one final bid for freedom, only to end up impaled on the fence outside.

With the death of Wan Chu, *Dangerous Encounter – 1st Kind* shifts its centre of gravity, but it has to tie up the fates of the three lads, and of the thriller/ triads subplot.[16] Thus, policeman Tan is hot on the case, determined to track down and bring to justice the killers of his sister Wan Chu (tho' his irritated superiors (Inspector Lui played by Ray Lui) order him to take some leave. There are several scenes where Tan explodes with frustration, including pouncing on some white guys in the street – who turn out to be Mormons).

The three youths have fled to the New Territories: *Dangerous Encounter – 1st Kind* stages its action climax in a large, rural cemetery in the foothills of the New Territories.[17] Cop Tan closes in on the bickering

---

15 As they tussle, the photograph of their dead father topples and the glass smashes.
16 There's a hilarious scene where Paul freaks out at the sight of a white guy at the bar – a foreigner! A white devil! (But even tho' Paul is playing up, over-reacting and running away, it's also a recurring gag in Hong Kong cinema – look out, there's a white man!).
17 Filmed during the day, probably for budgetary reasons, but it really should be a night sequence.

boys, mistaking them for his sister's murderers; when the N. American hoods turn up, the filmmakers mount an elaborate running fire-fight and cat-and-mouse chase.

The ending of *Dangerous Encounter – 1st Kind* has the quality of the nihilistic Westerns helmed by Sam Peckinpah, where everybody dies (and in a pathetic, hopeless manner). The action is brilliantly choreographed by Tony Ching Siu-tung (a low budget is no limit if you have a terrific imagination and a great stunt team who're willing to try anything).

This is one of the great action sequences in all of Tsui Hark's cinema – and he's delivered quite a few! What makes it soar is partly that the heroes/ anti-heroes are three kids, who, despite their big talk and posturing, are still three nerdy cowards from Hong Kong. Another significant ingredient is the desperation of the boys, as their lives seem to fall apart (they have tried drinking Dettol, in a sort of half-hearted suicide pact, which of course backfires). And the lads are pitted against serious hoods, fully armed. (That the boys accidentally shoot each other enhances the pathos. Ah Lung is shot to pieces in his hiding spot).

Guns, knives, pieces of wood, stones – the filmmakers throw everything into the mix, and it all pays off. This is Hong Kong action cinema in its rough-and-ready approach, where there's dust and grime and blood and sweat, and characters land hard on the ground. Look, for instance, at the details in the visuals: long shots of the cemetery with barbed wire snaking thru the sky; the kids dodging bullets behind the gravestones.

At the end, somehow having survived, Ko loses it, cackling and laughing as he fires a machine gun at the thousands of already-dead people in the graveyard. It's an end of chaos and despair, and the sound of gunfire continues over a short montage of b/w photographs of riots in Hong Kong in 1967 (adding an overtly political/ historical veneer to the narrative, which hardly needs it – we can see that it's war everywhere in this movie). [18]

This is a one-of-a-kind movie, and really worth seeking out.

.   .

18 Besides, the photos replay the motif of the war movie in the theatre scene.

2

PEKING OPERA BLUES

Dao Ma Daan

Peking Opera Blues (*Dao Ma Daan* in Mandarin = *Knife Horse Actresses*, 1986) was directed and co-produced by Tsui Hark; Raymond To Kwok-wai wrote the script; Claudie Chung Jan and Tsui were producers for Cinema City/ Film Workshop; David Wu Dai-wanwas editor; Hang-Sang Poon and Horace Wong Wing-hang were DPs; prod. des. by Kim-sing Ho, Chi-hing Leung and Vincent Wai; costumes by Bobo Bo-ling Ng and Peggy Cheung Siu-ping; hair by Lee Kin-tai; make-up by Fung Cho-tak; Tony Ching Siu-tung and Stephen Tung Wei were the action choreographers; music by James Wong and David Wu; it was distributed by Golden Princess.[19] Released Sept 6, 1986. 104 minutes.

Peking Opera Blues featured a stellar cast, many of whom were Tsui regulars: Brigitte Lin Ching-hsia, Sally Yeh Tse-man, Cherie Chung, Mark Cheng, Kenneth Tsang, Paul Chun Kong and veteran Wu Ma. Also in the cast were: Kwok Keung Cheung, Feng Ku, Po-Chih Leong, Ha Huang, Yin Szema, Ching Tien, and Dean Shek.

Peking Opera Blues is a 100% Tsui Hark classic movie: there's nothing not to like and enjoy in this slice of pure showbiz. *Peking Opera Blues* is a favourite with Hong Kong cinema fans,[20] regularly placed in fans' top tens: it's a terrific, feel-good movie (and a wonderful Christmas movie, too).

Peking Opera Blues is a historical movie, a nostalgic[21] movie, a backstage comedy, and an action-adventure spy story (with plenty of

19 Tsui Hark said that they had subtitled *Peking Opera Blues* for under $100 and in 2 days.
20 It was nominated for 6 awards at the Hong Kong Film Awards.
21 Several of Tsui Hark's movies benefitted from (and helped to create) the rise in the cinema of nostalgia of the late 1980s (with movies such as *Peking Opera Blues*).

action – Tony Ching Siu-tung and Stephen Tung Wei were the action directors). *Peking Opera Blues* happily skids between these genres, blending them and subverting them – which's one of the hallmarks of Tsui Hark's cinema (but genre-bending is also a hallmark of Hong Kong cinema – sometimes Hong Kong movies look as if they are entries in a competition to mix the most genres within a single movie).22

Tsui Hark has a thing for Peking Opera, and reckoned it would be good material for a comedy (LM, 70). The main titles features Peking Opera performers, costumes and props. (The film's title, like *Shanghai Blues*, emphasizes the links to the great movie centres of Chinese history).

Peking Opera Blues is also a reminder that *comedy* is a big part of Tsui Hark's cinema; this was the mid-1980s, of course, when Tsui had been working for Cinema City (a studio devoted to comedy), and had been involved with comedies such as *Aces Go Places* and *All the Wrong Clues*. But humour continued to play an important role in Tsui's output, whether it was in the *Once Upon a Time In China* series, or in movies that Tsui produced (such as *A Chinese Ghost Story* or the *Swordsman* series).

The background of *Peking Opera Blues* involves warlords vying for power during the regime of Yuan Shikai (the first President of the Republic), and his ambitions to expand his territory following the 1911 revolution in China. (It's set in Peking in 1913). A loan agreement between Chinese and foreign powers is one of the issues (and the documents of the loan form one of the MacGuffins).

Peking Opera Blues raises issues such as democracy, nationalism, government and politics in a self-conscious manner: *Peking Opera Blues* is not a history lesson, nor a message movie – it's primarily a piece of entertainment; but it is a satire on the Chinese ignorance of democracy, as Tsui Hark put it (and it contains sly digs at regimes such as the British in Hong Kong, and the People's Republic of China).

The celebrated 1993 movie *Farewell My Concubine* seems like a melodramatic sequel to *Peking Opera Blues* – *Farewell My Concubine* similarly focusses on a Peking Opera troupe to explore recent, Chinese history. Tsui Hark has adapted books by the author of *Farewell My Concubine,* Lilian Lee, and Tsui regular Leslie Cheung starred in it.

The stars of a movie like *Peking Opera Blues* include the production designs (Kim-Sing Ho, Chi-Hing Leung and Vincent Wai), the costume designers (Bobo Bo-Ling Ng and Peggy Cheung Siu-Ping), the hair (Lee Kin-Tai) and make-up (Fung Cho-Tak) supervisors, the DPs (Poon Hang-Sang and Horace Wong Wing-Hang), and the props guys (Lee Kuen-Long

22 *Project A* (1983) may have influenced the setting of *Peking Opera Blues*, and the female leads might've been inspired by *Golden Queen* (1984), which also starred Brigitte Lin and Sally Yeh.

and Cheung Foo-Wing).

Peking Opera Blues is *fast*, it's light, it's frothy and it's beautifully designed (a riot of colour, especially in the costumes). *Fast* – at the usual Tsui Hark rate of 1,000 miles-an-hour, and very nimble on its feet. There is a light touch to Tsui's comedies: the gags are not laboured over, and there's no pause built into the editing to allow the audience to laugh (but I bet this movie played like gangbusters in Hong Kong theatres).

Peking Opera Blues is another Tsui Hark movie which crams in several movies into 104 minutes, as well as careening around several genres. If only, the nay-sayers complain, Tsui could stick to a *few* issues and *one* genre and *one* stylistic approach. No, that's just not enough for Tsui! He'd be bored sick! Thus, *Peking Opera Blues* veers from bawdy slapstick comedy one minute (where Sheung Hung tries to grab a gun), to serious melodrama (which Tsao Yun cradles her dying father) the next, to full-on action cinema a moment later. For Lisa Morton, it's 'a film that created its own genre (the period-comedy-women's-actioner?)' (LM, 65).

Fast but not superficial, merely flashy, or incoherent: it's fast but always clear and readable: Hal Henson noted of the editing style in *Peking Opera Blues*:

> The action moves almost incomprehensibly fast, and the editing rhythms crackle like machine-gun fire. Not in a long time has a filmmaker made the screen jump with energy and wit and invention the way Hark does here. But though directed for speed, it doesn't have the sort of heedless acceleration that closes out beauty or coherence. (1988)

If you go back and look at (1) the shots in *Peking Opera Blues*, how they are staged, the information they convey, and then (2) look at how the beats are constructed, and then (3) consider how the beats are edited together to make mini-scenes, and then (4) see how those mini-scenes are placed end-to-end to form a whole scene, you will find that the construction, the selection of camera angles, the shot sizes, the lenses, the framing, and all of the other technical/ artistic choices are dead-on, are carefully worked-out, and, crucially, add up to a mesmerizing *flow*.

By contrast, if you look at rapid editing in films which don't work or flow, you can see that cutting quickly isn't the whole deal: it's about how the shots work in themselves, and together, to form a sequence. Some filmmakers are simply naturals at this construction (which is intuitive and instinctive).

There is plenty to enjoy in *Peking Opera Blues*: the enormous ensemble cast (which features a host of familiar faces in Hong Kong cinema); the sleek, sexy persona of Brigitte Lin Ching-hsia (here crossdressing for one of the first times of many in Chinese cinema); the breathless pace; the fizzy comedy; the dazzling visuals and designs (the production design and cinematography are outstanding); and of course the deftness and ingenuity of the action sequences.

And for those who need it or demand it (i.e., many Western film critics), *Peking Opera Blues* features political themes and subtexts a-plenty. Filmed in Hong Kong, set in Peking in a time of political unrest in the early years of the twentieth century (in 1913), *Peking Opera Blues* has everything a critic could desire in evoking political and ideological discourses.

If you like backstage comedies and backstage musicals (and who doesn't?!), *Peking Opera Blues* doesn't disappoint. *Peking Opera Blues* satisfies like the finest backstage musical comedies (such as, in the West, *42nd Street* or *Singin' In the Rain*). It's got the bitchy, very camp actors; it's got the exasperated veteran who runs the theatre and is focussed above all on keeping his business thriving; it's got the newbies who have to dress up and venture on stage to avoid detection; it's got performances going wrong; it's got crossdressing and disguises; and it's got the actors and the theatre being swept up in larger, political events.

The *exuberance* of this 1986 Cantonese movie, its panache, its all-out efforts to entertain, completely swamp the viewer. It's impossible not to be swept along by this artfully artificial confection.

A candy confection, admittedly, but one with blood and guts and a real passion for ideological and political issues. There's no doubting Tsao Yun's devotion to the political cause (or Ling Pak-hoi's), and how she will risk her life for it. There's no getting away from the fact that quite a bit of *Peking Opera Blues* is pretty gritty and hard-hitting: the torture scene, where Tsao Yun is whipped, is extremely nasty and intense (and *very long*, too). And when it's a woman being beaten and slathered over (and when that woman is played by Brigitte Lin),[23] the violence inherent in the scene (in the patriarchal system, you might say), is vividly manifested. (It's too much, really, and the movie doesn't need it – or to see this much of it).

Fluffy and romantic and nostalgic *Peking Opera Blues* might be at heart, but it doesn't draw a veil over the costs of political idealism when it's put into practice in the complicated, corrupt real world. The torture scene might come from another movie, and seems way over-the-top for this kind of backstage comedy mixed with a spy melodrama and a Shanghai-esque musical. (And, along the way, the other women also suffer, getting into all

23 Nobody wants to see Brigitte Lin being whipped and tortured.

sorts of scrapes).

Peking Opera Blues is a pæan to the movies that Tsui Hark grew up with, to the history of Chinese cinema, to an old-fashioned way of making movies, and to aspects of traditional, Chinese culture (such as the Peking Opera performance style). *Peking Opera Blues* is also an *hommage* to the live performances from the Peking Opera schools that Tsui would've seen in Hong Kong (Jackie Chan, Yuen Biao and Sammo Hung were famously part of the China Drama Academy of Peking Opera, which was portrayed in *Painted Faces*, released in 1988).

In *Peking Opera Blues*, Tsui Hark and his team are also exploring the past: around half of Tsui's films as director have been set in the past. In *Peking Opera Blues*, Tsui goes back to 1913, to a crucial period in the formation of modern China. That Tsui is dedicated to investigating Chinese history and culture everybody knows (it's positively a crusade for him): in *Peking Opera Blues*, the political and ideological aspects of this particular historical period are highlighted. It's a similar era to the *Once Upon a Time In China* series (the third *Once Upon a Time In China* movie is very close in its time period to *Peking Opera Blues*).

For some critics (such as Stephen Teo), *Peking Opera Blues* is more style over substance, with Tsui Hark and the team being absorbed by production and costume design, action choreography and movement, and the look of the whole thing, rather than with delivering a story with weight and characters with three dimensions.[24]

It's true that *Peking Opera Blues* has affinities with an M.G.M. musical comedy movie like *Singin' In the Rain* or *The Pirate*, but it also wants to dance away into multiple genres and forms, without being shackled by notions of classical structure and characterization. Even so, *Peking Opera Blues* is still telling a story all the time, and the narrative and the editing are firmly fixed to the characters and their goals (and when we look closely at the script we find that, yes, once again, it *is* classical in structure, as nearly all of Tsui's films are). There is a strong foundation to the narrative of *Peking Opera Blues*, despite how colourful and luxurious it is (and Hollywood musicals, too, are actually telling a story, and are classical structurally, no matter how much the filmmakers seem to be engrossed in camera moves or over-the-top costumes).

24 Stephen Teo suggests that the comedies of Frank Tashlin might be a Western equivalent.

WOMEN AND GENDER.

A reason that Tsui Hark often gives for the success of his movies is that he was able to cast certain actors at a certain time in their lives. Thus, he made *Peking Opera Blues* partly because he wanted to use the three actresses before they retired and got married: 'for that moment they are very fantastic and silly characters in the movie; probably later they would never have that chance again' (LM, 69).

In focussing on women, Tsui Hark's thinking was simple: 'I said, "Why don't we just make a movie with no guys, just women?"' (LM, 69). Not only would *Peking Opera Blues* be about women, it would be a period piece, and a comedy (there was resistance, Tsui recalled, to rendering important historical events in a comical style).

Gender is foregrounded in *Peking Opera Blues* from the outset: this was a movie in which, as with *Shanghai Blues*, Tsui Hark wanted to explore female protagonists, to see a story from a female/ feminine/ proto-feminist perspective. Hence the three women (Sally Yeh, Brigitte Lin and Cherie Chung) at the heart of *Peking Opera Blues*. Hence the setting of the Peking Opera theatre, where all the roles are played by men (as in many theatre traditions around the world and throughout history). Hence Tsao Yun dressing in a black suit with short hair as a man. Hence Sheung Hung being unable to dive into the dressing room to find the box of jewels. Hence a woman being thrown out of the dressing rooms. The gender issue is employed throughout *Peking Opera Blues* to create situations and to drive the narrative (as if the producers asked screenwriter Raymond To Kwok-wai to foreground gender as much as possible).

Part of the pleasure of *Peking Opera Blues* is simply that writer Raymond To Kwok-wai and the filmmakers have put women in roles usually taken by men (tho' it does take some finagling from To Kwok-wai to orchestrate scenarios where the women can convincingly do what male heroes usually do, and even more fiddling around with the mechanics of the plot to get the three women to work together and be in the same scenes together). But all of that hard work at the script meetings pays off (and thru much of the first act), because the most satisfying scenes are definitely those where the three women are adventuring as a trio.

Brigitte Lin is crossdressing in *Peking Opera Blues* and yet her gender is not disguised – this occurs throughout Tsui Hark's cinema. It's gender-bending with identity not obscured: altho' Tsao Yun would be played by a guy in most other movies, her femininity isn't hidden (LM, 68).

Splitting the heroine into three means that the filmmakers can explore several aspects of the key themes: Bai Niu/ Pat Neil (Sally Yeh Tse-man) is the performer, the artist, who wants to go on stage in her father's theatre; Xiang Hong/ Sheung Hung (Cherie Chung) is a woman on the make, with her eye on treasure (money, capitalism); Tsao Yun/ Wan (Brigitte Lin) is the political idealist, striving to do the right thing. You can regard the three women as aspects of China, of Hong Kong, of cinema, of politics in contemporary China, of contemporary youth in Canton, of anything you like.

Seeing each of the three actresses embody these issues and personalities is a treat. There's no doubt that Brigitte Lin steals the 1986 movie, that she is the heart and the conscience of *Peking Opera Blues*, and that she is the principal character (the narrative is most often following her, and is structured around her). Lin is sensational in *Peking Opera Blues* (is she ever less than sensational?!), and went on to become one of the greatest stars in Asian cinema (including essaying some key roles in the cinema of Tsui Hark, such as her Asia the Invincible in the *Swordsman* series).

Altho' the relationships between the three women Tsao Yun, Sheung Hung and Bai Niu are at heart of *Peking Opera Blues*, their relations with two young men (Ling Pak-hoi and Tung Man)[25] and two fathers (General Tsao and Boss Wong) are also significant. Much emotional juice, for instance, is squeezed out of Tsao Yun's relationship with her father (she is clearly a father's girl, and a woman with a father complex).[26] There are several touching scenes of tenderness between father and daughter, with Wan weeping, and feeling awful about betraying her father.

Meanwhile, Bai Niu/ Pat Neil exasperates her daddy, Boss Wong, with her ambitions to go on stage. And Sheung Hung gets to seduce Wong (played by the wonderful Wu Ma), in a comical scene which's delivered in a deliberately old-fashioned and stagey manner.

THE STORY, ACT BY ACT.

Much of the first act of *Peking Opera Blues* is set-up — not only is it exposition (as in any narrative-based movie), it is exposition designed to lead to the scenarios we see later. To keep the narrative set-up and exposition light and breezy, two MacGuffins are employed: first, and the easiest to grasp, is the box of jewels which Sheung Hung is desperate to get hold of; a simple treasure hunt plot, then, but one which gets Sheung into all sorts of situations (hiding in a car/ creeping around a mansion/ fainting at the sight of a bloody operation, etc).

25 However, the romantic subplots of the two women with the two youths are only lightly brushed in to the picture (which isn't that interested in them in the end).
26 At times, Tsao Yun's relationship with her pa threatens to over-shadow that between the three women.

The second MacGuffin of *Peking Opera Blues* is the more serious one, the political plot about the warlords, the Republic, the president, China and Peking: the loan documents involving foreign powers. Cleverly, writer Raymond To ties the two MacGuffins together when Sheung cadges a ride with Tsao Yun, and arrives at the general's manse (ending up in the same room as the safe where General Tsao has put the documents).

Act two of *Peking Opera Blues* continues the rapid to-ing and fro-ing of the charas and the 1,000 m.p.h. storytelling focusses on the Peking Opera performances at the theatre. The camera dwells lovingly on the actors in close-up with that stunning make-up (Fung Cho-tak was make-up head, with hair by Lee Kin-tai). Part of the time it seems as if *Peking Opera Blues* is stunned and delighted to have actresses such as Sally Yeh and Cherie Chung in full Peking Opera make-up and costume, and just wants to contemplate them at length in C.U.

And with the star of the Peking Opera show, Fa Kam-shu, leaving (after an ugly scene backstage where the mobster Liu seems intent on adding him to his collection of lovers), *Peking Opera Blues* makes the inevitable decision to put Sally Yeh on stage (to cover for Fa). Which's amazing enough – but then it tops that, by shoving Cherie Chung's Sheung Hung onto the stage, too (much to Bai Niu's father's dismay).

This is cinema at its most self-indulgent and glorious – and it's wholly in tune with Tsui Hark's project of reviving older forms of Chinese entertainment, history and mythology. And the balance of elements is perfect – because the second extraordinary, Peking Opera performance winds up with a massive fire-fight. It's acrobatic, comedic, and insanely fast (there's a great gag of the punters leaping onto the benches as the gunmen shoot it out on the floor, then ducking to the floor when the heavies stand up and fire).

It's scenes like this which encourage critics to rate *Peking Opera Blues* as the perfect Hong Kong (action) movie. It's got the lot.

And at the end of act two, *Peking Opera Blues* has put together the three female stars, Brigitte Lin, Cherie Chung and Sally Yeh, side-by-side (paying off that complicated script work in act one). In some movies, it's enjoyable to witness the formation of the trio or team, so to speak: *Peking Opera Blues* brings together the women legitimately and coherently.

And there's also the feeling that the filmmakers (and Tsui Hark in particular), are revelling in seeing the three girls together, when Tsao Yun, Sheung Hung and Bai Niu retire to Wan's place (after fleeing from the theatre), dressed in floaty, white, Western dresses (and getting drunk).

The action finale of *Peking Opera Blues* is a staggering *tour-de-force* of a fire-fight and chase across the nighttime rooftops of Peking.[27] Action director Tony Ching Siu-tung employs his customary elaborate and dazzling cable-work, encouraging the stunt team to ever-greater heights of acrobatics and daredevil stunts. 'An absolute masterpiece of Hong Kong action cinema' (Lisa Morton, 67). The finale of *Peking Opera Blues* is a joyous celebration of every trick that cinema can perform, but there's plenty of blood and near-deaths for our heroes, too (you don't really believe that the movie is going to sacrifice any of the three women or the two men, but sometimes it looks as if it might). Tsao Yun, for instance, is riddled with bullets.

CRITICS ON *PEKING OPERA BLUES*.

And the critics loved it.

If there is a 'best' Hong Kong picture, it is probably *Peking Opera Blues*, claimed Andy Klein (he had seen it over 20 times).[28] As Barbara Scharres noted of *Peking Opera Blues*, 'everything works'.[29] 'One of the most astonishing things about *Peking Opera Blues* is that its occasionally extreme tone shifts work so well' (Lisa Morton, 66). 'One of the best female action films' (Jenny Kwok Wah-Lau, 2005, 741). *Time Out* called *Peking Opera Blues* 'a speed-crazed riff on what happens when a spy melodrama meets a backstage comedy: Feydeau with blood at 150 beats per minute'. Howard Hampton wrote of *Peking Opera Blues*:

> Still unsurpassed. Tsui Hark recapitulates nearly the whole history of cinema – from slapstick farce to tragic heroism – in one gleeful, manic burst of inspiration. The last twenty minutes are so exhilarating, it's as though your entire moviegoing life flashed before your eyes.[30]

Ric Meyers on *Peking Opera Blues*: 'a soaring, romantic action-comedy, with loads of eye-popping color, French-farce-flavored set pieces, and high-octane cinematic imagination' (F. Dannen, 375).

---

27 The fighters employ the idea of 'crossing the sea' literally, taken from the play *Eight Fairies Cross the Sea*.
28 Quoted in F. Dannen, 351.
29 Ib., 401.
30 Ib., 339.

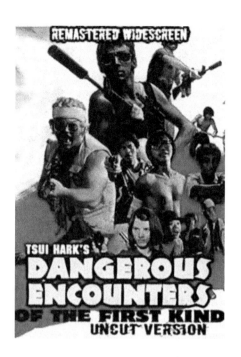

Dangerous Encounter – First Kind (1980).

Peking Opera Blues (1986).

3

A BETTER TOMORROW 2

Ying Hung Bun Sik II

A Better Tomorrow 2 (1987, *Jing Hung Bun Sik II* in Cantonese, *Ying Xiong Ben Se II* in Mandarin = *Heroic Character II*) was produced and co-written by Tsui Hark for Cinema City (Tsui has 'story by' credit), directed and co-written by John Woo (Ng Yu-sam), exec. prod. by Tony Chow Kwok-Chung, edited by David Wu, music by Joseph Koo,[1] Lowell Lo and David Wu (also music editor), action choreography by Tony Ching Siu-tung, art dir./ prod. des. by Andy Lee Yiu-Gwong, Chi Fung Lok and William Yam Wai-Leung, photography by Horace Wong Wing-hang and Bob Thompson, costumes by Pauline Lau Bo-Lam, Nancy Tong and Liu Mei-Chow, and starred Chow Yun-fat, Leslie Cheung, Ti Lung, Dean Shek, and Emily Chu. It was released on Dec 17, 1987. 104 mins.

Well, with those credits, *A Better Tomorrow 2* is going to be worth watching even if it stinks! Three major directors (Woo, Tsui and Ching), plus three great stars (Chow, Cheung and Lung)!

❀

The sequel seemed inevitable – because the first *Better Tomorrow* (1986) had been a big hit for all involved – the number one movie of 1986, with a gross in Canton of HK $34.6 million (the *Better Tomorrow* movies inspired cash-ins – such as *Hero of Tomorrow* (1988), *City War* (1989) and *Return To A Better Tomorrow* (Wong Jing, 1994)). The Hong Kong industry had been churning out gangster movies before *A Better Tomorrow*, of course, but when one comes along that proves a big hit with local audiences, and seem to develop a new cinematic style (and a hot star in

---

[1] Koo and James Wong Jim composed the theme song, performed by Leslie Cheung.

Chow Yun-fat), inevitably the rip-off movies pile in.

The first *Better Tomorrow* film (*Jing Hung Bun Sik* in Cantonese, *Ying Xiong Ben Se* in Mandarin = *Heroic Character*, a.k.a. *The Color of a Hero, Gangland Boss* and *True Colors of a Hero*) starred Chow Yun-fat, Ti Lung and Leslie Cheung. It was produced by Tsui Hark and Wan Ka Man for Cinema City and Film Workshop; written by Chan Hing-ka, Chan Shuk-dut and John Woo. It was a remake of *Story of a Discharged Prisoner* (a.k.a. *True Colors of a Hero,* 1967) and was inspired by *The Brothers* (1979), which was itself inspired by the Bollywood film *Deewaar* (1975). Released Aug 2, 1986. 95 mins.

Tsui Hark had invited John Woo to Hong Kong in 1985, to make *A Better Tomorrow* (Tsui had been appearing in *Run Tiger Run*, helmed by Woo, in Taiwan; at the same time, Tsui was preparing *A Chinese Ghost Story*, which starred Leslie Cheung, of course). According to Tsui's wife Nansun Shi, Tsui and Woo 'would go drinking, and tell stories, and pour their hearts out'. Woo said of *A Better Tomorrow* that 'a lot of the emotion behind the film reflects my friendship with Hark'.[2]

John Woo said he was feeling down because he was making comedies and he wanted to make character-driven dramas. Tsui Hark, Woo said, encouraged him to return from Taiwan to Hong Kong to direct *A Better Tomorrow*: 'he produced and helped me to write it'.

❀

There are four great performances in *A Better Tomorrow 2* – Leslie Cheung, Dean Shek, Ti Lung and Chow Yun-fat.[3] A movie can't go wrong with a cast like that – add to that action sequences choreographed by Tony Ching Siu-tung, and even if *A Better Tomorrow 2* reeked, it would have something worth watching. There is also a wonderful supporting cast, featuring many regulars in the Hong Kong movie business – Kenneth Tsang-kong and Shing Fui-on, for example, also pop up in the next film that John Woo directed, *The Killer*.

Among the many Woo-ian elements in *A Better Tomorrow 2*, apart from the mandatory ingredients of gun-play, brotherhood and old-fashioned chivalry, are a church (of course!), a hospital, a young girl who gets injured in a fire-fight, tearful reunions and sorrowful farewells.

Tsui Hark's input can be discerned in *A Better Tomorrow 2* in the introduction of not one significant female character, but two; in the romantic relationship surrounding Cantonese heartthrob Leslie Cheung; and in details such as the artist's studio featuring images of Chow Yun-Fat in his break-out role in the first *Better Tomorrow* movie (it's as if the

---

2 Woo has remarked that he drew on his friendship with Tsui Hark in the development of the relationships in *A Better Tomorrow*.
3 Chow is sensational in this movie.

audience is clamouring for Chow in the first act, we visit an artist who has produced numerous images of Chow's Mark in the Pop Art style, as if the movie is already selling its merchandize in the first act). In the third act, Ken appears in the studio, and dresses in Mark's gear: instead of being creepy and disturbing, it's played as a movie-movie moment (Ken poses beside an image of Mark in the same outfit. Hell, Ken even has a match in his *bouche*).

There were disagreements over *A Better Tomorrow 2*: John Woo said that he delivered a cut that ran to 2h 40m, which had to be reduced to two hours, within a week. So Tsui Hark also cut the movie [4] – he 'took half and I took half and we cut our parts separately. I didn't get to see the whole picture until its opening night. Naturally, the result was uneven and unsatisfying'. Woo complained that the two halves did not match up. Consequently, *A Better Tomorrow 2* is not one of Woo's favourites among his own movies.

❧

Most of the first act of *A Better Tomorrow 2* looks like it could've been directed by anybody, aside from only one or two Woo-ian flourishes (such as the over-done orchestral music, more suited to a day-time soap opera, and the long, lingering looks the men give each other. There are a few Woo-ian quirks in the editing, such as some freeze frames). Much of the first act of *A Better Tomorrow 2* is talky and low power, dramatically (the scenes are also lit flatly, without any texture or imagination). If John Woo's heart wasn't in doing this sequel, it certainly shows in act one. Dean Shek's Uncle Sei Lung is the focus, a man who's betrayed by his bosses (Shek is terrific in the scenes following his betrayal). And Leslie Cheung (as Kit/ Billie) is effortlessly wonderful, as always (was there ever a more luminous star in recent, Chinese cinema?). The focus in act one is also on Ti Lung in prison: the scenes deliver exposition and characterization.

Apart from a brief montage (which forms the nightmare of Sung-chi Ho (who's in jail), we don't see Chow Yun-fat until the start of act two of *A Better Tomorrow 2* (at around 26m). Here the action switches to Gotham,[5] where Chow is running a Chinese restaurant in Chinatown (Chow is basically the same character as Mark from *A Better Tomorrow*, tho' now he's Ken Lee, Mark's brother.[6] Ken is portrayed as the leader of a bunch of Chinese/ Chinese-Americans in New York City; they defer to him, and are distressed when he opts to return to China with Uncle Lung).

The face-off between Ken Lee and the Chinese restaurant employees

---

4 Seven editors are credited.
5 Aside from the second unit images of New York City (which might belong to any movie), the interior scenes look like we're back in Hong Kong.
6 Some accounts have Ken as Mark's cousin.

and the North American heavies who come demanding protection money re-plays familiar Asian vs. American conflicts (which Tsui Hark depicted in *Zu: Warriors From the Magic Mountain* and *The Master*): the *gweilos* ('white devils') are portrayed as crude, rude, and insanely aggressive, and the Chinese guys are polite and placatory (at first, at least, until they're pushed). Chow Yun-fat delivers a marvellous performance here, a lengthy monologue which uses rice/ food as a pretext for a riff on current issues (the movie lingers over a medium close-up of Ken, without bothering to include reverse angles of the criminal listening).

Following the customary action that climaxes act one (every Hong Kong action movie has a Big Scene to close the first act), *A Better Tomorrow 2* moves into some unusual territory, in particular the troubled relationship between Ken Lee and Uncle Sei Lung. *A Better Tomorrow 2* is more extreme than your usual crime/ gangster flick in not only having Lung undergo exile and suffering, he is also put into a strait jacket and installed in a hospital. Thus, for much of act two, Lung is played by Dean Shek as insane (and, this being directed by John Woo, it's a hysterical sort of portrayal of madness – he has hospital orderlies forcing food down him while he writhes on a bed).

In the second act, *A Better Tomorrow 2* cuts between the Hong Kong scenes, involving mob boss Ko and the gangsters, and Sung-chi Ho and Kit, and the Ken Lee and Lung Sei scenes in Gotham. There are many opportunities for action scenes – Ko and co. want to get rid of Lung, for instance, and send several teams of gunmen to the U.S.A. after him – but Lung has Ken as his heroic bodyguard (so no matter how many armed guys in suits lurk in corridors or stairways, Ken Lee manages to trounce them all). It's typical of the over-egged narrative style of Hong Kong action cinema that Uncle Lung should regain his senses smack in the middle of an action scene (and to help Ken, too, who's fallen to the ground as the heavies approach in a car).

There are bombs, too, which go off in the restaurant (when Ken Lee is looking after Uncle Lung). It's witnessing a girl being injured during one of the triad attacks on the restaurant that sends Lung over-the-edge into madness.

And there are action scenes back in China, too – in one, Kit manages to take advantage of a gangsters' hand-over, impressing mobster Ko's men. This is Leslie Cheung as James Bond, taking on hordes of armed henchmen when the hand-over of counterfeit money at night by the sea ⸱s in yet another shoot-out. Cheung's Kit is leaping about, and diving ⸱⸱er boat (boats and harbourside fire-fights occur in the next film in the John Woo canon, *The Killer*).

In the second nighttime, action scene, Sung-chi Ho is coerced to shoot Kit at close range (so that Boss Ko will trust him). It's certainly a very distressing scene – within the story of the movie, but also in seeing such a beloved actor as Leslie Cheung being shot twice. That is simply something you *don't* want to see. (And Ti Lung plays his remorse vividly, returning to the scene to hurry Kit to hospital. It's heavily ironic that Boss Ko used shooting Kit as an initiation test for Ho, after Ho comes to him looking for work. The scene is replayed in the finale, when Ken brings Kit to the hospital, and is met by Ho outside).

Inevitably, *A Better Tomorrow 2* moves back to Hong Kong for the resolution of the plot (and of course the blam-blam[7] shoot-out which you know is a dead certainty in a Woo-and-Tsui action movie): Uncle Lung and Ken muse on the concept of 'home' (a very poignant theme in both Woo's and Tsui's cinema), which has multiple resonances (of the 1997 Handover, of the Chinese abroad, of exiles, etc).

Wait – is that *Mark*? No, it's *Ken*. Both Kit and Sung-chi Ho are taken aback for a moment. Chow Yun-fat loudly, jokily insists that he's 'Ken, Ken', not Mark. Before the giant shoot-out, there's a charming scene set in a cemetery in sunlight: regardless of what the text or the subtext is saying in this scene, what impresses is observing these four great actors together within the same shot. For once they're not running around firing weapons while riddled with bullets, or crumpling to the floor in hysterical insanity, they're just talking. Scenes like this are as valuable as the action set-pieces. The scenes where Chow Yun-fat plays opposite Leslie Cheung are delightful, and to be treasured.

So *A Better Tomorrow 2* moves towards its shoot-out climax, in a plush manse up in the hills outside Hong Kong, where Boss Ko and his mob are celebrating the success of their money counterfeiting operation (out comes the Peter Gabriel music – for at least the third time). Ken suits up in Mark's old (bullet-ridden) duster coat and shades (hanging grenades inside it like he's a travelling salesman. Chow Yun-fat adds little bits of comical business here).

The finale of *A Better Tomorrow 2* is thus another stops-all-out, guns-'n'-grenades sequence, a men-with-guns smackdown, with one stunt after another – an explosion in slo-mo, a twisting dive, a two-pistol blammy moment, blood smeared on white walls, squibs bursting inside actor's shirts, and the sound of gunfire is mixed high.

---

7 The silent, cool assassin wearing shades uses a silencer – oh no, not on a John Woo movie, where every gun is fitted with a 'loudener'!

But the finale of *A Better Tomorrow 2* features so many henchmen, all of whom are absolutely useless in a fight, and so many gags and stunts, it's more like a parody (both Tony Ching Siu-tung and Tsui Hark are big on comedy, but John Woo isn't known for inserting much humour into his dramatic finales, even tho' he's directed comedies). For ex, the gunmen are endless, tumbling out of doors into corridors, in groups, so they're not human any more but objects to be shot by the heroes.[8] For ex, Sung-chi Ho snatches up a samurai sword, so we have some swordplay action for a few action beats (I bet that was Tony Ching's idea. Ti Lung, of course, had appeared in many swordplay pics). Ho uses the sword to dispatch Shing Fui-on (who's armed with an axe), then sets about some more heaves.

Three of the heroes survive (Lung, Ho and Ken) in *A Better Tomorrow 2*, but poor Kit bites the dust (halfway thru act three, prior to the mansion bust-up). In a moving scene (played for Maximum Tear Effect by Chow Yun-fat and Leslie Cheung), Kit speaks to his wife Jackie who's just given birth (while Ken stands beside him in a call-box. Kit can barely string two words together, but he does name the child just before he expires.

A woman giving birth is 100% of the time a wholly artificial dramatic-narrative device in movies of this kind (and 99.99% of the time in all other movies – consider how editor David Wu is cutting together the hospital, the mansion, Cheung and co.). Death and birth, the end and the beginning, loss and hope, the present and the future – there's no point complaining now, halfway through the final act of a movie! Especially about a film with such over-cooked melodrama! (and it's no use pointing out that stopping for a phone call instead of carrying straight on to the hospital is nuts. Kit is seriously injured, and they stop for a phone call!). So Kit dies – he's given a moving and protracted death scene, slipping to the ground as the camera moves backwards while Leslie Cheung sings on the soundtrack. (I can't be the only viewer who finds scenes where Leslie Cheung dies unsettling. I'm willing the movie – don't kill Cheung! He's too special).

✿

If you take *A Better Tomorrow 2* straight, it's very impressive; if you step back a little, it's ridiculous, comical and over-the-top; from the perspective of conservative politics, it's offensively violent, shamelessly crude and irritatingly stupid; from a feminist viewpoint, it's prehistoric and [from] a social realist standpoint, it has no relation to the real [world] and has little of value to say about society; from a liberal [view, A] Better Tomorrow 2 is ideologically backward, employing [politi]cs and mindless mayhem to convey garbled nonsense; [but in terms] of action cinema it's one of the great movies.

[th]em to clowns in a circus.

Sometimes contemplating a movie like the two *Better Tomorrows* and *The Killer* (which are not so much a trilogy as basically the same movie), I wonder if I'm watching: –

- A commercial *for guns* or a plea to *ban guns?*;
- Is it pro or anti violence?;
- Is it more than a morally murky cartoon about men running around buildings going *blam-blam, you're dead!* – just like kids in the playground?
- Is it a treatise on just how moronic humans really are, and the only hope for civilization is a bunch of rigthteous (self-righteous) crooks?
- Is it a movie about the corruption of the human soul via the technology of warfare?
- Are the heroes (actually, they're anti-heroes) different from their rivals (Boss Ko and his mob) just because they talk about being righteous?
- Is it a modern version of an Ancient Greek tragic play – Sophocles with guns instead of swords? (wait, there *is* a sword!).
- Is it a commercial for the return of fascism or for the Chinese Communist Party? (The MacGuffin is counterfeit money, after all; both fascists and Communists enshrine money, though for different reasons).

I guess I have to admit that part of me is thrilled by the brilliance of the filmmaking, entertained by actors as electric as Chow, Cheung, Shek and Lung, while another part of me is thinking, *this is garbage*. Ideologically, it's junk, and it's politically offensive. So it's classy trash, a corny cartoon (as hokey as the shooting star that Leslie Cheung reckons is an ill omen).

4

THE KILLER

Die Xie Shuang Xiong

The credits of *The Killer* (1989) tell us all we need to know:

TSUI HARK PRESENTS
A JOHN WOO FILM
STARRING CHOW YUN-FAT

Add to that a fantastic supporting cast, a brilliant technical crew, and some of the best action choreographers in the business (including Tony Ching Siu-tung and Yuen Cheung-yan), and you have one of the quintessential products of Hong Kong action cinema.

The Killer (*Dip Huet Seung Hung* in Cantonese, *Die Xue Shuang Xiong* in Mandarin = *Bloodshed Brothers*, 1989), was produced by Film Workshop/ Golden Princess/ Magnum, written by John Woo, produced by Tsui Hark, Peter Pau and Wong Wing-hang were DPs, the action was directed by Tony Ching Siu-tung, Alan Chui Chung San, Lau Chi Ho and Yuen Cheung-yan (with car stunts by Bruce Law),9 music by Lowell Lo, editor: Kung-Wing Fan, music editor: David Wu, art dir. by Man-Wah Luk, costumes: Shirley Chan, sound fx: Siu-Lung Ching, hair by Benny Chow, make-up by Yu Lai Cheng and Yvonne Yen, and in charge of production was Claudie Chung Jan. Box office: HK $18.25m. Released: July 6, 1989. 105 mins.

Chow Yun-fat, Danny Lee Sau-yin, Paul Chu (Chu Kong), Kenneth Tsang, Sally Yeh Tse-man, Shing Fui-on, Lam Chung, Wing-Cho Yip, Ricky Yi Faan-wai, Barry Wong Ping-yiu, Fan Wei-yee, Alan Ng, Tommy Wong, and Parkman Wong Pak-man starred (many were Tsui Hark regulars).

9 If there are car or motorbike stunts in a Hong Kong picture in the 1980s onwards, it's usual Bruce Law and his team.

Over the fall-out of Woo and Tsui on *The Killer*, Jasmine Chow (Chow Yun-fat's wife), explained that Tsui decided that he wasn't getting the recognition he thought he was due when *The Killer* started to receive plaudits. So Tsui argued with Woo over the ownership of the movie.

Tsui Hark said he didn't know exactly why he fell out with John Woo: when Woo received an award for *The Killer* and no one told Tsui, that rankled (and 'a lot of the people around him just got hostile', Tsui recalled).

❀

The Killer stars Chow Yun-Fat (never better) in a bold, brash, lush, baroque action thriller with religious and operatic overtones. A favourite with film critics (for all the obvious reasons – the religious themes, the brotherhood theme,10 the masculinity-in-crisis theme, etc), *The Killer* is also preposterous and over-cooked, and in many sections is as dumb (but fun) as a *James Bond* movie. (Episodes of the movie, you have to admit, are really adolescent or even childish – men running around go bang-bang! with guns).

The dramatic components of *The Killer* are clichéd, routine:11 the cold, distant, implacable and impossibly cool assassin Jeff, a.k.a. John a.k.a. Ah Jong (no ties, no family, an outsider and loner), a professional brilliant at his job (but his icy exterior hides a warm heart). Jenny, the woman (Sally Yeh, playing a nightclub singer) he maims by accident (blinding her),12 and falls for and protects. The one last job the killer promises to do before he retires to the coast (and to pay for Jenny's eye operation). His target, the powerful crime boss Tony Weng, and his nephew, Johnny (Shing Fui-on), who comes after him with hordes of henchmen. The unconventional cop Inspector Li Ying (Danny Lee Sau-yin) who gradually befriends the killer and fights beside him against Boss Weng and his crew. And finally the killer's faithful friend, the go-between, a retired, former hit man, Sidney Fung (Paul Chu Kong).

The Killer presents a series of brotherly relationships: Ah Jong and Fung, Ah Jong and Li, and Li and cop buddy, Chang (Kenneth Tsang). Inevitably for a John Woo-helmed picture, each of these brotherhoods overshadows the heterosexual liaison between Ah Jong and Jenny. Tsui Hark was partly responsible for bumping up the significance of the romance, though Woo was clearly not particularly enchanted by it. He prefers to stage scenes of men smouldering with dramatic conflict over issues such as loyalty to each other, and devotion to their profession (whether it's the police force or the crime syndicate. It's not the outfit,

10 The narcissism of gangsters is present and correct in *The Killer* (such as Ah Jong with his scarves), tho' Inspector Li seems dandyish in his striped linen suits.
11 John Woo recalled that the story was based on a *yakuza* picture of the 1960s starring Ken Takakura.
12 One wonders if that motif came from doing gun stunts, where blanks can be dangerous.

legal or illegal, that counts, so much as the loyalty towards it).

So *The Killer* is another of John Woo's explorations of the notions of brotherhood, of honour, of loyalty. You can see *The Killer* and similar crime movies as a contemporary-set version of portraying the *jiangzhu*, the 'martial arts world', in which the code of honour, of chivalry, of brotherhood, prevails. The code of living honourably is invoked in the *jiangzhu*.

The Killer obviously appropriates and reworks elements of North American and French thrillers, including the gangster thrillers directed by Martin Scorsese and Jean-Pierre Melville (in particular *Le Samourai*).[13] And it's also drawing on the cowboy genre, where men are real men, where disputes are conducted with blammy gun-fights and yelled insults, and where women are always on the sidelines. One critic claimed that *The Killer* was an amalgam of Martin Scorsese, Stanley Kubrick, Sergei Eisenstein, Alfred Hitchcock, Don Siegel, Robert Aldrich, Francis Coppola, David Lean, Jean-Pierre Melville, Akira Kurosawa, Sergio Leone, Chang Cheh and Masaki Kobayashi.[14] Maybe. Sure (John Woo happily renders his influences obvious, turning them into elaborate *hommages*). Actually, if you view *The Killer* as a Hong Kong movie, and as a Hong Kong action movie, it explains/ resolves everything.

❁

Altho' *The Killer* is usually set within the context of the cinema of John Woo (so it's 'John Woo did this' and 'John Woo did that'), you can also see it as a Tsui Hark picture. Among Tsui's influences are the casting of Sally Yeh Tse-man, for example (Yeh was a favourite actress of his in the 1980s – she's in the Tsui-produced films *I Love Maria, Diary of a Big Man* and *The Laser Man*, and Tsui's own favourite film of his as director, *Peking Opera Blues*. Yeh also sang the theme song of *The Killer*). There were Tsui regulars in the crew (such as Peter Pau, David Wu, Patrick Yip, Lowell Lo, Benny Chow, James Wong Jim, Patrick Leung, and Tony Ching Siu-tung). The Dragon Boat Race, a piece of traditional, Chinese culture, is likely a Tsui suggestion. It's possible that portraying Ah Jong and Sally as having a romantic relationship came from Tsui – Woo often holds back from man-woman romance, preferring to concentrate on the brotherhood theme.

And yet, *The Killer* can also be regarded as a 'Chow Yun-fat film': altho' both Tsui and Woo appear regularly in front of the camera in cameos, they are not (as they would admit!), superstar performers like Chow.

There's only one Chow Yun-fat, and altho' there are other action stars, in the West as well as in the East, who could've played this role, Chow makes it his own. When we see Ah Jong acting tenderly towards the little

---

13 John Woo's admiration for *Le Samouraï* is well-known: he has mined it on several occasions.
14 T. Williams, in Y. Tasker, 2002, 407.

girl who's caught in the crossfire on the beach, we buy it, even tho' it's ridiculously over-wrought. (This is a typical piece of Hong Kong Movie Cheese, and Woo-ian OTT melodrama – putting a cute moppet in the midst of a ferocious fire-fight is the kind of over-cooked drama that D.W. Griffith shamelessly exploited in film after film. That the injured kid echoes Jenny in the opening scene is delightfully simplistic thematic plotting).

Altho' Chow Yun-fat and Danny Lee Sau-yin rightly receive most of the plaudits for the acting (they had already worked together several times before), Paul Chu-kong is superb as Chow's triad cohort, suggesting, as with Chow and Lee, levels of suffering and angst beneath the surface (this movie features plenty of images of men brooding, and looking off into the distance. Sometimes the images resemble pop videos – even more so when Sally Yeh's songs drift over the top in the musical montages). And the supporting cast is excellent, too – from Kenneth Tsang's long-suffering cop sidekick to Inspector Li, to Shing Fui-on chewing the scenery as the mob boss Johnny Weng (Woo encourages Shing to go way over-the-top – plenty of action movie directors relish the opportunity to encourage out-size performances from the actors playing their villains). And not forgetting a huge number of henchmen and stunt guys, who're blown to bits by either Chow or Lee.

The cast of *The Killer* seems to include everybody who was in Hong Kong at the time – there are many familiar faces in the background characters. If you watch Hong Kong movies from the 80s and 90s, you will see them. (Often they're playing henchmen who get shot up by either Chow or Lee).

❁

Ultimately, *The Killer* is a Hong Kong action movie: for anybody who's seen more'n a few Cantonese flicks, everything in *The Killer* is familiar – the super-cool action hero, the hysterical melodrama, the inter-departmental rivalries in the police force, the political pressure from above (transmitted through the police chiefs), the wayward cop, the reformed villain, the men-being-men and male friendship themes, and of course the wild stunts and blammy fire-fights.

The Killer isn't a one-off masterpiece that exists in a space of its own (like, say, *Vampyr* (1932) or *Sunrise* (1927)), it's very much a part of the Hong Kong tradition of cinema, from its genre (it's one of a gazillion police thrillers), to its so-familiar settings (the harbour, downtown, the nightclub, the car lot, Causeway Bay, Stanley Beach, Horizon Drive – even the church).

However, it *is* true that filmmakers such as Tsui Hark and John Woo can elevate thrillers and gangster flicks way above the run-of-the-mill Hong Kong pic.

The dime-store melodrama is shameless in *The Killer*: this is a movie where the cop and the killer face off against each other right next to a team of doctors desperately trying to bring a girl back to life! Talk about over-done! But that, of course, is why we love Hong Kong cinema! (The thinking seems to be: we've done this shoot-out scene before, why don't we add some extra elements to wrench the audience's heart and nerves even further?). Holding pistols pointed each other is reprised several times – in front of Jenny in her apartment, for instance, or lying on the floor of the church in the finale.

And this is a movie where the super-cool anti-hero enters a nightclub in slow motion – this's *before* he's shown us that he can single-handed (single-gunnedly) take on a mobster and his henchmen, *before* we've seen him strut his stuff, and *before* he's established as a chilly, cool performer.

And that's why you cast Chow Yun-fat, a man who can walk into a nightclub (or thru a church) in slow motion and pull it off. So that, before he does anything, or says anything, or *is* anything, he's Chow Yun-fat!

❀

As an action film, *The Killer* doesn't disappoint: boat chases, car chases, car lot bust-ups, rooftop chases, tram chases, explosions, and some of the best shoot-outs ever put on celluloid (Bruce Law is a contributor, overseeing the car stunts). John Woo never uses one bullet where two hundred will do.[15] Only *Hard-Boiled* (1992), another Woo-directed extravaganza, employs more bullet hits, squibs and fake blood, more stunts and more slow motion (tho' other films of this period come to mind – like *Full Contact,* an astonishing, incendiary Ringo Lam-directed actioner from 1992 which also starred Chow Yun-fat).

The Killer also has religious motifs a-plenty (a favourite of John Woo's, who's a practising Catholic): the killer holes up in a rural church (thousands of candles, stained glass, a statue of the Virgin Mary and white doves), which is the site of the final, Alamo showdown.

> I spent a lot of money to make the perfect Virgin Mary statue, when it is shot to pieces, truth is destroyed by evil, and with it the spirit of chivalry displayed by ancient warriors. (2000, 66)

For some, John Woo's incorporation of Christian icons, such as an exploding statue of the Madonna,[16] is pretentious, over-wrought, and over-

---

15 There's the warrior code in *The Killer* of saving one last bullet – for yourself or your victim. Yes – but how can you count when you're firing 100s of rounds from a pistol that holds six bullets?!
16 Music editor David Wu put in Georg Frideric Handel's *Messiah* in this scene.

egged. For others, such as Martin Scorsese, it's part of Woo's exploration of the theme of guilt, vengeance and (Christian) redemption. (Over-wrought? Woo doesn't care! Over-wrought, over-cooked and over-the-top is what he does for a living! If you want meek, humble, timid, delicate storytelling, look elsewhere!).

❀

The first act of *The Killer* climaxes with the assassination of the triad politico at the Dragon Boat Race. Before that, we've seen Ah Jong performing multiple cold-blooded shootings, plus Danny Lee's cop Inspector Li Ying having his own adventures (including a superb downtown tram chase. This is part of the introduction of Lee's character, at the ten-minute mark: an unconventional but righteous policeman, Li goes undercover during the hand-over of weapons merchandize with some local hoods. It all goes wrong, inevitably, and Li is discovered, which cues another massive fire-fight followed by a chase on foot and tram. Mirroring Ah Jong's predicament of a bystander (Jenny) being injured by gun-play, a woman expires from a heart attack just as Li nails the gangleader on the tram. This part of *The Killer* features wonderful, atmospheric photography on the streets of downtown Hong Kong at night. No green screens here, and no boring city in Canada standing in for Hong Kong. It's the real Hong Kong, and the actors are really there, doing it all).

But after the act one climax, at the Dragon Boat Race, the 1989 film continues into a lengthy boat chase, followed by a fire-fight on a beach, followed by a car chase, followed by a face-off in a hospital – so it's really a continuous action sequence in the manner of a *James Bond* or *Indiana Jones* or *Die Hard* movie, where one whammo, as producer Joel Silver calls them, is topped by another. (And of course, like James Bond, Ah Jong escapes at the end).

The first act of *The Killer* closes, then, with the face-off at gun-point which brings Inspector Li and Ah Jong face-to-face in the hospital in a spectacular manner (a favourite location in Hong Kong action movies, a setting purpose-built for shoot-outs in labyrinthine corridors, for chases thru operating theatres, for stunts in stair-wells or elevators, and not forgetting the mandatory leaping out of windows. Add to that characters disguised as doctors, the inevitable romance when the heroine patches up the hero, and – if you want to see them – you have the grand themes of Life and Death).

❀

The second and third acts of *The Killer* don't sag, tho' there are, admittedly, rather too many scenes of slo-mo photography of Ah Jong looking introspective (and ultra-cool), and of Inspector Li following suit (using the facial expressions that Oliver Reed called 'Moody Three'). Acts 2 and 3 of *The Killer* are bolstered dramatically by complications with the triad gangs, with Sidney Fung's boss Johnny Weng, and with the order going out to get rid of Ah Jong ('kill him!' yells Weng as he hurries into his car in the parking lot). This is very familiar Hong Kong, action movie territory – about men being men, saving face, maintaining their pride/ dignity, and adhering to the quasi-chivalrous codes of gangsterdom. All of the gangster genre clichés are duly trotted out, but the sprightliness of the filmmaking, and the charisma of the lead actors, maintains interest (because there's no getting around the fact that we have seen this movie 100,000 times before).

The 2nd and 3rd acts of *The Killer* are also kept peppy by some action scenes – an attempt on Ah Jong's life at his apartment (where he blows away everybody with another gun fitted with unlimited ammo – where can we buy a gun like that?!); a car chase in a multi-level car lot (when Ah Jong messes up a bid to nobble Johnny Weng – the first time, apart from blinding Jenny, that we see him get it very wrong); an attempted collaring of Ah Jong at the airport (with Hitchcockian cat-and-mouse games); and another car lot shoot-out (this time involving Fung and Weng's heavies, with Chang getting shot. It's the same car lot as the first bust-up, but this time there's an abrupt cut to a rural highway, as the doggedly determined Chang, severly wounded, persists in performing his police duties, tailing the bad guys. Chang expires just after telling his boss the address of Ah Jong).

Another brilliantly inventive scene in *The Killer* has Ah Jong and cop Li Ying going literally head-to-head when Li ambushes Ah Jong at Jenny's apartment and they play the whole scene moving around the rooms with their guns pointed at each other's heads and hearts, while Jenny, unsuspecting, makes them tea. It's rightly played with a comical touch – because it's an absurd scenario; it's the farce version of a John Woo Mexican stand-off (one can spot the influence of Tsui Hark here). Anyhoo, no way are Inspector Li or Ah Jong going to open fire with Jenny right between them (not after she's been blinded once!). There's some amusing actorly bits of business – such as Jenny clutching Ah Jong and just missing the fact that he's holding a pistol at his new 'football friend' who's just dropped by, Inspector Li. These gags take *The Killer* into the farcical territory that Woo had explored in cheesy family fare such as *Run, Tiger Run* (1985). However, *The Killer* pulls back from the over-the-top jokes of *Run, Tiger Run*.

The flipside of loyalty is betrayal: *The Killer* presents several instances of one-time brothers betraying each other, such as Sidney Fung and Ah Jong. This occurs in act two, in a scorching scene where Fung visits Ah Jong, with the hit-man confronting his colleague about his collusion in the attempt to kill him after the Dragon Boat Race festival. Both Chow Yun-fat and Paul Chu are brilliant in this scene which includes, in the usual heightened-hysterical manner of John Woo's cinema, guns being held at faces (and fired – but Ah Jong took the bullets out of his gun).

No one can miss the physical, even erotic intimacy of these scenes, where masculinity-in-crisis is aligned with gun-play. This is John Woo's version of soap opera melodrama, where the hysterical histrionics of television soap opera acting are played out with guns pointing at heads or backs.

Sidney Fung gets his own big fight scene in *The Killer*, when, with the stubborn, suicidal diligence of a triad elder sticking to the old, chivalrous codes, he gets to shoot up Johnny Weng and his mob (demanding the money for Ah Jong! What a friend!). It's yet another one-man-in-a-nest-of-vipers scene, a one-man-army scene. Somehow, Weng and Fung both survive, even tho' they're perforated with bullets (there are plenty of suspend-your-disbelief-now moments, including hostage scenarios and gun-in-mouth scenarios. The flair for physical acting, for blocking scenes, for how people can interact within the confines of a small room, is striking: the filmmaking really comes alive when a bunch of very hostile people are crammed into a space, armed to the teeth). And then Fung, the schmuck, leads the hoods to the church, because he wants to deliver the $$$$ to Ah Jong! Ouch! Thereby damning himself, Ah Jong and many others in the subsequent fire-fight (Ah Jong puts Fung out of his misery, with a heroic bullet to the head, after Fung pleads that he doesn't want to die like a dog at the hands of the triads).

The philosophy of the 1989 movie is delivered in an impressive piece of parallel action. Editor Kung-Wing Fan is brilliant here, cutting between Sidney Fung's frustrating and very painful attempts to secure the money owed to Ah Jong from Johnny Weng and his heavies with Inspector Li and Ah Jong smoking and shooting the breeze beside a pool (this comes after Li has tended Ah Jong's wound – a role usually taken up by the girlfriend-of-the-hero or the female sidekick in action movies).

Thus, Li Ying and Ah Jong discuss the issues of ethics and honour while Sidney Fung is being beaten about by Johnny Weng's henchmen. However, it's not parallel cutting for irony, but to illustrate the ethical debate of Ah Jong and Li, and to demonstrate that notions of loyalty and honour are worth fighting for, and to show that the cost of upholding such out-dated concepts in the modern age can be high. Fung puts his life on the line to maintain honour and loyalty.

✦

The fourth act of *The Killer* starts by bringing together Inspector Li and Ah Jong at his fancy Horizon Drive digs where, once again, Johnny Weng's henchmen try to kill him. The result? Yet another over-the-top, non-stop fire-fight with an endless supply of bullets. No matter how many stunt guys you throw against Chow Yun-fat and Danny Lee, they are shot to pieces (however, Ah Jong is injured here – but by Li, not Johnny Weng's sadly expendable heavies). And the Woo-ian face-off is reprised – to make it even sillier, we have Jenny taking up a gun, so it's a three-way gun scene.

By this time, Inspector Li has found being a cop even more irksome (he's thrown off the case by his angry boss, and his buddy Chang dies), and that Ah Jong's sense of honour and ethics seem more appealing.

The finale of *The Killer* is the expected blammy, bang-bang ending, with men being men, and women're relegated to crawling around on the floor, wailing helplessly. Yes, if you're a *real man* in a John Woo movie, you get to (1) die heroically, (2) survive heroically (if you're lucky), or (3) expire in a hail of bullets (if you're a henchman).

Stunt choreographers Tony Ching Siu-tung, Yuen Cheung-yan *et al* invent all manner of ways of firing a gun and people dying: Ah Jong slides backwards on a chair, dives onto the ground and slides, leaps over seats, while the henchmen crash through windows, against walls, through balustrades, from balconies, onto candles, are blown up by gas/ fuel, in slow motion, and riddled with bullet hits. Cars burn, smoke blows, and the sound of the wind is mixed high (so the patch of ground in front of the church resembles a dust-blown desert out of a Spaghetti Western). To step away from the usual wardrobe of men in suits (a cliché of all gangster flicks which *The Killer* has already used), the henchmen are clad in white overalls.

Let's forget the flaws in the screenwriting and construction of the finale of *The Killer* (like how Sidney Fung leads the mob straight to the church! *Duh!*), and focus on the marvellous stunts orchestrated by Tony Ching Siu-tung, Alan Chui Chung San, Lau Chi Ho and Yuen Cheung-yan and their teams, on the hyper-melodramatic interactions between the leads (teary, sweaty, over-heated, grimacing, wild-eyed), on the lovely cinematography (by Peter Pau and Wong Wing-hang) which captures our heroes diving left, right and centre in glowing light, and on the preposterousness of the whole enterprise ('Woo at his most hysterically excessive', noted Stephen Teo [178]).

In case you've forgotten scenes that ran by your eyes 20 or 30 minutes earlier (the film assumes you're an idiot suffering from memory loss), *The Killer* reprises many oh-so poignant moments from the newly-formed brotherhood of Ah Jong and Inspector Li. We cut, for instance, from the fire-fight in the church to the cute male bonding during the tending-a-wound scene at the lake, between Ah Jong and Li. So touching! So bittersweet! Ah, just when Li discovers a new buddy, he loses him!

Because, of course, at the end of *The Killer*, Chow Yun-fat's assassin Ah Jong dies, pin-cushioned with bullets (from triad boss Johnny Weng, among others). It's the heroic immolation foreshadowed earlier, in a conversation between Ah Jong and Inspector Li. But, with bitter irony, Ah Jong's blinded by a bullet in the final confrontation with Weng. One of the (many) memorable images in this extraordinary film has Ah Jong and Jenny crawling across the ground looking for each other, both blinded, with the burning church behind them (is this a reference to the finale of *Duel In the Sun* (1946), another over-cooked, gun-and-passion melodrama?). They miss each other, and Ah Jong expires. Li shoots Weng in revenge, after the cops arrive, when Weng is pathetically pleading for protection from the police force. (Jenny, however, isn't given a proper final note or line in *The Killer* – the focus is on Li, who collapses in despair to the dirt, muttering Ah Jong's nickname, Shrimp Head).

❀

The Killer was criticized for its portrayal of the female character played by Sally Yeh Tse-man. Lisa Morton derides *The Killer* for its shallow, insensitive, 'callous treatment' of women:

> Woo seems incapable of creating a female character who is even remotely interesting or believable... *The Killer* marks a new low even for him... it's unforgivable that Woo simply never bothers to resolve her character... (LM, 163)

But according to John Woo in a 2007 interview, actress Sally Yeh let the film down by not offering enough of her schedule, forcing him to rewrite the story and focus more on the two men:

> I did try to make strong female characters in the past, but somehow, it never worked out. For example, when I was shooting *The Killer*, the original concept was a triangular love story, and the female character was supposed to be very strong, very brave and very smart, even

though she's blind. But the actress didn't concentrate on this movie, and she gave limited time to shoot. So that forced me to change the script...

Once again, let's remind ourselves that the director doesn't do everything in a movie. Tsui Hark was producer, for instance (and he makes his presence felt on every project he produces), and other important talents influenced *The Killer* (scheduling is the producer's responsibility, not the director's, for instance). Also, John Woo *doesn't* write all of his movies – but in the case of *The Killer*, yes he did write the script (with assistance from Tsui).

Stephen Teo remarked that

> the sum total of balletic violence and poetic meditations of killer and cop as they size each other up in almost transcendental terms, gives the impression that *The Killer* is more about sentiment and feeling. (177)

Paul Fonoroff wasn't convinced by *The Killer.*

> It's all very pretty and very phoney. *The Killer* seems to say that it is perfectly all right to commit murder as long as you hate truly evil people and act kindly to women and children caught in your cross-fire. (34)

Paul Fonoroff is one of the most unpleasable of Hong Kong film critics – very few films are enshrined by the Fonster. But Fonoroff is certainly right to call *The Killer* phoney. It is remarkably, even alarmingly cheesy and fake.

It's truly preposterous and cartoonish, too, and it's scary how many film critics take it all straight, accepting instantly the received view that John Woo's cinema is seriously tackling issues of brotherhood, friendship between men, loyalty and honour. Or life and death.

Is it because the filmmaking is so accomplished in its portrayals of over-the-top action? (There's no denying that this is amazing filmmaking). Is it because the film seems to really 'mean' it, is so earnest? (The film taking itself seriously). Is it because the actors are trying so hard to sell it all? (Even though the performances are also cheesily exaggerated at times). Is it because the accumulation of film criticism about John Woo's cinema over the years has persuaded all of us to view these movies straight and seriously? (When they are also ridiculous).

Film critics who adore the filmic output of John Woo have answers for this, too:

     – it's not ridiculous, it's 'operatic';

     – it's not violent and gory, it's a 'gun ballet';

     – it's not homoerotic, it's about brotherhood.

John Woo himself was happy with *The Killer* – it's one of the films of his own that he liked.

5

TWIN DRAGONS

Seong Lung Wiu

Twin Dragons (1992, a.k.a. *Double Dragons, Brother vs. Brother, When Dragons Collide, Duel of Dragons, Dragon Duo* and *When Dragons Meet; Shuang Long Hui* in Mandarin, *Seong Lung Wui* in Cantonese = *Double Dragon, Brother vs. Brother*), was exec. prod. by Ng See-yuen, produced by Teddy Robin, co-directed with Ringo Lam, co-written by Teddy Robin, Barry Long, Tung Cho Cheung, Wong Yik and Tsui Hark, music by Michael Wandmacher and Lowell Lo, DPs: Wong Wing-hang and Arthur Wong, editor: Marco Mak Chi-sin, costumes: Che Leung Chong, special effects and car stunts: Bruce Law, action choreographers: Tony Ching Siu-tung, Chris Lee, Siu-Hung Leung, Siu Ming Tsui, Wei Tung, Yuen Woo-ping and Jackie Chan.

 Twin Dragons featured Jackie Chan, Maggie Cheung Man-yuk, Teddy Robin, Nina Li-chi, Philip Chan, David Chiang, Guy Lai Ying Chau, Jamie Luk Kim Ming, James Wong Jim, Johnny Wang, Sylvia Chang, Mars, Eddie Fong, Kirk Wong and many others. Production by the Hong Kong Director's Guild/ Paragon Films/ Golden Harvest. Released Jan 25, 1992. 100 mins.[17]

 Twin Dragons was a benefit movie – this time for the Hong Kong Directors' Union,[18] who needed to buy land for a new HQ.[19] Consequently, it includes cameos from almost every Hong Kong film director,[20] including Kirk Wong, Teddy Robin, Clara Law, Raymond Lee, Ringo Lam, Gordon Chan, Lau Kar-leung, Wong Jing, Eric Tsang, John Woo[21] and many

---

17 The U.S. cut of 1999, from Dimension, had about 16 minutes left out.
18 *Twin Dragons* is also a re-make of *Double Impact*, a Jean-Claude Van Damme picture.
19 By 1997, the headquarters for the directors still hadn't been built.
20 Tsui has a cameo, along with Ringo Lam and producer Ng See-yuen, playing cards.
21 Playing a priest, of course.

others. Several other movies had been made in the era for benefits, charities, etc, including *The Banquet.*

One of the delights of *Twin Dragons* for Hong Kong cinema fans is playing Spot The Cameo – tho' for a global audience, the level of recognition is probably low (once again, this is a movie for a local audience: it's filmed in Hong Kong, it's filled with Hong Kongers, and the jokey cameos are from people in the Hong Kong film industry).

Tsui Hark said that Ringo Lam had directed most of the action in *Twin Dragons* (tho' no doubt Jackie Chan contributed, too, as he always does). Lam said he directed the second unit material. When Chan came aboard, the film shifted from action to comedy (B. Logan, 77).

✿

Twin Dragons is very much a Jackie Chan movie, rather than a Tsui Hark movie, or a Ringo Lam movie, or even a Hong Kong action comedy movie. Once Chan is headlining a movie, the productions always seem to become Jackie Chan Movies through and through. Chan is one of those performers who puts his stamp all over the movies he stars in (rather than taking a cameo). In *Twin Dragons* Chan is everywhere.

At this time in his career, Jackie Chan was an enormous star, able to command big budgets for his increasingly ambitious productions (he had recently completed the very costly, over-schedule and over-budget[22] *Armor of God 2: Operation Condor*). Chan's influence is all over the action, as expected: *Twin Dragons* is very much based in Chan's 'realistic' style of action choreography – that is, what can be achieved by the human body unaided by wires, trampolines and tricks (tho' of course, there *is* wire-work, and tricks all over). The action is big and loud; it's centred around Chan; Chan doesn't use guns; he employs numerous props; he tries to avoid confrontation, too; it includes Chan's distinctive form of comical action, where pain and suffering are empha-sized, where Chan isn't always the best fighter, where Chan undergoes numerous setbacks.

✿

The working-class Jackie Chan in *Twin Dragons* is teamed up with a sidekick, played by the famous Hong Kong celebrity Teddy Robin (who appeared in *All the Wrong Clues,* and who directed one of the sequels, which Tsui Hark produced). When Maggie Cheung Man-yuk[23] turns up in the first action scene, it's like a re-run of the *Police Story* films (where Cheung was the long-suffering girlfriend May of Chan's cop Ka-Kui). A scene's included to play to the Japanese market (Jackie Chan performs some rough-and-tumble stunts in front of a group of young, Japanese

22 Rumoured to have cost $12-15 million.
23 Even in an under-developed role as 'the Girlfriend of the Hero', Cheung lights up the screen.

girls).

Notice how, once he's performed his sidekick role, and the twins plot kicks in, Teddy Robin's Tarzan exits the picture (using the old staple of being chucked into hospital). Tarzan reappears in the finale, as the princess who must be rescued (he spends most of the finale hiding in cars).

In *Twin Dragons*, we have one of the longest pieces of black-and-white photography in Tsui Hark's *œuvre*, depicting the back-story of the twin Jackie Chans in the prologue which opens the 1992 movie. Here, Tsui goes back to the 1960s (to 1965),[24] instead of his more usual decades of the 1930s and 1940s, or back to the period of the *Once Upon a Time In China* movies (1890s-1910s). The prologue depicts the usual switch or loss (i.e., separation) of the twins in a twins narrative. So one boy grows up middle-class, affable, intellectual, artistic (the pianist and conductor), and one is a street tough, involved in minor crime, as well as working as a car mechanic.

The first act of *Twin Dragons* contains three big action sequences, with Jackie Chan front and centre of the second two: the first takes place in the prologue when the force that separates our heroes is a criminal who runs amok in a hospital. It's here that Bok Min (Wan Ma)[25] is discovered by a woman called Tsui (Wei Tung, portrayed as a good-time girl, first seen drunk).

The second action sequence is a typical Hong Kong action movie routine: one man against a mob of mobsters (set in a swanky hotel). We've seen this sort of caper many times – it is one of the default positions of the Hong Kong action movie, after all, and it appears throughout Tsui Hark's career as well as that of Jackie Chan (plenty of scenes in the whole *Once Upon a Time In China* series are just that: Jet Li or Vincent Zhao surrounded by bad guys). Glass tables which smash, TV sets hurled at hoods, a mic stand as a Shaolin Temple spear – it's Jackie Chan 101.

The third action sequence is a much bigger, more complex and more dangerous affair, which rounds off act one of *Twin Dragons*: a boat chase in Hong Kong harbour. The action sequence is mounted in the style of the Stanley Tong-helmed Jackie Chan pictures (such as *Rumble In the Bronx* or *Supercop 2*): *James Bond*-scale action of our heroes in a speed boat being pursued by henchmen in speed boats, while their boss yells into a cel phone, egging them on from a car following the chase.

24 The 1960s? Thus the movie shaves off eight or so years of Jackie Chan's age.
25 The U.S. cut has different names: John Ma and Boomer for the twins, Tammy for Tong Sum, Tyson for Tarzan, etc.

◆

Act two means complications, right? Two of the key complications in the narrative are Bok Min and Ma Yau switching round, so that Bok Min ends up conducting an orchestra for a prestigious concert, and Ma Yau is commanded to act as a getaway driver as the mob from earlier try to spring their boss from a cop wagon. This forms the big action set-piece which climaxes act two of *Twin Dragons* – it's a classic, Hong Kong action movie car and bus chase, with the cops closing in and Ma trying to do all he can to escape.

The second complication revolves around romance: it might be Tsui Hark's influence on this script, which clearly has many hands stirring the narrative pot, that two women – Maggie Cheung and Nina Li[26] – are foregrounded. While the romantic plots in an action comedy are, as usual, subplots, they are deftly handled by the filmmakers. For ex, consider the significance of music, as Ma woos Barbara by playing some Ludwig van Beethoven music at a grand piano, on the concert stage, while Cheung plays Barbara as a goofy girl who's swept away by music. Meanwhile, the more strait-laced and prim Tong Sum, Ma's girlfriend, enjoys some R. & R. with Bok Min. Action's included in the romantic subplots, too, as Nina Li's Neanderthal ex-boyfriend[27] turns up to make a fuss, and Chan's Bok Min shows his stuff once again (the shopping mall setting is a call-back to *Police Story*, 1985).

◆

The finale of *Twin Dragons* is the customary smackdown between the heroes and the villains, Hong Kong action movie-style: it's Jackie Chan and Jackie Chan versus countless hoods, with his sidekick Tarzan acting as the weasel who needs protecting. The first part of the finale is staged in a *milieu* we've seen plenty of times in Hong Kong flicks: the harbour. Which provides plenty of opportunity for gags with ropes, nets, boats, cranes, shipping containers, water, and of course men in suits running about wielding guns.

Jackie Chan and Tony Ching (and the many action directors) have been here before, and will revisit exactly the same territory again. And again.

The second part of the finale of *Twin Dragons* takes place in another staple of Hong Kong actioners: the warehouse/ factory (and, as it's a car testing centre, it combines the garage with the warehouse). The action is lengthy, intricate, fast, inventive and almost unduly complicated (how many times are Ma Yau or Bok Min going to run in and out of the rain room

26 Nina Li-chi was Butterfly in the third *Chinese Ghost Story*.
27 Don't ask why the daddy's girl Nina Li would date a gorilla.

and the hot room, switching places, one a great fighter, the other a coward?).

After that, the short *dénouement* is a double wedding to the two lovely girls, while the twins threaten to do a runner. Well, with multiple directors, producers, writers and the like, what did you expect? *Twin Dragons* is not the finest outing for anybody concerned in the production team, or among the cast, but so what? It's a pleasant enough hundred minutes.

Western critics found *Twin Dragons* a lesser Jackie Chan movie,[28] enjoying the visual effects and the stunts, but not so much the comedy (the clunky U.S. English dub (1999) doesn't help, even tho' Chan was dubbing himself into English – or 'Changlish', you could call it – Jackie speaks his own brand of English). Critics noted that *Twin Dragons* was a send-up of *Double Impact* (1991), which had starred Jean-Claude Van Damme.

Anyway, in Hong Kong, *Twin Dragons* did great business at Chinese New Year in 1992 – HK $33,225,134.

---

28 Chan himself wasn't happy with *Twin Dragons* – he found the comedy wasn't as funny as it should've been, and was disappointed with the visual effects (which he thought he oughta be good coming from Tsui Hark and co.).

A Better Tomorrow 2 (1987).

The Killer (1989).

Twin Dragons (1992).

6

NEW DRAGON GATE INN

San Lung Moon Haak Jaan

INTRO.

This is orgasmically, transcendentally fantastic filmmaking! This is an ecstatic movie! A movie so good you can't believe it! *Dragon Inn* (Raymond Lee Wai-man, 1992, in Mandarin: *Xin Long Menm Ke Zhan*, a.k.a. *New Dragon Gate Inn*) is a super-charged, 100% masterpiece of *wuxia pian*. This movie takes its place among the Top Ten of martial arts movies, alongside *Hero* (2002), *Enter the Dragon* (1973), *Crouching Tiger, Hidden Dragon* (2000) and *Once Upon a Time In China* (1991). For the finale alone, it's going to be a favourite with thousands of action fans.

New Dragon Gate Inn was produced by Film Workshop and Seasonal Films, and distributed thru Golden Harvest. The script was by Tsui Hark, Charcoal Tan and Hiu Wing. Tsui and Ng See-yuen were the producers. The music was by Philip Chan and Chow Gam-wing; editing by Poon Hung; the DPs were Arthur Wong and Tom Lau Moon-tong; action directors: Tony Ching Siu-tung, Cheng Yiu-sing, Wing Cho, Xiong Xin-xin and Yuen Bun; art direction: Chiu Gwok-San, Yee-Fung Chung, Chi-Hing Leung and William Chang Suk-Ping; sound (Cantonese): Angie Lam; first A.D.: Wing-Chiu Cheng; costumes by Poon Kwok-Wah and Ching Tin-Giu; make-up by Poon Man-Wa and Man Yun-Ling; hair by Siu-Mui Chau and Ho Yau Chun Heung; and vfx by Cinefex Workshop. The team are all regulars in the Tsui Hark Circus, making *New Dragon Gate Inn* very much a Tsui-led movie. Box office: HK $21 million. Released by Aug 27, 1992. 103 minutes.

This is a platinum movie, a masterwork of entertainment. The pacing is lively, the energy created is formidable and irresistible, the staging is enormously imaginative, the technical aspects are superb, the characters are fascinating, the story is compelling (with an unusual structure), the music (by Chan and Chow) is superb, the costumes and design are stellar, the locations (the Chinese desert) are lavish, and the tone is spot-on (with just enough comedy and romance to offer a change of pace from the thrills, suspense and action). Yes, *New Dragon Gate Inn* is another movie in which Tsui Hark and the filmmakers have thrown in *everything*.

Twenty-plus years after it was made, *New Dragon Gate Inn* still impresses as one of the greatest action movies in the history of cinema. Seeing it in a theatre in Beijing, Shanghai or Hong Kong in 1992 must've been extraordinary.

The level of energy and vitality on display in *New Dragon Gate Inn* is absolutely thrilling: everybody is working at the top of their game. Maybe the shift from Hong Kong to the deserts of Dunhuang in Northwest China for the exteriors freed everyone in the production team up, because they were *white-hot* when they produced this movie! (altho' most 'o the picture is filmed back on sets in Hong Kong).

New Dragon Gate Inn is a remake, as everyone knows. But it's a remake of a movie that's very highly regarded: *Dragon Gate Inn* (1967) was one of King Hu's big successes, critically as well as theatrically.[1] So Raymond Lee, Tsui Hark and Ng See-yuen were taking on an acknowledged hit movie. (That could be problematic for some viewers, who dislike remakes of masterpieces. Remake a minor movie, sure, but not a 100% masterwork).

In the defence of the movie, critics have pointed out that the 1992 version adds many new ingredients, reworks the original considerably, and is a new approach to the material.

Similarly, Tsui Hark insisted that his version of the *Dragon Gate Inn* mythology (of 2012) wasn't a remake of the 1992 movie. Tsui said rather than a remake, the new *Dragon Gate Inn* was a kind of sequel to the King Hu movie.[2] A wise remark, because the 1992 movie deserves a place on the list of the top ten action movies made in China (or perhaps anywhere). Anyhoo, this all means that the 1967 *Dragon Gate Inn* made a huge impression on the 17 year-old Tsui, for him to later rework it *twice*.

It's worth noting that the international cut of *Dragon Gate* is *not* the version the filmmakers preferred. Tsui Hark explained that the movie was meant to be 80-85 minutes (like many Hong Kong movies), but for the laserdisc release (which was used for later DVD and video releases), the

1 *Dragon Gate Inn* was King Hu's first big success. It was his first film made in Taiwan.
2 A sequel to *Dragon Gate Inn* had been considered, Tsui Hark recalled, soon after the 1992 movie, but due to conflicting schedules and other commitments, it didn't happen.

distributors added more scenes: they used master and cover shots of horse-riding, which weren't intended to be included. They added a voiceover. They re-dubbed the movie. And they changed the music. (The voiceover, for instance, explains about the Dong Chang and the historical context of the story – well, no Chinese audience needs a lecture about oppressive regimes! Meanwhile, there are too many horse-riding shots, which unbalances the pace of the narrative, extending the first act too much).

THE CAST.

Among the many, many marvellous elements in *New Dragon Gate Inn* is the incredible cast: *New Dragon Gate Inn* features pretty much every actor then working in Chinese movies. Many of the performers, for instance, also appeared in the *Once Upon a Time In China* movies, in *Tai Chi Master, Iron Monkey, The Blade, Police Story*, etc. The cast of *New Dragon Gate Inn* is a roll-call of your favourites from the period: Maggie Cheung Man-yuk, Brigitte Lin Ching-hsia,[3] Tony Leung Ka-Fai, Donnie Yen, Lau Shun, Yuen Bun, Elvis Tsui, Yuen Cheung-yan, Yen Shi-kwan, Xiong Xin-xin, Ngai Chung-wai and Lawrence Ng.

Everybody's here, and they're having a great time entertaining us with another old wives' tale from the *jianghzu*. (Except for one notable absence: Jet Li in the tailor-made role of the hero Zhao Huaian.[4] But he did essay the part in the remake of 2012, helmed by Tsui Hark). Brigitte Lin injured her eye[5] (deflecting arrows in a stunt at the Dunhuang location), and returned to a Hong Kong hospital. A double was used to film Lin's scenes (handily, Lin's warrior character is covered up with a scarf over her/ his face).

THE SCRIPT.

Scripts are routinely derided in Western critics' evaluation of Hong Kong movies – as if every North American movie has screenplays that exhibit the quality of *King Lear*. Yes, right! Every Summer, Hollywood releases twenty *King Lears*, fifteen *Hamlets* and ten friggin' *Othellos*!

But *New Dragon Gate Inn* has a fine script (by Tsui Hark, Charcoal Tan (co-writer of *Once Upon a Time In China 2* and *3*), and Hiu Wing) – and, yes, it's superior to most N. American, popcorn movies. For example, it orchestrates an enormous cast, and gives all of the principals things to

3 The characters of Brigitte Lin and Maggie Cheung were originally played in the 1967 *Dragon Gate Inn* by Polly Ling-feng and Cheng Pei-pei.
4 The remake of *Dragon Gate Inn* had been set up by Jet Li and his manager Jim Choi, with Michelle Yeoh to co-star, and filming to start in Beijing. However, when Choi was murdered, the production was scrapped, and the rival *Dragon Gate Inn* went ahead.
5 Tsui Hark recalled that he met Lin at the airport, on her way back to Hong Kong, feeling sorry for herself.

achieve and do. It provides proper introductions for the main protagonists. It elegantly (and quickly) sets up the relationships between the charas. There is plenty of detail in the screenplay, too – the foreshadowing of the storm in the dialogue (and songs) of Jade, for example (and the character of Zhao Huaian is built up, too, b4 we meet him).

Tracking the action and the plot reveals just how carefully *New Dragon Gate Inn* is worked out. The movie not only delivers all of the expected scenes, and sequences of scenes, for a *wuxia pian*, it includes 100s of details and minor gags. And the camera is right in there, capturing it all. (For instance, to add to the already stuffed plotting, there's a wedding night, a drinking competition, cannibalism, bits of business with wine which might be poisoned, etc). The film is also crammed with minor details which embellish the characters and their relationships, plus some recurring elements (such as the flute, the tunnels, and cannibalism).

New Dragon Gate Inn is unusual structurally: it doesn't have a single protagonist, for a start; the narrative focus shifts from character to character. Sometimes it follows the mysterious Swordswoman Yuan Mo-ya, and then her lover, Zhao Huaian. Sometimes we are with the two child hostages, and sometimes with the Chief Eunuch Cao. For much of the time, the script concentrates on Jade, mistress of the inn. For the creation of this character alone, the script of *New Dragon Gate Inn* is marvellous.

TECHNICAL ASPECTS.

Altho' there is sometimes confusion about who actually directed some movies which were produced by Tsui Hark but ostensibly helmed by someone else, much of *New Dragon Gate Inn* was directed by the credited director, Raymond Lee Wai-man (Li Hui Min – he also co-directed *The Swordsman* and co-directed *The Swordsman 3,* and co-produced *Iron Monkey, The Magic Crane, The Swordsman 3,* and *Wicked City* in this period). No doubt Tsui had his input on many areas of the production, and we know that Tsui is the kind of hands-on producer who can't stand back (!).

According to Tsui Hark, however, about 80% of *New Dragon Gate Inn* was filmed by him – partly because they were under the gun with schedules, and thus split the filming into two units (Raymond Lee in Dunhuang and Tsui in Hong Kong):

> ...for *Dragon Inn*, I was actually involved in the shooting. I shot something like 80 percent of the movie because we were in the situation of having to meet the talent's schedules. We were caught in a tight schedule on location in Dunhuang.

Numerous aspects of *New Dragon Gate Inn* bear Tsui Hark's imprint, from the comedy (the cannibalism gags are pure Tsui – from *We're Going To Eat You*), to the remarkable characterization of Maggie Cheung Man-yuk as Jade. (You can see Tsui's influence all over the studio-bound scenes, filmed in Hong Kong).

The Dragon Gate Inn itself has a delightful border town atmosphere, where anything goes (very similar to a frontier town in a Western).[6] Bandits, bad food (don't eat the meat!), wine, and everybody is glaring at everybody else. There's an earthy, somewhat sleazy air to the place, so that it resembles one of those border towns[7] in a Sam Peckinpah Western movie. And with Jade in charge, anything is possible!

The Dragon Gate Inn itself is sited improbably in the deep desert – so deep and so remote there isn't anything nearby for miles. And no roads, either (if the inn is situated on a trading route, there isn't much of a road or even a trail!). But that is the whole point, of course: this is a place so far from anywhere that anything goes. (including cannibalism!).

The production design – by Chiu Gwok-San, Yee-Fung Chung, Chi-Hing Leung and William Chang Suk-Ping – is marvellous, filling the inn with rich textures and details. The cinematography (from Arthur Wong and Tom Lau Moon-tong) lights the inn set every which way (once again, the night photography in a Hong Kong movie is especially fine: on top of everything else, *New Dragon Gate Inn* is a very *beautiful* movie. The photography, for instance, exploits the desert locations to maximum effect – it was worth every cent going out there).[8]

The inn has an intricate plan, comprising a large dining hall, upper balconies, pillars, basement kitchens, shadowy bedrooms, and secret tunnels. The action explores every part of the building over the course of the picture (including using the pillars and roof supports for staging the fights).

Many of the night exteriors are not filmed in the desert, however (where lighting large areas at night is a massive undertaking): it's that all-purpose spot in the New Territories, a patch of ground filled with smoke which many movies in the 1980s and 1990s used.

The outstanding score for *New Dragon Gate Inn* is a traditional Chinese piece, by Philip Chan and Chow Gam-wing,[9] featuring the sort of classical, Chinese music you might hear in the old Shaw Brothers movies. Pounding percussion, squealing woodwind, and jagged strings occur

---

6 *Dragon Gate Inn* has been called a riff on *Casablanca*.
7 The movie makes a big deal out of crossing a border.
8 You can see, too, that it was a tough shoot at times – stuntmen are performing difficult gags on hard, stony ground.
9 'It's probably the finest non-James Wong-composed score in all of Tsui Hark's films' (Lisa Morton, 95).

throughout. There's also a moment for lyrical flute music (played by Yuan Mo-ya to call her lover Zhao Huaian across the desert sands on his camels).

Later, a short but illuminating beat shows Yuan Mo-ya holding the flute, and closing her eyes; Zhao Huaian see her doing that, and closes his, too. it's a kind of romance-as-meditation scene. *New Dragon Gate Inn* is filled with subtle evocations of love, as well as the Jade-led, bawdy kind. (Yes, let's not forget that Jade sings several ribald songs, about red and white candles, and she's introduced (as the Dragon Gate Inn itself) with a song about a girl in the desert who loves men).

And while we're raving about *New Dragon Gate Inn* from a technical point-of-view, let's not forget an oft-overlooked aspect of filmmaking: costume design. All of the *wuxia pian* and *kung fu* pictures of the Chinese New Wave are wild costume extravaganzas, offering a fantasy vision of Ancient China. *New Dragon Gate Inn* is no exception: Poon Kwok-Wah and Ching Tin-Giu orchestrate ornate costumes for Cao and the Dong Chang faction, with his officers in different, single colours (green, blue, red), and the crack warriors all in black, with wide-brimmed hats. Talking about hats – Brigitte Lin and her cohorts sport very wide straw hats (to protect against the sun – you see them everywhere in movies of this kind). The heroes're clad in sleek, black outfits,with white scarves and shirts (but all garments in *kung fu* and *wuxia pian* movies have to be loose enough for the actors and stunt team sto execute those all-important twirls and kicks).

In fact, the *sight* of clothes rippling in the high breeze is part of the effect of a Chinese action picture, and the *sound* of clothing flapping is also mixed high. Indeed, *kung fu* movies often use clothing as a weapon (outer garments dipped in water are employed as spears, for instance). And *New Dragon Gate Inn* includes an outrageous scene where the two heroines are undressing each other in the middle of a fight.

THE CHARACTERS.

With formidable competition from a host of very strong performers, the actor who steals *New Dragon Gate Inn* is Maggie Cheung Man-yuk. She is a revelation in this 1992 movie. She plays the mistress of the Dragon Gate Inn, Jade, with a fiery, impish, sexy energy. Cheung's Jade is one of those super-kinetic characters who simply can't keep still; Cheung rises to the challenge of delivering a sassy, young woman who's so bursting with energy, she's leaping on top of tables, flying down from the upper balcony, slinking around the inn like a snake, flirting with every customer, and flashing those camera-melting eyes (Cheung is *very* beautiful in this movie).

It's a *tour-de-force* of *physical* performance. It's not a performance that's in the script – most of it has been created on the set, in the interactions with other actors, in the way that Maggie Cheung has been directed by Raymond Lee, Tsui Hark (and Tony Ching Siu-tung *et al*), and in the lively approach to the filmmaking. Name any of the famous spikey, independent, no-nonsense women in North American Westerns (Joan Crawford in *Johnny Guitar* (1954) comes to mind), and Cheung is their equal (I mean, you don't really believe that Joan Crawford could wield a gun, but you sure can buy that Maggie Cheung can kick ass!).

There's a delight in bawdy, sexy scenes, too, in *New Dragon Gate Inn*, with Jade being introduced fooling around with a sweaty client upstairs in her chambers at the inn (until he's dispatched with Jade's weapon of choice – throwing stars). Again, the staging is incredibly physical, with the actors rarely at rest (Jade displays her ingenuity in running rings around men, as they grapple on the bed). The corpse is promptly thrown down a chute to the kitchen (via one of many secret tunnels in the inn), where the cook starts to prepare the meat for the buns (another (tasty) slice of cannibalism[11] – from *We're Going To Eat You* and *A Chinese Ghost Story 2*).

Downstairs, in the dining hall, Jade is flirting with every guy, including the General of the authorities, played by Elvis Tsui (they have a history). She's lifted onto tables, she spins around to evade lecherous advances, and as soon as Yuan Mo-ya enters the building, she is immediately intrigued. The characterzation of Jade foregrounds sex – there are many jokes about flutes and candles, for instance.

Watching Maggie Cheung take the movie into outer space with her performance is mesmerizing. Within the first act alone, Cheung has horsed around with a guy, then killed him, tussled in a near-naked lesbian dance with Brigitte Lin, flirted with the General (whom she's had a relationship with), encountered the hero while rolled up in a banner, had jealous fits, and even been the butt of jokes about menstruation in a circle of guys. Few actresses do so much in so short a time.

Meanwhile, Brigitte Lin plays Yuan Mo-ya as another of her crossdressing warriors. Her Mo-ya is also mysterious (another Lin speciality), yet also with powerful feelings underneath that cool, enigmatic ?or. The erotic interplay between Yuan Mo-ya and Zhao Huaian is

Teo has also compared *Dragon Inn* with *Johnny Guitar*, with its world of lone ?tlaws, lady bosses, and remote inns.
?en as shadows on a wall, is pure Tsui Hark: Ngai the cook (Xiong Xin-xin)
?m a corpse hanging from a hook, while he merrily sings a Daki song
?ated for us by Siu-chuen). And when the cook cuts up a roasted goat
?unny gag, but it also plays into the finale, when Ngai turns out to

beautifully evoked, and the depths of Mo-ya's emotions are comically but also tenderly portrayed in the scene where she gets very drunk when her man joins Jade in her chambers.

If you like seeing sexy women being sexy, the scene in *New Dragon Gate Inn* that gives the two beautiful stars Brigitte Lin and Maggie Cheung a chance to shine is the one.[12] Unlike any comparable scene in any movie made in the West, the scene upstairs in Yuan Mo-ya's room combines a fight with aerial acrobatics, a catty face-off between two super-bitches, and a romantically-oriented interplay of bodies, movement and nudity with the lesbian subtext brought out into the open. As they fly around the room, yanking off each other's clothing (with Mo-ya always besting Jade – Jade is stripped piece by piece by Mo-ya, ending up nude), they admire each other's bodies (while the camera frames the actresses so that the jiggly bits're always cleverly obscured).

Altho' this scene is 'fan service' – undressing the two attractive, female stars (in true, exploitation fashion in Hong Kong cinema) – it does have a dramatic component: the romantic rivalry between the two (Jade is miffed when any man ignores her, and Yuan Mo-ya does so as soon as 'he' enters the inn). So Jade wants to discover Mo-ya's identity. And anything in *New Dragon Gate Inn* is done physically, with movement – hence the undressing dance.

And even that isn't the end of it – because Jade ends up on the roof of the inn nearly naked. And just as Zhao Huaian is approaching across the desert on his camels (her response? Only to start singing!). So how does she find some clothes? Only by diving off the roof into the night, spinning thru the air, grabbing the Dragon Gate Inn's banner, and wrapping it around her body as she spins to the ground (a remarkable piece of invention). So she greets Zhao dressed in a flag (a couple of guys're in the background in these scenes, ogling her partially-nude body – that's pure Tsui Hark!). Jade is simply one of those girls who finds herself in such sticky situations all the time (and she's also one of those women who can talk their out of it, while retaining their dignity). And right away, she's flirting with Zhao.

SEX AND PLEASURE.

Sexy! *New Dragon Gate Inn* puts together two beautiful stars – Tony Leung Ka-Fai and Maggie Cheung – and gives them a wedding night scene (the wedding sequence is pure Tsui Hark – especially in the way that it instantly complicates the romantic triangle with Yuan Mo-ya). Jade is in heaven – dolling herself up (and somehow finding rolls of red cloth and red

12 The 'film's most famous scene... an astonishing scene, one as charged with eroticism as action' (Lisa Morton, 93).

lanterns to decorate the inn).

Swept up to Jade's chambers in Zhao Huaian's arms, the couple perform an erotically-charged tussle of body-on-body that's played for comedy as well as thrills. Because much of the scene is a fight! After all, what is a love scene in an action movie going to be, but a fight! Jade wants Zhao, but Zhao only wants to know where the secret tunnel[13] is to lead his crew out of the Dragon Gate Inn in one piece. The bawdy dialogue (Jade tells Zhao that her tunnel is right there, and it's easy to find, as she grapples him on top of her on the table – she's dying for his candle to light her tunnel), is only part of the delight of this over-the-top honeymoon sequence. (Meanwhile, Yuan Mo-ya is drowning her sorrows with wine with the boys during the drinking competition, imagining that her lover Zhao really is falling for the slinky, sexy vixen Jade – she spotted Jade fiddling with the flute she gave Zhao, which Zhao also notices; much to Zhao's irritation, Jade snitched the flute, and dared him to get it back). When an erotic triangle is played with this amount of pizzazz, from a trio of incredible performers, you can't help but be won over.

There's a bawdy running gag about candles (the sort of gag that William Shakespeare couldn't resist – the Bard, bless him, was very fond of phallic jokes), candles and weiners and lighting the fire (meanwhile, the love object that's passed between Zhao Huaian and Yuan Mo-ya is a flute! Which Mo-ya puts to her pretty lips and plays, sending Zhao into paroxysms of delight!).

But even without that raunchy dialogue and phallic symbolism, *New Dragon Gate Inn* is a supremely *sexual* movie: just look at how many times bodies are tussling or grappling each other or spinning around each other or flying thru the air. There is an ecstatic freedom to the movement of the body in this hyper-kinetic *wuxia pian*.

This also applies to many *kung fu* and *wuxia* movies – they are often sexier and way more sensual than pornography. The emphasis on textures, on atmospheres, on clothing, on bodies, on bodies in contact and in motion, lends Chinese action movies a highly charged eroticism. It's the pleasures of a musical movie and a dance movie combined with exaggerated melodrama, passions running on ten, and an imaginative, operatic approach to filmmaking.

You can see where Chinese action movies are coming from, and where they are headed (pleasure – entertainment – show business), and you can't help but surrendering. The energy or *chi* flowing thru the movies is so high, so colourful, it makes many other movies seem like catatonic patients dying on a hospital bed in a lonely, suburban town. By comparison

13 The tunnel is discovered by Zhao later – it's the one in, where else?, the bed.

with a Chinese action movie, many another picture appears like someone in a coma.

Many of the details in the erotic triangle in the middle act of *New Dragon Gate Inn* are very Tsui Harkian – we've seen these looks of longing and jealousy before in films such as *Shanghai Blues* and *Peking Opera Blues*. Indeed, this part of *New Dragon Gate Inn* is like *Peking Opera Blues* in the desert.

Tsui Hark is never happier than when he's got some of his favourite actors and actresses on a single, large, multi-level set, divided into groups, where the characters have social obligations that tussle with unspoken desires, where their sense of duty to the group (plus their political affiliations) are at odds with their personal dreams and impulses.

ACTION.

With Tony Ching Siu-tung, Cheng Yiu-sing, Wing Cho, Xin Xin Xiong and Yuen Bun overseeing the action, *New Dragon Gate Inn* is a *tour-de-force* of imaginative action scenes. Like many a *wuxia pian* and *kung fu* movie, *New Dragon Gate Inn* frontloads the picture with a series of visceral encounters, many featuring terrific horse riding stunts and falls (filmed in the Chinese desert at Dunhuang). That is a mere prelude, however, to the key action sequence in act one, where Cao and his army ambush our heroes rescuing the hostage children.

Altho' it is very much a Hong Kong action picture, *New Dragon Gate Inn* was filmed in Mandarin and in Mainland China, in the deserts of Dunhuang. The locations alone are worth the price of the ticket – landscapes so impressive, you can point the camera in any direction and come up with gold. No computer-assisted aimgery here, no blue screens or green screens – you can't beat being out in the real desert under the burning sun and riding across stones and sand. And, like all of Tsui Hark's historical movies, there is fire, smoke, rain, wind and lightning blowing and crackling throughout the picture.

One of the marks of genius of Hong Kong stunt teams is their uncanny, almost miraculous ability to mix actors who aren't martial artists with stunt doubles. In your average action movie in the West, it's easy as pie to see where the joins are, where the doubles replace the actors. In Hong Kong action cinema, the staging, choreography, camera angles and editing make it seamless.

Maggie Cheung, Brigitte Lin and Tony Leung are not martial artists (tho' they have appeared in many action movies), but Tony Ching Siu-tung, Cheng Yiu-sing, Wing Cho, Xiong Xin-xin and Yuen Bun and the stunt team smake them look like the *kung fu* masters they are supposed to be.

A LOOK AT EACH ACT.

In many respects *New Dragon Gate Inn* is an 'Eastern Western', a replaying of the North American cowboy genre within an Oriental, *jiangzhu* context (plus some King Hu, some Hong Kong action, and 'a distinctly Tsui Hark spin').[14] The movie opens with very lengthy scenes of horses and riders in spectacular landscapes (more shots than the filmmakers intended – added by the distributors). The voiceover explains the set-up: the Imperial regime of Cao Shaoqin and Dong Chang is capturing and punishing anybody who steps in their way. Loading the front of the movie with hugely impressive production value scenes, the filmmakers create the world of *New Dragon Gate Inn:* a ruthless Imperial regime in the more remote, dustier, tougher regions of the Ming Dynasty.

There are many scenes of Imperial majesty and power for some ten minutes – soldiers on horseback carrying banners, Cao seated on a throne, with his minions arranged below him, and many deaths as the Dong Chang try out their new weaponry (including a 'phoenix arrow' that can fly around corners, a very Tsui Harkian gag).

The prologue of *New Dragon Gate Inn* is all about the villains: the training exercises of the élite, ninja-esque Black Flag squad, who practise their bow and arrow techniques on live (condemned) prisoners on horseback; the excessive torture of Defense Minister Yang Yu-xuan (Yen Shi Kwan); and, presiding over it all, the effete Chief Eunuch Cao[15] (played with vulpine relish by Donnie Yen, cast against type). In his eagerness to quash all opposition to his regime, Cao lets the children of Yang go free, using them as bait so that he can crush all those who aid the hostages in one fell swoop.

Evoking a corrupt regime is pretty much mandatory in *kung fu* and swordplay movies, in any era of cinema. So that when we are eventually introduced to our heroes (after quite some time – the main titles of *New Dragon Gate Inn* don't appear until some 8 minutes into the movie), we have a very good idea of what they're up against, and how anyone who opposes the totalitarian regime will be punished severely (thus also typing our heroes as social rebels). Of course, some critics linked the oppressive and violent regime of Cao and Dong Chang to the People's Republic of China's government (and the vicious political suppression embodied in the Tiananmen Square massacre).

---

14 Lisa Morton, 92.
15 In Chinese cinema, eunuchs have exchanged their male 'essence' for supernatural power (eunuchs are typically ambitious, political characters, part of the Imperial court). There are jokes about Cao's eunuch status in the 1967 *Dragon Gate Inn,* which the 1992 movie doesn't use.

The first act of *New Dragon Gate Inn* depicts the Dong Chang (= East Factory/ East Wing/ East Agents/ Gestapo) regime in the first half, building up to the rescue and the ambush in the middle of the act. In the second half, we're introduced to the Dragon Gate Inn itself (with a song, suitably, from Jade as the first thing we hear, about a girl in the desert who loves men). The first act climaxes with the arrival by camel of Zhao Huaian – a superb introduction for the hero (so now all of the pieces are in place).

❁

Riveting, compelling, thrilling, enchanting, yearning – *New Dragon Gate Inn* has everything, and *then some*. The second act often sags in an action movie, doesn't it?, for good reasons (try writing an action movie script, and you'll soon discover all of the reasons!).[16] But not in *New Dragon Gate Inn*: it has enough complexly entangled sexual desire, honour, ambition, greed, beauty, magic, scares, twists, buffoonery, and action for ten movies. There are ninja-swift dartings to and fro, around and on top of the Dragon Gate Inn;[17] there's a fierce rainstorm; there's a wine drinking contest (with no one wanting to lose face);[18] there's a fantastic bout of sex and comedy in the wedding night scene; and everybody is so jumpy they're clutching their swords and leaping up at the slightest slights.

Because everyone is in pretending to be someone else, and the stakes are high (arrest or maybe instant execution), nerves are at a jangly pitch.[19] Each group is jostling for position, while Jade attempts to keep the peace (and stop them destroying her inn!). Jade's flaring temper is incredible to see, as she flings wine at people,[20] berates the Dong Chang officials for creating a mess, and yells at everybody (except Zhao Huaian, of course).

The second act of *New Dragon Gate Inn* is filled with short but delightful two-hander scenes: Jade and Zhao, Jade and Cha, Zhao and Cha, Zhao and Yuan Mo-ya. Each scene is performed and cut at a sprightly pace, and staged with very dynamic movements. Some are romantic scenes (Jade and Zhao, Zhao and Mo-Ya), some are combative scenes between opposing sides (Cha and Zhao), and some are political manœuvring scenes (Jade and Cha, Cha and Zhao).

Cha and his Dong Chang cronies appear in the midst of the storm,

---

16 In fact, if you wanted to develop your enjoyment and appreciation of cinema and television (which, in the West, you might spend 4 hours a day watching), I'd recommend writing a script and having a go at editing. Working out the structure of a movie on paper will tell you plenty about how difficult it is, and cutting some scenes together will show you how many tricks and sleights of hand are involved in everything thing you've ever seen in film and TV.
17 Including two of the Dong Chang guys getting frazzled by lightning – they turn up next morning as breakfast!
18 The rebels cleverly water down their wine.
19 There are many scenes where characters, desperate not to reveal their identity, pretend to act cool and casual.
20 But she happily accepts several bribes, slipping them into her cleavage.

posing as merchants, but they're really after Zhao Huaian and his rebels. There are many scenes where characters jostle for position, pretending to laugh good-naturedly, while under the tables they're getting ready to throw darts.

The second act climaxes with a series of short but intense action scenes, inside the bedrooms of the Dragon Gate Inn: Zhao Huaian and Cha (fighting under and over a roofbeam), Zhao and Siu-chuen (whom he immobilizes at a pressure point), Cha and Jade (she rumbles him, he tries to enlist her aid in snaring Zhao & co.), and Zhao and Yuan Mo-ya (they share a moment of meditation amidst memories and flute music).

This really is perfect filmmaking: a great cast, colourful, rounded characters, a fascinating scenario, an exotic setting, beautiful music, and all building suspense. The shifting positions in the endless cat-and-mouse manœuvres are deftly tracked, as each group tries to gain the upper hand, without knowing quite the others are up to. And Jade, who seems to be everywhere, tries to keep on top of it all.

The audience has already seen several action scenes, and it knows that more are coming up – but the movie teases the audience by leading up to a smackdown, then edging away from it. For example, in the dining hall, Zhao Huaian berates Cha and the oppressive regime of the Emperor, and it seems as if the film is going to dive into another massive brawl. Tables are smashed with fists in ferocious anger, eyes glare at each other, and impish Jade flits between the opposing sides, sprinkling water on the faces, trying to cool everyone down.

The arrival of the General and his boys, still looking for the wanted rebels Zhao Huaian and co., complicates the middle act once more. Here the Dong Chang are out-foxed, when Yuan Mo-ya secretly shows the General their authorized, Imperial papers (pretending to be Dong Chang, working undercover).

The tension mounts and mounts in the middle act of *New Dragon Gate Inn* (using the three-act model), with editor Poon Hung controlling the pacing and the delights with supreme judgement. Incredibly, *everyone* gets their moment to shine (incredible partly because they are so many characters), and, also incredibly, the movie is clever and skilful enough to take a breather from the shenanigans inside the Dragon Gate Inn. So there's a lyrical interlude shot against the sunset outside when Zhao Huaian wonders when all of this is going to be over (not for a few more hours, I hope!), and even the child hostages enjoy a moment of relaxation on the roof of the inn (that scene is beautifully empty of action and incident: the kids eat fruit, and look at the moon, and they talk about their mom. That's all. And in an action movie thrill-ride, it's marvellous to be able to stop the headlong rush like that for something pretty inconsequential. However, let's not forget, too, that the two moppets are what is at stake in *New Dragon Gate Inn*).

❁

As *New Dragon Gate Inn* moves towards its finale, the suspense keeps mounting: there are multiple events taking place simultaneously (such as the drinking contest continuing downstairs, and Jade and Zhao Huaian tussling upstairs), with the 1992 movie cutting repeatedly to Chief Eunuch Cao approaching on horseback with his army of expert warriors in black (we know that Donnie Yen as Cao has yet to reveal his true colours and go into battle. You don't cast Yen in an action movie and not have him go to work! So the audience knows that the fight is coming up).

It builds and builds – like foreplay not even the gods could resist (!) – until it explodes. You are waiting for it to happen, and the filmmakers tease us by having the impatient Ho Fu smash his cup of wine on the floor in frustration, and everybody draws their swords, but then, no, they settle down again.

One of the heroes (Ho Fu) and the chief villain (Cha) begin the smackdown, and then it's all swords drawn and a full-on brawl and sword fight. Inside the inn, there are numerous action beats to delight the audience: Yuan Mo-ya swirling like a dervish, the Dong Chang crew tussling with everyone, and even Jade leaps into the fray. Especially satisfying is to see Jade have a moment to shine when she demolishes the evil, smug Cha: first, she duels with Cha's chief lieutenant, Siu-chuen, pushing him back until he's squished gorily between some mill wheels. Then (this is pure Tsui Hark!), she takes a bucket of blood that drips from the corpse, scurries over the dining hall, and throws it in Cha's face, yelling at him to eat his own blood. Then she runs him through with a sword. Blood and guts this vicious is seldom seen in Western movies perpetrated by female stars – and with such venom (thus the Dong Chang are dealt with).

Yuan Mo-ya tells Ho Fu and Iron to flee with the kids in their baskets – but they run into a hail of arrows from some of the Dong Chang outriders, arriving at night.[21] The death of Jin and Ho (crouched over the kids, to protect them, as with the death of Cha and his crew, indicates that the stakes are so much higher now (with about fifteen minutes still to run).

Without a doubt, the finale of *New Dragon Gate Inn* is one of the greatest action scenes ever filmed. Action directors Tony Ching Siu-tung, Cheng Yiu-sing, Wing Cho, Xiong Xin-xin and Yuen Bun and the stunt team

---

21 This is probably the scene where Brigitte Lin injured her eye.

go absolutely nuts with spins, kicks, leaps, acrobatics, thrusts, swipes, punches, and every possible combination of sword-on-sword action imaginable. Even by Hong Kong standards, the finale of *New Dragon Gate Inn* is simply tremendous. It's as if nothing could hold back the filmmakers, nothing could get in their way, and nothing could stop them from delivering this sensational mix of action, comedy and thrills.

It really is beautiful to witness, and awe-inspiring, too: you can see how *on fire* the filmmakers were in this period of cinema in China (there's a similar energy running thru most of the Chinese action movies of the early 1990s). The giant bust-up in the Dragon Gate Inn would be enough for many a movie (it's like watching a summary of thousands of Shaw Brothers movies!), but that's only *part* of the climax of this mind-boggingly wonderful movie!

Because Chief Eunuch Cao and the villains are hurtling towards the Dragon Gate Inn across the desert on horseback in clouds of dust. The attack begins with a remarkable sequence of arrows shot into the inn, as the horsemen encircle the building.[22] Horse riders storm into the inn (and onto the roof). Yuan Mo-ya goes into overdrive as the spinning, magical swordswoman who decapitates two villains while zipping thru the air, flying on a red banner (coming to the aid of Jade, who's taken on the riders and been thrown to the floor).

The editing of *New Dragon Gate Inn* (by Poon Hung) is blisteringly good, the staging is fabulously imaginative, and the visceral thrill is profound – to see Maggie Cheung and Brigitte Lin going supernova with their anger and battle frenzy is simply amazing (and yet the movie even has time for Jade to rescue the flute and hand it back to Yuan Mo-ya. *New Dragon Gate Inn* is full of poignant moments like that).

When the heroes try to break away from the inn during the Dong Chang assault, making a bid for freedom, they are cut down. Characters that we seem to have spent a long time with (and grown to like) are expiring all over the place, made into human pin-cushions by the arrows.

But even this is not the end of the finale of *New Dragon Gate Inn* – the incendiary action keeps on coming! And the filmmakers aren't out of imagination and playfulness and wit yet! Because we still haven't had the long-expected clash between the chief villain (Chief Eunuch Cao) and the surviving heroes: Jade, Zhao Huaian and Yuan Mo-ya. (Cao is alerted to the presence of the heroes when the red scarf of one of the kids blows free in the high wind. As soon as it falls, Cao leaps out of his wagon and onto the back of a horse, in hot pursuit).

The four-way sword fight that tops the finale of *New Dragon Gate Inn*

22 Cao signals the attack by just lifting his finger.

is like no sword fight in *any* Western movie (before 1992 – or since!), and like few in Hong Kong cinema, for its ferocity, its invention, its daring, its audacity and its flair ('one of the greatest in the martial arts cinema', reckoned Lisa Morton [LM, 95]).

You can see the stamp of action choreographer Tony Ching Siu-tung all over this majestic piece of cinema (Ching would use very similar techniques in movies like *Hero, A Chinese Ghost Story, The Curse of the Golden Flower* and *House of Flying Daggers*).[23] Ching gets his combatants into the air, and spinning and kicking, with his team's unsurpassed use of wires (it's as if there is simply *nothing* that Ching and his team can't do!). The fight contains literally 100s of beats and moves, which flash by with the speed of a slashing blade, yet the staging and the editing keeps the movements clear and readable.

The setting certainly helps plenty: here's a Hong Kong *wuxia pian* that leaves behind the forest and the bamboo and the stony land of the New Territories (or the village back-lot sets), for the bright, merciless light and choking dust of the desert.[24] The implacable violence of the desert is employed throughout *New Dragon Gate Inn* (the characters can't leave during the storm, for instance), and pays off again when a dust storm buries the remaining characters in sand. In one incredible shot (of many shots in this exhilarating sequence), the camera is tracking laterally across a stony slope while the combatants duel, tumble and run, barely seen in the clouds of dust.

That Yuan Mo-ya is mortally wounded by Cao and sinks to her death in quicksand adds an extra level of desperation and tragedy to the finale, partly because Mo-ya is played by one of the stars, Brigitte Lin (in this movie, only three people survive: Jade, Zhao Huaian and Ngai the cook. But the movie makes sure that the children had been led far away by Ngai).

Meanwhile, the element of sorcery in fighting techniques that Cao possesses is just enough to be scary without going overboard. But he is matched, unexpectedly, by the Daki character, Ngai (played by Xiong Xin-xin), still clinging to his beloved meat cleaver (!). It's a real crowd-pleaser that Ngai is able to slice away Cao's leg and his arm to the bone and to burrow underground (seen in other movies of the time, like Jacky Cheung's character Autumn in *A Chinese Ghost Story 2*). But it still takes all three of the remaining heroes to dispatch Cao (he manages to wound all of them

---

23 The final swordplay scenes feature many of Ching's flourishes, such as swords drawing energy lines on the ground, and swordsman descending in the air directly above their victim.
24 You can be sure that the performers found this a tough sequence to shoot – bone-hard stones to land on, dust and dirt, and that very hot sun. Also, many actors filmed other movies at the same time – but there's no chance of that in the Gobi desert far from a studio. Which perhaps meant that even more time and energy was focussed on this single movie than usual.

pretty badly). Zhao deals the killing blow with a smaller sword cleverly buried inside his blade (shoved into Cao's neck).

And the *dénouement* of *New Dragon Gate Inn* is perfect: brief but poignant. First, the aftermath of the ferocious battle, with the combatants recovering on the desert floor, to the sounds of the flute music (which evokes Yuan Mo-ya – we see a C.U. of the flute on the sand, the only thing left of Mo-ya).

Second, Zhao Huaian opts to leave the desert (on his camels, with the children), and Jade and Ngai later decide to join him – by burning down the Dragon Gate Inn. Out comes the wine, doused on the walls, and the building is torched with satisfaction by Jade. Cut to the wide, high angle shot of the inn in flames, with Jade and Ngai on horseback riding off to catch up Zhao (accompanied by a plangent piece of ethnic music).

Thus ends one of the greatest movies ever made.

New Dragon Gate Inn (1992).
(This page and over).

7

MOON WARRIORS
Zin San Cyun Syut

Moon Warriors (Cantonese: *Zin San Cyun Syut,* Mandarin: *Zhàn Shén Chuán Shuo*, 1992) is a marvellous period action movie with no less than five directors (Sammo Hung, Tony Ching Siu-tung, Corey Yuen (Yuen Kwai)[1] and the pairing of Alex Law and Mabel Cheung), and a superb cast headed up by Andy Lau Tak-wah,[2] and featuring two superstars of Chinese cinema, Anita Mui and Maggie Cheung Man-yuk. Kenny Bee, Chang Yi, Kelvin Wong, Chin Ka-lok, Heung Lui, Tam Waia and Ng Biu-chuen also appeared. With a cast and crew like that, it can't fail!

Teamwork Production made the movie; Alex Law scripted; Jessica Chan produced; Kam Ma edited; Arthur Wong, Peter Pau, Tam Chi-wai and Cheung Man-po photographed it; with music by James Wong Jim,[3] Mark Lui and Sherman Chow. Released Dec 19, 1992. 83 mins.

Kenny Bee was unusual casting as the Thirteenth Prince and disposed Emperor – Bee was best known as a singer, and for his comical roles.

The production of *Moon Warriors* required many stand-ins and doubles because of the hectic schedules of many of the main players. Maggie Cheung Man-yuk, for instance, apparently filmed all over her close-ups in two days, because she couldn't spare any more time. In addition to the complexity of the script, these added complications meant that the filmmakers had to keep track of all sorts of continuity issues. Hong Kong

---

1 According to Alex Law, *Moon Warriors* was edited by the main editors, with the action directors coming into fine tune their sections.
2 Andy Lau's Teamwork Motion Pictures produced *Moon Warriors*, and his star power probably helped to gather together the amazing production crew.
3 James Wong Jim also wrote the theme song, which was, of course, sung by Andy Lau.

filmmakers are of course geniuses at exploiting doubles, making non-martial artists such as Maggie Cheung look amazing. The technique needed to be exploited to the full to accommodate the tight schedules of the principal actors.

❖

Moon Warriors is pure pleasure from start to finish, like the finest Hong Kong action movies, and like so many Hong Kong movies of this period (*New Dragon Gate Inn, Once Upon a Time In China, Full Contact, The Swordsman, Fong Sai-yuk*, etc). As one would expect from a movie staged by three big name action choreographers, there is wealth of action and stuntwork in *Moon Warriors* (indeed, one of the treats of *Moon Warriors* is that you can compare the different styles of Sammo Hung, who liked realistic moves down on the ground, that a person was really capable of doing, and the up-in-the-air, all-out fantasy wire-work of Tony Ching, and the more technical approach of Corey Yuen Kwai, within the same movie. According to DP Arthur Wong, the production split into three units, to save time and schedules: thus, Hung handled the action in the forest, Ching oversaw the cave/ studio scenes, and Law and Cheung directed the dramatic scenes. According to Law, they would liaise with the action directors, then hand over to them when the action started up, as usual in Hong Kong cinema).

Moon Warriors features several big sets (the tombs, the cave, the fishing village), but it also cleverly suggests grandeur and scale for many other elements we'd expect to see in a Chinese, historical movie without showing them. For instance, we don't see the palace of 14th Prince – instead, we see him presiding over nighttime games of archery and chess in a field. Similarly, we don't see Yuet's palace; instead, we see another outdoor field for games (this time, kite-flying). We don't see the castle in the prologue, only the gateway of it on fire. And instead of large armies in full costume, we see the smaller groups of guards for the high and mighty, often on the move.

The giant (expensive) set for the finale of *Moon Warriors* is cleverly used in several other scenes: it's the tombs of Yen's ancestors, which he explains to Fei; Yen and his cohorts flee there to escape the villains (this is where Yen's royalty is revealed); and it's used for the pre-battle conflab. It's a multi-level set, featuring areas of water, raised platforms, ornate pillars – i.e., with plenty of opportunities for staging action (and it's beautifully designed[4] by James Leung Wah-sing and expertly lit by Arthur

---

[4] The wall carvings and the statuary receive some attention – usually, in *kung fu* movies, the set is merely the background for the constant action.

Wong).5

Many of the locations in *Moon Warriors* are the familiar ones in the New Territories, which we've seen in numerous Hong Kong flicks: the track in the hills below some cliffs (often used for galloping horse scenes); the tangled trees and vines (used for the thorn forest); the waterfall; and the cliffs which form the entrance to the tombs (seen in *Duel To the Death*).

The music – by James Wong Jim, Mark Lui and Sherman Chow – is also worth mentioning – a delightful mix of traditional, Chinese sounds with pounding percussion and, for the spooky scenes (like the forest of thorns), or the jade jewellery scene on the beach at night, some electronica.

Also notable in *Moon Warriors* are several musical interludes, common in Hong Kong cinema (Sally Yip and Andy Lau sing some of the songs, such as 'You and I Are the Most Freedom' and 'Let Spring Show My Smile', which were composed by James Wong Jim). As in many *wuxia pian*, the songs selected are melancholy and nostalgic, ruminating on lost times and evanescent life. And they are played over montages of characters in moody scenes. (In one montage, we see Yuet sadly contemplating her red wedding dress, as she ponders on her upcoming marriage to Yen – after falling for Fei).

An evil emperor who's ousted the decent, true ruler from the throne... a king in exile... black-masked ninjas... a simple, poor, working class youth who hooks up with an innocent princess... *Moon Warriors* happily delivers a raft of fairy tale and folklore clichés from Chinese mythology and history (which draws on motifs going back to the Ching dynasty), combining them with state-of-the-art action choreography and the miraculous cinematography by the legendary Arthur Wong (like many Chinese movies of this 1990s period, *Moon Warriors* looks absolutely sensational).

There are four main characters in *Moon Warriors*:

Fei   Andy Lau
Yuet   Anita Mui
Yen   Kenny Bee
Mo-sin Maggie Cheung

Plus the villain, the 14th Prince, played by Kelvin Wong.

Moon Warriors is a story in which everybody loves someone who

5 The tombs should fall to pieces at the end, but that event is handled in the cheapest way possible – in voiceover.

doesn't return their advances: Mo-sin secretly pines for Yen, but he prefers Yuet (their marriage is arranged), yet Yuet falls for Fei (who wouldn't, when he's played by Andy Lau?).

The political background of *Moon Warriors* is the usual one of Chinese, historical movies, especially those in the run-up to the Hand-over of Hong Kong in '97: an oppressive regime. The ruling powers are aggressive, cruel, and corrupt (they attained power illegally or immorally). So it's up to a small band of rebels, grouped around the ousted 13th Prince, to fight back.

Fei is drawn into this conflict, altho' he prefers to stay in his fishing village, to fish every day and make shark-and-pepper soup (as he tells Yuet). *Moon Warriors* evokes the familiar oppositions of folk and fairy tales: peasants and kings, the simple life and the courtly life, life in the country and life in the capital, etc.

In the finale, it's the villagers who're caught in the middle of the power games of the lords and emperors: some 89 people are massacred by the troops of the 14th Prince, including a young child.

❀

Maggie Cheung Man-yuk was cast against type: Anita Mui takes up the role of the girl who gets the guy – who has the romance with Andy Lau; so, instead, Cheung is the long-suffering acolyte of the ousted Emperor, Yen, and the double agent for the 14th Prince. Mo-sin is thus caught in the middle between the two fierce political rivals. She decides that she can't go thru with her task of nobbling Yen, yet she remains uncertain to the end. Inevitably, it's her boss, 14th Prince, who kills her, in the finale.

Not one fight, but a whole series of fights! The action scenes pile up thick and fast in *Moon Warriors,* and do not disappoint. Pretty much everything the finest action directors in the world can dream up is included in *Moon Warriors* (every Hong Kong action movie feels like a greatest hits package of action favourites). The fury, the speed, the elegance, and the complexity of the action is simply awesome.

There's an outstanding battle between Fei and Yuet and a mysterious, fearsome ninja in a darkened cave (with a magical use of firelight and flying cinders like fireflies, the sudden glows revealing where the participants are); an ærial battle in thorny undergrowth; an ambush in a bamboo forest[6] (with the assailants erupting from the ground); several running battles in sandy woodland; and of course the multiple action sequences of the finale.

Some sections of *Moon Warriors* involve lots of action followed by

6 Battles in bamboo forests are one of Ching's specialities, but this one was choreographed by Corey Yuen Kwai.

manic scenes of galloping on horses followed by more action. Our heroes are ambushed multiple times, split up, meet up again. They are forever leaping on or off horses.

The villains are introduced in the familiar high fantasy manner: practising archery at night in a grand, feudal setting outdoors. So we have flickering torchlight, fluttering banners, guards, a throne on a raised platform (royalty is always literally at a higher level than anyone else in Chinese, historical dramas). The Fourteenth Prince, the brother who usurped the throne of the hero, is given a ridiculous piece of over-the-top gore to portray his villainy: an underling (Leo Tsang) brings bad news, so he decapitates him with a bow, soars into the air, and fires an arrow which pierces the skull. As it flies thru the air to land on the wooden target board, the head passes thru a torch. In a trice all of the arrows fired by 14th Prince catch fire – together, from a distance, they spell the word, 'Heaven and Earth'. (The action is the kind of over-the-top, comical gore that Corey Yuen Kwai as well as Ching Siu-tung liked to cook up. It demonstrates that 14th Prince is a brilliant martial artist, and a vile commander).

Yet *Moon Warriors* also finds time (principally in the second act) to slow the movie down and explore the characters a little. So they are not one or two dimensional, but have depth. Anita Mui's Princess Yuet-nga, for instance, is not a killer, and is wracked with anguish when she is forced to kill attacking warriors, to save her life (in the aftermath scene, when Fei and Yuet-nga have escaped on horseback to a distant waterfall and pool, Yuet-nga is desperately trying to wash out the blood from her pure white gown).

To emphasize that Yuet is not a conventional warrior, but a princess primarily, Anita Mui is first shown (quite late in the running time) playing with kites with her maids in a field (filmed in the dreamy manner of childhood play). Yuet has led a sheltered life, and hasn't had any experiences like the ones that she later endures. In a brutal move by the assassins, the maids are all killed when Yuet sends them off to pick up the fallen kites. (The scene doesn't completely convince, but it works as an unsettling dramatic device, and it does allow the soldiers to get close to their target before they're detected).

This section of *Moon Warriors* has Andy Lau and Anit Mui playing the familiar bickering princess and warrior of a million movies.[7] *Moon Warriors* includes many of the stages in the development of the relationship, which starts out as animosity, moves into bonding thru adventures, and the warming of the princess for the warrior (when he defends her against the relentless ninja). Yuet is an innocent, clad in white, a princess spoilt and

7 *The Hidden Fortress* (1958) is one obvious reference.

indulged by her father, and knows little of the tough, outside world.

There are numerous quieter interludes in *Moon Warriors,* which flesh out the characters, so the 1992 movie is not hareing from one action scene to another, but building up a story. In one touching scene, the ousted ruler, the 13th Prince (Kenny Bee), talks with Fei on a jetty at night, and Fei tells him how he leaves part of the net open, so that some of the fish have a chance of escaping. Yuet tends Fei's wounds with magic, sparkling sand (from shellfish), in a romantic setting on the beach by firelight and moonlight (where the biggest special effect is the simple close-up – when you have actors as beautiful as Anita Mui and Andy Lau to look at, you don't need much else. However, Arthur Wong's photography is luxuriously romanticized).

The MacGuffin of *Moon Warriors* is a love token and a symbol of political union, a jade pendant, which chimes on its own and, when it's united with its other half, makes a swishy, mysterious sound. That pendant pays its way in the movie with several symbolic appearances (including the final one, when Fuet expires in Fei's arms, and the pendant falls and symbolically breaks on the stone floor of the tombs).

Andy Lau Tak-wah's Fei is a prince-in-the-making in *Moon Warriors,* a simple fisherman from a fishing village, the young, true Hans character of fairy tales, and the young Arthur from Arthurian legends (*Moon Warriors* was written by Mabel Cheung and Alex Law, who had studied English Literature in Hong Kong, and the Western influences, including Arthurian myths, can be discerned in their reworking of Ancient Chinese mythology. Part of the romantic triangle featuring Arthur, Lancelot and Guinevere remains in the script (between Yen, Yuet and Fei); there is also a second romantic triangle, with Yen at the centre, and Yuet and Mo-sin on either side).

One of the most remarkable scenes in recent Chinese cinema has Andy Lau Tak-wah swimming with a killer whale called Wei in *Moon Warrior:* it's a real film star swimming with a real whale! The footage is brilliantly filmed, with nary a hint of crappy computer-assisted animation or green screens – and this is the film's star and producer leaping out of the water with the world's fiercest predator! It's not something you will see from virtually any major film star anywhere on the planet. (The footage was shot at Ocean Park, a theme park in Canton).

Andy Lau Tak-wah is sensational in *Moon Warriors* – an actor who looks amazing, can really act, and can do many of his own stunts. At this time, in the early 1990s, Lau was one of a number of actors and filmmakers who were working so hard they were going from movie to movie at a breakneck pace (sometimes filming two or more different movies on the same day, and sometimes sleeping in their cars). The intensity of the filmmaking environment in Hong Kong of the late 1980s/ early 1990s no doubt adds to the quality of the movies.

❂

So *Moon Warriors* ends with the multiple deaths of Ancient Greek tragedy. In the final smackdown, four of the five principals die: Mo-sin, the double-crossing ninja, is dispatched by 14th Prince (in a gruesome manner), and dies in the arms of Yen, whom she loved; the fearsome rival also wastes his brother Yen, and also manages (tho' blinded) to find and attack the hero Fei with a spear. Unfortunately, Yuet-nga (Anita Mui) also expires, torn between her love for Fei and Yen.

As in similar stories of grand passions set in Imperial China, there is a dramatic logic and poetry to the multiple murders. A fantasy element has Wei the killer whale returning for a final appearance: the fish blasts out of the water in the tombs and swats the villain with its tail, sending him flying (the introduction of the whale occurs with one of Ching Siu-tung's specialities – explosions of water achieved using barrels, creating a wall of water behind the actors).

Even that isn't enough to finish off the 14th Prince – Yuet blinds him with her sword, but he still revives enough to hurl himself at Fei. But he's blind, right? Cleverly, that jade MacGuffin is revived once more: Yuet asks to hear it, and the tinkly, chimey sound guides the sightless villain. (14th Prince also stabs Fei in the shoulder, but in doing so a tablet of his ancestors falls on top of him and he expires).

The finale of *Moon Warriors* includes a superb sword duel between the two girls, Yuet and Mo-sin: it is a classic slice of Chingian swordplay, with graceful, flowing movements. As usual, Ching Siu-tung has the performers using the environment (such as the pillars, and the upper story of the grand colonnade. The outcome is deferred, when 13th Prince intervenes (the deaths are saved for the end of the finale).

The fishing village set built in the New Territories is exploited to the full for the traumatic scene of invasion and attack by 14th Prince's troops. Fei rushes around, fighting soldiers, trying to prevent a massacre. He fails – even children are dispatched on screen. This sequence, choreographed by Sammo Hung, is fast and ferocious, with the villagers overwhelmed by numbers (and they are peasants, with only Fei displaying notable martial arts. Just where or how he learned them isn't explained. No need – he's a hero in a Hong Kong action movie!).

In the *dénouement,* our hero Fei walks off into the sunset in the field of flowers, now dressed in white (the colour of the moon, and of purification). The setting is where he and Yuet enjoyed one of their lighter moments (tho' now it's forlorn, overcast, with the sound of the breeze). The voiceover explains what happened in the end, and places the action in the past (there's a statue tangled with vines, suggesting the passing of time). The final shot is the traditional boom up, to show the hero walking away from the camera.

This part of *Moon Warriors* features some voiceover to butter over scenes we usually expect to see but don't, such as the destruction of the tombs, and the burial of the main characters. A costly sequence is thus simply summarized by Fei's narration. Similarly, we don't see Fei's miraculous escape (despite being speared to a stone tablet).

There were rumours that the ending was deemed too downbeat, and the distributors wanted something a little lighter, where not every main chara dies, bar Andy Lau. According to Alex Law, no other ending was shot or even conceived.

8

ROYAL TRAMP

Lu Ding Ji

Royal Tramp (*Lu Ding Ji*, 1992) was a hugely enjoyable romp in the form of a broad, often crude pantomime spoofing the recent spate of swordplay movies in Hong Kong, and the *Swordsman* films (1990-1993) in particular. *Royal Tramp* was a massive hit in Canton (with over HK $40 million at the box office), and a sequel was rapidly produced – it was released less than two months later (and imitations appeared, as usual).

Royal Tramp was very much a Wong Jing production – Wong produced, directed and wrote the film (though Gordon Chan was an uncredited co-director; some sources credit Tony Ching with co-direction. Certainly some of the action scenes are staged in Ching's style. As we know, Wong was happy to hand over the direction of the action scenes in his movies completely to Ching). This was common in Hong Kong.

Louis Cha (Jin Yong, d. 2018) provided the story, from his book *The Deer and the Cauldron* (a.k.a. *The Duke of Mount Deer*). Prod. by Jimmy Heung and Stephen Shui for Win's Movie Productions, and distributor Golden Harvest, David Chung and Joe Chan were DPs, Jason Mok was art dir., Kenneth Yee Chung-man and Shirley Chan were costume designers, Chuen Chi edited, William Wu composed the score, and the action dirs. were Tony Ching, Yuen Bun, Dion Lam, Ma Yeuk-sing and Yeung Ching-ching. Released July 30, 1992. 106 mins.

The cast is an all-star line-up that included Sharla Cheung-man, Deric Wan Siu-lun, Chingmy Yau Suk-ching, Ng Man-tat, Elvis Tsui Kam-kong, Damian Lau Chung-yan, Sandra Ng Kwun-yu, Vivian Chen Te-yung, Fennie Yuen Kit-ying, Nat Chan Pak-cheung, and Brigitte Lin Ching-hsia.[8]

---

8 Lin appears at the end, advertizing the sequel, when the Empress Dowager escapes.

Headlining the movie is of course Chow Sing-chi, a.k.a. Stephen Chow. *Royal Tramp* is a star vehicle, with Chow dominating the movie and appearing in most scenes. Chow plays the familiar cowardly goof in the midst of mayhem, a seemingly ordinary guy thrust into extraordinary circumstances, the kind of role that Bob Hope played, or Woody Allen in his early comedies (the funny ones). It works – because the character is easy to identify with – he might be anybody – and he plays off every group of characters (and scores laughs off them, too, of course).

The *Royal Tramp* movies were based on *The Deer and the Cauldron* by Louis Cha (Jin Yong) which had already been adapted, and were adapted again in movies and television series (in fact, one occurred the year after *Royal Tramp*, starring Tony Leung). Films appeared in 1983, 1993 and 2011, and TV shows in 1978, two in 1984, 1998, 2001, 2008, and 2014.

❦

The premise of *Royal Tramp* is an appealing hook: Stephen Chow plays an undercover agent (called Wilson Bond a.k.a. Wai Siu-bo) in Ming Dynasty China (1368-1644), as rival organizations and governments vie for power (the fallen Ming Dynasty versus the invading Ching Dynasty). Bond ends up working as a double agent – for Chan Kan-nam from the Heaven and Earth Society and for the Kang Xi Emperor. There's a special book in the mix, too – the Buddhist text *The Sutra of Forty-two Chapters*. The background and the story is in part, as usual in Hong Kong comedy cinema, a pretext or coat hanger for a series of skits and set-pieces. However, the story is also worked out and makes sense: one of the foundations for a successful comedy movie is that the audience buys into the characters, the story and the premise. (For Western audiences the primary plot may seem a little too complicated).

Royal Tramp was full of Wong Jingsms – nonsensical humour, crude jokes, pretty girls, overblown action scenes, and parodies of contemporary Hong Kong movies (Wong's movies send up local products far more often than Western or Hollywood films). *Royal Tramp* is Wong's familiar let's-please-everybody cookery approach: give the audience a bit of everything. It's a movie like a big pile of Chinese food placed on hot plates in front of a crowd in a restaurant, with the chef and his assistant eager to please. If you don't like chicken, there's beef; if you don't like noodles, there's rice. It's a movie with one over-riding goal: to entertain.

This is a movie that's easy to like, and easy to watch. Oh, and it's very funny. There's no question that the combination of Wong Jing and Stephen Chow is cinematic gold dust. *Royal Tramp* is a very confident film comedy: it knows how to deliver this material. And it also seems that the actors and the crew are enjoying themselves (even if they actually weren't, because this was a period on Hong Kong film history when everybody was extremely over-worked. The sequel, for example, came out less than two months after this movie, with much of the same crew and cast).

There are some very enjoyable turns from the cast – Chingmy Yau Suk-ching is at her kittenish best as the Emperor's sister, Princess Kin-ning; Stephen Chow's regular straight man Ng Man-tat is terrific as the effete eunuch Hoi Da-fu, as is another stalwart comic of this era, Nat Chan Pak-cheung as Duran; Sharla Cheung is delightfully imperious and nasty as the fake Empress Dowager, Lung'er; Elvis Tsui chews the scenery as the arch villain O'Brian (a.k.a. Oboi); and Fennie Yuen and Vivian Chen Te-yung are an adolescent sexual fantasy as the twin Seung-yee bodyguards for the hero.

Meanwhile, some roles are played straight, to make the plot work in *Royal Tramp* (and because not everybody can be goofing off) – such as Damian Lau Chung-yan, dependable and righteous as Swordsman Chan Kan-nam; and Deric Wan Siu-lin as the earnest, young Emperor Kang Xi.

❖

The humour is pure Wong Jing at his schoolboy naughtiest – not one joke about penises, but many; eunuchs and castration are running gags, too. For example, Wilson Bond examines a bunch of animal members in glass jars on a shelf, including the penis of the eunuch Hoi (he uses a magnifying glass to see it, looking right into the camera). In *Goldfinger* (1964) James Bond was strapped to a table with a giant circular saw – in *Royal Tramp*, Wilson Bond is tied down with a bunch of guys about to castrate him.

Wong Jing staples such as brothels and prostitutes, group sex, and eunuchs also appear in *Royal Tramp*. It's not all frantic action or frantic comedy, however – parts of *Royal Tramp* are extended farcical scenarios, like Wilson Bond being given lovely twins to act as his bodyguards (Nam Seung-yee and her sister). As expected from Wong Jing, the twins feel what the other one is feeling, so there are gags featuring erotic play (massages, etc), and a lengthy scene where Princess Kin-ning visits Bond and he hides the girls behind him in his bed, but they act as his arms as he pretends to be alone.

Stephen Chow and Ng Man-tat milk the sleazy aspects of being a eunuch repeatedly in scenes featuring the two of them at Hoi Da-fu's digs. This is giggly, teenage humour, unapologetically crude (characters grab each other's crotches, for example, to check on their castrated status).

The action in *Royal Tramp* is in the over-the-top, Peking Opera style, which suits the broad, vaudeville approach of the movie – moves are swishy, exaggerated. *Royal Tramp* opens with a massive scene filmed in the familiar quarry in the New Territories, announcing the vibrant pageant of the movie (with colourful red and yellow costumes), the time period, and the warring groups. The scene introduces the super-villain of the piece, O'Brian (played by Hong Kong regular Elvis Tsui) and his ability to take on hordes of assailants with just his thumbnail (there are some gross gags, too – cutting a guy's head open, mass decapitations, and victims torn to pieces). Shots where five or six performers are flying on wires are pure Tony Ching in this scene, as are the images of multiple explosions in the ground detonated one after another, the ground collapsing, and soldiers being bayonetted on bamboo spikes. (Notice the dramatic structure of the movie – once this intense violence has been delivered, the movie steps away from it, and doesn't return to it for some time. In other words, the grotesque action in the opening scene is a function of the plot, to demonstrate the political threat and what's at stake, and to provide a narrative engine to make the story work. But the movie isn't actually interested it – we are waiting for Stephen Chow to make his entrance, which he does soon after the main titles, entertaining an audience at a brothel with his tall tales).

In *Royal Tramp*, Tony Ching and fellow choreographers such as Yuen Bun and Dion Lam send up the work they were performing for directors at the time such as Tsui Hark, John Woo, Derek Yee and Ringo Lam. Thus, the action has a loose, anarchic feel (even though the stuntwork and wire-work can be even more difficult to achieve for comedy as for straight drama).

Several action scenes climax *Royal Tramp*, including a classic Tony Ching sequence: it's night, smoke wafts about, there are multiple performers in the air, swords flash, unusual weaponry is deployed (here, brass, Tibetan cymbals), and there are gross-out gags. To thicken the mix of the action – which is essentially the heroes taking on O'Brian and his mob (paying off the prologue) – the production added some warriors from Tibet. In true, Chingian style, the Tibetans (clad in red and yellow costumes) are soon flying about all over the place, and performing familiar, Chingian stunt gags, such as standing atop each other like circus acrobats, riding on the cymbals which they throw, and using the cymbals to chop up their victims (animation adds some pizzazz to the movement of the cymbals).

In addition, the duel between Swordsman Chan and O'Brian reprises gags that Tony Ching has been using throughout his career (going back to his first film as director, *Duel To the Death*), such as a swordsman descending from on high upside-down, sword extended. 27 years after *Royal Tramp*, in 2019, the same gags appeared in *Jade Dynasty*.

9

ROYAL TRAMP 2

Lu Ding Ji 2 Zhi Shen Long Jiao

INTRO.

Royal Tramp 2 (*Lu Ding Ji 2 Zhi Shen Long Jiao,* 1992) was prod. by Win's Movie Productions and Golden Harvest. Prod. by Stephen Shiu and Jimmy Hueng, wr. and dir. by Wong Jing (some sources have Tony Ching co-directing both *Royal Tramp* movies, and some credit Gordan Chan with co-direction), from a story (*The Deer and the Cauldron*) by Louis Cha (Jin Yong). DP: David Chung. Music: Williams Hu. Art dir: Jason Mok Siu-Kei. Costumes: Kenneth Yee Chung-Man and Shirley Chan Koo-Fong. Sound editor: Benny Chu Chi-Ha. Editor: Chuen Chi. Action director: Tony Ching Siu-tung (plus five assistants).[9] Released Sept 24, 1992. 93 mins.

Colourful, fast-paced, and very silly, *Royal Tramp 2* boasts a superb cast which includes Stephen Chow Sing-chi, Damian Lau Chung-yan, Deric Wan, Paul Chun Kong, Law Lan Kent Tong, and an amazing number of leading ladies in Hong Kong cinema: Brigitte Lin Ching-hsia, Sharla Cheung-man, Natalis Chan, Chingmy Yau Suk-ching, Sandra Ng, Fennie Yuen, Vivian Chan, and Michelle Reiss.

Royal Tramp 2 was the follow-up to *Royal Tramp,* released earlier in the year, on July 30, '92. Both *Royal Tramp* movies were huge hits locally.

Royal Tramp 2 is a Stephen Chow comedy – which tells you all you need to know about the movie; thus, the star is in almost every scene, and is allowed to dominate the proceedings (Chow also carries most of the humour, as superstars usually do in comic star vehicles). Chow is once again playing Wilson Bond (Duke Wai Siu-bo in Chinese), an undercover agent (the role gives his character legitimate reasons for being in the

---

9 Yuen Bun, Ma Yuk-Sing, Yeung Ching-Ching, Dion Lam Dik-On and Cheung Yiu-Sing.

middle of rival factions and different groups).

Whether or not Wong Jing actually directed all of the two *Royal Tramp* movies, or did some of it, or used assistants, they are very enjoyable and highly accomplished productions. Wong surely deserves some of the credit for these two great movies.

The demands of the screenwriting are considerable: first, the cast is huge, and requires a *lot* of planning and thought to keep track of all of them, and to give them all something significant to do (and don't underestimate the egos of some of the actors involved!). Second, the superstar (Stephen Chow Sing-chi) has to be kept centre stage throughout. Third, the film has to deliver a lavish historical costume piece. Fourth, action and spectacle have to be integrated at regular intervals. Fifth, and above all, it has to be *funny*, it has to spoof *wuxia pian* like the *Swordsman* movies.

Royal Tramp 2 is partly a send-up of the *Swordsman* movies, like 1993's *Holy Weapon* (also a collaboration between Tony Ching and Wong Jing, among others). So there is plenty of mistaken identity comedy, and cross-dressing, and brothel and hooker jokes, and lusts scuppered by circumstances, and authority figures brought down to size, and people not being what you thought they were.

The political background of *Royal Tramp 2* is the very familiar one of a more liberal, easy-going community being threatened by stern, unforgiving Manchu/ Imperial authorities. If you wish, it can be related in the simplistic terms of: Hong Kong versus the People's Republic of China.

Our man, Tony Ching Siu-tung, was one of the action directors for *Royal Tramp 2* and displays his remarkable talents throughout the picture. The *Royal Tramp* movies, for action, are the equal of many other Hong Kong movies. As *Royal Tramp 2* has a historical setting (in the Qing Dynasty), the style of the action is in the usual swordplay genre, and in the usual Chingian manner of flamboyant wire-work, rapid sword slashes, fluttering robes, explosions, props that smash, and iconic poses.

As to Tony Ching Siu-tung's input in *Royal Tramp 2*, it's found in the many action sequences, and also in the action within otherwise dramatic scenes. *Royal Tramp 2* is another of those Hong Kong historical pictures where physical acting is emphasized: it's one of the delights of Hong Kong cinema: actors don't just stand there and mouth dialogue, they are in movement. (If you want to watch actors simply standing there and speaking, look at any Western television show. Hong Kong cinema is *more* than that).

Of the stand-out action scenes in *Royal Tramp 2*, there's an amazing ambush of the Imperial caravan in the countryside (filmed in the New

Territories, again). It's a chaotic sequence of flying swordsmen and slashing blades.

THE FIRST ACT.

Royal Tramp 2 is a movie where, in the opening exposition scene, Sharla Cheung-man turns into Brigitte Lin Ching-hisa! Lin's Lung'er is the leader of the St Dragon Sect, hoping to gain power again (she has martial arts powers which will be lost to the man who takes her virginity).

The political background of Emperors and governments and dynasties and warring factions in *Royal Tramp 2* is just that – a background for a Stephen Chow comedy. And yet, *Royal Tramp 2* is also an impressively mounted production, with some marvellous costumes and settings. Or is it that Chinese cinema, and Hong Kong cinema, has been churning out historical films for so long, and at such a high rate, that everybody in the production can do this sort of movie in their sleep? Even the tea boy or the script girl could probably step into the director's shoes at a moment's notice and direct a costume picture (we know that many people behind the camera can – and have – replaced the director. In Hong Kong non-unionized cinema, members of the crew take up other jobs as necessary).

THE MIDDLE ACT.

So in the middle act of *Royal Tramp 2* of course Stephen Chow Sing-chi gets a love scene with Brigitte Lin Ching-hsia (Lin who was formerly Sharla Cheung-man – a transformation from one Hong Kong super-babe into another). Lung'er, you see, has been poisoned, and can only be healed by lerrrve (it's another Wong Jingian potions/ poisons plot).[10] And Lin, after lovemaking, becomes the coy, simpering girl we always knew she was underneath the haughty exterior she usually projects (every movie featuring Lin pursues this uncovering of her 'true' persona).

Even the build-up to the love scene is couched within action cinema terms: Lung'er unfurls long, white banners in all directions, becoming a spider-woman for a moment (a favourite motif in Hong Kong fantasy cinema): it's woman as witch, predator, untameable nature.

As a visual motif, the sight of pieces of white cloth zooming thru the night air is something peculiar to Hong Kong movies (if there's a chance to include some billowing cloth blown by fans or the breeze, it will always be taken. Tony Ching Siu-tung is especially fond of fluttering material).

In an inspired beat, the white banners merge to form a cocoon in which

10 Wong Jing is very fond of gimmicks such as aphrodisiacs: they're always given or taken by the wrong person, or aimed at the wrong person. Also magical potions and poisons. It's typical in a Wong picture that the victim has to make love by a certain time, as here in *Royal Tramp 2*.

the lovers do what lovers do. (Next morning, the structure, composed now of leaves, looks like an Andy Goldsworthy sculpture).

THE FINAL ACT.

The finale of *Royal Tramp 2* is of course a series of big set-pieces, where the main characters get to fight each other. Yen Shi-kwan as Fung Sek-fan is introduced halfway thru *Royal Tramp 2* to provide a villain for the hero to go up against (Yen often plays heavies – he's familiar from his customary villainous cackle).

So Fung Sek-fan encounters Wilson Bond in a rural setting for their second smackdown in *Royal Tramp 2* (they have already fought once, with Fung retreating for the time being. That action scene is also remarkable – the one in the countryside replays it, but bigger and wilder. There's a classic piece of Tony Ching's use of props – the henchmen wield large gold hoops, like a circus juggling act).

In a send-up of *The Swordsman 2*, Wilson Bond is dressed as Brigitte Lin Ching-hsia in perhaps her most famous role, as Invincible Asia. Thus, the tussle with Fung Sek-tan and his scarlet-clad henchmen is played for laughs at first. And now that Bond possesses 80% of Lung'er's powers, there's no way he can lose (well, he's also Stephen Chow, and he's the hero of this movie, so it's impossible for him to be defeated in any way).

So Tony Ching Siu-tung gets to spoof his own movie *The Swordsman 2* with some silly bits of business in amongst the flying, the wire-work, and the flashing, slashing swordplay (such as Wilson Bond twisting the nipples of the hapless henchmen). Props, swords and stuntmen are soaring about all over the place, as usual in a Ching set-piece, and this sequence would be enough for many action movies, but *Royal Tramp 2* goes further, adding one more Big Set and one more Big Fight.

So, falling thru a hole in the ground (made by Fung Sek-fan being hurled by the high energy of Wilson Bond), the action shifts into a studio set. It's that favourite of historical action movies – an underground palace/ chamber/ lair. So we have the flickering torches, elaborate statuary, a mound of gold, and pools on each side of a walkway.

The action escalates from astonishing, acrobatic swordplay (where the combatants are in constant motion, moving across the screen, and performing tumbles and spins at the same time), to wizardly bolts of energy being hurled at each other.

In one highpoint, there's a Ching Siu-tung speciality – fountains of water exploding upwards from the pools (water placed inside oil barrels filled with explosives). Ching's team had deployed this gag with amazing effect in the *Chinese Ghost Story* movies as well as the *Swordsman* series.

In the end, Fung Sek-fan is impaled fatally upon a statue. Cleverly, Wilson Bond and his chums use the body of Fung to stand in for his master, Chan Kan-nam, at an execution.

In the customary *dénouement* scene (set in the customary location – on horseback in the countryside), everyone congratulates themselves for being so wonderful (or something like that). Wilson Bond is accompanied by several wives (i's tough being the hero), for the Ride Off Into the Sunset.

10

CITY HUNTER

Sing Si Lip Ya

INTRODUCTION.

City Hunter (*Sing Si Lip Ya,* 1993) was a brash, bright, colourful action comedy based on a Japanese *manga*[11] published in *Shonen Jump*[12] (1985) by Tsukasa Hojo,[13] starring Jackie Chan, and directed and written by Wong Jing. It was a perfect fit[14] – Chan's brand of broad comedy, posing and action cinema and the over-the-top approach to storytelling of Japanese comicbooks. The scenario – a cruise liner is taken over by terrorists, and agent Ryu Saeba has to Save The Day – is merely a paltry hook for a series of skits and gags. *City Hunter* is funny – it's designed for a late night crowd that wants some dumb but fun entertainment. Forget political 'messages', or solemn ruminations on the 1997 Hand-over, this is 100% popcorn and fries. It's certainly one of the most entertaining of Chan's mid-period comedies.

The cast of *City Hunter* included Joey Wong Jo-yin, Chingmy Yau Suk-ching, Richard Norton, Kumiko Gotoh, Gary Daniels, Leon Lai and Johnny Lo. It was written and directed by Wong Jing and produced by Chua Lam for Golden Harvest/ Golden Way Films/ Paragon Films. DPs: Tom Lau Moon-tong, Ma Gam-cheung and Gigo Lee. Music: James Wong Jim and Romeo Diaz. Editors: Peter Cheung and Cheng Ka-fai. Released Jan 14, 1993. 105 mins.

11 The *manga* led to 140 episodes of animation over 4 TV series. There was also a Korean TV series in 2011.
12 The biggest magazine in the world of *manga* (and one of the biggest magazines in the world) is *Weekly Boys' Jump* (*Shukan Shonen Jump*), with sales of 5-6 million (in the 1990s), and 2 million in the 2000s.
13 *Saviour of the Soul* (Corey Yuen and David Lau, 1991) was also based on *City Hunter.*
14 'Chan was born to play a real-life cartoon character', noted Bey Logan (81).

City Hunter was filmed on a ship at sea, at Golden Harvest (it was a Golden Harvest/ Golden Way/ Paragon movie), and at Shaw Brothers (where the giant casino set was constructed). The setting is one of those cruise ships (the *Fuji Maru*) that sails into international waters so the guests can legally gamble. It was a big hit at the local box office at New Year's.

Gadgets, guns, flashy cars,[15] luxury cruisers, beautiful women and a hi-tech city are some of the many *James Bond*-ian elements in *City Hunter*. Every time Ryu Saeba does something cool, the *City Hunter* theme music is played, *à la James Bond*, with the actors preening for the camera (sung by Jackie Chan, of course).

Visually, *City Hunter* was filmed in Pop Art colours, reminiscent of Walt Disney's 1990 *Dick Tracy* or Jean-Luc Godard's 1960s pictures (with red and white predominating). Jackie Chan moves thru the picture dressed in pale, loose-fitting clothes (Chan would often wear white after *City Hunter*, and he has favoured baggy clothing for a long time).[16] The comicbook stylization extends to sound effects, actors speaking to camera, cartoony animation, and speech bubbles *à la Batman*.

WONG JING AND JACKIE CHAN.

City Hunter was also a Wong Jing movie – and that meant plenty of cheap gags, crude humour,[17] movie spoofs, T. & A., and a fast, furious pace. Wong included many elements for which he is famous: movie spoofs (a *God of Gamblers* send-up starring Cantopop icon Leon Lai, as Kao Ta the Wanderer),[18] a giant dance number (in a suitably vast set), a completely gratuitous 'fan service' scene where 100s of women cavort around a swimming pool in bathing costumes, another T. & A. moment where City Hunter's surrounded by young women pretending to celebrate his birthday (pretty girls are sprinkled throughout *City Hunter*), crude humour and plain silly humour.

If there's a cheap joke that can be made in a scene, director Wong Jing will take it! Wong has been compared to Roger Corman (in terms of his low budget, high productivity), but perhaps Mel Brooks or Russ Meyer is a better comparison. Or the spoof flicks of the 2000s helmed by Jason Friedberg and Aaron Seltzer, such as *Date Movie* and *Vampires Suck*. (In the swimming pool scene, the starving[19] City Hunter stares at a woman

---

15 Mitsubishi again.
16 City Hunter's pad is modelled partly on Jackie Chan's own place (a similar room would crop up in *Gorgeous*).
17 The humour in *City Hunter* is really broad, reminiscent of the *Naked Gun* or *Scary Movie* or *Airplane* series.
18 Wong Jing produced some sequels to the Chow Yun-fat *God of Gamblers* movie around this time.
19 The hunger motif comes from the *manga*.

standing before him, turning her boobs into spinning hamburgers and her limbs into chicken legs!).

City Hunter contains not one but three pretty girls (a Jackie Chan movie – and a Wong Jing movie! – often has a high cute girl factor). And, true to form, there is some vacillation between each girl: Ryu Saeba is saving a Japanese millionaire's daughter Shizuko (Kumiko Goto), has an on-off girlfriend Kaori Makimura (Joey Wong), and also flirts with undercover cop Saeko Nogami (Chingmy Yau).

There was bound to be some friction between Jackie Chan the control freak and a fast and loose director like Wong Jing (who doesn't have time or money for going to 2,900 takes! Not if he's making five pictures a year! And directing two pictures at the same time!). Chan has expressed his displeasure over *City Hunter* (there were rumours that Chan tried to have Wong thrown off the set). However, some of the action scenes were co-ordinated by Chan, of course.

THE STUNTS.

The stunts are outrageous in *City Hunter* – one of the biggest has Jackie Chan fleeing down a corridor from multiple explosions on either side of him. A very dangerous stunt, it is played in both regular time and slo-mo, with the dive over the handrail at the end being repeated. It's another of those super-stunts, which Chan reckons his fans enjoy (and which no North American star would perform).

In addition, there are many more pyrotechnic gags in *City Hunter* (the super-villain blows stuff up in the finale), including one of Tony Ching's hallmarks, explosions in oil barrels hidden underwater. (Handily, all of the henchmen wear scarlet jackets with hoods, so that the same stunt guys can pop up time after time after being shot to pieces).

There's a scene where Jackie Chan comes face to face with Bruce Lee in *Game of Death* (where City Hunter, battling some more heavies in a cinema, fights them while *Game of Death* plays on the screen. Tho' why the theatre is empty is sort of bizarre). Fans of Chan will know that he is often compared to Lee, and that he resented being marketed as 'the next Bruce Lee' in the 1970s.[20] In *City Hunter*, Saeba takes some tips on how to defeat very tall, black guys from Lee when he fights Kareem Abdul-Jabbar in *Game of Death*.

The face-off between Ryu Saeba and the chief villain Colonel Don MacDonald (Richard Norton) took 6 weeks to film. And you can see why: it is stuffed with complex gags and a back-and-forth timing with the hits and

20 'Chan's movies in the 80s were practically alone in preserving Bruce Lee's tradition of kung fu as an instinctive but disciplined art linked to a cultural and national identity', remarked Stephen Teo (122).

punches which's lightning-fast. The duel runs thru numerous beats. In scenes like this, you can see why Jackie Chan is the number one action star in the world. (Ryu Saeba doesn't finish off the super-villain – he does that himself, when he accidentally steps on the remote control for his bombs).

Joey Wong Jo-yin plays City Hunter's sidekick, the on-off, jealous girlfriend Kaori Makimura. It's a delight to see Wong let off the leash and being encouraged to play some broad comedy. She's great in *City Hunter*, a huge departure from her role as the ghostly, mysterious woman of the *Chinese Ghost Story* and similar movies. Later, Japanese actress Kumiko Gotoh becomes City Hunter's sidekick, Shizuko Imamura (she's a millionaire's daughter who's on the run, that Saeba has to protect). There are also two super-babes (Chingmy Yau Suk-ching as Saeko Nogami and Carol Wan as her friend) who provide further 'fan service' (Yau had been sensational in *Naked Killer*, another Wong Jing picture – she's another Hong Kong actress who looks amazing wielding guns in tight black costumes – firing as she dives. At one point Yau's Saeko strips down to shorts, with pistols in thigh holsters. This leads to a dance-and-action sequence with Jackie Chan spinning Yau around him so she can fire the guns strapped to her legs. Yau's undercover cop in *City Hunter* might've had a spin-off movie of her own).

Gary Daniels (as Kim) also spars with Jackie Chan in a scene that's filled with a flurry of fists. Here, Chan saves his on-off girlfriend Joey Wong from Daniels' clutches. The comical riff on a seduction and possible rape scenario between Daniels and Wong is pure Wong Jing.

A massive musical sequence caps act one, staged in the casino of the ship: it's a combination of rap and dance-as-martial-arts choreography, filmed in a pop promo style. This is typical of Hong Kong movies, and of Wong Jing's goal of producing movies as a mix of flavours: some romance, some drama, some action, some thrills, and plenty of comedy. In the dance number, the main characters join in and perform the routine. Right after that, the musical sequence segues into an action scene which shifts from replaying a gambling scenario into action (where playing cards are using as weapons like ninja throwing stars). It's the 'God of Gamblers' motif again, which Wong has exploited to the full. This time, it's pop idol Leon Lai who strikes the cool poses and hurls cards which embed themselves in victims' faces and necks. (The scene is reprised in the corridor setting, the same set where Jackie Chan out-runs a series of explosions).

Tony Ching Siu-tung was the action director for *City Hunter* (as well as

Jackie Chan, of course). Ching was responsible, for instance, for the wild *Streetfighter* video game spoof. The *Streetfighter* computer game send-up is a delight (it's one of Wong Jing's passions – video games also appear his other films, such as *Future Cops*, which also contains *Streetfighter*). So Chan goes up against heavy Gary Daniels while dressed as a bunch of characters from the *Streetfighter* arcade game (including a woman – Chan is terrific when he's in drag, which goes back to his Peking Opera days). Assisted by wire-work, the *Streetfighter* spoof is deliciously dumb (everything is speeded-up and accompanied by loud sound effects).

HUMOUR.

City Hunter is also cheaply violent, with characters being gunned down all over the place once the action hots up in the finale. In one scene City Hunter flies thru the air on a dolphin, spraying the bad guys with a machine gun.

A wacky, 'anything goes' comedy is a great form for cinema because, well, anything goes, and anything can be tried if it's funny. And *City Hunter* definitely has many funny moments: one of the best is where Carol Wan's wannabe doofus boyfriend demonstrates a secret martial arts technique up the ass of a henchman who's trapped on the floor, bent over (a chair covers the act). 'That's disgusting!' someone quips. It is! (This occurs in the midst of a girl fight, when all of the girls set upon the heavy).

Some of the humour becomes madly violent – a henchman repeatedly punches a woman in the stomach. Poor Joey Wong gets hurled around and thrown to the floor (in a joky seduction scene with Gary Daniels). There's gay bashing humour in *City Hunter*, too. In a Wong Jing movie, no target is too sacred that it can't be attacked.

11

BUTTERFLY AND SWORD

San Lau Sing Wu Dip Gim

Butterfly and Sword (*San Lau Sing Wu Dip Gim* , 1993) was made by Chang-Hong Channel Film & Video Co.; exec. prod. by Hui Pooi-Yung and Dun Wu; Yen-Ping Chu was prod.; dir. by Michael Mak; wr. by John Chong; action dir. by Tony Ching Siu-tung (some credit Ching with co-direction), Yiu-Sing Cheung and Ma Yuk-Sing; music[21] by Chris Babida and Chin Yung Shing; Jung-Shu Chen was DP; ed. by Chung Yiu Ma, Tung-Lit Mui and Jing-Chang Wang; art dir. by Yiu Gwong Lee; costumes by Bobo Bo-Ling Ng; make-up by Hei-Ke Tsai; and hair by Yi-Ling Choi. It had a great cast that included Michelle Yeoh Chu-kheng, Tony Leung Chiu-wai, Joey Wong Jo-yin, Donnie Yen, Elvis Tsui and Jimmy Lin. Released: Jan 16, 1993. 88 mins.

Based on *Comet Butterfly and Sword* by Gu Long (which had been filmed at Shaws – Tony Ching was the chief martial arts adviser on the TV series *Meteor, Butterfly, Sword*, 1979), *Butterfly and Sword* is a swordplay picture made in the heyday of the Hong Kong New Wave (in nineteen ninety-three), when it seemed that a martial arts or costume pic or *kung fu* bust-up was being released every week.

Jimmy Lin is a Chinese pop star handed a cameo role[22] (as Prince Cha) in *Butterfly and Sword* as a glamorous martial artist. Lin's role has the appearance of someone ordering that Lin be assigned a cameo at a late stage in the production.

Meanwhile, the Prince pops into scenes, goofs around, fails at martial

---

21 There is too much music in *Butterfly and Sword* and too much of it simply doesn't fit the scenes. In the finale, for ex, there are dreamy electronic washes which would be more suited to a yoga exercise video.
22 Maybe the pop star's manager did a deal with the producers.

arts moves, and exits shame-faced. Master Suen is embarrassed, the other characters don't know what to make of him, and the plot continues following his exit.

The background plot of *Butterfly and Sword* involves ageing patriarchs such as Master Suen and the eunuch Tsao (Chang Kuo-chu), and the attempt to steal a special letter (a mission given to Sister Ko by Tsao). A third woman, Ho Ching (Yip Chuen-chan), a former member of the Happy Forest clan (and a former ex of Star's who disappeared), is also involved (Star and Ho Ching are wed at Suen's behest. But Ho dies, trying to retrieve the letter – thus upping the stakes).

❀

Butterfly and Sword is easy to like and easy to enjoy – after all, it has two of the top female stars of the era, Michelle Yeoh Chu-kheng and Joey Wong Jo-yin, and two of the top male stars, Donnie Yen and Tony Leung Chiu-wai. All four are charming, attractive people that the camera loves. And the 1993 movie provides plenty of opportunities to contemplate these stars at length. Tony Leung has the tough job of having his back bathed by Joey Wong (a difficult task, but someone had to do it), and Michelle Yeoh has the partially naked Donnie Yen at her mercy as she heals him. (Mild but welcome nods towards proto-feminism, perhaps, and the kind of reversals that flatter the audience. After all, Hong Kong movies are constructed to play to the female audience – they are aware that many women also go the movies as well as guys, and that often it's women who pick the movie if they go together on a date).

Butterfly and Sword's plot – of a crew of martial artists, the Happy Forest gang, battling a rival clan from the Elite Villa led by Master Suen Yuk-pa (Elvis Tsui) – is almost beside the point in a movie which features a lengthy sequence at the start of act two which might be titled *At Home With Tony Leung and Joey Wong*.[23] She cooks for him, he fishes in the river,[24] they look at the moon together like lovelorn teenagers, she washes his back, they kiss, he writes her a comical, ridiculously long farewell letter…[25] and all the while Butterfly looks as astonishing as only Joey Wong Jo-yin can look, and Star (a.k.a. Meng Sing-Wan) remains the goofy, adorable 'Little Tony' Leung.

Four great stars and chocolate box imagery – *Butterfly and Sword* is another instance where Hong Kong cinema portrays romance and drama in the form of a Hollywood musical movie, but with martial arts choreography replacing conventional dance routines. Consider the scene where

23 The location is incredible: a wooden house built over a raging river. And, this being overblown melodrama, of course the building is torched by the villains (nooo!).
24 In classic Tony Ching Siu-tung style – by sliding across the surface of the water and literally beating the fish out of the torrent.
25 Don't stay up late, work hard, remember to eat well, don't talk to dolls, etc.

Butterfly and Star meet, in act one: it is pure Tony Ching Siu-tung. For a start, not one foot is on the ground (or on a bed) – the characters are flying around the trees (why meet in a café or on a street corner when you can be zooming about a sunny woodland?). When Butterfly ascends up to a branch, she doesn't simply rise, she is also spinning. The lovers are flying on vines, à la Tarzan, they are rescuing birds dislodged from nests, they are giving each other pink flowers…

Love triangles are inevitable in this sort of flick: the main one in *Butterfly and Sword* comprises Joey Wong's Butterfly and Michelle Yeo's Lady Ko tussling over Tony Leung's Star. Star loves Butterfly, and thinks of Ko as a big sister. Meanwhile, Donnie Yen's Yip Cheung is seen as a little brother by Lady Ko, tho' Butterfly teases Ko repeatedly about Yip (and about Ko being older than she is).

Butterfly and Sword is not all-out action, or one wild set-piece following another. Several sections feature rather leisurely storytelling (by Hong Kong cinema standards), with plenty of evocations of romantic longings, teenage embarrassments and misunderstandings, and goofy comedy. These are the elements in a Hong Kong costumer that critics tend to gloss over, because they seem so unspectacular or compelling compared to the grand, political themes or the insanely over-the-top action sequences. But romance is absolutely fundamental to the conception of a costume movie in Chinese cinema – if there's a subplot in this sort of genre movie, it will usually be about erotic/ romantic desire. Meanwhile, comedy - and tragedy sometimes – are not far behind romance.

So in *Butterfly and Sword* we have Butterfly teasing Lady Ko about being much older, Yip kissing the drawing of Ko (while Butterfly spies on him), Star writing a letter on a scroll thirty feet long to Butterfly, and so on.

❀

With Tony Ching Siu-tung, Yiu-Sing Cheung and Ma Yuk-Sing overseeing the action, *Butterfly and Sword* is another wild action movie. Ching, the King of Cables, can make anything fly. You want a procession of warriors to fly thru the treetops while carrying a palanquin? *No sweat.* You want Michelle Yeoh to make an airborne entrance in a forest with an explosion of blue banners of cloth in the moonlight? *Done.* You want swordsmen slicing whole bodies in half in mid-air? *You got it.*

There is nothing that Tony Ching Siu-tung and company cannot do: if a writer or a director can imagine it, Ching and the team will find a way of making it happen. As his best, Ching's style of action delivers a miraculous world of weightlessness that *should* exist, even if some people insist that it doesn't and never did.

When the action isn't delineating a love triangle (or square) via acrobatic gestures in the treetops in *Butterfly and Sword*, it delivers some startlingly violent smackdowns – decapitations, bodies slashed in half, etc. But the deaths are very swift and fantastically portrayed (no showers of blood here – they're saved for the finale).

The wire-work is some of Tony Ching Siu-tung's finest of this era: a chase on horseback with Star launching himself thru the air, and palanquins zooming thru the treetops (the 'best of' montage over the end credits reminds us of the many action scenes).

The bust-up in the bamboo forest in *Butterfly and Sword* was reproduced wholesale in *The House of Flying Daggers* in 2004 (Tony Ching Siu-tung happily recycles his work just as everybody does in any film industry anywhere). In fact, other elements of *Butterfly and Sword* chime with *Flying Daggers* (released four months later).

Butterfly and Sword climaxes with the customary multiple duels – the Happy Forest crew versus Master Suen, then the Happy Foresters versus eunuch Li, and so on. Eunuch Li turns out to have killed eunuch Tsao and impersonated him, to set the clans against each other. Eunuch Li is one of those wizened but dangerous mandarins who can deploy cruel magic in conflicts: Lady Ko and Star are injured but survive (you can't kill Michelle Yeoh or Tony Leung!), and it takes *a lot* of effort to nobble eunuch Li. There are some big stunts in the finale, as is customary – like eunuch Li grabbing a column to use as a weapon (which causes the collapse of Elite Villa, delivering the expected explosive scenes). And some silly gags, like Lady Ko stretching a banner between her feet and using it as a bow to fire Star as an arrow at the villains. And like Prince Cha using a football as a weapon. (The finale adds blood – victims are pin-cushioned by lightning-quick swords thrusts, and eunuch Li is decapitated with a soccer kick).

And thus our doughty heroes bring down the corrupt Imperial authorities who continue to lead China stray. (However, the *dénouement* of *Butterfly and Sword* is too short, probably because the producers reckoned that the cinema audience would be rushing towards the exits because the Big Action Finale is over. So the romantic aspects of the plot of *Butterfly and Sword* are too hastily resolved. And poor Sister Ko is the loser: Star leaps to save Butterfly, and remains with her, leaving Ko to weep and turn towards the ocean in sorrow. Only one gal can get Tony Leung – and Michelle Yeoh loses out to Joey Wong. But what about Yip, who's always loved Ko from afar? Surely a mating of Ko with Yip would resolve the love square satisfactorily? Especially when Yip is played by Donnie Yen? But no, the movie declines to show that).

12

HOLY WEAPON

Mou Hap Cat Gung Zyu

INTRO.

Holy Weapon (*Mou Hap Cat Gung Zyu* = *Seven Princesses of Martial Arts,* a.k.a. *Seven Maidens,* 1993) was produced by Wong Jing's Workshop Ltd/ Regal Films Co. Ltd/ Scholar Films Co., Ltd, written by Lam Wai-lun, directed by Wong Jing,[26] produced by Thomas Ng and Pooi Cheungchuen, with music by Danny Chung, DP: Gigo Lee, edited by Keung Chuen-tak and Chun Yu, and action dirs. Ching Siu-tung, Dion Lam Dik On and Ma Yuk Sing. Category IIB. Released: June 3, 1993. 98 mins.

The cast of *Holy Weapon* is outstanding: Michelle Yeoh Chu-kheng, Maggie Cheung Man-yuk, Damian Lau Chung-yan, Simon Yam, Sandra Ng, Dodo Cheng, Sharla Cheung-man, Dickey Cheung, Carol Cheng Yu-ling, Charine Chan Ka-ling and Ng Mang-tai.

So *Holy Weapon* sees another collaboration between Tony Ching Siu-tung and the infamous, quite wonderful Wong Jing. Yes, it's another Wong Jing action comedy, an all-star affair in Ming Dynasty costumes. That is, it's not just any Hong Kong comedy, it's a *Wong Jing comedy*, which is, as we know, a genre all of its own (and this one is particularly goofy).

The background context of *Holy Weapon* concerns the age-old rivalry between China and Japan, embodied in the swordsmen of China pitted against Japanese ninja, and two special swords: the Heaven's Sword of China versus the Japanese Super Sword, and the two magical sword techniques: Yuen Tin Swords Technique, where seven virgins combine energies to defeat the Super Sword.

---

26 Dennis Chan is apparently an uncredited director.

Maybe *Holy Weapon* doesn't have the most compelling story or characters of the greatest movies from Hong Kong, but it does have several elements which make it highly entertaining: 1. A fabulous cast. 2. Fantastic action. 3. It's very funny.

THE CHARACTERS.

The golden couple at the heart of *Holy Weapon* are Damian Lau Chung-yan and Michelle Yeoh Chu-kheng, as the warriors Mo Kake and Mon Ching-sze separated by evil Super Sword (Mo Kake spends 3 years in recuperation at the hands of Ghost Doctor. In classic comical style, he's encased in a barrel of liquid).

In amongst many talented performers, Sandra Ng steals the movie, as Yam Kin-fai, the bodyguard to Princess Tin Heung (it's another crossdressing role). Yam Kin-fai succumbs to the magical spells and potions awash in the middle act of *Holy Weapon* and falls for Doll, Ng Tung's scary wife. Ng performs numerous outrageous bits of comical acting (including writhing on the ground, flailing about, taking lots of punches to the face, etc. It's very rare to find an equivalent performance from an actress in the West).

Maggie Cheung Man-yuk plays a pouty, spoilt princess, Princess Tin Heung (it's typecasting! – Cheung can pout and sulk as impressively as anyone in cinema). We first meet Cheung in a palanquin, with her crossdressing aide, Yam Kin-fai: soon Mon Ching-sze enters the frame, to protect Ng Tung, and challenge Yam to a duel.

Dicky Cheung's Ng Tung is harassed by his shrewish wife Doll (Carol Cheng): this section, also introduced in act one of *Holy Weapon*, doesn't really fit in with the previous scenes. Until, that is, we remember that this is a Wong Jing production – i.e., throw in everything you can think of.

The buffooning of Dicky Cheung, Carol Cheng and co. seems to come from a different movie – several scenes in *Holy Weapon* are historical, farcical comedy, where actors in silly costumes deliver the familiar sex comedy *shtick* of Hong Kong cinema.

Overseeing some of the mystical-medical goings-on is Ghost Doctor, played very OTT by Ng Man-tat in an over-bushy, white fright wig. Ghost Doctor is one of the many wise men in swordplay pictures, dispensing advice, healing the wounded, and rallying the troops to fight the enemy. Ghost Doctor is an important character in terms of the script – he is the one who clarifies the goals of the heroines, encouraging them to contribute to being part of the team of seven princesses needed to nobble Super Sword (so it's sad to see him bite the dust in *Holy Weapon*'s finale).

Simon Yam Tak-wah camps it up as the super-villain of *Holy Weapon*, Super Sword, a corrupt, Japanese swordsman. When he returns, after three years, he reveals his evil side during a sequence where he threatens to rape his underlings Spider (Sharla Cheung-man) and Butterfly (Charine Chan). They manage to flee his lair (tho' wounded by Super Sword), and encounter our heroes in the nighttime forest. After some mistaken identity comedy and melodramatic effusions (and a romantic clinch between Spider and Mon Ching-sze), the ninja refugees from Japan join forces with the Chinese heroines.

THE COMEDY.

Often the humour in Hong Kong cinema doesn't quite get conveyed to Western audiences – both solutions aren't adequate: subtitles plus the original language, or dubbing into the audience's language. In *Holy Weapon*, the humour transcends cultural boundaries: this is a very funny movie.

Humour is everywhere in *Holy Weapon* – after all, it's a Wong Jing film, which, even at their most serious and dramatic, Wong's flicks always contain comedy (let's remember, tho', that the writer was not Wong this time, but Lam Wai-lun). Among the humorous bits in *Holy Weapon* are jokes about swords (well, it's a story featuring 'super swords' and 'holy weapons'), a man taking a bath gag, a talking penis,[27] women-on-women love scenes, crossdressing, and quite a few magical potions and aphrodisiacs.

Holy Weapon is full of crossdressing, mistaken identity and disguises – the basic meat and gruel of farces and sex comedies. So Michelle Yeoh is dressed as a guy, as are other women, such as Sandra Ng (again, in Hong Kong cinema, there is always that suspension of disbelief that anybody could mistake superstar actresses like Brigitte Lin or Michelle Yeoh or Fennie Yuen for guys).

Anyway, in *Holy Weapon*, we have plenty of humorous scenes where Michelle Yeoh's Mon Ching-sze and Sharla Cheung's Spider are getting intimate in a bed, delivering the familiar lesbian clinch under the guise of farcical comedy (a comical device that Wong Jing and Hong Kong cinema has mined extensively. When Wong brings a whole bunch of lovely actresses together, he seems to prefer they get it on with each other, rather than with some male hunk).

Much of the comedy and farce in *Holy Weapon* occurs in the second act, always the saggy, tricky act in Hong Kong cinema (and in all cinema):

---

27 Ng Tung begs his penis, played by an actor in white in a dark space, not to leave when he mistakenly imbibes Ghost Doctor's feminine potion.

there's plenty of running about at night, characters mistaking each other, while others look on askance.

THE ACTION.

Early in act one of *Holy Weapon* we have a typical Tony Ching Siu-tung action set-piece in the grand manner: the opening duel of the 1993 movie, between the Japanese sword wielder Super Sword, played by the ever-wonderful Simon Yam Tak-wah, and the hero Mo Kake, played by the equally wonderful Damian Lau (the hero of *Duel To the Death*).

The ingredients in this over-the-top set-piece including victims tied to a wheel of torture and burnt alive (in the aftermath of a battle), other victims hanging from a giant, wooden cross, flying ninja on wings (more 'Chinjas'), and of course severed limbs on the soil everywhere.[28] And it's another practical effects extravaganza – a horse is decapitated, Super Sword wields the cross like an enormous *katana*, and in the final gag, the two ninja are hurled at each other in the air, exploding – as bodies always do – in sprays of blood and offal.

The joky-fun tone doesn't disguise the fact that this is ridiculously violent. But super-violence is OK in a cartoony context, right? I guess. (The aftermath of the battle is covered in a single, complicated take, tracking and craning across the corpses strewn across the battlefield).

Also in act one we have the sight of Michelle Yeoh Chu-kheng going into action – in drag, as Swordsman Mon Ching-sze (crossdressing and gender-bending is a recurring motif in *Holy Weapon*). Yeoh is truly a beautiful vision of movement and high kicks – you can sense the action directors in Hong Kong cinema going to town with Yeoh, because she is a performer who really can deliver some of the action required (Yeoh looks amazing soaring through the air performing a kick – not every actor does!). The setting is the usual bustling town, mandatory at the beginning of any historical movie.

The farcical approach to gender-bending in *Holy Weapon* is also a spoof of 1990s Hong Kong cinema, in particular the *Swordsman* series (also directed and action directed by Tony Ching Siu-tung), where Brigitte Lin Ching-hsia appeared as the formidable Asia the Invincible.

In the central act of *Holy Weapon* one of Tony Ching Siu-tung's outrageous set-pieces unfurls in that favourite location of Hong Kong swordplay cinema: a forest at night. Sharla Cheung, one of the Japanese ninjas under Super Sword's command, has a special ability – to transform into a spider. In this remarkable and imaginative scene, an enormous rope

---

28 The setting is the quarry area in the New Territories hills which has been used in numerous Hong Kong movies.

spider's web is strung between the trees, where Spider catches her flies – which're hapless guys, of course. Once again, there are numerous Chingian flourishes, of flight, movement, timing, rhythm and flapping-cloth flamboyance. (And some gore, of course – Spider devours her victims, caught in her net, and, in a brilliant, macabre touch, the whole net turns red as the blood from the victim spills over and runs everywhere).[29]

THE FINALE.

The finale of *Holy Weapon* is one of Tony Ching Siu-tung's outrageous set-pieces which looked like it took as long as filming the rest of the movie put together to set up, to rig, to rehearse, and to shoot. It brings together all of the surviving charas: the revived swordsman Mo Kake, Ng Tung, the seven virginal warrior women, Super Sword and his minions. To add some suspense, Super Sword has the seventh maiden, Princess Tin Heung (Maggie Cheung), needed for the Yuen Tin Swords Technique to work, captured and strung up in a net (where she watches the proceedings in screaming frustration).

To up the stakes, the Ghost Doctor is killed by Super Sword. It's sad to see the doctor, the key helper figure in the story, meet his demise at the hand of the Japanese super-warrior (despite Ng Tung trying to save him).

The climax of *Holy Weapon* plays out narratively as expected: following the customary exchange of insults and boasts, the smackdown commences; Super Sword appears to be in the ascendant, beating up our heroes savagely. There are multiple attempts at taking him down (and his henchmen are fighting, too). In a final move, maidens gather together to fuse into a giant, standing on each other's shoulders. It's an acrobatic, Peking Opera version of a Japanese transforming robot.

Super Sword is ultimately defeated – when the maidens are joined by Ng Tung, who has now become female (by drinking one of the Ghost Doctor's potions). Thus, Ng Tung makes up for the imprisoned Princess Tin Heung. Super Sword ends up looking like a pin cushion, with seven swords stuck in his torso, until he explodes.

Holy Weapon is surely one of Tony Ching Siu-tung's teams finest achievements – including Ching's more recent outings, such as *Hero* or *An Empress and the Warriors*. At several points in the climax, there are over ten performers flying thru the air, *plus* props like logs or rocks spinning. It's quite remarkable.

At a practical level, you can see that it must've been an absolute bitch to achieve – like doing a hundred work-outs for everybody on the set. And

29 Once again, the technicians who put together these scenes practically, creating elaborate rigs to fly actors and props, impresses.

very tough on the stunt guys and actors.

As well as the maiden-made giant, there are extraordinary images of the warriors smashing thru a wooden structure, of each swordswoman slashing their swords at the super-villain in close-up, of the warriors crashing through stone walls, of rocks hurtling in the air and hitting fighters, and of the virgins, now clad in fluttering, white robes, descending upon Super Sword *en masse.*

Holy Weapon is a superb demonstration of the Tony Ching action style – fantastical, beautiful, incredibly rapid (and rapidly cut), and completely free in its airborne stunts. Again, very few action directors can make the body in movement look so exquisite or heroic. For poses, for placing actors in inventive and memorable positions in the frame, Ching is in a class of his own.

And the editing (by Keung Chuen-tak and Chun Yu) is masterful – the poised build-ups to the action, the sudden flurries into movement, the quick spins in the air followed by a cut to the actor turning on the spot, arms open, in a crouch, sword held high. Wow! The depiction of motion, the length of the shots, the fusion of multiple camera angles, and the logical (yet fantastical) flow of movement is both completely solid (earthy, physical), and ultra-poetic. This is pure cinema, purely cinematic, and quite, quite magnificent.

13

FLYING DAGGER

San Ging Dou Jyu Fei Tin Maan

And so to *Flying Dagger* (*San Ging Dou Jyu Fei Tin Maau*, 1993).

For the purposes of a study of the ecstatic cinema of Tony Ching Siu-tung, only two things need to be pointed out:

It was written by Wong Jing.

It was action directed by Tony Ching Siu-tung.

For the rest of the credits, *Flying Dagger* features a stellar cast: Maggie Cheung Man-yuk, Tony Leung Ka-fai, Jacky Cheung Hok-yau, Gloria Yip, Sharla Cheung-man, Ng Man-tat, Chan Hung-lit, Kingdom Yuen, Yuen Cheung-yan, Lee Ka-ting, Lo Lieh, Pauline Chan, David Wu and Ku Pao-ming.

Flying Dagger was made by Chang Hong Channel Film & Video. Prod. by Hui Pooi-yung. Dir. by Kevin Chu Yen-ping (Tony Ching has worked with Chu several times). Music:[30] Chan Daai-lik and Foo Laap. DP: Chan Wing-shu. Ed. by Ma Chung-yiu. Released May 6, 1993. 86 mins.

Flying Dagger is a comedy scripted by Wong Jing,[31] the king of crude humour, tasteless jokes, and sexploitation. It's a parody of all the *wuxia* movies that the Hong Kong industry was churning out at the time. All of the participants in *Flying Dagger* had been involved in them; the cast seems to enjoy sending up their screen personas. *Flying Dagger* is of the order of a *Carry On* comedy or a Mel Brooks spoof. It's a pantomime of a martial arts movie, reminding us that many *wuxia pian* are actually utterly ridiculous if you examine them closely – even the ones celebrated by the crrritics as

---

30 The score comprises cuts from existing film music – from *Heathers*, *Death Becomes Her*, *A Fish Called Wanda*, *Maniac*, *Quigley Down Under*, etc.
31 Wong produced, directed or wrote other send-ups of *kung fu* movies and *wuxia pian* in this era, such as *Last Hero In China* and *Kung Fu Cult Master*.

Great Works of Cinema.

So, no, *Flying Dagger* is *not* about the anxieties in the colony in the run-up to the Handover to Mainland Chinese rule; it is *not* a savage critique of the ruling powers in the People's Republic of China; it is *not* a postmodern analysis of gender in contemporary Asia; and it is *not* a Maoist, revolutionary call-to-arms. It's a comedy.

Once again, several Western critics (the usual suspects) took *Flying Dagger* too straight, expecting (or desiring) an action movie with comical moments sprinkled on top, instead of what is clearly a comedy at its foundation, a pantomime of Ye Olde China, a Peking Opera routine (tho' a comedy with incredible action scenes). A movie where a severed hand runs amok and gooses Tony Leung is not a serious movie! A picture where Jacky Cheung farts in the faces of Gloria Yip and Sharla Cheung is not a sombre Work of Art!

The story of *Flying Dagger* is simple: two pairs of bounty hunters compete with each other to nobble the Nine-Tailed Fox (Jacky Cheung). That's it. One couple is the Hon (Dagger) brothers, Chung a.k.a. Big Dagger (Tony Leung) and Lam a.k.a. Little Dagger (Jimmy Lin). The other couple are the Fung (Bewitchment) sisters, Lady Fung (Sharla Cheung) and Ling (Gloria Yip). Oh, and Maggie Cheung Man-yuk plays the Fox's wife, Flying Cat.

Many clichés from *wuxia pian* are parodied in *Flying Dagger*. The humour is coarse in the Wong Jingian manner: Nine-Tailed Fox farts at the sisters trying to capture him – they collapse unconscious on the floor. The severed hand of a bandito called Never Die (Yuen Cheung-yan – one of the Yuen family) pinches Chung on the butt.[32]

As for the action and Tony Ching Siu-tung's input as choreographer, *Flying Dagger* contains many action sequences, including several with the famous Chingian flourishes. Like palanquins riding incredible distances through the air. Like furious swordplay amidst dust, smoke, trees and billowing robes. Like rapid flights amongst huge trees, a Chingian speciality. Like multiple warriors in the air at the same time, all performing different moves. Like swordsmen flying and spinning rapidly. Like victims being slashed apart into a series of cloth rags and body parts. Like assailants erupting from the ground.

The opening sequence of *Flying Dagger* is of course an action sequence (some 7 or 8 minutes long). And of course it takes place at night, in a town street. Hundreds of Chingian flourishes are hurled at the

---

32 Flying Cat catches up on what's been happening in the movie so far with a primitive print-out of sketches (drawn by an aged artist in the next room).

viewer. No need for the exposition to be unrolled in a slow crawl in the titles, because it's yelled out between the Hon Dagger team as they fight swordsmen. (The setting, the costumes, the make-up, and fun items like Tony Leung's silly hair-do, all set the scene).

Who says that Wong Jing can't write?! Of course he can! For ex, in those 7-8 minutes of screen time, in amongst furious and astonishing action, we discover that the Hons are bounty hunters, that they receive money for corpses, that they have fearsome rivals in the form of the Fung (Bewitchment) sisters, that Big Dagger doesn't like being called 'Uncle' in public, that there is an erotic interplay between Fung and Chung and Lam and Ling, etc.

And, courtesy of Tony Ching Siu-tung and the stunt team, we also see that the two pairs of bounty hunters are amazing sword fighters, and each is used to getting their own way (they are fighting one of those wild-haired, old guys called Eagle). We are also introduced to four of the top-billed stars (the third pair, Jacky Leung and Maggie Cheung (Nine-tailed Fox and Flying Cat), are introduced in the second half of act one).

Meanwhile, the scene where the bounty hunters are given their task (by the authority figure Emperor Tsao, whose daughter was killed by the Nine-tailed Fox), is delivered with just enough information. This movie simply doesn't bother with hanging around for, say, intriguing character-izations, or with weighty bits of thematic material. Instead, it's: *go kill the Nine-tailed Fox.* And off they hurry, galloping thru the forest.

In the usual Wong Jing manner, Nine-tailed Fox and Flying Cat are introduced in bed, in a send-up of using a sex book like the *Kama Sutra*. They are an unusual husband and wife team (to say the least!). There's never a dull moment when these two are around – they both have egos the size of Mount Everest. Further erotic interplay sees them boasting about their swords – which cues a marital spat in the form of a sword fight.

The two groups of characters are brought together when the two teams of bounty hunters converge on the Nine-tailed Fox's lair, pursued by Never Die. That means another action sequence, of course. In a Wongian twist, Never Die is so prudish he withers – literally – when he hears suggestive words. Never Die is thus dispatched by the cast acting lewdly.

Flying Dagger continues to visit all of the usual sites in a *wuxia pian* – the restaurant/ hotel, the forest again, and a bordello[33] (mandatory in a Wong Jing picture).

For the third act and the finale, three villains are brought in solely for

---

[33] Where Nine-Tailed Fox cavorts with a bevy of women – until his irate wife Flying Cat shows up.

the purpose of providing antagonists for the heroes (they haven't been mentioned previously. They reprise the political Chinese<->Japanese antagonism subplot). Crude gags abound, characters yell at each other before fighting, and bodies're ripped apart in mid-flight.

Yes, Tony Ching Siu-tung and co. deliver another airborne finale – this time exploiting the possibilities for colourful banners to look pretty as they're deployed as weaponry. And they do – several shots in slo-mo catch the red, yellow and blue banners falling in tatters like blossom, while swordsmen and swordswomen soar gracefully, robes fluttering. (*Hero* used flapping colourful banners in the throne room – a bigger version of this scene).

This is one of those sequences in the cinema of Tony Ching which deploys an enormous number of cables – not only for the performers, but also to puppeteer the set, to yank all of those banners all over the place, and to tear apart victims. In one scene, *Flying Dagger* has four warriors bursting out of a roof into the air; in another, they are tussling with rapidfire swordplay on a platform under the banners. The magician sucks up everything in his path (including wounds in the heroes); the hand of Never Die performs the rescue, by attacking Tsao.

❁

Flying Dagger might amount to nothing much for some – but if you've watched it, it's already served its purpose. *Flying Dagger* is fairly typical Hong Kong film fare – it's fast, loud, crude, stupid, and fantastical. It boasts a finer cast than 1,000s of other movies, and the action is directed by a genius.

The finale of *Flying Dagger* in particular is a marvel of action choreography and wire-work: only two or three people on Earth at the time could've pulled this off (and they're all in Hong Kong). It is fiendishly complicated, and could only be achieved by a team which had worked together for years, which had performers who could do it all (in take after take), which had the schedule that allowed for such intricacy, and which had developed the gear, harnesses and rigs to deliver the effects.

The 1993 movie is lighthearted fluff that doesn't take itself seriously. It's a burlesque of Mythical China. But that doesn't mean that aspects of it aren't outstanding, such as the action choreography. Nowhere else on Earth at the time could these scenes have been achieved.

Moon Warriors (1992).

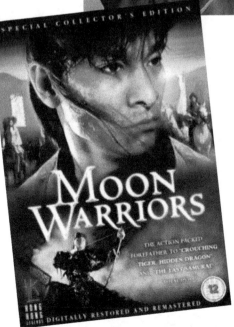

Royal Tramp 1
(above & left).
Royal Tramp 2
(below).
Both 1992.

This is the son of Ping Shi Ruler,
Wu-Sun-Gwei.

Damn it! Whose shoes are they?

City Hunter (1993).

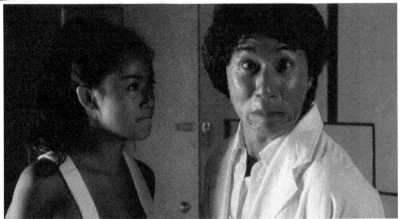

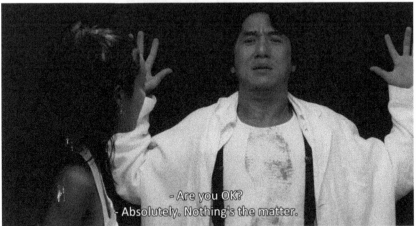

- Are you OK?
- Absolutely. Nothing's the matter.

Butterfly and Sword (1993).

Holy Weapon (1993).

Flying Dagger (1993).

14

FUTURE COPS

Chiu Kap Hok Hau Ba Wong

Future Cops (a.k.a. *Chiu Kap Hok Hau Ba Wong,* 1993), was prod. by Wong Jing's Workshop and Fantasy Productions Inc., prod. by John Higgins, exec. prod. by Sherman Wong Shui-Hin, wr. and dir. by Wong Jing, DP: Andrew Lau Wai-tung, art dirs.: Jason Mok and Raymond Gwok, costumes: Man Yun-Mei and Cheung Toi, ed. by Poon Hung, action dirs.: Tony Ching Siu-tung, Dion Lam Dik-On and Ma Yuk-Sing. Released July 15, 1993. 95 mins.

Future Cops is a Wong Jing extravaganza. It boasts an amazing cast: Andy Lau Tak-wah, Chingmy Yau Suk-ching, Jacky Cheung, Andy Hui, Simon Yam Tak-wah, Dicky Cheung, Aaron Kwok, Kingdom Yuen, and Richard Ng. Instead of Stephen Chow Sing-chi in the lead role of the hapless guy (as we might expect), we have Dicky Cheung. It was remade in 2010 as *Future X-Cops*.

Future Cops is one of those Hong Kong comedies which exists solely to entertain – it is not 'about' anything, doesn't have anything 'to say', and doesn't even contain a theme. Rather, *Future Cops* is one set-piece after another, one narrative beat after another, one comical bit after another comical bit.

The story of *Future Cops* does make sense – characters from the future visit the present day to alter fate – but this film is not about the background story at all. And with this stellar cast, it doesn't matter, either: this is the Hong Kong comedy movie as a pantomime, like the *Lucky Stars* flicks, or many a New Year's comedy.

Future Cops is a try-anything comedy. So we've got Andy Lau and

Chingmy Yau as a cute couple who visit an arcade and disappear inside a video game. In this riff on *City Hunter*, the Jackie Chan action comedy (which Tony Ching also action directed), Lau and Yau fool about in a set designed in the storybook colours and pantomime fakery of a children's TV show.

Future Cops is delivered in the wild style of a Hong Kong action comedy: performances are broad, aiming for the laugh every time. We're talking silly costumes, and ridiculous hairstyles (Jacky Cheung's *Bride of Frankenstein* bouffant is the wackiest; the costumes were by Cheung Toi and Man Yun-mei). It's a Wong Jing movie, so it's meant to entertain all-round. (So, don't think, don't analyze it, don't expect *War and Peace*).

The Wong Jingisms in *Future Cops* include the skirts of the schoolgirls being blown by the breeze as the superheroes zoom by; and Kingdom Yuen camping it up with Richard Ng as a horny, older woman.

A good deal of *Future Cops* is played as small-scale farce – frantically rapid comical shtick set in a single locale (the home of the hero), between two actors (Lau and Yau, for instance). In other words, it's cheap – it's two performers, a room, and some silly props (much is made of Lau's future cop's magical abilities).

Future Cops draws on time travel flicks like *The Terminator* and the *Back To the Future* series, where characters havet to travel back from the future to fix something in the present day (here, nobble a juror). *Future Cops* also shamelessly steals from *Fight Back To School* (the Stephen Chow Sing-chi comedy of 1991, which Wong Jing produced), with a lengthy sequence set in a school (St. Yuk Keung Secondary School).

The futuristic narrative device is just that – a narrative device. Most of the movie is set in the present day (i.e., in 1993). That's cheaper, for a start (recreating the future can be pricey).

The hapless hero's in his late twenties (which handily explains how he can still be at school, studying[1]), with a bitchy sister (Chingmy Yau), a cute, naïve sort of girlfriend (Charlie Yeung), and a sex-hungry mom (Kingdom Yuen). Richard Ng plays one of his mom's new beaus (when he speaks in English turns her on – maybe a reference to *A Fish Called Wanda*[2]).

Jacky Cheung Hok-yau, one of the four Cantopop stars, gets his own musical number, in a scene where he's teaching a class. One of his students fantasizes about romancing Cheung, with visions of a sprawling family of their children.

---

[1] The scenario is also artificial as *Fight Back To School*, where Stephen Chow was a cop going undercover.
[2] Wong Jing is certainly a film buff – he seems to have seen every big film coming out of the West.

✻

Future Cops opens with an extraordinary. stops-all-out action sequence, which employs every stunt and gag in the Hong Kong action cinema repertoire. It's a Tony Ching scene, with wire-work everywhere, as cops on flying scooters chase down their quarry thru a docklands area (which handily allows for explosions and fire gags).

This might be comedy, but the action is still frenetic and the stunts potentially dangerous, as characters dive to the ground, zoom down from on high on flying machines, flee from walls of fire, etc.

The opening sequence of *Future Cops*, however (clearly not directed by Wong Jing), is a mislead: most of the 1993 movie takes place in the familiar, present-day Hong Kong, in the daytime, and in schools and homes where regular people live.

✻

The finale of *Future Cops* is just what you'd expect: frantic action.[3] The General from the future turns up to battle our heroes, plus the future cops, providing a suitably formidable foe for the smackdowns. Also, the hero and his sister have been superhero-ized: Chingmy Yau turns into a Japanese loli, mom is a prancing courtesan, her new boyfriend (Richard Ng), is a green lion, and Dicky Cheung is a pint-sized Superman.

Chimgmy Yau Suk-ching in her superhero mode is impressive: she spins upside-down very rapidly with her legs out-stretched, to kick opponents. Richard Ng's green lion collapses into a spinning ball of mayhem.

Ching Siu-tung orchestrates multiple duels at the school: walls are crumbling as characters smash into them (and ceilings, and floors); characters blast flames at each other; characters are flying up and down and horizontally all the time; and of course stuff blows up.

Every piece of action is played for laughs – nobody gets seriously hurt[4] (except the General from the future, but he is a robot, so it doesn't matter when he's skewered thru the torso, and then blown to pieces).

The action won't be celebrated as the finest examples in the *œuvre* of Tony Ching simply because *Future Cops* is a throwaway, lighthearted comedy. *Future Cops* isn't played seriously, like *Hero* or *House of Flying Daggers*. It's fluff. But as stunt people know well, a comedy can be as difficult to achieve – and just as dangerous[5] – as a dramatic story.

---

3 The film is speeded up – for comic effect (way beyond the usual 22 f.p.s. projected at 24 f.p.s.)
4 Within the film, but you can bet that some of the stunt folk were injured.
5 And sometimes even more hazardous.

15

THE STUNTWOMAN

Ah Kam

The Stuntwoman (a.k.a. *Ah Kam* and *Ah Kam: Story of a Stuntwoman*, 1996) is an unusual movie in several respects: films about stunt folk are rare;[6] a film about stunt people directed by a woman is very rare; a film about stunt people directed by a woman and about a stunt woman is almost unknown. *The Stuntwoman* is also unusual in being a movie about movie production in the Cantonese business (in Hong Kong cinema, self-reflexive films tend to focus on the stars, or celebrity culture (such as *Viva Erotica*, 1996), but not on the nuts and bolts of film production behind the scenes).

The Stuntwoman was a star vehicle for Michelle Yeoh Chu-kheng, playing a stunt performer in the contemporary world of Hong Kong filmmaking. Ironically, this film about stunt people included a stunt that went wrong and damaged the film itself.

The Stuntwoman boasts a fine cast which includes Sammo Hung Kam-bo as the second top-billed name, Crystal Kwok Kam-yan, Jimmy Wong Ka-lok, Satoshi Okada, Ken Lo Wing-hang, Michael Lam Wai-leung, Nick Cheung Ka-fai, Richard Ng and Meng Hoi (many of the cast are well-known in Hong Kong cinema, including some appearing in cameos).

Golden Harvest and D.A.C.A. Entertainment produced; Chan Man-keung and John Chan scripted; Anne Hui On-wah directed; and Tony Ching and Lam Wai-ming were the action choreographers. Released: Oct 10, 1996. 96 mins.

The Stuntwoman was helmed by Ann Hui On-wah (b. May 23, 1947, Anshan, Manchuria), one of the original Hong Kong 'New Wave' directors

---

6 Though there are documentaries.

(*The Spooky Bunch, Boat People*), who went on to make *The Romance of Book and Sword, Sing of the Exile, Zodiac Killers, Ordinary, July Rhapsody, The Way We Are, Night and Fog, A Simple Life, The Golden Era* and *Summer Snow.* Hui debuted in features in 1979, along with Tsui Hark, Alex Cheung and Peter Yung, with *The Secret*. Hui is known for alternating between genre or commercial pictures (like *The Stuntwoman*) and socially conscious or political works (such as her early Vietnam film trilogy – *Boy From Vietnam, The Story of Woo Viet* and *Boat People*). Hui is not only one of the few significant female, Chinese directors, her works have been showered with awards: for example, she has won the Hong Kong Film Award for Best Director six times so far[7] (that's more than most of the other famous Hong Kong directors).

✳

Michelle Yeoh Chu-kheng is a charming presence on camera, as ever – she plays Ah Kam as a self-effacing, hard-working, somewhat shy woman. Yeoh plays Ah Kam ten or more years younger than her age (34 at the time). But Yeoh always seems amazingly youthful.

There's something very appealing about Sammo Hung Kam-bo when he's acting in a sort of everyday role (rather than being a wizard, a clown, or an action hero). But whoever Hung plays, you can't take your eyes off him. He is a unique actor in cinema. (Hung as Tung is not quite an ordinary guy – he is the authority on set, when the director or producer isn't around, and the crew call him Master).

Ah Long (Ken Lo Wing-hang) is a curious ingredient in *The Stuntwoman*: a bratty, mouthy teenager, the son of the Chief, Tung (making Tung a single parent). The rather obvious plotting has Ah Kam stepping into the shoes of the mother that Ah Long misses but hides under a strikingly vivid line in hostile banter.

✳

The Stuntwoman is a fascinating glimpse at the state of Hong Kong movie-making in the mid-Nineties. Even though, as with all movies about movie production (and all movies in general), everything is faked and dressed for the cameras, there is plenty of atmosphere and texture about ⌐ ⌐lms are created in the Hong Kong industry. How much of the practical ⌐f setting up stunts and filming them is accurate in relation to the ⌐ion of Tony Ching is uncertain. For example, sometimes the ⌐ *Stuntwoman* takes the angle of the filming itself, and ⌐he point-of-view of the production team watching the

⌐uction presented in *The Stuntwoman* are spot-on:
⌐ Best Director three times.

the work ethic, for example. As action director Tung points out, they have to work to make money. No one has a trailer or is pampered on set. Jobs are shared (with no unionized demarcation). Filmmaking in Canton is thoroughly masculinist: it's a boys' kingdom, with women relegated to the sidelines. Injuries are common, as well as spells in hospital. There is a *lot* of eating and drinking (but is there a film production centre anywhere on Earth who doesn't indulge in a lot of food and alcohol?). Ah Kam drinks, too (and has drinking competitions with Tung). Plenty of joshing amongst the crew (many have nicknames – Scarface, Copy, etc). People make sure they're getting paid. The stunties complain of shooting three nights in a row. Ah Kam is always so tired when she returns home she collapses on the bed. Ah Kam's lifestyle is fairly typical: she shares a tiny apartment with her roommate Crystal Kwok. (Many aspects of filmmaking are streamlined or ignored, as usual in the movie-making sub-genre. Getting into everything that film production entails would result in a movie fifteen weeks long).

The martial arts co-ordinator played by Sammo Hung Kam-bo (Tung) might be typical of the Hong Kong film business, but he is not Tony Ching (or Hung himself). Ching, however, delivers some entertaining versions of his stock repertoire, and of the typical Cantonese, action film. In the first act, for example, the crew are depicted shooting a swordplay movie, featuring flying swordsmen, big stunts with breakaway sets, elaborate aerial moves, and explosives. (The film can't resist caricaturing some of the crew members, such as the pyrotechnics guy.)

Tony Ching and Lam Wai-ming also choreographed action that took place outside of the movie productions. One of the subplots has business rivalry erupting in brawls (such as in a pool hall, where Tung is smashed on the head). In the second act of *The Stuntwoman*, when some heavies arrive to intimidate the bar where Ah Kam is now working, she uses her martial arts training, and trounces them. This is reprised (Ah Kam versus the hoods) in the third act finale, in the usual manner of Hong Kong action pictures.

The Stuntwoman is in part a backstage comedy about film production: it even includes staples of the sub-genre such as the bitchy rivalry between actresses, and one actress upstaging another or deliberately causing trouble (during a stunt, which injures Ah Kam in the first act).

❋

Early on, Tung asks the standard seduction lines: is she single? does she have a boyfriend? is she gay? We have to buy that Michelle Yeoh Chu-kheng is indeed single, as we always do: somehow, beautiful movie s always happen to be single and possibly available. (We know, though, that Yeoh was pursued by several high-powered individuals, including movie producers and film directors).

✳

In act two (*The Stuntwoman* is a three-act movie, like most Hong Kong movies), the focus shifts to Ah Kam's personal life: a romance begins between Ah Kam and Sam (Jimmy Wong Ga-lok). This was apparently added when Michelle Yeoh suffered a real injury during a stunt, and the film was reworked.

Sam invites Ah Kam to join him running his new bar. The characterization of Sam comes across as Any Guy: Jimmy Wong plays a man who's handsome but seems to lack any sort of personality. he's just a guy, the guy that Ah Kam eventually falls for (after resisting his aggressive advances).

The love story not only shifts attention away from the entertaining world of movie-making depicted in the first act, it seems too pat, and too cheesy.

✳

The Stuntwoman was a low-point in Tony Ching's professional career, when the film's star (and a much-loved actress) was seriously injured performing a stunt (it involved a high leap from a bridge onto a truck).[8] Footage of the stunt was included in the end credits (in the manner of the outtakes in a Jackie Chan film) – you can see Ching amongst the guys helping Michelle Yeoh as she recovers on a mattress. Putting the failed stunt into the credits helps to explain why the film boasts an unsatisfying plot in its later stages.

Following the strong first act, *The Stuntwoman* becomes increasingly erratic. It might be a film that Michelle Yeoh, Sammo Hung, Tony Ching and director Ann Hui would prefer to forget, and not only due to the injury that Yeoh sustained.

✳

The third act of *The Stuntwoman* is a reworking of the script following the injury of Michelle Yeoh. If you're kind about the film, it continues to explore melodramatic issues: Ah Kam, for example, discovers that Sam is seeing another woman, and their relationship founders. If you view the movie less sympathetically, it's a shambles.

The third act of *The Stuntwoman* is patched up and rescued in numerous ways. Several big events are not covered satisfactorily – foremost among these incidents is the death of the Chief, stuntmaster Tung. Only part of the murder is seen, the rest is explained in voiceover

8 Ching and Yeoh had worked together on *The Heroic Trio* and *The Executioners*.

(one of the clear signs that a movie is making up for unmade footage or plot holes. It looks like only one side of the confrontation with the hoods was filmed, for instance, with the reverse angles being planned for another time. But that didn't happen).

The death of Sammo Hung Kam-bo, who's been such a larger-than-life presence in *The Stuntwoman*, should be a major sequence. Anyway, the 1996 film does cover the fall-out from the murder, with both Ah Kam and Ah Long feeling his absence strongly, and the stunt crew hoping for payback.

The action finale of *The Stuntwoman* is thus very scrappy, unconvincing, and unsatisfying: it features Ah Long being kidnapped by the people who topped Tung (led by the narcissistic, foolish gang leader, Chan – Jack Wong Wai-leung), and tortured at a fairground. Ah Kam comes to the rescue, fighting off Chan and his henchmen at the funfair.

This is definitely one of the poorest fight sequences in a production that Tony Ching oversaw as action choreographer (along with Lam Wai-ming). Considering too that a major director was helming the show – Ann Hui On-wah – the whole thing is shabby. But *The Stuntwoman* wasn't written by Hui; the writers – Chan Man-keung and John Chan – might've come up with something more fulfilling than this. After all, writers in a film industry based on a guerrilla style of film production have to be nimble, have to be able to react to changing circumstances (earlier in the film, for instance, there's a scene where a production is cancelled and there's no money).

The 1996 film closes with bitty scenes of Ah Kam in an unlikely pairing with Ah Long, now a surrogate mother to him. Evocations of leaving, and a trip, don't satisfy on any level.

As for the critics, the reception was mixed: 'as fascinating as it is disapointing' (Almar Haflidason, British Broadcasting Corporation); 'fails as a whole' (Asian Movie Pulse). Paul Fonoroff really disliked it (but htis is his standard response to most movies in Hong Kong. Fonoroff gives a positive review to about one film in five).

16

WARRIORS OF VIRTUE

Wu Xing Zhan Shi

Produced by the family of Laws (Joseph, Ronald, Dennis K., Jeremy and Christopher Law), along with producers Yoram Barzilai, Lyle Howry and Patricia Ruben, for the companies I.J.L Creations and China Film Co-Production Corporation, with Metro Goldwyn Mayer handling distribution, *Warriors of Virtue* (*Wu Xing Zhan Shi,* 1997) was directed by Ronny Yu Ya-tai, and written by Michael Vickerman and Hugh Kelley. Prod. des. by Joseph Lucky and Eugenio Zanetti, editor: David Wu, DP: Peter Pau, casting by Felicia Fasano, music by Don Davis, and costumes by Shirley Chan. Released May 2, 1997. 101 mins.

In the cast were Angus Macfadyen, Mario Yedidia, Marley Shelton, Chao Li Chi, Jack Tate, Doug Jones, Don Lewis, J. Todd Adams, Adriene Corcoran and Michael Anderson. The film appeared in several dubs – English, Cantonese, Kangaroo, etc. Much of the film was made in English.

Warriors of Virtue was filmed in Beijing and Vancouver – largely, like many fantasy productions of this type, in the studio. With superstar cinematographer Peter Pau lighting the show, it looks great; however, the brilliant production designer, Eugenio Zanetti,[9] gives the film too derivative a look, for the main, village set (Zanetti and Joseph Lucky have more fun with the super-villain's compound, usually the biggest, most intricate set in an action-adventure movie).

Warriors of Virtue was a massive visual effects show, involving companies such as Buzz FX, Northwest Imaging, Gajdecki, Prospero, Asia Cinema, Rainmaker *et al*, with animatronic effects by Alterian

---

9 Zanetti designed *What Dreams May Come* and *Restoration*.

Studios.

＊

Unfortunately, *Warriors of Virtue* (1997) was a clunker. Despite the highly accomplished technical crew (editing by David Wu, photography by Peter Pau, production design by Eugenio Zanetti (along with Joseph Lucky), and action choreography[10] by Tony Ching), *Warriors of Virtue* is painful to watch in some sections. You might think, what a waste of talent – and of $36 million (!).

With all of those resources – the sets, the costumes, the animatronics, the cast, the film crew – it would be possible to create a decent movie. Indeed, one can imagine an independent film crew going in there after hours and filming a different, far better movie (in the Roger Corman manner, of re-using film sets and facilities).

Warriors of Virtue was spoilt technically by several elements: too much music (played by the Colorado Symphony Orchestra and scored by Don Davis), uneven pacing and editing, over-done slanted camera angles, and an over-reliance on step-motion and slow motion (step-printing in particular was over-used. Occurring once or twice, often for flashbacks or dream sequences, step-motion is a striking tool. But *Warriors of Virtue* is filled with it). The self-conscious trickery with cinematic basics such as the camera and the cutting (the angles, the step-motion) gets in the way of the storytelling.

The main problem with *Warriors of Virtue*, as with almost all failures in movies of this type, is the concept and the script. Add to that the lack of stars, and the too-derivative nature of the project. Critics complained that *Warriors of Virtue* was too similar to children's franchises such as *The Power Rangers* and *The Mutant Ninja Turtles*.[11]

The budget was too high for a movie coming from a group of filmmakers without a track record. $36 million is at the level of the famous over-budget productions and flops. It's a shame – you are willing this family-produced movie to succeed. Spending far less money on the negative costs and using the money instead to hire some crack writers to rework the screenplay from the ground up would have helped, plus allocating some cash for one or two stars.

The 1997 movie might've performed poorly at the box office, but it led to a sequel in 2002 (tho' direct to video): *Warriors of Virtue: The Return To Tao.*

Yet there *are* some aspects of *Warriors of Virtue* that're worth something – the slick, rapid, airborne action, one or two of the jokes, and

---

10 The other stunt co-ordinators were Marc Akerstream and Siu Ming-tsui.
11 The half-animal-half-human warriors are certainly very similar to the Turtles.

Angus Macfadyen's over-the-top performance.

❋

The story of the making of *Warriors of Virtue* is much more interesting than the film itself.[12] It was financed largely by a family of doctors from Colorado, the Law brothers (with distribution thru M.G.M., who spent a rumoured $20 million on P. & A.). And this isn't a small movie, a small-scale thriller, say, costing under one million dollars, which might be made by a group of friends all contributing: the budget was $36 million; it included huge sets, a large cast, visual effects, etc.

The Law brothers set about making a movie of their own in 1995: they came up with the story of *kung fu* kangaroos and hired a Hollywood screenwriter (who at the time hadn't had a script produced) to write the script. The Laws then pursued securing finance and deals for the project, ending up paying for much of it themselves (Hollywood wasn't that interested). But they also had experience with selling merchandize, and toys were manufactured to tie in with the movie.

The Laws reckoned their movie wasn't positioned correctly in the market – it should've been a 'PG-13', rather than a 'PG', but they wanted to produce a film for children. Also, it didn't have stars – if it had come from a Hollywood studio, some of the roles (such as the village master) would've been cast with recognizable names. *Warriors of Virtue* wasn't a recognizable property, either – many kiddie pics are adapted from well-known books, plays, TV shows, cartoons, etc.

❋

Warriors of Virtue is one of those fantasy adventure flicks aimed simultaneously at early teens and their parents who'll take them to the theatre. But it's too derivative of 1,000s of other movies, and doesn't carve out its own niche. *Warriors of Virtue* is not *The Princess Bride*, *Return of the Jedi*, or the movies of Jim Henson and his company. It's Disney Lite, George Lucas Lite, but doesn't have its own vision.

Fantasy adventure movies like this are a big challenge to get right – you can see why *Warriors of Virtue* cost $36 million: it has the giant sets (with huge trees, pools of water, boats, multiple levels like the Ewok Village in *Return of the Jedi* crossed with a generic jungle set); it has a large cast, plus extras, an enormous production team, and tons of visual effects, etc (but not, however, a starry cast. Angus Macfadyen is about the only recognizable face in *Warriors of Virtue*). But it comes across as a cheapo TV movie at times.

The warriors of the film's title are a bunch of guys (or girls) wearing

12 See this excellent article: T.R. Witcher: "Everybody Wasn't Kung Fu Fighting", *Westword*, Denver, CO, Jan 14, 1999.

animatronic animal heads, playing *kung fu* fighting kangaroos (dubbed 'rooz' in the publicity). They're first intro'd performing *wushu* routines (aided by wires, of course), while the village's chief, Master Chung (Chao-Li Chi), explains this new world to the pint-sized teenager. This is where the movie comes to life a little, altho' we have to wait a *long time* for it.

Before we reach the mythic realm of Tao, we have to endure a whole ten minutes in the company of the incredibly boring boy protagonist, Ryan Jeffers (Mario Yedidia). He's one of those cute, bland, All-American kids who act as the audience identification figure. Whenever we meet these characters who're dramatic devices to bridge the 'real', contemporary world with the fantasy world, our spirits sink: you mean we've got to stay with this wimpy twerp for the prologue *and* the epilogue? And we'll probably have to spend more time with him during the adventure? (As everything is explained to him, and the audience is introduced to the world of the story through him).

And the next ten minutes of *Warriors of Virtue* feature a lacklustre sequence of dares and joshing among the teens that Jeffers and his buddy Chucky encounter at night. So it's over 20 minutes before we reach the fantasy realm of Studio B (a.k.a. Tao).

At home, with Daddy absent (Jeffers is of course a father complex boy), the kid's given a surrogate father figure in the unlikely form of a cook who owns a Chinese restaurant (echoes of *The Karate Kid*). Ignoring the usual avuncular guff that Ming (Dennis Dun) delivers, it's fun to see a comedy Chinese cooking skit in a North American movie.

※

Lord Komodo, the super-villain of the piece, is played with a camp quirkiness and bursts of roaring venom by Angus Macfadyen, a kind of cross between Tim Curry in *The Rocky Horror Picture Show* and a pantomime dame.

The MacGuffin of *Warriors of Virtue* – the fabled manuscript – turns out to be empty, with nothing written on the pages. Jeffers, commanded by Lord Komodo to read what's written in it, comes up eventually (after much persuasion) with the motto: 'shit happens'.

The finale of *Warriors of Virtue* features multiple duels, inevitably: if there are five kangaroo warriors, but only one super-villain, how will that work? Simple: Lord Komodo splits into five versions of himself. Each of the 'rooz' gets their moment to shine, battling Komodo up on the walkways, leaping from the balcony, over the pools, slammed against trees, the works.

The ending of *Warriors of Virtue* plays out exactly as expected:

Komodo is defeated (tho' not, ultimately, killed off, perhaps a nod to this being a family movie), the warriors unite to fight, Ryan does his bit with the book, everyone is forgiven, and Komodo's bunch're invited back to the village. And Ryan returns to Earth. With the sweet *dénouement* of Ryan telling his mom he loves her, the movie ends.

17

THE DUEL

Jue Zhan Zi Jin Zhi Dian

The Duel (*Jue Zhan Zi Jin Zhi Dian*, 2000) was an all-star, New Year's swordplay fantasy comedy,[13] with action direction by Tony Ching Siu-tung. *Juezhan Qianhou* by Gu Long (from the *Lu Xiaofeng* novel series) was the basis for the script.

Win's Entertainment produced. Andy Lau Tak-wah, Ekin Cheng, Kristy Yeung, Nick Cheung and Zhao Wei headed up a terrific cast, which included Patrick Tam, Elvis Tsui, Jerry Lamb, David Lee, and Norman Chu. Manfred Wong scripted, Wong Jing and Manfred Wong produced, Andrew Lau Wai-keung (the other Andy Lau) directed (and was one of the DPs), ed. by Marco Mak Chi-sin, and music by Chan Kwong-Wing. Released Feb 3, 2000. 106 mins.

The Duel is another movie very much in the Tsui Hark mode: a joky tone, a historical/ mythological, Chinese setting, a martial arts literary basis, traditional, Chinese music, an all-star Hong Kong cast, flashy visuals, rapid cutting, special effects, and dynamic action.

The Duel in fact looks like a combination of the directing styles of Wong Jing (stars, comedy, farce), and Tsui Hark (stars, comedy, vfx, action, tradition). (At this point, director Andy Lau, who has photographed films for Tsui, was hitting the big time with *The Storm Riders* (1998), another distinctly Tsui-ian action-adventure movie, of the year before. But you wouldn't class Lau as an *auteur* director, with themes, motifs, concerns and the like. Nevertheless, Lau's movies have bags of style, and, like the best Hong Kong movies, an irresistible energy).

13 Other *wuxia pian comedies* similar to *The Duel* include *The Eagle Shooting Heroes*, Stephen Chow comedies like *Royal Tramp* and Wong Jing's many *wuxia* send-ups.

Manfred Wong shares the writing credit with Wong Jing – and the two Wongs were the film producers.

So, yes, we are back in Ye Olde Oriente for this swordplay romp of the millennium year: the stars are very familiar, the Imperial settings are very familiar (*The Duel* filmed in all the usual spots in Beijing for historical flicks), the comedy is very familiar, and the action is very familiar.

But also very enjoyable: it's impossible not to warm to this sort of movie. You'd have to be a really grumpy, old sod not to find this fun. It's Hong Kong cinema as pure entertainment, a movie as a pantomime, as putting on a show (there's even a bit of Peking Opera theatre in there, plus a New Year's celebration – this was a New Year's release).

The story – of two super-ace swordsmen ('Sword Saint' Yip and 'Sword Deity' Simon Snow) announcing they'll duel on top of the Forbidden Palace at the full moon – is used by Manfred Wong and Wong Jing (both very talented writers)[14] to stage a series of farcical/ romantic/ action sequences (there is drama here, but comedy is uppermost. No one is taking any of this seriously). We've got riotous brothel scenes, we've got one of the heroes (Dragon 9) in a bath with his favourite courtesan, Jade (Tien Hsin), we've got the buffoonish Imperial agents (who'd rather play mahjong), we've got the cowardly patricians, and for action fans, we've got the finest action choreographers in the world delivering outrageous set-pieces.

Tony Ching Siu-tung, remember, is as happy to oversee action scenes which're humorous and OTT as well as action sequences which're serious and OTT. Ching has choreographed *lots* of comedy films (the most well-known, at an international level, are the Stephen Chow comedies like Jackie Chan's *City Hunter, Royal Tramp* and *Shaolin Soccer*). And many of the hyphenated films are half comedies: *A Chinese Ghost Story* is comedy-horror, the *Swordsman* is action-comedy, etc.

But because *Hero, The House of Flying Daggers* and *The Curse of the Golden Flower* are 'serious', prestige pictures, they overshadow Tony Ching's work in action-comedies like *The Duel.* (Yet the action choreography is just as complicated for a comedy as for a drama, and sometimes even more dangerous, partly because comedies require exaggeration. Look at the wire-work in *Holy Weapon* or the *Royal Tramp* films).

Anyway, *The Duel* is a New Year's swordplay comedy, and Nick Cheung steals the show with his playing-to-the-gods turn as the pervy, exasperated Imperial agent, Dragon 9. (Cheung is dressed in dreads and

---

14 The two Wongs are perhaps the true stars of *The Duel* – the script is an elegant and genuinely funny riff thru martial arts literature.

round sunglasses – yes, *The Duel* riffs on *The Matrix* of the year before, when Hollywood ripped off Hong Kong action cinema. I mean, *ahem*, not 'ripped off', but when Hollywood cleverly hired Yuen Woo-ping and his team to spice up a lame sci-fi thriller with Yuen's state-of-the-art action). Hong Kong continued to milk the *Matrix* motherlode, with Ching Siu-tung supervising the action on *Shaolin Soccer* and *Invincible*, among others.

Canto-pop star Andy Lau smoulders with those famous cheekbones as Swordsman Yip; the equally lovely Ekin Cheng smoulders equally hotly as the silent, withdrawn Swordsman Snow; Zhao Wei is a delight as the naïve, perky, meddlesome Princess Phoenix (she became a favourite with Tsui Hark, and a big star); and the two women in the lives of Snow and Dragon 9, Jade and Ye Ziqing, are winningly played by Tien Hsin and Kristy Yeung.

Halfway thru, *The Duel* reduces the comedy in favour of intrigue and drama at the Imperial court.[15] With Snow absent for much of the time, the emphasis is on Princess Phoenix and Dragon 9. The plot moves into murder mystery territory, as the duo try to discover who's behind the series of deaths surrounding Swordsman Yip.

Tony Ching Siu-tung delivers most of the well-known set-pieces of his action choreographic art: giant, practical gags involving things blowing up, falling apart and collapsing; gloriously flamboyant swordplay (combined with vfx); endlessly inventive ways of using weapons; puppeteered object gags; the descending circle of warriors (used here for Swordsman Yip's 'heavenly fairy' martial arts); and of course characters flying everywhere in space.

The classic, Hong Kong cinematography (heightened colours, nights bluer than the sea, rapidly mobile camerawork), is also in the Chingian style. (However, you can see the filmmakers struggling with the low Winter sun in the exteriors filmed in the Chinese capital.[16] Not many hours of light a day, so filming is pushed into twilight and re-lit to match).

---

15 In fact, act three (of four acts) looks like the script was revised to accommodate the tight schedule, and the production was scaled down. Thus, the action scenes are far fewer, and many scenes comprise two actors talking in a room.
16 It was very cold – minus 13. So no need for fake snow.

18

SHAOLIN SOCCER

Siu Lam

INTRO.

Tony Ching said he didn't know much about soccer. But *Shaolin Soccer* was good for Ching – he won a Golden Horse for his action choreography (the film received many other awards, including from the Hong Kong Film Awards – best film, best director, best actor, best supporting actor, best sound, and best vfx). *Shaolin Soccer* was thus one of the big successes of Ching's amazing career.

Shaolin Soccer (*Siu Lam* in Cantonese, *Shàolín Zúqiú* in Mandarin) was produced by Universe Entertainment and Star Overseas, prod. by Yeung Kwok-Fai, wr. by Tsang Kan-cheung, Steven Fung Ming-hang, Lo Mei, Andrew Fung Chih-chiang and Stephen Chow Sing-chi , co-directed by Lee Lik-chi and Chow, with music by Lowell Lo and Raymond Wong, DPs: Kwen Pak-Huen and Kwong Ting-wo, editing by Kai Kit-Wai, costumes by Choi Yim-man, and action direction by Tony Ching. Released: July 12, 2001. 112 mins.

In the cast were Stephen Chow Sing-chi, Ng Man-tat, Zhao Wei, Patrick Tse, Vincent Kok, Wong Yat-fei and Danny Chan Kwok-kwan.

In Hong Kong, *Shaolin Soccer* was a mega-hit, grossing more than 60 million at the box office Hong Kong dollars (= US $7.8m). For a movie that cost some US $10 million, and grossed US $42 million around the world, this was amazing business.[17]

Shaolin Soccer was one of those few Asian movies that enjoyed a wide release in the Western world (I saw it at my local cinema). Even if

---

[17] *Shaolin Soccer*'s success would mean immediate cash-ins and rip-offs, but two factors made that more challenging than usual: the intricate visual effects, and the high budget.

Western audiences had no idea who Stephen Chow was, they knew soccer, and they knew *kung fu*.

STEPHEN CHOW.

Shaolin Soccer was another comedy which put together sport and *kung fu*, in this case, football and martial arts. Beyond that, *Shaolin Soccer* is a Stephen Chow Sing-chi movie – that's all you need to know: it's a Stephen Chow comedy. A superstar in Asia, Chow Sing-chi is a nobody in the West: like too many other Chinese stars, Chow simply hasn't made much impact on Western pop culture.

At 39, Chow Sing-chi was far too old for his role in *Shaolin Soccer*, but, somehow, Chow, a tiny, skinny figure, manages to get away with it (similarly, he had played a schoolboy in *Fight Back To School*[18]). And the audience accepts it, too – because it's Stephen Chow. A comedy star who generates a lot of good will in an audience will be indulged (as with Charlie Chaplin, Bob Hope, the Marx Brothers, etc).

With *Shaolin Soccer*, Stephen Chow moved into film direction and production; his career shifted towards fewer projects, which tended to be bigger budget, prestige productions. Chow stepped back too from appearing in 100s of movies per year of the early-to-mid Nineties.

VISUAL EFFECTS.

The concept of mixing sport and martial arts within a comical context was a strong hook or gimmick for *Shaolin Soccer*. Added to the mix was an extensive use of visual effects[19] – that is, effects added in post-production, not in front of the camera (the usual method in Hong Kong and Chinese cinema). Ken Law and Ronald To were the vfx supervisors.

Yes, for *Shaolin Soccer*, a large proportion of the budget went on visual effects. The most noticeable visual effects in *Shaolin Soccer* included digital animation (basically cartoons, but in a photo-realistic style), digital doubles for human characters, and digital props and environments.

Shaolin Soccer is also full of 'invisible' vfx, such as the removal of wires, rigs, supports, buildings, and crew members. These are the effects that seldom receive attention from film-goers, but for movie-makers they are perhaps even more valuable than the eye candy of animated monsters or faces, which attract the attention.

Shaolin Soccer took a slapstick, knockabout approach to the comedy and to the visual effects. Movements were exaggerated in the squash-

18 Chow required a lot of make-up, however.
19 Centro Digital Pictures was among the vfx houses working on *Shaolin Soccer*.

and-stretch manner of traditional animation. Characters were flung about like dolls. Thus, the visual effects didn't need to be perfectly photo-realistic, in the Western/ Hollywood manner, because with comedy you get a lot more lee-way. In a comedy, you can have silly sets – and cheesy effects.

The digital animation included familiar additions in the traditional, Chinese manner to the *kung fu* moves of the Shaolin Soccer Team – tigers, occasional demons, walls of flame, and wind and lightning for the *tai chi* moves.

SCRIPT AND STRUCTURE.

Shaolin Soccer is an underdog comedy, a losers comedy – all of the young charas are failures, many of them on the edges of society, with no wealth or social agency. So it's a self-empowerment comedy, a you-can-do-it comedy. It's striking that most of the characters in *Shaolin Soccer* are poor, scrabbling for survival, living in lean-to shelters, and doing the crummiest of jobs (cleaning restrooms).

The core relationship in *Shaolin Soccer* was between Sing (Chow) and Golden Leg Fung, the coach (Ng – Chow and Ng have often been paired in movies). Patrick Tse played Hung, the arrogant, cool villain, and Zhao Wei was the scarred girlfriend of the hero, Mui.

Among the secondary characters, Wong Yat-fei was great as the hapless, useless Iron Head,[20] and Cecilia Cheung and Karen Mok made an appealing pair of rival *kung fu* players, dressing up as boys with whiskers (from Team Dragon).

Structurally and generically, *Shaolin Soccer* follows the familiar pattern of the sports genre and of comedies in the sports genre. It has the team coach with issues, the utterly useless team that can't possibly succeed, the numerous training sessions, the big competition, the fierce rivalry, and the over-riding aspirations to overcome against all odds.

Shaolin Soccer is composed in three acts, although, running at 1h 52m, it's a little longer than many comedies (it's lengthier partly because it includes more straightish drama than a typical comedy film). The narrative structure of the 2001 picture follows the expected pattern of the genre (this is a formulaic film, as far as films can follow a 'formula' – some critics don't believe any film can be formulaized). Anyway, *Shaolin Soccer* is a classically structured script. For instance, there are climaxes that close each act (the memorable bust-up between the Shaolin Soccer team and the local gang ends act two, for example).

The finale of *Shaolin Soccer*, set at the Chinese Football open cut

20 Well, all of the Shaolin Soccer team were hapless and useless.

championship, had the Shaolin Soccer Team battling it out with Team Evil, managed by the villain of *Shaolin Soccer*, Hung. The shifting power between the two teams followed the usual format of sports films, with our heroes, after a sound beating, emerging triumphant.

HUMOUR AND GAGS.

Much of the humour in *Shaolin Soccer* comes not from Stephen Chow Sing-chi but from the surrounding group of characters. This is often the case with a Chow comedy movie: it's the settings, the other characters, and the situations which do much of the dramatic (= comedic) work. *Shaolin Soccer*, as a Chow comedy movie, cleverly includes a range of characters that surround the hero, plus some cameos from well-known actors, and of course it's Chow that gets the girl (Mui – she's much younger (14 years), as usual in movies).

Some of the humour in *Shaolin Soccer* is crude, as often in a Hong Kong comical movie, so that in part *Shaolin Soccer* is like a 'gross-out' comedy. *Shaolin Soccer* takes an almost sadistic delight in portraying its characters as hopeless and unappealing as possible. Some of the characters undergo extreme degradations (such as coach Golden Leg Fung or Iron Head).

But the overriding tone of *Shaolin Soccer* is sweet and goofy and cartoonish. A sports narrative is typically aspirational and romantic, poeticizing everything in its sights, including poverty and failure. Life is harsh in the Big, Bad City, but you can raise yourself out of the gutter with some hard work, a modicum of talent, some inspiring thoughts, some encouragement – oh, and more hard work.

One of the running gags in *Shaolin Soccer* is how to develop ways of making martial arts appealing to a young audience. Sing and his chums try *kung fu* merged with song and dance.[21]

The football field turning into a war zone is a great gag, with Stephen Chow's Sing turning into a soldier under heavy fire.

ACTION.

Tony Ching's stunt team were hired by *Shaolin Soccer* to recreate the exaggerated abilities of the *kung fu* soccer team. This meant that when a ball is kicked, it flies for miles, or moves with extreme force; it meant players flying up in the air, or executing impossible moves; it meant, in short, applying *wushu* and cartoon-like exaggerations to regular movements.

---

21 There's a funky dance number, choreographed by Danny Chan, at the steamed bun stand.

One of the challenges of *Shaolin Soccer* was working with a young cast, some of whom had never been involved with complex stunts or wire-work (or on such a big production). On screen, the results of the action choreography are winningly energetic – you can't resist some of the silly jokes. The dust-up that climaxes act two is an enjoyable send-up of typical martial arts movieness, with the Shaolin Soccer team performing spoofs of the clichés of swordplay and *kung fu* cinema.

Whether it's comedy or drama, for an action director the stunts still require enormous skill to pull off (and many takes). Comedy can be just as dangerous as drama (sometimes more so). Configuring the stunts for the post-production visual effects and digital animation that *Shaolin Soccer* deployed in spades was an added challenge. But, as we know, Tony Ching was using intricate cinematic effects from early in his career. After you've produced movies such as the *Chinese Ghost Story* and the *Swordsman* series, which are fiendishly complicated, you can take on pretty much anything.

'GIRLFRIEND OF THE HERO'.

The only significant female chara in *Shaolin Soccer* is played by Zhao Wei. Zhao (a.k.a. Vicky Zhao) was born in 1976; she is one of China's mega-stars (one of four renowned female stars in China – Zhang Ziyi, Xu Jinglei, and Zhou Xun are the others), appearing in movies such as *Painted Skin, Mulan, The Banquet, Suzhou River, Balzac and the Little Chinese Seamstress, The Emperor and the Assassin, Red Cliff,* and many hit TV shows. Zhao is known for her philanthropic work, and has also directed movies. Zhao is a favourite with Tsui Hark (she appeared in *Flying Swords of Dragon Gate* and *All About Women*).

In *Shaolin Soccer*, Zhao Wei's celebrated pixie-ish beauty is undercut with a ridiculously ugly make-up (the casting supercedes the make-up, however – we know that underneath the pustules and greasy fringe lies Zhao's wide-eyed radiance). Zhao's role is the usual 'girlfriend of the hero', this time given an extreme characterization: not only shy and quiet and misunderstood and anxious but incredibly ugly, too.

The romantic subplot is undercut several times in *Shaolin Soccer*. For ex, Sing and Mui don't form a romantic couple, and the expected kiss doesn't occur. Instead, Sing announces that they'll be friends forever (however, Mui is more inclined to take their relationship further).[22]

Meanwhile, the shy, timid personality of Mui, hiding behind the curtain of a fringe, is the subject of a running gag about changing her appearance.

[22] In the *Time* magazine billboard, however, shown at the very end, it seems that they are a couple.

First, she turns up as a caricature of feminine beauty, with 1980s shoulder pads and garish make-up (courtesy of what seems to be a tranny beautician). In the finale, Mui pops up again, this time bald like an alien (at least this silly gag allowed us to get a glimpse of the famous Zhao Wei peepers).

If the romantic subplot ends unresolved (Sing seems to care more about footie than girls), *Shaolin Soccer* does at least allow Mui to perform the role of the substitute who Saves The Game. (And Mui also unleashes a memorable *tai chi* version of soccer, with the sort of control of energy and the natural elements that we saw Jet Li perform in *Tai Chi Master*, 1993).

19

INVINCIBLE

Invincible (2001)[23] was a feature-length pilot film for a television series (for T.B.S.). The writers were Carey Hayes and Chad Hayes (written by credit) and Michael Brandt, Derek Haas, and Jeffrey Levy (teleplay credit). Steven Chasman, Janine Coughlin and Jim Lemley (producers), Bruce Davey, Mel Gibson, Jet Li, and John Morayniss (exec. prods.), plus four supervising/ line/ assoc. producers. Jefrey Levy (dir.), John McCarthy Photek (m.), John Stokes (DP), Keith Salmon (ed.), Michelle McGahey (prod. des.), Penny Ellers and Faith Martin (casting), Marta McElroy (set dec.), Chris Batson (art dir.), Noreen Landry and Terry Ryan (costumes), Pete Kneser (sound des.), and Chris Anderson (stunt co-ordinator). Released Nov 18, 2001. 87 minutes.

In the cast were Billy Zane, Byron Mann, Stacy Oversier, Tory Kittles, Dominic Purcell, Michelle Comerford, David Field and Simone McAullay.

Invincible looks as if a TV executive, puffing on a cigar in an office in L.A.'s Century City or Midtown Manhattan, announced to an assembly of filmmakers:

> I wanna produce a TV series that looks as cool as *The Matrix* but for a fraction of the price [*names an unrealistic low figure per episode*], ready for this air-date [*gives a too-soon date*], and within this time frame [*announces an impossible-to-achieve schedule*].

Yes, *Invincible* is certainly a *Matrix*-clone in part: flashy visuals, shiny, black clothing, cool, bald, monk-like teachers, Hong Kong action, a Save-The-World plot, cardboard heroes vs. villains, and cereal packet moralizing.

---

23 Werner Herzog also had a movie released in 2001 titled *Invincible*. Actually, it's one of those vaguely cool titles that's been used elsewhere.

So in *Invincible*, Billy Zane (the cad in *Titanic*), plays Os (as in 'Oz'? Or 'O.S.' = 'Operating System'?), a bald martial arts master (and former 'shadow-man') whose job seems to be trying to look cool. He's got the dark glasses, the black clothing, and the smooth, enigmatic demeanour of a chara in a typical Hollywood, hi-tech thriller.

The background plot in *Invincible* is easy to understand: Save The World. The MacGuffin is a set of ancient tablets with mysterious powers. Os brings together a team of four people (representing the four elements) to achieve the world-saving.

If Jet Li was involved (as executive producer), it suggests that he had considered appearing in the project (presumably as the Zen Buddhist-cool leader of the heroes, Os).

✳

Tony Ching Siu-tung was hired as the action director. The DVD notes relate that Ching put the cast into a two-week martial arts training programme (only a couple of the performers had dabbled in martial arts).[24] Similar training regimes had been run for Western/ American actors on productions like *The Matrix* and *Charlie's Angels*.

Unfortunately, if you are looking for some fireworks in the action choreography from Tony Ching Siu-tung and his team, you will be very disappointed. There *is* some action,[25] but it's over too quickly and awkwardly edited. And the whole middle act of *Invincible* comprises a tiresome lecture by Billy Zane about love (yes, folks, *loooove*!).

From the perspective of a study of Tony Ching Siu-tung's cinema, *Invincible* is a crude and disappointing venture: but let's remember that Ching was brought in to direct the action – he didn't originate the production, or co-write it, or cast it, and he wasn't the overall director. It seems, too, that Ching wasn't involved with the editing, which fiddles around with the action choreography too much, giving it video game sound effects and varied film speeds.

✳

In all, *Invincible* is a muddled mess of elements which don't gel and sure as hell don't compel.[26] *Invincible* is probably the sorriest project that Tony Ching Siu-tung has been involved in – and, sad to say, the two weeks that the actors undertook in the martial arts training camp were utterly wasted.

Add it all together, and you have:

• a boring concept, which is

24 And found they didn't know that much after all.
25 Os using the CDs from the disc jockey in the nightclub is pure Tony Ching Siu-tung – he loves props like that (such as the gold rings in *Royal Tramp 2*).
26 The response to *Invincible* seems to have been under-whelming (it didn't lead to a TV series. But then, 100s of pilots don't, either).

- over-written, too talky, and
- flabbily, messily conveyed by
- very dull, paper-thin characters, who're hampered by
- static staging and indifferent direction, which also adds
- gimmicks, effects and endless slo-mo, which results
- in a poor piece of television/ cinema.

All of those writers (five – count 'em!)... and all of those producers (eleven – count 'em!) couldn't do anything with this miserable garbage.

⁎

On the downside, the set-up in *Invincible* is muffed – despite the voiceover from Billy Zane, and the montages of Discovery Channel images, the threat to Planet Earth isn't really laid out clearly. And nor is the back-story of the 'shadow-men' and their nefarious aims.

That doesn't matter too much – because this is very generic, predictable fare. I mean, it's North American television, right? Which means being able to pick up the plot every few minutes, or in between watching ten other channels at the same time, plus commercials, plus checking yoiur phone, etc.

Let's not skewer North American TV here – one of its great strengths is to deliver clear stories – which *Invincible* stumbles over. And to deliver compelling characters, which *Invincible* doesn't do. If *Invincible* is intended as a team show (which it is), it needs to have fascinating characterizations (which it doesn't).

Yes, the characterizations of the four humans – and Os, the leader – is way too ordinary to suggest the riches that might be enjoyed if this pilot TV movie was given the green light.

Also, *Invincible* is visually and editorially far too gimmicky – slow motion is everywhere (at different speeds), plus step-motion, plus other editing tricks which try to spice up the proceedings. And the dreaded whooshes that accompany every action.

All of which fragments the fight choreography into self-consciously flashy filmmaking, and subverts its impact and beauty. Tony Ching Siu-tung insists that you have to stay youthful and be contemporary to stay in the film business, but not like this.

From an action perspective, *Invincible* is too much of an uneasy and unsatisfying mix between West and East, between Hollywood and Hong Kong, between Asian mythology and action and American television æsthetics (recalling similar fare of this 2000-2001 period, such as *The One*, which starred Jet Li).

The dissatisfying fusion also applies to *Invincible* as a whole: it's an attempt at mixing Eastern and Western sensibilities in cinema and television.

※

The finale of *Invincible* is dreadfully disappointing: just when it should be ramping up to all-out action, it relies on scrimp-and-save measures all over the place. It's also spoilt by ridiculous shaky camerawork, neurotic editing, and those bleeding flashing lights. (Yes, there is a lightning storm during the finale – *duh!* – to justify light flashing outside, but in the arena where Slate (David Field) stages the opening of the vortex, there are swivelling spotlights and which resemble a nightclub. Why?)

The irritating editing, the stupid flashing lights, the shaky camera-work, and the incoherent flow of action make for a truly tatty finale.

For instance, the 'vortex' opens up. But what *is* this vortex? The floor of the warehouse cracks and a fissure opens up and of course white light streams out (thank you, Steven Spielberg, the man responsible for white light appearing in any movie where anything weird occurs). And that's it! It opens, Os and Slate fight, then... uh... err... umm...

Action-wise, the climax of *Invincible* is a textbook of what *not* to do: it looks as if the producers have demanded a Hong Kong action finale but they decided at the last minute that they won't pay for it, and they haven't accounted for it in the schedule. They are asking for a Big Action Scene which would take three weeks to shoot but they've only allocated two nights.

※

Invincible is hopelessly over-written, as if each of the many writers had a clause in their contract that guaranteed (on pain of death) that at least 2,000 words of their dialogue could reach the screen. So Os talks in voiceover. Then he talks some more. Then – how about this?! – he *repeats* what he's already said (just in case we don't get it), and then *repeats it again*.

My dear, dear filmmakers, there is *no time* in a 90-minute movie for dialogue to be repeated like this, and so often! Even crazier, Os is talking about – guess what?! – love. Yes, *lerrrve*. According to Mr Slaphead, love is your greatest weapon, love can defeat any enemy, and all is good in the universe because of love.

So, yeah, *right* – Billy Zane is also <u>Lord Buddha</u> on top of everything else! – preaching *Fire Sermons* about love and compassion! Maybe coming from Jet Li in a far, far better movie, it might sneak by us without inducing mass-vomiting. But not here, not in this movie. (*Invincible* commits the mistake that's everywhere in television: it *tells* us things, but doesn't *show* us. Os talks about love, but it's empty rhetoric because there's no attempt to dramatize anything).

Invincible is useful for revealing the limitations and idiocies of North American television (or of all television): because the script is over-written, and because the staging is so static, the show resorts to numerous post-production video effects: shots flash to white, or judder, or have selective focus and blurs added to them, etc.

All of this post-production trickery is applied to *Invincible* because the footage is *so boring.* Because Os is delivering his lectures on a bicycle riding around in that stupid shallow pool. Because the filmmakers can't think of any other ways in which spice up the proceedings. So they add video effects, and flashing lights on the edge of the pool,[27] and blurs, and flashes, and – of course, oh no – let's not forget that all-important televisual effect: slow motion.

Thus, to counter a low budget, or to achieve a *Matrix*-like (actually Japanese animation-like) coolness, *Invincible* employs a lot of cheap effects in the editing (they probably utilized every video effect in the library of the digital editing software they were using).

Actually, *Invincible* looks a bit like a kid trying out a computer package like Photoshop or Final Cut Pro for the first time – you know, when kids try all of the gimmicky effects which nobody actually, seriously uses (but which computer software designers always insert into software, so they can brag 'comes with 1,000 video effects!').

On a minor note, the look of *Invincible* is horrible: production design (Michelle McGahey), set dec. (Marta McElroy), art dir. (Chris Batson), and the costumes are ugly (Noreen Landry and Terry Ryan). The sets look like very minimally re-dressed warehouses, and those shiny suits and jackets are just vile.

Indeed, *Invincible* looks like the budget was reduced during preproduction by hundreds of thousands of dollars, with the team having to scurry about desperately, trying to make a budget of 75 cents look like $100 million.

---

27 Why the hell does the hero have banks of flashing lights round his pool?

Future Cops (1993).

The Stuntwoman (1996).

Warriors of Virtue (1997).

The Duel (2000).

Shaolin Soccer (2001).

Invincible (2001)

20

SPIDER-MAN

Spider-man (Sam Raimi, 2002) was an important franchise for Sony/ Columbia – they wanted a blockbuster superhero franchise of their own which could rival Warner Bros.' *Batman* series in terms of generating $$$ and selling merchandizing. The result was *Spider-man*, based on the Stan Lee/ Steve Ditko/ Marvel Comics superhero of the early 1960s (Sony/ Columbia even employed some of the same personnel as *Batman*, such as composer Danny Elfman, who delivered a fantastic score).

Starring Tobey Maguire,[1] Kirsten Dunst, Jess Franco and Willem Dafoe, with a script by David Koepp and production by Laura Ziskin and Ian Bryce for Marvel/ Columbia/ Laura Ziskin Prods., *Spider-man* was released on May 3, 2002. 121 mins.

The journey of *Spider-man* to the screen was very long and involved writers and producers coming and going, and the inevitable legal battles (the property passed from Canon Films to Carolco, with James Cameron attached, then to M.G.M. in 1996, back to Marvel in 1998, who sold it to Sony in 1999). For Sony/ Columbia, the wrangling was protracted but it was worth it in the end.

Sony/ Columbia got what they wanted – a hit movie and the start of an important franchise. The 2002 led to sequels, of course – the first (2004) was a fantastic romp (with Doctor Octopus (Alfred Molina) as the super-villain), but the second sequel (2007) was a bloated disaster. Apart from the enormous cost of *Spider-man 3* (at least $270 million and possibly up to $350 million!), it was a troubled production which was subject to reworking (and the death of a construction worker). The *Spider-man* series went seriously off the rails with the third installment. (The next sequel was

---

1 The actors were too old to play teens, but that's typical. You try finding real teenagers who can play the levels of drama required on the roles – and have some star quality.

also problematic, and was cancelled).

Spider-man 1 took $403.7 million at the domestic box office, and $821 million globally, making it the biggest movie that Tony Ching had been associated with. Shooting ran from Aug 1 - Dec 6, 2001 (112 days). The production budget was $139 million. There was strong competition in the same blockbuster movie arena for *Spider-man* in 2002, including: *The Lord of the Rings: The Two Towers, Harry Potter and the Chamber of Secrets* and *Star Wars: Attack of the Clones.*

From its outstanding opening credits sequence (animated web and spidery forms backed by one of Danny Elfman's bold musical cues), *Spider-man* established itself as a solid, entertaining spin on the superhero movie model. It's a cracking movie with only a few missteps.

Spider-man was a mega-budget blockbuster movie which got the tone and the attitude just right – earnest but also comical, action-packed but with dramatic subplots and issues, fantastical but also grounded in scenes of high school and home.

The story of *Spider-man* charted Peter Parker's rise as a superhero and his battles with villains and rivals – i.e., it's the usual superhero outing. Along the way, the 2002 movie had time for popping fun at the whole superhero concept and how ridiculous it was (for example, with Parker struggling to fashion his own Spider-suit).

Thus, the most appealing parts of the *Spider-man* movie were the early scenes: Peter Parker was depicted as the high school loser, the smart but lame geek who wears glasses and wanders about taking photographs (so he's also a wannabe photographer – or film director). He looks longingly at M.J. from afar (she already has a boyfriend and is way out of his league, and doesn't consider him as boyfriend material), suffers being the class punchbag, and generally hasn't got a clue. Tobey Maguire plays this aspect of Parker brilliantly, with a blank, bug-eyed bemusement at everything. Maguire convinces as a youth who's completely clueless about girls, and has no idea what to say to M.J. For a big, superhero movie, there's a pleasing amount of screen-time allotted to the romantic sub-plot, to the romantic triangle between Parker, M.J. and his friend Harry.

Spider-man is a superhero movie, but it does have time to portray some of the problems of being young – M.J.'s troubled home life, for example, and Harry Osborn's uneasy relationship with his over-achieving, domineering father, are contrasted with Peter Parker's loving home with his Aunt and Uncle.

Spider-man was released in the wake of the 9/11 terrorist attacks.

Altho' they are not mentioned directly in the movie, there is famous line of dialogue, which Uncle Ben (Cliff Robertson) tells Parker: 'with great power comes great responsibility'. The line is universal (or vague) enough to apply to any superhero scenario, but it has an enhanced meaning after 9/11.

The look of *Spider-man* is a bright, colourful comicbook: it's a bold, muscular movie, confident enough to forget dialogue and dot-to-dot storytelling, and allow for several montages. Some of these portray Parker's evolving superhero powers. One montage sees him sketching out ideas for a good superhero costume. *Spider-man's* montages are enhanced greatly by one of the stars of recent, Hollywood scoring, Danny Elfman; he provides his customary choral cues that draw on the scores of Hollywood movies of the 1950s. Part-Hollywood cheese, part-religious movie choral warbling, part-B-movie sci-fi, and always delightfully self-conscious, Elfman's *Spider-man* score is brilliant at maintaining a balance between being too earnest and ironic, between playing it straight and playing it as a self-aware commentary, between underscoring the drama and action straight, and gently sending it up. Elfman's scores are always doing several things at the same time. And Elfman certainly earned his high fee ($2 million) for the score of *Spider-man* : the music is *really* helping to sell the scenes, and it definitely enhances the excitement.2

★

Spider-man is stuffed with action sequences, and demanded a huge stunt team. One of the big set-pieces is the Times Square festival, where dignitaries watch a procession from a balcony. It's Oscorp's version of a Macy's Day Parade (a similar sene was portrayed in *Batman*, 1989). This is where the Green Goblin makes his first appearance to the general public, flying in to throw pumpkin bombs at the board members at Oscorp who ousted his other self, Osbourn, from his own company. A very complicated sequence like the Times Square set-piece in *Spider-man* demonstrates why blockbuster productions such as this cost millions of dollars.

As to the contribution of our man Tony Ching: the action sequences required wire-work to depict the aerial acrobatics of Spider-man and his antagonist, the Green Goblin (along with puppeteering of parts of the sets and props). The early 2000s was a period when Hollywood cinema was starting to hire Hong Kong action directors more often (*Charlie's Angels*, *The Matrix*, *The Three Musketeers*, etc): Ching was part of that trend, though he did less than contemporaries of his such as Yuen Woo-ping.

The scenes where the Green Goblin is flying his glider low above the

---

2 The music and composer costs amounted to $5m.

ground and chasing Spider-man look like the work of Tony Ching; and the cable-work that helps to stage the scene with the crumbling balcony in Times Square also looks like Ching.

The finale of *Spider-man* is a highly artificial game of moral choices, when the Green Goblin captures both M.J. and a cable car of children at the Roosevelt Island Tram. The Goblin forces Spider-man to choose between his dream girl and some kids. Of course, being a superhero, Spider-man saves both. A nice touch has the citizens of Noo Yoik adding their bit, throwing refuse (and insults) at the Green Goblin.

Spider-man is surprisingly melodramatic and melancholy for a popcorn superhero movie: for exmaple, two boys lose their fathers (Uncle Ben is a father figure to Peter Parker); there are funeral scenes; and Parker at the end rejects the girl of his dreams fin favour of a career as a superhero protecting the Great American Dream. The movie explores the Sins of the Fathers yet agian, with the younger generation at odds with the older generation (which's actually one of the primary themes of Chinese movies). Osborn embodies the Sins of the Fathers *par excellence* – in his relationship with Parker as well as his own son Harry. But Parker rejects Osborn, too – and he pursues a path of righteousness.

21

HERO

Yingxiong

THE PRODUCTION.

Hero[3] (2002, Mandarin: *Yingxiong;* Cantonese: *Jing Hung*) was produced by China Film Co-Production Corporation/ Elite Group Enterprises/ Zhang Yimou Studio/ Metropole Organisation/ Miramax Films/ Beijing New Picture Film. The producers were: Shoufang Dou and Weiping Zhang (executive producers), Bill Kong, Sook Yhun and Zhang Yimou (producers), Philip Lee (line producer) and Zhenyan Zhang (assoc. producer). The script was by Feng Li, Zhang Yimou and Bin Wang. Costumes by Emi Wada and Huang Bao-Rong, hair by Tam Ying-Kwan and Chau Siu-Mui, make-up by Yang Shu-Dong, Ji Wei-Hua, Yang Xiao-Hai and Kwan Lee-Na, prod. des. by Tingxiao Huo and Zhenzhou Yi, action choreography by Ching Siu-tung, Li Cai and Stephen Tung Wei, sound by Tao Jing, editing by Angie Lam and Ru Zhai, DP: Chris Doyle, music: Tan Dun, with visual effects by Tweak Films, the Orphanage and Animal Logic. Category IIB. Released Oct 24, 2002. 99 minutes.[4]

Hero was a big hit in China and Hong Kong, and a hit too in the West. It achieved one of the healthiest theatrical grosses for a foreign language film around the world: $177 million (in US dollars). The film received many awards and nominations, including the Golden Rooster, 100 Flowers and Berlin Film Festival. (The Chinese government supported the movie by suppressing rival films from theatres, encouraging *Hero* to become the most successful film in Mandarin to date).

---

3 *Hero* is a common title in movies, of course; half of swordplay movies might be subtitled *Hero*. There was a great Yuen Biao movie called *Hero* of 1997, for instance (helmed by Corey Yuen Kwai).
4 There are slightly longer cuts of *Hero* (some 8 mins extra), plus a restored version (of 2008).

Hero was released in the U.S.A. on Aug 27, 2004 (by Miramax). It was a big success, grossing $53 million. Unusually, it was released uncut (Miramax and subsidiaries such as Dimension are notorious for altering cuts, music, dialogue, etc, sometimes terribly).

The production was based at the Hengdian World Studios[5] in Dongyang, also seen in *The Forbidden Kingdom* and *Young Detective Dee: Rise of the Sea Dragon* (and many other productions). *Hero* certainly got its money's worth, exploiting Hengdian to the max – especially for the grandeur of Imperial scenery (the Imperial Palace, built in the Qin and Han style, is one of the chief areas of Hengdian World Studios).

Before this, filmmakers often went to film in Beijing – where audiences saw the same courtyards, archways, staircases, statuary, etc, as other Chinese, historical pictures. The beauty of Hengdian World Studios was that it was a purpose-built film studio (founded in the 1990s), which could be redressed more extensively than the historical sites in China's capital. Other locations used in *Hero* included: Dunhuang, Gansu; Hangzhou, Zhejiang; Jiu-zhaigou, Sichuan; and Inner Mongolia.

Produced in the Western world, a film as prestigous as *Hero* would be a two-hour twenty-minute movie (or longer). Produced in China, it comes in at a trim 99 minutes, like most Hong Kong action movies (this is one of their great appeals). There are some additional scenes (running to some 8 minutes, included on the home releases).

❅

Hero is one my contenders for the title of Best Martial Arts Movie Ever, or Best Swordplay Movie Ever. It's one of those seemingly miraculous movies where everything works, from the concept thru the script and casting to the performances, the technical elements, the music, you name it.

Hero is a top quality production across the board: top flight cast, celebrated director, incredible action director, fantastic composer (Tan Dun), great DP (Chris Doyle), veteran editor (Angie Lam),[6] and so on and on.

For some Western critics, *Hero* was put into the same category as *Crouching Tiger, Hidden Dragon*, one of the few Chinese, martial arts movies to make a significant impression upon Occidental audiences. *Hero* has numerous affinities with *Crouching Tiger, Hidden Dragon,* from some of the same cast (Zhang Ziyi), the same composer (Tan Dun), to the same sort of material (swordplay in the *jiangzhu*), the same totems (swords), and the same character types. (However, *Hero* had been in development

---

5 Dubbed 'Chinawood'.
6 Angie Lam has cut numerous Hong Kong pics, including many for Tsui Hark.

before *Crouching Tiger* was filmed, let alone released).

Hero was one of a group of films which were essentially Hong Kong action movies but with new additions to make them appealing to both a Mainland Chinese audience, and the international market: big stars; a bigger budget; a straightforward story (tho' not told in a straightforward manner); a Hong Kong and Mainland Chinese crew; filming in Mainland China; filming in Mandarin; and computer-aided visual effects.

Crouching Tiger, Hidden Dragon was among the most well-known of movies of this type to cross over into Western markets, but there were many others: *The Storm Riders*, the *Zu: Warriors From the Magic Mountain* remake, *Shaolin Soccer* and *Kung Fu Hustle*.

Thus, *Hero* was very much a Hong Kong, swordplay flick but with more money to spend, more extras, some digital visual effects, and some impressive location shooting (however, Hong Kong movies had been filming in Mainland China for decades. Swordplay movies made in Hong Kong went to China for deserts and mountains, exotic locations that aren't available in the New Territories – if there was time and money available, of course. In the days of Shaw Brothers, when movies were being churned out at a rapid rate, there was no time for lengthy treks in the desert).

Certainly, all of the cast and the crew had been involved with this sort of movie before (some of them, like Ching Siu-tung, many, many times). But that helped the film enormously: you can make a film like this only if you have veteran filmmakers who *really* know what they're doing.

Only Jet Li and Donnie Yen among the main cast were martial artists. the rest of the principal actors – Zhang Ziyi, Tony Leung Chiu-wai.*/*, Maggie Cheung Man-yuk *et al* – were not *kung fu* experts. But Chinese action choreographers can make them all look amazing in the action scenes (Ching Siu-tung had worked with most of the actors and many of the crew before).

All of the six principal actors are terrific in *Hero*, but Jet Li is probably the stand-out performance. He is magnificent, a genuine superstar.

To bump up the female presence in what would historically have been a thoroughly manly story, *Hero* includes two radiant stars of Chinese cinema, Maggie Cheung Man-yuk and Zhang Ziyi (one of director Zhang Yimou's protegés). Both are portrayed, like the other principals, as warriors of superhero abilities.

Zhang Ziyi (b. 1979, Beijing), known as the 'Yimou Girl', for her association with director Zhang Yimou, was one of the rising stars of Asian cinema at the time – making her name in the West with *Crouching Tiger, Hidden Dragon,* and continuing with historical epics such as *The Legend of*

Zu in 2001, *Hero* in 2002, *Memoirs of a Geisha* and *Princess Raccoon* in 2005, and *The Banquet* in 2006, plus *Rush Hour 2* in 2001.

Hero explores a historical period and political moment which has been seen many times in Chinese and Hong Kong television and movies: it's the Warring States era, when China was split into rival factions and clans, where warlords clashed with each other, vying for supremacy. The leader of Qin has a vision of uniting all of the states, to become a vast empire (with himself, of course, as Top Dog). Qin, the First Emperor of China, has been portrayed many times in Chinese cinema – and in several movies since *Hero*.

King Qin was born in 259 B.C. as Zheng (meaning 'Correct'/ 'Upright'), during the Warring States period (475-221 B.C.); he became King Zheng of Qin at 13, following his father's (King Zuang Xiang) death in 246 B.C.; he became Emperor in 221 B.C. until his death in 210 B.C.; he had more than 20 children. The assassination attempt on King Qin occurred in 227 B.C.

In 221 B.C., Qin became 'Qin Shihuangdi', the 'First August Emperor': aided by his legalist minister, Li Si, he devoured his enemies 'like a silkworm devours a mulberry leaf'. Qin unified the Warring States into an Empire, and launched initiatives such as road building, expanding the Great Wall, standardizing weights, measurements and currency, and a single written script (forming the basis of 'all future developments in writing', as Ann Paludan put it [20]). Qin's palace in the movie *Hero* is enormous – but his A-fang Palace really was colossal. Qin's is famous for his lavish tomb and the Terracotta Army of 7,000 figures (discovered in Xian in 1974).

Qin Shihuangdi also exhibited many traits which were taken up by cinema's portrayal of Chinese Emperors: he was very superstitious, terrified of death, sought immortality (he had a spectacular tomb built), and feared assassination (there were several attempts on his life – he slept in a different place each night, and travelled in two carriages so attackers wouldn't know which one). Some of King Qin's controversial acts included the Burning of the Books, and the ruthless suppression of dissenters (460 victims were buried alive during the Burning of the Books episode).

Chinese and Asian audiences would be familiar with the story, set in Ancient China, but as this movie was aimed at an international audience too, there was some scene-setting at the beginning.

For Zhang Yimou, *Hero* was about heroes – the concept of a hero, the age of chivalry, of giving yourself up to a bigger cause. Hence there weren't giant battles (except one), and the focus was on the well-known philo-sophical attributes of *wuxia pian*.

Hero was criticized for its apparent right-wing political message, which some critics saw as aligned with the government of the People's Republic of China. Actually, pretty much *all* swordplay movies, *all* martial arts movies, *all* kung fu movies and even *all* action-adventure movies – from the West or the East – promote a right-wing, conservative, traditional ideology and politics.

Hero perhaps slightly more obviously enshrines right-wing ideology[7] with its portrait of King Qin who went on to unite Ancient China (and how the assassins, including Nameless Warrior, decide that maybe King Qin is right in the end, and decline to kill him).

Director Zhang Yimou maintained that *Hero* wasn't intended to carry any political messages – but a story about assassination attempts on a future Emperor is automatically explicitly political. Zhang did relate *Hero* to a post-9/11 political climate, however (the film was in production not long after 9.11.2001).

HERO AND TONY CHING.

Hero features numerous elements from the action cinema of Ching Siu-tung – like many of Ching's films as director, it's really a compendium of all of his favourite moves, shapes, gestures and sequences. The flowing, graceful choreography, the frozen poses, the loose, flapping clothing, the extensive wire-work, the slow motion, the use of vivid colour, the innovations of technology for weaponry, and the heightened, romantic stylizations – all these and more are central ingredients of the Chingian approach to cinema.

So many of the motifs of the later historical films directed by Zhang Yimou – *Hero, House of Flying Daggers*, etc – can be found in classics of the Hong Kong New Wave cinema such as *The Terracotta Warrior*, the *Swordsman* series, the *Once Upon a Time In China* series, etc. The floating leaves, the dripping water, the rainfall, the billowing hangings of white and red cloth, the slow motion, etc. Many of these visual elements were developed by Ching Siu-tung.

The invasion of King Qin's forces into Zhao boasts several distinctly Chingian motifs: one is the unusual methods of firing arrows – by having soldiers lie on their backs with their legs raised, holding the bows on the soles of their feet. That is a classic, Chingian invention – in *An Empress and the Warriors*, for instance, Ching had soldiers rapidly assuming a ramp-like formation, so they could topple the enemy's chariots.

Indeed, according to director/ producer Wong Jing, it was Tony Ching

---

[7] Some commentators drew attention to the pro-authority elements in *Hero* – in the end, it was all about worshipping the Emperor.

who really directed much of the three action films of Zhang Yimou:

> Take Zhang Yimou's last three action films [Wong said in 2007].
> Actually, he just sat there and Ching Siu-tung did everything. Zhang
> didn't put his brain on it. He did nothing on the set.[8]

Hero is a Zhang Yimou movie, for sure – he has co-writer, co-producer and director credits on it, and it's full of Zhang's distinctive approaches to movies (the stylizations of colour, the meticulous attention to detail, the lavish designs and costumes, the long lens photography,[9] the melo-dramatic performances, etc). But about the most memorable aspect of *Hero* – the action – comes very much from Ching Siu-tung (even tho' Ching was one of several action directors on the production (the other action choreographers were Li Cai and Stephen Tung Wei). Most movies of this scale require a few action directors, because there is so much to do. It's not only a question of organizing the principals, but also of training the extras).

There was a dispute between Tony Ching's team and the production, resulting in Ching's folk walking off the picture. A brief excerpt of Ching berating a production manager is seen in the *Hero* documentary. Apparently, things were smoothed over, and Ching and co. returned the next day. (This occurred during the filming of the lake duel, and also during the making of *Belly of the Beast*).

THE SET-UP AND THE SCRIPT.

The narrative set-up of *Hero* has Nameless Warrior arriving at King Qin's capital bringing the swords of Sky, Snow and Broken Sword with him, and claiming that he's killed them (each one is a famous warrior). After being strip-searched for hidden weapons, Nameless Warrior is admitted to the King's audience chamber for his rewards.

There are six main characters in *Hero*:

Nameless Warrior	Jet Li
Sky/ Long Sky	Donnie Yen
Snow/ Flying Snow	Maggie Cheung
Broken Sword	Tony Leung
Moon	Zhang Ziyi
Qin/ the King	Chen Daoming

---

8 Wong Jing, interview with Thomas Podvin, *Hong Kong Cinemagic*, 2007.
9 Some of the desert scenes look a little TV ad agency.

The narrative structure[10] of *Hero* is not 'simple' at all: it is a *rondo* format in part – A-B-A-C-A-D-A-E, etc, with the 'A' part comprising the conflabs between Nameless Warrior and King Qin in the present tense, and the back-stories and episodes as the new ingredients.[11] We keep returning to the palace scenes, to comment on the preceding episodes, to modify them.

However, after the account of Snow, Broken Sword and Nameless Warrior in Zhao, at the calligraphy school, King Qin accuses Nameless of lying, and it's revealed that some of the episodes didn't happen like that. Thus, *Hero* is in part a kind of storytelling contest.

The scenes with Nameless Warrior and King Qin are also part of an assassination plot. A clever device has King Qin allowing Nameless to approach him in stages. The closer Nameless gets, the better chance he'll have of nobbling King Qin with his lethal attack that works at ten paces. So it's also a game of chess, a battle of wits, as the men size each other up.

The scenes in the palace reception hall are essentially two people talking. Yes, it's two heads talking, the basic dramatic unit of all television and cinema – but it's in the grandest of settings. Most of the shots are big close-ups of Jet Li and Chen Daoming, with some variations. The battery of candles, the only thing lying between the assassin and the King, are employed as literal breathers for the pauses in the scene, when a draft blows them.

The characters in *Hero* repeatedly wound or kill each other: Snow attacks Broken Sword several times, and Nameless Warrior and Snow duel in the parade ground repeatedly. The first time that Snow attacks Broken Sword, in Nameless's invented story, it's in a fit of jealous rage; the second time, it's because Broken Sword refuses to go along with Nameless's plan. Each time, Snow immediately rushes to tend Broken Sword's wounds. In the present tense, during the finale, following Nameless's failure to dispatch King Qin, Snow kills Broken Sword for real.

Hero contains a good deal of narration – from Jet Li, and also from Chen Daoming (and some from Tony Leung); they narrate parts of the episodes, and provide links between the segments. The device is introduced early on, in the carriage carrying Nameless at top speed to Qin's kingdom (Jet Li speaks in his native Mandarin. It's good to hear Li, instead of a dubbed voice, which occurred thru much of his film career).

KING QIN.

Hero depicts a group of assassins who argue over the means and

10 *Hero* draws on the multiple level narrative structure of *Rashomon*.
11 Splitting the structure into self-contained episodes cleverly allows the film to stage each one with its own look and approach.

motives and goals of their work. The arguments concern three people in particular: Nameless Warrior, who hopes to vanquish King Qin (his family in Zhao was killed by King Qin's invasion); Snow, who is impressed by Nameless (and it takes a lot to impress Snow), goes along with his plans; and Broken Sword, who opposes both of them (with Moon as his passionate disciple). Initially, Sword too hoped to kill the soon-to-be-Emperor (his family was also from Zhao), but stops himself at the last moment.

Hero takes the group of assassins and links them to the wider, political context of Ancient China. The 2002 film aligns the audience with the small band of rebels who hope to overthrow a huge, oppressive regime (it's the familiar geopolitical background of the action-adventure film genre, and of many swordplay movies).

However, *Hero* doesn't depict the would-be Emperor Qin as a demonic, depraved, corrupt, violent and insane character, as many swordplay movies do. Hong Kong New Wave cinema of the early 1990s revelled in portraying Han/ Mandarin/ Imperial delegates and officials as psychotic eunuchs who aim to crush rebels mercilessly (as in *New Dragon Gate Inn* and the *Swordsman* series, for instance).

Rather, King Qin is seen as a suave, commanding, stern yet occasionally amiable personality, who listens carefully to Nameless Warrior's tales. He might be the C.E.O. of a conglomerate who's hearing out the sales pitch of an underling (or a studio boss considering the story pitch of a film producer).

This goes beyond the usual dramatic gesture of 'humanizing' the rival or the opponent (giving them some handicap or trauma which encourages the audience's sympathy) – King Qin is simply not portrayed as a villain in the first place. He comes across as a firm but reasonable man, making Nameless Warrior's aim of killing him seem misplaced (isn't Qin precisely the sort of firm but fair leader that a country in political turmoil needs? the movie asks).

STYLE.

Each of the episodes in *Hero* has its own visual and design theme: reds for the calligraphy school; rain and stone for the Chess Hall; Autumn leaves and trees for duel between Snow and Moon; blues for the Library demonstration of Nameless Warrior's powers and the Snow-Nameless duel; then white for the reworking of the same material; then green for the assassination bid on King Qin by Snow and Sky, and so on.

The use of colour across the three stories extending from the costumes by Huang Bao-Rong and Emi Wada[12] into the sets by Tingxiao Huo and Zhenzhou Yi, the props and so on, has a theatrical quality, the sort of self-conscious artifice found in musical movies (if Vincente Minnelli or Stanley Donen had directed a *wuxia pian*, it might look like *Hero*. M.G.M. musical movies were famous for taking a colour scheme from the costumes and accessories into the furniture, the walls, the decor, etc). As the stories progress, the colour stylizations continue, but move towards a more naturalistic approach (as we got closer to the truth).

The music, composed by Tan Dun, develops the approach of *Crouching Tiger, Hidden Dragon* (and makes much use of Itzhak Perlman playing the violin and fiddle). Percussion is a recurring motif, with drums pounding away during some of the action sequences. *Hero* is also notable for including some unusual solo voices (Faye Wong sang the theme song, composed by Zhang Yadong and Lin Xi).

SCENES AND ACTS.

The first Big Action Sequence in *Hero* (occurring around 10 mins into the film), is rightly between the two most notable martial artists among the principal cast – Jet Li and Donnie Yen (they had previously sparred in the stupendous finale of *Once Upon a Time In China 2*). It takes place at a Chess Hall in Zhao, where the *mise-en-scène* comprises stone and rain (stone walls and floors and constant, dripping water).

Here we have the first of several mini-lectures on swordsmanship in *Hero* – very familiar to Chinese and Asian audiences, but perhaps not so much to Western audiences (tho' there are equivalences with, for ex, the age of chivalry in mediæval pics, or with the codes of honour among cowboys in Westerns). Here, it's swordplay and music[13] – interweaving complex melodies and rhythms (it's Nameless Warrior who asks the musician (Shou Xin Wang) to continue to play the *guqin*, knowing that Sky enjoys music).[14]

The Li-Yen duel also introduced some of the visual devices early on that the 2002 film will employ later: slow motion (lots), wire-work (lots), visual effects (the drops of water controlled by energy), and cinematic stylizations (such as black-and-white photography).

The Nameless Warrior<->Sky duel is also an editor's piece, where veteran editor Angie Lam (along with Ru Zhai) explore ways of cutting back and forth between the warriors remembering parts of their fight – shown in black-and-white – and the present. *Hero* boldly states that we are already in an unusual cinematic realm: it's the first big fight of the film, but we slip

12 Wada has worked with Akira Kurosawa.
13 Jackie Chan often compares action cinema to dance choreography or jazz.
14 Played by Liu Li.

into a series of flashbacks (a kind of edited highlights of the duel). And this doesn't occur later, when the victor (Nameless Warrior) is remembering the duel, but right in the middle of it, with the two combatants standing in the rain with their eyes closed. (Later, Nameless explains that he didn't kill Sky – he wounded him with a near-fatal thrust).

Alas, following the remarkable duel with Jet Li in the Chess Room, Donnie Yen disappears from the movie, tho' his character – Sky – is mentioned often (and his totem, his sword (spear-head), is seen).

It might've made more sense to cast Donnie Yen as Broken Sword, as the character has many more martial arts scenes than Sky in *Hero*, but Yen, tho' brilliant, is not often cast as a romantic lead. Hence 'Little Tony' – Tony Leung – took that role.

Indeed, the subplot involving Sky recedes into the background as the movie progresses, and the focus is on the three assassins, the sidekick (Moon) and the Emperor.

❉

The second Big Action Sequence in *Hero* is set in, of all places, a calligraphy school. Here, in amongst art direction where everything is red, scarlet, crimson and 1,000 other shades of red, we're introduced to the charas of Flying Snow, Broken Sword and Moon. Before we get into the love triangle (which focusses on the bitter rivalry between an older woman and a younger woman over a man), there are disquisitions on the relations between swordplay and calligraphy (the sword and the brush). In the middle of the King Qin siege, for instance, we see Broken Sword manipulating a giant brush loaded with ink (it's red, of course), like a sword or spear. (This is the calligraphy which's hung up behind King Qin in his audience chamber).

Hero's calligraphy school is that familiar locale in Chinese, historical pictures: the self-enclosed, hierarchical institution, where the students are so devoted to the cause, they sit at their desks and continue to practise their art even when they're being bombarded by 10,000,000 arrows! Yes, *that's* dedication! *That's* what students should be doing! No slacking off – even in the midst of a lethal barrage!

The action sequence at the school is superbly handled – the practical effects of the arrows smacking into wood (and people) are marvellously achieved (w2ith echoes *Throne of Blood*, 1957). This is also when we see Maggie Cheung as Snow in action, using her long sleeves to deflect and gather the arrows. (One of her skills is to manipulate energy – used to great effect in her duel with Moon in the forest).

The calligraphy school introduces the first of the romantic tangles in

Hero: here's Tony Leung as the long-haired hunk Broken Sword, the cool, laid-back dude that the girls're fighting over; here's Maggie Cheung as the ice-cold warrior Flying Snow (no one, but no one, can out-pout and out-sulk Cheung! She is marvellous in this role, which cuts down dialogue and relies a good deal on looks and performance); and here's Zhang Ziyi, in a kind of development of her break-out role in *Crouching Tiger, Hidden Dragon*, as the too-beautiful, awkward and angry rival for Broken Sword's affection.

Nothing in the calligraphy school menagerie surprises us: *Hero* is not inventing new forms of storytelling, at least in terms of the character-izations and the relationships between the charas. We have seen this erotic triangle before, but the way that it's filmed is flamboyant and fun. (For instance, how the Steadicam camera careens off-kilter down the corridors to suggest the deranged mental states of the lovers). And altho' the narrative scenario is soapy, it's played by three terrific actors.

❀

As it continues into the middle act (*Hero* comprises three acts of the usual 25-30 minutes each), the complications include Broken Sword's opposition to Nameless Warrior's scheme, disagreements over who will receive the near-fatal blow (and so pretend to die, like Sky did), Moon's support of her master (Broken Sword), and so on.

Thus, in the repetitions of the Library scene, we have Moon attacking Nameless Warrior after Snow has stabbed Broken Sword (again), and in the repetitions of the scene in the parade ground, we have Nameless and Snow duelling each other (each time Nameless is victorious, as planned).

So that it seems as if everyone has fought everyone else. But not quite: the duel between Nameless Warrior and Broken Sword, which seems inevitable, doesn't occur. Instead, there's an argument in the desert (following the storming of the palace in King Qin by Broken Sword and Flying Snow, which climaxes act two). Broken Sword tries to persuade Nameless not to try to kill the King. Broken Sword could try to get his point across literally, by drawing his blade. In a movie genre where conflicts are resolved by duelling, it's notable that Nameless and Sword don't fight.

❀

Moon attacks Flying Snow in an Autumnal forest,[15] where Fall leaves are used for several impressive visual effects (some practical, some digital). The swirling leaves are a vivid manifestation of Snow's ability to control *chi*. Neither Cheung or Ziyi are professional martial artists, but once again the interweaving of the principals with doubles is seamless. The sequence is pure Tony Ching, too – the flowing movements, the slow motion, the attacks from above, the floating over long distances, etc.

15 The forest in Autumn extends the red colour scheme of the calligraphy school.

(In the making of documentary, you can see Ching Siu-tung in his usual place – operating the camera – and encouraging the performers. At one point in the production of *Hero*, Ching was summoned from Hong Kong to oversee the Fall forest duel between Snow and Moon. At short notice, and with no preparation, Ching arrived and got to work. But then, if anyone can orchestrate a grand, passionate duel between swordswomen at the drop of a hat, it's Tony Ching).

❊

So Flying Snow offers herself up willingly to undergo a near-death experience at the hands and sword of Nameless Warrior – Snow seems to possess a more hardened resolve than Broken Sword in this respect, and is constantly chiding him (and stabbing him!) for being weaker, as she sees it.

In one of the versions, Snow's seeming death has her placed on a bier in a lake, like Snow White in the glass coffin, while Sword and Nameless Warrior go through the motions of duelling. This is one of Ching Siu-tung's most extravagant action scenes, which draws on his work with the *Swordsman* series, where characters fly and run above water (as Jet Li does in *The Swordsman 2*, when he's drunkenly cavorting with Asia the Invincible).

Ching Siu-tung loves to stage warriors flying over *huge* distances thru the air, as here in the exquisite lake scene. Not a one step exaggerated slightly with wire-work, but long leaps. This is action choreography as a poetic dance, where it's all about the flowing movements, the rapid spins, the flapping clothing, the swords tapping the surface of the lake, and the camera angles looking up under the water. Drops of water are a recurring motif, along with swords and feet touching the lake. The banks of the lake're forested. It's action as a Chinese landscape painting (the visual approach flattens the perspectives to emulate landscape art of Ancient China, as if we're looking at an animated, Chinese scroll).

The stylization is extreme – the lake sequence is a good example of Ching Siu-tung's fundamentally romantic approach to cinema:

> I like beautiful, romantic things, and have an almost extreme and
> idealized sense of perfectionism regarding the films I make, and strive
> to achieve the kind of poeticism found in traditional Chinese paintings.
> ❊

Another outstanding action sequence has Broken Sword and Flying Snow storming the King's palace on their own, a two-person army against hordes of guards (this is a common motif in swordplay pictures, where it's usually one person versus thousands. Jet Li has appeared in this sort of scene several times – famously in the *Once Upon a Time In China* series, where Wong Fei-hung takes on mobs of henchmen).

The way that Snow and Broken Sword lash out at everyone on all sides to fight their way thru to King Qin's audience chamber is marvellous to behold (they cut thru shields, swords and spears like butter, and soldiers're sent flying).

The reception hall is reworked again by furnishing it with green hangings, to add some visual spice to the duel. Here we see Broken Sword clearly getting the better of King Qin (sending his sword spinning away), but letting him off with only a scratch. Qin (and Snow) are gobsmacked. But this is what Nameless Warrior will also do, three years later.

❉

To convince Nameless Warrior, Broken Sword's last act of calligraphy (achieved with his sword in the desert sand), is *tianxia* (= 'all under heaven', i.e., the world).[16] We don't see what Broken Sword writes – partly because it's saved for when Nameless tells King Qin (and partly because you won't see much in gritty sand and high wind).

The finale of *Hero* comprises failure, defeat, heroic sacrifice and the deaths of the principal characters – the kind of tragic, poignant ending that occurs often in historical, Chinese dramas, which are very fond of a rise and fall narrative structure – or, even better, a fall and fall). Nameless fails to kill the future Emperor, and is executed, and Snow kills Broken Sword then herself (and all the while Itzhak Perlman continues to saw away on the violin in the background). Moon's hoarse cries of despair, as she hurries back to the desert, say it all (like Snow's scream of agony as Broken Sword expires. This time, after repeated possible plots, she really does kill him (tho' that attack is ambiguous, when Broken Sword opts not to parry Snow's blade). And she really does expire, too – on the same sword).

The finale of *Hero* is beautifully staged, with an emphasis on meticulously composed, static, symmetrical, long lens shots (no need for fancy camera moves here), and slow-paced editing.

So Nameless Warrior sacrifices himself for the greater political cause (for 'all under heaven'), as does Sword. Jet Li walking out of the audience chamber as cool and implacable as fate or time itself and and facing a hail of hundreds of arrows in the main courtyard of the King's palace is a suitably grandiose ending to this remarkable movie.

Nameless Warrior receives a funeral with full honours (from the Imperial guard). But the final image of *Hero* is of King Qin in the audience

---

16 In the Western subtitles, *tianxia* became 'our land', which was taken to mean China, and was criticized for not meaning the same as 'all under heaven'.

chamber, alone, still reeling from Nameless's act of giving up his life.

THE MAKING OF *HERO*.

Hero was the subject of a behind the scenes documentary – *Cause: The Birth of Hero* (2002), produced by Noble Entertainment/ Xuan Liu Documentary Film Studio and dir. by Gan Lu. It was a fly-on-the-wall style documentary. Unfortunately, *Cause: The Birth of Hero* was shoddily made, technically inept (bad sound, terrible camerawork), and despite its long running time (over two-and-a-half hours), it doesn't tell us much about the making of *Hero* (and little more than we could've guessed if we know anything about filmmaking).

The *Hero* documentary looks like the girlfriend of one of the producers was given a camera and told to shadow the filmmakers. So she got a friend to help out, and away they went. Well, we've all seen 100s of documentaries about movies, but *Cause: The Birth of Hero* is just feeble.

A pity, it's a missed opportunity, because *Hero* was a grand production, boasting two great directors,[17] a terrific cast, and exotic locations. Many of the people we'd love to hear from, in detail, with proper interviews, were missing. A five-minute segment could explain something of how Hong Kong wire-work is deployed (instead of the boring montages of the Happy, Smiling, Film Crew, or the repetitive montages of people hugging). And of course, like most film documentaries, there was little to nothing about how movies like this are financed, nothing about money or fees, nothing about the complexity of mounting a production involving hundreds of people.

There were some veteran filmmakers on the team for *Hero*, but we don't get to hear from them at all. Producer Bill Kong, for instance, is glimpsed in passing but nothing more. We see Angie Lam working on the editing of *Hero* in a hotel room, but never hear from her (and she's a genius who's cut so many of our favourite Hong Kong movies). Luckily, Ching Siu-tung is one of the very few among the production who has significant screen time (chiefly in his conflabs with Zhang' Yimous team).

---

17 The *Hero* documentary is really more of a director's notebook, as it focusses chiefly on Zhang Yimou, to the exclusion of many others in the production.

22

HOUSE OF FLYING DAGGERS

Shí Miàn Mái Fú

INTRO.

Production credits for *House of Flying Daggers* (*Shí Miàn Mái Fú,* 2004) include: the companies: China Film Co-Production Corporation/ E.D.K.O. Films/ Elite Group/ Zhang Yimou Studio/ Beijing New Pictures; writers: Wang Bin, Li Feng, Peter Wu and Zhang Yimou; exec. prod.: Weiping Zhang; producers: William Kong, Zhenyan Zhang and Zhang Yimou; action dir.: Tony Ching Siu-tung;[18] DP: Zhao Xiaoding; music: Shigeru Umebayashi; Huang Bao-Rongitor: costumes; Long Cheng: ed.; prod. des.: Tingxiao Huo; costumes: Emi Wada and Huang Bao-Rong; sup. art dirs.: Zhong Han and Huo Ting-Xiao; hair: Siu-Mui Chau; make-up: Lee-Na Kwan and Xiaohai Yang; sound: Tao Jing; sound sup.: Roger Savage; visual effects by Digital Pictures Iloura, Fuel VFX, Digital Pictures, Animal Logic and Mendfond. Released July 15, 2004. 119 mins.

In the cast were: Zhang Ziyi, Andy Lau Tak-wah, Takeshi Kaneshiro, Dandan Song, Hongfei Zhao, Jun Guo, Shu Zhang, Jiusheng Wang, Zhengyong Zhang and Yongxin Wang.

Meanwhile, Andy Lau Tak-wah and Takeshi Kaneshiro were, by 2004, two of the biggest stars in Chinese cinema; Lau had by then appeared in just about everything, making many movies per year (and sleeping in his car to save time between shooting days), not to mention an impressive musical career.

Location shooting for *House of Flying Daggers* was based in Kosiv in Russia, with filming in Hutsul Region National Park (for the forests

---

18 Martial arts coordinator: Cai Li.

scenes). The bamboo wood was in China. *House of Flying Daggers* was made in Mandarin (and looped). Principal photography began in Sept, 2003.

The budget was US $12 million (which seems completely impossible for a movie of this scale, in period costume, with many vfx shots, and 70 days filming on location. But that is one of the great strengths of Hong Kong and Chinese cinema).

House of Flying Daggers is a very traditional movie through and through – after all, it's a romantic drama/ tragedy which is about as conservative a narrative form as possible. The political aspects of some of Zhang Yimou's other films (and Tony Ching Siu-tung's) are left aside for the telling of a traditional love story. (There *is* a political element in *House of Flying Daggers*, of course – the Flying Daggers clan are fighting the oppressive authorities, so the movie sides with the rebels against authority figures, which could be linked to the People's Republic of China).

So *House of Flying Daggers* is not inventing the wheel narratively – it is unashamedly telling a very familiar yarn, but with an appealing cast, gorgeous visuals, intricate visual effects, and stupendous action choreography.

❄

SCRIPT AND THEMES.

There are three main characters in *House of Flying Daggers* -

Xiao Mei	Zhang Ziyi
Leo	Andy Lau
Jin	Takeshi Kaneshiro

In other words: it's one woman and two guys. Yes, it's a romantic triangle plot set within a swordplay plot, with the rivalries in love mixing with the political intrigue, the pursuit of the Flying Dagger clan, etc.

One of the inspirations for *House of Flying Daggers* was a poem by Li Yannian (Han Dynasty). The poem is quoted by Xiao Mei[19] when she dances for Jin in the Peony Pavilion:

In the North there is a beauty; unique and independent,
A glance from her will overthrow a city; another glance will overthrow a nation.
One would rather not know whether it will be a city or a nation that will be overthrown.
As it would be difficult to behold such a beauty again.

---

19 Zhang Ziyi sings it on the soundtrack album.

House of Flying Daggers is another big budget, Mainland Chinese version of the sort of movie that Hong Kong (and China) has been making for decades, right back to the 1920s. It is also a version of the movies of the 1980s and 1990s, which established Hong Kong cinema as an important influence on world cinema. The actors and the crew have all been here before (some of them many times – like Tony Ching Siu-tung and Zhang Yimou, the two directors. Indeed, Ching was involved with a movie called *Flying Dagger*, in 1993, which Ching action directed).

House of Flying Daggers, structurally, is a film of rhymes and doubles: the same scenarios repeat and are doubled (including the same shots and compositions). In addition, layers and disguises are peeled away, as each new revelation re-aligns the characters and the plot (similar to *Hero*).

Xiao Mei being blind is a gimmick – but we know that Hong Kong cinema is very fond of gimmicks (such as one-armed swordsmen). And it's a rather extreme gimmick for a story where everybody is in disguise: *House of Flying Daggers* is one of those movies where later revelations make you re-assess all you've seen, and where watching it again changes the narrative.

House of Flying Daggers is dedicated to Anita Mui, one of the great actresses of Hong Kong cinema, the 'Madonna of Hong Kong', who died in 2003, before filming her role (the script was altered accordingly). It's likely that Mui would've played Nia, the leader of the Flying Daggers clan (Nia does appear, but instead she's called Yee, played by Song Dandan). As Mui has been paired romantically with Andy Lau before, the missing plot might've involved a liaison for Lau's Leo, as a counterpart to Kaneshiro falling for Xiao Mei. (Nia's role in the movie seems much reduced from a character that Mui would play).

❈

There's an immature, retrogressive aspect to the psychology of romance represented in *House of Flying Daggers*. Altho' these two guys are middle-aged (or at least in their 30s),[20] they both act like teenage boys. The way that Leo conducts himself in the bamboo grove at the Flying Daggers HQ is especially adolescent: how he sulkily confesses to Xiao Mei that he's been in hell for three years since they parted. And, in a passive-aggressive switch, how he tries to rape Mei. And finally how he slopes off in disgrace with a knife in his back! (That it's *Andy Lau* who's playing someone half his age makes it all the more unsettling).

But this of course plays into one of the themes of *House of Flying Daggers*: love makes fools of us all. Or: love turns men into gibbering boys. Or: why do guys get so stupid around women?

---
20 Andy Lau was 42.

No one can miss the proto-feminism is having the Flying Daggers Society being run by women (and seeming to comprise mainly women). Again, Chinese martial arts cinema since the 1960s has placed female warriors in the foreground (sometimes as a gimmick to help to sell the same martial arts stories to audiences which by then had already seen everything).

ACTION AND SCENES.

House of Flying Daggers opens with the introduction of the two male stars, Andy Lau Tak-wah and Takeshi Kaneshiro, sitting opposite each other, on either side of the screen, in the police headquarters. The composition of this shot is a classic way of hinting at the equality of the pair, as well as their rivalry. We also see that they know each other (probably well), and both have the same job.

The exposition about the Flying Daggers sect is given here, plus the initial quest of the 2004 movie: to investigate the member of the sect supposedly hiding in the Peony Pavilion. And when we cut to said Pavilion, we're rapidly introduced to the third star of *House of Flying Daggers*, Zhang Ziyi, appearing as a blind courtesan.

The Peony Pavilion is the astonishingly elaborate[21] setting for a series of scenes exploring the three main characters: Xiao Mei the blind dancer, Jin the visiting captain (introduced as a drunk client fooling around with some of the prostitutes), and the stern captain, Leo, who arrives to arrest Mei.

A lengthy song and dance number from Zhang Ziyi introduces the theme of the 2004 movie: love – or, rather, love and war (love and politics). The song is sung in the plaintive, yearning style that is peculiarly Chinese. The themes of emotion and politics intertwine throughout *House of Flying Daggers* in the usual manner of Chinese, historical movies.

The 'echo game' is the second set-piece, where a series of drums on poles are placed in a circle around the chamber. It's a ballet of sound and music and movement – as Xiao Mei follows the sound of the beans hitting the drums (the scene is a gift to the sound department). Again, the scene appears self-consciously obscure and Chinese. And it's artificial, yet performed with a Peking Opera feeling for motion and sound.

When Xiao Mei attacks Leo with a flying sword, the second set-piece shifts rapidly into the third: the mandatory Big Sword Fight at the beginning of a swordplay epic. The gimmick here of one participant being blind (and female) is played out with some grand, acrobatic moves. Only later, when

21 Fabulous, colourful, wooden structures here – but the production gets its money's worth with this set.

some of the disguises and pretences are lifted, do we realize that these are two old lovers.

Leo subdues Mei with some *kung fu* that emulates erotic acts – the final beat has Leo grasping Mei by the neck and hurling her into a pool and under the water, in slow motion. Again, in retrospect some of Leo's actions are explained: he's the spurned lover, angry and resentful, who sadistically enjoys arresting Mei and showing her the torture machine where she's hung up like an animal. (That Andy Lau is partly playing against type – being a major pop idol and star in Asia – enhances the drama).

When Jin springs Mei from the police jail (another action sequence of ninja-like rapidity), the movie gets moving with a chase and road movie motif (which continues for some time).

✻

The bamboo forest ambush in *House of Flying Daggers* is a familiar set-piece in the history of martial arts cinema (the King Hu classic *wuxia pian A Touch of Zen* features a famous example). Tony Ching Siu-tung had already been involved in two bamboo forest scenes in 1993 alone as action director (in *Flying Dagger* and *Moon Warriors*). In *House of Flying Daggers*, the bamboo action sequence is very much a Ching affair: it looks as if Zhang Yimou and the producers handed over this particular scene to Ching. In the 'making of' documentary, you can see Ching directing the stunt guys and performers (showing Zhang Ziyi how to waste the heavies with a split bamboo pole, for instance. Ching doesn't tell her how to do it, he demonstrates it for her).

The bamboo action sequence is stuffed with Chingisms – from shots of the soldiers running thru the air at the tops of the bamboo trees to the elaborate traps placed by the soldiers (split bamboo shoots in the ground).

Every gag you can think of set in a bamboo forest is deployed: soldiers running up trees; sliding down trees upside-down; Xiao Mei braced between two trees; running across the tree-tops; bamboo used as staffs (in the *wushu*, Jet Li manner); and finally bamboo thrown as spears to entrap the heroes in a cage of stalks.

As if one bamboo forest setting wasn't enough, *House of Flying Daggers* also placed the secret den of the Flying Daggers Society in a bamboo copse, so that the encounter between Leo and Xiao Mei echoes that of Mei and Jin earlier.[22]

✻

The attack on the travelling heroes in a meadow is another staple of

22 The colour grading here, though, is all-out green – the green of Leo's jealousy for Xiao Mei and Jin, perhaps?

the martial arts genre (tho' this time the landscape doesn't look like the familiar spots in the New Territories). The long grass is exploited for visual possibilities (already established when Jin collects flowers for Xiao Mei in a ridiculously OTT fashion – on horseback, with plenty of horse-riding stunts. Well, this *is* a romantic movie after all).

The meadow sequence reveals the stakes getting higher, with Jin forced to maim his fellow soldiers (tho' narratively it simply repeats the bust-up in the forest. Then, tho', Jin is able to shoot arrows thru clothing, to trick us as well as Mei that they're killed). The next beat, in the bamboo forest, ups the stakes even further (i.e., more soldiers, and bigger obstacles).

Again, it's the *rhythm* and the *timing* of the flow of the action that's very typical of Tony Ching Siu-tung's style of action choreography – and of Chinese martial arts cinema. How, for instance, like a dance number in a musical the combatants all start running at the same time, and stop all at once, swords raised.

The meadow battle is the first time we see the flying daggers of the film's title used to deadly effect: this becomes a recurring device in *House of Flying Daggers*, with the conflict stopped at a key moment by a hurled knife or two.

Point-of-view shots of arrows and daggers are a recurring motif in *House of Flying Daggers* – some of the shots are visual effects shots. However, weapon p.o.v.'s had already been part of the visual arsenal of Hong Kong action cinema for decades.

❊

There's a lull of several minutes before the Big Finale (which we know will include lots of action). Shots of Xiao Mei in the forest are match-cut with images of Jin in a different part of the forest (don't those Russian woodlands look incredible?). Plenty of meaningful looks, agonized looks, and teary-eyed looks (each of the three actors are required by weep *a lot* in *House of Flying Daggers*. Even by the standards of Chinese and Hong Kong cinema, there are waterworks a-plenty in the *Flying Daggers House*).

Script-wise, narrative-wise, this can look like padding: Jin wants Xiao Mei to come with him; Mei refuses; he weeps and leaves; she stands there and weeps; he halts, miles away; she decides to run after him anyway… and so on and on.

Throughout, the score (by Shigeru Umebayashi) dips in and out, with lots of the pity-making, poignant violin music that all historical, Chinese movies must include by law. (Umebayashi's[23] score is doing a *lot* of

---

[23] A Japanese composer, note. For sheer, operatic emotion, Japanese film composers can compete with anybody.

dramatic work in *House of Flying Daggers*: if the looks of longing and anxiety from the actors don't do the trick, the lovely score will).

❋

House of Flying Daggers culminates with – what else? – a giant swordfight. With some rather obvious and artificial tinkering with the script in order to get the three protagonists into the same arena, there is a Big Sword Fight between Leo and Jin. In action terms, this is what *House of Flying Daggers* has boiled down to, and what the film seems most interested in: a romantic triangle. And, this being a Chinese action movie, the triangle is played out in excessive and glorious action. (The Flying Daggers Society subplot is mentioned, but pretty much forgotten: this is all about three lovers – two guys and one woman. There is a shot, however, cutting away from the field to some soldiers advancing, swords raised (a pure, Chingian touch) on the Flying Daggers clan's HQ in the bamboo forest).

Everybody remembers the sword duel in the snow – as the 'making of' documentaries reveal, it started to snow during the filming of the finale (too early for the season). Instead of clearing away the snow (possible but time-consuming – because it would have to be done every day for possibly weeks), the production decided to use the weather to enhance the scene.

Thus, there are two or three visual effects shots towards the beginning of the duel, to demonstrate how the snow is falling near-horizontally (in high wind), and covering the characters in white magic. Snow can be added after the fact (with digital technology offering even more visual possibilities), but it helps here that the setting is a location, and not a stage.

Anyhoo, several aspects of the Big Sword Fight are worth noting: first, and most obviously, Xiao Mei has been left out of it: at the start, she is thwacked in the heart (of course!) by a flying dagger from Leo. That puts her out of the running, so that she is now relegated to the role of weeping, swooning, near-dead heroine (which's a pity, as we've seen that Mei is a formidable fighter herself).

So, secondly, that leaves Leo and Jin to go at it in a classic Tony Ching Siu-tung slice of swordplay. This is why you hire Ching, to come up with marvellous choreography like this. The intensity of the action is exaggerated by having the lads roaring at each other and hurling themselves at each other. The snow, which wasn't planned for, is used by the team on the hoof to make make the swordplay even tougher, as the guys stumble and roll about. (It's difficult enough walking in deep snow, let alone fighting for your life!).

Thirdly, a whole raft of cinematic devices are deployed to enhance the confrontation – not only slo-mo (as expected), and cables (as expected), but digitally added wounds and gushes of blood (one wonders if this influenced *300* (2007)). And a shift into animalistic noises, rapid zooms, and glaring close-ups, as the soldiers're descending to the level of beasts.

This is majestic filmmaking, shamelessly over-the-top and operatic – it's drops of blood on white snow, it's swirling snowstorms enveloping humans so they disappear in the wilderness, it's Xiao Mei fluttering her eyes open for one last time before she expires.........

.........And of course there is a reprise of the poem/ song from the opening scenes, about that fatal beauty in the North who will bring down cities and whole nations (it is whispered-sung by Jin, and then reprised by, presumably, Xiao Mei, singing from beyond death).

So *House of Flying Daggers* didn't invent a whole new form of cinema, or topple the government of the People's Republic of China with an incendiary calls-to-arms, but it did deliver a cracking piece of very old-fashioned, indulgent entertainment. Cinema as Peking Opera.

23

KRRISH

Krrish (2006): first, the credits: six writers (Sanjay Masoomi, Sachin Bhowmick, Rakesh Roshan, Akash Khurana, Honey Irani and Robin Bhatt), dir. and prod. by Rakesh Roshan, music by Salim Sulaiman, Salim Merchant, and Rajesh Roshan, Santosh Thundiyil (DPs), Amitabh Shukla (ed.), Farah Khan (choreographer), Manish Malhotra (costumes), Samir Chanda and Sham Kaushal (art dirs.), Baylon Fonesca and Nakul Kamte (sound designers), and Dhananjay Prajapati and Nahush Pise (make-up). Filmkraft Productions was the production company. As well as Tony Ching, vfx supervisors from Hollywood were brought in for *Krrish* (Marc Kolbe and Craig Mumma). Released June 23, 2006. 175 mins.

Krrish starred Hrithik Roshan as Krishna Mehra, Naseeruddin Shah, Priyanka Chopra, Rekha, Manini Mishra, Sharat Saxena, Archana Puran Singh, Bin Xia, Hemant Pandey and Puneet Issar. (It was another Roshan[24] family production, with the director's son as the star and his brother (Rajesh Roshan) as the composer of the songs, along with Salim Sulaiman).

There is a long tradition in Bollywood cinema (going back to the 1970s) of introducing Hong Kong martial arts (Bruce Lee's films made a big impression), so it's no surprise that Indian cinema hires specialists from the Hong Kong industry, such as Tony Ching.

Krrish was part of a series re-telling and updating Indian mythology using superhero motifs, intense colour, visual effects, and plenty of romance and comedy. It was the second movie in the series which began with *Koi... Mil Gaya* (2003), from the same team. The *Krrish* movies developed into a franchise – with two cartoon/ live-action TV series, *Kid Krrish* (2013) and *J Bole Toh Jadoo* (2003), comics, and video games. A

---

[24] Roshan has a huge list of credits, going back to the mid-1970s.

fourth movie was announced for 2020 (and teased in 2021).

One of the most amazing things about *Krrish* is the budget, which was 45 crore = U.S. $7 million (other sources say $6.1 million)! A figure impossibly low for a similar product made in the West (in N. America, it would be $150 million or more). The average Bollywood movie budget in the 2010s was 25-50 crore (50 crore = U.S. $7.6 million). *Krrish* was filmed between Sept and Nov, 2005, in India and Singapore.

Heavily merchandized and marketed, *Krrish* was a hit in India (tho' local reviews were mixed – the main film critics found *Krrish* too kiddie movie-ish for their tastes. It is! But that's what great about it). Critics acknowledged the importance of *Krrish* as a movie produced in India which could compete with overseas blockbuster movies.

❉

Krrish is a bit-of-everything – it's a *masala* (= spice) film – a cinematic form which mixes action, comedy, romance, spectacle, music and melo-drama. So *Krrish* is Bollywood schmaltz and romance, it's Bollywood songs-and-dances, it's Indian mythology re-done using North American superheroism, it's very sentimental and soapy Indian forms, it's Spielbergian sci-fi and computers, it's Hong Kong action set-pieces, it's exotic travelogues, and it's goofy comedy.

If you don't enjoy one genre riff, you know they'll be another one along in a few minutes, as *Krrish* happily changes tack, swinging ʼnle movie genres and forms. An intense argument in a living is overtaken by a sci-fi flashback the next; one minute ᵗical number which's all white, toothy smiles, pastel ᵃ moves, and the next it's a smoky, Hong

filmmaking – no matter how pulpy/
paper-thin the characteriz-
ative the politics and
song and dance
the *mise-en-*
would be,
g Siu-tung).
try anything to
of these movies

e cinematography by
amazing locations in the
music, and a charming
errific job with that tiny budget.

and
is a
ts fired
on news.
om Hrithik
he sings, he
ts wushu solo,
do everything in
etic performance.
onu Nigam, Shreya
others who deliver the
ard: like North American
ey make Singapore look super-
, and the National Library.

NG ❉ 494

central relationship between the golden couple, Hrithik Roshan and Priyanka Chopra. (That's the first half – the second half is downtown Singaporean[26] settings[27] and futuristic, indoor sets, blue lighting, and black, superhero cloaks).

❈

The *Krrish* movie franchise is derivative of 100s of Hollywood movies – as many critics pointed out. But *every* superhero movie is derived from other superhero movies, and in fact, *all* North American movies of the action-adventure type are cannibalized from parts of other movies, just like the robots in *Transformers* or the junk machines in *The Road Warrior*. (Even the very rare blockbuster movies which claim to be 'new' or fresh are, on closer inspection, reworkings of previous movies).

Krrish was significant, however, in being a home-grown superhero, a character drawing on Indian mythology, and not merely another outing from Marvel or Detective Comics, which regularly update and rework their superhero franchises in the movie industry just as they do with the same superhero characters in comics publishing, or video games, or toys and merchandizing. For Marvel and Detective Comics, superhero franchises are simply products to be exploited.

❈

Priyanka Chopra and Hrithik Roshan make an appealing, romantic couple at the heart of *Krrish* (Roshan has been told to smile, smile, smile in every single scene, Which he does, like professional dancers smile when they perform. And Chopra's famous beauty lights up the screen. Also, *Krrish* doesn't make Priya the stay-at-home girlfriend/ wife (from the first movie) – she has a career as a TV journalist for Aaj Tak). Alas, Preity Zinta was not in the movie, this being about the son of Rohit.

One of the minor subplots in the *Krrish* movies is amusing (perhaps takes its cue from Sony's *Spider-man*): that altho' Krishn superhero, in ordinary life he has a string of crummy jobs (and he g repeatedly). Meanwhile, Priya has a classy job, working in televis

Krrish is a *tour-de-force*, once-in-a-lifetime performance Roshan (b. 1974, Mumbai), one of the biggest stars in India dances (very well), he does stunts, he performs a martial a he's the romantic lead, and he's a superhero. He gets to *Krrish*, and then some. It's a winning, hugely ener (However, the singing is not Roshan – in *Krrish*, it's Ghoshal, Shreya Ghoshal, Rafaqat Ali Khan, and

26 The *Krrish* movies were aided by the Singaporean tourist b superhero movies with Gotham, Washington, DC and L.A.; th sleek and attractive.
27 Including the Zoo, Robinson Road, the Gateway buildin Mumbai and Manali were other locations.

TONY CHING SIU-TU

vocals).

The family is an important thematic ingredient in the *Krrish* movies. The superhero genre often pivots around parents (usually the father, as in most fantasy genres), but in these Indian, superhero movies, it's the family as a unit, and as the reflection of the core of contemporary society in India. *Krrish*, for instance, features Krishna's grandmother Sonia in a prominent role as well as his father Rohit.

Krrish also includes some shamelessly over-the-top melodrama – a common component in Asian cinema (Chinese and Japanese movies specialize in it), but far, far too out-there and weepy for a North American and European audience. So many moments of charas gazing soulfully at each other or into the distance, or hugging, or sobbing (accompanied by too-sweet string cues).

Every time this happens in a North American movie, the sidekick'll deliver a quip to cut thru the treacle. Not in Bollywood! They really do mean it!

You lose count in the *Krrish* movies of the number of times we see extreme close-ups of teary eyes. Of sorrowful eyes. And sometimes of angry eyes. Slow zooms into the eyes. Sudden cuts to the eyes. So many eyes!

And then the Bollywood, musical elements kick in – the charming musical numbers, filmed in the showy manner of M.T.V. with the camera craning and careening all over the place, aided some ultra-romantic choreography by Farah Khan. The dance number in the big top circus in Singapore is outstanding: the movie really delivers in terms of all-out, Broadwayesque staging and entertainment. (The cutting *is* rapid in the musical numbers in *Krrish*, but thankfully not accelerated into irritation, like some recent musical movies. And there're plenty of full-body shots, which're held, so we get to see the body moving in space as a whole, rather than bitty fragments. In fact, many of the dance numbers are filmed in formal long shots).

Superman, Batman, X-Men, Avengers – yeah, yeah, all wonderful superheroes, but do they sing? No. Do they dance? No! In *Krrish*, we have a superhero who can do everything that Batman and Superman can do – *and* he can dance and sing! It's amazing! (And it's refreshing to see superhero antics taking place in colourful, faraway lands like India and Singapore, instead of the usual sarcastic, gloomy Gotham).

(Actually, North American blockbuster movies do occasionally have musical interludes – a montage cut to a tie-in pop song, for instance, to depict the courtship of the two leads. But they don't sing, and they don't dance. Instead, they're walking in Central Park or on the beach at Santa Monica, etc).

❊

Several of the action sequences in in *Krrish* look like the filmmakers handed them over totally to Tony Ching Siu-tung and his team. After all, Ching is not just a world-class action director, he's also the director of two of the finest fantasy adventure series ever: *A Chinese Ghost Story* and *The Swordsman*.

The scene where Krishna and Priya are buzzed by the motorcyle gang[28] in Singapore is completely Chingian, as is the smackdown where Krishna, now as Krrish the superhero, enacts his revenge. This scene could be spliced into a Hong Kong action movie without anyone noticing – the same sort of set-pieces featuring hoodlums on bikes being trounced by superheroes in black pop up in the *Black Mask* movies and the *Heroic Trio* flicks, for instance (the latter were choreographed by Ching). Flying, spinning motorcycles are one of Ching's specialities. Another totally Chingian set-piece is the one-man-versus-many-henchmen set in a forest on Dr Arya's secret island: from the appearance of the heavies descending on cables all at once, to surround the hero, to the many stunt gags, this is a replay of the bamboo forest set-pieces in *Butterfly and Sword* and *House of Flying Daggers*.

The action choreography by Tony Ching Siu-tung[29] required plenty of wire-work to create the illusion of Krrish flying: if you want an actor to zip thru tree-tops, forty feet above the ground, Ching is your man. Partly because *Krrish* is so long, and partly because Krishna as the superhero Krrish does a *lot* of running and flying, there is probably more travelling wire-work across great distances in *Krrish* than any other Ching movie. The stage-hands must've carted the heavy cable rigs, pulleys and cranes all over Singapore to capture the shots.

❊

Krrish is too long – it clocks in at nearly three hours (tho' there is an interval). If this picture really is aimed at kids, as many critics have asserted, that is far too long. *Krrish* is simply in no hurry to tell its story: it spends close to sixty minutes charting the gradual romance between the two leads, for example. It's after an hour's gone by that Priya and her chums leave the mountains and return to Singapore, where they live.

The villain of *Krrish* is Dr Siddhant Arya (played by Naseeruddin Shah), who works on the super-computer with Krishna's father Rohit[30] (who's been kept alive). The plot driven by Arya (world domination, the

---

28 A reprise of similar scenes in the first *Krrish* movie, but much, much better.
29 Sham Kaushal was assistant action director.
30 Roshan plays his father, too – in a film directed by his own father.

ability to be God granted by a computer that predicts the future, etc), is probably too pat, too routine, and too derivative to compel much;[31] but it does provide for a spectacular finish to the movie.

As the Arya/ computer/ superhero/ Krrish plot kicks in (in the second half of *Krrish*), unfortunately there's less time for Priya, Krishna's mom Sonia, and the romantic subplot (and, boo-hoo, no more musical numbers!). Now it's all about Krishna doing his duty as the superhero Krrish to Save The World from evil Doctor Arya.

The finale of *Krrish* is an extended rampage thru all of the expected action-adventure movie clichés, with the emotional beats in particular milked to the max (this *is* a Bollywood movie, after all). Intense stares, eyes welling up, anxious reaction shots, sweaty faces, people waving guns, lots of running, etc.

❈

One of the attractive elements of *Krrish* is that it *doesn't* deliver the usual 'America Über Alles' ideology of all North American superhero movies. Yes folks, every North American superhero flick features not only commercials for the U.S. military-industrial complex (which spends $798 billion on the military), plus ads for the U.S. forces at home and abroad, they all promulgate the Great America Way of Life. Yes, the only way to live is the North American Way, and only North America can Save The World. Sometimes the ideology of 'America Über Alles' is so aggressive it's offensive and sickening.

Thankfully, and marvellously, this Bollywood, superhero fantasy is free of that. It's a breath of fresh air for the superhero movie genre. Krishna is saving the world, true – as all superheroes do – but not to propagate the Great American Way of Life, and not by using the U.S. military. (However, the narrative form of *Krrish* does contain enough of the North American, superhero movie form for it to also be didactic and aggressive).

---

31 And you do get tired of seeing the super-villain Arya smugly being smug.

Koi... Mil Gaya (a.k.a. *I Found Someone,* 2003) was the first entry in the *Krrish* franchise. It was wr. by Honey Irani, Sachin Bhowmick, Robin Bhatt and Rakesh Roshan, with dialogue by Javed Siddiqui, prod. by Roshan, Rajesh Shah and Been Shah for Filmkraft, and dir. by Roshan. Music:[32] Rajesh Roshan, lyrics: Dev Kohli, DPs: Sameer Arya and Ravi K. Chandran, and ed. by Sanjay Verma. Released Aug 8, 2003. 166 mins.

I Found Someone was a hit with audiences, and with many critics. It also received many awards. It was filmed in Canada, Bhimtal, Kasauli, and Nanital. The budget was between INR 250 million to INR 350 million, which equals $3.3 million to US $4.6 million.

Oh, *come on!* Four and a half million American bucks for a movie made in 2003 with this many locations, actors, props, vehicles, sets, costumes, practical effects, visual effects, night shoots, etc – it just ain't possible!

I Found Someone is a cute tale that mixes Bollywood musical segments, science fiction in the Spielbergian manner, soap opera/ melodrama in the familiar, over-cooked Hindi mode, and action-adventure elements from children's cinema.

It's pointless resisting[33] a movie such as *I Found Someone* – this is a movie where two soon-to-be-lovers dance in the rain on a date, where the hero is surrounded by cutie kids on scooters (tho' he's 20 years older), and where every scene takes place in a Theme Park India, an India that's as fake and chocolate-box-pretty as anything produced by the Walt Disney company. (The first half of *I Found Someone* is filmed on sets that look exactly like an amusement park (complete with prominent product placement – Nescafe, Coca-Cola, etc), combined with filming in a national park or two up in the mountains. It seems as if *I Found Someone* was supported by local tourist offices).

❀

I Found Someone is the story of Rohit Mehra, a youth with arrested development: he's an adult with the mental age of 8. That's a motif occasionally taken up by Western cinema (Hollywood has delivered many versions of the child-like man, such as *Rain Man, Forrest Gump, Big, Elf* and *Edward Scissorhands*). In part, the child-man scenario allows for a *tour-de-force* turn from actors such as Johnny Depp, Dustin Hoffman and Tom Hanks. *I Found Someone* is the same: this is Hrithik Roshan's movie, thru and thru. He's in most every scene, and it's his story. (True, Roshan

---

32 The singers include Alka Yagnik and Udit Narayan (voicing the lovers), plus Taz, Shaan, Adnan Sami, etc.
33 As with a Hollywood musical movie, you can't judge or critique this sort of film in the same way as many other films.

fills his characterization of Rohit with tics and quirks and a bobbling head that might irritate some viewers. It *is* a self-conscious performance – but then, Hoffman and Depp,[34] among many Hollywood stars, also go the self-conscious route when they play disabled folk or just plain weirdos).

It's an outstanding turn by Roshan as Rohit, which he developed to even greater heights in the *Krrish* sequels (playing Krishna, and Krrish and his dad, Rohit). He had already been in hit films by the time of *Koi Mil Gaya*. And Zinta, who had appeared with Roshan in *Mission Kashmir* (2000), is a delight as the chipper, feisty girlfriend of the hero. Like Roshan, Zinta gives the role her all – the only way to perform in a movie like this.

There are only three other main characters in *I Found Someone*: super-mom (Sonia Mehra), played by Rekha, the love interest (Nisha), played by Preity Zinta, and the chief rival, Raj, was played by Rajat Bedi.

Director Rakesh Roshan appears in a cameo as the hero's father (he's also the father of the star, Hrithik Roshan). He's the scientist who makes the initial contact with the aliens until he exits the movie in a spectacular car crash.

The main plot in *I Found Someone* is the story of Rohit the mentally challenged youth, rather than his encounter with a friendly alien, which counts as a secondary plot. Meanwhile, the other subplot, the romantic triangle, assumes so much significance it's virtually the central spine of the movie. Thus, Raj, the spoilt, bratty rich kid, is one of the chief obstacles in the romance of Rohit and Nisha. (This romantic triangle in *I Found Someone* is portrayed in a thoroughly child-like manner, as if everything in Rohit's life is at a playground level).

❄

I Found Someone shamelessly raided Western/ Hollywood cinema: we've got *Close Encounters of the Third Kind, Independence Day* and *Contact* (aliens, U.F.O.s, even communicating with extraterrestrials using sound and music),[35] we've got *E.T. The Extraterrestrial*, we've got comedy sports matches from *Shaolin Soccer,* and we've got extravagant pop promos for the musical numbers *à la* M.T.V. (The 1967 unproduced film *The Alien*, dir. by Satyajit Ray, was also cited by some critics as an influence).

Altho' director Rakesh Roshan asserted that *I Found Someone* was *not* an Indian version of *E.T.*, the movie contained many elements instantly recognizable from the 1982 Universal film, even down to particular shots. If you wanted to distance yourself from Hollywood cinema even while competing with Hollywood, it seems ill-judged to replicate many ingredients so precisely (and from a much-loved and very well-known

34 Indeed,Johnny Depp irritates the hell out of some viewers – *viz*. his Mad Hatter, his Willy Wonka, his Edward Scissorhands, his Captain Jack Sparrow.
35 Tho' here it's the Hindu word 'OM'.

movie, too).

So Jadoo is our cute, blue alien: short, stocky, with huge eyes, blue skin and a pouty mouth. (In among so many wildly expressive performers, who can all weep, yell, dance and sing on cue, the animatronic eyes and features of li'l Jadoo seem really limited).

Jadoo's chief act in *I Found Someone* is to lift the curse, in fairy tale terms, on Rohit: that is, to take away his mental instability (and also to give him special powers). Rohit zooms from being a disabled dweeb, pushed around by the local thugs, and cast aside at school, to a superhero, turning into a great basketball player, dancer, and all-round hero.

Like the other entries in the *Krrish* franchise, *I Found Someone* is in no hurry to tell its tale: it's 166 minutes long! Close to three hours for a kids' movie! Thus, act one depicts the character of Rohit as a mentally challenged child (at school, at home, at play); and act two portrays the budding romance with Nisha.

So it's not until act three of *I Found Someone* – over an hour into the piece – when the alien plot returns (after being introduced in the prologue). There's no need to rush, I guess, when you've got goofy comedy to deliver, plus gentle scenes of children playing, plus an unbelievable and cheesy romance (where the sweetness and sentimentality overwhelms all of your resistance, cynicism and bitterness), and not forgetting the mandatory scenes in any Bollywood film of weepy over-acting and out-size melodrama. Plus the singing and the dancing.

The songs in *I Found Someone* are gloriously cheesy – and the choreography is wonderfully exuberant. (Cheesy – but the soundtrack was a massive hit, selling some 21 million copies in India alone).

The stand-out musical number in *I Found Someone* is the nightclub scene (there's one in each *Krrish* movie), where Rohit stuns everybody with his amazing moves. The energy in the scene is impossible to withstand (but why would you resist in the first place?). Choreographer Farah Khan leads the ensemble in some delightful dances – and comically places Nisha in the middle of the scene as the girl who's embarrassed and can't dance. Like the later romantic duo in the national park in the mountains, this is all about pure entertainment, movement for the sake of movement, colour for the sake of colour (and music, of course, for the sake of music). The greatest special effect in movies is the face and the body – why doesn't every movie have a big dance number like this?

❉

Certainly, *I Found Someone* is too long – and the subsequent *Krrish* films also happily skittered past the two hour mark (nay, the two and a half hour mark!). Can you have too much of a good thing? Not here, in this mix of dopey melodrama, ditzy comedy, romance, dance and alien encounters.

Just when you thought the movie was approaching an ending, or closure of some kind, it gleefully slips into *another* romantic song-and-dance number (filmed in the mountains). You thought the romantic subplot was over, tied up, done with? Oh no! Here are the lovers gushing over each other once again, telling each other with shining eyes and brilliant smiles how much they are dazzled by each other. They nudge each other, bounce together then apart, twist around each other, chase each other, embrace then fly apart – again and again. By a waterfall, on a bridge, on a walkway, on a stony shore.

This is Bollywood as Hollywood – the Bollywood musical taking up the Hollywood musical trope of using a dance scene to stand in for a love scene. No need for a lovemaking scene when you've got actors and choreographers who can come up with move after move, and a film crew willing to drive up into the mountains to photograph them bouncing about day after day.

Bollywood cinema is fabulously *expressive* cinema – like Japanese animation, like Hong Kong action cinema. Why *speak* a scene when you can *express* it with the body and with movement? Most Western television and Western cinema consists of talking heads, people standing or sitting and talking (it's filmed radio, as Alfred Hitchcock pointed out). Hong Kong action cinema, like Japanese *anime* and Bollywood cinema, does so much more.

There's a common crossover from Hong Kong action cinema to Bollywood adventure/ fantasy cinema. Both employ exaggerated performances, very stylized cinematic forms, saturated colour, pop promo visuals, exotic locales, and a passion to entertain.

And both film forms don't apologize or hold back: what's the point in holding back when you're trying to entertain? (Or trying to persuade punters to visit a movie theatre). These sorts of movies are all-out, where actors're weeping and emoting like mad, where cars don't just crash, they explode, where musical interludes punctuate the narrative, and where the camera performs elaborate, sweeping moves.

Spider-man
(2002).

Hero (2002), this page and over.

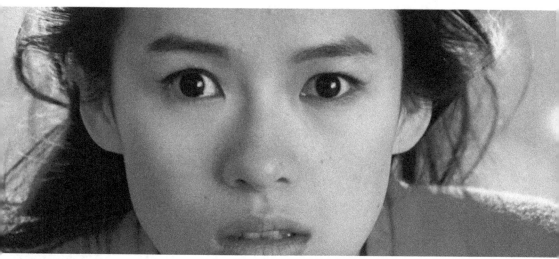

House of Flying Daggers (2004), this page and over.

You know how to hold your drink.

Krrish (2006).

24

CURSE OF THE GOLDEN FLOWER

Manchéng Jìndài Huángjinjia

Tony Ching Siu-tung was the action director for another collaboration with director Zhang Yimou, *Curse of the Golden Flower* (*Manchéng Jìndài Huángjinjia*, a.k.a. *The City of Golden Armor,* a.k.a. *Autumn Remembrance,* 2006). Filmed in Mandarin, on the Mainland of the People's Republic of China, with a very high budget of U.S. $45 million, *Curse of the Golden Flower* was produced by Zhang Weiping, William Kong and Zhang Yimou for E.D.K.O. Film/ Bejing New Pictures Film/ Elite Group Enterprises, wr. by Zhihong Bian, Nan Wu, and Zhang, dir. by Zhang, sound design by Tao Jing and Roger Savage, vfx by Cheuk Wah, art dir. by Huo Tingxiao, supervising art direction by Bin Zhao, costumes by Kenneth Yee Chung-man and Jessie Dai, DP: Zhao Xiaoding, with music by Shigeru Umebayashi. Jay Chou sang the theme songs. In the cast were Chow Yun-fat, Gong Li, Jay Chou, Qin Junjie, Liu Ye, Ni Dahong, Chen Jin and Li Man. Released Dec 21, 2006. 114 mins.

Curse of the Golden Flower was based on Cao Yu's 1934 play *Thunderstorm.* The caption A.D. 928 was used for the overseas print of *Curse of the Golden Flower,* but the movie might also be set in the Later Tang or the Later Shu dynasties.

The stellar cast of *Curse of the Golden Flower* is topped by two superstars that we can watch from now until the next millennium: Chow Yun-fat and Gong Li. If you're going to cast a Chinese Emperor in a prestige, historical movie, you can't do better than Chow, an emperor among actors (Tony Ching had worked with Chow many times before). Gong Li is as ageless and attractive as Chow (tho' now she's portraying a mom with grown-up sons). And Jay Chou is impressive as the righteous, loyal son – he's waiting in the wings for much of the movie, but gets several all-out action scenes in the finale. (Ching worked with Chou later, in *Kung Fu Dunk*).

The movie was a big hit, with US $37.8 million at the Chinese box office. It took advantage of the huge increase in box office takings of the 2000s ($336 million in 2006).

Curse of the Golden Flower is a historical romp in the Grand, Chinese Manner: it features all of the elements we've come to expect from a big, Chinese, historical movie: spectacle (and more spectacle), an aggressively enforced social and political hierarchy, back-biting and courtly intrigue, revenge fantasies, poison, suppressed eroticism and secret ambitions. Add in Zhang Yimou's motifs – saturated colour, attention to detail, camp over-acting, and melodramatic (even soap opera-ish) relationships.

So we're in the Tang Dynasty in a flamboyant but corrupt regime. We've got power struggles behind the throne between warring groups, we've got the Emperor Ping asserting his influence ruthlessly at times, and we've got seething resentments, desires and ambitions that're barely hidden.

All of this is familiar material in a Chinese, historical movie about an Imperial regime. The implied critique of contemporary People's Republic of China is there is you want to take it up. As are the nods towards proto-feminism. Otherwise, you can sit back and relish this stops-all-out recreation of a China that never existed (or, if it did, certainly never existed looking like this!).

At the centre of *Curse of the Golden Flower* is the Imperial family, comprising:

The Emperor	the Empress
Prince Jai	Crown Prince Wan
Prince Yu	

And the characters who become involved with them:

Imperial Physician	His wife, Jiang-shi
	His daughter, Jiang Chan

So it's two families that become entangled, the Emperor's family and the doctor's family. Crown Prince Wan has romantic liaisons with both the

Empress and Jiang Chan. Meanwhile, Jiang-shi is revealed as the mother of Wan, from an affair with the Emperor. The hidden secrets revolve around parentage, adultery, and incest.

Critics pointed out that the terms for the characters might meant 'king' and 'queen' rather than 'emperor' and 'empress': that is, the Emperor depicted in *Curse of the Golden Flower* is not the ruler of all of China, but only one of the kingdoms. The point is important, but doesn't alter the movie much.

The viewpoint in *Curse of the Golden Flower* is chiefly with the Empress Phoenix – she is what's at stake, the bird in a cage, the victim of the oppressive regime of the Imperial family.[1] But this is movie-making as a pageant, as opera, as a visual feast, and the characters are types. There is little characterization or subtlety in the characters, once they've been established. All we need to know is, oh, he's the Emperor, right, and she's the Empress, and that must be the Handmaiden. I get it.

The golden flowers of the title are chrysanthemums – a multivalent symbol, which you can interpret any way you fancy. That the Empress spends much of her time embroidering chrysanths tells you all you need to know about how the symbol is deployed in the movie.

The 2006 picture is filled with many melodramatic flourishes – an operatic version of soap opera. For ex, to illustrate the oppressive regime of the Imperial court, Empress Phoenix is subjected to a programme of medicine which's making her very ill. It's a crude and clunky way of expressing the oppression in the political system (and also the subjugation of humanity, and of women in particular. The irony is that it's the handmaids of the Empress who administer the slow poison).

Curse of the Golden Flower gives us an assured, vivid (tho' thoroughly stylized) vision of life in the Imperial Palace: every hour is announced by a touring band of time-keepers (*the hour of the snake! the hour of the tiger! get your gold armour here! very good price! no refunds!*), every part of the day is run by clockwork (and is heavily ritualized), and even breathing is done to the beat of a gong or a bell (if you breathe out of turn, it's 50 lashes).

✦

Curse of the Golden Flower is one of those movies about royalty and power where every single scene comprises a main character entering a (luxurious) room where another main character waits for them, and the handmaids and servants are dismissed. While the main characters wait for the servants to melt obsequiously into the shadows, that wastes twenty or thirty seconds in every scene, before they get to the meat of the scene.

[1] The Empress's emblem is the phoenix, while the Emperor's is of course the dragon.

(The source material being a theatrical play perhaps accounts for this sort of staging. But it's very common in pageant films).

Another common scene in *Curse of the Golden Flower* is a character striding down a corridor – yes, those multi-hued, glass passageways are exploited to the full, with the Steadicam tracking either behind the actors or in front. Gong Li seems to have spent half of principal photography walking down the rainbow-coloured corridors at Hengdian World Studios (but not Chow Yun-Fat – he is carried, if he's seen in the corridors at all. More often, he's ensconced on his beloved steam-bath chair).

And there's another repeated dramatic motif in *Curse*: the lingering, emotional look. Yes, following each new reveal of buried feelings, Gong Li stares into space, welling up with exquisite, delicate, quivering Imperial tears. The camera holds and holds (and the editor holds and holds), until 'cut!' is called. This is to drive home those emotions, just in case we missed them during the scene. Thus, the Empress cogitates *a lot* on what just happened – for the audience, it means we are spending *a lot* of time looking at the Empress staring into space.

This brings us to another dramatic device, probably over-used: actors playing their roles on the brink of tears. Boys cry, men cry, women cry – this is one of the hallmarks of Chinese, historical movies (actually, of many contemporary, Chinese movies, too – actors are always teary-eyed in the modern-day thrillers of John Woo *et al*. Chow Yun-fat has spent plenty of time on the set of Woo's gangster flicks in tears).

The acting style is highly wrought, suiting the stylized approach which is part-Peking Opera and part-Western opera and part-television soap opera (i.e., it's all the operas, from the high art of classical opera to the low art of soapy dramas on telly).

It's cheese. It's camp. But it's also grand and over-cooked (and the performers and the audience know it, and revel in it). There isn't really an equivalent for this acting style in the Western world; well, not anymore. Maybe in Hollywood, between 1930 and 1950, say, when American actors declaimed in historical pictures in their version of what they thought theatre actors should sound like (or what they reckoned British stage actors were like).

✦

We're back in the studios at Dongyang again, the famous Hengdian World Studios where *Hero, Forbidden Kingdom* and *Detective Dee* were filmed, as well as the film studios in the Chinese capital. Despite the location work, and the odd scene outside in one colossal courtyard or another, most of *Curse of the Golden Flower* is studio-bound (like most movies about courtly/ palace shenanigans).

Curse of the Golden Flower is a costume movie *par excellence*, with pride of place going to the Dragon costume and the Phoenix costume worn by the Emperor and Empress.[2] There's gold[3] and red everywhere, and every costume is as fancy as can be (the full-body armour is astonishing,[4] for instance). To emphasize the opulence of everything in the Imperial court, some of the wardrobe is shamelessly anachronistic (like giving all of the female characters bulging cleavages. Well, Hollywood does it all the time, so why not Beijing?). Certainly, *Golden Flower* is a triumph for costume designers Jessie Dai and Kenneth Yee Chung-man, whose work is foregrounded in many scenes. And the hair and make-up people should be mentioned: chief hair stylists: Siu Mui Chau, Emily Lin and Ying Kwan Tam and chief make-up artists: JianPing Liu and YunLing Man.

Golden Flower's signature colours are red/ crimson and gold, as often in an Imperial-era romp in Chinese cinema. The colour design of reds and golds runs throughout the art direction, too (by Huo Tingxiao and Bin Zhao). The stand-out feature of the art direction might be the coloured glass used for the Palace interiors.

Zhao Xiaoding heads up a marvellous photography team which deliver stupendous visuals, as excessive as everything else in this 2006 movie. Especially impressive are the remote camera and wire shots: many filmmakers have used these new toys, but seldom as deftly as this (the overhead shots on cables zooming through the tunnels and gateways of the Imperial Palace are outstanding.

Another over-the-top element in *Curse of the Golden Flower* is the score by Shigeru Umebayashi (b. 1950), who also wrote the music for *House of Flying Daggers*. For *Curse of the Golden Flower,* Umebayashi went the whole hog with choirs that quiver and tremble even more than Gong Li's over-wrought performance: some of the choral cues are Asian equivalents of Hollywood schmaltz, while some are self-consciously operatic, Chinese versions of Giacomo Puccini or Giuseppe Verdi.

✦

As we're in the realm of the *wuxia pian*, there's a swordplay scene after ten minutes, when the Emperor meets his son Prince Jai. In the confines of a small audience chamber, father and son go at it in their very fancy full-body armour (Daddy in gold, Sonny in silver).

The swordplay action hints at what's to come, the father-son conflict (where soldiers in gold armour are pitted against soldiers in silver armour in

2 It took 40 people over 1,000 years to create the costumes.
3 Golden armour is mentioned in the poem by Huang Chao, from the Qi Dynasty ('the whole city will be clothed in golden armour').
4 Tony Ching employed it two years later for his own venture into Ancient Chinese history and courtly intrigue in *An Empress and the Warriors*.

the finale); and it's a little taster of action, because the rest of act one of *Curse of the Golden Flower* is rather stagey and talky. It does, of course, express the characterizations of father and son: the Emperor might be pushed around the Imperial Palace in a super-regal version of a wheelchair, he might take long, herbal baths, but he can also wield a sword when necessary. (And he likes to test his offspring). It also shows off the armour itself, in a series of abstract close-ups with zingy, grating sound fx that enhance the swords sliding over the metal.

✦

As the second act unfurls, the Imperial Doctor and his family becomes embroiled in the in-fighting behind the throne. Romantic attachments – the Doctor's daughter (Jiang Chan) is secretly seeing the Crown Prince – are just one of the strands linking the charas.

Act two climaxes with a truly astonishing shot of adrenalin, in the form of one of Tony Ching's most impressive action scenes: the ninja raid on the Inn. It's so intense and so rapidly staged, it really comes from another movie. Tony Ching certainly is the King of Ninja Scenes on film, and here in 2006 he gets to stage several big *shinobi* sequences (there are more that follow this one at the Inn). Ching has delivered variations on this scene before, but the budget is considerably larger than the typical Hong Kong action flick of the 1970s through 2000s (or the many TV series that Ching has action choreographed).

For four or so minutes, *Curse of the Golden Flower* becomes a completely different movie, as we take a welcome break from the over-heated tussling in the Imperial Palace. The scene is a compendium of some of Tony Ching's favourite *shinobi* gags – the sliding down wires, *en masse*, the tumbling, scurrying movements, the vicious, bladed weaponry on chains, etc. And instead of an all-out slaughter, the bodyguards of the Imperial Doctor at the Inn put up some resistance, and the family is thrown into the chaos of a running battle. It's gloriously over-the-top, and segues in the blink of the film editor's cut into a horse chase thru a narrow canyon (and the ninja are still on cables, zooming up behind the galloping horse).

There's a reprise of the band of the Emperor's black-garbed assassins – they materialize in the Imperial audience chamber to take on Prince Yu's bodyguards (whom they vanquish); they appear in several clashes with Prince Jai's guards; and they run down the Jiangs, mother and daughter, Jiang-shi and Jiang Chan, as they flee the Palace.

✦

Curse of the Golden Flower is a three-act movie, with the final act running on for 45-50 minutes (although the movie is 114 minutes, and would normally be split into four acts, this time it's three acts).

This is because the third act of *Curse of the Golden Flower* is stuffed with events which pay off the previous two acts: all of the courtly intrigue comes out into the open (the betrayals, the warring factions), along with the explosive secrets (like incest), and the giant insurrection led by Prince Jai.

The battle in the Imperial Palace is one of the stand-out sequences in the ecstatic action cinema of Tony Ching. It's a storming, big budget scene of extraordinary moments, captured in many formal, high angle shots, as well as the usual medium close-ups down in the fray. The staging uses bold visual devices: many symmetrical compositions; key figures (such as Prince Jai) are framed centrally; the silver armour of Prince Jai's rebellion is pitted against the gold armour of the Imperial guards; the sea of yellow flowers cover the entire courtyard of the Imperial Palace; a wall of grey shields hem in the Prince's army.

Filming at night added to the atmosphere, but no doubt made this sequence even more challenging to shoot. Even with multiple cameras, and a battalion of assistant directors, it would still take many nights to complete. Partly because the battle is split into numerous bits of business: instead of a rush of soldiers smashing into each other on both sides, the production has opted for a staging emphasizing chilly, military strategy. Prince Jai's rebellion army might rush into the Imperial Palace, but the wily Emperor has already gauged their numbers, predicted their tactics, and prepared things accordingly (such as the walls of shields).

The Emperor has cunning, age, experience, and a deadly will on his side, which Prince Jai cannot match: this was expressed in their duel in the first act (where Jai seemed to have the Emperor beaten down, but his father has some tricks up his gold-armoured sleeve).

Indeed, one of the striking aspects about the giant battle in *Curse of the Golden Flower* is that the Emperor himself doesn't lead his forces. He doesn't even go outside to observe the conflict from on high, while sipping a Martini. No, the Emperor is still in the audience chamber, beating his youngest son Prince Yu to death.

The two narrative elements of *Curse of the Golden Flower* – the courtly intrigue inside the Imperial Palace, all filmed in the studio, and the larger, political events (filmed on the big, outdoor sets at Hengdian World Studios) – echo each other. And there's just as much dramatic intensity in the scenes in the Palace.

The multiple revelations and subsequent betrayals and deaths evoke William Shakespeare's tragedies, such as *Hamlet,* and the tragic plays of

Ancient Greece. Prince Yu stabs the Crown Prince Wan and subsequently tries to force his father to give up the throne. Like a father with a naughty child, the Emperor takes off his belt to punish his son – only in this type of over-heated melodrama, that means killing him. (The moral? Do not raise your sword against Daddy, or the ruling powers).

The Empress's lack of agency is vividly portrayed by Gong Li as a character who is unable to act effectively: everything she tries seems doomed to failure. The series of revelations and the resulting acts of betrayal and death do not alter the status quo one iota. The Emperor is still the Emperor, and the political regime of the Imperial Palace remains the same.

This is brilliantly portrayed in perhaps the most incisive political commentary in *Curse of the Golden Flower* when the entire battlefield, the corpses, the blood, the weaponry and everything else, are briskly and efficiently whisked away. It's as if nothing ever happened: 100s of flunkies bring out fresh, yellow chrysanthemums and place the pots in the courtyard.

The Double Ninth Festival *will* go ahead, political power will *not* be disrupted – and life at the Imperial Palace continues as planned. Is this a critique of the government of the People's Republic of China and its attitude towards political subversion in the form of the Tiananmen Square protests, which were soundly and aggressively quashed? Maybe. But the director of this film, Zhang Yimou, was asked by the Chinese government to oversee events at the Olympic Games two years later, in 2008.

✦

We've seen this movie before (in China, you can probably see a version of this movie every single day on television). But we enjoy seeing it again when it's delivered with such panache and skill. Certainly it's a movie to see in a theatre (and *Curse of the Golden Flower* made it to the West, to theatres. I saw it at my local theatre).

The critical response admired the look, the two glamorous stars, and the melodrama of the piece, but reckoned it was a poor show in relation to Zhang Yimou's other work. For the critics who didn't like *Curse of the Golden Flower*, it was Zhang and co. going over material they've done before, and better. For those who *really* didn't go for *Curse of the Golden Flower*, it was dramatically over-cooked and psychologically shallow.

✦

What is the moral message of *Curse of the Golden Flower*? Don't attempt a rebellion against authorities, or against the Chinese authorities? (It will be aggressively suppressed). Even if the rulers of China are corrupt, are they still the ruling class? (And must be obeyed and respected). Or the family must be protected at all costs?

In a typical *wuxia pian*, the oppressors and the rulers are defeated – or one of their official representatives is, and the rebels and the liberals are triumphant (even if only for the moment). In *Curse of the Golden Flower*, the regime ruling the land remains in place, and the Emperor lives on (which they usually do in historical, Chinese romps like this – the Imperial structure isn't overthrown and a new, democratic, liberal government isn't put in its place).

25

DORORO

Dororo (2007) was a live-action version of an animated television series of 1969, which in turn was based on a 1967 comic by the 'god of *manga*', Osamu Tezuka. The *animé* of *Dororo* was produced by Osamu Tezuka's company Mushi Productions in 1969, and broadcast on Fuji TV. The show, prod. by Tatsuo Shibayama, wr. by Yoshitake Suzuki and dir. by Gisaburo Sugii, ran to 26 episodes (two seasons). The *manga* was published in *Weekly Shonen Sunday* and *Bokeno* from 1967 to 1969. A further *animé* series appeared in 2019.

The 2007 adaptation of *Dororo* was prod. by Toho/ Tokyo Broadcasting System/ Twins Japan/ Yahoo Japan/ W.O.W.O.W./ Universal/ Dentsu/ Mainichi Broadcasting System/ Hokkaido Broadcasting Company/ Asahi Shimbun/ Stardust Pictures, prod. by Takashi Hirano and Atsuyuki Shimoda, wr. by Masa Nakamura and Akihiko Shiota, and dir. by Akihiko Shiota. Art dir. by Ken Turner, DP: Takahide Shibanushi, costumes by Kazuko Kurosawa, music by Goro Yasukawa and Yutaka Fukuoka, and ed. by Toshihide Fukano. Hiroyuki Yoshida was action director – Ching Siu-tung is credited as action instructor. Released Mch 15, 2007. 139 mins.

Dororo starred Satoshi Tsumabuki, Ko Shibasaki, Kiichi Nakai, Yoshio Harada, Eita, Mieko Harada, and Katsuo Nakamura.

Dororo re-imagines the mythical Olde Japan, the world of monsters and demons, temples and wayside shrines, mountains and country roads, bamboo forests and quaint villages. It's the Nippon that never existed, but which Osamu Tezuka helped to revive.

Dororo was produced for a home audience, in Japanese, like most Japanese movies (in fact, most movies everywhere are produced for home audiences, and only a small percentage get released in other territories, and some don't even get released in their home country).

Altho' there is plenty of action in *Dororo*, it is a contemplative, supernatural outing, enlivened by some comedy. The performance style is familiar from other live-action, Japanese fare: slightly hysterical, indulgently sentimental, and *very* Japanese (that is, *Dororo* doesn't angle itself at an international audience, altho' parts of it were filmed in New Zealand).

Dororo is a charming slice of Ye Olde Nippone, lovingly evoked, and spoilt a little by the irritating, bratty and one-note performance of pop singer Ko Shibasaki as Dororo, and the rather leaden turn by Satoshi Tsumabuki as the cursed swordsman Hyakkimaru. However, altho' they are the two main charas, the world they inhabit is full of other elements (and two uninspiring lead charas don't automatically weaken a movie).

The cursed youth, Hyakkimaru, and his sidekick thief, Dororo, are familiar characters in Japanese pop culture: the youth is silent, brooding, always serious, and a brilliant *ronin*, while the sidekick girl adds earthy humour (and exposition). Hyakkimaru's goal is to slay the 48 demons who took parts of his body in the Faustian pact his father, the warlord Daigo Kagemitsu, conducted in order to gain power.

Hyakkimaru and Dororo make an unlikely pair as they wander archaic Japan, searching for demons to kill. (The girl,[5] who dresses as a boy, tags along with Hyakkimaru, hoping for a big score when he regains his body and can take over the world, or at least snaffle some treasure).

✦

Gods, demons and Japanese warriors within a high fantasy context seems perfect for the action cinema of Ching Siu-tung. Ching's contribution included some swordplay scenes (of course), and several battles between the swordsman and demons. *Dororo,* being chiefly a slice of Japanese folklore, featured some unusual monsters (some were updated with digital effects, but some were the usual monsters of all movies everywhere – a guy in a suit).[6]

The action scenes overseen by Ching Siu-tung include an impressive battle against a spider-woman in the opening act, which sets the tone for the following adventures. Here the combination of digital animation and live-action elements is skilfully handled (increasingly in the 21st century, Hong Kong action directors have to blend their live-action work on set with animation added later miles away, or in other countries, by the geeks at their computers).

The mid-film action sequence in *Dororo* sees Hyakkimaru battling a

5 In the comic she's only revealed as a girl in the final section.
6 The reptile inevitably recalled Godzilla.

series of monsters – in a rocky grassland, and in a forest (Ching Siu-tung must've staged more action scenes in woodland than most action directors). And if we're in a forest, we must have the usual Chingian motifs (like characters scurrying up or down tree trunks, high falls, trees being split apart, etc).

In the sandy grassland there's an impressive tussle between our heroes and a reptile (achieved partly with digital animation, partly with animatronics, and partly with a guy in a monster suit). This section included the beastie extending an enormous tongue – Ching Siu-tung must be one of the very few directors who has been there, done that with giant tongues (in the *Chinese Ghost Story* movies).

A huge amount of wire-work was employed in *Dororo* to achieve the marvellous mid-air battle between Hyakkimaru and a winged demon, which extended across a large area. This sequence looked like it was tough to stage – the setting included many uneven, irregular rocks.

The finale of *Dororo* was by far the most exciting section, where the Faustian plot reaches its hysterical climax amid multiple deaths (and some demonic reanimations of corpses). It's all about the Law of the Father, about fathers and sons, as usual in all Japanese folk tales (and in all samurai yarns): so it's about Hyakkimaru challenging his father (and his brother), with women being sidelined completely (Hyakkimaru knocks out Dororo so she can't interfere, but his father, Daigo Kagemitsu, cuts down his mother and kills her).

✦

Sidenote on Osamu Tezuka: Osamu Tezuka (1928-89) has probably had more influence on Japanese animation (and *manga*) than any other single individual – Fred Schodt reckons that Japanese *manga* and *animé* would be unthinkable without Tezuka, and that *every* major *manga* artist has been inspired by him.

While animators work under the shadow of Walt Disney in the West, in Japan, it's Osamu Tezuka. Known as the 'god of *manga*', Tezuka is of course one of the major figures in Japanese *animé*, creator/ director of *Astro Boy, Arabian Nights, Princess Knight, Triton of the Sea, Kimba the White Lion, Buddha, Bix X, Black Jack, Dororo, Jungle Emperor Leo,* and *Phoenix.*[7]

Osamu Tezuka was very successful very quickly: by his early twenties, he was 'the biggest selling *manga* artist in Japan'.[8] And he was immensely prolific, creating thousands of pages of *manga* (as well as developing *animé* and running production companies).

7 As well as 21 TV series and twelve TV specials, Tezuka also produced 700 stories and around 17,000 *manga* pages (C, 30).
8 H. McCarthy, 1993, 13.

26

IN THE NAME OF THE KING

In the Name of the King (2007) was a Canadian-German-American co-production based on a computer game, *Dungeon Siege* (made by Gas Powered Games). Produced by Brightlight Pictures/ Boll K.G. Product-ions/ Herold Productions. Producers: Uwe Boll, Dan Clarke, Shawn Williamson and Wolfgang Herold, wr. by Doug Taylor and dir. by Uwe Boll. *In the Name of the King* starred Jason Statham, Claire Forlani, Leelee Sobieski, Ron Perlman, John Rhys-Davies, Burt Reynolds and Ray Liotta. Released April 11, 2007. 127 mins.

In the Name of the King has a terrible reputation among film critics and viewers – it was trashed on release.[9] So what? It's a reasonably effective flick in the fantasy adventure/ sword 'n' sorcery/ dungeons 'n' dragons mode. Sure, it has clichéd characters, bog standard villains, and all sorts of dumb elements – but then so does 99% of the output of most film production centres around the globe (not only Hollywood – *all* of them churn out dreck. No film production centre makes *only* exquisite, prestige, award-winning items). And sword-and-sorcery movies are notorious (and loved) for ropey acting, dodgy casting, silly ideas, and sinister ideology.

Anyhoo, it has become a favourite sport among film critics to attack director Uwe Boll personally, as with hated directors such as Jason Frieberg and Aaron Seltzer (the spoof movie masters), Michael Bay, Michael Winner, Joel Schumacher,[10] Paul W.S. Anderson, M. Night Shyamalan, Kevin Smith, Danny Boyle, McG, Lars von Trier, Mike Leigh, Michael Cimino, Ken Loach, Roland Emmerich, and Ken Russell.

And, yes, each one of the critics who guillotined *In the Name of the King* in their film reviews have scripted a hundred classic movies of their

9 But sold close to a million units in home release formats.
10 Joel Schumacher was blamed by fans for 'ruining' the *Batman* franchise with the two entries, of 1995 and 1997. But those are both wonderful, very entertaining movies!

own. And all of the critics who attacked the film contributed their own ideas on how to improve it.

Uwe Boll (b. 1965) was certainly a character: his movies were routinely rubbished by film critics, to the point where Boll offered to have boxing matches with his fiercest critics (which he did!). Filmmakers often joke about something like that, but hardly any have actually done it! Boll is also a despised director, like Michael Bay or M. Night Shyamalan, a director that people love to hate. So there have been petitions to stop Boll making more films.

Critics also complained that *In the Name of the King* stole from movies like the *Lord of the Rings* franchise of 2001-2003, forgetting that all movies steal from each other, and that the *Lord of the Rings* film series shamelessly snitched material from 100s of movies (*Star Wars*, Ray Harryhausen, Tim Burton, Disney, *The Wizard of Oz*, *Conan*, *Indiana Jones*, *Titanic*, *Braveheart*, *The Last of the Mohicans*, disaster movies, WWII movies, Hong Kong action cinema, you name it – and the *Rings* films were also remakes).

But it's true that Ray Liotta and Burt Reynolds look like they've strayed in from a movie about Las Vegas and gangsters (Liotta, a truly feeble super-villain here in *In the Name of the King*, resembles Tony Curtis in the 1950s, and also his *GoodFellas*, wise guy character). Leelee Sobieski looks quite out of place, too (Sobieski wearing full battle armour is not the thrill you'd hope for). And some of the rest of the players in *In the Name of the King* are miscast (one dodgy casting choice can slip by, but not so many!). And the music is crudely and horribly over-used (this is one of the worst uses of music in a movie ever. The score – by Jessica de Rooij and Henning Lohner – is already mediocre, but to plaster it absolutely everywhere is painful).

But the cast of *In the Name of the King* has some good names, even if they're not particularly convincing playing their characters (well, they've been good in other material). However, Jason Statham, as 'Farmer', hoarse whispers his lines to bizarre effect. (Plus you do get a little tired of his constant petulant/ cranky/ antsy attitude to all and everything except his family. He's basically the family man and very reluctant warrior that Mel Gibson played in *Braveheart* (1995). But the dramatic device[11] of the unwilling warrior lasts here until after halfway thru the movie, and becomes so tiresome. Just get on the horse and kick some ass already, Farmer Boy!).

As to the involvement of Tony Ching Siu-tung in *In the Name of the King* – the action is filled with rough and tumble fighting, and a massive

---
11 A favourite device with screenwriters who enshrine Joseph Campbell.

amount of stunts, featuring an array of mediæval weaponry and the odd bit of magic. The henchmen (who're orcs ripped off from J.R.R. Tolkien's fiction in all but name), topple as easily as all movie henchmen do,[12] and the heroes barely get out of breath. But that's perfectly OK in any action-adventure flick.

One of Tony Ching Siu-tung's trademark action scenes occurs halfway through in *In the Name of the King*, in the giant battle in the forest: ninja-like swordsmen scrambling up and down very tall trees. It's not a Ching action scene unless a squad of warriors are descending on wires in a circle, simultaneously (it worked 20 years ago, in *A Chinese Ghost Story*, so why not here, in Canada, in 2007?). It does seem that film producers, when they hire Ching, ask him for some of his famous gags.

Tony Ching Siu-tung's wire-work team also had fun with the elf-like women in the forest: babes in leather slide down vines from tall trees in swirls of falling leaves to attack victims. (It was a Chinese martial arts variation on the way that elves and sprites are usually depicted in Western fantasy flicks).

On a technical level, there are many impressive ærial shots in *In the Name of the King*, filmed by cameramen strapped to flying dragons. (The beasts were paid by the dead goat. Unfortunately, a cameraman from New Jersey was also eaten).

Some critics carped that the production values in *In the Name of the King* were shoddy? Eh? This movie cost $60 million, had whole villages built specially, included a large cast (plus costumes), filmed a good deal on location, included a massive battle at night (with rain machines), and featured pricey ærial footage and vfx). In Hong Kong, of course, exactly the same movie (but probably much better) would cost US $6 million (and in India, $3 million).

---

12 They can barely move under all that armour, weaponry, prosthetics, make-up, etc.

27

THE WARLORDS

Tau Ming Song

The Warlords (*Tau Ming Song,* 2007), also known as *The Blood Brothers,* was produced by Media Asia/ China Film Group/ Morgan & Chan. Andre Morgan and Peter Chan produced, dir. by Chan, and no less than *eight* writers are credited: Xu Lan, Chun Tin-nam, Aubery Lam, Huang Jianxin, Jojo Hui, He Jiping, Guo Junli and James Yuen. DP: Arthur Wong. Music: Peter Kam, Chan Kwong-wing, Leon Ko and Chatchai Pongprapaphan. Editor: Wenders Li. Art directors: Kenneth Yee Chung-man, Yi Zheng-zhou and Pater Wong. Costumes: Kenneth Yee Chung-man and Jessie Dai, Lee Pik-kwan. Vfx: Ng Yuen-fai. Sound design: Sunit Asvinikul and Nakorn Kositpaisal. Released Dec 12, 2007. 127 mins.

The budget was U.S. $40 million (*very* high for a Chinese movie), with apparently $15 million going to Jet Li ($6m to Andy Lau Tak-wah and $2 to Takeshi Kaneshiro). It was filmed in Shanghai, Beijing and Hengdian World Studios, between early Dec, 2006 and Mch 28, 2007.

The movie was given splashy publicity and multiple premieres in China (Beijing, Shanghai, Hong Kong, etc), with the actors and director attending press conferences. *The Warlords* won many awards, including the top prizes at the Hong Kong Film Awards and the Golden Horse Awards (and was nominated for many more. Tony Ching was nominated though didn't win).

In the cast were Jet Li, Andy Lau Tak-wah, Jinglei Xu, Takeshi Kaneshiro, Xiadong Guo, Jacky Heung and Zongwan Wei. The three brothers are:

Jet Li   Qingyun (General Pang)

| Andy Lau | Zhao Erhu |
| Takeshi Kaneshiro | Wuyang |

Many great talents in the Chinese movie industry worked on *The Warlords*, such as top, much-revered cinematographer Arthur Wong, whose credits include: *Painted Skin, The Soong Sisters, Aces Go Places, Armour of God, Eastern Condors, A Chinese Ghost Story, Moon Warriors, Iron Monkey, Hitman, Once Upon a Time In China* and *New Dragon Gate Inn*.

This movie is one of the great achievements of Tony Ching Siu-tung – he took on the action direction of *The Warlords*, and might be regarded as co-director. Peter Chan (b. 1962) was best-known for comedies and dramas about relationships (*He Ain't Heavy, He's My Father, He's a Man, She's a Woman, The Love Letter, The Age of Miracles*, etc). Chan hadn't made a movie of this scale before.

The 'making of' documentary demonstrates that this was a challenging production for the cast and crew, with some tough location shooting thru the Winter of 2006-2007. Principal photography wended on for some 117 days, which is very long for a Chinese movie (and in Hong Kong, you could make five films in that time).

The Warlords is a big, historical Chinese movie in the manner of *The Curse of the Golden Flower* and *Hero*, but although it stars the eternally wonderful Jet Li, it's not a martial arts movie (though it does feature some astounding martial arts scenes, choreographed by Tony Ching). Rather, *The Warlords* is a slice of recent, Chinese history (the 1860s, to be precise), focussing on the brotherhood of three soldiers, played by Jet Li, Andy Lau Tak-wah and Takeshi Kenshiro, big stars on the Asian film scene (Ching had worked with them before, many times – Kaneshiro and Li appeared in *Dr Wai* in 1996, for example).

The Warlords is a remake of *The Blood Brothers* (Chang Cheh, 1973). *The Warlords* was set in the late Qing dynasty, in the late 19th century, during the Taiping Rebellion. Peter Chan said he was inspired by *A Better Tomorrow* and John Woo's concept of brotherhood and loyalty. (Incidentally, Woo was helming a prestige historical picture at the same time, *Red Cliff*).

✦

The Warlords is about brotherhood, heroism, war, sacrifice, and the creation of modern China. The struggles for survival and the battles between warring armies and leaders is familiar material, which cinema has been mining since the days of D.W. Griffith. That's the bigger picture, as the story widens from small-scale conflicts to bigger operations, such as Suzhou and Nanking, with the action finally ending up in Beijing.

Sweeping vistas caught with widescreen photography,[13] a lush orchestral score,[14] thousands of extras, lovely historical buildings such as palaces and castles, it might be a movie from any year from the 1950s to today. But the dramatic focus of *The Warlords*, the concentration on the interaction of the three warriors, and the way the roles're written, and the way they're played and directed, means this can only be a product of contemporary, Chinese cinema. No other filmmaking centre produces movies quite like this, where the allegiance of the three brothers is depicted in such a fierce, serious manner (there are several explosive scenes for the actors, when they are required to really let rip. And they do. This is also a movie of weeping men – numerous scenes are performed with the characters on the edge of breaking down).

The Warlords is another example of the Chinese film industry producing the finest and most impressive historical dramas (in live-action; but in animation, it's the Japanese *animé* industry – *Moribito, Barefoot Gen, Nobunaga the Fool, Drifters, Princess Mononoke*). In the best Chinese, historical movies, everything is raised up a degree that nowhere else can match in recent times. Chinese, historical movies know how to present the epic sweep of history like no other movies, including the productions of France, Italy, Germany, Russia or America (and there's a genuine sensuality to the filmmaking in *The Warlords* – you can feel the sunlight, the dirt, the rain, and the cold).[15]

Of course, there is action a-plenty in *The Warlords*, from a stunning ambush sequence in a canyon (where the bait army proves itself), to vast battles with horses, dirt, swords, spears, blood and 100s of nasty gags involving stunts and more blood. And as Jet Li is the star, there is plenty of opportunity for Li to let loose big-time. Which he does, including one of his trademark moves, taking out hordes of soldiers with a very long staff. (This is a form of *wushu*-style action that Li has performed several times in Chinese movies – and also variations on it. For instance, in the *Wong Fei-hung* movies, he uses an umbrella).

Instead of Tony Ching's famous wire-work and flying swordsmen (and ninjas), the action is ground-based, and consists mainly what humans are capable of without summoning *chi* or magic. It's the down-and-dirty style of action, with handheld camerawork capturing combatants slamming into each other. (The action is covered with numerous   cinematic devices,

---

13 Inevitably, the cinematography follows a recent trend in world cinema for gritty, dirty photography, with the colours selected to favour greys, blacks, blues and creams.
14 With heavy percussion for some of the dramatic scenes.
15 Like so many Chinese movies, you can see it is very cold in the night scenes.

such as slow motion, subjective viewpoints, and unusual camera angles. One of the inspirations is the opening act of Saving Private Ryan, 1998).

The hand-to-hand duels in the finale are especially impressive – when Jet Li and Takeshi Kaneshiro have to grapple with each other in Beijing, when General Qingyun is about to accept his new job as the governor of Nanking.

There are some departures from the usual Jet Li vehicle, too, in The Warlords: one is Li having an obviously sexual relationship with a woman, Liansheng (played by Jinglei Xu, the only significant female character in this very boysy outing).16 Liansheng helps tend Qingyun after the opening battle, and they make love that night. That Liansheng is also Qingyun's lover doesn't, in the end, play out as you might expect (there is no revelation scene of the erotic triangle between Li, Lau and Xu, for instance, which is set up in the first half of the first act). And Li's Qingyun dies at the end (which he has done b4, of course – in Hero, most spectacularly – but not as in The Warlords. Here, the brotherhood plot comes to fruition, and Wuyang attacks Qingyun on his way to accept his new job in Beijing, resulting in an incredibly painful, bone-snapping duel (literally bone-breaking). Wuyang thinks it is because Qingyun has betrayed the blood oath, and had Erhu murdered. He has – but the movie also suggests that it was the Imperial Court who wanted Qingyun taken care of, using General Ho as their intermediary).

Halfway thru act one of The Warlords the oath of blood is undertaken by the three brothers. This is the turning-point, and the narrative set-up of the movie. In a typically excessive turn, the oath requires that a victim is killed by each of the brothers, thus damning the participants.

It's Qingyun who suggests that a way out of the poverty of the community (and to sidestep it being vulnerable to attacks) is to join the independent loyalist army. Bandit Wuyang reluctantly agrees, leading to the blood oath.

The Warlords is filled with highly dramatic scenes. The most intense is definitely the sequence where 4,000 soldiers are killed in a courtyard by their fellow countrymen. It's the kind of over-cooked and impossible scenario that Chinese cinema relishes, and The Warlords milks it for every ounce of emotion (Wuyang thinks that General Qingyun is correct and orders the archers to fire, while Erhu is chained up on the ground and writhes and screams in protest. Nothing in this movie holds back!).

The inclusion of a woman in amongst all of the macho histrionics,

16 It's reassuring that for once the producers and casting directors haven't cast a too-pretty young woman in her early 20s or late teens to play against Jet Li (in his mid-forties) – Jinglei Xu was born in 1974 – which filmmakers too often do. However, the romantic plot is still definitely a sub-plot. Jinglei Xu was one of the 'Four Dan Actresses of China' (the other three were Zhou Xun, Zhao Wei and Zhang Ziyi).

bloodshed and war-mongering is rather contrived: Liansheng is introduced early on in *The Warlords* (not long after Jet Li's Qingyun), but her presence is dramatically artificial (though no more so than many cheesy, Hollywood flicks). In addition, Liansheng isn't given much of a personality or identity beyond her relationship with either Qingyun or Erhu. When we cut back to the village from time to time, for example, she is sitting on the wall overlooking the route into the community, typing her as the war bride who waits longingly for her beloved, staring off into the distance.

Qingyun, meanwhile, might be a veteran warrior, but he acts a little like a teenage kid where a woman is concerned – he wonders, as in a pop song, if the one night they shared ever really happened. While Liansheng might be torn between the two men, Qingyun and Erhu, the Qingster is smitten (she means more to him than he does to her, it seems).

The Warlords builds to a tragic finale: Chinese cinema adores nothing better than an all-out piece of sustained tragedy. You get the feeling that if Chinese movies could cut straight to act three – when all is chaos and howling and weeping and multiple deaths and high opera – they would. So Erhu is ambushed and pricked with arrows (alone, at night, in heavy rain), expiring face-down in the mud; so Wuyang stalks into Liansheng's chambers and kills her (he hopes to persuade Qingyun that he doesn't have to take care of Erhu now); and finally Wuyang attacks Qingyun.

28

KUNG FU DUNK

Gongfu Guanlan

akehiko Inoue's *manga Slam Dunk* (1990-96) is one of the biggest
sses in Japanese comicbook culture. Published in *Weekly Shonen*
had huge sales (of 170 million copies). *Kung Fu Dunk* is a loose
Slam Dunk (as the movie was originally titled). Thus, *Kung Fu*
her adaptation of Japanese comics by Hong Kong cinema
k is a Chinese-Taiwanese-Hong Kong production).

1967, Okuchi) is a superstar *mangaka* – his
n in 1998) is an epic about the famous samurai
more perfect for a Hong Kong make-over
rld is so rich and remarkable, it doesn't
ng Fu Dunk also clearly draws on the
Chow comedy which was a huge
ed the 2001 movie.

n Cantonese,[17] 2008), we
c youth, surly rivals,
on/ coach-protegé

from Tony
Ching had
nanghai Film
prod. by Albert
ao Xiaoding, Pengle
hu Yen Ping, You-Chen

tory in
act one
any gags
action with
e sent flying
ction is looser
as over-the-top
ang Shi-jie as a
can perform the
er suited Ching Siu-
re, in *Kung Fu Dunk*
n scenes required immense

530

Wang and Lam Chiu Wing, music by Ko Ishikawa, DP: Zhao Xiaoding, ed. by Po-Wen Chen, costumes by Shirley Chan, prod. des. by Kenneth Yee Chung-man, and sound by Duu-Chih Tu. *Kung Fu Dunk* was filmed in Shanghai (the location for the school was the Shanghai Science and Technology Museum in Pudong). Released: Feb 7, 2008. 98 mins.

In the cast, Eric Tsang Chi-wai stole the movie from the lead, Jay Chou, and everybody else – Tsang is a delight throughout *Kung Fu Dunk*, with comical skills honed from decades in the trenches of Hong Kong cinema, going back to the goofy Cinema City comedies of the early Eighties. Chou, meanwhile (Tony Ching had directed him in *Curse of the Golden Flower*), is impressive as the boy from the wrong side of the tracks (a foundling), who becomes a *kung fu* star (and trouble-maker), and basketball whizzkid. (Indeed, the relationship between Fang Shi-jie and Uncle Wang Li is the backbone of the 2008 movie, with the other plots and subplots being left on the bench at the edge of the basketball court – like the rivalry with other team members, or with the rival sports teams, or Fang's parental quest, or the romantic subplot that goes nowhere).

Also in the cast were Charlene Choi (she worked with Tony Ching in *The Butterfly Lovers* and *The Emperor and the White Snake*), Bolin Chen, Baron Chen, Wang Gang, Will Liu, Ng Man-tat, Eddy Ko and Kenneth Tsang.

Kung Fu Dunk is a charming and modest slice of Chinese hokum freighted with an appealing young cast, some veteran actors, a thoroughly familiar script, many humorous moments, and Tony Ching's solid and inventive action choreography. It's a market-driven movie, yes, shamelessly incorporating a batch of elements designed to appeal to mul target audiences.

Sure, for Tony Ching, *Kung Fu Dunk* is re-treading familiar terr terms of action direction – from the bust-up in the swanky club in to the numerous gags on the basketball court (which reprise m from *Shaolin Soccer* and similar fare). Combining *kung fu* basketball sports means plenty of wire-work, as the teens a all over the place.[18] As this is fundamentally a comedy, the a and broader than some of Ching's other movies (tho' not as some of his work with Wong Jing!). Besides, we see hotshot martial arts master first, so we know he weightlessness of *kung fu* before he takes up basketb

The broad, comical approach of *Shaolin Socc* tung's style of action choreography, and it does h

18 As the behind-the-scenes footage demonstrates, the actio patience, as shots were taken again and again.

going back to films such as *The Terracotta Warrior* and *A Chinese Ghost Story*, Ching has been happy to come up with very silly stunts and bits of martial arts business. The cinematic approach of Hong Kong film rightly doesn't take itself too seriously – it cuts loose far, far more than equivalent movies in the Western arena.

✦

Kung Fu Dunk is lightweight throughout, ticking off a host of clichés and stereotypes, from the outcast, underdog hero to the wise, crafty parental figures, the drunken rivals, and the too-sweet, too-cute potential girlfriend. *Kung Fu Dunk* is a market-driven movie, a producer's movie (like most Hong Kong productions), a movie which's been developed to cater to certain sectors of the global audience. Before the actors're cast, the director hired, or the crew signed up (or even the script written), this production has been carefully developed to hit a bunch of commercial targets.

It works. And it gets away with being so mechanically formulaic partly due to the canny casting of Jay Chou and Eric Tsang Chi-wai, who hold this piece of fluff together. The other roles are under-written (look at what the older character actors can do with a thin, bitty characterization in the script compared to the young cast, who lack the acting experience to fill out their one-dimensional characters). Indeed, some of the young cast seem adrift somewhat in *Kung Fu Dunk*: they're playing secondary roles, sure, but there doesn't seem to be much investment in them as characters.

Cinematically, being such a mechanical and by-the-numbers script, the clever casting is aided by some flashy visuals and a rapid form of editing in many scenes (by editor Po-Wen Chen) – which contrasts strongly with the heart of the movie – the duologues between Fang Shi-jie and Uncle Wang Li.

You can't be out-of-date or unfashionable, Tony Ching insists, if you're going to keep producing movies. *Kung Fu Dunk* certainly tries to remain fresh and sparkly in its visual style. The selections of pop songs, too, are part of that drive by the producers to be contemporary and relevant. (The pop music elements also cross over into the casting of pop singer Jay Chou in the lead role – Hong Kong cinema has been using pop stars for a long time).

Kung Fu Dunk is partly a commentary on stardom and celebrity, as Uncle Wang Li tries to turn Fang Shi-jie into a star. Wang Li is a svengali with his ear permanently glued to a cel phone, working deals and drumming up publicity from journalists, while he peruses the papers or the web.

◆

The upmarket club bust-up in *Kung Fu Dunk*'s act one, where Fang Shi-jie takes on a host of heavies, is amusingly choreographed and edited to the song 'Hero Chou' (a shameless piece of marketing, this tie-in piece is reprised in the finale). The presentation is in the self-consciously gimmicky manner of many recent, Hong Kong action movies (using speed ramping, for example, and many flashy editing effects).

The finale of *Kung Fu Dunk* brings the expected Giant Smackdown, as our boys're pitted against a bunch of basketball thugs (they resort to dirty tricks). The arrival of the four *sifus* from Fang's martial arts *dojo* provides a comical interlude in amongst the frowns and slow motion leaps. By the end of the sequence, every player on the court seems to be flying (courtesy of Ching Siu-tung's team).19

The finale of *Kung Fu Dunk* is followed by a little too much cheese, as the movie milks melodrama and sentiment to the max. This is an indulgent movie – when other films would've been wrapping up the proceedings, *Kung Fu Dunk* shifts into several moody scenes in slo-mo, accompanied musically by – you guessed it – plinky plonky solo piano (the go-to music across the *entire* world for sappy, emotional scenes. Yes, it's not just Hollywood cinema, it's also found in Japanese *animé*, in Bollywood musicals, in Euro-art films, etc. And it should be outlawed).

---

19 Now we see why the interiors of many martial arts movies have to have high ceilings – to fit in those giant cranes to perform the wire-work.

29

THE BUTTERFLY LOVERS

Jian Die

The Butterfly Lovers (a.k.a. *Jian Die* and *The Assassin's Blade*, 2008) saw Tony Ching working as the action choreographer on a *wuxia pian* interpretation of the Ancient Chinese legend of the doomed lovers Liang Shanbo and Zhu Yingtai.

The Butterfly Lovers was helmed by Jingle Ma Choh-shing (a Hong Kong director and cinematographer – *Mulan, Tokyo Raiders, Prison On Fire, Fong Sai-yuk, Viva Erotica* and several Jackie Chan pictures),[20] prod. by Catherine Hun Ga-jan for Brilliant Idea Group/ China Film Co-Production Corp./ Different Digital Design Ltd./ Xian Mei Ah Culture Communciation Ltd, and wr. by Chris Ng Ka-keung, Yeung Sin-ling, Wong Nga-man, Jingle Ma and Chan Po-chun. DPs: Jingle Ma, Chan Kwok-hung and Thomas Yeung Yiu-fai. Costumes: Petra Kwok Suk-man. Image designer: Bruce Yu Ka-on. Sound design: George Lee Yiu-keung and Kinson Tsang King-cheung. Art dir.: Tony Yu Hing-wah. Ed.: Eric Kwong Chi-leung. Music: Ronald Fu Yuen-wai and Chiu Tsang-hei (Charlene Choi sang the theme song). Released Oct 9, 2008. 102 mins.

Some of the cast and crew had worked with Tony Ching (and Tsui Hark) before – such as Xiong Xin-xin (here playing a tough *sifu* at the *dojo*, costume designer Bruce Yu, and Ti Lung from *A Better Tomorrow* and a zillion other Hong Kong movies). In the cast were Charlene Choi Cheuk-yin, Wu Chun, Hu Ge, Ti Lung, Harlem Yu, Li Qunqin and Xiong Xin-xin.

✦

The story of the lovers Liang Shanbo and Zhu Yingtai, sometimes

---

20 Jingle Ma filmed several Jackie Chan movies as DP, including *First Strike, Drunken Master 2* and *Rumble In the Bronx*.

termed the Chinese *Romeo and Juliet*, goes back to at least the Tang Dynasty. It has been filmed many times before in cinema and television (as well as operas and stage plays).

The approach in the 2008 interpretation was in part a remake of the 1994 movie *The Lovers*, directed by Tsui Hark (the characterization of Zhu Yingtai, for example, clearly draws on the way the character was played by Charlie Yeung). Like *The Lovers*, *The Butterfly Lovers* mounted much of the story as lighthearted comedy (in the first half, before the tale becomes tragic), making much of the crossdressing of Yingtai (with the usual misunderstandings and embarrassments stemming from a girl dressing up as a guy).

Charlene Choi Cheuk-yin steals the 2008 movie as Zhu Yingtai – she plays Yingtai as Charlie Yeung performed the character – a naïve, vulnerable but plucky young girl. Harlmen Yu Ching-hing as the herbalist (Teacher Herbal Head) provides solid support as a kindly guide for both Yingtai and Liang Shanbo. Choi appeared in another folktale, *The Emperor and the White Snake*, as Green Snake.

✦

As you'd expect from a director who was (and still is) a cinematographer, *The Butterfly Lovers* looks wonderful: it features many camera techniques which photographers are fond of, such as mounting long scenes in two shots, and using selective focus to shift attention from one actor to another (in *The Butterfly Lovers*, several scenes are staged with both actors facing the camera, but with one actor with their back to the other).

✦

As *The Butterfly Lovers* was a *wuxia pian* approach to the *Romeo and Juliet* legend, there were many action scenes – even though the story didn't quite need them, being at its heart a tale of tragic love. Thus Tony Ching was hired to stage some of his famous martial arts choreography – and Chingian choreography fits in perfectly with a romantic drama clad in period costumes.

The Butterfly Lovers announced that it would be featuring some big action scenes in this particular take on the legend by starting out with a rough-and-tumble street brawl in the opening sequence. Among the subsequent action scenes was a classic ,Chingian nighttime duel, with Ma Chengen clad in ninja black (you can spot the way that Ching handles the camera himself in this sequence, selecting low angles and tilting the camera).

The school that the characters attend in *The Butterfly Lovers* is a martial arts *dojo* in Ancient China, and that means several group scenes of children practising *kung fu*, overseen by their *sifu*. That also means some comedy is extracted from the sight of tiny Charlene Choi trying to wield heavy weaponry (some she can't even lift). Actually, that's an important point: real metal weapons are *very heavy* (try picking up a real sword and swinging it).

The second half of *The Butterfly Lovers* moves into the familiar tragic mode of a zillion romantic dramas and tragedies – not only in China, but around the world. It's one girl and two boys, it's an arranged marriage, and it's the fates or destiny or the gods overtaking the lovers, so that no matter what they do, they are doomed.

Dramatically, love stories like this seem childishly 'simple', yet that is their very appeal. Audiences know that the characters in a tragedy such as this are condemned (by circumstance, by destiny, by fate, by tradition, by patriarchy, whatever). But the mechanisms of the tragedy remain powerful. These stories have endured for a good reason: *they work.*

Anyway, in the second half of *The Butterfly Lovers,* the staging and pacing slows down, with scenes played with many pauses in between the dialogue, with looks of longing and sadness, caught in lingering close-ups of the three principal actors.

By the time we reach the finale of *The Butterfly Lovers,* there are several action set-pieces strung together, focussed on Liang Shanbo, as he struggles to stop the tide of patriarchal power and tradition in Ancient China single-handed. It's a losing battle, of course – everything is lined up against Liang, from his subordinate class status and his lack of a family and support on his side, to centuries-old tradition, and to the kind of power and influence that the aristocracy can wield.

Variations on the one-man-versus-an-army scenario are rolled out in *The Butterfly Lovers'* finale (Tony Ching has delivered so many of these scenes) – the first being when Cao Fang (Liu Kai), Ma Chengen's lieutenant, comes to arrest Liang Shanbo with his lackeys. An exciting rooftop chase ensues (the soldiers have spears and bows and arrows, while Liang of course wields the primary weapon of martial arts movies, a sword).[21] Liang is caught by sniping archers (but somehow, he manages to continue his struggle even with two arrows in his back).

The Butterfly Lovers' climax occurs in a heavy rainstorm, with Liang Shanpo still on the war-path, taking on Ma Chengen's guards in the mansion still decorated with red wedding lamps. The poses and the moves of the duel with Cao Fang are pure Tony Ching – how Cao lunges with his

---

21 And it's a sword that Zhu has decorated with butterflies. On a poetic note, those butter-flies flutter off the sword at the end, away from the dead lovers.

spear towards Liang in slow motion, for example, while flying thru the air, and how the camera focusses on the guys' boots hitting the ground, splashing water (similar shots occurred in *Hero*, for example, in the fight between Jet Li and Donnie Yen, and Wu Chun resembles a young Yen).

✦

The Butterfly Lovers is not a movie to fight – it's pointless trying to resist, or trying to turn it into a different movie. It's entertainment, and it's entertaining. Maybe it should have more of this, or less of that. Maybe it should be more lighthearted, or maybe it should be more dramatic. Maybe it shouldn't include so much action. Maybe it should've cast this actor instead of that one. Maybe – but you can always go and make your own version of the legend of Liang Shanbo and Zhu Yingtai, can't you?

The Butterfly Lovers is a confection, and you have to submit to it (or not). *The Butterfly Lovers* is a handsome production, with some appealing actors and performances. The action sequences and swordplay are not essential, but they add some thrills and rapid pacing to the romance and the tragedy.

30

THE TREASURE HUNTER

Ci Ling

The Treasure Hunter (*Ci Lung,* 2009) was a Taiwanese/ Hong Kong production, prod. by Chang Hong Channel Film & Video. The producers were: Han Sanping, Han Xiaoli, Jiang Tai, Raymond Lee, Pei Gin-yam, Du Yang, Ding Li, Dong Zhengrong and Han Xiao, wr. by Charcoal Cheung Tan, Yip Wan-chiu, Lam Chiu-wing, Lam Ching-yan and Shao Huiting, and dir. by Chu Yen Ping (a.k.a. Kevin Chu). Tony Ching Siu-tung acted as action director (along with Wong Ming Kin). Ching had worked with director Chu previously on films such as *Flying Dagger* and *Kung Fu Dunk* the previous year. Released Dec 9, 2009. 105 mins.

Heading up the cast was Jay Chou, as the cool, rebellious 'Eagle of the Desert', Qiao Fei,[22] the wonderful Eric Tsang Chi-wai provided expert comic relief as greedy, tubby Pork Rib, and Lin Chi-ling was the romantic interest, Lan Ting (Chou and Tsang had been the central duo of *Kung Fu Dunk*).

The rest of the cast in *The Treasure Hunter* included: Baron Chen Chu-he, Chen Dao-ming, Miao Pu, Will Liu Keng-hung, Kenneth Tsang-kong, Wong Yat-fei, Peng Bo and Teddy Lin Wai-kin. Jay Chou plays the cool hero with an appealing, wry quality (i.e., he under-plays). Lin Chi-ling seems somewhat out of her depth, tho', as if the filmmakers haven't decided how to portray her character.[23] For much of the movie, Lin plays the damsel in distress, clinging to the hero as he pilots a motorbike thru the TV ad vistas of the desert, but she is given a secondary role – she's a writer! (So, Lan Ting sort of book-ends the movie: at the outset, she's

22 Or, rather, the hero who walks away from being the Eagle of the Desert.
23 Yes, Lan Ting is beautiful, and just happens to be single.

struggling with a looming deadline, and being pressured by a bullying book editor, and at the end she's surrounded by adoring fans of her new book, and happily rejects the new contract offered by her editor. Lan Ting also, unusually, provides the opening narration/ exposition).

The Treasure Hunter was an old-fashioned, action-adventure fantasy, obviously drawing on the *Indiana Jones* series and the numerous *Indy* imitators (such as the *Mummy* series and the *National Treasure* flicks). *The Treasure Hunter* also drew on Hong Kong movies such as 1996's *Dr Wai* (which Tony Ching Siu-tung had directed), and Tsui Hark movies such as *New Dragon Gate Inn* and *The Blade*. (There are numerous links to *Dr Wai* – the archæologist-treasure hunter motifs, the desert setting, the lost city, and Lan Ting is even a novelist of adventure fiction). Indeed, *The Treasure Hunter* comes across as an amalgam of the output of both Ching and Tsui.

An old-fashioned, treasure hunt narrative, then, with the familiar groups of noble hunters (preferring to leave ancient artefacts alone), greedy, grasping hunters (Eric Tsang and co.), and the mysterious guardians of the desert (the Sandstorm Legion and their leader, Dao-dao).

Story-wise, much of *The Treasure Hunter* is hokey and contrived, but so are most action-adventure movies, including nearly all of the classic movies in the genre. It doesn't matter a jot, because the jokey tone, the exotic locales, the appealing cast, and of course the outstanding action makes up for any deficiencies in the narrative.

So we're back in the Chinese desert yet again (where we've spent a lot of time in Chinese action movies since the 1980s), with staple ingredients of the action-adventure genre like buried treasure, rival groups of hunters, an underground city of ancient times, fearsome peasant folk, betrayals and all the rest.

Very striking in *The Treasure Hunter,* however, is how much the issue of the past haunts the present tense. Every group of charas in *The Treasure Hunter* has a past which they can't escape from, and which they are coming to terms with. The ghosts of the fathers float through this movie – and they literally appear in the finale, as spectres of old men who battle our heroes. The Law of the Father permeates this movie. Much is made of the death of Lan Ting's pa (which occurs off-screen). It's also the conflict between the younger generation and the older generation, with the Sins of the Fathers being enacted on the younger generation.

Master Hua Ding-bang (Chen Dao-ming (the Emperor in *Hero*) is troubled by being the only survivor of a previous archæological expedition to the lost city (where he ate his dead fellows in order to survive). Master

Hua never recovered from the experience. The hero of *The Treasure Hunter*, Qiao Fei, has an unsettled past with the heroine, Lan Ting, and also walked out on everybody ten years ago (his sister Dao-dao remonstrates with him).

The subtext in *The Treasure Hunter* of people trying to make good their past mistakes or failures is very strong – taking precedence over the usual subplot in action-adventure movies, of romance. While the characterizations are pretty thin, the emotions generated are genuine: they are the familiar ones of fleeting life in Asian cinema. In case you weren't aware, dear reader, time is passing, death is approaching, and life is suffering (we don't need movies to tell us that, but they do anyway. Yes, folks, the 'treasure' in *The Treasure Hunter* is of course life itself – so chuck away those bars of gold, Eric Tsang, and hurry for the exit before the whole place collapses! As it always does).[24]

The middle act (of three) in *The Treasure Hunter* is livened up with the funkily-cast and art-directed 'travellers' village', a settlement of Mongolian nomads in the desert. It's the watering hole section of *The Treasure Hunter,* where all of the characters converge. The second female presence in *The Treasure Hunter* is introduced here, Dao-dao (Miao Pu)[25] – as, rather improbably, the leader of the Sandstorm Legion, a bunch of ethnic heavies with the usual tattoos and punky haircuts. (Dao-dao is also improbably Qiao Fei's long-lost sister).

✦

The direction of *The Treasure Hunter* is solid (tho' rather flashy), the visuals are of the M.T.V./ pop promo/ TV commercial sort (long lenses, backlight, smoke), the music is the usual orchestral grandeur for an action-adventure flick,[26] and the editing incorporates plenty of gimmicks.

As to the action in *The Treasure Hunter,* it is masterclass – the highlight is the climax of act one, when the Sandstorm Legion lay siege to the desert inn where our heroes are holed up. The scene, which consciously evokes films such as *Hero* and *New Dragon Gate Inn* (both of which Tony Ching Siu-tung worked on), is a wild ride of horses, arrows, swords, and numerous stunts, culminating in the wholesale destruction of the inn, followed by a rough-and-tumble pursuit across the desert by motorcycle and car. Technically breathtaking, the action sequence includes some remarkable stunts featuring galloping horses amidst explosives. (The movie, from a practical point-of-view, seems to draw on Ching's work as choreographer in the previous year's *An Empress and the*

---

24 Jay Chou picks up the mystical pearl from the skeleton in the tomb, and it turns to ash, as we all do.
25 Looking like a young Michelle Yeoh.
26 And of course plinky piano for emo scenes.

Warriors, which staged some very impressive mass battles, including charges with horses).

As with many of Tony Ching Siu-tung's movies as action director, pretty much every sort of action is featured – from fierce open-handed combat on the floor to out-size stunts involving collapsing buildings and motorcycles. Ching seems to approach each new project with the ambition to throw in all he can (so he does – *The Treasure Hunter* contains the whole arsenal of Chingisms).

Again, there is no let-up in the energy in filming the action, and no feeling that the momentum is lost. This is a lively movie, nimble on its feet. Some of the pretexts for the conflicts are flaky even by Hong Kong cinema standards (i.e., charas start fighting for shaky reasons), but it doesn't matter too much against the over-arching context of a treasure hunt.

31

JUST CALL ME NOBODY

Da Xiao Jiang Hu

Tony Ching performed action director duties on a 2010 adventure comedy entitled *Just Call My Nobody* (= *Da Xiao Jiang Hu,* a.k.a. *Kung Fu Shuffle*). Produced: Polybona Film Distribution Co.,Ltd; the producers were Kevin Chu Yen-ping, Don Yu-dong, Fargo Pi, Maxx Tsai, Jeffrey Chan and Zhao Benshan; Ning Cai Shen wrote the script, with direction by Kevin Chu Yen-ping. In the cast were: Xiao Shen-yang, Kelly Lin Hsi-lei, Banny (Julian) Chen Zhi-pen, Zhao Benshan, Eric Tsang Chi-wai, Norman Chu Siu-keung, Jacky Wu Tsung-hsien, and Xiao-xiao Bin. Released Dec 3, 2010. 94 mins.

Tony Ching has worked with Kevin Chu Yen-ping several times (going back to films such as *Flying Dagger,* 1993). This was their third film in three years. *Just Call My Nobody* is a similar sort of movie as the comedies of the 1990s, though this one is filmed in Mandarin and aimed at a Mainland Chinese audience. Plus it has pop culture references, including video games and TV game shows.

Xiao Shen-yang heads up a strong cast of Chinese regulars in a comical adventure yarn set in the *jiangzhu,* the martial arts world of yore. This time, however, the emphasis is on sending up the well-worn genre: Wu Di is mad about *kung fu,* and gleans most of his knowledge from black-and-white picture books (sold in a local market[27]), rather than a *sifu* (instead of movies, the internet and cel phones, fan-boys get their fix of *kung fu* action from an early and primitive form of comics. In one scene, the pages are flipped rapidly, forming a flick-book effect). *Just Call My Nobody*

---

27 So we have a market scene early in act one, the usual place for a production value scene.

spoofs old chestnuts of the swordplay genre such as magical scrolls containing the secrets of special techniques (video games are included, game show commentators, and quotes from *Star Wars* – 'may the Force be with you').

Just Call My Nobody is built around a popular character type in comedies: the Idiot. Bumbling jerks have been central to comedy films for at least 120 years, and *Just Call My Nobody* is no different. Xiao Shen-yang steals the 2010 movie as the dim cobbler Wu Di. The family set-up is a simple fairy tale: Daddy has gone to war, while mommy works and tries her best to keep her stupid son in check (when things get tough, she locks him in at home so he won't get into mischief).

As *Just Call My Nobody* is a broad comedy, much of Tony Ching's work comprises concocting humorous action which sends up the swordplay genre (which he has done many times before). But sometimes a genuinely intense piece of sword fighting is required (such as in the first act, when Wu Di encounters the swordswoman Lady Moon (a.k.a. Ue-lou, from Qin Mountain) and somehow seems to defeat her tormentor, Lonesome (Pirate Dugu – Zhao Benshan). However, Swordsman Lonesome and his crusty, idiotic sidekick Horse Ray (Pirate Ma Chou-tzu – Cheng Ye) pop up later, so it seems that Wu Di didn't kill them after all).

Just Call My Nobody is not all broad comedy, however: the movie shifts into a much quieter mode halfway through for a lengthy and intimate two-hander between Wu Di and Lady Moon (when Kelly Lin disappeared from the movie in act one, we knew, as she was one of the top-billed stars, that she would be back). The conversation delves into back-story for both characters, and inevitably becomes mildly flirtatious (Lady Moon confesses that she had been persuaded to marry by her parents, but fled).

The finale of *Just Call My Nobody* features the expected Giant Action Sequence: it is set at the Imperial Palace and involves the principal actors. Lady Moon has been captured, the Imperial Eunuch Cheng (Norman Chu) is angling for the Top Spot in the kingdom, attacking the Emperor (Banny Chen). Among the numerous bits of business – clearly overseen by Tony Ching, and feauturing many of his signature motifs – the highpoint is the sword fight between the hero, Wu Di, and the super-villain, Eunuch Cheng. As we are now in the digital cinema age (it's 2010), computer-aided animation has been added all over the place (giving Wu DI extendible legs, for example).

✦

The chemistry between Kelly Lin and Xiao Shen-yang is one of the highpoints of *Just Call My Nobody* – following the set-up of the possible romance in the middle act, the movie indulges in some all-out romantic mushiness after the finale. *Just Call My Nobody* shifts into one of the standard filmic devices of Chinese cinema: the musical montage. As usual, it's a ballad (and a love ballad), depicting the two potential lovers on their own (with Wu Di looning for Lady Moon). So, after the Big Fight Scene at the Imperial Palace, and the inevitable separation of the couple (Lady Moon is betrothed to the Emperor, no less, reprising the arranged marriage motif), the song ('Just Call Me Nobody') runs. The Emperor is a softie, unusually, instead of the usual Tyrant Who Must Be Obeyed, and he gives up Lady Moon, knowing that she's unhappy (as they sit on their wedding bed).

Now a Chinese movie can play it two ways: if it's a tragedy, the lovers are forever parted (one dies, say, or one is a ghost). And if it's a comedy, as here, the lovers can be re-united (though in a comical manner, with some guff about a phoenix's egg which Wu Di has stumbled upon).

Just Call My Nobody is happy to be an old-fashioned and traditional sort of martial arts comedy film (which both Ching Siu-tung and Kevin Chu have delivered many times before), but it has been updated with numerous contemporary pop culture references, with cinematic tricks like digital animation, and with a new, young cast. Yes, *Just Call My Nobody* is 'Old Stories With New Actors', but then that comprises 99% of cinema anywhere at any time in film history.

32

KRRISH 3

Krrish 3 (2013) – the sequel to *Krrish* (2006) – was More Of The Same (like most sequels). Many folk behind and in front of the camera from the 2006 movie were back. Once again, it was a Roshan family affair. Rakesh Roshan, Akash Khurana, Honey Irani, Sanjay Masoomm, Irfan Kamal, David Benullo, Rajshri Sudhakar and Robin Bhatt wrote the script, exec., prod. by Shammi Saini, prod. by Sunaina Roshan and Rakesh Roshan, dir. by Rakesh Roshan, music by Salim-Sulaiman, Rajesh Roshan and Salim Merchant, S. Tirru (DP), Chandan Arora (ed.), Farah Khan (choreographer), Dipika Lal and Anirudh Singh (costumes), Sabu Cyril and Suresh Selvarajan (art dirs.), Baylon Fonesca and Udit Duseja (sound designers), and Jaideep Sen (1st A.D.). Filmkraft Productions was the production company. Released Nov 1, 2013. 152 mins.

In the cast were: Hrithik Roshan, Vivek Oberoi, Priyanka Chopra, Kangana Ranaut, Arif Zakaria, Raju Kher, Rajpal Yadav and Rakhi Vijayan. Filming took place in Jordan, the Swiss Alps, Singapore, Hyderada film studios, and Mumbai; the production was based in Mumbai at the Filmistan Studios.

✦

Krrish 3 is pretty much the same movie as *Krrish* – the same super-villain with his revolting schemes for world domination (this time a plague), the same sort of action beats, the same sort of set-pieces, the same sort of designs and *mise-en-scène*, etc.

But none of that matters, because the filmmaking is still completely confident, the production is sparklingly bright and assured, the players are appealing, and the storytelling romps along like, well, a tireless superhero.[28]

Yes, *Krrish 3* is too long (like *Krrish*, it has an intermission). Yes, 2h30m or more of running time is too long for a superhero movie, for a fantasy movie, for a musical, and for a movie aimed at early teens. But this movie has energy to spare, and we go along for the ride.

With its too-long running time, *Krrish 3* is able to extend the narrative structure a tad by including a second subplot: Kaya falling for Krishna. The other subplot – of Priya having a baby – is simply a reworking of the usual romantic subplot in all action-adventure movies (it's a standard ploy in sequels to introduce offspring of the heroes). So slinky, shape-changing Kaya, with her rubberized, form-fitting costume[29] and black contact lenses, has several romantic scenes with Krishna (including a sweet encounter in the desert). Kangana Ranaut was terrific as Kaya.

You'll notice that Krishna's grandmother Sonia is absent – now his father Rohit takes up all of the familial themes, which're so important in these Indian versions of the superhero movie genre.

The *Krrish* movies are cartoony – there's always a vast cityscape outside a window, or a molten sunset. Helicopter shots over modern cities. Sleek skyscrapers of concrete and glass. Even the scuzzy parts of town are meticulously art directed (by Sabu Cyril and Suresh Selvarajan), with the graffiti on the back alley walls being spray-painted *just so*.

Krrish 3 features another *tour-de-force* performance from lead actor Hrithik Roshan. Once again, he gets to do everything (and then some), and you can't take your eyes off him (even when other strong actors are competing for your attention). Gene Kelly and Fred Astaire could sing *and* dance *and* act, but Roshan does all three – *and* he does action! (Well, yes, Kelly could do action mightily well, in flicks such as *The Pirate* and *The Three Musketeers*).[30] Like Kelly and Astaire, Roshan has immense charisma, a winning screen persona, and a physical grace which's hypnotic. And the comparisons with Kelly and Astaire are fully justified.

And Hrithik Roshan is doing everything twice, too – he also plays his father, as in *Krrish* (and many scenes feature both characters). Playing Krishna and Krrish and his father Rohit is one of those roles where you have to be at the top of your game, feeling super-fit, very focussed, and you have to commit 100%. Like actors in a Hong Kong action movie, Roshan throuws himself into the role eagerly.

✦

As to action, Tony Ching Siu-tung and his team deliver the expected

28 How many cloaks were crafted in the making of this film? How many gallons of glycerine were used to create all those tears? How many slabs of foam rock did the art dept. produce?
29 Director Roshan said they looked to *Batman* for inspiration. Yes, it's another costume inspired by the incredible costume designer Bob Ringwood.
30 But Kelly never flew around on wires quite like this!

high-wire, rapidly-cut shenanigans: we've go the bust-up in an alley with heavy objects being hurled by the participants, we've got one man versus multiple assailants, we've got numerous examples of characters soaring up into the air or landing in a *kung fu* crouch on the ground, we've got glass shattering and windows caving in, we've got the henchmen invading the hero's home at night, we've got the hero dashing into the villain's compound to Save His Girl, we've got the epic duel of the hero and the super-villain (which runs thru multiple beats), and we've got the seamless amalgamations of in-front-of-the-camera effects with post-production visual effects.

Many of the action scenes in *Krrish 3* are wholly Chingian – the emphasis on free-floating movement, the frozen poses, the cloaks blowing in the breeze, the blends of vfx with practical effects, and always, always ensuring that everything has that heightened, romantic feel, and looks great. For sheer beauty, no one among Tony Ching's contemporaries can compare – maybe because none of Ching's cohorts among action choreographers are quite as consumed by beauty and romance as Ching is. Ching adds layers of mystery and romance to his action sequences which're over and above the requirements of the scene: consider the action beats in *Hero* or *A Chinese Ghost Story*, for instance. (Ching reveres the poetry of action, and his action scenes always contains elements of intense romanticization).

Action-wise, *Krrish 3* literally soars like its superhero hero. By now it seems as if Tony Ching Siu-tung and co. can do anything, and they have developed a very sophisticated way of working. (Actually, they had already achieved that way back in films such as *Duel To the Death* in 1983).

As with *Krrish* n 2006, the 2013 sequel looks just like a Hong Kong action movie in many places. The action scenes are constructed just like Hong Kong film sequences, from the build-up and the explanation of the narrative set-up, to the introduction of the villains, the flow of action, and of course the pay-offs and climaxes. The full, golden light of Singapore, Mumbai and India enhances the exotic look of the *Krrish* films.

✦

As with *Krrish,* the shift into full-on superheroics in the finale of *Krrish 3* is the least compelling section of the piece, even tho' the spectacle is impressive, and the levels of action and incident are intense. The finale is given a jolt of emotion when Rohit gives up his life for his son, Krishna. In a moving scene, Daddy wishes his Son farewell, reminding him that he is never alone and that he lives on in his son and his memories.

The motifs that link divinity and Hindu deities to light and the sun in Indian religion are used here, in Rohit's scientific invention of utilizing solar energy, reflected from multiple mirrors and concentrated on one point. It makes for a memorable image of crisscrossed beams of light, with the sun shining through the window behind. The trope is employed again in the superhero duel, when Krrish uses it to dispatch the super-villain Kaal in a blaze of heat.

In the finale, we spend rather too much time with super-villain Kaal (Vivek Oberoi) – because in the end he is not particularly compelling. For ex, he has the same nefarious schemes as every other super-villain, his goals are just as stupid and badly thought-out as all super-villains, and we don't sympathize with him at all (even if he's made disabled, wheelchair-bound, and also the half-brother of Krishna).

Why are the villains' schemes in *all* action-adventure movies absolutely rubbish?

Here, as in all superhero flicks, the chief villain Kaal is merely a function of the plot, to get the movie moving, to give the heroes something to fight against (and for)... and blah blah. No one's that interested in them – which drives super-villains into jealous huffs, and makes them shout even louder. We don't care – we know that they will not prevail.

✦

Once again, the insertion of Bollywood songs and dances into the middle of a fantasy/ comedy/ action/ adventure is absolutely delightful. What could be more fun at a surprise birthday party for Krishna in a nightclub than having the entire crowd dancing? (Yes, *everybody* dances, not only the principals. It's a reprise of the scene in *I Found Someone*).

It works. The form of the *Krrish* movies is big enough to include songs and dances as well as all of the usual elements of an action-adventure flick (and extra Bollywood ingredients, such as OTT emotion and melodrama).

The blossoming romance between the villainness Kaya and Krishna is also given a song and dance number (turning the movie into a romantic triangle). For no particular reason – other than it looks fantastic – we cut to sun-drenched desert settings (and the famous exterior in the cliff at Petra in Turkey). Here Krishna and Kaya slink and sway, emote and sing, while the camera booms and soars around them.

The dance numbers are as effective and lavish as any of the visual effects set-pieces or the action sequences in *Krrish 3*. Enormous troupes of dancers take the stage, performing some glorious choreography.

This is a movie as a circus show, a variety show, the finale of a vaudeville show or Oscars night. In the N. American superhero idiom, only spoof movies allow themselves permission to feature vast dance numbers (spoof movies of recent times are especially fond of musical/ dance sequences).31 But in Bollywood cinema, nobody needs much encouragements to break out into singing and dancing.

As in *Krrish*, the *energy* in the sequel sweeps you along. Who cares if some of the plot is clichéd, if the characterizations are decidedly thin and formulaic, if there are too many steals from North American movies? Not when there is so much else going on.

You can complain about this or that element in a movie if there isn't enough happening elsewhere to make up for it. But the *Krrish* movies jam so much in, there's plenty of entertainment to go around.

These are movies to surrender to, not to fight, not to sit back with arms folded, scowling, and grumpily muttering, 'so impress me'. Sure, not every element in *Krrish 3* soars, some of the transitions are clunky, and the movie repeats a *lot* of the second movie (but what sequel doesn't?). But the action, the spectacle and music-and-dance elements and all are plenty to be going on with.

Filled with clichés and delightfully dumb gags, and with derivative material rehashed from 100s of other movies and TV shows, *Krrish 3* nevertheless delivers many striking images and scenes.

Yes, all superhero movies rework all other superhero movies (and *Krrish 3* is no different), until one comes along which jolts the genre with new energy and fresh ideas, like *Superman* (1978) or *Batman* (1989) or *Spider-man* (2002).

---

31 Such as *Date Movie, Meet the Spartans, Dance Flick, Disaster Movie*, etc.

Curse of the Golden Flower (2006).

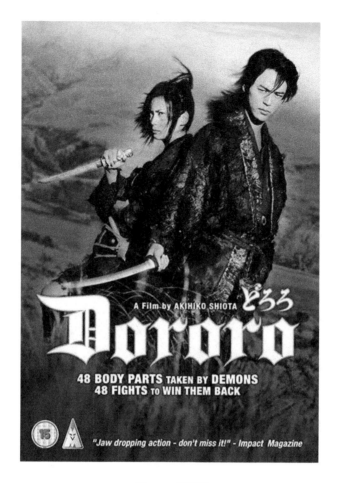

Dororo (2007).

In the Name of the King (2007).

The Warlords (2007).

He told me later that he
didn't believe in the pledge.

Kung Fu Dunk (a.k.a. Shaolin Basket, 2008).

蔡卓妍　吴尊

导演·编剧 马楚成

动作导演 程小东

剑蝶

BUTTERFLY LOVERS

剑行江湖　蝶化梁祝

Butterfly Lovers (2008).

Krrish 3 (2013).

33

OTHER MOVIES AND TV SHOWS
ACTION DIRECTED BY
TONY CHING SIU-TUNG

THE SWORD.

The Sword (*Jian* a.k.a. *Ming Jian,* 1980) was prod. by Raymond Chow Man-wai for Golden Harvest, wr. by Lau Shing-Hon, Clifford Choi Gai-Gwong, Wong Ying, Patrick Tam Kar-Ming, Lo Chi-Keung and Lau Tin-Chi, and dir. by Patrick Tam Kar-ming. Action dirs.: Tang Tak-Cheung and Tony Ching. In the cast were Adam Cheng Siu-chow, Norman Chiu Siu-keung, Tien Feng, Lau Siu-Ming, Eddy Ko Hung, Bonnie Ngai Chau-Wah, JoJo Chan Kei-Kei and Chui Git. Ching would later cast Norman Chiu in one of the two main roles (as well as Eddy Ko Hung) in *Duel To the Death*. Released: Aug 14, 1980. 84 mins.

The Sword is a swordplay movie of the early New Wave of Hong Kong cinema. Like *Duel To the Death*, *The Sword* deserves to be much better known in the West. It displays Tony Ching's fantastic choreography in full effect, with some of his most sublime work in portraying duels using swords (you can see how Ching's work led directly into his first feature two years later, *Duel To the Death*). The action in *The Sword* is frenetic and acrobatic, with the performers bouncing into every part of the frame, and every area of the set. Blades flash, the sound effects editors add the familiar swishes, and the participants duck and weave with incredible speed.

TWINKLE TWINKLE LITTLE STAR.

Twinkle Twinkle Little Star (*Xing Ji Dun Tai,* 1983) was a Shaw Brothers comedy prod. by Mona Fong Yat-wah, wr. by Alex Cheung Kwok-ming, Manfred Wong Man-jun, John Au Wa-hon, Sandy Shaw Lai-king, Lawrence Cheng Tan-shui and Yuen Gai-chi and dir. by Alex Cheung Kwok-ming. Tony Ching and Dang Tak-cheung were the action directors. In the cast were: Cherie Chung Chor-hung, James Yi-lui, David Lo Dai-wai, Leung Tin, Tam Tin-nam, Cheng Miu, Lau Yat-fan, Fung Fung and Ha Ping. Released: Feb 12, 1983. 93 mins.

Twinkle Twinkle Little Star is an 'anything goes' comedy flick (have a look at the trailer). No attempts at 'logic' or 'realism' here – this is a thoroughly Hong Kongian, over-the-top comedy, with Tony Ching providing the action direction for the inevitable physical comedy scenes.

NEW HEAVENLY SWORD AND DRAGON SABRE.

New Heavenly Sword and Dragon Sabre (Ji Tin Tou Lung Gei, 1986) was based on the novel The Heaven Sword and Dragon Sabre by Louis Cha (Jin Yong). It was a T.V.B. television series broadcast from Nov 3 to Dec 30, 1986. 40 episodes.

It was prod. by Wong Tin-lam. The script was by Lo Hon-wah, Lee Yin-ping, Lau Bak-nung and Kwan Chin-bok. Directed by Benny Chan, Johnnie To, Nelson Cheung, Wong Kam-tin, Fung Pay-yuen and Ng Chun-shing. Music: Michael Lai.

The enormous cast was headed up by many familiar faces, including: Tony Leung, Kitty Lai Mei-xian, Sheren Tang, Newton Lai, Maggie Shiu, Simon Yam, Carol Cheng, Kenneth Tsang, Lau Kong, Liu Kai-chi, and Lau Dan.

I LOVE MARIA.

I Love Maria (a.k.a. Roboforce, 1988) was a Hong Kong version of RoboCop (1987), co-produced by Tsui Hark with John Sham Kim-fun, written by Yuen Kai-chi, directed by David Chung Chi-man, starring Sally Yeh, Tsui Hark, John Sham and Tony Leung. Tony Ching Siu-tung was 2nd unit director. Released: Mch 10, 1988. 96 mins.

JUST HEROES.

Just Heroes (a.k.a. Tragic Heroes, 1989) was a benefit movie for the Hong Kong directors' union. Production by Magnum Films. Producers: Alan Ng, David Chiang, Danny Lee, and Tsui Hark. Exec. prod. by Chang Cheh. It starred a host of names, including David Chiang, Danny Lee, Chen Kuan-tai, Stephen Chow Sing-chi, Lo Lieh, Ti Lung, Cally Kwong, Wu Ma, Shing Fui-on, James Wong, Bill Tung, Zhao Lei and Tien Niu. Sept 14, 1989. 97 mins.

THE BANQUET.

The Banquet (*Hao Men Ye Yan*, 1991) was one of several benefit movies that Ching Siu-tung has been involved with – this one was made to help the victims of flooding in Mainland China in 1991. Tsui Hark is one of several directors in *The Banquet*. Ng See-yuen and John Sham Kim-fun produced. Written by Choi Ting-ting.

The cast included pretty much everybody in Hong Kong movies, such as Eric Tsang, Maggie Cheung, Jacky Cheung, Anita Mui, Gong Li, Michael Hui, Andy Lau Tak-wah, Sammo Hung Kam-bo, Aaron Kwok, Leon Lai, Leslie Cheung, etc. Released: Nov 30, 1991. 97 mins.

THE MAD MONK.

The Mad Monk (*Ji Gong,* 1993) was prod. by Cosmopolitan Film Productions, produced by Mona Fong Yat-wah, wr. by Sandy Shaw Lai-king, directed by Johnnie To, and action choreographed by Tony Ching Siu-tung. The cast included: Stephen Chow Sing-chi, Ng Man Tat, Anita Mui, Philip Chan, Maggie Cheung, Anthony Wong and Kirk Wong. Released: July 29, 1993. 88 mins.

The Mad Monk was a Stephen Chow comedy about the Robin Hood figure Chai Kung (Ji Gong), already the subject of many Chinese comedies. Much of the action is distinctly Chingian – the movie opens with elaborate wire-work depicting a gathering of the gods amidst the Chingian setting of dry ice, smoke, breezes and floaty costumes.

LOVE ON DELIVERY.

Love On Delivery (*Po Huai Zhi Wang*, a.k.a. *King Of Destruction,* 1994) was a contemporary-set Stephen Chow Sing-chi comedy. Tony Ching provided the action direction (along with Deon Lam Dik-on and Lau Gar-ho). *Love On Delivery* was prod. by Cosmopolitan Films, produced by Mona Fong Yat-wah, wr. by Vincent Kok Tak-chiu; dir. by Chow and Lee Lik-Chi; some credits have Ching as co-director with Lee (not Chow). Alongside Chow, the cast featured Ng Man Tat, Jacky Cheung, Joey Leung, Christy Chung, Philip Chan and Joe Cheng. Released at Chinese New Year (Feb 3), 1994. 100 mins.

A CHINESE ODYSSEY.

A Chinese Odyssey was an adaptation of *Journey To the West* starring Stephen Chow Sing-chi, released during New Year's in 1995. Yeung Kwok-fai produced for Xi'an Film Studio and Choi Sing Film Company, Wu Cheng-en scripted, and Jeffrey Lau directed.

The film was split into two installments: *A Chinese Odyssey Part One: Pandora's Box* and *A Chinese Odyssey Part Two: Cinderella*. Tony Ching was action director. In the cast were: Stephen Chow, Athena Chu, Ng Man-tat, Yammie Lam, Karen Mok, Law Kar-ying, Jeffrey Lau and Lu Shuming. Released: Jan 21, 1995 and Feb 4, 1995. 87 and 95 mins.

BLACKSHEEP AFFAIR.

Blacksheep Affair (1998, a.k.a. *Meltdown 2, Another Meltdown* and *Bi Xie Lan Tian*) was made by Win's Entertainment/ Eastern Film Production, prod. by Alex Law Kai-yui, presenters: Charles Heung Wah-keung and Chui Po-chu, wr. by Roy Szeto and Alex Law, and dir. by Lam Wai-lun. Tony Ching, Ma Yuk-sing, Tony Tam Chun-to and Xiong Xin-xin were the action directors. In the cast were Vincent Chiu Man-chuk, Andrew Lin Hoi, Shu Qi, Kenneth Tsang-kong and Lau Shun. Released: Feb 14, 1998. 90 mins.

L'AME-STRAM-GRAM.

L'Âme-Stram-Gram (1999) was a music video directed by Tony Ching for French pop star Mylène Farmer (b. 1961). With a budget of 900,000 Euros,[1] and filmed in Beijing, *L'Âme-Stram-Gram* was an eight-minute extravaganza featuring the pop star Farmer in a setting drawing on *A Chinese Ghost Story*. Farmer plays twin sisters, one of whom is captured by bandits (in a night-time setting familiar from many Hong Kong movies).

Many Hong Kong action movies and fantasy movies were filmed like pop promos, and *A Chinese Ghost Story* is a supreme example (the *L'Âme-Stram-Gram* promo was lit by superstar cinematographer Arthur Wong). *L'Âme-Stram-Gram* boasts many Chingian elements – floaty dresses, colourful banners, bandits, slow motion, stunts and of course wire-work (if you're going to hire Ching to direct your pop promo, you probably want to fly). *L'Âme-Stram-Gram* is all about the mood and the visuals, matching the somewhat dreamy song (altho' the lyrics have sexual ingredients).

WIND AND CLOUD.

Wind and Cloud (a.k.a. *Fung Wan* a.k.a. *The Storm Riders*, 2002) was the television series version of *The Stormriders*, a 1998 movie based on the same *manhua* (comic) by Ma Wing-shing, entitled *Fung Wan*. The Taiwanese TV series ran on China Television Company, comprising 44 ~~l~~ong (= 45-minute) episodes. Tony Ching oversaw the action ~~directi~~on.

~~…~~ong Zheng, Zhou Wu, Huang Jianxin, Cai Yuling, Zhu Cheng and Liu

[1] Euros is about the budget of the whole of the first *Chinese Ghost Story* movie!

Xiaozhong executive produced; Han Sanping, Yang Fan, Zhu Yunhong, Zhong Conghai and Zhang Yuwei produced; Wen Lifang scripted; and Hsu Chin-liang directed. In the enormous cast were Sonny Chiba, Vincent Zhao, Peter Ho, Wong Hei, Tao Hong, Annie Wu, Jiang Qinqin, Sun Xing, and Li Qi.

The *Stormriders* movie was a big hit in Hong Kong; it was a swordplay fantasy outing with a gloriously OTT, highly melodramatic, very colourful, pan-Asian/ Chinese approach to the historical martial arts genre. *The Stormriders* was produced by Golden Harvest/ Centro Digital Pictures/ B.O.B./ Tian Shan Film Studio, John Chu Ka-Yan and Jessinta Liu Fung-Ping were producers, Manfred Wong scripted (and co-produced), and Andrew Lau Wai-keung directed.

Wind and Cloud drew on *The Stormriders* heavily – it featured cast members such as Sonny Chiba, and employed the same approach to the visual effects, and some of the same locations. However, the main cast differed. Chiba is an astonishing screen presence in *Wind and Cloud*, as he was in *The Stormriders*. When Chiba's on screen you don't look at anyone else; he has an Emperor Ming quality, fearsome and commanding. A Japanese speaker, Chiba was dubbed (but so were many of the roles in *Wind and Cloud*; the low, gravelly voice of actor Wai Wong is perfectly suited to Chiba's out-size performance).

Wind and Cloud was a typical, Chinese television series: filmed on video (which meant bright, over-lit scenes, as in most TV), with a rapid pace, a huge cast, cheesy and melodramatic scenes, lashings of sentiment, plentiful dubbing[2] of dialogue, and a very stylized approach to the action and the visual effects.

As to Tony Ching's contribution to *Wind and Cloud*, his style of very swift swordplay and graceful, wire-assisted choreography was employed as the basic stylistic approach to action (whether or not Ching actually oversaw all of the action is uncertain – this was a huge series, running to forty-four episodes, requiring assistants). The first show, for example, contained a duel set in a bamboo forest, a classic, Chingian locale, where Xiongba takes on Whispering Prince (instead of swords, they snap off bamboo stalks and go at it very intensely). Xiongba steals away Prince's wife (boo-hiss!), and there's a second round of the smackdown two years later (again, atop the giant, sandstone, Buddha statue, as in *The Stormriders*).

After some (not especially memorable) scenes that flash back to the early childhoods of the principal cast (full of cute kids), episode one of

2 It's a pity that so little time in the factory-like schedule of TV allows for more care to be taken with the sound and the looping.

Wind and Cloud introduces the actors who'll appear through the run of 44 shows: Vincent Zhao, Peter Ho, and Wong Hei. The context for establishing the characters is a series of martial arts games, overseen by Xiongba. Here, each of the principals displays their special *kung fu* skills.

THE ROYAL SWORDSMEN.

The Royal Swordsmen (*Tian Xià Dì Yi,* 2005) was a TV series of 40 episodes, scripted by Wong Jing and Lin Qiang, prod. by Wong Jing, Wang Dapeng, Chen Beibei, Huang Jinmei and Chen Jingxia for Jing's Production/ First Media Corporation, and and dir. by Deng Yancheng and Wei Liyuan. Tony Ching provided the action choreography.

LEGEND OF THE SHAOLIN KUNGFU 1: HEROES IN TROUBLED TIMES.

Legend of the Shaolin Kungfu 1 (*Shao Lin Si Zhuan Qi,* 2007) was a *wuxia* TV series which Ching Siu-tung worked on as action director. It was wr. by Liu Qi, dir. by Du Xiao, and starred Bao Guo-an, Tse Miu, Li Yuan, Wu Man, Yu Cheng-hui, Chen Jia-jia, Ji Chun-hua and Guo Da. 42 episodes.

THE IRON FORT'S FURIOUS LION.

Irumbukkottai Murattu Singam (= *The Iron Fort's Furious Lion,* 2010) was an action comedy made in Tamil which had Tony Ching working as action director. *The Iron Fort's Furious Lion,* was prod. by Kalpathi S. Aghoram, Kalpathi S. Ganesh and Kalpathi S. Suresh for A.G.S. Entertainment, and wr. and dir. by Chimbu Deven. In the cast were Lawrence Raghavendra, Padmapriya, Lakshmi Rai, Sandhya, Nassar, Sai Kumar and M. S. Bhaskar. Released: May 7, 2010. 140 mins.

FUTURE X-COPS.

Future X-Cops (*Wei Lai Jing Cha,* 2010) was a remake of the 1993 *Future Cops*, with Wong Jing again writing and directing; prod. by Ken Nickel, Haicheng Zhao, Ming Li, Sanping Han, Jason Han and Venus Keung (also DP); Raymond Wong composed the score; with Tony Ching as action director. In the cast were Andy Lau Tak-wah, Barbie Hsu Hsi-yuan, Fan Siu-wong, Xu Jiao, Eric Tsang Chi-wai, Louis Fan, Jacky Wu Zong-xian, Dylan Kuo Pin-chao, Fan Bing-bing, Natalie Meng-yao and Mike He Jun-xiang. Released: Apl 15, 2010. 101 mins.

Future X-Cops was a visual effects movie, as many Hong Kong movies actually are (tho' usually more on-set special effects and practical effects, rather than visual effects manufactured in post-production). *Future X-Cops* was delayed due to the creation of the visual effects (Wong Jing denied that one of the investors was having money troubles).

Future X-Cops is delivered in a broad, bold and fun manner in terms of the action sequences (which Wong Jing handed over to Tony Ching, as usual). The out-size, comicbook style of the action is demonstrated in the first big action sequence, when the enemy materializes from underground, using a giant screw machine (Ching is fond of characters travelling under the Earth). They are a motley crew furnished with superhero-style, hi-tech augmentations: giant bat-wings, steel claws, Hydra-snakes, cat claws, etc (they resemble the mutants in *Black Mask 2* (2002), and clearly draw on American superhero titles such as *X-Men* and *Avengers*).

As usual, Wong Jing will have his eye on what is successful at the U.S. box office (and in the decade 2000-2010, superhero movies certainly made a lot of $$$$, particularly those from Marvel and Detective Comics). Wong's business method is simple: he will reproduce what the U.S. movie industry does, but at fraction of the cost. And he will angle his movies towards the Asian market. And he'll add his trademark Wongisms: humour, crudity, and exaggerations.

So Andy Lau Tak-wah's cop Zhou Zhihao and his colleagues take on the bad guys with guns, but they're out-matched: Kalong's (Louis Fan) crew swoop about, chewing them up. The choreography of the action required careful collaboration with the visual effects teams, who added all of the superhero gadgets.

Future X-Cops reworks the 1993 movie, adding elements such as some cute schoolkids. Andy Lau isn't always his usual brilliant-at-everything hero, but also a bungling doofus (but when he dons his special body armour, courtesy of visual effects animation, and jumps into his flying platform, he becomes the familiar superhero).

FILMOGRAPHY

TONY CHING SIU-TUNG

MOVIES AS DIRECTOR

Duel To the Death (1983)
The Witch From Nepal (1986)
A Chinese Ghost Story (1987)
The Terracotta Warrior (1989)
The Swordsman (1990 – co-directed)
A Chinese Ghost Story 2 (1990)
The Raid (1991 – co-directed)
A Chinese Ghost Story 3 (1991)
Swordsman 2 (1992)
Swordsman 3 (1993 – co-directed)
The Heroic Trio (1993, co-directed)
The Executioners (1993, co-directed)
Wonder Seven (1994)
Dr. Wai In "The Scripture With No Words" (1996)
The Longest Day (1997)
Conman In Tokyo (2000)
Naked Weapon (2002)
Belly of the Beast (2003)
An Empress and the Warriors (2008)
The Sorcerer and the White Snake (2011)
Jade Dynasty (2019)

The Fourteen Amazons (1972)
The Rats (1972)
Love and Vengeance (1973)
Shaolin Boxer (1974)
The Tea House (1974)
Kidnap (1974)
Lady of the Law (1975)
Negotiation (1977)
He Who Never Dies (1979)
Monkey Kung Fu (1979)
The Bastard Swordsman (1979)
The Sentimental Swordsman (1979)
Dangerous Encounter - 1st Kind (1980)
The Spooky Bunch (1980)
The Sword (1980)
The Master Strikes (1980)
Gambler's Delight (1981)
Return of the Deadly Blade (1981)
Sword of Justice (1981)
The Story of Woo Viet (1981)
Rolls, Rolls, I Love You (1982)
Once Upon a Rainbow (1982)
Swordsman Adventure (1983)
Twinkle Twinkle Little Star (1983)
Cherie (1984)
Happy Ghost 3 (1986)
Peking Opera Blues (1986)
A Better Tomorrow 2 (1987)
The Eighth Happiness (1988)
I Love Maria (1988)
The Killer (1989)
All About Ah-Long (1989)
The Fun, the Luck and the Tycoon (1990)
Casino Raiders 2 (1991)
Son On the Run (1991)
New Dragon Gate Inn (1992 – co-directed)
Moon Warriors (1992)
Twin Dragons (1992)
Royal Tramp (1992)
Royal Tramp 2 (1992)
Gambling Soul (1992)
Justice, My Foot! (1992)
Lucky Encounter (1992)
Flying Dagger (1993)
Future Cops (1993)

Holy Weapon (1993)
The Mad Monk (1993)
Butterfly and Sword (1993)
City Hunter (1993)
Love On Delivery (1994)
A Chinese Odyssey I: Pandora's Box (1995)
A Chinese Odyssey 2: Cinderella (1995)
The Stuntwoman (1996)
Warriors of Virtue (1997)
Hong Niang (1998)
The Blacksheep Affair (1998)
The Assassin Swordsman (2000)
The Duel (2000)
My School Mate, the Barbarian (2001)
Invincible (2001)
Shaolin Soccer (2001)
Hero (2002)
Spider-Man (2002 – uncredited)
House of Flying Daggers (2004)
The Curse of the Golden Flower (2006)
Krrish (2006)
In the Name of the King: A Dungeon Siege Tale (2007)
The Warlords (2007)
Dororo (2007)
Legend of Shaolin Kungfu I: Heroes in Troubled Times (2007)
Butterfly Lovers (2008)
Kung Fu Dunk (2008)
The Treasure Hunter (2009)
Future X-Cops (2010)
Just Call Me Nobody (2010)
Legend of Shaolin Kungfu 3: Heroes of the Great Desert (2011)
Krrish 3 (2013)

TV SERIES

The Spirit of the Sword (1978)
It Takes a Thief (1979)
The Roving Swordsman (1979)
Reincarnated (1979)
Reincarnated 2 (1979)
Dynasty (1980)
Dynasty 2 (1980)
Legend of the Condor Heroes (1983)
The Return of the Condor Heroes (1983)
The New Adventures of Chor Lau Heung (1984)
The Duke of Mount Deer (1984)
The Return of Luk Siu Fung (1986)
The New Heaven Sword and Dragon Sabre (1986)
The Storm Riders (a.k.a. *Wind and Cloud,* 2002)
The Storm Riders 2 (a.k.a. *Wind and Cloud 2,* 2004)
The Royal Swordsmen (2005)

FILMOGRAPHY

TONY CHING SIU-TUNG

FILMS AS DIRECTOR

DUEL TO THE DEATH, 1983

(A.k.a. *Sang Sei Kyu/ Sheng Si Jue*). Production: Paragon Films. Distributor: Golden Harvest. Producers: Raymond Chow Man-Wai and Catherine Chang Si-kan. Script: David Lai, Manfred Wong and Ching Siu-tung. Released: Jan 13, 1983. 86 mins.

THE WITCH FROM NEPAL, 1986

(*Qi Yuan* in Mandarin, a.k.a. *The Nepal Affair/ Affair From Nepal/ A Touch of Love*). Production: Golden Harvest/ Paragon Films. Producer: Anthony Chow. Script: Chui Jing-Hong. Released: Feb 27, 1986. 89 mins.

THE TERRACOTTA WARRIOR, 1989

(*Chin Yung/ Gu Gam Daai Zin/ Yon Qing* in Cantonese, a.k.a. *Fight and Love With a Terracotta Warrior*). Production: Art & Talent Group Inc. Exec. producer: Kam Kwok-Leung. Producers: Tsui Hark, Zhu Mu and Hon Pau-chu. Script: Pik Wah Lee. Released: Apl 12, 1990. 106 mins. (145 mins).

THE RAID, 1991

(*Choi Suk Ji Wang Siu Chin Gwan*). Production: Film Workshop and Cinema City. Producer: Tsui Hark. Script: Tsui Hark and Yuen Kai-chi. Story: Michael Hui Koon-Man. Co-directed with Tsui Hark. Released: Mch 28, 1991. 100 mins.

THE HEROIC TRIO, 1993

(*Dung Fong Saam Hap*). Production: China Entertainment Films and Paka Hill Productions. Producer: Tony Ching. Script: Sandy Shaw Lai-King. Co-directed with Johnny To Ke-fung. Released: Feb 12, 1993. 83 mins.

THE EXECUTIONERS, 1993

(*Xian Dai Hao Xia Zhuan*, a.k.a. *The Heroic Trio 2*). Production: China Entertainment Films and Paka Hill Film. Producers: Johnnie To Ke-fung, Tony Ching and Yeung Kwok-fai. Script: Susanne Chan and Sandy Shaw Lai-King. Co-directed with Johnnie To Ke-fung. Released: Sept 30, 1993. 97 mins.

WONDER SEVEN, 1994

(*7 Jin Gong*). Production: China Entertainment Films. Producer: Catherine Hun. Script: Charcoal Tan Cheung, Elsa Tang Bikyin and Tony Ching. Story: Manfred Wong Man-Chun. Released: Apl 1, 1994. 88 mins.

DR WAI IN "THE SCRIPTURE WITH NO WORDS", 1996

(*Yale: Mo Him Wong*, a.k.a. *Mao Xian Wang*). Production: Win's Entertainment and Eastern Production. Producers: Tsai Mu-ho, Wong Sing-ping, Charles Heung Wah-keung and Tiffany Chen Ming-Ying. Script: Lam Wai-Lun, Roy Szeto and Sandy Shaw Lai-King. Released: Mch 14, 1996. 87/ 91 mins.

CONMAN IN TOKYO, 2000

(*Zung Waa Dou Hap*). Production: Star East and Best of the Best and Partners. Producer: Wong Jing. Script: Law Yiu-fai. Released: Aug 31, 2000. 103 mins.

NAKED WEAPON, 2002

(*Chek Law Dak Gung*). Production: Media Asia/ Jing Productions. Producers: Wong Jing and John Chong. Script: Wong Jing. Released: Nov 15, 2002. 92 mins.

BELLY OF THE BEAST, 2003

Production: G.F.T. Entertainment/ Salon Films/ Studio Eight Productions/ Emmett/ Furla Films. Producers: George Furla, Gary Howsam, Jamie Brown, Randall Emmett, Steven Seagal and Charles Wang. Script: Thomas Fenton and James Townsend. Released: Dec 30,

2003. 91 mins.

AN EMPRESS AND THE WARRIORS, 2008

(*Jiang Shan Mei Ren* = *The Kingdom and a Beauty*). Production: Beijing Polyabana Publishing Co./ United Filmmakers Organization/ China Film Co-Production Corp./ Big Pictures, Ltd. Execuive producers: Eric Tsang and Kuo Hsing Li. Producers: Claudie Chung Jan, Gin Lau Sin-hing, Peter Chan and Dong Yu. Script: James Yuen, Tan Cheung and Tin Nam Chun. Released: Mch 19, 2008. 99 mins.

THE SORCERER AND THE WHITE SNAKE, 2011

(*Baak Se Cyun Syut Zi Faat Hoi*, a.k.a. *The Emperor and the White Snake*, a.k.a. *Madame White Snake*, a.k.a. *It's Love*). Production: China Juli Entertainment Media/ Distribution Workshop/ Different Digital Design Ltd. Exec. producer: Pang Yau-Fong. Producers: Chui Po Chu, Chi Wan Tse and Yang Zi. Script: Charcoal Tan, Tsang Kan Cheung and Roy Szeto Cheuk Hon. Released: Sept 28, 2011. 100 mins.

JADE DYNASTY, 2019

(*Zhu Xian*). Production: Huxia Film Distribution/ New Classics Pictures/ Shanghai Taopiaopiao Film Culture/ Youku Pictures/ I.Q.I.Y.I. Pictures. Producer: Ning Li. Line producers: Huang Qunfei, Jia Xu and Tony Ching. Script: Shen Jie and Song Chaoyun. Released: Sept 13, 2019. 101 mins.

TONY CHING SIU-TUNG

FILMS AS ACTION DIRECTOR

THE SWORD, 1980

(*Jian* a.k.a. *Ming Jian*). Production: Golden Harvest. Producer: Raymond Chow Man-Wai. Script: Lau Shing-Hon, Clifford Choi Gai-Gwong, Wong Ying, Patrick Tam Kar-Ming, Lo Chi-Keung and Lau Tin-Chi. Direction: Patrick Tam Kar-ming. Released: Aug 14, 1980. 84 mins.

DANGEROUS ENCOUNTER – 1ST KIND, 1980

(*Diyi Leixing Weixian = First Kind of Danger,* a.k.a. *Dangerous Encounter of the First Kind, Don't Play With Fire* and *Playing With Fire*). Production: Fotocine Film Production Ltd. Producer: Thomas Wing-Fat Fung. Script: Tsui Hark and Roy Szeto Cheuk-hon. Direction: Tsui Hark. Released: Dec 4, 1980. 92 mins.

TWINKLE TWINKLE LITTLE STAR, 1983

(*Xing Ji Dun Tai*). Production: Shaw Brothers. Producer: by Mona Fong Yat-wah. Script: Alex Cheung Kwok-ming, Manfred Wong Man-jun, John Au Wa-hon, Sandy Shaw Lai-king, Lawrence Cheng Tan-shui and Yuen Gai-chi. Direction: Alex Cheung Kwok-ming. Released: Feb 12, 1983. 93 mins.

PEKING OPERA BLUES, 1986

(*Dao Ma Dan = Knife Horse Actresses*). Production: Cinema City/ Film Workshop. Producers: Claudie Chung-jan and Tsui Hark. Script: Raymond To Kwok-wai. Direction: Tsui Hark. Released: Sept 6, 1986. 104 mins.

A BETTER TOMORROW 2, 1987

(*Jing Hung Bun Sik II* in Cantonese, *Ying Xiong Ben Se II* in Mandarin = *Heroic Character II*). Production: Cinema City. Producer: Tsui Hark. Script: Tsui Hark and John Woo. Direction: John Woo (Ng Yu-sam). Released: Dec 17, 1987. 104 mins.

I LOVE MARIA, 1988

(*Roboforce*). Producers: Tsui Hark and John Sham. Script: Yuen Kai-chi. Direction: David Chung Chi-man. Released: Mch 10, 1988. 96 mins.

THE KILLER, 1989

(*Dip Huet Seung Hung* in Cantonese, *Die Xue Shuang Xiong* in Mandarin = *Bloodshed Brothers*, 1989). Production: Film Workshop/ Golden Princess/ Magnum. Script: John Woo. Producer: Tsui Hark. Direction: John Woo. Released: July 6, 1989. 105 mins.

JUST HEROES, 1989

(A.k.a. *Tragic Heroes*, *Yi Dan Qun Ying* in Cantonese). Production by Magnum Films. Producers: Alan Ng, David Chiang, Danny Lee, and Tsui Hark. Exec. prod. by Chang Cheh. Script: Ni Kuang, Tommy Hau and Yiu Yau Hung. Direction: John Woo and Wu Ma. Released: Sept 14, 1989. 97 mins.

THE BANQUET, 1991

(*Hao Men Ye Yan*). Producers: Ng See-yuen and John Sham. Script: Choi Ting-ting. Direction: Clifton Ko-chi, Alfred Sum, Joe Tin, Kin Cheung and Tung Cheung Cho. Released: Nov 30, 1991. 97 mins.

NEW DRAGON GATE INN, 1992

(*Xin Long Menm Ke Zhan* in Mandarin). Production: Film Workshop and Seasonal Films. Producers: Tsui Hark and Ng See-yuen. Script: Tsui Hark, Charcoal Tan and Hiu Wing. Direction: Raymond Lee Wai-man and Tsui Hark. Released: by Aug 27, 1992. 103 mins.

CITY HUNTER, 1993

(*Sing Si Lip Ya*). Production: Golden Harvest/ Golden Way Films/ Paragon Films. Producer: Chua Lam. Script and direction: Wong Jing. Released: Jan 14, 1993. 105 mins.

THE MAD MONK, 1993

(*Ji Gong*). Production: Cosmopolitan Film Productions. Producer: Mona Fong Yat-wah. Script: Sandy Shaw Lai-king. Direction: Johnnie To. Released: July 29, 1993. 85 mins.

FUTURE COPS, 1993

(*Chiu Kap Hok Hau Ba Wong*). Production: Wong Jing's Workshop and Fantasy Productions Inc.. Producers: John Higgins and Sherman Wong Shui-Hin. Script and direction: Wong Jing. Released: July 15, 1993. 95 mins.

LOVE ON DELIVERY, 1994

(*Po Huai Zhi Wang,* a.k.a. *King Of Destruction*). Production: Cosmopolitan Films. Script: Vincent Kok Tak-chiu. Direction: Stephen Chow Sing-chi and Lee Lik-Chi. Some credits have Tony Ching as co-director with Lee. Released: Feb 3, 1994. 100 mins.

A CHINESE ODYSSEY, 1995

(*Daiwah Saiyau* and *Sai Yau Gei: Daai Git Guk Ji-Sin Leui Kei Yun*). Production: Xi'an Film Studio and Choi Sing Film Company. Producer: Yeung Kwok-fai. Script: Wu Cheng-en. Direction: Jeffrey Lau. Released: Jan 21, 1995 and Feb 4, 1995. 87 and 95 mins.

WARRIOR OF VIRTUE, 1997

(*Wu Xing Zhan Shi*). Production: Joseph, Ronald, Dennis K., Jeremy and Christopher Law, Yoram Barzilai, Lyle Howry and Patricia Ruben. Distribution: Metro Goldwyn Mayer. Script: Michael Vickerman and Hugh Kelley. Direction: Ronny Yu. Released: May 2, 1997. 101 mins.

BLACKSHEEP AFFAIR, 1998

(*Meltdown 2, Another Meltdown* and *Bi Xie Lan Tian*). Production: Win's Entertaiment/ Eastern Film Production. Producer: Alex Law Kai-yui. Presenters: Charles Heung Wah-keung and Chui Po-chu. Script: Roy Szeto and Alex Law. Direction: Lam Wai-lun. Released: Feb 14, 1998. 90 mins.

THE DUEL, 2000

(*Jue Zhan Zi Jin Zhi Dian*). Production: Win's Entertainment. Producers: Wong Jing and Manfred Wong. Script: Manfred Wong. Direction: Andy Lau Wai-keung. Released: Feb 3, 2000. 106 mins.

SHAOLIN SOCCER, 2001

(*Siu Lam* in Cantonese, *Shàolín Zúqiú* in Mandarin). Production: Universe Entertainment and Star Overseas. Producer: Yeung Kwok-Fai. Script: Tsang Kan-cheung and Stephen Chow Sing-chi. Direction: Lee Lik-chi and Stephen Chow. Released: July 12, 2001. 112 mins.

INVINCIBLE, 2001

Production: T.B.S. Producers: Steven Chasman, Janine Coughlin and Jim Lemley. Executive producers: Bruce Davey, Mel Gibson, Jet Li, and John Morayniss. Script: Carey Hayes, Chad Hayes, Michael Brandt, Derek Haas, and Jefrey Levy. Direction: Jefrey Levy. Released: Nov 18, 2001. 87 mins.

SPIDER-MAN, 2002

Production: Marvel/ Columbia/ Laura Ziskin Prods. Producers: Laura Ziskin and Ian Bryce. Script: David Koepp. Direction: Sam Raimi. Released: May 3, 2002. 121 mins.

HERO, 2002

(Mandarin: *Yingxiong;* Cantonese: *Jing Hung*). Production: China Film Co-Production Corporation/ Elite Group Enterprises/ Zhang Yimou Studio/ Metropole Organisation/ Miramax Films/ Beijing New Picture Film. Executive producers: Shoufang Dou and Weiping Zhang. Producers: Bill Kong, Sook Yhun and Zhang Yimou. Script: Feng Li, Zhang Yimou and Bin Wang. Direction: Zhang Yimou. Released: Oct 24, 2002. 99 mins.

HOUSE OF FLYING DAGGERS, 2004

(*Shí Miàn Mái Fú*). Production: China Film Co-Production Corporation/ E.D.K.O. Films/ Elite Group/ Zhang Yimou Studio/ Beijing New Pictures. Executive producer: Weiping Zhang. Producers: Bill Kong, Zhenyan Zhang and Zhang Yimou. Script: Bin Wang, Li Feng, Peter Wu and Zhang Yimou. Direction: Zhang Yimou. Released: July 15, 2004. 119 mins.

KRRISH, 2006

Production: Filmkraft Productions. Producer: Rakesh Roshan. Script: Sanjay Masoomi, Sachin Bhowmick, Rakesh Roshan, Akash Khurana, Honey Irani and Robin Bhatt. Direction: Rakesh Roshan. Released: June 23, 2006. 175 mins.

CURSE OF THE GOLDEN FLOWER, 2006

(*Manchéng Jìndài Huángjinjia*, a.k.a. *The City of Golden Armor,* a.k.a. *Autumn Remembrance*). Production: E.D.K.O. Film/ Bejing New Pictures Film/ Elite Group Enterprises. Producers: Zhang Weiping, Bill Kong and Zhang Yimou. Script: Zhihong Bian, Nan Wu, and Zhang Yimou. Direction: Zhang Yimou. Released: Dec 21, 2006. 114 mins.

THE WARLORDS, 2007

(*Tau Ming Song* a.k.a. *The Blood Brothers*). Production: Media Asia/ China Film Group/ Morgan & Chan. Producers: Andre Morgan and Peter Chan. Script: Xu Lan, Chun Tin-nam, Aubery Lam, Huang Jianxin, Jojo Hui, He Jiping, Guo Junli and James Yuen. Direction: Peter Chan. Released: Dec 12, 2007. 127 mins.

IN THE NAME OF THE KING, 2007

Production: Brightlight Pictures/ Boll K.G. Productions/ Herold Productions. Producers: Dan Clarke, Shawn Williamson, Uwe Boll and Wolfgang Herold. Script: Doug Taylor. Direction: Uwe Boll. Released: April 11, 2007. 127 mins.

DORORO, 2007

Production: Toho/ Tokyo Broadcasting System/ Twins Japan/ Yahoo Japan/ W.O.W.O.W./ Universal/ Dentsu/ Mainichi Broadcasting System/ Hokkaido Broadcasting Company/ Asahi Shimbun/ Stardust Pictures. Producers: Takashi Hirano and Atsuyuki Shimoda. Script: Osamu Tezuka, Masa Nakamura and Akihiko Shiota. Direction: Akihiko Shiota. Released: Mch 15, 2007. 139 mins.

THE BUTTERFLY LOVERS, 2008

(*Jian Die*). Production: Brilliant Idea Group/ China Film Co-Production Corp./ Xian Mei Ah Culture Communciation Ltd. Producer: Catherine Hun. Script: Chris Ng Ka-keung, Yeung Sin-ling, Wong Nga-man, Jingle Ma Choh-shing and Chan Po-chun. Direction: Jingle Ma Choh-shing. Released: Oct 9, 2008. 102 mins.

KUNG FU DUNK, 2008

(*Gonfu* or *Guanlan* in Cantonese). Production: Shanghai Film Group/ Emperor Motion Pictures/ MediaCorp Raintree. Executive producers: Albert Yeung, Zhonglun Ren and Wu Tun. Producers: Zhao Xiaoding, Pengle Xu, Albert Lee and Yiu Kay Wah. Script: Kevin Chu Yen Ping, You-Chen Wang and Lam Chiu Wing. Direction: Kevin Chu Yen-ping. Released:

Feb 7, 2008. 98 mins.

THE TREASURE HUNTER, 2009

(*Ci Lung*). Production: Chang Hong Channel Film & Video. Producers: Han Sanping, Han Xiaoli, Jiang Tai, Raymond Lee, Pei Gin-yam, Du Yang, Ding Li, Dong Zhengrong and Han Xiao. Script: Charcoal Cheung Tan, Yip Wan-chiu, Lam Chiu-wing, Lam Ching-yan and Shao Huiting. Direction: Kevin Chu Yen-ping. Released: Dec 9, 2009. 105 mins.

FUTURE X-COPS, 2010

(*Wei Lai Jing Cha*). Production: China Film Group Corp. Producers: Ken Nickel, Haicheng Zhao, Ming Li, Sanping Han, Jason Han and Venus Keung. Direction and script: Wong Jing. Released: Apl 15, 2010. 101 mins.

THE IRON FORT'S FURIOUS LION, 2010

(*Irumbukkottai Murattu Singam*). Production: A.G.S. Entertainment. Producers: Kalpathi S. Aghoram, Kalpathi S. Ganesh and Kalpathi S. Suresh. Script and direction: Chimbu Deven. Released: May 7, 2010. 140 mins.

JUST CALL ME NOBODY, 2010

(*Da Xiao Jiang Hu*). Production: Polybona Film Distribution Co.,Ltd. Producers: Kevin Chu Yen-ping, Don Yu-dong, Maxx Tsai, Jeffrey Chan and Zhao Benshan. Script: Ning Cai Shen. Direction Kevin Chu Yen-ping. Released: Dec 3, 2010. 94 mins.

KRRISH 3, 2013

Production: Filmkraft Productions. Executive producer: Shammi Saini. Producers: Sunaina Roshan and Rakesh Roshan. Script: Rakesh Roshan, Akash Khurana, Honey Irani, Sanjay Masoomi, Irfan Kamal, David Benullo, Rajshri Sudhakar and Robin Bhatt. Direction: Rakesh Roshan. Released: Nov 1, 2013. 152 mins.

RECOMMENDED BOOKS
AND WEBSITES

One of the finest general introductions to the history of Hong Kong cinema, and a great place to start, is *Hong Kong Cinema* (1997) by Stephen Teo. David Bordwell and Kristin Thompson are consistently excellent commentators on film, in books such as *Film History: An Introduction* (2010) and Bordwell's account of Hong Kong cinema, *Planet Hong Kong: Popular Cinema and the Art of Entertainment* (2000).

Bey Logan's *Hong Kong Action Cinema* (1995) is an entertaining introduction to the action side of Hong Kong cinema (with many valuable illustrations). *Kung-fu Cult Masters: From Bruce Lee To 'Crouching Tiger'* (2003) takes a more theoretical approach to the same subject.

For surveys of films, Jeff Yang's *Once Upon a Time In China* (2003) is superb, as is *Hong Kong Babylon* (1997) by F. Dannen & B. Long (this book also features many interviews with the key players in the Hong Kong industry). Lisa Morton's *The Cinema of Tsui Hark* (2001) is an important early study.

Jackie Chan has attracted many studies and biographies, including *Jackie Chan* by C. Gentry (1997), *The Essential Jackie Chan Sourcebook* by J. Rovin & K. Tracy (1997), and *Dying For Action: The Life and Times of Jackie Chan* by R. Witterstaetter (1997). And Chan's own memoirs: *I Am Jackie Chan* (1998) and *Never Grow Up* (2018).

Among critical essays, I would recommend *At Full Speed: Hong Kong Cinema In a Borderless World* (1998, edited by E.C.M. Yau) and *The Cinema of Hong Kong* (2002), edited by P. Fu & D. Desser.

WEBSITES

Hong Kong Movie Database
Hong Kong Cinemagic
Love Hong Kong Film
Film Workshop
Jet Li   jetli.com

BIBLIOGRAPHY

A. Abbas. *Hong Kong*, University of Minnesota Press, Minneapolis, 1997
J. Abert. *A Knight At the Movies: Medieval History On Film,* Routledge, London, 2003
R. Altman, ed. *Sound Theory, Sound Practice*, Routledge, London, 1992
—. *Film/ Genre*, British Film Institute, London, 1999
G. Andrew. *The Film Handbook*, Longman, London, 1989
—. *Stranger Than Paradise: Maverick Filmmakers In Recent American Cinema*, Prion, 1998
A. Assister & A. Carol, eds. *Bad Girls and Dirty Pictures: The Challenge To Reclaim Feminism*, Pluto Press, London, 1993
R. Baker & T. Russell. *The Essential Guide To Hong Kong Movies*, Eastern Heroes, London, 1994
—. *The Essential Guide To the Best of Eastern Heroes*, Eastern Heroes, London, 1995
—. *The Essential Guide To Deadly China Dolls*, Eastern Heroes, London, 1996
M. Barker, ed. *The Video Nasties: Freedom and Censorship In the Media*, Pluto Press, London, 1984
—. & J. Petley, eds. *Ill Effects: The Media/ Violence Debate*, Routledge, London, 1997
L. Bawden, ed. *The Oxford Companion To Film*, Oxford University Press, Oxford, 1976
R. Bergan & R. Karney. *Bloomsbury Foreign Film Guide*, Bloomsbury, London, 1988
C. Berry. *Perspectives On Chinese Cinema*, BFI, London, 1991
P. Biskind. *Easy Riders, Raging Bulls: How the Sex 'n' Drugs 'n' Rock 'n' Roll Generation Saved Hollywood*, Bloomsbury, London, 1998
—. *Down and Dirty Pictures: Miramax, Sundance and the Rise of Independent Film*, Bloomsbury, London, 2004
M. Bliss. *Between the Bullets: The Spiritual Cinema of John Woo*, Scarecrow Press, Lanham, MD, 2002
D. Bordwell & K. Thompson. *Film Art: An Introduction*, McGraw-Hill Publishing Company, New York, NY, 1979
—. *et al. The Classical Hollywood Cinema: Film Style and Mode of Production To 1960*, Routledge, London, 1985
—. *Narration In the Fiction Film*, Routledge, London, 1988
—. *Making Meaning*, Harvard University Press, Cambridge, MA, 1989
—. & N. Caroll, eds. *Post-Theory: Reconstructing Film Studies*, University of Wisconsin Press, Madison, WI, 1996
—. *Planet Hong Kong: Popular Cinema and the Art of Entertainment*, Harvard University Press, 2000
—. "Aesthetics in Action: *Kungfu*, Gunplay and Cinematic Expressivity", in E. Yau, 2001
—. *The Way Hollywood Tells It*, University of California Press, Berkeley, CA, 2006
J. Bower, ed. *The Cinema of Japan and Korea*, Wallflower Press, London, 2004
D. Breskin. *Inner Voices: Filmmakers In Conversation*, Da Capo, New York, 1997
A. Britton *et al. American Nightmare: Essays On the Horror Film*, Toronto, 1979
R. Brody. *Everything Is Cinema: The Working Life of Jean-Luc Godard*, Faber, London, 2008
A. Brown. *Directing Hong Kong: The Political Cinema of John Woo and Wong Kar-Wai*, Routledge/ Curzon, 2001
R. Brown. *Overtones and Undertones: Reading Film Music*, University of California Press, Berkeley, CA, 1994
N. Browne *et al*, eds. *New Chinese Cinema*, Cambridge University Press, 1994
S. Bukatman. *Terminal Identity: The Virtual Subject In Postmodern Science Fiction*, Duke University Press, Durham, NC, 1993
G. Burt. *The Art of Film Music*, Northeastern University Press, 1994
J. Chan. *I Am Jackie Chan*, with Jeff Yang, Pan Books, 1998
—. *Never Grow Up*, Simon & Schuster, London, 2018
J. Charles. *The Hong Kong Filmography: 1977-1997*, McFarland, 2000
R. Chu. "*Swordman II* and *The East Is Red*", Bright Lights, 13, 1994
C. Chun-shu & Shelley Hsueh-lun Chang. *Redefining History: Ghosts, Spirits, and Human*

Society in Pu Sung-ling's World, 1640–1715, Ann Arbor: University of Michigan Press, 1998

D. Chute & Cheng-Sim Lim, eds. *Heroic Grace: The Chinese Martial Arts Film,* University of California, Los Angeles, Film and Television Archive, 2003

P. Clark. *Chinese Cinema: Culture and Politics Since 1949,* Cambridge University Press, 1987

J. Clements & H. McCarthy, eds. *The Anime Encyclopedia,* Stone Bridge Press, Berekeley, CA, 2001/ 2007/ 2015

S. Cohan & I.R. Hark, eds. *Screening the Male: Exploring Masculinities In Hollywood Cinema,* Routledge, London, 1993

J. Collins *et al,* eds. *Film Theory Goes To the Movies,* Routledge, New York, NY, 1993

D.A. Cook. *A History of Narrative Film,* W.W. Norton, New York, NY, 1981, 1990, 1996

P. Cook, ed. *The Cinema Book,* British Film Institute, London, 1985/ 1999

S. Cornelius & I. Smith. *New Chinese Cinema,* Wallflower Press, London, 2002

J. Crist, ed. *Take 22: Moviemakers On Moviemaking,* Continuum, New York, NY, 1991

F. Dannen & B. Long. *Hong Kong Babylon,* Faber, London, 1997

C. Desjardins. *Outlaw Masters of Japanese Film,* I.B. Tauris, London, 2005

D. Desser. *Eros Plus Massacre: An Introduction to the Japanese New Wave Cinema,* Indiana University Press, Bloomington, IN, 1988

L. Dittmar & G. Michael. *From Hanoi To Hollywood,* Rutgers University Press, NJ, 1991

J. Donald, ed. *Fantasy and the Cinema,* British Film Institute, London, 1989

K.J. Donnelly, ed. *Film Music,* Edinburgh University Press, Edinburgh, 2001

C. Ducker & Stuart Cutler. *The HKS Guide To Jet Li,* Hong Kong Superstars, London, 2000

A. Easthope, ed. *Contemporary Film Theory,* Longman, London, 1993

P. Ettedgui. *Production Design & Art Direction,* RotoVision, 1999

D. Fairservice. *Film Editing,* Manchester University Press, Manchester, 2001

K. Fang. *John Woo's A Better Tomorrow, The New Hong Kong Cinema,* Hong Kong University Press, Hong Kong, 2004

C. Finch. *Special Effects,* Abbeville, 1984

J. Finler. *The Movie Director's Story,* Octopus Books, London, 1985

—. *The Hollywood Story,* Wallflower Press, London, 2003

J. Fletcher & A. Benjamin, eds. *Abjection, Melancholia and Love: The Work of Julia Kristeva,* Routledge, London, 1990

K. Fowkes. *Giving Up the Ghost: Spirits, Ghosts and Angels In Mainstream Comedy Films,* Wayne State University Press, Detroit, MI, 1998

A. Frank. *Horror Films,* Hamlyn, London, 1977

—. *The Horror Film Handbook,* Barnes & Noble, 1982

K. French, ed. *Screen Violence,* Bloomsbury, London, 1996

P. Fu & D. Desser, eds. *The Cinema of Hong Kong,* Cambridge University Press, Cambridge, 2002

Lisa Funnell. *Warrior Women: Gender, Race, and the Transnational Chinese Action Star,* State University of New York Press, 2014

M. Gallagher. "Masculinity In Translation: Jackie Chan", *Velvet Light Trap,* 39, 1997

—. *Tony Leung Chiu-wai,* British Film Instititute, 2018

L. Gamman & M. Marshment, eds. *The Female Gaze: Women as Viewers of Popular Culture,* Women's Press, London, 1988

J. Geiger & R. Rutsky, eds. *Film Analysis,* Norton & Company, New York, NY, 2005

K. Gelder & S. Thornton, eds. *The Subcultures Reader,* Routledge, London, 1997

—. ed. *The Horror Reader,* Routledge, London, 2000

J. Gelmis. *The Film Director as Superstar,* Penguin, London, 1974

C. Gentry. *Jackie Chan,* Taylor, Dallas, TX, 1997

Jean-Luc Godard. *Godard on Godard,* eds. J. Narobi & T. Milne, Da Capo, New York, NY, 1986

—. *Interviews,* ed. D. Sterritt, University of Mississippi Press, Jackson, 1998

M. Goodwin & N. Wise. *On the Edge: The Life and Times of Francis Coppola,* William Morrow, New York, NY, 1989

B.K. Grant, ed. *Film Genre,* Scarecrow Press, Metuchen, NJ, 1977

—. *Planks of Reason: Essays on the Horror Film,* Scarecrow Press, Metuchen, NJ, 1984

—. *Film Genre Reader II,* University of Texas Press, Austin, TX, 1995

—. ed. *The Dread of Difference: Gender and the Horror Film,* University of Texas Press, Austin, TX, 1996

E. Grosz. *Sexual Subversions,* Allen & Unwin, London, 1989

—. *Jacques Lacan: A Feminist Introduction,* Routledge, London, 1990

—. *Volatile Bodies,* Indiana University Press, Bloomington, IN, 1994

—. *Space, Time and Perversion,* Routledge, London, 1995

K. Hall. *John Woo: The Films,* McFarland & Co., Jefferson, N.C., 1999

L. Halliwell. *Halliwell's Filmgoer's Companion,* 7th edition, Granada, London, 1980

D. Hamamoto & S. Liu, eds. *Countervision: Asian-American Film Criticism,* Temple University Press, Philadelphia, PA, 2000

S. Hammond. *Hollywood East,* Contemporary Books, Lincoln, IL, 2000

P. Hardy, ed. *The Aurum Encyclopedia of Science Fiction,* Aurum, London, 1991

C. Heard. *Ten Thousand Bullets: The Cinematic Journey of John Woo*, Lone Eagle Publishing Co., L.A., 2000

S. & N. Hibbin. *The Official James Bond Movie Book*, Hamlyn, London, 1989

G. Hickenlooper. *Reel Conversations: Candid Interviews With Film's Foremost Directors and Critics*, Citadel, New York, NY, 1991

J. Hillier. *The New Hollywood*, Studio Vista, London, 1992

—. *American Independent Cinema: A Sight & Sound Reader*, British Film Institute, London, 2001

L.C. Hillstrom, ed. *International Dictionary of Films and Filmmakers: Directors*, St James Press, London, 1997

Hal Hinson. "*Peking Opera Blues*," *Washington Post*, Oct 14, 1988

Sam Ho, ed. *The Swordsman and His Juang Hu: Tsui Hark and Hong Kong Film*, Hong Kong University Press, Hong Kong, 2002

Hong Kong Film Archive. *The Making of Martial Arts Films*, Hong Kong Provisional Urban Council, 1999

Hong Kong International Film Festival. *Hong Kong Panorama*, Leisure and Cultural Services Department

Hong Kong International Film Festival. *Hong Kong New Wave: Twenty Years After*, Provisional Urban Council of Hong Kong, 1999

Hong Kong International Film Festival. *Hong Kong Cinema '79-'89*, Leisure and Cultural Services Department, 2000

D. Hudson. *Draculas, Vampires, and Other Undead Forms*, Rowman & Littlefield, 2009

D. Hughes. *Comic Book Movies*, Virgin, London, 2003

L. Hughes. *The Rough Guide To Gangster Movies*, Penguin, 2005

L. Hunt. "Once Upon a Time In China: Kung Fu From Bruce Lee To Jet Li", *Framework*, 40, 1999

—. *Kung-fu Cult Masters: From Bruce Lee To 'Crouching Tiger'*, Wallflower Press, London, 2003

J. Hunter. *Eros In Hell: Sex, Blood and Madness In Japanese Cinema*, Creation Books, London, 1998

J. Inverne. *Musicals*, Faber, London, 2009

L. Irigaray. *The Irigaray Reader*, ed. M. Whitford, Blackwell, Oxford, 1991

S. Jaworzyn, ed. *Shock: The Essential Guide To Exploitation Cinema*, Titan Books, London, 1996

S. Jeffords. *Hard Bodies: Hollywood Masculinity In the Reagan Era*, Rutgers University Press, New Brunswick, NJ, 1994

E. Jeffreys, Elaine & L. Edwards, eds. *Celebrity in China*, Hong Kong University Press, Hong Kong, 2010

B.F. Kawin. *Mindscreen: Bergman, Godard and First-Person Film*, Princeton University Press, Princeton, NJ, 1978

—. *How Movies Work*, Macmillan, New York, NY, 1987

P. Keough, ed. *Flesh and Blood: The National Society of Film Critics on Sex, Violence, and Censorship*, Mercury House, San Francisco, CA, 1995

P. Kolker. *The Altering Eye: Contemporary International Cinema*, Oxford University Press, New York, NY, 1983

—. *A Cinema of Loneliness: Penn, Stone, Kubrick, Scorsese, Spielberg, Altman*, Oxford University Press, New York, NY, 2000

P. Kramer. *The Big Picture: Hollywood Cinema From Star Wars To Titanic*, British Film Institute, London, 2001

—. *The New Hollywood*, Wallflower Press, London, 2005

J. Kristeva. *About Chinese Women*, tr. A. Barrows, Marion Boyars, London, 1977

—. *Desire In Language: A Semiotic Approach To Literature and Art*, ed. L.S. Roudiez, tr. T. Gora *et al*, Blackwell 1982

—. *Powers of Horror: An Essay on Abjection*, tr. L.S. Roudiez, Columbia University Press, New York, NY, 1982

—. *Revolution In Poetic Language*, tr. M. Walker, Columbia University Press, New York, NY, 1984

—. *The Kristeva Reader*, ed. T. Moi, Blackwell, Oxford, 1986

—. *Tales of Love*, tr. L.S. Roudiez, Columbia University Press, New York, NY, 1987

—. *Black Sun: Depression and Melancholy*, tr. L.S. Roudiez, Columbia University Press, New York, NY, 1989

—. *Strangers To Ourselves*, tr. L.S. Roudiez, Harvester Wheatsheaf 1991

J. Kwok Wah Lau. "Imploding Genre, Gender and History: *Peking Opera Blues*", in J. Geiger, 2005

M. Lanning. *Vietnam At the Movies*, Fawcett Columbine, New York, NY, 1994

R. Lapsley & M. Westlake, eds. *Film Theory: An Introduction*, Manchester University Press, Manchester, 1988

Shing-hou Lau, ed. *A Study of the Hong Kong Martial Arts Film*, Hong Kong International Film Festival, 1980

—. *A Study of the Hong Kong Swordplay Film, 1945-80*, Hong Kong International Film Festival, 1981

Law Kar, ed. *Fifty Years of Elecric Shadows*, Hong Kong International Film Festival, 1997

M. Lee. *"Once Upon a Time In China"*, Criterion, 2021

J. Lent. *The Asian Film Industry*, Austin, TX, 1990

T. Leung Siu-hung. "Mastering Action", Hong Kong Cinemagic, March, 2006

E. Levy. *Cinema of Outsiders: The Rise of American Independent Film,* New York University Press, New York, NY, 1999

J. Lewis. *The Road To Romance and Ruin: Teen Films and Youth Culture*, Routledge, London, 1992

—. ed. *New American Cinema*, Duke University Press, Durham, NC, 1998

—. *Hollywood v. Hard Core: How the Struggle Over Censorship Created the Modern Film Industry,* New York University Press, New York, NY, 2000

J. Leyda. ed. *Film Makers Speak: Voices of Film Experience*, Da Capo, New York, NY, 1977

V. LoBrutto. *Sound-On-Film*, Praeger, New York, NY, 1994

B. Logan. *Hong Kong Action Cinema*, Titan, London, 1995

S. Lu, ed. *Transnational Chinese Cinemas*, University of Hawaii Press, Honolulu, 1997

H. Ludi. *Movie Worlds: Production Design In Film*, Mengers, Stuttgart, 2000

The Making of A Chinese Ghost Story: The Tsui Hark Animation, Hong Kong, 1997

R. Maltby. *Harmless Entertainment: Hollywood and the Ideology of Consensus*, Scarecrow Press, Metuchen, NJ, 1983

—. *Hollywood Cinema*, 2nd ed., Blackwell, Oxford, 2003

E. Marks & I. de Courtivron, eds. *New French Feminisms: an anthology*, Harvester Wheatsheaf, Hemel Hempstead, 1981

G. Mast *et al*, eds. *Film Theory and Criticism: Introductory Readings*, Oxford University Press, New York, NY, 1992a

—. & B Kawin, *A Short History of the Movies*, Macmillan, New York, NY, 1992b

C. Marx. *Jet Li*, Martial Arts Masters, Rosen Publishing Group, 2002

T.D. Matthews. *Censored*, Chatto & Windus, London, 1994

B. McCabe. *The Rough Guide To Comedy Movies*, Rough Guides, London, 2005

S.Y. McDougal. *Made Into Movies: From Literature To Film*, Holt, Rinehart and Winston, New York, NY, 1985

R. Meyers. *Martial Arts Movies*, Citadel Press, NJ, 1985

—. *Great Martial Arts Movies*, Citadel Press, NJ, 2001

D. Millar. *Cinema Secrets: Special Effects*, Apple Press, 1990

T. Miller *et al*, eds. *Global Hollywood*, British Film Institute, London, 2001

T. Moi. *Sexual/ Textual Politics: Feminist Literary Theory*, Methuen, London, 1983

J. Monaco. *The New Wave: Truffaut, Godard, Chabrol, Rohmer, Rivette*, Oxford University Press, New York, NY, 1977

—. *American Film Now*, New American Library, London, 1979

—. *How To Read a Film*, Oxford University Press, Oxford, 1981

L. Morton. *The Cinema of Tsui Hark*, McFarland, Jefferson, North Carolina, 2001

R. Murray. *Images In the Dark: An Encyclopedia of Gay and Lesbian Film and Video*, Titan Books, London, 1998

S. Neale. *Cinema and Technology*, Macmillan, London, 1985

—. & M. Smith, eds. *Contemporary Hollywood Cinema*, Routledge, London, 1998

—. *Genre and Contemporary Hollywood*, Routledge, London, 2002

J. Nelmes, ed. *An Introduction To Film Studies*, Routledge, London, 1996

D. Neumann, ed. *Film Architecture: From Metropolis To Blade Runner*, Prestel-Verlag, New York, NY, 1996

K. Newman. *Nightmare Movies*, Harmony, New York, NY, 1988

—. *Millennium Movies*, Titan Books, London, 1999

G. Nowell-Smith, ed. *The Oxford History of World Cinema*, Oxford University Press, Oxford, 1996

D. O'Brien. *Spooky Encounters: A Gwailo's Guide To Hong Kong Horror*, Headpress, 2004

T. Ohanian & M. Phillips. *Digital Filmmaking*, 2nd ed., Focal Press, Boston, MA, 2000

J. Orr. *Contemporary Cinema*, Edinburgh University Press, Edinburgh, 1998

B. Palmer *et al*. *The Encyclopedia of Martial Arts Movies*, Scarecrow Press, NJ, 1995

A. Paludan. *Chronicle of the Chinese Emperors*, Thames & Hudson, 1998

L. Pang. *Masculinities and Hong Kong Cinema,* Kent State University Press, 2005

D. Parkinson. *The Rough Guide To Film Musicals*, Penguin, London, 2007

J. Parish. *Jet Li: A Biography*, Thunder's Mouth Press, New York, 2002

D. Peary & G. Peary, eds. *The American Animated Cartoon*, Dutton, New York, NY, 1980

—. *Cult Movies 2*, Vermilion, London, 1984

—. *Cult Movies 3*, Sigwick & Jackson, London, 1989

P. Phillips. *Understanding Film Texts*, British Film Institute, London, 2000

M. Pierson. *Special Effects*, Columbia University Press, New York, NY, 2002

L. Pietropaolo & A. Testaferri, eds. *Feminisms In the Cinema*, Indiana University Press, Bloomington, IN, 1995

D. Pollock. *Skywalking: The Life and Films of George Lucas*, Crown, New York, NY, 1983, 1990, 2000

M. Polly. *Bruce Lee*, Simon & Schuster, New York, 2018

S. Prince, ed. *Screening Violence*, Athlone Press, London, 2000

N. Proferes. *Film Directing Fundamentals*, Focal Press, Boston, MA, 2001

M. Pye & Lynda Myles. *The Movie Brats: How the Film Generation Took Over Hollywood*, Faber, London, 1979

T. Reeves. *The Worldwide Guide To Movie Locations*, Titan Books, London, 2003

P. Rice & P. Waugh, eds. *Modern Literary Theory: A Reader*, Arnold, London, 1992

D. Richie. *The Films of Akira Kurosawa*, University of California Press, Berkeley, CA, 1965

R. Rickitt. *Special Effects*, Aurum, London, 2006

B. Robb. *Screams and Nightmares*, Titan Books, London, 1998

D. Robinson. *World Cinema*, Methuen, London, 1981

W.H. Rockett. *Devouring Whirlwind: Terror and Transcendence In the Cinema of Cruelty*, Greenwood Press, New York, NY, 1988

J. Romney & A. Wootton, eds. *Celluloid Jukebox: Popular Music and the Movies Since the 50s*, British Film Institute, London, 1995

P. Rosen, ed. *Narrative, Apparatus, Ideology: A Film Theory Reader*, Columbia University Press, New York, NY, 1986

J. Rosenbaum. *Placing Movies*, University of California Press, Berkeley, CA, 1995

R. Rosenblum & R. Karen. *When the Shooting Stops... The Cutting Begins: A Film Editor's Story*, Da Capo Press, New York, NY, 1979

J. Ross. *The Incredibly Strange Film Book: An Alternative History of Cinema*, Simon and Schuster, 1993

The Rough Guide To China, Penguin, 2017

R. Roud. *Jean-Luc Godard*, Thames & Hudson, London, 1970

J. Rovin & K. Tracy. *The Essential Jackie Chan Sourcebook*, Pocket Books, New York, 1997

M. Rubin. *Thrillers*, Cambridge University Press, Cambridge, 1999

V. Russo. *The Celluloid Closet: Homosexuality In the Movies*, Harper & Row, New York, NY, 1981

A. Sarris. *The American Cinema*, Dutton, New York, NY, 1968

T. Sato. *Currents In Japanese Cinema*, Kodansha, New York, 1982

D. Schaefer & L. Salvato, eds. *Masters of Light*, University of California Press, Berkeley, CA, 1984

T. Schatz. *Hollywood Genres,* Random House, New York, NY, 1981

—. *The Genius of the System: Hollywood Filmmaking In the Studio Era*, Pantheon, New York, NY 1988

F. Schodt. *Manga! Manga! The World of Japanese Magazines*, Kodansha International, London, 1997

—. *Dreamland Japan: Writings On Modern Manga*, Stone Bridge Press, Berkeley, CA, 2002

A. Schroeder. *Tsui Hark's Zu: Warriors From the Magic Mountain*, Hong Kong: Hong Kong University Press, Hong Kong, 2004

R. Schubart. *Super Bitches and Action Babes: The Female Hero in Popular Cinema, 1970-2006*, McFarland, 2007

Screen Reader I: Cinema/ Ideology/ Politics, Society for Education in Film & TV, 1977

Screen Reader II: Cinema and Semiotics, British Film Institute, London, 1982

C. Sharrett, ed. *Crisis Cinema*, Maisonneuve Press, Washington, DC, 1993

—. *Mythologies of Violence In Postmodern Media*, Wayne State University Press, 1999

T. Shone. *Blockbuster: How the Jaws and Jedi Generation Turned Hollywood Into a Boom-Town*, Scribner, London, 2005

E. Showalter, ed. *The New Feminist Criticism*, Virago, London, 1986

L. Sider *et al*, eds. *Soundscapes: The School of Sound Lectures 1998-2001*, Wallflower Press, London, 2003

M. Singer. *A History of the American Avant-Garde Cinema*, American Federation of the Arts, New York, NY, 1976

P. Adams Sitney, ed. *The Film Culture Reader*, Praeger, New York, NY, 1970

—. ed. *The Avant-Garde Film: A Reader of Theory and Criticism*, New York University Press, New York, NY, 1978

—. *Visionary Film: The American Avant-Garde, 1943-1978*, 2nd ed., Oxford University Press, New York, NY, 1979

G. Smith. *Epic Films*, McFarland, Jefferson, NC, 1991

T.G. Smith. *Industrial Light and Magic: The Art of Special Effects*, Columbus Books, 1986

E. Smoodin, ed. *Disney Discourse: Producing the Magic Kingdom*, Routledge, London, 1994

V. Sobchack. *The Limits of Infinity: The American Science Fiction Film*, A.S. Barnes, New York, NY, 1980

—. *Screening Space: The American Science Fiction Film*, Ungar, New York, NY, 1987/ 1993

J. Squire, ed. *The Movie Business Book*, Fireside, New York, NY, 1992

J. Staiger. *Interpreting Films*, Princeton University Press, Princeton, NJ, 1992

—. *Perverse Spectators: The Practices of Film Reception*, New York University Press, New York, NY, 2000

N. Stair. *Michelle Yeoh*, Rosen Publishing Group, 2001

D. Sterritt. *The Films of Jean-Luc Godard*, Cambridge University Press, Cambridge, 1999

G. Stewart. *Between Film and Screen: Modernism's Photo Synthesis*, University of Chicago

Press, Chicago, IL, 1999

M. Stokes & R. Maltby, eds. *Identifying Hollywood Audiences*, British Film Institute, London, 1999

J. Storey, ed. *Cultural Theory and Popular Culture*, Harvester Wheatsheaf, Hemel Hempstead, 1994

J.M. Straczynski. *The Complete Book of Scriptwriting*, Titan Books, London, 1997

J. Stringer. "Problems With the Treatment of Hong Kong Cinema As Camp", *Asian Cinema*, 8, 2, 1996

—. ed. *Movie Blockbusters*, Routledge, London, 2003

C. Sylvester, ed. *The Penguin Book of Hollywood*, Penguin, London, 1999

K. Tam & W. Dissanayake. *New Chinese Cinema*, Oxford University Press, Hong Kong, 1998

S. Tan. "Ban(g)! Ban(g)! *Dangerous Encounter – 1st Kind*", *Asian Cinema*, 8, 1, 1996

C. Tashiro. *Pretty Pictures: Production Design and the History Film*, University of Texas Press, 1998

Y. Tasker. *Spectacular Bodies: Gender, Genre and the Action Cinema*, Routledge, London, 1993

S. Teo. *Hong Kong Cinema*, British Film Institute, London, 1997

—. "Tsui Hark", in C. Yau, 1998

—. "Tsui Hark: Filmography", *Senses of Cinema* 17

B. Thomas. *Video Hound's Dragon: Asian Action and Cult Flicks*, Visible Ink Press, 2003

K. Thompson & D. Bordwell. *Film History: An Introduction*, McGraw-Hill, New York, NY, 1994/ 2010

—. *Storytelling In the New Hollywood*, Harvard University Press, Cambridge, MA, 1999

D. Thomson. *A Biographical Dictionary of Film*, Deutsch, London, 1995

S. Thrower, ed. *Eyeball: Compendium: Sex and Horror, Art and Exploitation*, FAB Press, Godalming, Surrey, 2003

C. Tohill & P. Tombs. *Immoral Tales: Sex and Horror Cinema In Europe 1956-1984*, Titan Books, London, 1995

K. Van Gunden. *Fantasy Films*, McFarland, Jefferson, NC 1989

M.C. Vaz. *From Star Wars To Indiana Jones*, Chronicle, San Francisco, CA, 1994

—. & P.R. Duignan. *Industrial Light & Magic*, Virgin, London, 1996

G. Vincendeau, ed. *Encyclopedia of European Cinema*, British Film Institute, London, 1995

—. ed. *Film/ Literature/ Heritage: A Sight & Sound Reader*, British Film Institute, London, 2001

P. Virillio. *War and Cinema*, Verso, London, 1992

D. Vivier & T. Podvin. "Through the Lens of Arthur Wong", Hong Kong Cinemagic, Jan 2005

C. Vogler. *The Writer's Journey: Mythic Structure For Storytellers and Screenwriters*, Pan, London, 1998

J. Wasko. *Movies and Money*, Ablex, NJ, 1982

—. *Hollywood In the Information Age*, Polity Press, Cambridge, 1994

E. Weiss. & J. Belton, eds. *Film Sound: Theory and Practice*, Columbia University Press, New York, NY, 1989

T. Weisser. *Asian Cult Cinema*, Boulevard Books, New York, NY, 1997

D. West. *Chasing Dragons: An Introduction To the Martial Arts Film*, I.B. Tauris, London, 2006

T. Williams. "To Live and Die In Hong Kong", *Cineaction*, 36, 1995

—. "Kwan Tak-hing and the New Generation", *Asian Cinema*, 10, 1, 1998

—. "Space, Place and Spectacle: the Crisis Cinema of John Woo", in P. Yu, 2002

R. Witterstaetter, *Dying For Action: The Life and Times of Jackie Chan*, Warner Books, New York, 1997

J. Woo. Interview, in J. Arroyo, 2000

—. *Interviews; Conversations With Filmmakers Series*, ed. R. Elder, University Press of Mississippi, 2005

M. Wood. *Cine East: Hong Kong Cinema Through the Looking Glass*, FAB Press, 1998

R. Wood. *Hollywood From Vietnam To Reagan... and Beyond*, Columbia University Press, New York, NY, 2003

T. Woods. *Beginning Postmodernism,* Manchester University Press, Manchester, 1999

J. Yang *et al. Eastern Standard Time: A Guide To Asian Influence on American Culture*, Houghton Mifflin, Boston, MA, 1997

—. *Once Upon a Time In China*, Atria Books, New York, NY, 2003

E.C.M. Yau, ed. *At Full Speed: Hong Kong Cinema In a Borderless World,* University of Minnesota Press, Minneapolis, MN, 1998

Z. Yimou. *Zhang Yimou: Interviews, Conversations With Filmmakers Series,* ed. F. Gateward, University Press of Mississippi, 2001

Judith T. Zeitlin. *Historian of the Strange Pu Songling and the Chinese Classical Tale*, Stanford University Press, Stanford, CA, 1993

Y. Zhang & X. Zhiwei, eds. *Encyclopedia of Chinese Film*, Routledge, 1998

J. Zipes. *The Enchanted Screen: The Unknown History of Fairy-tale Films*, Routledge, New York, NY, 2011

S. Zizek. *Enjoy Your Symptom Jacques Lacan In Hollywood and Out*, Routledge, New York,

NY, 1992

—. *The Fright of Real Tears: The Uses and Misuses of Lacan In Film Theory*, British Film Institute, London, 1999

JEREMY ROBINSON has published poetry, fiction, and studies of J.R.R. Tolkien, Samuel Beckett, Thomas Hardy, André Gide and D.H. Lawrence. Robinson has edited poetry books by Novalis, Ursula Le Guin, Friedrich Hölderlin, Francesco Petrarch, Dante Alighieri, Arseny Tarkovsky, and Rainer Maria Rilke.

Books on film and animation include: *The Akira Book • The Art of Katsuhiro Otomo • The Art of Masamune Shirow • The Ghost In the Shell Book • Fullmetal Alchemist • Cowboy Bebop: The Anime and Movie • The Cinema of Hayao Miyazaki • Hayao Miyazaki: Pocket Guide • Princess Mononoke: Pocket Movie Guide • Spirited Away: Pocket Movie Guide • Blade Runner and the Cinema of Philip K. Dick • Blade Runner: Pocket Movie Guide • The Cinema of Donald Cammell • Performance: Donald Cammell: Nic Roeg: Pocket Movie Guide • Pasolini: Il Cinema di Poesia/ The Cinema of Poetry • Salo: Pocket Movie Guide • The Trilogy of Life Movies: Pocket Movie Guide • The Gospel According To Matthew: Pocket Movie Guide • The Ecstatic Cinema of Tony Ching Siu-tung • Tsui Hark: The Dragon Master of Chinese Cinema • The Swordsman: Pocket Movie Guide • A Chinese Ghost Story: Pocket Movie Guide • Ken Russell: England's Great Visionary Film Director and Music Lover • Tommy: Ken Russell: The Who: Pocket Movie Guide • Women In Love: Ken Russell: D.H. Lawrence: Pocket Movie Guide • The Devils: Ken Russell: Pocket Movie Guide • Walerian Borowczyk: Cinema of Erotic Dreams • The Beast: Pocket Movie Guide • The Lord of the Rings Movies • The Fellowship of the Ring: Pocket Movie Guide • The Two Towers: Pocket Movie Guide • The Return of the King: Pocket Movie Guide • Jean-Luc Godard: The Passion of Cinema • The Sacred Cinema of Andrei Tarkovsky • Andrei Tarkovsky: Pocket Guide.*

'It's amazing for me to see my work treated with such passion and respect. There is nothing resembling it in the U.S. in relation to my work.'
(Andrea Dworkin)

'This model monograph – it is an exemplary job, and I'm very proud that he has accorded me a couple of mentions… The subject matter of his book is beautifully organised and dead on beam.'
(Lawrence Durrell, on *The Light Eternal: A Study of J.M.W. Turner*)

'Jeremy Robinson's poetry is certainly jammed with ideas, and I find it very interesting for that reason. It's certainly a strong imprint of his personality.'
(Colin Wilson)

'*Sex-Magic-Poetry-Cornwall* is a very rich essay... It is a very good piece… vastly stimulating and insightful.'
(Peter Redgrove)

CRESCENT MOON PUBLISHING

web: www.crmoon.com e-mail: cresmopub@yahoo.co.uk

ARTS, PAINTING, SCULPTURE

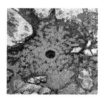

The Art of Andy Goldsworthy
Andy Goldsworthy: Touching Nature
Andy Goldsworthy in Close-Up
Andy Goldsworthy: Pocket Guide
Andy Goldsworthy In America
Land Art: A Complete Guide
The Art of Richard Long
Richard Long: Pocket Guide
Land Art In the UK
Land Art in Close-Up
Land Art In the U.S.A.
Land Art: Pocket Guide
Installation Art in Close-Up
Minimal Art and Artists In the 1960s and After
Colourfield Painting
Land Art DVD, TV documentary
Andy Goldsworthy DVD, TV documentary
The Erotic Object: Sexuality in Sculpture From Prehistory to the Present Day
Sex in Art: Pornography and Pleasure in Painting and Sculpture
Postwar Art
Sacred Gardens: The Garden in Myth, Religion and Art
Glorification: Religious Abstraction in Renaissance and 20th Century Art
Early Netherlandish Painting
Leonardo da Vinci
Piero della Francesca
Giovanni Bellini
Fra Angelico: Art and Religion in the Renaissance
Mark Rothko: The Art of Transcendence
Frank Stella: American Abstract Artist
Jasper Johns
Brice Marden
Alison Wilding: The Embrace of Sculpture
Vincent van Gogh: Visionary Landscapes
Eric Gill: Nuptials of God
Constantin Brancusi: Sculpting the Essence of Things
Max Beckmann
Caravaggio
Gustave Moreau
Egon Schiele: Sex and Death In Purple Stockings
Delizioso Fotografico Fervore: Works In Process 1
Sacro Cuore: Works In Process 2
The Light Eternal: J.M.W. Turner
The Madonna Glorified: Karen Arthurs

LITERATURE

J.R.R. Tolkien: The Books, The Films, The Whole Cultural Phenomenon
J.R.R. Tolkien: Pocket Guide
Tolkien's Heroic Quest
The *Earthsea* Books of Ursula Le Guin
Beauties, Beasts and Enchantment: Classic French Fairy Tales
German Popular Stories by the Brothers Grimm
Philip Pullman and *His Dark Materials*
Sexing Hardy: Thomas Hardy and Feminism
Thomas Hardy's *Tess of the d'Urbervilles*
Thomas Hardy's *Jude the Obscure*
Thomas Hardy: The Tragic Novels
Love and Tragedy: Thomas Hardy
The Poetry of Landscape in Hardy
Wessex Revisited: Thomas Hardy and John Cowper Powys
Wolfgang Iser: Essays and Interviews
Petrarch, Dante and the Troubadours
Maurice Sendak and the Art of Children's Book Illustration
Andrea Dworkin
Cixous, Irigaray, Kristeva: The *Jouissance* of French Feminism
Julia Kristeva: Art, Love, Melancholy, Philosophy, Semiotics and Psychoanalysis
Hélène Cixous I Love You: The *Jouissance* of Writing
Luce Irigaray: Lips, Kissing, and the Politics of Sexual Difference
Peter Redgrove: Here Comes the Flood
Peter Redgrove: Sex-Magic-Poetry-Cornwall
Lawrence Durrell: Between Love and Death, East and West
Love, Culture & Poetry: Lawrence Durrell
Cavafy: Anatomy of a Soul
German Romantic Poetry: Goethe, Novalis, Heine, Hölderlin
Feminism and Shakespeare
Shakespeare: Love, Poetry & Magic
The Passion of D.H. Lawrence
D.H. Lawrence: Symbolic Landscapes
D.H. Lawrence: Infinite Sensual Violence
Rimbaud: Arthur Rimbaud and the Magic of Poetry
The Ecstasies of John Cowper Powys
Sensualism and Mythology: The Wessex Novels of John Cowper Powys
Amorous Life: John Cowper Powys and the Manifestation of Affectivity (H.W. Fawkner)
Postmodern Powys: New Essays on John Cowper Powys (Joe Boulter)
Rethinking Powys: Critical Essays on John Cowper Powys
Paul Bowles & Bernardo Bertolucci
Rainer Maria Rilke
Joseph Conrad: *Heart of Darkness*
In the Dim Void: Samuel Beckett
Samuel Beckett Goes into the Silence
André Gide: Fiction and Fervour
Jackie Collins and the Blockbuster Novel
Blinded By Her Light: The Love-Poetry of Robert Graves
The Passion of Colours: Travels In Mediterranean Lands
Poetic Forms

POETRY

Ursula Le Guin: Walking In Cornwall
Peter Redgrove: Here Comes The Flood
Peter Redgrove: Sex-Magic-Poetry-Cornwall
Dante: Selections From the Vita Nuova
Petrarch, Dante and the Troubadours
William Shakespeare: Sonnets
William Shakespeare: Complete Poems
Blinded By Her Light: The Love-Poetry of Robert Graves
Emily Dickinson: Selected Poems
Emily Brontë: Poems
Thomas Hardy: Selected Poems
Percy Bysshe Shelley: Poems
John Keats: Selected Poems
Joh n Keats: Poems of 1820
D.H. Lawrence: Selected Poems
Edmund Spenser: Poems
Edmund Spenser: Amoretti
John Donne: Poems
Henry Vaughan: Poems
Sir Thomas Wyatt: Poems
Robert Herrick: Selected Poems
Rilke: Space, Essence and Angels in the Poetry of Rainer Maria Rilke
Rainer Maria Rilke: Selected Poems
Friedrich Hölderlin: Selected Poems
Arseny Tarkovsky: Selected Poems
Arthur Rimbaud: Selected Poems
Arthur Rimbaud: A Season in Hell
Arthur Rimbaud and the Magic of Poetry
Novalis: Hymns To the Night
German Romantic Poetry
Paul Verlaine: Selected Poems
Elizaethan Sonnet Cycles
D.J. Enright: By-Blows
Jeremy Reed: Brigitte's Blue Heart
Jeremy Reed: Claudia Schiffer's Red Shoes
Gorgeous Little Orpheus
Radiance: New Poems
Crescent Moon Book of Nature Poetry
Crescent Moon Book of Love Poetry
Crescent Moon Book of Mystical Poetry
Crescent Moon Book of Elizabethan Love Poetry
Crescent Moon Book of Metaphysical Poetry
Crescent Moon Book of Romantic Poetry
Pagan America: New American Poetry

MEDIA, CINEMA, FEMINISM and CULTURAL STUDIES

J.R.R. Tolkien: The Books, The Films, The Whole Cultural Phenomenon
J.R.R. Tolkien: Pocket Guide
The *Lord of the Rings* Movies: Pocket Guide
The Cinema of Hayao Miyazaki
Hayao Miyazaki: *Princess Mononoke*: Pocket Movie Guide
Hayao Miyazaki: *Spirited Away*: Pocket Movie Guide
Tim Burton : Hallowe'en For Hollywood
Ken Russell
Ken Russell: *Tommy*: Pocket Movie Guide
The Ghost Dance: The Origins of Religion
The Peyote Cult

Cixous, Irigaray, Kristeva: The *Jouissance* of French Feminism
Julia Kristeva: Art, Love, Melancholy, Philosophy, Semiotics and Psychoanalysis
Luce Irigaray: Lips, Kissing, and the Politics of Sexual Difference
Hélène Cixous I Love You: The *Jouissance* of Writing
Andrea Dworkin
'Cosmo Woman': The World of Women's Magazines
Women in Pop Music
HomeGround: The Kate Bush Anthology
Discovering the Goddess (Geoffrey Ashe)
The Poetry of Cinema
The Sacred Cinema of Andrei Tarkovsky
Andrei Tarkovsky: Pocket Guide
Andrei Tarkovsky: *Mirror*: Pocket Movie Guide
Andrei Tarkovsky: *The Sacrifice*: Pocket Movie Guide
Walerian Borowczyk: Cinema of Erotic Dreams
Jean-Luc Godard: The Passion of Cinema
Jean-Luc Godard: *Hail Mary*: Pocket Movie Guide
Jean-Luc Godard: *Contempt*: Pocket Movie Guide
Jean-Luc Godard: *Pierrot le Fou*: Pocket Movie Guide
John Hughes and Eighties Cinema
Ferris Bueller's Day Off: Pocket Movie Guide
Jean-Luc Godard: Pocket Guide
The Cinema of Richard Linklater
Liv Tyler: Star In Ascendance
Blade Runner and the Films of Philip K. Dick
Paul Bowles and Bernardo Bertolucci
Media Hell: Radio, TV and the Press
An Open Letter to the BBC
Detonation Britain: Nuclear War in the UK
Feminism and Shakespeare
Wild Zones: Pornography, Art and Feminism
Sex in Art: Pornography and Pleasure in Painting and Sculpture
Sexing Hardy: Thomas Hardy and Feminism

The Light Eternal is a model monograph, an exemplary job. The subject matter of the book is beautifully
organised and dead on beam. (Lawrence Durrell)
It is amazing for me to see my work treated with such passion and respect. (Andrea Dworkin)

CRESCENT MOON PUBLISHING
P.O. Box 1312, Maidstone, Kent, ME14 5XU, Great Britain. www.crmoon.com

cresmopub@yahoo.co.uk   www.crescentmoon.org.uk

Printed in the USA
CPSIA information can be obtained
at www.ICGtesting.com
LVHW022047081224
798639LV00003B/521